DATE DUE

			PRINTED IN U.S.A.

· THE ·

International

ENCYCLOPEDIA

OF SEXUALITY

Edited by

ROBERT T. FRANCOEUR

———⇒•◦•⇐———

Preface by

TIMOTHY PERPER

———⇒•◦•⇐———

Introduction by

IRA L. REISS

· T H E ·

International

ENCYCLOPEDIA

OF SEXUALITY

VOLUME II

India to South Africa

CONTINUUM · NEW YORK

1998

The Continuum Publishing Company
370 Lexington Avenue
New York, NY 10017

Typography, Design Coordination, and Computer Graphics by
Ray Noonan, ParaGraphic Artists, NYC

Printed in the United States of America

Library of Congress Cataloging-in-Publication Data

The international encyclopedia of sexuality / edited by Robert T.
  Francoeur ; foreword by Timothy Perper ; preface by Ira L. Reiss.
    v. cm.
    Includes bibliographical references and index.
    ISBN 0-8264-0838-9 (v. 1 : alk. paper)
    1. Sex—Encyclopedias.   2. Sex customs—Encyclopedias.
  I. Francoeur, Robert T.
  HQ21.I68   1997
  306.7'03—dc20   95-16481
                                                           CIP

3-Volume Set ISBN 0-8264-0841-9

Vol. 2 ISBN 0-8264-0839-7

CONTENTS

VOLUME THREE

India
(*Bharat*)

Jayaji Krishna Nath, M.D., and Vishwarath R. Nayar

Contents

Demographics and a Historical Perspective

A. Demographics

India, with an area of 1.26 million square miles (3.29 million kilometers), is the largest democratic country in the world. The country has about 16 percent of the world's total population and 2.4 percent of the global land area. India is one third the size of the United States and occupies most of the Indian subcontinent in south Asia. Next to China, India is the most populous country in the world, with a 1995 population of 950 million. India's urban population accounts for 28 percent of the country's total population. In 1991, one third of the 12.6 million inhabitants of Bombay were homeless, living on the streets or in squatters' camps built on putrid landfills. Bombay, India's most populous city, has 100,000 people per square kilometer.

The 1995 age distribution showed that 36.8 percent of the population were under 15 years of age; the working age group (15 to 64) was 69 percent; and the aged population (65 and over) was about 4 percent. The 1995 life expectancy at birth for males was 58 years and for females 60 years. The birthrate was twenty-eight per 1,000 population and the death rate ten per 1,000 population, giving a natural annual growth rate of 1.8 percent. The 1995 infant mortality rate was 76 per 1,000 live births. The sex ratio showed 929 females to 1,000 males. India has one hospital bed per 1,357 persons, and one physician per 2,189 persons. The 1993 literacy level was estimated at about 50 percent, with schooling compulsory to age 14; the literacy rate is significantly lower for females than males. The per capita gross domestic product in 1995 was $1,300.

India's neighbors are Pakistan on the west, China, Nepal, and Bhutan on the north, Bangladesh and Myanmar on the east, and the Indian Ocean on the south. Below the Indo-Ganges plain, which extends from the Bay of Bengal on the east to the Afghan frontier and Arabian Sea on the west, the land is fertile and one of the most densely populated regions of the world. The three great rivers, the Ganges, Indus, and Brahmaputra, have their origins in the Himalayas. With one quarter of the land forested, the climate varies from tropical in the south to near-Arctic in the north. The Rajasthan Desert is in the northwest; in the northeast, the Assam Hills receive 400 inches of rain a year.

B. A Brief Historical Perspective

Modern India is one of the oldest civilizations in the world. Excavations in the Indus valley trace civilization there back for at least 5,000 years. India's cultural history includes prehistoric mountain cave paintings in Ajanta, the exquisite beauty of the Taj Mahal in Agra, the rare sensitivity and warm emotions of the erotic Hindu temple sculptures of the nineth-century Chandella rulers, and the Kutab Minar in Delhi.

Around 1500 B.C.E., Sanskrit-speaking Aryan tribes invaded the Indus valley from the northwest, and blended with the earlier inhabitants to create the classical Indian civilization. Asoka ruled most of the Indian subcontinent in the third century B.C.E. and established Buddhism, but Hinduism experienced a revival and became the dominant religious tradition. The Gupta kingdom, in the fourth to sixth centuries of the Common Era, enjoyed a golden age of science, literature, and the arts. In the eighth century, Arab invaders brought the Muslim faith to the west, and Turkish Moslems gained control of north India by 1200. Vasco de Gama established Portuguese trading posts in 1503, and the Dutch followed soon after. Between 1526 and 1857, India was ruled by the Mongul emperors. In 1609, the British East India Company sought concessions for spices and textiles from the Mongul emperor, and subsequently gained control of most of India. The British curbed the rule of the rajahs around 1830 and supported the native rulers in the mutiny of the Sepoy troops in 1857-1858.

After World War II, the Indian National Congress joined with the Muslim League. Mohandas K. Gandhi, who had launched opposition to the British in 1930, emerged as the leader of the independence movement. In 1935, the British partitioned British India, giving India its own constitution and bicameral federal congress and establishing India as a self-governing member of the British Commonwealth. The partition created an independent Pakistan, triggering a mass migration of more than twelve million Hindu and Moslem refugees that was often violent and set the stage for a war in 1971-1973. This time, the massive migration involved some ten million refugees. Kashmir, a predominately Moslem region in the northwest, which has been in dispute with Pakistan and India since 1947, was divided in 1949, with Pakistan incorporating one third of Kashmir and India two thirds. India's new territory became the states of Jammu and Kashmir with internal autonomy. In 1952-1954, France peacefully yielded to India the five colonies of former French India, Pondicherry, Karikal, Mahe, Yanaon, and Chandernagor.

Ethnic violence accompanied several Sikh uprisings in the 1980s—the former British protectorate of Sikkim had become a protectorate of India in 1950 and was absorbed into India in 1974. Violence also broke out in the Pungab in 1988, and Assam in 1993. The biggest wave of criminal violence in Indian history jolted Bombay and Calcutta with devastating bombings in 1993.

1. Basic Sexological Premises

A. Gender Roles

The family in Indian society provides for the satisfaction of the fundamental biopsychic drives of hunger and sex, and makes it possible to perpetuate the species through reproduction and the social heritage through the handing down of traditions from generation to generation. The function of preserving language, customs, and traditions is normally performed in collaboration with other social groups. Husband and wife, though, contribute to the maintenance of the family. There is a clear division of labor based on sex. The sex roles of a person consist of the behavior that is socially defined and expected of that person because of his or her role as a male or female. Rigid, mutually exclusive, conceptualization of appropriate abilities or activities, tasks, characteristics, and attitudes are assigned differently to man and woman in all Indian cultures. Due to rapid social and technological changes, it is observed that in the recent period, traditional gender-role differentiation is breaking down, especially in the fields of education and work. The historical analysis of the status of women shows that in Vedic India, as revealed by its literature, women were treated with grace and consideration. However in the postvedic age, there was a slow but steady decline of their importance in the home and society. A decline, indeed a distinct degeneration in their status, is visible in medieval India. The purdah system of female seclusion, the *sati* tradition of immolating the widow on the husband pyre, dowry, and child marriages were obvious in the preindependence period. Following independence from England, however, there was a distinct, if uneven, and gradual liberal change in the attitude toward and status of women.

> [In India's] male-dominated tradition, and everywhere in Vedic, classical, medieval, and modern Hinduism, the paradigms in myths, rituals, doctrines, and symbols are masculine. But just as goddess traditions encroached successfully on the territory of masculine deities, so too has the impact of women's religious activity, the ritual life in particular, been of increasing significance in the overall scale of Hindu tradition. To put this another way, in traditional life the unlettered folk have always shaped Hinduism, and half of them have been women. It is not feminine roles in Hinduism that have been lacking but rather the acknowledgment of such in literature, the arts, and institutions such as the priesthood and temple and monastic administrations. Only now, in a world rapidly changing because of education opportunities, are such institutions and media beginning to reflect accurately the total picture of Hindu class, caste, gender, and regional life. (Knipe 1991, 10-11)

The urban/suburban environment has given birth to a fascinating mix of traditional and new male/female roles and role models among the affluent middle class. Bombay films are much more influential in creating new role models than the Hollywood films were in their early days in the United States. While the United States had one example of a film star succeeding in presidential politics, India has seen many famous film stars, both male and female, achieve political prominence. In 1966, Indira Gandi became prime minister of India, at a time when few Western nations would have accepted a woman head of state. And yet India remains a very male-dominated society.

Despite new currents, very often in Indian culture, a woman's body is not seen as an object of pride or pleasure, but as something that is made impure every day, an abode of sinfulness. Thus, a muted yet extremely powerful theme can be found in Hindu marriages: "the cultural unease, indeed, the fear of woman as woman." Women, as reflected in popular novels and clinical practice, frequently view their sexuality as a capacity to redress a lopsided distribution of power between the sexes (Kakar 1989:13). The age-old, yet still persisting, cultural splitting of the wife into a mother and a whore, which underlies the husband-wife relationship and which explains the often contradictory Hindu views of the woman, is hardly unique to Indian culture, though it may be more pervasive here than in other cultures (Kakar 1989, 17).

The social context determines whether the woman is viewed as divine, good, or bad—as partner in ritual, as mother, or as whore. In the context of ritual, women are honored and respected. In her maternal aspect, actual or potential, woman is again a person deserving all reverence. "It is only just as a woman, as a female sexual being, that the patriarchal culture's horror and scorn are heaped upon the hapless wife" (Kakar 1989, 17).

B. Sociolegal Status of Males and Females

While it is mostly the husbands who are breadwinners, the women generally take care of the household activities, besides bearing and rearing children. However, due to widespread educational programs and improvement of educational facilities for girls, women nowadays are accepting jobs outside the home, and thus contributing financially to the family budget. Also, because of constant efforts in making women aware of their rights and the importance of their involvement in day-to-day family matters, the status of women has increased significantly. Due to all these measures, women nowadays actively participate not only in their family affairs, but also in social and political activities in the communities.

The occupations that were earlier monopolized by men are gradually being shared by women. Similarly, various professional courses like engineering, architecture, and allied disciplines are also studied by women. In spite of these changes initiated for the benefit of women in India, the people's attitude to equal status for women has not changed significantly in actual practice, and in this regard various educational programs for men are still in great need of changing their outlook. For instance, although the legal age of marriage for girls is set by the government at 18 years, people, especially in rural and tribal India, encourage early marriage for girls, mostly within a short time of their attaining puberty. Similarly, in the educational development, the dropout rate among females is very high.

C. General Concepts of Sexuality and Love

Adult marriage is generally the rule in India. Usually it is expected that a husband must be in a position to earn a living and his wife must be able to run the home, which they set up after marriage. The influence of the Hindu religion has resulted in some prepuberty marriages. The vast majority of regular marriages are still parent-made, arranged marriages. Irregular marriages do occur with the increasing influence of Western concepts of romantic love in the mass media of magazines and movies. In one form of irregular marriage, the two lovers run away and stay away until they are accepted by their families, which is done as a matter of course. In a second form, known as "Intrusion," a girl confronts her chosen husband and his parents and presses their acceptance of her by living in the house. A third form involves "forcible application of vermilion," when a young man takes the opportunity at some fair or festival to place a vermilion scarf on his chosen girl's head. Sometimes a betrothal ceremony takes place before the marriage proper is solemnized. Legally, marriage take place only between those who have passed the puberty stage. At the marriage ceremony, the local priest is required to officiate and prayers and offerings are made to the gods.

Due to modernization and the influence of Western culture, arranged marriages are becoming less popular and common, especially in metropolitan cities. In its place, marriages based on the couple's choice, often crossing caste and/or religious boundaries, are becoming more common.

While sexual urges had to be subordinated to social norms in the joint-family system, except for rare rebellious behavior or outbursts, the present newly found freedom has instigated more openness and casualness in matters of sexual behavior. Expressions and feelings that would have been termed scandalous and in need of being tamed to adhere to socially accepted rules, values, and practices, are now accepted as natural.

Individualism, in its Western Euroamerican consciousness is foreign to the traditional Indian social consciousness and experience. However, this is changing. Sudhir Kakar, a distinguished psychoanalyst who has taught at the Universities of Harvard, Chicago, and Vienna, and written extensively on Indian sexuality, notes that "individualism even now stirs but faintly" in India (Kakar 1989:4).

Traditional Indian folklore and stories, as well as modern novels, provide an important theme—the perennial, cosmic-based conflict between man and woman—that flows through much of male-female relationships in Indian culture and domestic life. Margaret Egnor sums this theme up in her study of *The Ideology of Love in a Tamil Family*. Based on her research in Tamil Nadu, Egnor observed that:

> Within the household, as well as in the domain of paid labor, there was a strong spirit of rivalry between many women and their husbands. Wives would not automatically accept submission. Neither would their husbands. Consequently, their relationship was often, from what I was able to observe, disputatious. . . . The eternal conflict between spouses is abundantly reflected in Indian mythology, especially Tamil which debates the issues of male vs female superiority back and forth endlessly on a cosmic level in the form of battles and contests between deities or demons and their real or would-be mates. (Egnor 1986).

In Indian folklore, Shiva and Parvati argue interminably about who is the better dancer, while Vishnu and Lakshmi are constantly debating which is the greater divinity.

In most regions of the country, male folk wisdom traces the reasons for man's perennial war with woman to the belief that the female sex lacks both sexual morality and intelligence. The Punjabis and Gujaratis agree that "The intelligence of a woman is in her heels." Tamils maintain that "No matter how educated a woman is, her intelligence is always of the lowest order." The Malayalis warn that "One who heeds the advice of a woman will be reduced to beggary."

Men in southern India seem more resigned and willing to acknowledge their helplessness in the face of "general female cussedness and constant provocation." Kannada and Telugu men admit that "Wind can be held in a bag, but not the tongue of a shrew," while Telugu males confess that "Neither the husband nor the brother-in-law can control a pugnacious woman." By contrast, in the northern regions of India, folk sayings place "singularly greater emphasis on the employment of force and physical chastisement to correct perceived female shortcomings." "The place of a horse and a woman is under the thighs." Two proverbs from Gujarati echo this view: "Barley and millet improve by addition of salt; women through a beating by a pestle," and "Better to keep the race of women under the heel of a shoe" (Kakar 1989, 6).

Faced with this perennial conflict between husband and wife, the object of the wife's affectional and sensual currents traditionally has been the husband's younger brother in the joint or extended Indian family.

For a time in Indian social history, the custom of *nigora* officially recognized the erotic importance of the brother-in-law—in the sense that he would or could have sexual relations with his elder's brother's widow. The *nigora* custom has been traced back to the times of the Rig-veda where a man, identified by the commentators as the brother-in-law, is described as extending his hand in promised marriage to a widow inclined to share her husband's funeral pyre.

Although the custom gradually fell into disuse, especially with the prohibition of widow remarriage, the psychological core of *niyoga*, namely the mutual awareness of a married woman and her younger brother-in-law as potential or actual sexual partners, remains very much an actuality even today (Kakar 1989, 13).

Kakar has added a perspective from clinical practice, noting that women who are on terms of sexual intimacy with a brother-in-law rarely express any feelings of guilt. Their anxiety is occasioned more by his leaving home or his impending marriage, which the woman perceives as an end to her sensual and emotional life (Kakar 1989, 13-14).

The fate of sexuality within marriage is likely to come under an evil constellation of stars. Physical love will tend to be a shame-ridden affair, a sharp stabbing of lust with little love and even less passion. Indeed the code of sexual conduct for the householder-husband fully endorses this expectation. Stated concisely in the *smritis* (the Law codes), elaborated in the *puranas* which are not only collections of myths, but also contain chapters on the correct coduct of daily life), modified for local usage by the various kinds of religiosi, the thrust of the message seems to be "No sex in marriage, we're Indian." Kakar 1989:19).

According to Hindu tradition, a husband should only approach his wife sexually during her *ritu* (season), a period of sixteen days within the menstrual cycle. But intercourse is forbidden on six of these sixteen days, the first four days, and the eleventh and thirteenth. This leaves only ten days for conjugal relations, but since the all-important sons are conceived only on even nights and daughters on uneven nights, the days for conjugal relations shrinks to five. Then there are the parvas, the moonless nights and those of the full moon when sexual relations lead either to the birth of atheist sons (*Brahma Purana*) or the "hell of feces and urine" (*Vishnu Purana*). Add to these taboos, the many festival days for gods and ancestors when erotic pleasures are forbidden. Sex is also beyond the pale during the day.

There is a general disapproval of the erotic aspect of married life, a disapproval that cannot be disregarded as a mere medieval relic; this general disapproval of the erotic, even in marriage, continues to inform contemporary attitudes. This is quite understandable since changes in sexuality occur at a more gradual pace than transformations in the political and social sphere; sexual time, as Kakar suggests, beats at a considerably slower pace than its chronological counterpart. Sexual taboos are still so strong in some Hindu communities that many women, especially those in the higher castes, do not have a name for their genitals (Kakar 1989, 20).

Cultural taboos may not, despite their pervasive presence in Indian society, affect the sexual expressions of men and women across the economic and caste spectra of India. But they can, and apparently do increase the conflicts around sexuality, sour it for many, and generally contribute to its impoverishment. This can effectively block many men and women from a deep, fulfilling experience of sexual love. Accordingly, the considerable sexual misery one can deduce as being reflected in the Indian marriage and family from cultural ideals, prohibitions, and modern fiction, the sexual woes expressed by middle- and upper-class women who seek relief in psychotherapy is also evidenced in the interviews Sudhir Kakar and others have conducted with low-caste, "untouchable" women in the poorest areas of Delhi.

Most of these women portrayed their experiences with sexual intercourse as a furtive act in a cramped and crowded room, lasting barely a few minutes and with a marked absence of physical or emotional caressing. It was a duty, an experience to be submitted to, often from a fear of beating. None of the women removed their clothes during intercourse since it is considered shameful to do so (Kakar 1989, 21).

Despite these pervasive negative images of the conflict between the sexes in marriage, and the negative view of women and sexuality, it must be pointed out that Indian sexual relations are not devoid of regular pauses in the conflict between man and woman. Tenderness, whether this be an affair with the soul of a Mukesh song, that is much quieter than a plunge into the depths of erotic passion known in Western culture, or sexual ecstasy of a husband and wife who have found their way through the forest of sexual taboos, does exist in India (Kakar 1989, 22-23).

2. Religious and Ethnic Factors Affecting Sexuality

A. Source and Character of Religious Values

India is a multiethnic and multilingual society with wide variations in demographic situations and socioeconomic conditions. People in India practice different religions, and there are numerous cultural identities. The religious composition of India shows that a majority, 82 percent, are Hindu. The other religious groups are Muslim, 11.7 percent; Christians, 2.4 percent; Sihks, 1.9 percent; and other religious groups, 2 percent.

In a nation as religiously and ethnically diverse as India—the nation is commonly described as "a jumble of possibilities"—the people follow a wide variety of customs, and have varied beliefs that ultimately mold their lifestyles. In the life of a Hindu male, for instance, marriage is regarded as necessary, because without a wife he cannot enter the *Grihasthasrama* (the life stage of a householder). In addition, without marriage there can be no offspring, and without a son no release from the chain of reincarnation in birth-death-rebirth. According to Hindu custom, which still prevails in most families, marriage must take place within one's caste or Varna, although marriages between members of different castes and communities are gaining acceptance. Hindu marriage, being a religious sacrament, is indissoluble.

The purdah system still prevails in the Muslim northern region of the country, where a female has to cover her face in front of other males and elders, but this custom is also slowly fading out. The Muslim male, who is allowed to have four wives, subject to specified conditions, is also realizing the wisdom in small families and monogamy (more so the educated, urban Muslim male). Marriage is solemnized by signing a legal document and can be dissolved. Divorce is almost exclusively the husband's privilege, although a divorcing husband has to pay the "Dower," a settlement made to the wife out of her husband's property to compensate her in the event of death and divorce.

Indian Christians are also influenced by the social practices of the region, but they tend to follow the pattern of a family as an independent unit, in which their lifestyles and interactions revolve around the community and the local church. They have more freedom in their general outlook and easily adapt to local conditions and trends.

The tribal people of India have varied religious and social practices, often with a more natural approach to sexuality and age-old practices of premarital sex and premarital experimental cohabitation.

Although there is a decreasing acceptance of orthodox beliefs and religious practices among India's younger generation, each of India's religious traditions maintains its own forms of observations of various practices starting with birth and regulating life through marriage to the death ceremonies. The lifestyles of the people, including their sexual behavior, are generally governed by these prescribed practices.

B. Source and Character of Ethnic Values

India's dominant ethnic element is the Indo-Aryan peoples with 72 percent of the population. The Aryans invaded India from the northwest between 2400 and 1500 B.C.E. and intermingled with already well-civilized native people. The Australoid Dravidans, including the Tamils, constitute 25 percent of the total population and dominate in southern India. Arab invaders established a Moslem foothold in the western part of the country in the eighth century, and Turkish Moslems gained control of northern India by 1200. These Muslim were in part responsible for the decline of the Chandella culture that dominated in northern India from c. 200 B.C.E. to C.E. 1200. The great "love temples" of northern India, including Khajuraho, were built in the eleventh century and in part destroyed by the invading Moslems (Deva 1986). In 1526, Moslem invaders founded the great Mongul empire centered in Delhi. This empire lasted, at least in name, until 1857. Today, 3 percent of Indians are of Mongoloid ancestry.

The Portuguese influence in Bombay and the Indian subcontinent dominated trade with Europe in the 1500s. In 1612, the English influence began to spread with the founding of the East India Trade Company. In 1687, the English took over Bombay, setting the stage for their defeat of the French and Islamic armies, and laying the foundation for the incorporation of India into the British Empire in 1858. English Victorian views of sexuality remain a strong influence in urban India.

In 1947, the Indian Independence Act was passed, and a new constitution establishing India as an independent democratic country adopted in 1949. In the 1970s, a war in the north between East and West Pakistan ended with Indian intervention and establishment of East Pakistan as the new nation of Bangladesh.

3. Sexual Knowledge and Education

A. Government Policies and Programs for Sex Education

Present-day children in India are more exposed to new areas of knowledge than their parents were. As a matter of fact, young people are simply deluged these days with movies, magazines, and books—all prime sources of sexual information and stimulation. Young people nowadays want to know more about pros and cons of marriage, premarital and extramarital sexual relationships, venereal diseases, etc. In a survey of college students conducted by the All India Educational and Vocational Guidance Association, it was reported that 54 percent of male students and 42 percent of female students stated that they did not have adequate knowledge regarding matters of sex. Though parents have the primary responsibility of imparting sex education to their children, it has been found that a majority of young people in India derive their information about sex and sex behavior largely from companions, street-corner conversation, movies, and magazines. The government is seriously contemplating introducing sex education as a part of the curriculum from the secondary school level onwards. One important reason for giving the school responsibility for sex education is that many parents feel unable to handle this task themselves. Many have inhibitions about discussing sex with their children; others admit that they do not have the technical knowledge to answer all the questions their children ask. In this situation, the teacher is a major factor in determining the success of any sex-education program. Serious efforts are under way in specifying the contents and components of sex education and the level at which this has to be taught. No information is available on the provision of sex education in special schools such as those for mentally handicapped persons.

B. Informal Sources of Sexual Knowledge

Parents give their young children sex education many years before they can begin to convey sex information verbally. The mother's behavior, attitudes, and roles are a clear model for the growing girl. Similarly, the father provides a role model for a son. The relationship, warmth, and responsiveness between parents provides for all children a model for their later marriage. By observing their parents, children see the basic qualities that make men and women different. Similarly, when the child is in the company of his friends, he/she learns through them the various facets of their life. The other important informal sources of sexual information for the child are peer group influence, teachers, books, movies, magazines, and siblings.

Fifteen million Indians attend the cinema every day. Hindi cinema, perhaps more than the cinema of many other countries, provides fantasy, the stuff that dreams are made of. The cinema is the major shaper of an emerging, pan-Indian popular culture. As such, the mix of fantasy and reality, dreams and hopes, that permeates Hindi cinema is already a major factor in the remolding of Indian sexual values, expectations, and attitudes, as well as gender relations, marriage, and the family (Kakar, 1989, 25-41).

4. Autoerotic Behaviors and Patterns

Masturbation is generally unacceptable among girls. For boys however it is considered a preparation for mature sex life. Though boys at the younger ages may masturbate together without shame, at little more mature ages, they all give it up. This seems to be particularly so in the case of married men. In recent years, the availability of sexually explicit books, magazines, and videos has also acted as major contributory factor for male autoerotic activities.

5. Interpersonal Heterosexual Behaviors

A. Children

Indian children are pampered as much as possible, often until age six or seven. Before puberty, a natural approach to sexuality and nudity prevails, especially in rural areas. Daughters and sons are carefully prepared for their future domestic roles as mothers and fathers. Women are considered to be much more skilled than males in love and sexual pleasures. At puberty, most boys and girls are segregated. In some regions of India, pubescent girls are not even allowed to enter a house where a single young man is present.

Sexual views and behavior are somewhat more natural and less inhibited in India's rural villages, according to Dr. Promilla Kapur, a research psychologist and sociologist at New Delhi's India International Center. Some tribal groups practice totally free sex among adolescents.

Nowadays, with the advent of various satellite television programs, children are exposed at their early ages to various programs, including considerable sexually related material. This exposure often results in conflicting responses for girls raised in a society that represses or ignores female sexuality. In rural areas, adults sometimes talk loudly about their sexual experiences in the presence of children, and this provides opportunities for the young men to think more about sex. In urban areas, especially cities where housing shortage is very acute, adults in public places like parks and cinema theaters generally satisfy their sexual feeling through hugging or other noncoital sexual practices. These acts also provide learning opportunities for the younger ones. Sexual play, such as looking at another child's buttocks or genitals, genital touching games, sharing a bed with a child of the opposite sex, etc., likewise provides children with opportunities for sexual exploration; the parents would not necessarily be aware of these acts of their children.

B. Adolescents

Adolescents in India today face a number of problems related to changing value systems and social expectations. The sexual world of adolescents is becoming increasingly complex. In traditional Indian society, adolescents were initiated into their sexual roles, more or less, in a clearly defined period and by a series of ceremonies and rites. As in some other cultures, these included instruction on their sex roles, marriage customs, sexual morality, and acceptable sexual behavior. But with the influence of Western culture, the present generation of youth are facing a number of problems that are ultimately forcing them to violate the traditional norms as laid down by the society.

When Kakar and Chowdhary (1970) examined some aspects of sexual behavior among young men prior to marriage, they found that a lack of adequate information and opportunities prompted these young people to turn to literature (often pornographic), to experimentation with prostitutes, friends, or relatives of the opposite or same sex, to covert observation of sexual activities of others, and to masturbation. Reddy and his colleagues, in a 1983 study of young people, found that the sample youth had their first sexual experience between the ages of 15 and 24 years. Homosexual activities were also reported in this study: 38 percentage of women in the sample reported that their first sexual activity had been with a partner of the same sex. The Family Planning Foundation of India undertook a study in 1990 among teenagers (between 14 and 17 years) and found that about one fourth of them expressed their acceptance of premarital sexual contact, "if the boy and the girl were actually in love." While a good number of respondents were aware of at least one contraceptive method, they had very little precise knowledge. Men were found to be more liberal in their views than women.

Mane and Maitra (1992) have rightly inferred that "relatively little is known about the sexual behavior and attitudes towards different aspects and forms of sexual activity in India." With changing conditions in India, the opportunities for risk-taking behavior among adolescents seem to be increasing. Coping with sex is a growing problem for young people. Today's teenagers are faced with an ever-widening gap between the age at which they are physically ready to have sexual intercourse and the age at which it is culturally acceptable for them to do so. Youngsters are in fact often sandwiched between a near-obsessive preoccupation with sex in the media and a veritable wall of silence from other sources of information on the subject. Sex education, including family planning and reproductive health management, has to be the cornerstone of any youth program that is attempted. The social, psychological, and emotional consequences to early sexual involvement also need to be carefully explained.

C. Adults

Premarital Courtship, Dating, and Relationships

The marital bond involves a social sanction generally in the form of a civil or/and religious ceremony authorizing two persons of the opposite sex to engage in sexual relations and assume the consequent and correlated socioeconomic relationships and responsibilities society maintains for a married couple. Under the kind of social structure that caste has given rise to in India, there are certain restrictions in the limits beyond which the parents, in the case of an arranged marriage, and a man and a woman, in the case of a love marriage, cannot go in choosing a spouse; he/she must invariably marry outside his or her own *gotra*. (*Gotra* is the name of the ancestral head or father of the family.) A decision to marry is usually marked by an "engagement" where the elders of both the parties announce their intention to conduct the marriage to their family and friends.

Traditionally, premarital sex activity was controlled in India. As the marriages were mostly arranged by elders, premarital sex was not the accepted practice. Although premarital sex among the tribal societies of India has been widely reported, there is very little if any reliable data on this topic in either the rural or urban areas.

A recent study by Savara and Sridhar in 1992 showed that 30 percent of the respondents had experienced premarital sex, while 41 percent of unmarried men and 33 percent of married men had their first intercourse before attaining 20 years. In another study, they found that about one quarter of married women had sex with their husbands before marriage. Other premarital sexual partners for women were mostly friends, relatives, and work acquaintances. A majority of the respondents—43 percent— agreed that casual sex is all right, and it is acceptable to sleep with someone you have no plan to marry. It is clear that, although premarital sexual relationship is considered generally as immoral in contemporary India, the majority of the young generation do not find it objectionable. A gradual increasing openness about sex in films, video music, television, magazines, etc., is clearly influencing the young in India to be more adventurous about premarital sex than their parents and elders were.

Single Adults

Since marriage is strongly endorsed for all adults in India, the number of men and women remaining unmarried is very negligible. With the rapid increase in urbanization and industrialization, more and more young people are moving out of the rural areas into the urban areas, mainly in search of a livelihood. Mostly they move to urban areas by leaving their families, sometimes including a spouse, in their place of origin, because of the lack of proper housing facilities and the high cost of living in their new home. In the absence of their spouses, many married men turn to the brothel houses for satisfying their sexual urges. In so doing, they face many health problems like STD and HIV.

Marriage and Divorce

Despite an increasing modernization and shift to love-based marriages, most marriages in India are still arranged by parents. Family concerns take precedence over the interests of young couples, because Indian parents strongly believe that a marriage will be good only if the bride and groom come from similar backgrounds. The impetus for arranged marriages is respect for the wisdom of one's elders. To assure that their offspring marry within their own community or caste, many Indian parents use the classi- fied advertisement sections of newspapers to make contact and arrange marriages for their children. In the villages and rural areas, distinctions in the caste system are much stronger and sharper than they are in the cities.

Although the tradition of arranged marriages has a practical value in preserving family traditions and values, it encounters some opposition as young Indian men and women learn of the Western tradition of romance and love. Urban middle-class Indians are most affected. Most Indian men and women attending college outside India are careful not to compromise their prospects back home by letting their family or parents know they have dated a foreigner.

While marriage is a sacred arrangement made in the presence of elders, divorce is legally possible. The incidence of divorce was very negligible in the past, mainly because of the low status of women in the society and the very low level of educational background of females, which left divorced women incapable of supporting themselves. Current trends show that the divorce rate is increasing in the recent past, especially in urban areas. This clearly indicates that women are becoming more aware of their rights, and more assertive in maintaining their individual identity in their employment and personal earnings without being submissive to men.

The joint or extended Hindu family, which dominated in the past, is gradually disintegrating. In the traditional Hindu extended family, the eldest male governed the entire family; the daily life of its members revolved round this huge family. The family head, in consultation with other elder males, arranged marriages in which the youngsters had little say. The females lived behind closed doors—"within the four walls" environs. Festive occasions were the only times when they had the opportunity to interact with others in the neighborhood or relatives. With the disintegration of this family unit into individual families, the problems of insecurity and social influences of the neighborhood have become common. This is indeed leading to the assertion of individual freedom in the choice of marital partners and lifestyles.

Family Size

In India, the demographic transition is at the middle stage where both birth and death rates are showing a declining trend, but the death rate is declining at a faster rate, while the fertility rate is not declining as fast as expected. As marriage is almost universal, in almost all religious groups the age at marriage—especially of females—is very low. For instance, the average age for females at marriage is 18.3 years; for males, it is 23.3 years. Because women have a long reproductive span, Indian couples tend to have large families. The total fertility rate in India is 4.5 and the total marital fertility rate is 5.4. Various factors, such as a strong preference for a son, the low status of women, a high infant mortality, high illiteracy level, inadequate health-care facilities, and irregular follow-up services provided by the health staff play a major role in keeping couples from accepting contraception.

More than 80 percent of deliveries in India, especially in rural and tribal areas, are conducted by the traditional birth attendants, locally called

"*Dais.*" In the absence of a formal health care system within their reach in times of need, people in general depend on these indigenous people for their deliveries. These older women generally have very high credibility and act as good change agents in the community. Though in traditional societies, a joint family system is more commonly observed, nuclear families have become more common in the recent decades due mainly to changes in the occupational structure and dispersal of family members in search of livelihood and their movements into urban areas.

Sexuality and the Physically Disabled and Elderly

There are no organized attempts made so far to assess Indian attitudes about the sexuality of physically and mentally handicapped persons and elderly. Very little attention has been paid so far in sexuality training for the teachers and health personnel who work with these disadvantaged groups. Furthermore, there is no effort made by the institutions that serve these people to deal with the sexual needs of their residents.

Incidence of Oral and Anal Sex

Vaginal intercourse is the norm for marital sexual activity. The incidence of fellatio and cunnilingus is not known in Indian context. However oral sex appears to be relatively uncommon.

6. Homoerotic, Homosexual, and Ambisexual Behaviors

Heterosexual acts, the only socially acceptable sexual expression, is based primarily on the much wider contact and more common relationships between males and females in society. The family is promoted as the early valid social unit. Although homosexuals existed even in ancient India, they never attained social approval in any section of the Indian population. There was a reference to such practices in the *Kamasutra*, written by Vatsyayana more than 1,500 years ago and long admired as an extraordinary analytic treatise on sex and love.

Very little is known about the current practice of male or female homosexuality in India. Homosexuality is slowly gaining acceptance, in part due to the efforts of one or two organized groups in metro cities that are affiliated with a couple of activist homosexual groups connected to international bodies of gays. A regular voice of one organization, and of its homosexual members, is published in Bombay, titled *Bombay Dost*, or "Bombay Friend."

Savara and Shridhar (1992) reported that 12 percent of unmarried men and 8 percent of married men reported that their first sexual experience was with another man and most of them had it before they were 20 years of age. About two fifths of them had a homosexual experience with one or two persons, while over a fifth had such experiences with more than ten persons. In their homosexual acts, only 21 percent of them had used condoms. Ahmed (1992), in his study of truck drivers, found that 15 percent of them admitted previous homosexual experience. Parasuraman et al. (1992), from a study in Madras, found that 3 percent of the homosexuals earned their livings as dancers and/or sex workers. It is further reported in this study that most of the men were between the ages of 21 and 30, and took both active and passive roles in unprotected anal and oral intercourse.

7. Gender Conflicted Persons

Gender-conflicted persons are generally regarded as homosexuals. Traditional Indian society did not provide for special gender roles. In the case of transsexuals, it is not possible to alter one's birth certificate to change the sex designated at birth.

The *hijras*—an Urdu word for eunuchs—are the most notable example of gender variance in India (Jaffrey 1996). *Hijra*, who live predominantly in the larger cities, belong to a Hindu caste of males who dress as females. Their religious role is to perform as mediums for female goddesses, hence their role at weddings. Usually, they leave their families in their teen years to join adult *hijras* in large city. Some may finalize their gender status by castration. Their societal role, and means of making a livelihood, involves providing entertainment at weddings and other festivals, sometimes uninvited but always expecting to be paid. They may also engage in sexual activity with men for money or to satisfy their own sexual desires. The most commonly used technique of the *hijras* is the anal-intercourse passive role without the use of condoms. Characteristically, according the Walter Williams (1986, 258-259), *hijra* are bitchy like American gay drag-queens—heterosexual transvestites are rarely or never bitchy. Insistent and bad-tempered, they wear no underwear and lift their skirts to expose themselves to the embarrassed guests if not paid. They tend to complain and frequently make demands on others in public, such as demanding (rather than politely asking) rich women for their clothes on the street (Weinrich 1987, 96).

8. Significant Unconventional Sexual Behaviors

A. Coercive Sex

Sexual abuse

Due to pressures of social change and the loss of the holding power of traditional taboos, child sexual abuse seems to be increasing in India. However, there is a growing awareness about child sexual abuse in the society. Girls who are near to attaining their puberty, or have just attained it, are often objects of older men's attention.

Although it is socially disapproved, some instances have been reported where parents, because of their poverty, accept a bride price for the marriage of a very young daughter to an older man seeking a young girl as a second wife. In spite of rigorous efforts by the government in educating the people, it is still an accepted practice, especially in rural areas, to arrange marriages of young girls.

Incest

Repressed sexuality has also been a factor in what in the West might be considered widespread incest. In India's extended family system, sex between brothers-in-law and sisters-in-law, for example, or between cousins, or uncles and nieces, or aunts and nephews is common, although hard statistics are not available. See Section 2C for the tradition of *niyoga*, describing the relationship between a wife and the younger brother of her husband.

Sexual Harassment

Poverty forces many rural girls around 10 years of age to be employed as housemaids in rich and middle-class homes. In addition to the economic exploitation, some of these girls also face sexual harassment by males in these households. Since these girls are in no position to resist sexual advances, most sexual harassment acts are not reported or complained about to the police. College girls and young working girls face the problems of harassment. The problem of "Eve-teasing"—old-fashioned pinching, fondling, and other sexual harassment of women on the street—has become so serious in recent years that the government has had to promulgate a law prohibiting this behavior.

One small but significant incident that may signal a change in the pervasive acceptance of sexual harassment in Indian culture occurred in mid-1996, when a 61-year-old Punjab state official was convicted of "outraging the modesty" of a woman in public by slapping the backside of another senior Punjab official at a public event in 1988. After eight years of delays and alleged government cover-ups for the defendant, the court unexpectedly convicted the defendant, the former general of police for the Punjab district and a national hero for his suppression of the Sikh rebellion. While the sentence appeared insignificant, a mere three months in jail and a $20 fine, the court did stipulate that the defendant be subjected to what is known in India as "rigorous imprisionment," a harsh regimen generally reserved for serious criminals and hardly befitting a national hero. While recognizing this verdict as a small measure of justice, women's groups in India hailed it as a landmark because of the prominence of those involved, and the fact that appeals will keep this harassment case in the public view for some years to come.

Rape

Sexual exploitation of girls is another problem faced by females in India. Data on the crime of rape shows that a total of 4,919 rape cases were registered in the country in 1981, with an increase of 12.8 percent from 1980.

Few cases of rape are actually reported to the police because of the negative consequences to the future life of rape victims. Young Indian women who are known to be victims of rape are viewed as outcasts and their families disgraced, even though they were not in any way responsible for the attack. The spread of Western culture, the disruption of urbanization, exposure to films with lots of sex scenes, and pornographic materials are all contributory factors in the increasing the number of rape cases in India.

Marital Violence

See Sections 2A and 2C.

Dowry Deaths

The centuries-old marital tradition of the dowry has recently become troublesome among some young married couples. Since females historically could not inherit property, parents would give their daughters money and property, a dowry, when they married. Young men came to depend on a good-sized dowry to start them off in a comfortable middle-class life. Although dowries were outlawed in the 1947 Constitution and in subsequent laws passed by the Indian Parliament in the 1970s, the new law has created serious problems for brides whose parents refuse to give a sizable gift—the equivalent of the traditional dowry—to the groom. In such cases, some new husbands and their families conspire to drive the young bride to suicide, or if this fails, even murder her. In this way, a young man might marry several times and eventually accumulate enough in illegal dowries to live comfortably. But dowries remain important for Indian women today. Even though they can inherit and no longer depend on the dowry for financial security, Indian women still consider the dowry their right. In the mobile social strata of the cities, the size of a woman's dowry definitely affects her social status. In West Bengal, the groom and his family may demand dowry payments of as much as 60,000 rupees or nearly $2,000, more than ten times the annual income of many rural families.

Effective enforcement of the antidowry law and protection of brides from abuse is difficult, despite the efforts of women's rights groups and special courts set up by the government. Many believe the only hope for permanent improvement lies in changing social attitudes, including the promotion of marriages based on love instead of arranged marriages.

B. Prostitution

Prostitution, the indulgence in promiscuous sexual relations for money or other favors, is an age-old institution in India. Purchasing young girls and dedicating them to temples, the Devadasi system, was an established custom in India by 300 C.E. These girls often served as objects of sexual pleasure for temple priests and pilgrims. The current knowledge about female sex workers is mostly gained from studies done in the red-light districts of metropolitan cities. Generally, prostitutes tend to come from the less-educated class of women, including single abandoned girls, and economically distressed women. Some of the studies on prostitutes in India revealed that a majority of them had STDs, tuberculosis, chronic infections, anemia, scabies, and parasite infestation. Most of them were treated by the local medical practitioner who are quacks in their profession. Most of these women were either forced by gang members and others to take up this profession or were betrayed with false promises of a job. Both the central government and the state governments have enacted statutes to repress and abolish prostitution. The central act, The Suppression of Immoral Traffic in Women and Girls Act (SITA), 1956, has been amended as The Immoral Traffic (Prevention) Act (ITPA), 1956. However, these statutes have made little impact on the increasing traffic in persons and sexual exploitation and abuse (Pawar 1991).

[According to investigative reporter Robert I. Friedman (1996), there are more than 100,000 female commercial sex workers in Bombay, which he describes as "Asia's largest sex bazaar." In all of India, there are as many as 10 million commercial sex workers. According to human rights groups, about 90 percent of the Bombay prostitutes are indentured servants, with close to half trafficked from Nepal. One in five of Bombay's sex workers are under age 18—the government is aware of child prostitution but generally ignores the problem. Child sex workers as young as 9 are sold at auctions where wealthy Arabs from the Persian Gulf compete with wealthy Indian males who believe that having sexual intercourse with a virgin cures syphilis and gonorrhea. A major motivation in the bidding for and slavery of child virgins is the fear of AIDS. In this context, child virgins often bring up to 60,000 rupees, the equivalent of $2,000. (See also Section 11 on HIV/AIDS).

[The commercial sex district of Bombay is actually two interconnected neighborhoods in the south central part of the city, approximately three square kilometers sandwiched between immense Muslim and Hindu slums. It is also the home of the largest organized crime family in Asia. This red-light district is well served by two major railway stations just a half kilometer away, and twenty-five bus routes. The district is laid out with twenty-four lanes of wooden frame brothels with gilded balconies interspersed with car repair shops, small restaurants, liquor stories,

200 bars, numerous flophouses, massive tenements, three police stations, and a municipal school from which only 5 percent of the students graduate.

[Two thousand *hijras* work on Eunuch Lane. Dressed in short black leather skirts or saris, they are virtually indistinguishable from the female prostitutes, except many are extremely beautiful. Shilpa, a 30-year-old social worker with five years experience working in the red-light district, provides a fair description of this aspect of Bombay's sex workers:

> [The eunuchs, or *hijras*, have deep roots in Hinduism. As young boys they were abandoned or sold by their families to a sex cult; the boys are taken into the jungle, where a priest cuts off their genitals in a ceremony called *nirvana*. The priest then folds back a strip of flesh to create an artificial vagina. Eunuchs are generally more ready to perform high-risk sex than female prostitutes, and some Indian men believe they can't contract HIV from them (Quoted by Friedman 1996:14).

[Female sex workers are often harassed by the police, although their madams pay the police weekly bribes to look the other way. To protect themselves, each girl services several police for free.

> [Though on average the girls see six customers a day, who pay between $1.10 and $2 per sex act, the madam gets the money up front. By the time the madam deducts for food, electricity, and rent, as well as payment—with interest—on her purchase price, there is almost nothing left. So to pay for movies, clothes, makeup, and extra food to supplement a bland diet of rice and dal, the girls have to borrow from moneylenders at an interest rate of up to 500 percent. They are perpetually in hock (Friedman 1996:16).

[Bombay's flesh trade is an efficient business, controlled by four separate, harmonious crime groups. One group controls police payoffs, a second controls moneylending, and the third, which maintains the district's internal law and order. The fourth group, the most powerful, manages the procurement of women in a vast network that stretches from South India to the Himalayas (Friedman 1996:18). (Editor)]

C. Pornography

All forms of sexually oriented publications are illegal in India. The government-appointed Central Board has the power to make cuts or ban the indecent or obscene scenes in films. Although pornographic books, magazines, and videos are illegal, their display and sales are casually noticed in urban areas, especially in the major cities.

9. Contraception, Abortion, and Population Planning

A. Contraception

Contraception and Population Control

As wide differences exist among different regions of the country, the population distribution is also not uniform among these regions. Despite the wide variations of existing customs, beliefs, and socioeconomic development among India's 866 million, the people generally favor a large family size and thereby are not in favor of adopting modern methods of contraception. India is the first country in the world to realize the importance of controlling the population growth and thereby initiated The Family Planning Program as far back as 1952.

There are nearly 145 million married couples with wives in the reproductive age group of 15 to 44 years. Assessment of the Family Planning Program performance reveals that nearly 40 percent of the eligible couples were effectively protected by one of the contraceptive methods. The Family Planning Program in India is being promoted on a voluntary basis as a people's movement in keeping with the democratic tradition of the country. The services of the program are offered through Health Care Delivery System. The program makes extensive use of various mass-media sources including television, radio, newspapers, posters, and pamphlets, besides interpersonal communication, in its strategies for explaining the various methods of contraception and removing the sociocultural barriers that work against the program.

Since the majority of the population lives in rural areas, which lack a good infrastructure of health-care facilities and an adequate Social Security System, these people almost universally perceive children and large families as an asset. Added to this is a strong preference for a son that acts as a barrier in limiting the family size. In spite of the availability of various contraceptive methods like sterilization, IUD, condoms, hormonal pills, and other temporary methods, the adopters of the program mostly opt for sterilization, more often tubal ligation or tubectomy.

Because of widely varying customs, beliefs, and the very low level of involvement of the wife in the decision-making process, it is the women who ultimately are adopting the method of contraception. It is not surprising to know in a male-dominated society, especially in rural areas, that people generally perceive that the program is mostly meant for the women folk as they are bearers of the children. Some common beliefs, like "using a contraception reduces a man's masculinity" and "contraception impairs the health of working men," also acts as a barrier for the adoption of the program by men. Methodwise data of adopters generally reveals that the temporary methods are mostly utilized by people with relatively high educational backgrounds and those living in urban areas. The condom, a simple reversible and nonchemical method of contraception, is widely accepted by couples in the younger age group, mostly for spacing pregnancies.

The government has adopted a primary health-care approach that uses various indigenous and local medical practitioners, traditional birth attendants, and religious and community leaders as change-agents in convincing the eligible couples to adopt family planning. The medical termination of pregnancy, which is legalized in the country, is also considered as one of the methods of family planning. In spite of vast investments in a supportive infrastructure and manpower, the achievements of the Family Planning Program have fallen short of its targets. Rigorous efforts are needed to implement the program more effectively.

Selective Female Abortion and Infanticide

Census counts in India have shown a disturbing pattern, moving from 972 females for every thousand males in 1901, to 934 in 1981 and 927 in 1991. In Haryana, a populous northern state surrounding Delhi, there were only 874 females for every thousand men, an unprecedented disproportion.

A law passed in 1994 by the Indian Parliament provides penalties of three years in prison and a fine of about $320 for those found guilty of administering or taking prenatal tests—mainly ultrasound scans and amniocentesis, solely to ascertain the sex of the fetus. The new law focuses on hospitals and clinics, but leaves the operators of mobile van clinics outside the law's purview. Charges for fetal screening tests can run as low as 150 rupees, about $5, in poor rural areas to ten times as much or more in more affluent urban areas. Under Indian law, ending a pregnancy only because the fetus is female was illegal even before the 1994 law was enacted, even though the practice remains common. No reliable figures are available on the number of abortions performed every year solely to prevent the birth of girls. But, with some clinics in major cities like Delhi and Bombay admitting to conducting as many as 60,000 sex-determination tests a year, child welfare organizations estimate the nationwide figure at tens of thousands every year, possibly higher (Burns 1994).

Another concern among women's groups has been the fear that curbing sex-determination tests will drive many families back to the centuries-old practice of killing baby girls soon after birth, or so favoring boys with scarce supplies of food that girls die young. In a 1993 survey conducted by the National Foundation of India, a private group working on child welfare issues, it was estimated that 300,000 newborn girls die annually from what it called "gender discrimination" (Burns 1994).

B. Teenage Pregnancies

Sexual activity at an early age but within marriage is common in India. The most obvious health risk of teenage sex among the young is pregnancy for girls who are not yet physically matured. Further, if the pregnancy is unwanted or illegitimate, the health hazards are likely to be compounded by the social, psychological, and economic consequences. In their study of infant and childhood mortality, K. Mahadevan et al. (1985) found that the mean age of women at first conception was only 16 years; further, they found that infant mortality was very high for the first, followed by the second birth order, and then tapered down subsequently. The findings reveal that the high incidence of infant mortality among the first two birth orders may be mainly due to teenage pregnancy and childbirth. In traditional societies where mothers marry young, there is family support for the young parents although medical risks remain high. But in today's transitional society, the family support is gone, and many times the teenage pregnancies lead to abortion and thus have dangerous consequences.

C. Abortion

Abortion is not considered a method of contraception in the strict sense, although it is treated as one of the methods of family planning because of its dramatic impact on birthrates. The Medical Termination of Pregnancy Act (1971) has great importance. Attempts are continuously made to induce all women seeking abortion to accept a suitable method of family planning, although abortion is mostly advocated on health grounds. The main health reasons for recommending an abortion are: (1) when continuance of the pregnancy would involve a risk to the life of the pregnant woman or of grave injury to her physical or mental health; and (2) when there is a substantial risk the child, if born, would suffer from such physical or mental abnormalities as to be seriously handicapped. Since the inception of the 1971 Act, the annual number of abortions is around 7.6 million. Despite legalisation of abortion, the lack of trained health personnel and termination by local *Dais* who abort by using unscientific instruments, the death rates for women who have undergone termination of their pregnancies are also high, especially in the remote rural and tribal areas. It is also observed that young unmarried girls who experience a premarital pregnancy and approach unqualified charlatans seeking an abortion also experience similar high risks of mortality and morbidity. Though official statistics on these situations are not available, these situations are common, and their incidence may well be in an upward trend because of modernization and Westernization.

D. Population Control Efforts

See Section 9A.

10. Sexually Transmitted Diseases

The spread of sexually transmitted diseases is affected by sexual promiscuity resulting from marital maladjustment, and in some distinct inadequacies in the social and economic life of India and its health care system. Gonorrhea, syphilis, and other sexually transmitted infections are major problems for young people, especially in urban India where social change is rapid, marriage tends to be delayed, and traditional restraints on premarital intercourse are reduced. Many cases of STD infections remain untreated, especially in the large urban areas, mainly because the sufferers do not know that they are affected, and also because they fear revealing their problem. The lack of scientific knowledge about the diseases among the infected also adds to the misery of the victims. In some communities, parents act as a major source of information on sex for their sons and daughters, but for most of the communities in India, sex is a taboo topic, and parents generally avoid communicating it to their offspring. Among most of the young people in India, even in urban areas, ignorance of the most basic facts about sexuality, conception, and contraception still continues to be the norm. The combination of the rapid social change in India and the ignorance on the basic information about sexuality are creating major and widespred health problems for the young generation.

11. HIV/AIDS

The first confirmed evidence of AIDS infection in India came in April 1986, when six prostitutes from Tamil Nadu tested positive for HIV antibodies. Subsequent findings indicate that between October 1, 1985, and September 30, 1993, a total of 459 AIDS cases have been detected in India, of which 444 are Indians and 15 are foreigners. Data available in early 1995 indicate that thus far 1,898,670 persons have been screened for the HIV virus, and 13,254 were found positive to HIV by the Western-Blot test. The seropositive rate is 6.98 per thousand.

An indication of the population at risk for HIV infection can be found in the millions of STD cases occurring in the country. In addition to being a marker for behavioral vulnerability to HIV infection, untreated STD cases facilitate HIV transmission. In Pune, the HIV infection rate among people seeking treatment for STD has increased from about 9 percent in 1991 to 17 percent in 1992. An infection rate of up to 25 percent was reported in 1992 from surveys among prostitutes in Bombay. Meanwhile, there is little public support for or interest in promoting safer sex practices and condom use among the prostitutes, who are generally viewed as outcasts in India's caste-bound society and deserving of any ills that befall them. Among Bombay's estimated 100,000 prostitutes, the HIV rates shot up to 52 percent in 1994, from 2 percent in 1988. The sale of young girls into sexual slavery in the Persian Gulf complicates the situation (Burns 1996).

The prevalence of HIV infection among the 5 million long-route truck drivers is also very high. Health officials believe that the drivers are at the center of an imminent explosion of AIDS among India's 970 million people. The problem is evident at Petrapole, 75 miles from Calcutta, on the main road between India and Bangladesh. While grimy trucks line up fender to fender for miles, often waiting a week or more to cross the Broken Boat River, thousands of drivers, helpers, and hawkers mix with local women and teenage girls willing to engage in sex for as little as 10 rupees, about 28 cents. It is common for these men to buy sex every day, and sometimes several times a day, while they wait. Researchers estimate that the truck drivers average 150 to 200 sexual encounters with sex workers a year. A single sex encounter can earn a woman enough to feed her family for a day. They seldom use condoms. In late 1996, experts estimated 30 percent of India's long-distance truck drivers were HIV-positive. The impact on the family is already evidence. In a 1994 study by the National AIDS Research Institute in Pune, 100 miles southeast of Bombay, 14 percent of the married women who reported no sexual contact with anyone other than their husband tested HIV-positive (Burns 1996).

The United Nations estimates that by the end of this century, over a million Indians will be sick with full-blown AIDS, and 10 million will be HIV infected. A quarter of the world's projected infected will be in India. Some Indian experts paint a still grimmer picture, estimating that between 20 and 50 million Indians will be infected by HIV by the year 2000. In this event, there will be more AIDS patients in India than there are hospital beds (Burns 1996).

While the principle mode for transmission of HIV infection in India is by heterosexual promiscuity, the prevalence of the disease is also high in intravenous drug users who share syringes and needles. In Manipur state, in India's far northeast, bordering with Burma (Myanmar), Laos, and Thailand, where studies have been conducted by the field-practice unit at the surveillance center for HIV infection in Imphal. The results show that the situation in this area is different from the rest of the country, primarily because injectable heroin is easily available here. After the first seropositive case in Manipur appeared in 1989, HIV infections soared among drug users to 54 percent within six months, By the beginning of 1992, 1,600 HIV-positive cases had been detected, most of them being intravenous drug users.

Apart from unprotected sexual intercourse and intravenous drug injections, contaminated blood transfusion is one of the main sources of infection. In India, the sale of blood for transfusion and for preparation of blood products is a big business and subject to very little control. Estimates of the incidents of HIV-infected mothers transmitting the virus to their children during pregnancy and delivery shows that (Ramachandran 1992) every year twenty thousand out of twenty-four million deliveries in India are likely to occur in HIV-positive women.

More than half of Bombay's sex workers are HIV-positive, according to Dr. Subhash Hira, an Indian-American, who runs as AIDS clinic in Bombay. Currently an estimated 5 million people in India are HIV-positive. Hira predicts that by the year 2000, as many as 20 million Indians will be HIV-positive. However, with the incidence of the virus currently doubling every year, it is more likely that the figure for HIV-infected people in India will be about 15 percent, or 160 million. This, according to Dr. I. S. Gilada, a leading Indian expert on AIDS, could bring a collapse in India's economy, set the country back at least 50 years, and pull it "into a black hole of despair unlike anything seen in this century" (Quoted by Friedman, 1996:12). India's national politicians and public health officials refuse to recognize or discuss this crisis, often considering sex workers as an expendable commodity.

The government has proposed to set up a resort for AIDS Rehabilitation and Control as a preparatory measure to cope with the AIDS threat looming large over the Indian horizon. However, the nation's annual AIDS budget is only about $20 million, or slightly more than two cents a person. Despite an $85 million World Bank loan to set up a national AIDS control organization, India's expendures for the control AIDS is woefully inadequate. In late 1996, with only a year of the program left to run, only $35 million of the $85 had be spent (Burns 1996).

Opponents of spending money on AIDS prevention, including many politicians and other opinion makers, argue that the government should give top priority to controlling diseases like malaria and tuberculosis which kill tens of thousands of Indians every year. In a nation which spends six tenths of one percent of its $50 billion annual budget on all health care, there is little money for educational publicity and free condoms. Some programs have been able to distribute packets of four condoms at two rupees (three cents), about half the usual cost. There is no money for AZT and other drugs (Burns 1996).

Although the HIV virus apparently did not begin to circulate in the Indian subcontinent until about a decade after it arrived in the United States, where the disease was first recognized in 1981, the virus has spread much more rapidly in India than elsewhere. According to a July 1996 report at the eleventh international meeting on AIDS, well over three million Indians were HIV-positive. This number easily surpassed South Africa with 1.8 million cases, Uganda with 1.4, Nigeria with 1.2, and Kenya with 1.1 million.

12. Sexual Dysfunctions, Counseling, and Therapies

A. Concepts of Sexual Dysfunction

The concept of sexual dysfunction in Indian context is defined differently with reference to the persons socioeconomic and demographic backgrounds. Generally, it is differentiated for men and women, young and old, rich and poor, and able-bodied and disabled persons.

B. Availability of Counseling, Diagnosis, and Treatment

There are no legal or other restrictions on who may practice as a psychosocial or sexual therapist in India. Most of the persons with sexual problems who feel that they need some treatment, seek help related to their symptoms. What sexual therapy there is available deals with symptom relief and is generally regarded as successful if this is the outcome. Though there is no clear-cut, government-funded, psychosexual therapy services available in India, most of the health and family planning clinics provide one or more of these services to their clients. Counseling by some of the marriage counseling services, especially in cities, are also widely reported in the society. Quacks who pose as very knowledgeable in sexual therapy, and widely advertise about the effectiveness of their treatment, are commonly seen, especially in rural areas and small towns. Because many people do not understand the need for qualified training of sexual therapists, these fraudulent therapists and their clinics attract many of those who need proper counseling and cash in on their weaknesses.

A prevailing Victorian sexual repression, left over from colonial times, still makes it impossible for many married couples to function well sexually, or even to function at all. Sex clinics around New Delhi and other large cities typically cater mostly to men, and offer advice, hormone injections, and herbal remedies at a cost of up to about $500 for a full course of treatment.

There is no organized data available on such incidences, nor on the effectiveness of their treatments. Moreover, with the topic of sex being a taboo in Indian society, people generally do not discuss their problems openly with others. In the process, they easily become victims of such quacks in their communities.

13. Sexual Research and Advanced Education

There is very little sexological research being carried out in India thus far. Very few institutions have concentrated any effort in this area of research or undertaken any formal program on this important topic. Although there is no graduate or postgraduate program on sexuality in any of the educational institutions, because of the recent widespread discussions of HIV/AIDS, sexually transmitted diseases, and a host of other problems like bride burning and marital violence, there is a growing inclination to undertake research in the area of sexuality, and to impart proper sex education for the people in the society.

The National Institute for Research in Sex Education, Counseling and Therapy (NIRSECT) is the only official professional organization devoted to sexual research in India. Its address is: Saiprasad-C5/11/02, Sector-4,

C.B.D. New Bombay, 4990615, India. The director is Dr. J. K. Nath, first author of this chapter.

Other important sexological organizations are:

Sex Education, Counseling, Research Training Centre (SECRT). Family Planning Association of India (FPAI). Fifth Floor, Cecil Court, Mahakavi Bhushan Marg, Bombay 400 039, India (Phone: 91-22/287-4689).

Indian Association of Sex Educators, Counselors, and Therapists (IASECT) 203 Sukhsagar, N.S. Patkar Marg., Bombay 400 007, India (Phone: 91-22/361-2027; Fax: 91 -22/204-8488).

Parivar Seva Sanstha. 28 Defence Colony Market, New Delhi 110-024. (Phone: 91-11/461-7712; Fax: 91-11/462-0785).

Acknowledgments

The authors wish to aknowledge the assistance of Dr. S. N. Kadam, M.R.C.P.; J. V. Bhatt, M.D.; Dr. V. C. Prabhu, M.B.B.S.; Shirish Patil, M.D.; C. Prakasam, Ph.D.; M. C. Watsa, M.D.; Mrs. S. J. Nath; Mrs. S. V. Nayar; Mr. Khan at the MGM Medical College; Mr. V. S. Rajan; Ms. Chandra Prabha, and M. S. Pawar, Ph.D.

References and Suggested Readings

Ahmed, Swed. I. 1992. "Truck Drivers Are Vulnerable Group in North-East India." An abstract published in the Second Intermational Congress on AIDS in Asia and the Pacific. Randwick, Australia: AIDS Society of Asia and the Pacific.

Bhende, Asha A. 1994. "A Study of Sexuality of Adolescent Girls and Boys in Under-priviledged Groups in Bombay. *Indian Journal of Social Work*, 55(4). Bombay: Tata Institute of Social Sciences.

Bhende, Asha A., and Lata Kanitkar. 1978. *Principles of Population Studies*. Bombay: Himalaya Publishing House.

Burns, John F. 1996 (September 22). "Denial and Taboo Blinding India to the Horror of Its AIDS Scourge." *The New York Times*, pp. 1 and 16.

Burns, John F. August 27, 1994. "India Fights Abortion of Female Fetuses." *The New York Times*.

Chowdhry, D. Paul. 1992. *Women's Welfare and Development*. New Delhi: Inter India Publications.

Department of Family Welfare. 1992. *Family Welfare Programme in India*. New Delhi: Government of India, Ministry of Health and Family Welfare, Department of Family Welfare.

Deva, Krishna. 1986. *Khajuraho*. New Delhi: Brijbasi Printers Private, Ltd.

D'Souza, Anthony A. 1979. *Sex Education and Personality Development*. New Delhi: Usha Publications.

Egnor, Margaret T. 1986. *The Ideology of Love in a Tamil Family*. Hobart and Smith College, unpublished. Cited by Sudhir Kakar, *Intimate Relations*, (1989:11).

Family Planning Association of India (F.P.A.I.). 1990. *Attitude and Perceptions of Educated, Urban Youth to Marriage and Sex.* Bombay: S.E.C.R.T. (Sex Education Counseling Research Therapy Training) F.P.A.I.

Friedman, R. I. 1996 (April 8). "India's Shame: Sexual Slavery and Political Corruption Are Leading to an AIDS Catastrophe." *The Nation*, pp. 11-20.

Jaffrey, Zia. 1996. *The Invisibles: A Tale of the Eunuchs of India.* New York: Pantheon Books.

Kakar, Sudhir. 1989. *Intimate Relations: Exploring Indian Sexuality.* Chicago: University of Chicago Press. New Delhi: Penguin Books India (P) Ltd.

Kakar, Sudhir, and K. Chowdhary. 1970. *Conflict and Choice: Indian Youth in a Changing Society.* Bombay: Somaiya Publications.

Kapur, Promilla. 1973. *Love, Marriage, and Sex.* Delhi: Vikas Publishing House.

Knipe, D. M. 1991. *Hinduism.* New York/San Francisco/London: Harper/Collins.

Mahadevan, K., N. S. Murthy, P. R. Reddy, P. J. Reddy, V. Gowri, and S. Sivaraju. 1985. *Infant and Childhood Mortality in India.* Delhi: Mittal Publications.

Majumdar, N., and T. N. Madan. 1956. *Social Anthropology.* Bombay: Himalaya Publishing House.

Mane, P., and S. A. Maitra. 1992. *AIDS Prevention: The Socio-Cultural Context in India.* Bombay: Tata Institute of Social Sciences.

Nair, P. S., Muralidhar Vemuri, and Fanjdar Ram. 1989. *Indian Youth.* New Delhi: Mittal Publications.

Narayan, S. 1988. *Social Anthropology.* Delhi: Gian Publishing House.

Parasuraman, R., et al. 1992. "STD and AIDS in Homosexuals." *Abstracts of the Second International Congress on AIDS in Asia and the Pacific.* Rand Wick, Australia: AIDS Society of Asia and the Pacific, p. 200.

Pawar, M. S. 1991. "Prostitution and the Girl Child." *Indian Journal of Social Work,* 52(1).

Ramachandran, Prema. 1992. "Women's Vulnerability." *Seminar*, 396:21-25.

Reddy, G., D. Narayana, P. Eswar, and A. K. Sreedharan. 1983. "A Report on Urban (Madras) College Students' Attitudes Towards Sex." *Antiseptic*, September, pp. 1-5.

Savara, Mira, and C. R. Shridhar. 1992. "Sexual Behaviour of Urban Educated Indian Women. Results of a Survey." *Journal of Family Welfare*, 38(1):30-43.

Tata Institute of Social Sciences. October 1994. *Indian Journal of Social Work. Bombay*, 55(4).

Registrar General and Census Commissioner India. 1991. *Provisional Population Totals (Rural-Urban Distribution)*, (New Delhi), paper number 2 of 1991.

Watts, Alan. 1974. *Erotic Spirituality: The Vision of Konarak.* New York: Collier Books.

Weinrich, James D. 1987. *Sexual Landscapes: Why We Are What We Are, Why We Love Whom We Love.* New York: Scribners.

Williams, Walter. 1986. *The Spirit and the Flesh: Sexual Diversity in American Indian Culture.* Boston: Beacon Press.

Indonesia
(*Republik Indonesia*)

Wimpie Pangkahila, M.D., and J. Alex Pangkahila, M.D.

Contents

Demographics and a Historical Perspective

A. Demographics

Located in the archipelago southeast of Asia along the equator, Indonesia comprises some 13,700 islands, including Java, one of the most densely populated areas of the world, with 2,108 persons per square mile. Besides Java, Indonesia includes four other major islands: Sumatra, Kalimantan (most of Borneo), Sulawesi (formerly Celebes), and Irian Jaya (the western half of New Guinea). Bali, known as the "paradise island," is also part of Indonesia. The mountains and plateaus on the major islands have a cooler climate than the tropical lowlands.

In 1997, Indonesia had over 200 million people with more than 300 ethnic groups. The age distribution of the population was: under age 15, 39.2 percent, 15 to 59, 56.5 percent, and 5.3 percent over age 60, and a population density of 262 per square mile. Life expectancy at birth in 1995 was 59 for males and 63 for females. The 1995 birthrate was twenty-four per 1,000 and the death rate eight per 1,000, for a natural annual increase of 1.6 percent. The infant mortality was sixty-five per 1,000 live births. Indonesia has one hopital bed per 1,643 persons, and one physician per 6,861 persons. The literacy rate is 78 percent, and 97 percent attend primary school.

Indonesia is a developing country with major problems in the social and economic areas. Most people still have a low subsistence standard of living. However, the small middle- and upper-class populations have a very good standard of life. It is estimated that the country will join the developed countries in the near future. The 1995 per capita gross domestic product was $2,900.

B. A Brief Historical Perspective

It is generally believed that the earliest inhabitants of the Indonesian archipelago came from India or Burma (Myanmar). Later immigrants, known as Malays, came from southern China and Indochina. This later group is believed to have populated the archipelago gradually over several thousand years. Hindu and Buddhist civilizations reached Indonesia about 2,000 years ago, taking root mainly on the island of Java. In the fifteenth century, Islam spread along the maritime trade routes and became dominant in the sixteenth century. In the seventeenth century, the Dutch replaced the Portuguese as the dominant European power in the area. The Dutch gained control over Java by the mid-1700s, but the outer islands were not subdued until the early 1900s, when most of the current territory of Indonesia came under Dutch rule.

After the Japanese occupation of 1942-1945, nationalists fought four years until the Dutch granted Indonesia its independence. Indonesia declared itself a republic in 1950. In 1957, Indonesia invaded Dutch controlled West Irian (the western half of New Guinea); in 1969, tribal leaders voted to become part of Indonesia, a move sanctioned by the United Nations. East Timor became the twenty-seventh province of Indonesia after tribal and political leaders declared integration in 1975. Since 1965, after the fall of the Communist Party and the late President Sukarno, the government has been led by President Suharto.

1. Basic Sexological Premises

A. Character of Gender Roles

In the traditional Indonesian society, women clearly occupy a lower social status than men. This is still the dominant value in Indonesian culture. The idea that the female's place is in the kitchen is still easy to find, especially in the villages. The husband-wife relationship is a chief-assistant relationship rather than a partnership.

Nevertheless, the role of women is improving in modern Indonesian society. Many women work outside the home, particularly in restaurants, garment, and cigarette factories, even though their wages are lower than those of males. Many female physicians, notaries, and lawyers are found in modern Indonesia. A few women have achieved high political positions as cabinet and parliament members.

B. Sociolegal Status of Males and Females

From the standpoint of national law, males and females enjoy the same rights in schooling and careers. However, in some areas, traditional laws discriminate against females. Only males, for instance, have a right to receive a legacy from their parents. This contributes to a higher status for males. Another consequence of traditional values is that parents insist on having a son, even though the government has proclaimed a limit of only two children per family, regardless of sex. Many pregnant women come to clinics seeking male-sex preselection, even though there is no method that can give a 100-percent guarantee of having a male child.

C. General Concepts of Sexuality and Love

Traditionally, Indonesian women connected sexuality with love, and engaged in sexual activities only with the male they loved, i.e., their husband. Women, it was believed, were not able to have sex with a male unless she loved him. In contrast, the traditional view fully accepted males as having sex with any female they liked. In essence, females were only sexual objects, designed for male pleasure.

This traditional view is changing in modern Indonesia. For many, sex and love are easy to separate and are frequently viewed as two different things. Many females, especially among the young, want to engage in sexual intercourse with anybody they like without the necessity of loving that person. This concept, of course, is not well received by the older generation.

2. Religious and Ethnic Factors Affecting Sexuality

A. Source and Character of Religious Values

During the first few centuries of the Christian era, most of the islands came under the influence of Hindu priests and traders, who spread their religion and culture. Moslem invasions began in the thirteenth century and most of the area was Moslem by the fifteenth. Today, 88 percent of Indonesians are Moslem, with Hindu, Buddhist, and both Protestant and Catholic Christian minorities. There is a commendable degree of religious tolerance among the people.

Christian Portuguese traders arrived early in the sixteenth century, but were ousted by the Dutch around 1595. After Napoleon conquered the Netherlands homeland in 1811, the British seized the islands but returned them to the Dutch in 1816. After the Japanese occupation during World War II ended, nationalists declared Indonesian independence from the Dutch. After a year's fighting, a treaty was signed, political stability returned, and economic development began.

In the past, conservative religious and cultural values had a strong influence on sexual attitudes and behaviors. For instance, it was taboo for male and female adolescents to walk together in public. A daughter who became pregnant before marriage posed a disaster for her whole family.

However, the influence of religious and traditional cultural values has decreased in recent decades, most noticeably since 1980. This is evident in the fantastic changes in the sexual attitudes and behaviors of the people, especially among the young.

B. Source and Character of Ethnic Values

Each ethnic group has its own culture and sexual values. The Javanese and Balinese, for instance, are more modern than the Dyaks and other tribal cultures of Borneo. In general, however, sex is considered something private and even secret. Sex is appropriate only between husband and wife. Women are like maids, there for their husband's benefit. Wives are subservient to their husbands in everything including sexual contact. Some men who engage regularly in homosexual behavior do so because they believe that they have supernatural powers that will disappear if they have sexual contact with women.

In today's globalization trends, sexual attitudes and behaviors are changing rapidly in all the cultures of Indonesia. Premarital sex, for example, is now common among adolescents. Even premarital pregnancy is easy to find and, for many parents, it is no longer the disaster it was only a generation or two ago.

3. Sexual Knowledge and Education

A. Government Policies and Programs

Sex education is not a priority in the government's program. School curricula do not offer students any education on sexual topics or issues. However, the Department of Education and Culture has recommended a book, *About the Sexual Problem in the Family*, by Wimpie Pangkahila, as a source of sexual information for high school students. This 1988 book discusses many sexual problems that occur in Indonesian families as a result of misinformation, misunderstanding, and myths, such as the belief in the harmful consequences of self-pleasuring or the impossibility of pregnancy if sexual intercourse occurs only once a month. This 152-page book is available in many bookstores and some libraries.

The Indonesian Health Department and the National Coordinating Board of Family Planning have a program for Reproductive Health Education. This program, designed for young people, provides seminars on topics of reproductive and sexual health.

In recent years, some secondary high schools have introduced a small segment of sex education as part of their extracurricular offerings. Outside experts are invited to talk about sexuality in these seminars.

B. Informal Sources of Sexual Knowledge

Despite the public reticence about sexuality, the Indonesian people are eager for and need more information about the subject. Hence the popularity of public and semiprivate seminars on sexual topics. Many social organizations for young people, and women's organizations, sponsor seminars for their members with outside experts invited to speak about sexuality.

Some magazines, newspapers, and radio broadcasts also have columns or programs in which sexuality and sexual problems are discussed. Readers and listeners write or call in asking about some sexual issue or problem they are facing. Many people, however, still express a negative reaction to these forms of informal sexual education.

4. Autoerotic Behaviors and Patterns

A. Children and Adolescents

Autoeroticism is common among children in the phallic stage of their psychosexual development. Although some parents report that they watch their children pleasuring themselves to orgasm, many parents are afraid when they discover their children self-pleasuring because they believe this to be an abnormal act.

Autoeroticism is also common among adolescents as a way of tension release. One study by Wimpie Pangkahila found that 81 percent of male adolescents and 18 percent of female adolescents aged 15 to 20 years old engaged in self-pleasuring. Most reported using their fingers, sometimes lubricated with a liquid. Some rubbed against a pillow or mattress. Only a few females reported using a vibrator.

B. Adults

Autoeroticism is very common among adults, especially single adults. The pattern is the same as among adolescents. However, many people still believe that autoeroticism is morally wrong and will result in harmful physical and mental consequences, such as sterility, impotence, and a decrease in memory ability.

5. Interpersonal Heterosexual Behaviors

A. Children

Sexual exploration and sex rehearsal play are common among children as a natural part of their psychosexual development. However, many parents are afraid of such behavior, believing that it results in sexual abnormalities.

B. Adolescents

Puberty Rituals

Some ethnic groups, especially in the remote areas and among tribal people, have ritual ceremonies for adolescents, especially for the female on the occasion of her first menstruation. These ceremonies differ greatly from one ethnic culture to another.

Premarital Sexual Activities and Relationships

Premarital sexual activities are considered taboo. In general, older persons and parents oppose all sexual activities engaged in before marriage. However, during the past decade, there has been a change in sexual attitudes and behaviors among adolescents. Some studies in a few Indonesian cities reveal a growing trend among adolescents to engage in premarital sexual activities such as necking, petting, and even intercourse.

Knowing that parents and the older generation oppose premarital sexual activities, young people hide their activities from them. On the other hand, parents frequently give their children more opportunities to be alone with their boy- or girlfriends. And many adolescents take advantage of these opportunities for sexual activities.

C. Adults

Premarital Courtship, Dating, and Relationships

Dating and premarital sexual relations among adults are very common in modern Indonesian society. The culture requires a particular kind of courtship when a couple wants to marry. In this courtship, the parents and family of the male approach the parents of the female to make the arrangements. In some ethnic groups, a courtship document is signed when presents, such as cows, buffalos, gold, and jewelry, are given. For many people in these groups, this custom is very expensive, because they have to collect enough money to buy the presents for courtship.

Sexual Behavior and Relationships of Single Adults

Self-pleasuring is a common sexual behavior among single adults, even though it is not allowed by religious and moral values. Sexual relationships among male and female single adults are also taboo. However, some data show that many couples engage in sexual relations before they marry. A study by Wimpie Pangkahila suggested a rate of 53 percent for urban couples. Another study of rural, pregnant women found a premarital intercourse incidence of 27 percent.

Many single adult males have sexual contact with prostitutes. Prostitution exists in many places in Indonesia, whether it is legal or illegal. The range of services comes in various classes from low-cheap to high-expensive.

Marriage and the Family

Indonesia has had a marital code to regulate marriages since 1974. The law requires that a marriage be performed in a religious ceremony and then be registered in the civil act office for Christians, Buddhists, and Hindus. The marriages of Moslems are registered in the Moslem Religion Affairs Office.

Extramarital intercourse is common, especially among males. Many married men seek prostitutes or have sexual relations with single or married women. Extramarital intercourse is also found among married women, but in a lower incidence than among husbands. Although married women do have sexual relations with single and married men, most people consider this very bad and unacceptable behavior. In a typical, double moral standard, extramarital sex by males is considered something usual, even though it is forbidden by religion, morality, and law.

Sexuality and the Physically Disabled and Aged

Most Indonesians believe that sex is only for the physically normal and young people. Most feel uncomfortable when a disabled or aged person still thinks about or expresses an interest in sexual activities. However, marriages do occur between disabled persons, or between a disabled and an able-bodied person. Some disabled and many aged people do come to sexual clinics with their sexual problems for counseling and treatment.

Incidence of Oral and Anal Sex

Generally Indonesians do not accept fellatio, cunnilingus, and anal sex as foreplay or sexual outlets. Most people consider these behaviors as abnormal or sinful. On the other hand, many people do engage in fellatio and cunnilingus.

Many men seek out prostitutes only for fellatio, because they enjoy that outlet, but their wives refuse to engage in it. Some women do like to have cunnilingus, but refuse to perform fellatio for their husbands. Still, many couples enjoy both fellatio and cunnilingus as a part of their sexual activities.

Fellatio and cunnilingus are becoming popular among young people as a sexual alternative to vaginal intercourse. Cunnilingus is preferred especially by and for females, because it does not tear the hymen, which many still believe is a mark of virginity. Very few couples engage in anal sex.

6. Homoerotic, Homosexual, and Ambisexual Behaviors

A. Children and Adolescents

Homoerotic or homosexual activities are not common among Indonesian children, although some sexual exploration involving exhibiting the genitals is known to occur.

Some adolescents engage in homosexual activities as a sexual outlet, while others engage in this activity for material gain as homosexual male prostitutes. In one Java society of traditional artists, known as Reog Ponorogo, some adolescents engage in homosexual activities to serve adult males who are believed to have supernatural powers (See Section 1B above).

B. Adults

In general, Indonesians consider homosexuality and bisexuality as abnormal acts forbidden by morality and religions. Despite this taboo, thousands of adults engage in homosexual and bisexual relationships. A Functional Group for Gays and Lesbians exists with branches in some large cities. Most gays and lesbians, however, hide their orientation and activities because they know that most people oppose homosexual behavior.

Since homosexual marriage is illegal, homosexual persons are limited to living-together arrangements and cohabitation. Sexual outlets among homosexual, lesbian, and bisexual-oriented adults include oral sex, anal sex, and mutual self-pleasuring. Some lesbians use vibrators.

7. Gender Conflicted Persons

There are no precise statistics on the incidence of gender conflicted persons. It is estimated that there are thousands of male transsexuals. *Waria*, an abbreviation of *Wanita* (female), and *Pria* (male), are popular terms for gender conflicted persons in Indonesia. In Surabaya, capital city of East Java, Perkumpulan Waria Kotamadya Surabaya or the Association of Waria in Surabaya provides members with support, education, and career training as beauticians, artists, or dancers. These skills hopefully allow *Waria* to support themselves and avoid a life of prostitution. Support groups also provide information about AIDS prevention. Many transsexuals work as prostitutes.

Only a few male transsexuals, usually well-known artists, can afford to have surgery to change their sexual anatomy. The average cost for such surgery is the equivalent of 330 to 400 percent of a middle-class worker's monthly income, about $1,500 to $2,000 in American money.

8. Significant Unconventional Sexual Behaviors

A. Coercive Sex

Sexual Abuse, Incest, and Pedophilia

There is no research on child sexual abuse, incest, or pedophilia. What is known about these issues comes from reports in the newspapers detailing some incidents of coercive sex involving children. Legal penalties exist for persons convicted of child sexual abuse, incest, and pedophilia. The social response to these acts is very negative, and the perpetrators are viewed as criminals.

Sexual Harassment

Even though there is no significant data about sexual harassment, it is believed that it happens very often. Many women who work in factories or offices, or walk along the street suffer from a variety of sexual harassments, although few women realize they are victims of sexual harassment that is contrary to the law. The penalty for sexual harassment may range from three to six months in prison.

Fortunately, in recent years, some women leaders have been trying to educate women that sexual harassment is illegal, and that women have the right to prosecute those who engage in it.

Rape

As with other forms of sexual coercion, there is no significant data on the incidence of rape in Indonesia. Rape incidents perpetrated by an acquaintance, boyfriend, or stranger, and rapes that end in murder are reported in the newspapers. Marital rape is not reported in the news media, although some wives in counseling or therapy do report being raped by their husbands when they refuse to have sexual intercourse.

B. Prostitution

Prostitution is widespread and occurs in many locations from small to large cities. In some jurisdictions and cities, where prostitution is illegal, the law may prosecute either the prostitutes or those who manage the business of prostitution. Childhood prostitution is supported by wealthy sex tourists from the Middle East, Europe, Japan, and other countries, but it is not the extensive problem it is in neighboring nations, like Thailand, Cambodia, Myanmar, and Vietnam (Kristof 1996).

C. Pornography and Erotica

In keeping with conservative tradition, pornography is illegal throughout Indonesia. However, it is not difficult to find blue or hard-core video material. Some people sell pornographic books, magazines, and pictures, despite their being illegal.

9. Contraception, Abortion, and Population Planning

A. Contraception

Indonesia has a national program promoting contraception to help married couples plan their families. This program addresses only married people, and not adolescents or unmarried adults. Information on contraception is provided through women's social organizations, newspapers, radio, and television broadcasts.

In the early 1980s, the government provided free contraceptives at public health centers. In 1988, with an improving economic situation and people recognizing the need for family planning, the government gradually began reducing its support, encouraging people who could afford them to obtain contraceptives from physicians in private practice or midwives with reasonable fees. The poor can still obtain free contraceptive services at public health centers where the only charge is for an inexpensive admission ticket.

The most popular contraceptive is the oral hormonal pill. Women have to be examined by a physician before they can obtain a prescription for it, but renewal of such prescriptions is not limited. Intrauterine contraceptive devices are also popular, followed by hormonal implants.

Despite this limitation of contraceptive information to married women, some adolescents and unmarried adults also use contraceptives. They are available in pharmacies (apothacaries or chemists), and include the condom and vaginal film (tissue). Often the hormonal pill can be obtained without a physician's prescription.

In general, the people do not agree that unmarried people should have access to and use contraceptives. Thus, there is no formal education in the schools about contraceptives for adolescents. Sexually active adolescents and single adults have only informal sources of information about contraceptives: newspapers, television, radio programs, and seminars sponsored by interested social groups.

B. Teenage Unmarried Pregnancies

Unmarried pregnancies are not uncommon, but data is nonexistent. What little information is available simply documents the number of unmarried pregnancies in different years. One urban clinic, for instance, reported 473 unmarried pregnant women seeking aid in 1985-86, a second clinic served 418 pregnant unmarried women in 1983-86, and a third clinic reported 693 unmarried pregnancies in 1984-90. These reports provide only raw data with no perspective, and the frequency and incidence of unmarried pregnancies are much higher than the few studies indicate. Likewise, there are no data that would allow one to compare the incidence of unmarried pregnancies in the cities and rural areas. However, the incidence of abortions performed by traditional healers suggests that unmarried pregnancies are not uncommon in the rural areas.

C. Abortion

Abortion is illegal throughout Indonesia, except for some medical cases to save a mother's life. However, some abortions are performed in clinics in certain cities. It is impossible to obtain any realistic number of abortions performed in Indonesia, simply because it is illegal. In Jakarta, with a population in 1988 of an estimated 8.8 million, one clinic reported 500 abortions per month, while a Bali clinic reported 7 to 10 abortions per day. Abortions are also performed by native healers who use traditional, often unsafe methods that sometimes result in complications.

D. Population Control Efforts

The success of Indonesia's national program of family planning was recognized in 1989 when the United Nations Organization gave its Population Award to the President of Indonesia. Efforts are being made to achieve zero population growth in the near future. These efforts are particularly important considering that the island of Java is one of the most densely populated areas of the world with 2,100 persons per square mile, over 100 million people on an island of 51,023 square miles. By comparison, the states of New York, North Carolina, and Mississippi are each roughly the same size as Java, but have only 18, 6.6, and 2.5 million people respectively.

10. Sexually Transmitted Diseases

Sexually transmitted disease are often found among adolescents and young adults, indicating that the taboos against premarital sex are not observed. The incidence is highest in ages 20 to 24, lower in ages 25 to

29, and in 15- to 19-year-olds. As would be expected given the social customs, the incidence among males is higher than it is among females. The most commonly reported STDs are nonspecific urethritis and gonorrhea. Syphilis is no longer common, although it appears to be increasing in recent years.

Treatment for STDs is available at all health clinics throughout the country. Some years ago, the government sponsored a program to prevent the spread of STDs by providing prostitutes with penicillin injections. Other prevention efforts focus on providing information in group-sponsored seminars and the mass media, newspapers, radio, and television.

11. HIV/AIDS

At the end of January 1997, Indonesia reported 509 cases of HIV infection, and AIDS cases have been reported. Most of the cases were heterosexual persons ranging from adolescence to old age. The real number of HIV-positive and AIDS cases is believed to be much higher than this report.

Prevention efforts have focused on high-risk groups, particularly prostitutes, both female and male, and people who work in the tourism industry. Most of the HIV and AIDS cases in Indonesia have resulted from sexual contact. Prostitutes are one source of infection, but it is estimated that many HIV-positive tourists have come to popular tourist centers like Bali, and some have introduced the virus through sexual contact with local people. Prevention efforts involve providing information on how to reduce the spread of AIDS and blood tests for HIV infection. Campaigns to popularize the use of condoms are conducted in some areas where prostitution is common. Unfortunately, these education efforts do not deter people from unprotected sexual contact with prostitutes. Consequently, cases of HIV and AIDS will likely explode in Indonesia in the near future.

12. Sexual Dysfunctions, Counseling, and Therapies

The diagnostic paradigm used by Indonesian sexologists is basically that of William Masters and Virginia Johnson, with presenting cases of inhibited male arousal (impotence), early (premature) ejaculation, inhibited (retarded) ejaculation, male and female dyspareunia, inhibited female orgasm, and vaginal spasms. A common psychological sequela for males with a sexual dysfunction is a feeling of inferiority with regard to the partner. This feeling is often what brings the male into seek treatment. Many women, on the other hand, tend to hide their sexual problems and feel shy about seeking treatment. Many married women never have orgasm and never tell their husbands. At the same time, many husbands are unaware or do not even suspect that their wives never have orgasm.

Diagnosis and treatment for sexual dysfunctions are available in only a few clinics.

13. Sexual Research and Advanced Education

The Andrology Program at Airlannga University has a postgraduate program (segment) in sexology. The Andrology postgraduate program requires a two-and-a-half-year study in spermatology, experimental reproductive biology, reproductive endocrinology, infertility management, and sexology. Instruction in the sexology specialization includes sexual dysfunction, sexual deviation, and premarital and marital counseling. Some Indonesian sexologists have finished their education and training in the United States, Belgium, and other countries. A few studies of sexuality are currently in process, including management of impotence using intracavernosal injection, and a comparison of sexual perception and behavior in young and old subjects.

At Udayana University Medical School there are two organizations studying sexology as a part of their programs. The mailing addresses for these organizations are:

The Study Group on Human Reproduction. Udayana University Medical School. Attention: Wimpie Pangkahila, M.D., Jl.Panglima Sudirman, Denpasar, Bali, Indonesia

The Indonesian Society of Andrology, c/o Laboratory of Pathology, Udayana University Medical School, Jl.Panglima Sudirman, Denpasar, Bali, Indonesia

Iran
(*Jomhoori-Islam-Iran*)

Paula E. Drew, Ph.D.*

Contents

Demographics and a Historical Perspective

[*Note:* Of all the countries examined in this *Encyclopedia,* Iran is among the most controversial. Major factors in Western/Iranian misunderstandings include the history of British imperial expansionism into Iran, influence struggles between the Soviet Union and the West over oil-rich territories, post-World War II efforts of Iran to nationalize its oil production, and several decades of armed and unarmed conflict between Iran and the United States. Another factor in Iran's negative image in the West has been the

---

*Additional comments by F. A. Sadeghpour, a historian and social researcher, are provided in brackets with the attribution (Sadeghpour); other commentators asked to remain anonymous. The editor's comments are enclosed in brackets with (Editor) at the end.

Salman Rushdie affair. These circumstances conspire to make an objective and scholarly study of sexuality in Iran very difficult.

[Fluent in Farsi, Dr. Paula Drew is a British-born-and-educated cultural anthropologist. While married to an Iranian, she held consecutive tenured positions at the University of Tabriz in northern Iran and the National University of Teheran between 1964 and the fall of the Shah in 1978. In these universities, she taught Iranian women French, German, English, and psychology. For three years, she served as academic and personal advisor to female students in the humanities. She also ran a clinic for mothers and babies in an Iranian oasis community for almost ten years. Her field-note observations formed the basis for her doctoral thesis in anthropology on arranging marriages in Iran. Dr. Drew presents her view of a society torn by modernization, yearnings for traditionalism, undertows of ancient customs, conflicts between urban and rural segments, tensions between newly affluent classes and the historically poor, and the influx of petro dollars, all of these surmounted by intensely complex religio-political conflict and warfare. Since Dr. Drew left Iran in the late 1970s, Iran has seen a revolution, a major war with Iraq, and an upsurge in Islamic activism.

[Several Iranian commentators, all men, reacted strongly to Dr. Drew's depiction of sexuality and gender in Iran. They provided important clarifications and alternative viewpoints. As Dr. Drew's essay makes clear, sexuality and gender have been crucially affected by large-scale changes in Iran's modern history. In a world torn as painfully as Iran, it is probably impossible to attain consensus about the recent tidal changes in sexuality, women's roles, and gender in Iran. In the editor's view, these disagreements exist in a matrix of conflicts between West/Middle East, developed/developing economies, native/foreign, Judeo-Christian/Islamic, and male/female perspectives. There is also a strong overtone of national pride in Iran and its achievements, both under the Shah and the Ayatollah.

[This chapter represents a starting point for disentangling the web of changes that have affected sexuality, gender, women, and reproduction in Iran. (Editor)]

A. Demographics

The Islamic Republic of Iran occupies 636,363 square miles of mainly salt desert area, with many oases and forest areas surrounded by high mountains. Iran is bordered by the former Soviet republics of Azerbaijan, Turkmenistan, and Uzbekistan in the north, by Turkey and Iraq in the west, Afghanistan and Pakistan to the east, and the Persian Gulf on the south. It is slightly larger than the state of Alaska.

Ninety-three percent of Iran's 65 million population are Shi'ite Muslims. An estimated 4 to 6 million Iranians reside outside the country, the majority of these in the United States. Forty percent of Iranians live in rural villages and oasis communities. Sixty percent of Iranians are concentrated in the cities; the north and northwest, and south and southwest are heavily populated. The population density is 92 per square mile. The 1995 age distribution of Iranians was 44.4 percent under age 15; ages 15 to 59, 50.3 percent; and over age 60, 5.2 percent. Life expectancy at birth in 1995 was 66 for males and 68 for females. The 1991 birthrate was thirty-five per 1,000 population; the death rate, seven per 1,000, for a 2.8 percent annual natural increase. The 1992 literacy rate was in the range of 54 percent. Iran has one hospital bed per 650 persons, one physician per 2,000 persons, and an infant mortality rate of 55 per 1,000 live births. The per capital gross domestic product in 1995 was $4,780.

B. A Brief Historical Perspective

Iran, once known as Persia, emerged in the second millennium B.C.E., when an Indo-European group supplanted an earlier agricultural civilization in the Fertile Crescent of the Tires and Euphrates Rivers. In 549 B.C.E., Cyrus the Great united the Medes and Persians in the Persian Empire. Alexander the Great conquered Persia in 333 B.C.E., but the Persians regained their independence in the next century.

When Mohammed died suddenly in 632, he had designated no successor (caliph). Despite the ensuing struggle over religious leadership, the second caliph, Umar (in office 634-644), captured the ancient city of Damascus, defeated the Byzantine Emperor Heraclitus, and annexed all of Syria. Jerusalem and all of Palestine fell to the Muslims in 638; Egypt in 639-641. Islam arrived in Iraq in 637, and in Iran between 640 and 649, replacing the indigenous Zoroastrian faith. After Persian cultural and political autonomy was restored in the ninth century, the arts and sciences flourished for several centuries while Europe was in the Dark Ages. The Caliphs of the Umayyad dynasty (661-750), who ruled from their capital in Damascus, masterminded and extended the great Arab-Islamic conquests of Palestine, Syria, Iraq, Egypt, across North Africa, through Spain, and into France in the west. In south and central Asia, the Caliphs extended their rule to the Indus and as far north as the Jaxartes River. Turks and Mongols ruled Persia in turn from the eleventh century until 1502 when a native dynasty reasserted itself. In the nineteenth century, the Russian and British empires vied for influence; Britain separated Afghanistan from Persia in 1857 (Denny 1987:32-39; Noss and Noss 1990:552-556).

When Reza Khan abdicated as Shah in 1941, his son, Mohammed Reza Pahlavi succeeded him. Under Pahlavi's rule, Iran underwent major economic and social change, strongly influenced by Western culture. Despite the repression of political opposition, conservative Muslim protests led to violence in 1978. The Shah left Iran January 16, 1979, and was replaced two weeks later by Ayatollah Ruhollah Khomeini, an exiled conservative religious leader. An Islamic Constitution was adopted, setting up a theocracy with the Ayatollah Khomeini as the final authority, the sole contemporary representative of the last divinely guided Imam. The complete takeover by very conservative Islamic clerics brought revolts among the ethnic minorities, a halt to Western influences in society, and a tension between the clerics and Westernized intellectuals and liberals that continues to the present. The new regime quickly revoked the Family Protection Act which, under the Shah, allowed mothers some custody rights of their children in cases of divorce, and restored the *Shar'ia* provisions giving child custody to the father. The war with Iraq (1980-1988) was particularly devastating to Iran. In addition to the death of thousands of young males, Iran's economy suffered severely following the 1979-1981 seizure of the American embassy and the break in international diplomatic relations.

Following the Persian Gulf War in 1991, some one million Kurds fled across Iran's northern border into Turkey to escape persecution. Following the 1989 death of the Ayatollah Khomeini, the Islamic authorities were faced with pressure from the business community and middle class to moderate somewhat their opposition to Western influences. In the 1992 Parliamentary elections, President Rafsanjani and his supporters easily won control of the government against the anti-Western opposition.

1. Basic Sexological Premises

A. Character of Gender Roles

Gender roles in Iran must be discussed in terms of different stages of the life cycle and in terms of different kin roles: mother, father, aunt, son-in-law, daughter-in-law, etc. Iran is a dependency culture.

B. Sociolegal Status of Males and Females

Children are raised to be dependent on other family members and to remain so throughout their lives. Children are taught to contribute their labor to the family as part of their duty with no expectation of financial reward or praise. Teenage boys help their father, uncles, or grandfathers in their business. Girls help in the home and with the care of younger siblings. They make few choices with regard to their clothing or the way they spend their time, and have little or no access to money. Working outside the family is frowned upon.

At a suitable age, determined by the parents and other older kin, a husband or wife will be selected for a daughter or son by the mother. She will investigate the health, wealth, and character of the proposed spouse and bring about the agreement of the person's parents that the marriage will take place. She will also ensure the compliance of her son or daughter. The father will negotiate with the proposed spouse's male kin with regard to all financial aspects of the marriage.

Since loss of virginity invalidates these financial agreements, female offspring are physically supervised by older relatives from cradle until the post-nuptial proof of a hitherto-intact hymen. It is thus part of the female role, in the capacity of mother, aunt, or grandmother to participate in the continual supervision of younger females, leaving no opportunity for behavior that might jeopardize nuptial agreements. Once the marriage occurs, the mother-in-law takes over from the bride's mother the responsibilities of supervising her new daughter-in-law, ensuring her fidelity as a wife. The importance of this particular role depends both on the education level of the groom son and the residential situation, i.e., whether patrilocal or neolocal. As a wife, a woman is subordinate to her husband and his older kin, particularly his parents and older sisters. Regardless of her age, a woman's friendships with males are confined to those with her father, brothers, and sons. This is particularly true for upper-class women; the greater her family's wealth, the more likely the female is to be controlled and supervised. At the same time, there is a strong emotional component in father-daughter and brother-sister relationships, including familar touches Westerners would likely consider somewhat erotic, if not lightly sexual.

Like the female, the male has a set of gender-defined kin roles. He remains subordinate to his father, uncles, and grandfathers until the age when his own children are marriageable. As he ages, he acquires more say in the financial affairs of the family. His major arena of power until well into middle age is the control of his wife. His mother, maternal aunts, and older sisters act as allies in enforcing his rules when he is away from home. This makes opportunities for shirking household duties, unmonitored phone calls, or unaccompanied shopping expeditions highly unlikely—let alone opportunities for infidelity. In the 1970s, wives in college and the work force were more often than not accompanied to and from their places of study or business by an older relative or the husband. At the National University of Iran, the guard at the gate would not allow a father or brother to escort a daughter or sister to class within the enclosed campus.

As a father, uncle, and father-in-law, a man's power of veto in family decisions increases with age. He is likely to exercise strong veto over the education of his daughters and the way they dress. In this respect, he sets the rules and his wife carries out the necessary supervision. The gender roles are thus closely tied to maintaining the rules and upholding the honor of the extended family unit.

When the Shah of Iran was ousted in February 1979, the country reverted from a legal system, based on that of Switzerland, to the *Shar'ia* or Islamic law, under which females are not considered legally or mentally the equal of males. A woman must be represented in all legal transactions by a man, by her father or brother if she is unmarried, or by her husband if she is married.

At any time, a woman is at risk of repudiation. Divorce—male-initiated, incontestable, and brought about in a matter of days—can bring the immediate loss of her children to the husband's family. Children under Islamic law are perceived as the "substance of the male," merely incubated by the female body without any biological or genetic contribution. Children thus belong to the male, and Islamic law reflects this by allocating custody of children to the father. It is thus part of a woman's concept of her own sexuality that it is inextricably linked with the production of children; she will love them but forever risk losing them through repudiation. To keep her children, she must not risk repudiation by her husband. In a culture that has not encouraged romantic attachments leading to marriage, and discourages affection and companionship between spouses, the fear of losing her children often sustains the woman's efforts—culinary, domestic, and sexual—to please the husband, at least until the children are into their 20s. This fear of repudiation is stronger today, because of the 1979 restoration of the father's rights to child custody.

This fear of repudiation is further exacerbated by the lack of acceptable societal slots for divorced women. In a country where houses are not rented to single people, especially female, a repudiated woman must inevitably return to the home and control of her parents. Remarriage usually means becoming the wife of a man with custody of children from a previous marriage, who will often address her and refer to her by the title *zan baba*, "Daddy's woman/wife." If the children by an earlier marriage are on friendly terms with the new wife, they may refer to her by her first name or a more appropriate title.

Legal adulthood has little practical meaning because children are always the responsibility of the father, regardless of their age. The war with Iraq (1980-88) saw compulsory conscription to active combat of all males over the age of 12, other than only sons of widows. If a man dies, his brother automatically takes on the financial burden and social responsibilities of the widow and children. In this dependency culture, custom, not law, compels him in this.

If children do not like the arrangements made for them, it is not their place to comment, nor are there social agencies to which they could appeal. Kinship binds more strongly than law. There is also little infrastructure concerned with legalities other than blatant criminality or property disputes.

It is apparent to the careful observer that the legal and social status and rights of Iranian women are very much in transition, creating an unexpected blend of "traditional Islamic" and modern Western values. While the government still warns against a return to the near-Western freedoms that women experienced in Iran under the Shah, the strict fundamentalist practices introduced by the 1979 Islamic Revolution have undergone a major shift. Iranian women are still subject to fines, and sometimes flogging, for not wearing the *chador* (veil); they also suffer from the persistent denial of gender equality in Islamic law. Still, many Iranian women maintain that wearing the *chador* is not repressive, but in fact protects them from sexual harassment when they go out in public.

[In November 1994, thousands of Iranian women marched in a Teheran stadium to celebrate Women's Week and show their support for women's rights and a shift in government policy which started in 1991. The celebrations for the 1994 Women's Week included exhibitions by female artists, award ceremonies for female factory workers, and amnesty for 190 women prisoners. In recent years, a dormant family-planning program has been restarted. State-approved prenuptial contracts allow women the right to initiate divorce proceedings. Restrictions banning women from higher education to become engineers and assistant to judges have been lifted. As a result of these and other developments, the number of women in the workplace and in institutions of higher education have increased. In 1994, 30 percent of government employees were women as were 40 percent of university students, up from about 12 percent in 1978.

[Faezeh Hashemi, the Iranian President's oldest daughter, has become the chief spokeswoman for the emerging women's movement. In 1993, the 31-year-old former volleyball coach organized the first Islamic Women's Olympics in Teheran in 1993. "Our goal was to give women a sense of self-confidence," Ms. Hashemi announced. "In most of the Islamic world, women have cultural problems. They are regarded as a commodity. For Iranian women, the values have changed." She does not see restrictions such as wearing the *chador* as necessarily impeding a woman's career.

[Iranian secularists are not satisfied by this slow return to women's freedoms. They compare an event like the Women's Olympics, which attracted 700 athletes from eleven countries, but was closed to men and photographers, as a continuation of harem seclusion. Meanwhile, fundamentalists are equally unhappy, warning against the subversion of traditional Islamic values by "obscene Western values."

[The younger generation among Iranian government officials and administrators, who are more open to the West, are working to create their own complete and comprehensive version of Islamic fundamentalism that will rival Western liberalism and be viewed as better than it and other alternatives (*The New York Times* 1994). (Editor)]

C. General Concepts of Sexuality and Love

Iranian culture is quite comfortable with speaking openly about all the physical aspects of sexuality and sexual responses. This includes open teasing about the physical side of sexuality. There is, however, a strong taboo when it comes to mentioning or discussing the emotional aspects of relationships.

The onset of attraction to the opposite sex is generally spoken of in physical terms. Teenage boys are openly subjected by older kin to routine inquiries as to their health and capacity for erections, as soon as hair appears on the upper lip. "Your mustache is beginning to sprout. Do you need a wife yet?" is a more coy version of the same inquiry. The physical maturation status for young girls is measured by the onset of menarche.

Among young people, feelings of love for a person of the opposite sex are, if suspected by older kin, thought of as something to be ignored or ridiculed away rather than respected and indulged. Such feelings are only considered if they are directed towards a person found suitable for marriage after investigation by the older kin. Love is not considered a basis or prerequisite for marriage, which in turn is the only acceptable social matrix for sex.

Popular Iranian songs speak of love. Soap operas on Teheran television make much of love matches thwarted by economically more viable arrangements made by parents. Both songs and soap operas reflect the social reality. Young people see and are attracted by the face and form of members of the opposite sex, but such feelings cannot be nurtured and encouraged by dating into a situation where emotional and physical inclinations coalesce, unless there is social and financial eligibility for an imminent marriage approved by the older kin on both sides.

Even where a boy and girl meet these requirements, they will be most carefully watched to make sure they do not anticipate financial settlements. A girl who loses her virginity before such financial matters are agreed upon is not considered as having behaved immorally, but as having given the other side an advantage in negotiations, in that the girl's parents cannot now threaten to withdraw from the match, however poor the terms offered. Emotional attachment in marriage is considered desirable on the part of the wife towards the husband, but not vice versa. The male's power and control over his wife is considered in jeopardy if he is overly fond of his wife. In the early months of marriage, the husband's father and older brothers will often set up competing demands on the young man's time should they become privy to any prior arrangements he has made with his new wife. A husband will be ridiculed if he shows the weakness of acceding to his wife's wishes. A man's mother and older sisters will also often erect barriers in the way of companionship and intimacy between spouses by their continual presence and superior claims on the husband's time.

2. Religious and Ethnic Factors Affecting Sexuality

A. Religious Factors

[Islam, the dominant faith of Iranians, has two traditions or divisions: Sunni and Shi'ite. The Shi'ites, who account for 93 percent of Iranians, regard 'Ali, the son-in-law of Muhammad, as the founder's proper successor, while Sunni Muslims follow the three caliphs who actually succeeded Muhammad. Shi'ite Muslims believe that God guides them through the divine light descending through 'Ali and several Imams, or divinely guided "leaders" of Shi'ism. Shi'ites have never ceased to exercise *ijtihad*, the intellectual "effort" of Muslim jurists to reach independent religio-legal decisions. Shi'ite Muslims are generally considerably more flexible and adaptive than the Sunni Muslims. However, both Shi'ite and Sunni Muslims consider each other to be members of the same tradition of faith, order, and community. To understand the connection between Islam and sexual attitudes and behavior, it is important the keep in mind that the worldwide Muslim community or *Umma* can be compared with a triangle whose sides represent history, the religious doctrine/ritual, and culture. In different historical eras in Iran's long history, as well as in other Muslim countries and communities, the balance between these three elements varies. At times, doctrine and ritual are emphasized over culture and history. At other times, cultural and ethnic identity within particular regions have been emphasized. At still other times, Muslims have emphasized the ideal of certain historical eras of Islam. Still, all three dimensions are essential to the *Umma*. (Denny 1987:5-12, 32-71; Noss and Noss 1990).

[While the number of Sunni Muslims in Iran is much smaller than that of the Shi'ites, they and other minorities of Christians, Jews, B'hai, Zoroastrians, Ismailies, Sikhs, and Buddhists quietly reside in isolated communities. There are also seven to eight million ethnic Kurds and Belouch, the majority of whom are Sunni Muslim (Denny 1987; Noss and Noss 1990). (Editor)]

Islam, like other monotheistic religions, prohibits pre- and extramarital sex. Sex between two adults married to others is condemned as the most serious of sins (*zina*)—under Islamic law, adultery and fornication incurs the penalty of stoning to death. Some Islamic countries have at different points in time lifted the death penalty for adulterous males, while retaining it for females. In Iran and probably most Islamic countries, adultery is rare, not because of Islamic prohibitions but because of social mores that segregate the sexes and allow no privacy. [F. A. Sadeghpour says, "In the upper classes, it is rampant, for both men and women!"] The Islamic sense of pollution, which prohibits all acts of worship under certain conditions of spiritual and physical uncleanliness, makes public—and therefore amenable to control—otherwise-private, biological events such as menarche, menstruation, sexual contact, and ejaculation.

Males who have ejaculated, females whose external or internal organs have had contact with seminal fluid, and females who are menstruating may not pray or touch a copy of the Qur'an without first performing ablutions. Since these ablutions were not possible in the majority of Iranian houses in the 1970s, these necessary ablutions had to be performed at public facilities and were therefore open to public scrutiny. Prayers were said individually within the home, but audibly and in full view of others at the prescribed times of the day. Thus anyone who, through fear of committing sacrilege, had to abstain from ritual recitation of prayers or from the obligatory periods of fasting set down by the Islamic calendar, would be subject to scrutiny and interrogation by older family members about the reason for such abstention.

Most Iranian housing consists of a one-story, single large room, or two-story, two-room, with-curtain-hung alcoves, a private courtyard enclosed by a high wall, and a toilet/bath in one corner of the courtyard. The wealthy can afford to live in moderate high-rise apartments, but these are limited because of the danger of earthquakes. This architecture and the desert environment makes privacy a premium.

Menarche announces itself to the entire household when a young girl is unable to recite her prayers. This is often the signal for parents to conclude marriage arrangements, so that the girl can be wed before her second menstruation. Intercourse between married members of the household is similarly monitored. Conception or failure to conceive is similarly apparent to all. The approximate time of any woman's ovulation can be informally calculated by interested parties. Wet dreams and visits to houses of prostitution can be surmised by the family in the same way, by watching who does and does not pray and when. Wash basins or pools for routine washing of the face, hands, and feet are set in full view of all household members in the hallway or yard. Bathing the body under a shower takes place at the neighborhood bathhouse where abundant hot water is available for a modest sum. Taking a shower, for the most part, is seen not so much as a hygienic measure, but as a way of ridding the body of anything that makes it spiritually unclean and the person unfit to participate in religious activities. The body parts are washed in ritualized sequence with prescribed prayers. The bathing practices of family members reveal a great deal of otherwise private information to those interested in monitoring them. The rituals of Islam thus abet the older members of the family in their task of controlling the sexual behavior of all those potentially reproductive or sexually active within the household.

There is a strong resistance among older women to the growing practice of installing hot water systems in the home. Although simplifying their dish-washing and laundry tasks, an automatic hot water system interferes with their ability to supervise the bathing practices of their husbands, offspring, and daughters-in-law, and thereby keeping tabs on their sexual behavior. Even in houses with a shower, the matriarch of the household often controls the means of igniting the hot water system. Similarly, she controls the supply of laundered undergarments and towels, keeping them tied up in bundles so that nobody can retrieve these essentials without her help.

Although the Qur'an does not prescribe the covering of the head for women nor the separation of men and women in public places, Iranians follow a style of dress and segregation of the sexes characteristic of Islamic societies of the Middle East. In Iran, some cities have always been more conservative than others in this regard, but the Ayatollah Khomeini did much to bring about conformity to the strictest code by making violations subject to immediate physical punishment at the hands of the young revolutionary guards, the Pastoran. [Commentators strongly agree with this observation.] The traditional veil or *chador*, which in many villages and towns often concealed only the back of the head and the general outline below the waist, is now supplemented with bandannas pulled low over the forehead, and thick stockings to conceal lower limbs not completely covered by loose pants. The outline of the ankle has to be obscured because its dimension is thought to be related to that of the vagina. The veil itself is pulled firmly across the face and chest, as was always the custom in Qum, Mashad, and most of Tabriz. Now "modesty" is a requirement for all girls over the age of 9. No hair must show around the face.

By custom, certain times of the day are "women's hours" on the streets and few men are about. At other times, only men throng the streets, so a woman would be conspicuous and likely to be harassed. Many stores have sex-segregated service lines, often with a curtain separating the two. Public baths have days for women and days for men, identified by the color of the flag hoisted above the establishment. Schools, too, are segregated to the point that girls' schools employ only female personnel at any level. Places of worship are divided into men's and women's quarters with separate entrances. Informal prayer meetings are only for one sex or the other. Many celebrations and funerals in private houses send males and females into separate rooms. Women are barred from many places, such as some cinemas, restaurants, and tea houses. Other places, such as swimming pools and ski areas, allow families to enter but not young men or women, either singly or in same-sex groups. Young multiage groups of cousins might be allowed into a cinema, if several of the older males are obviously in charge.

The Iranian culture, especially now with its conservatism bolstered by the Islamic regime, is not one in which people of the opposite sex can meet casually. Clandestine meetings, for which there are few arenas, are made dangerous by the pervasive armed guardians of Islamic law, the Pastoran, who demand to see marriage certificates of couples on the street, at beaches, and parks.

B. Ethnic Factors

Just over half of all Iranians are Persian, 25 percent Azerbaijani, and 9 percent Kurd. Although the vast majority of Iranians are Muslim, each has its own distinctive character with regard to the extent to which Islamic dress codes for women, and sexual segregation in streets and public buildings are enforced. [For instance, the Baktiari, Quashquai, and Lore tribes, who live in the Zagros Mountains in the west, do not follow the Islamic dress codes or the practice female segregation in public places. Although these tribes are Muslim, they do not comply with the Islamic regime's heavy handiness. (Sadeghpour)]

3. Sexual Knowledge and Education

A. Government Policies and Programs for Sex Education

Under the Shah's regime, which ended in 1978, the state school biology curriculum for the second year of high school included a section on human reproduction, showing the mechanics of meiosis, or egg and sperm production. Such information, revealing that males and females both contribute genetic material to the production of a fetus, runs counter to a central underpinning of Islamic law with regard to child custody, i.e., that the child is the product solely of male seed. When Islamic law was reinstated by the Ayatollah Khomeini, it was necessary to suppress any dissemination of the idea that males and females both contribute materially to the production of a child.

Even before the 1978 revolution, and despite the passage of the Compulsory Education Act of 1953, many female children were withdrawn from school before the onset of puberty. The Compulsory Education Act required children to remain in school until age 15. However, the birth of a newborn girl was commonly recorded as having occurred two years prior to her actual birth date among all but the educated elite. The parents then had government documentation in hand that their daughter was 15 and old enough to leave school, when in reality, she may not even have reached puberty. During the Shah's regime, efforts to curb this practice were frustrated by the fact that few births took place in a medical setting with personnel able to provide documentation.

The other chief formal source of information on human sexuality is provided by the compulsory religious instruction curriculum in the public schools. In religious instruction classes, students are taught the format of prayers to be said at the five daily prayer times prescribed by Islam, and the rules of purity and pollution surrounding them. Details of prerequisite ablutions of the genital and other orifices of the body provided information on anatomical differences between the sexes. Information is also given on the measures to be taken prior to prayer to counter the polluting effects of urination, defecation, expectoration, expulsion of nasal mucus, menstruation, childbirth, ejaculation, and penetration of the vagina (human and animal) to restore spiritual purity. These measures require that the student have detailed knowledge of the reproductive organs and sexual practices. The Islamic clergy, or Mullahs, also disseminate this type of information on television, in the mosque, and in the many informal neighborhood prayer meetings.

The general trend of this information, whether given by lay teachers or mullahs, is to present sexual behavior as the most polluting form of elimination, which renders the participant spiritually and physically unclean. Sexual behavior of any kind obstructs spiritual readiness. Whereas the polluting effects on the body and spirit of urination or defecation can be washed away in a bathroom with a sink or a shower, orgasm or sexual contact with a person or animal requires a more ritualized bathing with accompanying spiritually cleansing words.

Television programs in Iran regularly deal with the finer points of Islamic observance, such as determining the readiness or otherwise for prayer in ambiguous situations such as nursing mothers, sufferers from vaginal discharges, and males awaking in a state of sexual arousal. Often the format of the program is one in which viewers' letters are answered by experts in Islamic practice.

B. Informal Sources of Sexual Knowledge

The nature of Iranian family and social life offers a major informal source of sexual knowledge.

There is little coyness about the physical aspects of sex. Because it interrupts fasting and prayer schedules, menstruation is openly mentioned by men and women. Pregnancy's physical aspects are not only discussed in intimate detail, but the taboos against males' touching women are lifted during pregnancy, so that males can feel free to pat a pregnant woman approvingly on the abdomen. Breast feeding is also subject to few social taboos. Women breast-feed in public places and in mixed company in private houses with no attempt to cover the breasts. A little milk, believed to be stale, is usually expressed quiet openly from each breast before beginning to nurse. So although faces and limbs are assiduously covered, the nursing breast is displayed quite blatantly. [This is characteristic of provincial and lower-class urban Iranians. (Sadeghpour)]

Little girls of all ages are kept well covered. In many provincial towns, girl babies are hidden completely under their mother's *chador* on the street. Toddler girls wear *chadors* often with only a pacifier protruding from its folds.

Little boys are often bare from the waist down, obviating the need for diapers outside. At any age, males may urinate openly in the street or at the roadside. Older males often seek the partial privacy of a tree or wall. Most, however, orient themselves in a way so as to avoid the sacrilege of urinating while facing Mecca, even if it then means facing an audience. Many men, subsequent to urination, bend down and bathe the head of the penis in any convenient pool or stream of water, to avoid the spiritual defilement of a drop of urine before prayer. Females' visual knowledge of male anatomy is derived largely from seeing little boys unclad and males of all ages urinating and washing in public.

Prior to puberty, male children gain a much more extensive knowledge of female anatomy at all stages of the life cycle, and all stages of pregnancy and lactation, by virtue of the fact that their mothers take them to the public baths with them on "women's day." The public baths consist of waist-deep bathing pools for communal bathing and private shower rooms for families. No one bathes completely alone. Women of all ages are unclad. Most wear loose drawers in the public areas, but are otherwise nude. Within the privacy of the shower rooms, little boys therefore observe their grandmothers, mothers, aunts, sisters, and female cousins taking showers and being depilated of all body hair. Female bath attendants, who assist in applying the leefah and pumice stone, also assist in the removing of facial and leg hair with a kind of scissor made of twisted threads, and in the shaving of the pubic regions and armpits. The bath attendants enter the cubicles wearing a *chador*, which they then remove to work in the nude. They themselves are devoid of all body hair. It is up to the bath attendants to decide, based on their own observations, whether a young boy is too old to be present on women's day. Clearly men retain in adulthood images of what they saw in the bathhouse during childhood. Many speak openly, with disgust and derision, of the effects of pregnancy and the aging process on the female body. Females, however, lack this kind of longitudinal information on males, because fathers do not take children with them to bathe. [These observations do not apply to upper- and rich-class families, which commonly have showers in their homes. (Sadeghpour)]

Children are aware from an early age that an intrinsic part of wedding preparations is the setting out of the wedding night sleeping quarters for the bride and groom. The first night after the wedding has to be spent within the supervised setting of the family. Children learn too that something painful involving blood is going to happen to the bride, and that for her protection against excessive brutality on the part of the groom, older female kin have their bedding set out within earshot, often with only a curtain separating them from the bridal couple. (The prevalence of voyeurism, mentioned in Section 8 below, also provides a rich informal source of sexual knowledge.)

Another informal source of sexuality information is American and European adult magazines such as *Playboy* and *Penthouse*. Until the crackdown of the Islamic regime, these magazines were on sale everywhere and openly displayed in homes. They were a source of pictures to decorate the walls in private houses, particularly in the kitchen and areas of the house off-limits to formal visitors. Although the magazines can no longer be openly sold, back issues still abound and old centerfolds still adorn some family rooms.

In the absence of many other forms of recreation, watching television has become a major urban pastime. Since there are only three Government-run television channels, and since their regular scheduled programming is often supplanted, without announcement, by religious broadcasts, satellite-dish television keeps the general public aware that the position of women, and patterns of courtship, marriage, and sexual behavior, are much more liberal outside Iran. In 1994, Iranian-made satellite antennae cost $700 and small, low-tech antennae sold through the black market for as little as $400. An estimated 200,000 Iranian families have dishes, but it is common for several neighboring families to reduce the cost even more by tying in their television sets to a single jointly purchased dish.

For some years, Iranian satellite dishes were able to bring in everything from late-night soft pornography films from Turkey to the BBC news. Most satellite programs were handled by the Hong Kong-based Star TV. The most popular satellite programs were "Dynasty," "The Simpsons," "Baywatch," "Moonlighting," "Wrestlemania," professional American basketball, and an Asian version of MTV. The Donahue and Oprah Winfrey talk shows, which regularly deal with sexual and relationship issues, were also very popular in a society where a woman's ankle cannot be exposed in public. Until December 1994, when the Government outlawed satellite television antennae, this source of sexuality information encouraged the adoption of Western ideas of fashion and relationships. [For the rich, this has always been the norm. (Sadeghpour)] Of necessity, even before they were outlawed, satellite antennae were carefully hidden from the representatives and enforcers of religiously conservative dictates from the Ministry of Culture and Islamic Guidance.

In 1994, threatened with a loss of their captive audience, the mullahs fought back with Government efforts to jam the satellite reception. Members of the popular militia, known as *bassijis*, began barging into homes to smash satellite receivers (Hedges 1994). On December 25, 1994, after months of debate, the Iranian Parliament ratified a ban on satellite dishes. Once the ban is routinely approved by the Guardian Council, dish owners would have thirty days to remove them or face confiscation and trial with unspecified penalties. The Interior Ministry and Secret Service agencies were ordered to prevent the import, distribution, and use of satellite dishes "with all the necessary means." Some lawmakers warned that, if people refused to comply with the ban, the forceable removal of satellite dishes would violate their right to privacy and could lead to serious political repercussions for the Islamic Government.

In addition to their interest in controlling sexual information and sexually explicit material available to Iranians on satellite television, the government has very mixed feelings about allowing access to the Internet. *Sobh*, the monthly newspaper of the most puritanic clergy, has called for a ban on the Internet, similar to the ban on satellite-television antennae enacted in 1994. However, as of late 1996, the Parliament had yet to take up the issue. Rapid upgrading of telephone lines, growing pressure from scientists interested in communicating with colleagues around the world, and clergy interest in spreading the message of Islam by making computerized texts of both Sunni and Shi'ite law available on the World Wide Web are forcing the government to open up some access to the Internet. The government is trying to centralize all access through the Ministry of Posts and Telecommunications, which is struggling to screen the rapidly increasing number of sites on the World Wide Web, and block access to objectionable sites with a "firewall." The Ministry is constantly updating its list of banned Web sites and information, ranging from pornography sources like "playboy.com," to opposition groups like the Mujahedeen Khalq, based in Iraq, and abhorred religious faiths like the Bahai, as well as any information seen as Western propaganda (MacFarquhar 1996b).

Cost remains a major hurdle for most Iranians seeking information on the Internet. The Government charges large initiation fees, and bills Internet use at the same high rates as long-distance phone calls.

Outside the Government, a few services have established Internet links. Since 1994, much of the Iranian university system has depended on a trunk line established by the Institute for the Study of Mathematics and Science to a sister institution in Austria. But with an estimated 30,000 people having accounts, and the trunk line limited to six users at a time, getting through requires patience. There is also an ongoing feud between the universities and the Telecommunications Ministry over whether the universities will be allowed to keep their independent access once the government's system is operational. In 1996, Teheran's energetic Mayor, Gholam Hussein Karbaschi, had a municipal bulletin board and an e-mail system that forwarded messages internationally, but exchanges often took at least twenty-four hours. Professors and students were suspicious that messages sent and received on this municipal service were screened and deleted when found objectionable, but the Mayor denied messages were vetted, blaming the huge backlog for lost exchanges. Government officials have already admitted they cannot control access to objectionable information on the Internet mechanically, so the future of access to sexuality information on the Internet remains uncertain.

4. Autoerotic Behaviors and Patterns

The subject of self-pleasuring is apparently taboo or unacknowledged because its only reference appears to be within the context of preprayer ablutions requirements on the male after voluntary ejaculation.

5. Interpersonal Heterosexual Behaviors

A. Children

Children do not play unsupervised. An invitation to a child to play at the house of a neighbor or a schoolmate always includes the mother. Such invitations are in any case rare, as are all social interactions with nonkin. Children, in general, play with their cousins under the watchful eye of all mothers. Female children are watched very carefully. Access to information on sex-rehearsal play would be severely hampered by cultural taboos on admitting anything detrimental about one's children, especially to nonkin.

B. Adolescents

Puberty Rituals

The male puberty rite of circumcision, which formerly celebrated the onset of manhood, has for many years now been more customarily performed at the age of 5 or 6 for children born at home, and at two days old for those born in a medical setting. Boys circumcised after infancy wear a girl's skirt for several days, ostensibly to prevent chafing of the unhealed penis, but also to proclaim their status to others. By puberty, all Muslim Iranian boys must be circumcised if they are to participate fully in religious activities.

Female circumcision, common in African Muslim cultures, does not occur in Iran. For Iranian girls, there is some ambiguity about her societal status from the age of 9 on. In the Iranian brand of Shi'ite Islam, a girl of 9 is judged to have reached the age of understanding. She is therefore expected to say her prayers and abstain from food during periods of prescribed fasting. As a fully participating Muslima in many layers of society, she is expected to assume modest dress, i.e., the *chador*, if she has not already done so. More conservative Mullahs in Iran have construed the phrase "age of understanding" to mean age of readiness for marriage. The Islamic regime of the Ayatollah Khomeini has encouraged a return to this interpretation, promoting child marriages in which the 9-year-old girl joins her husband's household (patrilocal). The marriage, however, is not consummated until after her first menstruation. The child bride often shares a quilt at night with her mother-in-law, who, because of the prevalence of cousin marriage, is more often than not the bride's paternal or maternal aunt.

Premarital Sexual Activities and Relationships

It can be said that there are no societally approved premarital sexual activities. The sexes are separated by adolescence. Young single males join male kin for most social activities. Young single females stay with the women in the family. Many young girls are married immediately after menarche. [Several commentators questioned this broad generalization. (Editor)]

A young virgin who joins a household as a live-in maid, is often required by both her parents and her employers to submit to a medical examination to establish whether her hymen is intact. Written into her employment contract is the amount of cash penalty payable by the employer should she lose her virginity (as determined by a second medical examination) during her employment. This contract protects her from the advances of male members of the household, as well as from male visitors to the house, by placing the onus on her employer to protect her and supervise her. In her subordinate capacity, she is extremely vulnerable to rape and seduction. Households employing young girls are also vulnerable to extortion by her parents. Her certificates of pre- and postemployment virginity are also documents that feature in her own prenuptial negotiations. Despite these precautions, young servant girls are usually considered fair game for sexual advances and harassment by males in general.

C. Adults

Premarital Courtship, Dating, and Relationships

Courtship takes place in a supervised, formalized setting. All marriages are arranged, even those based on love matches and mutual inclination. Since male kin, especially the father, passes on the groom's portion of the family estate when he marries, the bride's kin have to know how much is involved before they consent to their daughter's betrothal. The older generation therefore controls all meetings between those seeking to marry each other.

A young man visits the girl he intends to marry accompanied by at least three older members of his family. He will be received in the dining room by her parents and relatives. The girl herself will often appear only fleetingly and not speak unless questioned directly. Marriage often follows betrothal by a matter of days. Often a contract is signed in the presence of a Mullah, making the couple legally married and all financial agreements legally binding. The wedding celebration for the families is held off for up to a year. In some families, especially in Teheran, the couple is allowed to go out together between the official signing of the marriage contract and the wedding celebration. Sometimes the groom's family and sometimes the bride's family will prohibit such contact because during negotiations proof of virginity has been spelled out as a prerequisite to the finalization of property transfers. Urban and landless families usually have no such considerations.

Mild public displays of affection are tolerated between urban middle-class couples during the prewedding period. The couple, however, is seldom completely alone, even when allowed to go to the cinema or an ice cream parlor. Usually there are siblings on either side in tow as a precaution against anything beyond hand holding or chaste kisses on the cheek.

Marriage and the Family

The Shah imposed severe legal restraints on the Islamic style and ideal of polygamy, four wives to one husband. During the 1960s, it was rare to find a polygamous household in which the multiple spouses were under the age of 55.

A form of temporary marriage (*mut'a*), thought unique to Iran, had been very common during the times when long religious pilgrimages were undertaken on foot or horseback. Males could take on for the duration of the trip a female traveling companion, whom they legally married, but only for a specific number of days or weeks, as spelled out in the marriage contract. Resulting offspring were then legitimate with a claim to the father's support and a right to his name on the birth certificate. This form of marriage became more and more rare over time though never officially delegalized. The form was repopularized during the Khomeini regime as a form of legalized prostitution for the destitute left by the Iran-Iraq war, and as a source of income for the Mullahs in their capacity as officiators at the signing of the temporary marriage contracts.

Monogamy, however, has long been established as the norm for both urban and rural households. Traditionally, newly married couples were given quarters in the household of the groom's parents. This pattern persists in rural areas. Young couples in the cities now often rent an apartment, usually in close proximity to the groom's parent's house. The groom's mother, and sometimes the bride's younger sister, stay with the newlyweds for the first few weeks of marriage. The groom's mother sets her guidelines for the way the house is to be run. From the beginning, everything serves to compartmentalize the aspects of the marriage relationship and prevent any spillover of feeling to be expressed in physical expressions of affection or the companionship of shared daytime activities.

The bride is prepared for her wedding night at a prenuptial bath in which her pubic hair is removed for the first time. Her mother-in-law and her own mother will sleep in close proximity to the marriage bed on the first night. Both will inspect the specially prepared handkerchief, which will provide evidence of both a broken hymen and ejaculation. If a honeymoon trip is undertaken, the couple will seldom travel alone, but be accompanied by a couple of younger siblings, or maybe an older sister. Honeymoon companions are particularly common for females of the middle class and among university students.

At home, the couple cannot retire until the groom's mother deems it is a fit hour for everyone. Generally, sleeping arrangements are such that the couple cannot rely on uninterrupted privacy. Iranian houses do not have rooms set aside exclusively as bedrooms. Nothing prevents a mother-in-law from setting up her bedding adjacent to that of her son and his wife, or in such a way that she has an excuse to walk by during the night en route to the kitchen or toilet. A pattern is then set for sex in marriage to be quick and almost furtive with ejaculation of the male as the prime or even sole goal.

Incidence of Oral and Anal

The general lack of privacy inhibits all but the most perfunctory intercourse. Anal penetration of the female is a common means both of birth control and avoidance of possible contamination with menses. Khomeini's writings provide guidelines for preprayer ablution after penetration of the anus and animals under separate headings, though he considered the latter practice unworthy of practicing Muslims.

6. Homoerotic, Homosexual, and Ambisexual Behaviors

In the same way that admissions about sexual behavior in children are impossible, homosexuality in a family member cannot be acknowledged. The derogatory term *cuni* (from *cun* = backside) is used to describe men outside the family, whose gait or voice is considered effeminate. Men who do not marry stay with their natal family all their life. Within the family, some such men are described as *na-mard* (not-men). Implicit in the term is a suggestion of phallic underdevelopment or dysfunction. Other older single men are described as not having found a wife yet, the implication being that they are physically normal but financially ineligible for marriage.

Male homosexuality is condemned by Islam and overt homosexuality is unknown. Just as most heterosexual relationships lack an emotional component, it is to be expected that homosexuality be predominantly physical and without an emotional component. Long-term, companionable homosexual relationships are rare. Two unmarried men (of whatever sexual orientation) would be unlikely to be able to set up house together, because of strong societal pressures against any unmarried person living beyond the pale of family control. However, since there are many exclusively male social arenas—tea houses, political and religious organizations, and men's days at the bathhouse—there are more opportunities both for male/male physical contact and for the setting up of clandestine meetings between males. Women, as noted earlier, do not have similar occasions for privacy in same-gender relationships. Iranian culture also allows men a great deal of public touching, embracing, kissing, and holding hands for prolonged periods while walking or in conversation.

Other than among siblings, women do not enjoy an equal freedom. Although a similar situation applies to females with regard to touching and embracing, most are married or have marriages already being arranged for them before they reach a stage of physical/hormonal development at which they are aware of their own sexual orientation. Homosexual orientation in females has therefore little chance for expression.

Lesbianism is reported to occur in one of the very few residential situations for unmarried women, nurses' training hostels. It is possible that homosexually oriented females select a nursing career as one that allows opportunities for intimate contact with other women.

7. Gender Conflicted Persons

Since each person's behavior is strictly controlled by older family members, no overt expression of gender conflict, such as transvestism, would be tolerated. A child suffering from a physical or emotional deviation from narrow, accepted norms is generally kept from public view. Expression of any kind of individualism in unconventional dress or hairstyle is almost impossible, because of the power and the control of access to funds of the parent generation throughout the life cycle of the offspring. The burlesque theater with its morality plays (*tazieh*) performed in the street or market place could provide a niche for gender-conflicted males, because female roles are played by tradesmen. This theater is largely thought of as a disreputable arena for the marginalized, providing a normal social framework for those without kin.This theater plays no part in upper-class mores.

8. Significant Unconventional Sexual Behaviors

A. Coercive Sex

Sexual Abuse

Since marriages can be contracted at any point after a girl has reached the age of 9, it is legally feasible for a very little girl to be married to a man of any age, and thus be physically at his mercy. This no doubt constitutes the broadest category of potential sexual abuse of children. One of the strongest arguments made in Iran against the custody of children, particularly girls, being given to the mother, is that on her remarriage, the children will be in danger of sexual abuse from the new husband.

Sexual abuse of children, particularly little girls, often occurs at the hands of uncles and cousins staying under the same roof. In such cases, the child's mother is inevitably blamed for leaving her child unguarded, and little outrage is directed at the abuser. Sexual abuse of children in a family setting is not the concern of the police, nor are there any relevant social agencies to which it could be reported. A young servant boy would be withdrawn from the household by his parents if he were the victim of abuse. Only in the case of a young servant girl could the police be implicated, and then only if her virginity had been certified prior to employment.

Incest

Incest always requires a cultural definition at two levels. To be considered incestuous behavior within a culture, the sexual behavior must take place between people of the opposite sex who are not allowed to marry because of genetic or affinial relatedness. Secondly, the behavior itself must be considered erotic in nature and somehow shocking by the members of that culture. In Iran, marriage between cousins is the norm. Even the marriage between the offspring of two sisters, considered incestuous in most cultures, is very common in Iran, as it prevents the splitting up of parcels of land inherited jointly by two sisters by passing it on to their children at marriage. Within the same generation in a family, only brothers and sisters are off-limits to each other as marriage partners.

In Western cultures, certain zones of the body are described as erogenous, and any touching of these zones by another person is generally interpreted as sexually motivated behavior. Similarly, slow dancing, with bodies touching and the arms of one partner about the neck of the other, would be assumed to be motivated by either sexual attraction or a desire on the part of one or both of the partners to stimulate themselves or the other. In Iran, however, fairly intimate touching is common between opposite-sex siblings, although such behavior would not be tolerated among those of the opposite sex more distantly related. Teenage siblings of the opposite sex, even those who are married, have the license for close "accidental-on-purpose" body contact in rough-and-tumble play. They often display physical affection, kissing on the face, lips, and neck that border on the erotic. They may be seen grooming each other and, for example, anointing each other with suntan oil in a sensuous way. Such behavior continues with siblings until late in life. At any age, touching high up on the inner thigh or on the outer periphery of the breasts between opposite-sex siblings is allowable in public as a way of drawing attention to points made in conversation, even though it would be deemed indecent public behavior between nonsiblings.

Similarly, in large family gatherings, weddings for example, Western-style dancing is often mixed with Iranian-style dancing. Married couples, fathers and daughters, brothers and sisters, and occasionally mothers and sons, may be seen dancing together very closely. An Iranian would not interpret this behavior as incestuous or in any way distasteful, and would probably find any such suggestion rather warped on the part of the observer. This, of course, raises very interesting questions about what is and is not sexual behavior.

Sexual Harassment

The general pattern of sex segregation makes opportunities for sexual harassment rare. Should it occur and be mentioned, the female, and more particularly her mother, would be blamed for affording anyone the opportunity. The most common forms of sexual harassment are those of frottage and furtive pinching in crowded shopping areas.

Rape

The legal concerns of rape are not connected in Iran with the indignities suffered by the victim, but with the financial damages incurred to the family as a result of rupture of the daughter's hymen.

Opportunities for rape are rare. When it does occur, it is likely to involve the police at the instigation of the girl's parents. The police are empowered to force a man who has robbed a girl of her virginity, with or without her assent, to marry her legally. He is allowed to divorce her immediately if he wishes, but the legal procedures and documentation of marriage must be followed through. A divorced woman is more marriageable than an unmarried girl with a ruptured hymen. In the case of a servant girl, her parents may choose between a cash settlement from her employer or a forced marriage between the employer and their daughter, even if he already has a wife. Under the law, a girl can force into legal marriage any man with whom she claims to have had intercourse. The procedure is swift and uncomplicated, involving simple arrest and handcuffs. However, since the girl must be represented in this by her father, few girls would initiate this procedure frivolously or maliciously. This is especially true because there would be few legal repercussions against a father who killed his daughter for dishonoring the family.

Marital rape is not a legal category, in that a woman is her husband's property. If a woman shows signs of physical abuse, her male kin, especially older brothers, will threaten or assault her husband. In general, it is the duty of different members of the kin group to protect the females in the group. In most instances of sexual violence, punishment will be dealt out by the group without fear of intervention from police.

B. Prostitution

Prostitution is one of the few subsistence slots available for women marginalized by the death of those kin vital to their functioning in society. Daughters of repudiated women and childless widows are particularly vulnerable. Every village seems to have its "fallen woman," who is rumored to serve as a prostitute. People speak too of brothels in the bazaar area of large towns. Veiled women can be seen at night walking alone on the outskirts of towns. A woman walking alone at any time, particularly after dusk, unless obviously bent on shopping or an urgent errand, would be assumed to be a prostitute. Maids commuting from their place of employment carry large totes, a pair of men's shoes, or a garment on a hanger in a dry cleaning bag, so as not to be mistaken for prostitutes and harassed.

C. Pornography and Erotica

During the Shah's regime, copies of American magazines such as *Playboy* and *Penthouse* were widely sold at newsstands, openly perused by men and women, and left lying around in full view in homes (see Section 3B). Despite the Khomeini regime's ban on all depictions of the unclad human form and the sale of such magazines, this material is still available.

Displays of belly dancing in restaurants and private weddings and parties were staple entertainment prior to the Islamic regime. Although the dancers often showed great skill, male members of the audience clearly viewed them as prostitutes, or at least women with whom liberties could be openly taken. In mixed family audiences, older males often greeted their performances with exaggerated leering and lip-smacking. Young males would be inhibited by the presence of their parents. Middle-aged men, however, would tuck bills into the spangled brassiere or the low-slung waistband of the fringed skirts of the dancer as she passed their table.

[In December of 1993, the Iranian Parliament approved legislation providing for capital punishment for the producers and distributors of pornographic video tapes. First offenders would receive a maximum five years' prison term and $100,000 in fines, "Principal promoters" face the death penalty. Experts doubt that this attack on the "Corrupters of the Earth" will discourage the immensely profitable business. Video tapes of Western and pornographic films are already widely available through a network of unlicensed distributors. Also feeding the trade, according to official statistics, are three million Iranian homes with video recorders and 25,000 satellite dishes—analysts say the real figure is more like six million and 50,000 respectively (Hedges 1994). (Editor)]

D. Domestic Sexual Controls

Living quarters in the cities are similar to private homes and apartments found in European countries. However, the traditional architecture of Iranian homes in small villages and the rural areas have curtained alcoves, rather than closets, for storing bedding and clothing. In these more traditional homes, people unroll mattresses and bedding from these alcoves to sleep at any convenient spot on the floor in any of the rooms, or on the roof or balcony. Often the choice seems to be dictated by the opportunity it provides for spying on others as they sleep or disrobe. Females, particularly those in their 30s, 40s, and 50s, seem particularly prone to spying on married couples, as well as on other women as they bathe, undress, or use the bathroom. Women gossip openly about information they have obviously garnered by such spying. Some intimate information is clearly used at times to discredit other females, as it is presented to listeners as if revealed by a male confidant with carnal knowledge.

There appears to be a strong interest, not only in details of other women's bodies and personal hygienic measures, but in the frequency and urgency with which they urinate. One who urinates often is spoken of in disparaging terms. Houses with outhouses often have no doors, with walls that conceal only the midsection of the occupant. It is considered a basic precaution to check that one is not being observed.

It is easy for a female to wander from room to room, from roof to balcony to yard without arousing suspicion as she goes about domestic tasks like rounding up soiled dishes and laundry. There are few internal doors in some Iranian house and any stealthiness can be explained away as consideration for those engaged in the national pastime of brief and frequent naps.

Males do not have such freedom of movement in the house, and thus male voyeurism is less of a day-to-day problem in the typical large multigenerational household. Male voyeurism more often takes place outside the home. It usually takes the form of the male wearing a woman's all-concealing veil to insinuate himself into female enclaves or the bathhouse on women's day. While the success of such endeavors appears to be largely hearsay, there seems to be an acceptance of voyeurism as a far-from-infrequent fact of life embedded into the culture.

9. Contraception, Abortion, and Population Planning

A. Contraception and Abortion

Condoms are openly sold on every street corner in the towns in Iran. Itinerant vendors display trays of condoms, together with cigarettes and chewing gum. Anal intercourse and coitus interruptus were previously the main male-initiated forms of contraception before the widespread distribution of condoms.

Abortion remains, in rural areas and among the urban poor, the most common female-initiated form of contraception. Untrained midwives induce abortion by introducing a chicken quill into the cervix. From the 1950s on, abortions were widely available in clinics, hospitals, and doctors' offices, restricted only by a woman's ability to pay. Neither male consent nor religious considerations seemed to be issues raised. The conceptus has neither legal nor spiritual status, nor for that matter, has an apparently nonviable term-born child. Efforts are often not made to succor a weak newborn in the home. Mothers often abandon sickly babies born in a hospital. Only a viable offspring becomes a male concern and an object of his proprietary rights.

Tubal ligations are the contraceptive method of choice among the urban middle class. Contraceptive pills are freely available without prescription and are in common use by young, urban married couples.

B. Population Control Efforts

Efforts on the part of the Iranian Women's Organization to educate women about safe contraception since the mid-1960s have been mainly aimed at improving female health rather than affecting the population size. Life for women among the rural and urban poor, until the 1960s, was more often than not one of an endless chain of pregnancies, spaced by prolonged and intensive nursing and unskilled, unsterile abortions. High infant-mortality rates in the villages, rather than contraception, kept the population size stable. The Shah set up a network of rural government clinics in the late 1960s and early 1970s to provide free primary health care, which included the distribution of contraceptive pills. This latter measure, together with the sudden widespread availability to all of antibiotics, had a dramatic effect both on the birthrates and the survival of those born.

[Between the Islamic revolution of 1979 and 1996, Iran's population almost doubled, from 35 million to more than 60 million. Faced with internal and external threats to the revolution, including the 1980-1988 war with Iraq, Iran's spiritual leaders regularly extolled large families as a way of preserving the revolution. The legal age of marriage was dropped to 9. Today, at least 43 percent of the population is under 17. Despite official support for larger families, many Iranians in the early 1980s found themselves faced with soaring inflation and eroding wages, a common deterrent to large families. Dr. Alireza Marandi, then Iran's Deputy Minister of Health and its current Minister of Health, recognized that Iran's population growth rate was rocketing out of control. At the time, considering the very conservative religious climate, Marandi did not deem it wise to bring the population issue into public debate. Instead, he quietly kept alive a prerevolutionary program of distributing free condoms and I.U.D.'s while maneuvering for an opening. One word from the Ayatollah Ruhollah Khomeini and all contraceptives would disappear throughout the country. In 1988, after the Cabinet approved birth control by a single vote, Marandi asked for a public statement supporting contraception. But the internal opposition was so strong, the Cabinet vote was not announced. Instead Ayatollah Khomeini suggested a public discussion that sent Muslim scholars digging through their texts for religious sanctions that could be cited in support of birth control.

[The debate culminated in a 1993 law that enshrined birth control and lifted subsidized health insurance and food coupons for any child after the third. Condoms, vasectomies, and the birth control pill are free. The state also introduced mandatory prenuptial birth control classes. Couples seeking a marriage license must submit a stamped form documenting their participation in an hour-long lecture on contraception. Abortion, however, remains illegal except when the mother's health is in danger. As a result, Iran's population growth rate, which in the 1980s was 4 percent—one of the highest growth rates seen anywhere—declined to about 2.5 percent. Rural families still tend to have many children. Despite the fact that the nation's growth rate is now below 2.5 percent, Iran's population will pass the 100 million mark early in the next century (MacFarquhar 1996a). (Editor)]

10. Sexually Transmitted Diseases

The major endemic sexually transmitted disease has for decades been syphilis, although it is suspected that the term syphilis has become a generic one in Iran to include all sexually transmitted diseases. It is assumed that men contract syphilis from prostitutes and then infect their wives. Many babies in the villages are born with syphilis, contracted during the birth process. Standard neonatal ward procedure in hospitals involves medicating the eyes of newborns against the onset of syphilis-related infections. Part of the prenuptial inspection of prospective brides by the mother-in-law in the bathhouse is a search for what are thought to be symptoms of syphilis, notably patchy skin and thinning hair. Treatment for syphilis is available in clinics, but there is no government attempt to eliminate or track down sources of infection.

11. HIV/AIDS

At present, there is no information on the prevalence or otherwise of AIDS in Iran. Although prostitution anywhere can bring about a spread of infection, there are cultural patterns in Iran that would minimize the spread of HIV infections. Consorting with prostitutes is not common for married men because of the strong cultural belief that variety adds nothing to the spice of sexual behavior. Since the main object of sex is seen as the relief of phallic tension, this goal is thought to be more safely achieved with one's wife. Advice to this effect is a common subject of sermons and religious writings. Visits to prostitutes are also seen as signs of immaturity, as "real men" have achieved the financial eligibility prerequisite to marriage and uninterrupted access to a woman.

12. Sexual Dysfunction, Counseling, and Therapies

A. Concepts of Sexual Dysfunctions

In Iran, there is generally very little concern and a great deal of impatience with psychological considerations. Children who receive regular meals and are kept clean are considered well looked after, regardless of how happy or unhappy they are. A woman who complains about having nothing to wear would be taken more seriously than one who complains that her husband never talks to her or approaches her sexually. Sexual functioning and satisfaction are similarly measured without regard to the emotional component. Tenderness and attention to the state of arousal of the female are not valid considerations.

A male is judged to be sexually adequate if he is capable of erection and ejaculation, as proven by the presence of both semen and blood from the ruptured hymen of his bride on the nuptial handkerchief used on his wedding night. A female is inspected before marriage by her prospective mother-in-law to check for mammary development, nipples sufficiently protruding for nursing, and the width of pelvis for childbirth. The main proof of sexual adequacy, however, is her ability to conceive. Failure to conceive within two years of marriage is grounds for repudiation.

B. Availability of Counseling, Diagnosis, and Treatment

Counseling in all marital matters is strictly a family affair. There is a strong taboo against discussing family problems of any kind with a nonfamily member. It is not even acceptable to admit, however casually, to a friend or person outside the circle of close kin, that anything is wrong with family, children, or finances. Iran is thus not very fertile ground for any kind of psychotherapy. On the one hand, the therapist would be perceived as a stranger and therefore not one to whom confidences should be made. Secondly, after long years of dictatorship under the Shah, backed up by the secret police, or S.A.V.A.K., and more than a decade of the repressive Islamic Republic with its brutal guardians of public morals, the Pastoran, no clear line would be seen between professionals of any kind asking questions and government officials collecting incriminating information.

Under the Shah's regime, gynecologists in Teheran and other major cities offered help to women with fertility problems. Western-trained medical personnel, however, for the most part fled from Iran after the ousting of the Shah. Most women in small towns and villages seek herbal and spiritual measures to overcome fertility problems. Bitter infusions, thought to aid conception, are concocted and drunk by the desperate. Large, old trees, thought in this mostly desert area to hold the power of fertility, often have their branches completely covered with little pieces of rag into which are knotted the prayers of supplicants who cannot conceive. Advice on the formulations of such potions and the text of such prayers is perhaps the closest one comes in Iran to therapy for sexual dysfunction.

13. Sexual Research and Advanced Education

Other than a concern with physical causes of infertility in women during the reign of the Shah, sexual research has been nonexistent in Iran. Surgical measures to correct reproductive dysfunction were widely available under the Shah. The psychosexual component of reproduction and sexuality itself were, even then, seldom considered to be of academic or medical interest.

Conclusion

Within the family, sexual activity between married people can be alluded to in a jocular way. In mixed company, men may be teased for looking tired as a result of suspected sexual activity. Members of households exchange innuendoes about suspicious sounds heard during the night. However, alluding to extramarital sex is considered to be in extremely bad taste and discussion of one's sex life absolutely taboo. Friendships with nonkin are rare. The composition of marital households and informal networks is such that most social contact involves in-laws within the group. Discussion of anything intimate is thus inhibited. There are strong cultural constraints on revealing anything of a personal nature within the family, and even stronger ones on mentioning anything to strangers. Because of this lack of exchange of information, there tends to be an overestimate of the strength and longevity of the human sex drive, and a wildly exaggerated sense of the amount of sexual behavior that occurs in places, such as the U.S.A. and Europe, where Islamic cultural constraints are not in effect. This belief serves to reinforce the notion that such constraints are vital.

Resources and Suggested Readings

Beck, Lois Grant, and Nikkie Keddie, eds. 1978. *Women in the Muslim World.* Cambridge, Massachusetts: Harvard University Press.

Bouhdiba, Abdelwahab. 1985. *Sexuality in Islam.* Translated by A. Sheridan. London: Routledge and Kegan Paul.

Brooks, G. 1995. *Nine Parts of Desire: The Hidden World of Islamic Women.* New York: Anchor Books/Doubleday.

Denny, F. M. 1987. *Islam and the Muslim Community.* New York: Harper & Row.

Haeri, Shahla. 1980. "Women, Law and Social Change in Iran." In J.I. Smith, ed. *Women in Contemporary Muslim Societies.* Cranbury, New Jersey: Associated University Presses.

Haeri, Shahla. 1983. "The Institution of Mut'a Marriage in Iran: A Formal and Historical Perspective." In Guita Nashat, ed. *Women and Revolution in Iran.* Boulder, Colorado: Wesyview Press.

Hedges, C. August 16 1994. "Satellite Dishes Adding Spice to Iran's TV Menu." *The New York Times,* p. A11.

Jalali, Behnaz. 1982. "Iranian Families." In M. McGoldrick, J. K. Pearce, and J. Giordano, eds. *Ethnicity and Family Therapy.* New York: Guilford Press.

MacFarquhar, N. 1996a (September 8). "With Iran Population Boom, Vasectomy Received Blessing." *The New York Times,* pp. 1, 14.

MacFarquhar, N. 1996b (October 8). "With Mixed Feelings, Iran Tiptoes to the Internet." *The New York Times* (International Section).

Mackey, Sandra. 1996. *The Iranians: Persia, Islam, and the Soul of a Nation.* New York: Dutton.

Mernissi, Fatima. 1993. *Islam and Democracy: Fear of the Modern World.* Reading, Massachusetts: Addison-Wesley.

Mernissi, Fatima. 1991. *The Veil and the Male Elite: A Feminist Interpretation of Women's Rights in Islam.* Reading, Massachusetts: Addison-Wesley

Naneh, Kitabi Kulsum. 1971. *Women of Persia: Customs and Manners of the Women of Persia.* Translated by J. Atkinson. New York: B. Franklin.

Nashat, Guita. ed. 1983. *Women and Revolution in Iran.* Boulder, Colorado: Westview Press.

The New York Times. 1994 (December 21). "Iran Offers an Islamic Way to Improve the Lot of Women," p. A11.

Noss, D. S., and J. B. Noss. 1990. *A History of the World's Great Religions* (8th ed.). New York: Macmillan.

Parrinder, G. 1980. *Sex in the World's Great Religions.* Don Mills, Ontario, Canada: General Publishing Company.

Ireland
(*Eire*)

Thomas Phelim Kelly, M.B.*

Contents

Demographics and a Historical Perspective

A. Demographics

Ireland—"Eire" in the Irish language—is an island of 32,000 square miles, about the size of the state of West Virginia, situated in the Atlantic Ocean, just west of Great Britain. The northeastern corner of the island is Northern Ireland, a part of the United Kingdom.

Ireland had slightly over 3.5 million people in 1995, with 57 percent of the population living in the cities. The age distribution was 26 percent 14 years of age or younger, 63 percent between ages 15 and 64, and 11 percent age 65 or older. Life expectancy at birth in 1995 was 73 for males and 79 for females. The birthrate was 154 per 1,000 and the death rate 8 per 1,000,

---

*Additional comments by Harry A. Walsh are enclosed thus [. . . (Walsh)]. Comments by the editor are bracketed as [. . . (Editor)].

giving a natural annual increase of 0.6 percent. The infant mortality rate was 7 per 1,000 live births. Ireland has one hospital bed per 255 persons and one physician per 681 persons. The literacy rate was 100 percent, with 96 percent attendance in nine years of compulsory school. The Republic of Ireland is considered one of the poorest of the European Community and has an unemployment rate, despite emigration, of 20 percent. The per capita gross domestic product in 1995 was $13,100.

B. A Brief Historical Perspective

Celtic tribes invaded what is now Ireland about the fourth century B.C.E., bringing their Gaelic culture and literature. St. Patrick brought Christianity to these Celts in the fifth century C.E. The Norse invasions, which began in the eighth century, ended in 1014 when the Irish King Brian Boru defeated the Danes. English invasions began in the twelfth century with bitter rebellions, famines, and savage repressions. The Easter Monday Rebellion (1916) failed, but was followed by guerrilla warfare and harsh repression by the English. When the Irish Parliament (Dail Eireann) reaffirmed their independence in 1919, the British offered dominion status to the six counties of Ulster and to the twenty-six counties of southern Ireland. The Irish Free State in the south adopted a constitution and dominion status in 1922, while northern Ireland remained a part of the United Kingdom. In 1937, a new constitution was adopted along with the declaration of Eire (Ireland) as a sovereign democratic state. In 1948, Eire withdrew from the Commonwealth declaring itself a republic. The British Parliament recognized both actions, but reaffirmed its control over the northeast six counties, a declaration Ireland has never recognized. Despite recurring violence and political shifts, both the British and the people of Ireland favor a peaceful resolution of the conflict.

1. Basic Sexological Premises

A. Gender Roles and Sociolegal Status of Males and Females.

The idea that there are definite and separate roles for the sexes pervades all aspects of Irish society. In this division of roles, the feminine is regarded as subordinate to the masculine. The society is a patriarchal one where social power and control are associated with masculinity. The 1937 Irish Constitution reflected what was considered the main role of Irish women thus: "In particular the State recognizes that by her life within the home, woman gives to the State a support without which the common good cannot be achieved." This provision, and the attitudes underlying it, have been used to deny women equality in all spheres of Irish life.

[The cult of the Virgin Mary is very strong in Ireland. Mary is depicted as a kind of Cinderella—confined to the kitchen with her dreams and fantasies. The model presented to the women of Ireland is seen at the Marian Shrine of Knock in western Ireland. In this vision, she was reported to have worn a long dress with a sash, a veil, and wearing the crown of a rich feudal lady. Yet, one of the best-selling prayer-cards at the shrine is "The Kitchen Prayer":

> Lord of all the pots and pans and things . . .
> Make me a saint by getting
> Meals and washing up plates.

[The image of the Virgin Mary held up before the eyes of Irish women reinforces the established cultural attitude: women can have their dreams, but their place is in the kitchen. (Walsh)]

However, since the advent of the women's movement and Ireland's joining with the European Community in 1973, a number of legal reforms have been brought about, giving women more or less legal equality. But socially, economically, and politically, women are far from equal, although the gap has narrowed somewhat in the past twenty years. Women make up about 30 percent of the workforce, but in industry, their average earnings are only 67 percent of the average male earnings. Ireland has the lowest employment rate in Europe for mothers with children under 5 years of age. In 1991, 16.7 percent of married women were in the labor force, compared with 50 percent in Germany. There are no publicly funded child-care facilities. Discrimination against women is widely practiced, and as yet they have no redress in law. The most powerful positions in politics, law, medicine, the military, police forces, industry, universities, and financial institutions are held almost exclusively by men. Although attitudes to equality have changed considerably in recent times, in the social sphere, actual practice lags far behind. For example, in a 1986 survey, 95 percent of the respondents agreed that men and women should share housework. In reality, women do the lion's share.

B. The Sociolegal Status of Males and Females

There are no differences between the legal status of male and female children. There are minor distinctions between male and female adolescents. For example, boys may work in bars at age 16 while women cannot work there until age 18. It is illegal for a male over age 14 years to have sexual intercourse with a girl under 17 years of age, but the girl commits no crime in the same situation. Homosexual acts under the age of 17 are illegal for males, but not for females. The government has recently promised legislation that will make discrimination on the grounds of sex illegal.

The social status of males and females is reflected in the gender roles demanded of each. From a very early age, girls begin to learn to prepare themselves for a traditionally feminine role in society and boys learn to prepare for a traditionally masculine role. The feminine role is regarded as having a sense of social value, while men regard themselves personally as superior to women. These attitudes are used as a justification for denying women equality and for the fact that political, social, and economic power is exercised by men.

C. General Concepts of Sexuality and Love

The socialization process and gender-role stereotyping generally demands that sexual expressions belong properly to the married state of heterosexual men and women. The proper expression of sexuality within the marital union is limited to the act of penile-vaginal intercourse. An inability or lack of inclination to engage in coitus can be grounds for annulment of a marriage. Childless marriages are generally frowned on and the childless couple is considered selfish. Any overt or suggested sexual expression outside the privacy of the marriage bed is, at the very least, disapproved of. Within marriage, women are expected to be sexually available and to play second fiddle to their husband's sexual desires.

Sexual activity outside marriage in heterosexual relationships is tolerated to some degree, especially if it appears that the couple may eventually marry. However, different standards exist for men and women. Males are seen as sexual go-getters with instinctive sexual urges they cannot control. They are neither encouraged nor expected to take responsibility for the consequences of their behavior. Females are seen as sexually passive and in need of a male to awaken their relatively weak sexual desires. Because females are seen as more in control, they are held responsible for both their own and the male's sexual behavior. A further twist to the tale is that women must never undermine the male's dominant role in sex.

Romantic love is idealized and this ideal is perpetuated in all media forms. Romantic novels outsell all other types of fiction. Most people would say they married because they were "in love." People who say they are still "in love" after many years of marriage say so with pride.

The sexuality of children, disabled persons, the chronically ill, the elderly, those who live in institutions, and single persons without an opposite-sex partner is hardly acknowledged, let alone recognized and respected.

2. Religious and Ethnic Factors Affecting Sexuality

A. Source and Character of Religious Values

The Irish are an outstandingly religious people. Over 90 percent of the population are Roman Catholic and 3 percent Protestant. Eighty percent attend church at least weekly and about 50 percent express a great deal of confidence in their Church. Among the younger generation, there is less acceptance of orthodox beliefs and religious practices, but the difference between generations is not nearly as great as that found in other Western countries.

Roman Catholicism greatly influences all aspects of Irish life. Since its foundation, the state laws have complemented Catholic Church laws. Until 1972, the Irish Constitution paid homage to the "special position" of the Catholic Church in Irish life. [This resulted, until recently, in an unresolved issue of Church annulments vis-à-vis the constitutional prohibition against divorce. After the constitutional prohibition against divorce was revoked in a November 1995 referencum, it became possible for the estimated 80,000 separated Irish couples to obtain a civil divorce. The Church has, in recent years, granted annulments, dubbed "divorce Irish-style," and permitted remarriage, but annulments were and remain difficult to obtain from church authorities. (Walsh)].

State schools, which the majority of children attend, are mainly run by religious organizations. [However, because of aging and a decline in vocations, many teaching and administrative positions in schools, once held by religious, are now filled by laity. This has caused some tension in recent years as lay educators become more conscious of having political clout. (Walsh)] Religious bodies also play a major role in the provision of the country's nonprimary health-care services.

This pervasive religious influence is reflected in the way sexuality is treated on political, social, and personal levels. It is reflected in the type of censorship of books, films, and television programs that prevails. It is reflected in the laws relating to human reproduction, the lack of sex education in the schools, and the absence of the study of sexuality in any academic institution.

On a personal level, sex is associated with fear and guilt for many people, and even in communal, single-sex showers, nudity is unusual. There is evidence, however, of some decline in religious influence over the past ten or so years.

The Irish people as a whole are characterized by conservativism—conservative in religion, in morality, in politics, and in their views on work, marriage and the family. Many Irish people are at ease with a republic that is traditional, nationalist, and Catholic. However, a growing number feel alienated in such a society.

[Ease of travel has made the young people of Ireland less insular and more impatient with the insular mentality of the older generation. The youth of Ireland think of London, Paris, Frankfurt, even Boston and New York, as "neighboring cities," and have exposure to lifestyles and value systems that their parents never had.

[Catholicism and nationalism were synonymous in the minds of the previous generation. To be Irish was to be Catholic. Some of Ireland's greatest writers went into exile because, although thoroughly Irish, they were not seen as Catholic enough. The young Irish today do not see Catholicism as a necessary component of self-identity. They seem to understand where culture leaves off and real faith begins. Consequently, they can discard elements of Catholic orthodoxy with greater ease and feel no guilt about being un-Irish when they do so. (Walsh)]

For some, the shift towards greater permissiveness and tolerance that began in the 1960s is progressing too quickly; for others too slowly. There is a constant tension between old and new ideologies, between Catholicism and nationalism on the one hand, and liberalism and materialism on the other. Until recently, the battle lines were clearly drawn, but now some are attempting a synthesis of these seemingly contradictory values. Foremost in this attempt is the Irish President, Mary Robinson.

B. Source and Character of Ethnic Values

[In the fourth century B.C., Celtic tribes invaded what is now Ireland where their Gaelic culture and literature flourished. The Celtic worldview was dualistic, dividing the world into two opposing subworlds, one of light, good, and spirit, and the other of darkness, evil, sin, and body. In the fifth century A.D., St. Patrick converted the Celts to Christianity. Some anthropologists have suggested that a major factor in the negative and repressive view of sexuality that pervades Irish culture may be traced to the adoption of the original Celtic dualistic philosophy by celibate Christian monks who found it congenial to their own apocalyptic vision. (Editor)]

[Monasticism introduced an ascetical element into Irish spirituality. To this day, thousands of Irish seek out the barrenness of mountains and islands to do penance for their sins of the flesh. Suffering is seen as meritorious, something to be "offered up" in union with Christ on the Cross, or for the release of "the poor souls in purgatory." Since suffering was seen as meritorious, it was natural that pleasure would be suspect. Sex was "a stolen pleasure." (Walsh)]

[In the seventeenth and eighteenth centuries, Irish youth were trained for the clergy in France where they were strongly influenced by another dualistic current, French Jansenism. The Jansenists saw the world torn between two opposing forces of good and evil. Jansenism stressed the corruptibility of human nature and its sinful, evil tendencies, associated the body and emotions with evil, and glorified the ascetic denial of all "worldly" desires (Messenger 1971; Francoeur 1982, 58-60).

[English invasions and colonization started in the twelfth century, and the resulting 700 years of struggle, marked by bitter rebellions and savage repressions, have left their mark on Irish culture. English taxation, limits on industrialization, and restrictions on the kinds of crops Irish farmers could raise helped create a society in which marriage of the offspring was delayed to provide manual labor for the farm and support for the parents. In the system of primogeniture, the first-born son inherited the entire paternal homestead, because dividing up the farmland among all the sons would leave none with a viable economic base. With few other economic opportunities available, the other offspring frequently became priests or nuns, or emigrated.

[This combination of religious dualism and economic pressures has resulted in a society strongly dominated by the clergy and religious, with late marriages for those who marry, and a sexually repressive value system that holds celibacy and sexual abstinence in great esteem (Stahl 1979).

[In 1922, Northern Ireland chose to remain part of the United Kingdom, while the Irish Free State adopted a constitution as a British dominion. In 1937, the Irish Free State rejected dominion status and declared itself a sovereign democratic state. In 1948, the Irish Free State withdrew from the British Commonwealth and declared itself a republic.

[*Note:* John C. Messenger has provided extensive ethnographic observations of "Sex and Repression in an Irish Folk Community" in a small island community of the Gaeltacht he calls Inis Baeg. See Marshall and Suggs, 1971. (Editor)]

3. Sexual Knowledge and Education

A. Government Policies and Programs for Sex Education

Prior to 1984, the government had no formal policies regarding sex education. In that year, a 15-year-old girl and her baby died during childbirth in a field in the middle of winter. She had not told anybody that she was pregnant. Following this tragic event, sex education became a matter of public and political debate. The Minister for Education planned a reform of secondary level education to include personal and social skills training, including sex education, in the new curriculum. The government's Health Education Bureau began training teachers to teach this new aspect of the curriculum. However, this reform was not implemented because of political, religious, and pressure-group opposition. Nonetheless, over 2,000 teachers have been trained so far to deal with sexuality and personal relationships. A criticism of this training has been that it does not place enough emphasis on how political, religious, economic, and social factors shape sexuality, values, and personal relationships.

In 1987, the Department of Education issued guidelines to postprimary schools recommending that sex and relationship education be integrated into all subjects. These guidelines also recommended that such education should not be secular and would require a religious input. Parents were to be fully involved in the process. Whether or not and how schools implement these guidelines is not known, but it appears that few schools have adopted them. In a *Green Paper on Education* (1992), the government proposed that future curricula will provide for "sexuality education appropriate to all levels of pupils, beginning in the early stages of primary education."

The government-controlled Eastern Health Board has initiated a Child Abuse Prevention Program in primary schools. The program encourages children to exercise control, to be assertive, and to seek help for any problem. Critics claim that it dwells on negative aspects of sexuality, is too narrow in its scope, and places responsibility for avoiding abuse on potential victims rather than on adults.

It appears that there is wide variation in the ways in which individual schools provide sex education. Some provide none, others set aside a particular day or days and provide expert speakers. More frequently, it is incorporated into one or two school subjects, usually science and/or religion. Surveys reveal that the majority want a more comprehensive school sex education that begins early in schooling and is independent of religious instruction.

No information is available on the provision of sex education in special schools such as those for mentally handicapped persons.

[Higher education was not available to most Irish in the first half of this century. The priests, school teachers, and local doctor, if the town had one, were the only ones with a higher education. This gave the clergy enormous power. Many of them were, for all practical purposes, mayors of the towns. With Irish universities turning out thousands of graduates today, the clergy have to deal with an educated youth. Older Irish people obeyed instinctively when the Church ruled on something. The young Irish today test the pronouncements to see if they make sense or not. If not, they say so. The older Irish were too superstitious to disagree with the Church ("God will get you for that"). The availability of higher education has resulted in young Irish men and women testing the ethical positions of Catholic orthodoxy. (Walsh)]

B. Informal Sources of Sexual Knowledge

The Durex Report—Ireland (1993), designed to be statistically representative of the adult population aged 17 to 49 years living in the Republic of Ireland, found that the following were the main sources of sexual information: own friends, 36 percent; mother, 23 percent; books and magazines, 12 percent; religious teacher, 10 percent; lay teacher, 10 percent; father, 5 percent; and sisters or brothers, 5 percent. Sixteen percent of this sample believed that the teaching of sex education should be directly influenced by their Church's teachings.

Another nationally representative survey carried out by *The Irish Times* (1990) found that 95 percent of urban dwellers and 92 percent of rural dwellers were in favor of providing sex education in the schools. A Health Education Bureau study in 1986 of a national random sample of 1,000 parents found that 64 percent learned about sex from friends, 37 percent from books, 23 percent from mother, 6 percent from both parents, 2 percent from father, and 11 percent from a teacher. Thirty-two percent stated that they had not themselves provided sex education for their children and one in three of these parents stated that they did not intend to do so.

Although sex education is firmly on the political and social agenda in Ireland, consensus has not yet been reached by those who control education on how it should be incorporated into the school curriculum. Meanwhile, the needs of children and adolescents go largely unheeded.

4. Autoerotic Behaviors and Patterns

A. Children and Adolescents

The first Irish study of childhood sexual behavior (Deehan and Fitzpatrick 1993) assessed sexual behavior of children as perceived by their parents. It was not nationally representative and had a middle-class bias. More than half of the parents reported that their child had shown no interest in his/her own genitals. Boys were much more likely to show such interest, as were younger children. Thirty-seven percent reported that their child played with his/her genitals. Most parents said this occurred openly in the home. Sixteen percent described such play as self-pleasuring, most regarding this as a comfort habit or "nervous fiddling." It is probable that much childhood autoerotic behavior does not come to the attention of parents.

The impression that autoerotic behavior is common in adolescence comes from the frequency with which it is condemned by the clergy reacting to the frequency with which this "sinful behavior" is confessed, the high proportion of letters to "Agony Aunts" on the subject, and the frequent usage of slang words for self-pleasuring, particularly among adolescent boys.

[Only fifty miles separate Ireland from England, the home of Victorianism. During Victorian times, Ireland was occupied by England. The Victorian frenzy about masturbation crossed the Irish Sea, and with it much of the inaccurate "scientific" information about the health risks to those who masturbate, the so-called degeneracy theory. Both the Church and the medical profession reflected Victorian attitudes to autoeroticism in Ireland. Even the language of Victorian England crossed the Irish Sea with masturbation being known as "self-abuse," "the solitary vice," etc. However, the Irish have a way of molding the English language. While churchmen and physicians spoke of the "solitary vice" and "self-abuse," the native Irish began to speak of "pulling the wire" and "playing the tea pot." (Walsh)].

B. Adults

No studies have been carried out to indicate the extent or diversity of adult autoerotic behavior. There are indications that some men who engage in self-pleasuring during adolescence stop doing so when they reach adulthood because of the stigma of immaturity attached to it. This seems to be particularly so in the case of married men. In contrast, there are some indications that many women engage in self-pleasuring for the first time in adulthood. In recent years, there has been an increasing market for vibrators and other sex toys in Ireland. Sexually explicit books, magazines, and videos have become increasingly available in recent years, and these undoubtedly sometimes play a part in autoerotic activities. Unusual auto-erotic practices sometimes come to light through the work of coroners and doctors. One of these is the use of asphyxiation techniques to heighten sensation during self-pleasuring. Other examples are the use of penile constricting devices, or "cock rings." It appears, too, that drug use is sometimes associated with autoerotic activities.

5. Interpersonal Heterosexual Behaviors

A. Children

In Deehan and Fitzpatrick's study, less than half the parents stated that their child had shown interest in the bodies of others. Where interest was shown, 46 percent mentioned the interest was in the mother's breasts or genital area; 25 percent mentioned sibling's genitals as the focus of interest. Sexualized play that involved looking at another child's buttocks or genitals was reported by 23 percent of parents. However, parents always qualified their answers by adding that this had only taken place in a situation where the child would need to be undressed.

When parents were read a list of possible sex games their child might have engaged in, 7 percent reported genital touching games and 4 percent said that their child had been lying on top another child in imitation of a sexual act. Simulated intercourse or kissing or licking of the genitals was not reported by any parents. Thirteen percent of the children were re-ported to share a bed, usually with siblings. This was distinguished from children going regularly to the parents' or sibling's bed, which was reported by 64 percent and 39 percent respectively. Bathing or showering with other family members occurred in 78 percent of 3- to 5-year-olds, 68 percent of 6- to 9-year-olds, and 33 percent of 10- to 12-year-olds. These situations provide opportunities for sexual exploration of which the parents would not necessarily be aware.

B. Adolescents

Puberty Rituals

There are no rituals to mark the milestone of puberty in Irish life. In the Deehan and Fitzpatrick study, parents reported having discussed breast development with 38 percent of daughters and 20 percent of sons, men-struation with 26 percent of daughters and 7 percent of sons, pubic hair development with 40 percent of daughters and 20 percent of sons, erections with 11 percent of sons and 5 percent of daughters, and wet dreams with

4 percent of sons and 3 percent of daughters. The vast majority of those children were prepubertal. An increasing number of primary school teachers are discussing puberty with their pupils.

Premarital Sexual Activities and Relationships

The only survey to date on premarital sexual activity in adolescence was conduced in 1991 by Ni Riordain among 2,000 female 12- to 17-year-old students in the province of Munster. It revealed that 25 percent of the 17-year-olds, 10 percent of the 15-year-olds, and 1 percent of the 12-year-olds had experienced sexual intercourse. In the same year, teenage extramarital births accounted for 26 percent of all extramarital births and 4.7 percent of all births. These figures suggest that the traditional religious and social taboos regarding premarital sex that were effective for so long are no longer so. It appears that adolescents are sexually active to a degree that would be unthinkable to their parents as adolescents. In addition to the change in adolescents' attitudes towards sex, there is the fact that today's teenagers also have greater freedom to meet and spend time with potential sexual partners. Mixed schools, teenage discos and other social events, trips away from home, and fewer social restrictions by parents provide sexual opportunities that were not heretofore available. The formation of couple relationships with an understanding of some degree of exclusivity seems to be occurring at a progressively earlier age.

C. Adults

Premarital Courtship, Dating, and Relationships

The most common pattern in premarital heterosexual relationships is that of a series of more or less "steady" relationships leading eventually to engagement and marriage. A "steady" relationship usually involves a high degree of mutual affection and sexual exclusivity. Partners usually get to know and socialize with one another's family and friends.

Dances, workplaces, colleges and other postsecondary educational institutions, and social networks, appear to provide the most opportunities for meeting prospective partners, but parents in particular are not slow in letting a son or daughter know that they consider a particular person to be an unsuitable partner.

Between "steady" relationships, there may be a series of short-lived relationships, and "one-night stands" seem to be increasingly common. Otherwise, there may be periods of varying length where people show no interest in close heterosexual relationships.

A decision to marry is usually marked by an "engagement," when the couple announce their intention to family and friends. Rings are usually exchanged and a celebration party held. Most couples in steady heterosexual relationships appear to engage in sexual intercourse, though this fact would rarely be openly acknowledged within their families. When such couples spend the night in a family home, they are usually shown to separate bedrooms. More and more couples are choosing to cohabit, often causing considerable conflict with family, particularly for women.

Single Adults

Little is known about the sexual behavior and relationships of single adults. The cultural imperative to marry is so strong that older single adults, especially women, are often referred to in pejorative terms. Despite this, more and more adults are remaining single. In 1986, 39 percent of the adult population were single.

Marriage, the Family, and Divorce

Until the 1960s, Ireland provided an example of Malthusian population, such that although fertility was high, population growth was controlled through the delaying or avoidance of marriage. Since then, Ireland has moved rapidly toward a neo-Malthusian type of population control, with generally increasing nuptiality and declining marital fertility. In 1961, the crude marriage rate was 5.4 per 1,000 population. This rose to 7.4 in 1973, but has been declining since to 4.6 in 1993. The median age of marriage shows a similar pattern. In 1945-46, this was 33.1 years for grooms and 28 years for brides. This fell to 25 and 23.2 respectively in 1977, but by 1990 had risen to 28.6 for grooms and 26.6 for brides.

The crude birthrate per 1,000 population remained more or less constant at around 22 until 1980. However, between 1961 and 1981, marital fertility declined 37 percent, with a corresponding increase in the extramarital birthrate. Since 1980, the crude birthrate has fallen dramatically to 15 per 1,000. The extramarital fertility rate has continued to increase, accounting for 16.6 percent of live births in 1991, with 28.6 percent of extramarital births being to teenagers. Marriage has declined in popularity in the past twenty years; women are having fewer children and having them at an earlier age.

As extramarital births increase, so have single-parent families. The 1991 census revealed at least 16 percent of households were single-parent families, with married couples with children making up 48 percent of the households. The vast majority of single parents are women. On average, they have lower incomes than other women with children and a higher risk of poverty. Most single parents are dependent on the state for their main or only source of income. Single mothers or fathers who cohabit are not classified as single parents.

Within two-parent households, there has been a change from the traditional pattern characterized by a dominant patriarchy, a rather severe authority system, and a generally nonexpressive emotional economy. There was a rigidly defined division of labor, with mothers specializing in emotionally supportive roles. The modern trend is toward a marriage where both husband and wife are expected to achieve a high degree of compatibilities based on shared interests and complementary differences. Rather than being defined and legitimized within closed communal systems, interpersonal relationships are geared toward individual self-development. Part of this trend is that an increasing number of married women are employed for wages, and more married men are assuming child-care and housekeeping duties.

The Durex Report—Ireland (1993) included questions regarding frequency of sexual intercourse, change in sexual behavior in relation to the awareness of AIDS, and the number of sexual partners in the previous twelve months. Daily coitus was reported by 2 percent of married and single adults. Forty-five percent of married and 25 percent of single people reported intercourse once or twice a week; 13 percent and 10 percent respectively reported a frequency of once or twice a month. Three percent of married and 36 percent of single people said they were not sexually active. Married men and women averaged 1.05 and 1.03 sexual partners respectively in the previous year. Single men averaged 2.72 partners and single women 1.25 partners in the previous twelve months.

Faithfulness within marriage is highly valued. In the 1983 *European Value Systems Survey*, 98 percent of the Irish respondents considered it as very important for a successful marriage. In the same study, 12 percent said they considered marriage to be an outdated institution; less than 1 percent were cohabiting. In law, a person may have only one husband or wife. Occasional instances of bigamy come to light.

In November 1995, Irish voters approved a referendum legalizing divorce. The original Irish Constitution had stated that "No law shall be enacted providing for the grant of a dissolution of marriage." A 1986 referendum on an amendment to allow divorce was rejected by 63.3 percent of the voters. Recent opinion polls suggest that the majority would now vote for such an amendment; the government proposed holding a second referendum in 1994. In the 1991 census, just over 2 percent of adults classified themselves as separated.

[In December 1993, after a Matrimonial Home Bill had been approved by parliament, the Republic's President, Mrs. Mary Robinson, sent the bill to the Supreme Court for a review of its constitutionality. This unexpected move appeared to be an effort to avoid a protracted battle in 1994, when the people were scheduled to vote again whether to legalize divorce. The matrimonial bill was intended to replace the traditional practice of almost always giving the home to the husband with joint ownership of homes in divorce settlements. After a year's delay, in November 1995, a scant majority of 0.4 percent of the voters, slightly over 9,100 votes out of more than 1.6 million votes cast in a country of 3.5 million people, legalized divorce. In mid-1996, the Supreme Court of Ireland rejected a challenge and confirmed the pro-divorce vote of November 1995. (Editor)]

Sexuality and the Physically Disabled and Elderly

Attitudes about the sexuality of physically and mentally handicapped persons and the elderly are generally negative. In the training of teachers and health personnel who work with the handicapped and the elderly, sexuality in given little or no attention. Institutions in general make little provision for the sexual needs of their residents.

Incidence of Oral and Anal Sex

The incidence of these sexual expressions is unknown. Oral sex appears to be relatively common and anal sex much less so. There are no legal restrictions on any of these activities.

6. Homoerotic, Homosexual, and Ambisexual Behaviors

Representation of heterosexuality as the only acceptable sexual expression is directly linked to the wider relationships between the sexes in society. The family, based on marriage, is promoted as the only valid social unit. Homosexual men and lesbian women are seen as a threat, and are marginalized, ostracized, and discriminated against. They can be, and are, dismissed from jobs and denied promotion. In custody proceedings, they can have their children taken from them on the basis of their sexual orientation. They cannot adopt children. They are the targets of pervasive social prejudice, often amounting to open hostility and physical assault.

The societal messages to which young people are exposed almost entirely omit the experiences, desires, and hopes of young lesbians and gay men, as they do with all minority groups. Those images that do occur are almost always negative stereotypes and caricatures. Young homosexuals face an even greater burden of sexual guilt and confusion than is the norm in other societies.

While little or no research has been carried out on homosexual experiences, it appears that these are common in adolescence, particularly for males. It may be just as common for girls, but the greater general tolerance for male sexual expression makes it more likely that one becomes aware of the male homosexual.

Gay men and lesbians tend to meet in particular bars, discos, saunas, and clubs. These are concentrated in cities, particularly in Dublin. Relationships formed can include brief, anonymous sexual encounters, a series of sexual friendships, an open relationship with a primary partner, or a closed monogamous relationship. Cruising, in which sexual partners are sought in public places such as parks and toilets, seems to be limited to gay men. Bisexual married men also appear to favor these outlets.

Telephone support and information lines are run in the major cities by gay and lesbian organizations. They also provide facilities for meetings and social events. Gay and lesbian publications are widely distributed, and publications by the Gay Health Action organization have been in the forefront in keeping all segments of the community informed about HIV infection and AIDS.

In 1993, the government repealed the existing law making homosexual acts between men in public or private illegal, giving all such acts the same legal status as heterosexual acts. The extent of the reform surprised many, since a more limited reform would have resolved a ruling by the European Court of Human Rights in 1988 that Ireland's laws on homosexuality were in breach of the European Convention on Human Rights. The government has also initiated introduction of specific legislation to outlaw discrimination on the grounds of sex and sexual orientation in both employment and social areas.

7. Gender Conflicted Persons

Transvestism and transsexualism are so marginalized as to be almost invisible. However, people are generally aware of both phenomena and transvestism appears to be quite common. There are a number of transsexual people, but all would have undergone gender reassignment surgery abroad. It is probable that most hospital ethical committees would not permit the procedure. At present, it is not possible to alter one's birth certificate to change the sex designated at birth. There are no legal restrictions on transvestism.

[Transvestites have a way of acting out their transvestism that is culturally accepted. They can join a fife-and-drum band, or belong to a troupe of traditional dancers, and wear kilts. (Walsh)]

8. Significant Unconventional Sexual Behaviors

A. Coercive Sex

Sexual Abuse, Incest, and Pedophilia

In the past decade, there has been a growing awareness that child sexual abuse is common and widespread in Ireland. A 1987 survey of Dublin adults revealed an incidence of 6 percent for males and females. However, this survey asked only about digital/genital and penile-genital contact. There has been much controversy and some denial concerning child sexual abuse, but there are now signs of official recognition of the problem. An integrated approach involving different disciplines is being developed in an effort to reduce its incidence and to treat victims. Following the success of a recent pilot project, plans are to introduce a full treatment program for abusers. A Child Abuse Prevention Program has been introduced in primary schools, but is not universally supported. One criticism has been that it places too much responsibility on children for prevention of such abuse.

A 1989 study of 512 confirmed cases of child sexual abuse in a health board area revealed only 55 criminal prosecutions (10.7 percent). Sentencing ranged from a seven-year jail term to application of the Probation Act. Police statistics for 1991 include only six reported or known incest offenses, a gross understatement of actual incidence. Legally, a male is prohibited from having sexual intercourse with his daughter, granddaughter, sister, or mother, and a female from having intercourse with her son, father, grandfather, or brother. When the victim is under 15 years of age, the maximum penalty for convicted males is life imprisonment and for convicted females, seven years imprisonment. When the victim is over age 15, the sentencing varies greatly.

There is very little public discussion of pedophilia and its incidence is not known.

Sexual Harassment

Irish legislation does not specifically address the problem of sexual harassment. The Minister for Equality and Law Reform has indicated that such legislation will be introduced. Since 1985, victims of sexual harassment can pursue claims against employers under the Employment Equality Act. A survey of personnel managers, conducted by the Dublin Rape Crisis Center in 1993, found that incidents of sexual harassment had been brought to the attention of management in 40 percent of the companies. Half of the companies did not have a specific sexual harassment policy and 55 percent of these had no plans to introduce one.

Rape

In 1991, 110 cases of rape were reported or known to the police, yet the Dublin Rape Crisis Center was aware of over 300 cases in the same year. Social and professional attitudes to victims of rape often encapsulate in stark form society's pervasive negative attitudes towards women. These very attitudes lead many victims not to report the crime. It is widely recognized that the number of rapes reported to the police represents a minority of the actual incidents.

The 1990 Criminal Law (Rape Amendment) Act extended the legal definition of rape to include penile penetration of the mouth or anus, and vaginal penetration with any object. This act also permits a married woman to charge her husband with marital rape. Conviction on charges of rape or other serious sexual assaults carries a maximum sentence of life imprisonment. Judges, however, possess complete discretion in sentencing, provided they take into account a Supreme Court ruling in 1988 that held that the normal sentence for rape should be a substantial prison sentence. Lenient sentencing is common and causes considerable public outrage.

B. Prostitution

Female, and to a much lesser extent male, prostitution is practiced in the main ports, cities, and towns. Contact between prostitutes and clients occurs on the street, in massage parlors, and through advertising. Some prostitution is controlled by pimps.

Prostitution is not a criminal offense, but associated activities such as soliciting in a public place, operating and managing a brothel, or creating a public nuisance are felonies. The government has recently indicated that it intends to amend the laws on prostitution to make clients liable to prosecution for soliciting and to make "curb crawling" an offense. There is a high degree of tolerance towards prostitution in Ireland, as long as it is out of sight and mind.

C. Pornography and Erotica

In 1926, the government appointed a Censorship Board with the power to prohibit the sale and distribution of material it considers indecent or obscene. Initially, books were its main focus of attention and many works of literary merit, such as James Joyce's *Ulysses*, were banned. In 1946, an appeals procedure was introduced, and in 1967, the duration of each ban was reduced to twelve years. Customs and Excise officers are empowered to confiscate material they consider indecent or obscene. Pornographic books, magazines, and videos, mainly imported, are widely available, though they are not openly displayed or easily accessible.

9. Contraception, Abortion, and Population Planning

A. Contraception

Until 1979, the law prohibited importation and sale of contraceptives, despite the fact that, in 1975, 71 percent of the adult Dublin population supported the view that birth control was a basic human right. *The Irish Times* survey in 1990 found that 88 percent of the 18- to 65-year-olds favored the provision of contraceptive information in health education courses in schools. For over twenty years, the discrepancy has been growing between Catholic Church teaching on contraception and the actual practice of many Catholics. Yet the progressive liberalization of contraception law since 1979 has lagged behind the changing public attitude.

The absence of a comprehensive school sex-education program, combined with the reluctance of most parents to discuss contraception with children and adolescents, means that many young people begin having sexual intercourse with little knowledge, and even less use, of contraception. Little attention has been paid to the needs of adolescents in this regard, mainly because, up to now, the focus has been on meeting the needs of adults.

According to *The Durex Report—Ireland* (1993) the main sources of information on contraception for 17- to 49-year-olds were: books and magazines, 31 percent; friends, 20 percent; television and films, 7 percent; and lay teachers, 6 percent. The preferred main sources of information were: parents, 35 percent; lay teachers, 22 percent; books and magazines; 10 percent; and government health agencies, 5 percent.

[Before the advent of "the pill" and condom, the most frequent form of contraception in Ireland was coitus interruptus. Many an Irish woman was shocked to find that she was pregnant even though "he pulled out in time." Also, men who could not get their hands on condoms were known to fashion their own from saran wrap. (Walsh)]

All contraceptive methods are currently available in Ireland, although a person may have to travel a considerable distance for some methods, such as the IUD, diaphragm, or sterilization. Furthermore, the majority must pay for contraceptive services and supplies. Family planning clinics in the main cities and towns are the principle providers of comprehensive family planning services. These receive no government funding except for some educational and research projects. Some clinics have been providing recognized training for doctors and nurses for twenty-some years, so that more and more family doctors are now providing fairly comprehensive family planning services.

A recent amendment to the family planning laws allows condoms to be sold to a person of any age with minimal restrictions. Male sterilization is provided in family planning clinics, some private and public hospitals, and by a few family doctors. Female sterilization is carried out in some private hospitals with varying preconditions. Many hospitals will not perform female sterilization for ethical reasons. Some voluntary organizations provide free instruction in natural contraceptive methods, the Billings cervical mucus, and related methods.

Respondents to *The Durex Report—Ireland* (1993) reported on contraceptive use as follows: condoms, 28 percent; the pill, 24 percent; natural methods, 9 percent; vasectomy and IUD, 3 percent each; female sterilization, 2 percent; diaphragm and other methods, 1 percent each. Fourteen percent reported using no contraception, and 12 percent reported not being sexually active. The condom is particularly popular among 25 to 29-year-olds, upper-social-class groups, and those living in urban areas. By contrast, natural methods are practiced almost exclusively by married couples over age 30 and those in rural areas. The pill is most popular among single women.

No comparable survey has been carried out among adolescents. However, surveys in individual family planning clinics have repeatedly found that a high proportion of teenage, first-time clients had been having unprotected sexual intercourse, sometimes for up to three years.

B. Teenage Unmarried Pregnancies

In 1992, there were 2,435 live births to unmarried teenagers, representing 26 percent of extramarital births and 4.7 percent of all births. There has been a continuous rise in both extramarital and teenage unmarried births since 1981, even though the proportion of teens in the population has remained at about 13.3 percent.

Official statistics show that 700 unmarried teenagers of Irish residence had abortions in England and Wales in 1991. In addition, other Irish teenagers commonly give an English or Welsh address. There is no way of knowing how many unmarried, pregnant teenagers had miscarriages, illegal abortions, or concealed the birth of their babies.

Whatever the actual figures, an appreciable number of Irish teenagers are experiencing unplanned pregnancies each year. In contrast to former times, most pregnant teenagers do not marry. Most have and rear the child themselves, usually with the help of the family and/or partner. About twenty percent have an abortion and a small number give up the baby for adoption. All unmarried parents are entitled to a means-tested state allowance. In 1984, 42 percent of Irish teenagers who had an abortion in England or Wales had not used contraception on most occasions when they had sexual intercourse, and 83.4 percent were not using contraception at the time they became pregnant.

C. Abortion

The Offenses Against the Person Act (1861) makes abortion illegal in Ireland. However, in 1992, the Irish Supreme Court ruled that abortion was permissible where pregnancy posed a real and substantial risk to the life of the pregnant woman. Both pro-choice and antiabortion groups campaigned for further action to clarify this ruling. A referendum followed in which the people rejected an amendment to the Irish Constitution that would allow abortion only where there was a real and substantial risk to the life of a pregnant woman, with the exception of a risk of suicide. At press time, legislation by the government was still pending to give effect to the Supreme Court ruling.

In 1983, the people had voted for an amendment to the Constitution that would have prevented any possible future legislation to allow abortion. Ironically, it was the wording of this amendment that facilitated the 1992 Supreme Court ruling.

Following the 1983 referendum, the court ruled that provision of information and counseling services concerning abortion were illegal. Legal opinion also held that a pregnant woman could be restrained from travelling abroad for an abortion. In 1992, an injunction was obtained prohibiting a pregnant 14-year-old alleged rape victim from having an abortion in England. This was appealed to the Supreme Court and led to the latest ruling mentioned above.

In the 1992 referendum, the people also voted in favor of amendments to the Constitution to allow dissemination of information on abortion and freedom to travel of pregnant women to travel abroad for an abortion. Legislation giving effect to these amendments is also awaited. Opinion polls have indicated that the majority of Irish adults approve of abortion where the pregnant woman's life or health is at risk.

In 1991, 4,154 women who gave Irish addresses had abortions in England and Wales. It is not known how many Irish women giving other addresses have abortions each year. The majority of these women go to private, fee-paying clinics. Because of the ban in Ireland on providing abortion information, counseling, and referral, many of these women travel abroad unaware of and unprepared for what is ahead of them. Many have never been outside Ireland previously. Despite the ban, some organizations and individuals continue to provide nondirective counseling and abortion referral, although these sources will be hard to find for many women in need of such information. It is probable that many women experiencing complications following an abortion are afraid to seek help from medical personnel in Ireland.

D. Population Control Efforts

The Irish government has no stated position on population growth or reduction. With the exception of the period between 1961 and 1986, the population has been decreasing since figures were first officially recorded 150 years ago. A high emigration rate has more than offset the traditionally high fertility rates. Almost every family in Ireland has a personal experience with emigration. In the past, most emigration has been motivated by the prevailing economic and social conditions.

10. Sexually Transmitted Diseases

A. Incidence, Patterns, and Trends

All sexually transmitted diseases are officially reportable in Ireland. However, the number of cases reported to the Department of Health is low and widely acknowledged as representing only a small proportion of the total. A 1979 study by Freedman et al. estimated that reported cases of syphilis represented only 24 percent of the probable total and reported gonorrhea cases less than 10 percent of the probable total. The total number of reported STD cases increased from 1,823 in 1982 to 4,619 in 1988 before decreasing to 3,858 in 1991. Overall, there has been a rise of about 400 percent in the number of cases reported annually between 1972 and 1991. The majority of cases reported are those treated in STD clinics, and these represent a small proportion of all STD cases. Statistics from the city of Cork STD clinic show a decline in the number of new cases between 1985 and 1989, with a considerable increase each year since. Genital warts is the most common condition encountered in this clinic, increasing by 63 percent between 1985 and 1991, while gonorrhea decreased dramatically in the same period.

B. Treatment and Prevention Efforts

Treatment for STD is available free of charge at STD clinics in the main cities and towns. Treatment is also available from specialists in private practice and family doctors. Thirty percent of the population is entitled to free medical treatment by family doctors. Until the appointment of a full-time consultant in genitourinary medicine in 1988, clinic services were poorly developed, understaffed, and overcrowded. Since 1988, the situation has improved, but many parts of the country still have no clinical services.

Patients are encouraged to contact partners at risk. If they fail to do so, some clinics will make the contact themselves, with the patient's permission. In the 1979 Freedman et al. study, one in five family doctors was interviewed by phone about treatment of STDs. Six percent had seen no STD cases in the previous twelve months. The vast majority had not seen a single case of syphilis or gonorrhea in a woman and a very small number saw more than two cases in the prior twelve months. More than half saw at least one case of male gonorrhea; 4 percent saw ten or more cases. At the time the male/female ratio of syphilis and gonorrhea cases was 8.4:1 and 8.5:1 respectively. Over two thirds of the family doctors said they would diagnose and treat cases of STD themselves; 18 percent would use laboratory tests, and 51 percent would treat on the basis of clinical diagnosis alone. Unfortunately, there is no more current data on STD treatment in Ireland.

Only in very recent years has an effort been made to educate the public about STD symptoms, treatment facilities, and prevention. Leaflets on these topics are now produced by the Department of Health, STD, and Family Planning Clinics. STDs are sometimes discussed on radio programs.

11. HIV/AIDS

By April 1993, over 70,000 HIV tests had been administered in Ireland. Of these, 0.5 percent were positive, with intravenous (IV) drug users represented 52 percent of those who tested positive, homosexuals 18 percent, and heterosexuals 13 percent. Among the 341 persons diagnosed as having AIDS, 40 percent were IV drug users, 35 percent were homosexual or bisexual, 10.5 percent were heterosexual, 7 percent hemophiliac, and 2.8 percent were babies.

All blood donors have been tested for HIV since the mid-1980s. Since November 1992, women attending antenatal clinics and pregnant women having blood tests for rubella status have had anonymous (unlinked) HIV testing. Consideration is being given to similar testing of IV drug users and those attending STD clinics to ascertain the incidence of HIV infection in these populations.

The vast majority of those suffering from AIDS are treated at a Dublin hospital that is finding it more and more difficult to cope as the numbers increase. Efforts are now being made to concentrate medical care for AIDS patients in primary health-care settings.

In Ireland, the gay community reacted swiftly and effectively to the AIDS epidemic. A 1989 survey of gay men found that there had been a major swing to safer sex practices, and that this had resulted primarily from education and information campaigns initiated by the gay community. For IV drug users, the government has initiated a methadone-maintenance and needle-exchange program. This is concentrated in satellite clinics around Dublin. A national AIDS committee advises the Minister of Health on various aspects of AIDS. This has led to wider availability of condoms and government-sponsored advertising about HIV infection in the media. These prevention efforts are supplemented by school sex education programs, but the availability and effectiveness of these, as discussed earlier, is highly suspect. Many nongovernment bodies, such as trade unions, have initiated their own prevention programs.

12. Sexual Dysfunctions, Counseling, and Therapies

A. Concepts of Sexual Dysfunction

Irish society defines healthy sexuality differently in many respects for men and women, young and old, rich and poor, and able-bodied and disabled persons. Consequently, cultural definitions of sexual dysfunction depend on who is doing the defining and which people they are talking about. Those who define sexual dysfunctions are often the same people who treat it. In many instances, the definitions current in professional circles in Ireland reflect and reinforce cultural stereotypes of what is considered socially appropriate gender and sexual roles. Those seeking treatment are usually as culture-bound as professionals in their concept of what is sexually dysfunctional or unhealthy.

B. Availability of Counseling, Diagnosis, and Treatment

Kieran (1993) sent questionnaires to 201 organizations and individuals who appeared to practice psychosexual counseling and sex therapy. Psychologists, social workers, and doctors made up the majority of 75 respondents. Most worked in private practice settings and doctors were the most common source of referral. The responses are the only perspective on sexual therapy in Ireland.

While there are psychosexual therapists who practice a more psychosomatic approach; they are in a minority. The most common, shared theoretical element used by the respondents was a behavioral approach.

In the survey, sexual problems were defined in terms of symptoms, for example, vaginal spasms, erectile dysfunction, and early ejaculation. Symptom relief is regarded as a successful outcome in sexual therapy. This symptom-oriented approach is also evident in the enthusiastic manner in which many people have embraced the latest "cure" for "erectile dysfunction," namely, pharmacologically induced penile erections.

Government-funded psychosexual therapy services are not available, except on an ad hoc basis by some public health personnel. Most family planning clinics provide this service, as do organizations such as the Catholic Marriage Advisory Council and the nondenominational Marriage Counseling Services.

There are no legal or other restrictions on who may practice as a psychosexual therapist in Ireland. Although all respondents to Kieran's survey stated that they had undergone training in counseling, no indication of the quality of such training was given. Forty percent of the respondents had received no specific training in psychosexual counseling or sex therapy; 70 percent were receiving supervision. Training, professional standards, and accreditation were the most common concerns of the respondents.

13. Sexual Research and Advanced Education

Little sexological research is carried out in Ireland. No university or other tertiary educational institution has a graduate or postgraduate program on sexuality. Nor is there any formal program for sexological research in any of these institutions.

The only sexological organization working in Ireland is the Ireland Region of the British Association of Sexual and Marital Therapists. Address: 67 Pembroke Road, Dublin 4, Ireland.

References and Suggested Readings

A.I.D.S. Action News. August 1989. Dublin: Gay Health Action.

Cantillon, J., et al. April 1993. *Sexually Transmitted Diseases.* Newsletter of the Irish Association of Family Planning Doctors.

The Changing Family. 1984. Dublin: University College, Family Studies Unit.

Child Abuse Statistics 1983-1991. Dublin: Department of Health.

Child Sexual Abuse in Dublin (Pilot Survey Report). 1987. Dublin: Market Research Bureau of Ireland Ltd.

Child Sexual Abuse in the Eastern Health Board Region of Ireland in 1988. 1993. Dublin: Kieran McKeown Ltd.

Deehan, A., & C. Fritzpatrick. 1993. "Sexual Behaviour of Normal Children as Perceived by Their Parents. *Irish Medical Journal*, 4:130-32.

The Durex Report–Ireland. 1993.

First Report of the Second Joint Committee on Women's Rights. 1988. Dublin: Government Publications Office.

Francoeur, R. T. 1982. *Becoming a Sexual Person*. (1st ed.). New York: John Wiley & Son.

Freedman, D., et al. 1981. "Sexual Transmitted Diseases as Seen by General Practitioners in Ireland: Use of a Telephone Survey." *Sexually Transmitted Diseases*, 1:5-7.

Guidelines on the Development of Sex/Relationships Education. 1987. Dublin: Department of Education.

Irish Values and Attitudes: The Irish Report of the European Value Systems Study. 1984. Dublin: Dominican Publications.

The Irish Times/M.R.B.T. Poll. May 28, 1990. Dublin: *The Irish Times*.

Kiernan, K. 1992. *School Sex Education in Ireland*. Dublin: Trinity College. Thesis.

Kieran, P. 1993. *Psychosexual Counseling and Sex Therapy in the Republic of Ireland*. University College Cork. Thesis.

McGoldrick, Monica. 1982. "Irish Families." In M. McGoldrick, J. K. Pearce, and J. Giordano, eds. *Ethnicity and Family Therapy*. New York: Guilford.

Messenger, J. C. 1971. "Sex and Repression in an Irish Folk Community." In D. Marshall & R. Suggs. *Human Sexual Behavior*. Englewood Cliffs, New Jersey: Prentice-Hall.

Report of the Garda Commissioner. 1991. Dublin: Government Publications Office.

Sexual Harassment in the Workplace. 1993. Dublin: Dublin Rape Crisis Center.

Stahl, E. J. 1979. "A New Explanation of Sexual Repression in Ireland." *Central Issues in Anthropology (Journal of the Central States Anthropological Society)*, 1(1):37-67.

Summary of A.I.D.S./H.I.V. Statistics. March 1993. Dublin: Department of Health.

Sunday Press/Lansdowme Market Research Poll. June 20, 1993. Dublin: The Sunday Press.

Termination of Pregnancy: England, Women from the Republic of Ireland. 1984. Dublin: The Medico-Social Research Board.

Third Report of the Second Joint Committee on Women's Rights. 1991. Dublin: Government Publications Office.

Venereal Disease Statistics 1982-1991. Dublin: Department of Health.

Israel
(*Medinat Yisrael*)

Ronny A. Shtarkshall, Ph.D., and Minah Zemach, Ph.D.*

Contents

Demographics and a Historical Perspective

A. Demographics

At the eastern end of the Mediterranean Sea, Israel is a small nation, long and narrow in shape, about the size of the state of New Jersey. Its western border is the Mediterranean Sea. On all other sides are Arabic, predominantly Moslem, nations—Egypt, Syria, Jordan, and Lebanon, most of which are in a state of war with Israel since its declaration as a Jewish state in 1948.

---

*See the important comment by the *Encyclopedia* editor in his Foreword, pp. 10-11. Although most of this paper was prepared prior to March 1994, it was edited and corrected until just before publication, with some parts written or updated in the interval.

Israel's 7,847 square miles include a western, fertile, coastal plain, a well-watered central Judean Plateau, and the arid Negev desert in the south.

Its population was slightly above 5,200,000 as of the end of 1995. In that year, 83 percent of the population was Jewish, 13.9 percent Moslem Arabs, and 2.5 percent Christian—most of whom are also Arabs or Druzes—and 1.7 percent other. Ninety percent of the people live in towns or cities. The age distribution was 30 percent age 14 or younger, 61 percent between 15 and 64, and 9 percent over age 65. In seventy-five years, Israel's population has increased tenfold, while the Jewish population multiplied by fifty fold from about 85,000 Jews in 1918 to more than 4,140,000 Jews in 1992. The population density, usually a measure of urbanization and industrialization, rose from 106 in 1960 to 231 per square kilometer in 1991. Life expectancy for the Jewish population at birth in 1995 was 76 for males (second in the world after Japan) and 80 for females. The birth rate was 20 per 1,000 population and the death rate 6 per 1,000, for an annual natural increase of 1.4 percent. Israel has one hospital bed per 177 persons and one physician per 345 persons. Infant mortality is 8 per 1,000 live births. The per capita gross domestic product was $13,350. The literacy rate was 92 percent for Jews and 70 percent for Arabs.

Israel is the only country where the society is predominantly Jewish and the Jewish culture dominates. This is a source of difficulty in understanding sexuality in Israel. First, Western cultures do not always appreciate the extent to which Christian teachings differ from Jewish teachings in matters relating to sex and sexuality. (Outside of Israel, large Jewish communities living within dominant Christian cultures have acquired some of the host culture constructs.) This problem is aggravated by a methodological difficulty: Some of the common analytical tools and theoretical frames of reference used to explain sexual issues, especially gender ones, are somewhat lacking, because they are anchored in alien, mainly English-speaking, cultures.

B. A Brief Historical Perspective

In the southwest corner of the Middle East's ancient Fertile Crescent, the land of Israel contains some of the oldest evidence we have of agriculture and the earliest town life. By the third millenium before the Common Era, civilization had made significant advances in the area. The Hebrew people probably arrived sometime during the second millenium B.C.E. Judaism and the land of Judea prospered under King David and his successors between 1000 and 600 B.C.E. After being conquered by the Babylonians, Persians, and Greeks, Judea again became an independent kingdom in 168 B.C.E. However, within a century, the land was occupied by the Romans. Rome suppressed revolts in 70 and 135 of the Common Era, and renamed Judea Palestine, after the Phillistines who had inhabited the coastal land before the Hebrews arrived.

Arab invaders conquered the land in 636. Within a few centuries, Islam and the Arabic language became dominant and the Jewish community reduced to a minority. During the eleventh to thirteenth centuries, the country became a part of the Seljuk, Mamluk, and Ottoman empires, although the Christian Crusades provided some temporary relief from Islamic culture between 1098 and 1291.

During four centuries of Ottoman rule, the Jewish population declined to about a third of a million people in 1785. As the Ottoman empire collapsed in World War I, Britain took over control of the land in 1917; the Balfour Declaration pledged support for a Jewish national homeland there as anticipated by the Zionists. In 1922, the land east of the Jordan River was detached.

Jewish immigration, which began in the late nineteenth century, swelled in the 1930s as Jews fled the rising tide of Nazi persecutions. At the same time, Arab immigration from Syria and Lebanon also increased. Arab opposition to Jewish immigration erupted in violence in 1920, 1921, 1929, and 1936. After the turmoil of World War II, the United Nations General Assembly voted to partition Palestine into an Arab and a Jewish state. In 1948, Britain withdrew from the country and Israel declared itself an independent state. The Arab world rejected the new state, and Egypt, Syria, Jordan, Lebanon, Iraq, and Saudi Arabia invaded, but were defeated by Israel, which incorporated new territories. In separate armistices signed with the Arab nations in 1949, Jordan occupied the Left Bank of the Jordan and Egypt occupied the Gaza Strip in the south, although neither granted Palestinian autonomy.

An uneasy truce prevailed until the Six Day War of 1967 erupted when Egypt tried to reoccupy the Gaza Strip and closed the Gulf of Aqaba to Israeli shipping. The war ended with Israel taking the Gaza Strip and occupying the Sinai Penisula to the Suez Canal, and captured East Jerusalem, Syria's Golan Heights, and Jordan's West Bank.

Egypt and Syria attacked Israel on Yom Kippur of 1973. Israel drove the Syrians back and crossed the Suez Canal into Egypt. In the disengagement agreement of 1974, Israel withdrew from the Canal's West Bank. A second withdrawal followed in 1976, and Israel returned the Sinai to Egypt in 1982. In 1979, Egypt and Israel signed a peace treaty, ending thirty years of war. A 1978 terrorist attack from southern Lebanon led to an Israeli invasion. The violence and terrorism has continued, with Israel responding to the 1982 wounding of its ambassador to Great Britain by surrounding and entering West Beirut, a military occupation by Israel of the West Bank and Gaza Strip, and the 1996 assasination of Prime Minister Yitzhak Rabin by a fundamentalist Jew opposed to accommodations Israel was planning to gain peace in the area.

1. Basic Sexological Premises

A. Character of Gender Roles

Judaism paints an ambivalent attitudinal picture in regard to women. It is certainly patriarchal in nature. The prayer a man recites three times a day includes a blessing for not being made a woman. On the other hand, the *Shabbat* blessing includes a praise glorifying the woman of valor. She is described in a traditional role of wife, mother, and homemaker. When a person is commanded to honor his parents, mother and father are mentioned explicitly and not the general form or the masculine one. A man is ordered to leave his mother and father and literally "stick" to his wife, while she is never ordered to leave her parents.

Gender and gender roles are viewed in a more traditional manner in Israeli sociocultural reality than elsewhere in Europe or North America. Already mentioned are several unique conditions that contribute not only to the perception of gender roles and the division of labor that are the public domain of family life, but also to concepts of intimacy and roles in sexual relations.

Service in the army reserves also contributes to the fixation of traditional roles of men and women beyond the military service at young adulthood. Men serve in the reserve forces a significant part of their adult life, typically 7 to 8 percent, but some as much as 25 percent of their time, annually, until they reach the age of 45 to 50. This fact has to be coped with within the family, and essentially exerts its influence on the balance of family life emotionally, as well as on the division of labor within the family balance of power, and the burden of physical and emotional responsibility of women to the children. Many children grow up with the ongoing worry about the danger to the life of the father, but also with stories that include macho and aggressive overtones. The exemption of women from reserve service on their first pregnancy, understandable as it is, only stresses the role division (see also Section 5C).

B. Sociolegal Status of Males and Females

Children

Legally, the rights of male and female children are fully equal. They inherit equally, are viewed with no distinction in terms of rights for protection by state authorities, and have the same rights for education and welfare in case of need.

Another law that has a bearing on sexual and familial issues is the prevailing legal situation (both in civil code and religious law), that there is no flaw in the legal status of a child born out of wedlock. This is sometimes used by religious authorities as an additional argument against granting abortions for unmarried women.

The only gender difference in the legal status of children is part of the religious family law that favors giving custody over girls to the mothers, while favoring fathers in the case of boys over the age of 6.

Adolescents

During adolescence, the legal status of boys and girls becomes somewhat different, mainly in regard to age of consent for sexual intercourse and the legal age of marriage, while their basic sociolegal rights remain equal.

The differences are in statutory rape laws—a concept that does not exist for boys. This creates an anomalous situation when a boy, who is more than two to three years younger than a girl of 14 or 15, has intercourse with her, opening him to the charge of rape in strict legal terms.

Despite this, the law does not distinguish between minors when it comes to sexual intercourse or molestation by an authority figure such as parents, caretakers, and professionals like teachers, psychologists, or physicians. Both males and females are considered under the protection of the law until age 21.

Another difference is the explicit permission to grant a minor girl an abortion without the knowledge and consent of her parents (see Section 9C). The practice is an extension of the rule that allows physicians to give minor girls treatment for preventing abortions, i.e., contraceptives, without consent of their parents. This widespread interpretation of the law is never challenged in the courts.

Adults

The situation becomes more complicated when females and males reach adulthood. In addition to the complications of family law and the interaction between a predominantly nonobservant population with state-enacted and enforced orthodox laws and legal system mentioned above, there are several other issues of personal standing in which the issues of gender arise.

Only a few years ago, the income tax laws were changed so that the designation of "head of family" was struck and married women acquired independent standing. Prior to that, women's earning were treated as a joint income of the family. The term "head of family" was applied to the husband, unless it was a one-parent family headed by a woman.

An increased percentage of women participate in the labor force. While in 1967, only about 25 percent of the women worked outside their household, their number passed 40 percent in 1980 and reached 49 percent in 1992. Despite their increasing number in many economic branches, and higher positions, women still suffer from lower wages for equivalent work, and from lower chances for advancement within a specific area.

The equal opportunity law does not permit discrimination on the basis of gender, and even demands that advertisements for work be directed toward both genders.

There is a public campaign now for corrective or compensatory discrimination. Many men and women object to this proposal because they believe that women in Israel do have some offsetting advantage because they do not serve in the reserves, a fact that many employers appreciate.

Another point is the fact that several of the labor laws, especially those dealing with maternal leave, shorter working hours for mothers of small children, and the inability to fire pregnant women burden employers with additional expenses and restrict their ability to compete in an open market. This seems to be a case where what was perceived to be an advanced social law less than thirty years ago may be inappropriate in the new political climate.

Another economic burden and female advantage that both employers and politicians cite is the differences in the pension laws and regulations. Women whose life expectancy at birth is 79, 3.6 years longer than men (75.4), retire five years earlier than men at age 60. In the public campaign to change the rules, women won the right to choose their age of retirement, but men still have to work until age 65 in order to earn their pensions. Thus the time that pension funds expect to pay most women is almost nine years longer.

This condition is aggravated by the fact that pension rights to which the surviving member of a couple is entitled are strongly in favor of women, who can receive up to 40 percent of their partner's salary, while in the rarer cases of a men surviving his wife, he can receive about 15 percent of hers. Several advocates of labor reform claim that any such changes will need to deal at the same time with all the structural differences between men and women, otherwise the system will not be able to carry the economic burden, and will also move from one form of discrimination to another instead of toward egalitarianism.

2. Religious and Ethnic Factors Affecting Sexuality

A. Source and Character of Religious Values

The term "secular Jew" embodies the problematics and the uniqueness of the Israeli situation. One part of it—Jew—defines the national sociocultural and historical identity. The second part—secular—defines a relationship to Judaism as a religion and religious lifestyle, and the choice of humanistic or secular democratic frame of reference over a religious one. These two parts can be naturally linked together only within Israel, the Jews' national home.

Only about 30 percent of the Jews living in Israel define themselves as religious. Most of the other 70 percent define themselves as secular, while about seventeen to twenty-three percent define themselves as traditional. The latter observe a few selected rules of observance, mainly ritualistic ones, while living most of their lives according to secular lifestyle. Despite that, the culture is strongly influenced by traditional Jewish religious values.

Three examples—(1) Jewish thought and its vehicle, Hebrew language, (2) the role of religious values in a predominantly secular society, and (3) religious politics—will illustrate the extent in which Jewish culture influences sexual constructs.

The Hebrew Language and Jewish Thought

Language is the vehicle of abstract and analytical thought and therefore plays an important role in our psychosocial phenomena. Hebrew, the language of Jewish thought, exerts a very strong influence on Israeli Jewish thinking about sex and gender. The first expression of the place and meaning of sex in the world appears in the first chapters of the Old Testament, in a way diametrically divergent from Christian thought. In Genesis, the first time intercourse is mentioned in Jewish literature, the root of the verb used has multiple meanings: knowledge, consciousness, and intercourse. As far as is known, Hebrew is unique in using one root, and thus overlapping meanings, for sexual intercourse: knowledge and consciousness. The common root for knowledge, consciousness, and the verb for sexual intercourse indicates that sex is highly prominent in Jewish thought, and not necessarily in a negative way, especially when one recalls that Jews are known as the "people of the book."

This influence is apparent despite the fact that other layers were added over the biblical language and, until this century, Hebrew was only intermittently used as a spoken language for secular, nonritual, or nonreligious studies. In modern, largely secular, albeit Hebrew-speaking Israel, very few people use the biblical term for intercourse in daily life. Current terminology ranges from the intimate (make love) through the neutral (to perform sex or sexual relations, to lie with) to the aggressive equivalents of fuck, screw, shaft, etc.

Thus, unlike many Christian approaches, traditional Jewish thought views sex as intrinsically neutral. It is a human characteristic with an extremely strong potential (like knowledge and consciousness), which can be turned into either good or evil by three humanly determined acts of choice: the meaning one gives to sex (an act of piety), the context within which it is practiced (marriage), and the way one practices it (rules of conduct, including purity laws). In itself sex and the pleasure of sex is not a sin. The harmony of flesh and spirit, an important tenet of Jewish culture, is expressed in married heterosexual relations. Its consummation on a regular basis, not necessarily for procreation, is a *mitzvah*—a combination of an obligation and a privilege—and pleasure is an important part of it. Those who abstain in marriage run the risk of religious sanctions. As role models, community leaders are to be married with numerous children. There is no monasticism, and abstinence is frowned upon.

Despite this, one can also find strong ambivalence about sex and the expression of sexuality in Jewish thought throughout the ages. Its instinctual nature and extremely high potential for evil needs to be guarded and curbed at all times. Some strong Christian influences are also apparent, especially among the Jews living in Europe for the last two millennia.

Another example of the role of the historical language's influencing modern sexual constructs is the fact that Hebrew is almost a totally genderized language. All the forms of speech—nouns, pronouns, verbs in all tenses, adjectives, and adverbs—take a genderized form. In contrast, English, the language of international research, is neutral, except for a few nouns describing animate objects. A comparative study among children of three different countries found that the gender prominence and dichoto-mization was ordinal according to the gender differentiation within the language, Hebrew-speaking children having the highest gender awareness. Thus Jewish children learn with their first abstractions how important it is to identify the gender of each object/entity and to look for the characteristics that distinguish one gender from the other.

The Power of Religious Values in a Secular Society

The Judaic nature of the society is demonstrated by the role that even secular people ascribe to Judaism in the life of Israel. While most Jews are nonobservant in terms of Jewish orthodoxy, many of them define themselves as traditional. Debates on the relations between state and religion are a constant issue in Israeli politics and public life. Issues like the definition of the Jew in the law of returning, opening of public places, or the operation of public transportation on *Shabbat* (Saturday), support for religious educational systems, and the exemption of women and men studying in religious seminaries from army service, are argued regularly.

In many such debates, many secular people defer to religious demands, not as a surrender to their power politics, but because they view Judaism as having a special role in the life of the state. One of the basic tenets of Judaism is that it is a national religion with a role in both public and private life, with a unique historical role in preserving the Jews as a cohesive people. Sometimes there is a feeling that in relating to religious demands in public life, secular people place themselves in an inferior position. This closely relates to this topic because marital and gender issues are an important part of the discourse and the complex relationship between state and religion.

The Political Power of Religious Parties

The influence of Judaism on family, gender, and sexual issues is exerted not only through the subtler cultural and indirect sociocultural forces, but also through the political, social, and economic power of the religious minority of the population. While the political platforms of the religious parties are varied, they are united in their determination to preserve the power and lifestyle of Jewish orthodoxy in the public life of Israel. Their political leverage is far greater than their actual electoral power. While the left- and right-wing parties alternated as dominant political powers and formers of governments, religious elements have held the balance of power in all coalition governments due to a proportional electoral system.

In return for support on issues of defense, foreign affairs, and the economy, the secular parties give in to the demands of the religious parties on issues of secondary importance to them in many social areas, including those relating to family, sex, and gender. Thus the judicial system that determines family matters is religious, although some aspects can be dealt with also in civil court. The religious influence is obvious in the reform of laws regarding abortion, homosexuality, and censorship of pornography.

The combination of religious Halachic canons with a public that is largely secular creates a conflicted situation. The reason for this conflict lies in several religious laws that impose great hardship on men and women, especially on those who do not adhere to the religious lifestyle. These include the law that forbids men who are descendants of the priesthood families of the temple from marrying a divorcee or a widow; a law forbidding an adulterous woman from marrying her partner in sin, even after she is granted a divorce from the husband; and similar laws.

These situations cause hardship also for religious people, but they suffer them because they adhere to the basic religious tenets. For the secular majority who encounter them, they are an imposition. This is one of the reasons for the strong tensions between the religious and the secular sectors, but the fear of schism is so intense that most people will look for compromise solutions instead of cultural war.

Nevertheless while the secular and the religious parties have officially agreed to a token truce, the preservation of an ill-defined status quo, in reality there is a constant political war fought in separate skirmishes on different fronts: in parliament, the courts of law (especially the Supreme Court of Justice), local governments, and economic pressures. While many secular people feel that religion is gaining ground in public life, most of the religious sector feels on the defensive within the paradox of a secular Jewish state.

B. Source and Character of Ethnic Values

An Immigrant Society with Unifying Forces

Israel is an immigrant society with a common historical background and a melting-pot ethos acting as cohesive forces. The absorption of repeating masses of immigrants since the early 1950s has had a considerable impact on sexual behavior, sexual health, and public involvement in sexual issues. In 1990 and 1991, 400,000 people, 10 percent of the total Jewish population of Israel, immigrated from the former Soviet Union. Issues of increased rate of induced abortions, relatively low number of children, one-parent families, an alleged combination of alcohol consumption and sex, and a seemingly instrumental view of intercourse quickly surfaced.

Also in 1991, 15,000 Jews immigrated from Ethiopia over one weekend, confronting Israel with issues of traditional medical practices, ritual isolation of menstruating women, and increased incidence of infectious diseases including STDs and AIDS.

Unlike other societies where immigration leads mainly to social fragmentation, indications suggest that social cohesiveness forces within Israeli society also act in the opposite direction, as integrating agents even within the span of one generation (see below in marriage and fertility patterns). The melting-pot ideology is not just a whim. There are some strong basic and structural needs that contributed to its development: a belief in the continuity and unity of the Jewish people; a sense of threat of either political or physical annihilation or both; and, a sense of revival and modernization of an old culture that was suppressed or dormant by external conditions. Although many people perceive the melting-pot society not as a domination of one group over others, but as a continuous process of the evolvement in a new culture, others espouse a more pluralistic approach, advocating the preservation and even the development of ethnic characteristics.

In reality, one can see that many factors relating to dyadic relations and sexual behavior, fertility and fertility regulation, and other characteristics change in a relatively short time, and different studies show the emergence of common phenomena.

Israel's Political Situation

Israel's political situation has a strong impact on sexuality and sexual issues. This small country, with a total population less than that of New York City, has been surrounded by enemy states and hostile populations since its founding. Until the 1979 treaty with Egypt, there was no land border that an Israeli Jew could legally cross. Even in mid-1994 when ongoing political processes set the stage for reducing the siege, Israel requires a military service for all citizens that influences sexual and related issues beyond that requirement.

Siege feelings and the need to keep national unity make many people accept compromises in striving for change, or at least lower the tone. This often changes the perspectives about priorities and leads to personal inner conflict between personal aspirations and internalized collective ones.

The influence of wars and physical danger on the sexual behavior of people, their marriages, and their fertility patterns are understudied. It is proposed here that, in critically dangerous situations, sex—which is biopsychosocially still connected to reproduction—may serve as a means to symbolically negate personal death. Such a hypothesis was used in attempts to explain diverse phenomena, like the frequently discussed increase in reproduction following military engagement, and the divergence from normative sexual behavior during times of active warfare.

Recent analysis demonstrates that the first phenomenon is only a rumor based on impressions and does not exist in reality. As appealing as the symbolic explanation is, the anecdotally reported departure from normative behavior during times of peace could alternatively be explained by feelings of disintegration during wars and irrelevance of social norms in those times. However, if this explanation were true, one would also expect widespread occurrence of phenomena like rape of the conquered population, which did not materialize in the wars in which Israel conquered land and assumed rule over large Arab populations.

Military Service

Several characteristics of the general military service, which is dictated by the political realities, can affect, directly or indirectly, the nature of Israeli sexual constructs. The role of the Israel Defense Forces (IDF), both as an institution and as a life event for Israeli youth and adults, is larger than in other Western societies. Most people would view it as essential to both their physical and national existence. It is an existential event in the life of most Israelites, and most families are immediately involved with its realities and dangers.

(1) *Gender Roles and the Status of Women.* Military service in Israel is general and compulsory for both men and women at the age of 18. Exemptions are granted for physical and mental health reasons, low educational level, criminal record, and religious reasons, but rarely for conscientious objections. However, men serve for three years and continue to serve in the reserves for twenty-five to eighty days annually until they are 50 years old. Women serve for approximately two years and are retired from reserve service when they bear their first child. This in itself is both a reflection and an enhancer of the more traditional role still ascribed to women in Israel (discussed in greater detail below). Other characteristics of the military service tend to accentuate the traditional gender roles.

Despite compulsory service, there is a strong element of volunteering in the army, as youth compete, sometimes fiercely, for service in elite units or prestigious tasks. This entails additional physical and mental hardship during compulsory service and in many cases an obligation to serve as many as six additional years. There is a strong element of macho psychology involved here with both male status and preference by the young women at stake.

Women do not serve in combat, and their choice of professions is not only smaller, but also limited to the less prestigious tasks within the army. Being out of combat service also blocks them from advancing in the army to the higher levels of general staff commands.

As the IDF retires its generals at between the ages of 45 and 53, exemplary service in the army and a top-echelon position is one of the stepping stones to the higher levels of civil service, business, and political careers. This avenue for advancement is closed to women.

The hardships of service, especially in combat units, promote strong male camaraderie and individual friendships; annual service in the reserves to age 45 to 50 tends to reinforce them. These almost-exclusively male interactions can be transferred to civilian life in the form of enhanced networking and alliances.

It seems that the realities of the military can foster traditional gender roles in the minds of both men and women, and also influence their social positions. Other issues discussed below point in the same directions.

(2) *Social Mobilization and Meeting Ground.* Sociologists have noted the IDF's role as a unifying factor and as contributing to the relative high mobilization within the Israeli society.

The IDF is involved in absorbing immigrants and in educational projects for women and men who otherwise would be unfit to serve. It also serves as a common meeting ground for people from different ethnic groups, allowing them to mix socially, and in many cases sexually. Many marriages can be traced to relationships formed in the army.

All IDF officers start as rank and file. There is a strong emphasis on advancement based on merit and achievement, and excellence is measured by a combination of mental, physical, and social characteristics. A meritorious service record is viewed as a strong character reference; in civilian life, young men from less-privileged strata have another chance for mobility.

(3) *Rite of Passage or Moratorium?* It is hard to appreciate the influence of the IDF on sexual and family issues if one does not understand the role it plays in the general individual psychosocial development of Israeli youth, and its centrality in the life of many individuals. Most Israeli youth leave direct parental control to go into the army. This is only one factor that ties army service strongly to sexarche, choice of mates, and other sexual issues (see Section 5C). Developmentally, IDF service has some definite elements of a rite of passage—the physical and mental tests, the demand for initiative and resourcefulness judged by peers and veterans, the formation of group cohesion and social responsibility, the ability to deal with moral dilemmas in extreme conditions—and these serve to separate childhood from adulthood.

While not disputing the rite of passage elements in IDF service, or its positive effects, it was recently suggested that at the same time the nature of IDF service may also cause a long moratorium on the tasks of real life, and can even be viewed as causing some elements of infantile regression. These may have effects on dyadic relationships and gender roles within them (see below).

(4) *Internal Conflicts, Trauma, and Violence.* A possible negative aspect of the military service that may have a bearing on sexuality and family life involves the nature of military engagement in the civilian uprising in the disputed occupied territories during the last six years. This forced the soldiers to confront civilians, rather than enemy soldiers, in a manner previously unexperienced. These high-risk confrontations with civilians tend to create strong inner and normative conflicts. Those who raised the issue hypothesized long-lasting effects, among them proneness to violence (including

domestic violence) and posttraumatic stress disorders. Claims had been made that in such discussions, it is difficult to distinguish between political stands and professional opinions.

The possible contribution of these issues on the actual shaping of sexual and dyadic constructs will be discussed in several instances.

3. Sexual Knowledge and Education

A. Government Policies and Sex Education Programs

The educational system in Israel is divided between general educational system and religious ones. This necessitates separate discussion of the situation in the different sectors. Most of this discussion will be devoted to the secular educational sector.

The Early Years (1930s and 1940s)

Early attempts at sex education, in the late 1930s and early 1940s, were based on local initiatives. Although coming from two different directions, they converged around the dominant psychoeducational ideology of that period—the Freudian psychoanalytical thought. The theoretical concepts, which had little direct field application, were largely that of mental health hygiene of a "preventive" nature, and were concentrated around the Psychoanalytical Institute of Jerusalem and the Public Health Services of a voluntary health service of the Jewish Community (Hadassah).

At the same time, attempts were made to develop sex education programs at the educational institutions of the left-wing kibbutz movement "Hashomer Hatzair." The atmosphere in these institutions was highly experimental, and the issues of sex, sexuality, gender equality, and the control of individual urges and wishes—not only sexual ones—as part of socializing ethos, were central to the life of the movement at that time. For example, not only was the system coeducational, but boys and girls slept together in the same room, four to a room, until age 18, and bathed together until age 12 to 14. Contrary to the expected, this was a society with highly puritan values, at least when it came to youth, and the key concept of sex education and youth sexuality was borrowed from psychoanalytical literature—sublimation. There was high social control over behavior: purity and self-control were expected, not only in the area of sexuality, but also in areas like smoking and drinking. It is interesting to note that these two behaviors are clustered with precocious initiation of intercourse as "problem behaviors" in the modern research literature.

The 1960s

A revival of interest in sex education came in the early and mid-1960s, when several sex-education "guidebooks" were published by concerned professionals. These were not as yet part of an organized sex-education drive, but their almost simultaneous publication is significant, as was the foundation of the Israeli Family Planning Association in 1966. It seems that the main concerns during that period were the apparent increase of sexual behavior among youth and the alleged contribution of large families to low socio-economic status (SES) prospects and crime among young immigrants from Middle Eastern countries.

The 1970s and 1980s

The big organizational change happened in the early 1970s. Dominant among the incentives was the increase in the incidence of sexually trans-mitted diseases (STDs) among youth, following a wave of youth tourism to Israel after the 1967 war. This also coincided with some changes in the general ethos of the country from communal to individual, which may be attributed to filtration of the youth movements of the 1960s in Europe and North America, and with a relative economic boom following four years of recession.

A national study about sexual knowledge, attitudes, and practices was mandated and carried out in the early 1970s. The outcome of the delib-erations of a multisectorial committee was an outline for a comprehensive general curriculum arranged chronologically by content areas and skill formation, and the formation of a Unit of Family Life and Sex Education at the Ministry of Education.

The original conceptual framework for this experimental unit was a mixture of preventive health (implying a high potential for adverse effects of sexual behavior), a developmental outlook, and normative boundaries. Its mandate was very wide and flexible and included the development of educational programs, the training of sex educators, and the implementa-tion of nonmandatory sex education within the school system.

Two parallel units were formed, one to deal with the issues within the national-religious sector (which dropped the sex education out of its name) and the other one to deal with the same issue within the general (secular) national educational system.

The National (Secular) Sex Education Approach. The efforts concerning sex education in the secular (general) system developed in three main parallel directions: (1) the development of programs and educational materials for different content areas, ages, and skills; (2) training sex educators/facilita-tors; and (3) creating the infrastructure for the implementation of the programs within schools. The development of the programs and the training of sex educators was influenced by the humanistic approach to sex education of the Sexuality Information and Education Council of the United States (SIECUS), American Association of Sex Educators, Counselors, and Therapists (AASECT), and Society for the Scientific Study of Sexuality (SSSS) schools. Professionals from the United States of America, most notably Lester Kirkendall and Sol Gordon, helped with the first training courses and development programs in the late 1970s and early 1980s.

In 1978, the curriculum for family life and sex education was formally adopted and the unit ceased to be an experimental one. After several years of independent (precarious) existence, it was adopted administratively into the Psycho-Educational Services of the Ministry of Education. The infrastructure for supporting implementation of sex education now includes several regional trainers, with whom teachers can consult.

The appearance of AIDS on the Israeli scene in the mid-1980s was a mixed blessing for sex education. The rise in public interest in sexual behavior, the perception of youth as an at-risk group, and the feeling of inadequacy concerning sex education among many parents, acted together with other factors in 1989 to mandate sex education at least three times within the formal education span. In each stage, elementary, middle, and high school, pupils are to be given sixteen hours of sex education. Unfortunately, this mandate was not accompanied by the necessary budgetary or time allotment for this purpose, so that its implementation still depends on local arrangements, the priorities of principals, and the difficulties of the staff in dealing with the subject.

On the other hand, the public interest in sex education took a swing from the developmental-humanistic approach back to the preventive-medical ones. Also, parties less interested in education jumped on the bandwagon and attempted to lead campaigns by playing on the fears of the public.

The National-Religious Sector Approach (Excluding the Ultra Orthodox Approach). This educational system focuses on a moralistic approach and normative behavior within the boundaries of the religious framework. An integral part of this framework is the dichotomization between public and private behavior. While the Jewish practice allows for the fallibility of the individual and mitigating circumstances, it strongly forbids the a priori consideration or discussion of alternative behaviors. Thus, an educational discussion of the forces leading to premarital sexual behavior, decision making, and alternatives within such situations can be done only within a judgmental right-wrong framework in which abstinence is viewed as the only appropriate alternative.

Several religious educators have been dissatisfied with this approach and expressed their displeasure by participating in training courses for sex educators in the secular sector, contrary to administrative directives. They explain this by their wish to respond to the pressing needs of their pupils beyond the formal and normative guidelines and by a personal need for developing in this area.

Ultra Orthodox Educational Systems. There is only indirect and fragmentary knowledge about sex education within the "Independent Educational System," run by the ultra orthodox sector, because this system is not accountable to the administrator of the national curriculum (see Section 14 on Ultra Orthodox Jews [*Haredim*]).

B. Informal Sources of Information

Parents as a Source of Information

Findings of a national study of youth sexuality from the 1970s, augmented by some later studies using convenience samples and limited populations studies, show that between the ages of 14 through 17: (1) parents in general were viewed as a low source of information on sexual issues; (2) daughters consulted more than sons with parents; (3) mothers are a much more common information source than fathers; and (4) both parents were a very low source of information for sons, although sons also consulted more often with their mothers than with fathers. Finally, the tendency to view parents as a source of information decreased with age—youth in the tenth and eleventh grade were less likely to view their parents as a source of information than were eighth and ninth graders. This change was bigger for sons than for daughters. These results are supported by studies of unique populations such as youth from problem families residing in boarding high schools, kibbutz youth, and by youth general health studies that included sexuality components. Even when similar pictures are different in important details, this can be explained by the unique conditions of the studied populations.

A possible explanation for the findings that girls interact more than boys with their parents, especially their mothers, on sexual issues, can be that the interactions are not initiated by the girls but by the mothers, who are both more concerned with the expression of female sexuality and more comfortable in approaching their daughters.

This finding that daughters consult parents more than sons conflicts with the findings that their objective knowledge is lower when compared to male youth. An explanation might be that the interaction of daughters with their mothers is more on issues of attitudes and consent than on information, or that the higher ambivalence of female adolescents about their sexuality does not allow them to benefit from the higher amount of interactions with adults.

A recent study using a limited convenience sample found a different picture that could be very important, if replicated in a more generalizable form. In a high-middle-class senior high-school sample, parents were the second most important source of information for girls and third for boys.

This may indicate that urban middle-class parents are now finding it easier to talk with their children about sex. This may be part of the trend of increased acceptance of adolescent sexuality, or a reduction in the distance between parents and their adolescent offspring.

There is a question whether parents are an appropriate source of sexual knowledge for youth because of their emotional involvement and their heterogeneity in regard to reliable information. Popular sentiments, based on the general assumption that parental involvement in education is desired, regard as problematic the findings that parents are a low perceived source of information. Attempts are being made to change this situation by interventions directed toward both youth and their parents. However, the effort to increase parental involvement may also reflect adult ambivalence over youth sexuality and the desire to control it.

Even if one accepts the belief that increased parental involvement is desirable, these findings are insufficient grounds for designing interventions; many studies need to be deliberately targeted at more defined specific subgroups before intervention programs are designed. It may be worth investing in programs to help parents to increase their role as a resource for their children and to help fathers talk with and be more available to their sons, only if the recent findings from the urban middle class are confirmed and the explanatory assumptions hold.

The findings from the boarding schools may indicate that in dysfunctional families, a parental substitute may be needed as a reliable source of information, especially for boys whose fathers are either physically or mentally absent and whose mothers find it difficult to interact with male adolescents about sexual issues.

Other Sources of Information to Adolescents

Concern over parents' being a low resource is heightened when other sources of information are viewed. Peers and older adolescents are found to be the main source of information for both male and female adolescents. This may increase parental and adult perception of loss of control as these are potential sexual partners. In addition, the reliability of this information resource is questionable because of the limited knowledge among older adolescents and because it is biased by the agenda of the resource persons.

While information from peers is in many cases unreliable or incomplete, its language and tone are acceptable to adolescents and young adults. It may therefore be beneficial to invest more efforts into developing systems of peer education and peer training.

An important information source is the written and electronic media. Unfortunately, much of the material directed to adolescents is sensationalistic, commercial in nature, and/or caters to the lowest common denominator. Thus questions/answers sections in youth magazines rarely deal with ambiguities and some questions that have no definite or generalizable answers.

Another source of concern is the fact that more children and youth report exposure to pornographic videos, especially among males but also females, a result of cable television networks and the popularization of video. (Pornography is discussed in Section 8C.)

Extent and Reliability of Sexual Knowledge

Although knowledge is insufficient to assure healthy or responsible sexual behavior, it is essential for their attainment. Knowledge is also essential during puberty and adolescence to help prevent adverse sequels of sexual behavior, like unwanted pregnancies and sexually transmitted diseases.

It should be noted that, unfortunately, some of the studies mentioned above used what is considered unsatisfactory measures of knowledge, i.e., subjective perception of knowledge rather than measurable objective ones. Studies by Ronny A. Shtarkshall in convenience samples have shown a marked discrepancy between objective knowledge and the subjective perception of knowledge about contraception; e.g., the fact that 90 percent of adolescents in a large study reported familiarity with at least one contraceptive did not mean that they really had the knowledge they needed to use it.

When objective measures of knowledge were used, a low level of knowledge was found among high school students, many of whom were either sexually active or on the verge of initiating intercourse. Generally, male adolescents demonstrated higher objective knowledge. Female adolescents had higher score on signs of pregnancy and abortions, possibly because of the personal concern with an unexpected pregnancy.

It is unclear why females who reported more interactions with adults demonstrate lower knowledge. As was hypothesized earlier, this could be because their contacts are on issues of conduct, but also because they and the adults are more ambivalent about female sexuality and sexual behavior during adolescence. This hypothesis is supported by limited findings from a high-middle-class study that showed that positive feelings about sex were positively associated with higher objective knowledge.

Sexual Knowledge Among Professional Students

A study evaluating knowledge of professional students in medicine, social work, and law at the Hebrew University in their first and final years revealed rather alarming findings. First, medical school education had almost no effect on the knowledge of medical students; only one of five content areas, the biomedical, showed a positive effect. Second, the level of knowledge was rather low, especially considering the professional needs of physicians and social workers. Third, sexual experience was in marked and significant association with subjective perception of knowledge. Fourth, there were weak and inconsistent associations between sexual experience during adolescence and objective knowledge. The combination of the two findings is alarming. Since it is assumed that awareness of lack of knowledge is better than perceived knowledge that is erroneous, the finding that medical students are largely aware of their lack of knowledge was viewed as a mitigating sign. Finally, even at this stage, age was positively associated with both increased knowledge and a more adequate perception of knowledge.

Extrapolating for a younger age, this finding supports the hypothesis that older adolescents are more ready, both cognitively and mentally, to enter into the sexual arena.

Several studies by Shtarkshall evaluated the lack of knowledge apart from mistaken knowledge, assuming that people who are aware of their ignorance are in a better situation than those who do not know, but mistakenly think that they do. The finding that professional students were largely aware of their lack of knowledge was viewed as a positive sign.

4. Autoerotic Behaviors and Patterns

There are no known sources that document autoerotic behavior patterns in the general population in a quantitative way. Even a publication of a recent general population survey on sexual function and dysfunction does not fill this gap.

Sexual history interviews with a large biased sample of help-seeking individuals and couples show the following patterns. Among the nonreligious, more men than women report masturbating either prior to sexarche or after it. Also, more men than women report direct manual stimulation, while fewer report indirect stimulation like rubbing the thighs, or thrusting and rubbing against objects. These methods are more favored by women. There is a question whether this is a difference in practice or a reporting bias, but this question cannot be resolved on the basis of these reports in themselves. Among the orthodox, and certainly among the ultra orthodox, the issue of reporting bias is more pronounced, as male masturbation is a serious sin, while female masturbation is only frowned upon and considered unhealthy.

There are many lay beliefs concerning masturbation that are expressed mainly by adolescents and youth, either as questions or comments within sex-education sessions. These are mainly lay beliefs concerning general or reproductive health, and also the ability to identify a masturbating person. For men, the beliefs include depletion of the semen, blindness or short-sightedness, hirsutism on the palms, and an asymmetrical (bent) erectile penis. Among women, there are admonitions about weak sight and about giving birth to retarded children as a consequence of masturbation.

5. Interpersonal Heterosexual Behaviors

A/B. Children and Adolescents

Pubertal Rites of Passage

See remarks on IDF service as a kind of rite of passage for adolescents under Section 1B above.

General Lack of Data

Attempts to elucidate the patterns of sexuality, sexual behavior, dyadic relationships, and other sexual issues concerning adolescents and youth are hampered by sociopolitical restraints. The last study of sexual knowledge, attitudes, and practices in a national sample of youth was done in 1970. In 1991, a proposed study of adolescent sexuality was approved by a review system and then vetoed on educational and moral grounds by the Director General of the Ministry of Education and Culture, a political appointment of a religious minister. Even after the change of government at the end of 1992, a lengthy and tortuous negotiation process about the same study ended abruptly when the psychological services of the Ministry of Education "changed its research priorities" and excluded the survey from them.

Most of the available quantitative information is on secular youth with little on those who define themselves as traditional. All information about religious youth reported here is anecdotal, although it represents the cumulative shared experiences of a network of researchers, counselors, and educators.

Puberty, Adolescence, and Psychosocial Development

Very little research has been done on pubertal stages. All studies have used convenience samples of Jewish girls. The normal range for the onset of breast development in 1977 was from 8.22 to 12.38 years and the normal (corrected) age for pubic hair development 8.58 to 12.58 years. The normal range for reaching menarche is 11.09 to 15.49 years.

Several interesting effects associating pubertal stages and social class or ethnic origin have been observed. Girls from low socioeconomic class as defined by their fathers' occupations, whose mothers were poorly educated and who came from large families, reach the stages of puberty later than other girls. All three variables are highly and significantly associated with each other and with Middle Eastern/North African origin. Sample sizes did not allow a distinction between the contribution of ethnic origin (genetic) and social conditions (nurture) to this phenomenon.

It is possible that a secular trend is present, since a comparison of menarche in separate studies of similar populations have shown a drop of almost five months in mean age from 13.75 in the mid-1960s to 13.29 in the late 1970s. (This is not significant because of a large standard error in the more recent study.) During this period, there was a large increase in both the general standard of living and ethnic mixing.

The importance of individual and group differences in pubertal development in relation to psychosocial sexual development is well recognized but very difficult to study. Based on observations and anecdotal information, a hypothesis can be advanced that among Israeli female adolescents there is an inverted J curve relationship between age at puberty and the time gap between the onset of puberty and the first sexual intercourse or sexarche, i.e., girls who develop earlier and later than their peers may go faster through a scale of the stages of sexual behaviors. (Information about male adolescents is insufficient even for development of a hypothesis.)

As for social-class differences in puberty showing that girls of low socio-economic class reach pubertal stages and menarche at a later age, this may put some stressful pressure on them to act out sexually, especially in integrated schools, because the influence on psychosocial sexual development is exerted not through the abstract national norm, but through interactions with the significant peers. Another pressure on adolescents of low socioeconomic classes in schools, and especially in integrated ones, is the need to excel. There is enough information to suggest that low achievement, in comparison with a significant reference group, is associated with precocious sexual activity.

Premarital Sexual Activities and Relationships

This discussion of sexual practices among Israeli youth focuses on two main issues: premarital intercourse and the context within which it occurs, and on sexarche or age at first intercourse.

The issue of premarital intercourse during adolescence is more complex than that of premarital intercourse in general. It includes adult attitudes toward adolescents' sexual expression and adolescents' response to it, the interaction between adolescents, peers, and significant adults on issues of control, and separation. It is very hard to treat these different issues separately, and sometimes even to distinguish between them.

In general, studies up to the mid-1980s showed that attitudes of Israeli youth concerning premarital intercourse, self-pleasuring, homosexuality, and gender are more conservative than those of European and North American youth. Attitudes among adolescents towards premarital intercourse were associated with several independent variables: gender, age, modernity (socioeconomic status of the family of origin), and religiosity.

Degree of agreement with two extreme attitudes toward premarital intercourse—"Intercourse is forbidden before marriage" and "Intercourse is permitted if both partners want it" (not qualified by age, above 18, or by relationship status, in love or engaged)—are detailed in Figure 1. In general, younger adolescents are more conservative about premarital intercourse. Both younger boys and girls are more accepting of the forbidding message than older boys and girls, while the situation is reversed for both genders in relation to the permissive attitude.

The findings indicate that, in general, younger adolescents are more conservative about premarital intercourse. (1) As expected, acceptance of the permissive message increases and that of the restrictive message decreases with age for both genders. (2) Comparing genders, one sees that in various adolescent age groups, more boys than girls accept the permissive

Figure 1

Attitudes of Adolescents Toward Premarital Intercourse

Boys' Attitudes Toward Premarital Intercourse

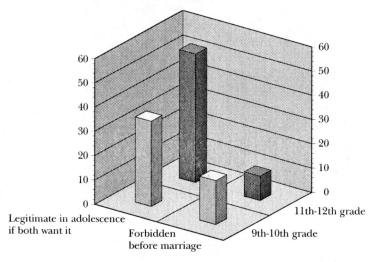

Girls' Attitudes Toward Premarital Intercourse

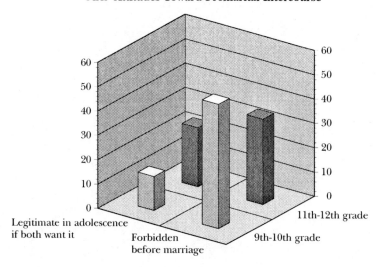

message and more girls than boys accept the restrictive one. (3) Both boys and girls are more accepting of premarital intercourse if there is an emotional commitment, and more so if there is a formal public one, i.e., engagement. The commitment is much more important to girls than to boys. (4) The discrepancy between boys and girls that supports a behavioral double standard is more pronounced when males and females report their attitudes towards virginity at marriage. Both genders express more permissive attitudes toward males' premarital intercourse. More than two thirds of females believe that girls should be virgins at marriage, while less than half expect this of their prospective partners. Among males, 10 percent believed that sex is forbidden before marriage, while 43 percent felt that a woman should be virgin at marriage. (5) There is also a discrepancy between attitudes and behaviors: Males are more permissive in their attitudes than their behavior and females more permissive in their behavior than their attitudes.

These differences in premarital sex attitudes is more pronounced if one compares older boys with younger girls. As this is usually the pattern of pair formation, it can be a source of tension and discontent in dyadic relationships, prior to initiation of intercourse and after initiating it.

Mechanisms like denial and externalization used to cope with these discrepancies can cause difficulties on the individual and social level, including coercive behavior and problems in contraceptive behavior. They can also lead to a reporting bias about intercourse.

In the religious sector, public norms are against any premarital sexual expression, not just intercourse. Many structural and social controls attempt to enforce these norms because of the common belief that, while adolescents have natural urges, they lack the self control of adults—such beliefs are also common among the more conservative elements of the secular sector. The result is sometimes paradoxical: the constant warnings and controls make people more aware of the temptation. The results may be dire when those who transgress do not possess the range of skills that enable them to protect their own needs while doing so. Those who transgress also have very little chance of parental or even peer social support.

Trends in Sexual Behavior, Premarital Intercourse, and Sexarche

Pooling the results of several different studies, one is able to conclude that the trend from the 1960s to the 1980s is for more youth to engage in premarital intercourse, and that a larger proportion of those who do so start at a younger age. The increase in the reported rate for younger women from the 1960s to the 1980s is three- to sixfold, the highest increase for both men and women of all ages.

Figure 2 shows the trend to earlier sexarche among urban women in one study. Caution is needed in using this study, the only one giving data about premarital intercourse among urban Jewish women prior to 1965. This study has all the limitations of retrospective studies; the time span between the occurrence of the events and the reporting point varies, and the reporting may be influenced by a memory bias. In addition, it was limited to married women in their first marriage, and thus it does not represent the whole Jewish population. Both nonmarrying and divorce may be associated in more than one way with the timing of first intercourse.

Figure 2

Cumulative Percentages of Women Initiating Intercourse at Different Ages, for Women Reaching Age 16 at Three Different Periods (Cumulative Percentages of Those Who Practiced Intercourse at a Calendar Year Prior to Their Marriage)

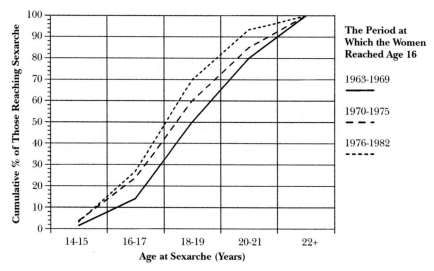

The differences between the three studied periods are significant at the $p = 0.001$ level.

Figure 2 also demonstrates an interesting phenomenon. All three groups of women show a rise in the slope of the curve between ages 16 to 17 and 18 to 19. Since most Israeli youth leave home at that age to go to the IDF, it seems that this is a critical age for the urban women.

In all studies of the urban population, more than 90 percent of the studied population—secular Jewish youth at high school, at any age more men than women—reported that they had already had sexual intercourse. However, the trend from the 1970s to the 1980s shows that the gender discrepancy in decreasing. The ratio of urban men/women reporting intercourse ranged from more than 8:1 for tenth grade and 3:1 in the twelfth grade in the 1970s, to 3-4:1 in the tenth grade and 2-3:1 in the twelfth grade in the late 1980s.

In the middle-late 1980s, between 12 and 30 percent of urban females and 40 to 55 percent of males had reached sexarche by the end of grade twelve; 2 to 11 percent of girls and 20 to 35 percent of boys were sexually active at the end of grade ten.

The discrepancy in proportions between men and women should be a source of concern. The three most widely used explanations in the literature are: (1) the presence of a small group of young women who engage in sex with many young men; (2) The initiation of young men into inter-course by older women; and, (3) reporting bias. As far as is known, the age gap between partners in most of the relationships among adolescents and young adults is either very small or in the opposite direction, the men being older than the women. There are no indications that there is a small group of women who initiate many men into sexual intercourse. Also, the tradition of initiation through sex-for-profit is relatively rare in Israel. It is thus probable that the normative pressures reported above are acting on youth of both genders to create reporting bias in the opposite direction: that is, more boys report having reached sexarche than those who actually do so, with fewer girls reporting it than those who do. An extensive experience with interactive sex education programs dealing with normative pressures and sexual behavior lend additional evidence to support this explanation.

The Context of Sexarche

In studies of the context within which intercourse is initiated during adolescence, a high proportion of youth reported that intercourse is started within a steady relationship. This is more true for females (95 percent of those reporting premarital intercourse in a large-scale study) than for males (46 percent in the same study). The same picture is apparent when com-paring the length of relationships: more girls initiate intercourse in longer relationships. Also, girls who were sexually active reported higher frequency of intercourse than boys, which would be the case if intercourse is practiced within a steady relationship.

Despite the general trend of initiating intercourse within a steady rela-tionship, a phenomenon of initiating intercourse with a "sex object" is encountered in significant numbers. Youth of both genders report that they chose a person for the sole purpose of losing their virginity, mainly because "it was time." Sometimes the chosen person is a different man or women from the one they are in a current dyadic relationship with. Sometimes this happens when they play the role of a sexually experienced person in the beginning of a relationship and do not find a way out of the role; at other times, they set out deliberately to find a person "to do it" with. Attention should be paid to this group even if it is small, as they may be considered an at-risk group. Because communications may be hampered by conflicting agendas and pretending experience that is not there, and the commitment between the sexual partners may be lower, it can be hypothesized that protection within this group would also be lower.

Experience shows that youth who are able to consult with parents or other significant adults, more often engage in protected intercourse. Un-fortunately, these are a minority, and those who do talk with adults are usually older and less in need of this support than the younger ones.

In looking at the length of relationship within which intercourse is initiated, a seemingly contradictory picture appears. A higher proportion of young women initiate intercourse within a steady relationship of more than thirteen months as compared to the young men—41 percent and 27 percent respectively.

Several factors, acting separately or in unison, could contribute to this phenomenon. First, the study was done among high school youth, and it is possible that the steady relationship of the young women is with older men who are already out of school. This does not fit with the higher proportion of males reporting the initiation of intercourse during adolescence. Second, the study may be dealing with a double-barreled reporting bias: young women, who feel that it is desirable to initiate intercourse within a relationship, tend to overreport the duration of the relationship, or those who start intercourse early in a relationship refrain from reporting it. An additional contribution to this discrepancy is that a higher proportion of casual relationships are between younger males and older females.

Premarital Courtship, Dating, and Relationships
and the Prospects of Military Service

The dyadic and sexual relations are highly influenced by the required military service, even long before they have to enter the IDF. Awareness of this future in the life of each and every youth comes in many ways, encroaching on the daily life of adolescents. Boys and girls are called for physical examinations at age 17. Many of the boys and some of the girls start even earlier on a road leading to one of the elite units or to a desirable military task. Membership in an elite unit means three things: first, a very high physical and mental competition requiring intense and long preparation; second, a much more strenuous and dangerous service; and third, a longer service, ranging from one to six years beyond the mandatory three years. Not all Israeli youth actually espouse this lifestyle; those who do are the pacesetters. The danger of getting killed or wounded in the army is small, higher in the combat units, and still higher in the elite units where even the training can be dangerous. The visibility and psychological impact on everyone are very high and out of proportion to the statistical reality when compared with road accidents or accidents in the workplace.

Working closely with youth and with facilitators of sex education, one frequently encounters two ways in which this reality influences youth in their midadolescence. First, lack of time to grow up and an unsure future are often brought up as reasons for hastening sexarche, mainly by boys but also by girls who find it hard to face these realities. Girls bring these facts up as looming in their mind even when the boys do not raise them. While it is possible that some young men use these as manipulative arguments, many of them are also strongly concerned. This effect is also documented in fiction and films, especially those by young artists. The summer before army service is part of the cultural terminology that carries with it connotations far beyond the surface.

Also encountered was an effect acting in the opposite direction, to postpone initiation of intercourse. Girls from some conservative environments, especially of Middle Eastern origin, may postpone sexarche in expectation of the time when the family and social controls will be lowered, and also out of regard for their parents' feelings, honoring family values by waiting until they are out of the home prior to initiating intercourse. Most of these girls will not go to college, but when they come back home after two years, the parents are already resigned to their new status.

Age of Consent: Lowering the Social Controls Over the Sexual Behavior of Youth

In the 1980s, the law of consent underwent a significant reform. Until then, the uniform age of consent—16—applied to women only. While some interpreted this as an expression of the wish to control the sexuality of women, others viewed it as expression of male threat to females' virtue. Toward the end of the 1980s, a change in the legal age of consent took into consideration some of the changes in the behavior of youth. While the age of consent remained 16—again only for women, intercourse between a girl aged 14 to 16 and a boy who was older than her by two year or less would not be considered statutory rape in the context of this relationship. On the other hand, the age of consent was elevated to 21 in cases of intercourse with someone under the guardianship or influence of a professional. The latter section applies to both men and women victims, but it is still not clear whether it applies to perpetrators of both genders.

C. Young Adults

Heterosexual Relations and IDF Service

Life within the IDF strongly influences sexual behavior, the formation of couples, marriage patterns, and gender issues.

By and large, the IDF is an institution of young people, outside regular parental and adult social controls, with its own sets of norms and pressures. Its immediate formal rules, which can be very restrictive, are usually set and administered by people who are between two to seven years older than those obeying them. For most youth, the regularity of military life is highly irregular when compared to their previous lifestyle. On the other hand, outside of defined training and active military duty, life in the military leaves them with unregulated and unsupervised time in the exclusive company of their peers. Despite being a male institution, the IDF includes a high proportion of young women.

There are no formal or social restrictions on fraternization between officers and soldiers, and very little emphasis on military formality and distancing that to outsiders sometimes looks alarmingly like anarchy. Since most youth serve in the army, and all officers rise from the ranks, they are essentially of the same class and traditions.

These circumstances that offer many chances for intimate and sexual encounters, combined with a rite-of-passage situation, tend to give those who are not sexually initiated a chance to be so. This is especially true for those who refrain from dyadic or sexual relations because of external restriction. Many girls growing up in traditional families or communities consciously postpone their sexual debut until the army, as an act of honoring their parents. They view sex away from home as less encroaching on the parental values. It seems that, by mutual consent, the question is not discussed between parents and daughters. Most of these girls will not go to college, but when they return home after two years, the parents are already resigned to their new status.

The conditions and situations within the army service are conducive not only to sexual relations, but also to pair formation and to experimentations in relationships (see Section D below). The IDF environment also creates two specific problems in regard to sexual behavior and gender roles.

First, the permissive environment can impose a strong hardship on youth from traditional backgrounds, especially those with lower educational achievements, who find it very difficult to deal with the relatively lowering of parental control over sexual behavior, coupled with increased opportunities and the company of eligible mates. This is especially true of some young women, mostly from families of Asian/African origin, who put a great value on virginity, and who, finding themselves in an environment much more permissive than their home atmosphere, lack the personal, experiential, and social skills to cope with controlling their own sexual behavior. Add to this the fact that those behaving permissively, including other women, are the ones with the prestigious jobs and high social status, and one gets a problematic situation. To resolve this conflicted situation requires internal controls and social skills that some of these women do not possess because of their traditional sheltered upbringing. For some who feel that once they have lost their virginity they are tainted, the result is promiscuous behavior. For others, it is a contributing factor to their inability to use contraceptives resulting from externalizing what they are doing. Internal conflicts regarding the fact that they are engaging in intercourse are sometimes resolved by the feeling of being repeatedly subjected to it "unintentionally," a solution that also precludes the use of contraceptives. The majority of soldiers applying for abortions through IDF come from this background.

To counter this, the IDF women's corps targets women with low educational achievement as a priority group for sex education programs. These programs attempt to strengthen their self-image and internal controls and to allow those who initiate intercourse to preserve both their self-respect and health.

A second factor is that Israel is a geographically small country. With very strong family ties, most soldiers in the combat units get home regularly every second or third week for a long weekend. It is rare that they will not get home for a month or more. It is thus possible to preserve dyadic relationships and meet with girlfriends on a regular basis. On such weekends, the soldiers, who are both tired physically and under a lot of emotional stress, try to cram in as much eating and sleeping together as they can. Their girlfriends accept the role of supporters and nourishers, a traditional motherly role, because they know how much hardship the boys have to take. There is also a tacit agreement not to raise disagreeable issues. This creates a situation in which the partners establish a pattern of separate traditional roles at the early stages in the relationship. It may also create regressive symbiotic dependence, where one is feeding into the relationship different components and relies on the other to supply the missing ones.

Cohabitation

Unmarried cohabitation has become more prevalent in recent years. Its frequency is unclear, but it is certainly much more visible and acceptable, mostly among middle-class, secular youth, either working or in higher education. This is a change from a generation ago when fewer couples cohabited, and then mostly after having decided to get married. Although this phenomenon has been little studied in Israel, the combination of anecdotal data and educational experiences suggest several points of interest:

1. While cohabitation is less binding than marriage and is often perceived as an experiment in dyadic relationships, the partners are expected to be monogamous.
2. Although somewhat more flexible than married ones, cohabiting couples adhere to traditional gender roles.
3. Cohabitation sometimes develops through an interim semi-communal stage, as when two or more boys or girls or a mixed gender group share an apartment for economic reasons. When one of them forms a liaison, the partner sometimes moves in and shares the bedroom in that communal arrangement. It is only at a later stage in the relationship that the couple sets out to find their own apartment. The initial stage is characterized many times by advertising it only among the peers and not sharing it with the parents, at least not immediately. The movement to the private apartment is usually done with parental knowledge and/or consent.
4. Parental consent, either implied or overt, is no refuge from the feelings of tensions or ambivalence on both sides. When interviewed, several women in such arrangements mentioned that either their father or mother had a difficulty in relating to either the bedroom or the shared bed when visiting their apartment.
5. It is possible that cohabitation is part of the larger phenomenon of extended moratorium that Israeli youth take after IDF service. Co-

habitation creates an interim stage between the public announcement of the relationship and creating a formal commitment.

6. Cohabiting young adults who eventually marry, although not necessarily with the cohabiting partner, suggest some ambivalent attitudes to marriage. On one hand, there is dissatisfaction with the parental model of marriage and reluctance to perpetuate a similar pattern. On the other hand, the idealization of marriage and attachment to it as an institution drives them to aspire to an improved version. This may act against the crystallization of traditional gender roles.

7. There are anecdotal indications that cohabiting is, for a growing number of couples, an expression of shunning the rabbinical religious ritual and a rejection of the legal ramifications that it entails. Resolution comes either by using one of the tolerated civil arrangements or in postponing the religious ritual until the last moment when they plan to have children.

8. Breaking up a cohabiting arrangement seems to be more difficult than breaking up a noncohabiting relationship, and the phenomenon of feeling entrapped in a relationship is encountered also by cohabiting couples.

9. When deciding to marry, couples express it as either taking another step along the road or as wanting to formalize the relationship in order to have children. Many cohabiting couples marry when the women are already pregnant.

D. Marriage Patterns

Legal Age of Marriage

The legal age of marriage is distinct from the age of consent. It applies only for women, and currently it is 17. Ronny A. Shtarkshall was involved as an expert witness in an attempt to apply both age of consent and legal age of marriage to men also. This was barred in a parliamentary committee by a representative of a human rights party on the grounds that this will complicate things and that, while women need protection from men, men do not need protection from women.

Age at First Marriage

In comparison to other Western industrial countries, Israelis marry relatively young. This is true even if one looks separately at the Jewish population. In 1990, the median age at first marriage for Jewish brides was 23.2 and for grooms 26.0. It seems reasonable that many marriages at the younger age were initiated by encounters within the service in the IDF. In 1990, roughly 25 percent of all the men who married for the first time did so between ages 20 and 23, and a third of the women marrying for the first time did so between ages 20 and 22, the years immediately following the service.

Among the Arabs, Moslem women marry for the first time at the median age of 20.0, more than 3 years younger than their Jewish counterparts, while the men marry at 24.4, only about a year and a half younger than Jewish men. Among the Christian Arabs, the median age is only a year younger for women, 22.5, but a year later for the men, 27.5.

In Figure 3, we show the changes in age at first marriage of the Jewish population over four decades. It is evident that between the early 1950s and mid-1970s there was a drop of more than two years in age at first marriage of Jewish grooms from 27 to 25. Among Jewish brides the phenomenon is very similar, but smaller, a drop of about one year (23 to 22). This drop is due to the mass immigration from Moslem countries in the mid-1950s and early 1960s. The tradition of these Jewish communities favored early marriage, similar to the Moslem host cultures. This effect on the mean marriage age of brides is less pronounced—and in the median age even nonexistent—because traditionally, brides were younger than the grooms and were married at a very young age, 14 to 16. The Israeli laws forbade such marriages, raising somewhat immediately the marriage age of brides.

Figure 3

Age at First Marriage of Jewish Men and Women

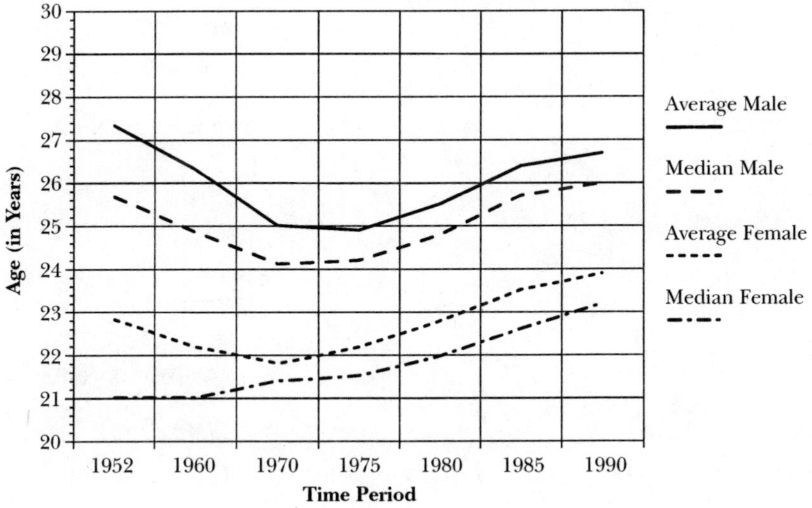

Since the mid-1970s, there is a steady rise in both mean and median age of first marriage for both brides and grooms. The rise is larger for women than for men. It is suggested that this rise is the result of educational changes, especially those affecting immigrants from Islamic countries that had a greater impact on women who were educationally underprivileged in comparison to men. It is also possible that the social acceptance of cohabitation has contributed to the rise in age at first marriage for both genders.

Marriage Formation

Among the Jewish population, most first marriages, especially those that do not deviate by more than a few years beyond the median age for first marriage, are based on personal choice and attachment. This is true for the secular, traditional, and orthodox segments of the Jewish population, the exceptions being the ultra orthodox and small groups of immigrants from Georgia, Ethiopia, and the Caucasus. Even among the immigrants, the pattern is changing, and many arranged marriages merely formalize previously formed attachments. Youths from some immigrant groups explain that they go through the motions in an attempt to preserve cultural traditions and avoid conflict within their families. The pattern of marriage formation among the ultra orthodox Jews and among Moslems, the largest group of non-Jews, will be discussed in the special sections dedicated to them at the end of this chapter.

At an indeterminate point beyond the median first marriage, the pressure on the unmarried to conform increases. Participation in family weddings becomes a burden, as many people use the traditional well-meaning but stress-generating blessing "Soon at your wedding." This is especially stressful to people with homosexual orientation and those whose self-image keeps them from initiating pair formation. At this point, families, especially mothers, sometimes turn to matchmakers and the young adults agree. The young adults themselves sometimes resort to meeting people through advertising in the newspapers. It seems that these channels are used by a minority of the population.

Interethnic Marriages Among the Jews

It is estimated that 15 to 20 percent of the marriages of secular and traditional Jews are among those who originate from different parts of the world, mainly Ashkenazi Jews, originating mainly in Europe, and Sephardic ones, who lived during the last 500 years in Islamic countries. The rate is somewhat lower among the orthodox and lowest among the ultra orthodox. The melting-pot ethos, high mobility of the Israeli society, and the strong mixing effect of the army all contribute to this.

Marital Variations: Polygamy

Polygamous marriages were prevalent among several Jewish ethnic groups, especially those immigrating from Islamic countries. During the peak immigration years of the 1950s, there was a great outrage about polygynous marriages, mainly from women's organizations, and they were outlawed almost immediately. This civil law contradicted both the Jewish Halachic law (as interpreted in these Jewish communities) and the Islamic law and tradition.

Common Law and Civil Arrangements

The courts recognize the status of a "common-law spouse" for the purpose of property division, inheritance, pension rights, and carrying a name. It also recognizes civil marriages enacted in foreign countries by citizens of Israel, and cohabitation contracts enacted according to the civil code, even when the religious courts ban these specific unions. As a matter of fact, these arrangements evolved in order to solve cases that rise from the conflicts that have already been referred to between the Halachic canons and the secular public.

Other patterns of marriage, like homosexual marriages, are not recognized by Israeli law, and single people find it very hard to adopt children.

Divorce

The Israeli divorce rate is lower than that of the U.S.A. and non-Catholic European countries. Still, the rates of divorce per 1,000 ever-married people aged 15 to 49 rose monotonously by 48 percent from 1973 to 1983 from 6.5 to 9.6 respectively for husbands and from 5.3 to 8.2 for wives. In 1983, the denominator was changed to 1,000 married at all ages; comparison between the two periods is difficult. Since 1983, the rate has fluctuated, rising from 5.8 in 1983 to 6.4 in 1991 (new rates), about a 10 percent increase.

A time series analysis of rates of divorce after specific duration of marriages reveal that the increase in rate of divorce is due only to increase in rate of "late divorce." It is the rates of divorce after nine and twelve years of marriage that are still on the rise. The rate of divorce after two years of marriage did not rise at all since the early 1960s and may even have come down slightly. The rate of divorce after six years of marriage has remained stable since the early 1970s; see Table 1. These findings are somewhat puzzling as formal marriages are almost universal, the percentage of secular people is similar to most western European countries, and the Jewish religion is more tolerant toward abortion than Catholic Christianity. The relative stability in Israeli marriages supports the claim that the family is a central theme in Israeli society.

One result of the increase of late divorce is an increase in the average duration of marriages that ended in divorce—a rise from 8.3 in the early 1960s to about 11 in the late 1980s and 11.9 in 1991. However, this increase in the duration of the divorcing marriages by almost 4 years was not accompanied by a similar increase of average age of divorce. For men, the average age at divorce for the same periods is 40.0, 38.6, and 39.4; for women it is 35.1, 35.2, and 35.8 respectively.

This means that the proportion of the couples who marry at a younger age among the divorcing couples is higher than among other couples. This

Table 1

Couples Who Married in Israel and Divorced, by Year of Marriage and Selected Periods of the Duration of the Marriage

	Cumulative Percentages of Divorcing Couples[1]			
Elapsed Time:	2 Years	6 Years	9 Years	12 Years
Years Married:				
1964-1967	2.7	6.0	7.5	8.9
1968-1969	2.4	5.4	7.5	8.8
1970-1971	2.4	5.6	7.5	9.2
1972-1973	2.4	5.8	7.9	9.6
1974-1975	2.6	6.6	8.7	10.4
1976-1977	2.5	6.9	8.9	10.7
1978-1979	2.9	7.2	9.4	11.0
1980-1981	2.7	6.9	9.3	
1982-1983	2.7	7.1		
1984-1985	2.6	6.6		
1986-1987	2.9			
1988-1989	2.2			

[1] The formula used is: Number of couples divorcing after the specified interval from marriage period divided by the number of couples who married in a specific period times 100.

is a sobering observation regarding marriage at a younger age if one regards stable marriages as desirable.

Extramarital Relations

Another measure for the quality of marriages is extramarital affairs. There is no reliable research evidence about the prevalence of extramarital affairs among married Israeli couples but anecdotal evidence, the reports in the newspapers about extramarital affairs of celebrities of all kinds, and the citations in divorce cases lead one to believe that the prevalence is rather high. Evidence from counseling, and from extensive education and information work among adults, leads one to believe that extramarital affairs, even known ones, are not in themselves sufficient to destabilize marriages.

E. Marital Law and the Status of Women

The law in Israel gives authority over personal issues to semiautonomous religious judicial systems of the recognized religious communities. Cases are tried according to the religious laws of each denomination. This is one of the reasons why conservative fundamentalist elements within the non-Jewish religions sometimes support Jewish religious parties, and even vote for them. Opponents of religious rule over personal issues sometimes refer to this as the unholy alliance.

Marriage and divorce issues of Jews are therefore largely determined by the religious Halachic law, although the civil law may also be resorted to in issues of division of property and custody of children. For a secular Jew, the patriarchal nature of the Halachic law creates an asymmetrical and undesirable power balance between the marriage partners.

This situation should not be fully attributed to the power of religious politics. They have at least the passive support of large segments of the secular majority. Attempts to create a situation in which secular civil marriages will be recognized under the law have been defeated several times under different governments. The claim of orthodox Jews, who are a minority, that this will create a schism within the nation that will end up in a disaster, strikes a chord in the heart of many nonobservant Jews. On the other hand, several developments suggest that the power of the religious establishment is diminishing (see below).

Jewish religious laws and the practice of the religious courts place women in a highly undesirable position for those who do not accept the canonic tenets. They cannot be judges in the rabbinical courts or even testify officially; they can only present their case. According to the Jewish religious laws, the men have more sexual freedom, even within a marriage. The husband is the grantor of a divorce and the wife is the acceptor. Even the religious courts cannot force a husband to receive a divorce against his will. On the other hand, there are several reasons why a divorce can be enforced on a women, one of them being adultery. As the duty to procreate is placed on the man, he may be granted permission to marry a second wife, when his first one is infertile and refuses to accept a divorce after ten years of marriage.

F. The Incidence of Oral and Anal Sex

Although anal intercourse was proscribed by law until recently, the restriction was almost never applied to heterosexual couples. A prosecution dealing with a heterosexual couple did result in a ruling by the then Legal Advisor and Chief Prosecutor, that strongly restricted the legal control of sexual issues (see below).

There is no collected data on the prevalence of these practices, but the experience of counselors and therapists point to the fact that all are practiced by significant numbers of couples. It is interesting to note that several subgroups in the Israeli population, Jews and non-Jews, practice heterosexual anal intercourse as a means of keeping an intact hymen and as a birth control measure, where the loss of one and the appearance of the other can be highly stigmatizing, damaging, or even dangerous.

The approach of orthodox Judaism is expressed in the fact that it frowns upon these practices but does not proscribe them. A Talmudic story illustrates this approach very clearly, although using metaphorical language. A woman approached one of the sages with a complaint: "I set a table for my husband and he turned it around." The sage answered: "What can I do, daughter, and the scriptures permits him." There is a question whether the story deals with the issue of anal sex or with vaginal rear entry, but at least some of the commentators agree that anal sex is the issue. This can be perceived on one hand as ambivalence, but on the other as a realistic view of human nature.

6. Homoerotic, Homosexual, and Ambisexual Behaviors

A. The Legal Situation

Until recently, homosexuality—or rather anal intercourse (sodomy) including heterosexual anal sex—was illegal in Israel. This was an inheritance of the British colonial penal code of 1936. According to gay organizations, victimization of homosexuals on the basis of this law was frequent.

Changes have occurred gradually and evolutionary, starting in the early 1960s. Despite the illegality of anal intercourse, the then Legal Advisor to the government and Chief Prosecutor and later Supreme Court Judge, H. Cohen, ruled that sexual intercourse between consenting adults, in private, cannot be a basis for prosecution. Since 1972, five attempts had been made by members of different parties to strike this sodomy statute from the penal code. In 1988, a political opportunity allowed its revocation. An amendment to the Equal Opportunity Law passed in 1990 also protects the rights of homosexuals to employment.

The attempts to change the law were accompanied by both public campaigns and many changes in public mood toward homosexuals and homosexuality. Until the mid-1970s, the IDF discharged homosexuals for psychiatric incompatibility and/or for being a security risk. This was changed prior to the 1988 legal change, and the IDF made several arrangements that allow homosexuals to serve without being exposed to undue difficulties.

Currently, several issues are being contested in the courts, mainly rights of cohabiting males that are usually granted to spouses under the rulings of common-law marriages. The issue is not as simple as it looks on first sight, especially when considering the regulations governing the pension rights of spouses when the principal owner of the rights dies. Male spouses have smaller pension rights as survivors than females. In the case of cohabiting gay men, this will give the couple an economic advantage over heterosexual couples.

B. Public Atmosphere Concerning Homosexuality

Several factors combine to make issues of homosexuality very difficult to cope with:

1. The political power of the orthodox-religious sector within the Jewish population and the opposition/respect ambivalence of the secular sector are major factors. While shifting from viewing homosexuality as a crime to medicalizing it, the orthodox religious still strongly opposes its public sanction.
2. The high sex-role polarization in Israel is part of the perceived centrality of gender differences that have both cultural origin and social importance. Tolerance of Israelis to homosexuality is inversely related to their sex-role polarization, and lower than that of American students living in Israel in proportion to the differences in sex-role polarization. Homosexuality, especially male homosexuality, threatens the world picture of two dichotomized genders.
3. Homosexuality is perceived as incompatible with the familial structure, which is of central importance within Israeli society.

In early 1993, a gay/lesbian conference was held in The Knesset (Israeli Parliament), despite strong protests from members of religious and right-wing parties. Public response to the conference, and to the personalities who discussed their difficulties, created further changes in both attitudes and practice.

A still problematic issue is that of open gay cohabitation. Although possible and prevalent, many people feel uncomfortable about it, and some express opinions that this is part of homosexual activism attempting to influence heterosexuals.

C. Homosexuality in Sex Education

Despite the fact that homosexuality is part of the sex-education curriculum and several units deal with homosexuality in general and with homophobia in particular, it seems that both school administrations and sex educators still find it uncomfortable to deal with the issues properly. Many youths, therefore, go through school without encountering issues of homosexuality in sex education, a fact that in itself constitutes a very strong message, to both homosexual and heterosexual youth, and especially to those who are still ambivalent about their orientation or wonder about it. Adolescents uncertain of their sexual orientation or gender identity will hardly find support within the school system, as there is no systematic training and recommendations on how to deal with these issues. Normative pressures to conform are high.

An interesting difficulty in facilitating issues of homosexuality in the schools was encountered during the training process of sex educators. Several educators justified their reluctance to deal with homosexuality, expressing fear of their own biases or stereotypical thoughts. Facilitators from the Association for Individual Rights, the Israeli equivalent of a gay task force, supported this position, claiming that only gay people are sufficiently unbiased and sensitive enough to facilitate educational programs on homosexuality.

7. Gender Conflicted Persons

Gender conflicted persons find it difficult to be evaluated and cared for in an organized and controlled way. There is not one center that has a comprehensive program for sexually conflicted people, and the authors know of several occasions that surgical interventions were accomplished without going through a protocol of evaluation/care/treatment. Other cases, where the psychiatric and psychosocial questions were resolved properly, had to go abroad for the surgical procedures. Professionals may be wary to raise the issues, for fear of invoking restrictive regulations that will even lower the ability to supply the needs of these people.

8. Significant Unconventional Sexual Behaviors

A. Coercive Sex

The categories in the criminal records of the *Statistical Abstracts* do not distinguish between subcategories of sexual crime and include sexual abuse, incest, and rape under sexual offenses. It is agreed by police, researchers, and activists alike that sexual offenses are probably one of the most underreported crimes. There is some disagreement as to the extent of underreporting as well as to the definition of criminal sexual offenses.

Sexual Harassment

The special circumstances of service in the army may create a convenient atmosphere and even stimulate sexual harassment. Since most officers in the three lowest ranks of IDF are not career soldiers, but extending their compulsory service, they are selected from the general mainstream of Israeli youth. Because IDF is in active combat, the selection of male noncommissioned officers (NCOs) and commissioned officers is based on, among other things, aggressiveness, charisma, initiative, and improvisation. These same officers, who are also in the closest working relationship with both men and women of the rank and file, are also older by two to five years, as compared to the compulsory service women—and in addition, are in a position of authority. Add to this the fact that IDF is organized mainly around values that are traditionally identified as male, and one gets an environment in which women are at a disadvantage. This creates situations that have a potential for sexual harassment on the one hand and manipulative relationships on the other.

There is another situation affecting older male officers of higher rank who are usually married. In combat units, the commanders are in direct daily contact with enlisted soldiers. As one of them phrased it in a group situation: "We grow older all the time, but they always remain at the same age, and we have to compete with them all the time." The context of this remark clearly indicated that women were part of the competition. It is unclear whether these officers are only in a power position or also in a very vulnerable one. Such environments and motivations have high potential for abuse of power.

The official stand of the army concerning harassment or misconduct, is strong, with several structural arrangements that attempt to counterbalance the potential for abuse. First, all women dormitories are out of bounds for men, including the officers commanding the camps. On any official supervisory visit, a male officer must be accompanied by an officer of the female corps. All female soldiers have direct access to an NCO or an officer of the female corps whose source of authority comes from an independent chain of command headed by a woman general. Complaints of sexual harassment, or any other issue of a sexual nature, are dealt with independently by the authority under which the woman is serving—the female corps—and if necessary, by the military police and prosecution. A highly publicized case is that of a general commanding the navy who was dismissed from the IDF for misconduct the day after he was acquitted in court of rape charges, for lack of supporting evidence.

Despite this, it seems that harassment is prevalent and is a source of concern to both women and the military establishment. In a structurally male, aggressively oriented organization, there is strong ambivalence in treating sexual harassment issues, and there are documented cases of attempted minimalizing of complaints, especially when they concern officers with high military potential.

The difficulty lies in what is construed as harassment in the eyes of male and female soldiers. Moreover, many young women find it very flattering, even important, that high-prestige men in the immediate environment are attracted to them. There are also cases where such situations are used manipulatively by the women, this mainly with younger officers.

Several educational efforts are now in process to inform both genders about their rights and about the feelings and points of view of the two genders on this issue. It is believed that legal as well as educational efforts are urgent because, beside the individual aspect, sexual harassment can be used as a means to keep a disadvantaging power balance.

Incest

In Jewish tradition, incest is such a heinous act, that according to the *Halachah,* it is one of the only three crimes that a person should prefer being killed rather than commit. This may explain the shroud of silence and shame covering the issue of incest. For many years, this was an un-heard-of crime.

In recent years, the changes in public climate, the establishment of child/youth investigators, and the change in the rules of evidence, allowing the investigator to testify for the child, have increased the number of cases in which incest is reported and prosecuted.

Unfortunately, charges of incest (like battering) are sometime used as weapons in attempts to get vacating orders and/or custody between divorc-ing couples.

There are some interesting research questions that need to be clarified, which will have strong bearings on preventive intervention and treatment: first, the differences between the legal definitions of family and of incest in different cultures prevailing in Israel; second, the contribution of the increase in nonbiological parents or siblings living together to the increase in the phenomenon.

Rape

A marked change in public attitude in Israel toward rape and rapists occurred in the 1980s and early 1990s. This is mainly due to the activities of rape-crisis centers founded by the feminist movement and to their political and public campaigns. These campaigns resulted in changes in the rape and sexual assault laws, mainly the abolition of the need for additional material or other evidence, to that of the victim, in order to convict a sexual offender, an increase in the punishment range given within the law, and a redefinition of grave assaults done with the help of a weapon or gang rape. There were also some changes in the rules of evidence, making it impossible to bring into the trial the previous sexual behavior of an accuser or a witness.

There were also changes in the treatment of survivors. Special examina-tion centers were arranged in emergency rooms in hospitals in each of the big urban centers in which the staff were trained both by police, by professionals, and by the volunteers of the rape-crisis centers. There are special courses for police investigators, and the volunteers of the centers are allowed to accompany survivors throughout the police investigations.

These changes, which are by and large positive, nevertheless raise some problematic points: first, how to maintain the right to a fair trial and the principle that people are innocent until their crime is proved beyond reasonable doubt; second, the mixing of political and educational work aimed at eradicating rape, with prevention work in a society were rape is still prevalent, with crisis intervention, and with treatment of survivors can create some confusion and ambivalent messages.

A study presented at an international conference on victimology found some interesting phenomena that could cause some concern in this direc-tion. The study compared the attitudes of two groups of professionals whose job was to treat rape survivors, police investigators, and emergency-room rape specialists, with those of helping-professions students and those of the volunteers of the rape-crisis centers. It was found that on several scales, the rape-crisis volunteers were more likely to take extreme positions, even when compared only to the women in the other groups. For example, they strongly disagreed with any assertion that there is a possible environmental involvement in the probability of rape, an attitude that seems to be problematic for prevention work. Despite the fact that they were one of the smallest groups, the standard deviation of their opinion scales was the smallest, indicating a very uniform norm. There is at least one case in which a woman who confessed in court that she had made false accusation of rape against a man cited the pressure by the volunteers as the reason for the filing of the complaint. One has to be careful with such an allegation, because it may be an attempt to lighten the personal load.

Another issue of concern, debated in public, was the slogan that "every man is a potential rapist" proposed for a public service announcement spot. When challenged, it turned out that the intended messages were that one cannot distinguish by appearances a rapist from other men, and that rapists are "ordinary" people. While in itself a political statement open to argument, this is a far cry from the initial message, which was understood by many men and women alike as stating that in every man there exists a potential for rape.

B. Prostitution

The Legal Situation

Israeli law on prostitution is somewhat complicated. Prostitution itself is not outlawed, but soliciting is, and so are the operating of an establishment used for prostitution and living off the proceeds of prostitution.

As a result, there are several arrangements through which sex workers sell their services and there are "classes" of sex workers. Lowest on the ladder are the "street" or outdoor prostitutes, many of whom also perform the sexual act outside. Higher up are sex workers operating in hotels, especially in tourist hotels, and those operating through some of the escort services that are currently freely publicized with advertisements on the fringe of legality. So, also, are massage parlors, which became a euphemism for sexual services with allusions to "relaxation."

There have been several media articles describing another kind of arrangement, which is reportedly limited to students, professionals, and middle-class women "supported" by a few men who are regular and exclusive clients. According to the reports, these arrangements are usually temporary, particularly among students.

Several attempts to change the legal situation by licensing prostitutes, putting them under medical surveillance, and allowing them to keep places of business, have failed mainly due to the opposition of the religious parties in the parliament.

Pimping: The Exploitation of Female Prostitutes

Although the pimps have traditionally belonged to the lower echelons of individual male criminals, they get most of the profits from prostitution. The women under their domination are kept in line by threats and the use of force.

There were several reports of specialists "hunting" young, runaway adolescents around the central urban bus stations, befriending them, and offering them shelter, and gradually moving them into prostitution. A more recent phenomenon in Israel involves importing women from the former USSR under forged papers and employing them in prostitution. This operation has many of the characteristics of organized crime, and the women are totally at the mercy of their "employers," as they are in a strange county with no valid documents.

Homosexual Prostitution

Several areas in the urban centers are known to be mainly or exclusively the territory of male prostitutes. Several reports have shown that, as with female prostitution, many of the sex workers are early or middle adolescents. Apparently, despite the fact that homosexuality is no longer a criminal offense, the police are checking constantly on these areas, and there were some reports of them keeping "pink lists" of male prostitutes. These reports were denied by the police authorities.

Transvestites

Several reports have revealed that some of the female sex workers are really male transvestites who are not gay and who do not cater to a gay clientele. These sex workers, some of whom have undergone hormonal treatment to grow breasts, pretend to their clients to be female prostitutes. They mainly provide fellatio; when asked to preform vaginal sex, they depend on their ability to stimulate the client to orgasm prior to penetration.

C. Pornography and Erotica

The Legal Situation

Until recently, Israel had at least nominal censorship on the theater and cinema. Written and audio materials were regulated only on grounds of security and not moral ones, and only public pressure created some restrictions. Abolishing censorship on the theater and cinema in 1990, part of an ongoing process of increasing the boundaries of freedom of expression as a basic human right, allows the production and dissemination of explicit sexual acts, and of violent ones, in print, film, and video formats.

Currently, despite the fact that there are less restrictions on moral grounds, there is a relatively recent law about displaying offensive materials in public that allows people to sue for damages if their feelings are hurt by specific items. Until now, the attempts to use this law have been restricted to religious issues. It seems that this does not include films or otherwise displayed for a fee, especially if the public is warned about the presence of sexual materials. This is still vague, since different aspects of the law have to be tried through a full cycle of litigation before its extent and effectiveness are established.

Restrictions on importing pornographic materials in commercial quantities by customs control are inefficient, and developments in satellite television and videotaping make them obsolete. This, combined with the rise in VCRs during the 1980s and cable television in the early 1990s, expose much wider segments of the population to both soft and hard pornography. Another prominent development concerning the public treatment of sexual issues is the increased commercialization of sex that started in the mid-1980s and intensified in the early 1990s.

Response of the Religious Sector

There is opposition to the increase of explicit materials aired in public from the religious sector. The more orthodox do not allow TV sets in homes and would shun those who do. Their reactions toward the treatment of sexual issues in public range from the economic boycotting of products promoted by what they consider offensive depictions in their advertisements (including dinosaurs!) to the defacing of commercial display windows and the burning down of bus stops. Because the glass/plastic walls of bus stops in Israel are used for displaying advertisements, conservative religious youths mounted a campaign of destroying bus stops displaying "offensive" ads. They later managed to persuade both advertisers and advertising firms, through boycotting, to change their policy and display different ads in areas where there is a large population of ultra orthodox.

The Response of the Secular Public

Secular Jews are mainly concerned with two other aspects of pornography: sexual depictions that are demeaning or threatening to segments of the population and the effects of pornography on children and adolescents.

The influence of pornography on children and early adolescents is a source of concern to some parents, psychologists, and educators. Because sex is a very private matter, children and adolescents who are exposed to pornography have no objective criteria to compare it to and may believe that many or most of the things shown are part of normative behavior of adults. This may cause some difficulties in their emotional reactions to adult and parental sexuality. They are also unaware of the manipulations that are done in making these films, and that can create problems of self-image or fear regarding the sexual organs. There has been speculation that several cases of sexual violence among adolescents, especially those involved with group sex, are related to pornography. Despite the fact that there is no hard evidence to support this assertion, it cannot be ignored and should be researched appropriately.

Two issues are at the core of the secular political discourse. First, which of the following is the most prominent feature of pornography: the commercialized and dehumanized treatment of the human body, the linking of sex and violence, or its use by heterosexual males to dominate women and to perpetuate a sexist and heterosexist society? The second issue focuses on how to counteract the pernicious effects of pornography and whether censorship or social control are a remedy, or a worse disease.

Sex Education and Pornography

Several efforts are being made to incorporate units dealing more effectively with pornography and its impact within the sex education programs in schools. The basic approach is that since there is very little hope of lowering the exposure of children and early adolescents to pornography unless there is a major social change, it is important to give them the skills to deal with its potential effects. The concern is focused on the explicitness of such units and on the claim that they may raise the interest in pornography or lower the barrier to exposure.

Paid Services by Telephone

Privatization of the telecommunication monopoly in 1990 brought with it many new initiatives for marketing new services. One of these was caller-paid telephone (056) numbers offering medical advice, astrology maps, practical information, and in the sexual area, advice, introduction services, party lines, and sexual-talk bulletin boards. Each of these meets the different needs of people with sexual interests.

At their best, sexual-advice services supply minimal sexual information and a referral service. Callers have no idea of the expertise, knowledge, or training of the persons who provide advice. Some services attempt to do counseling, not the crisis intervention of hot lines, but on a more extensive, sometimes therapeutic level. It is questionable how helpful these procedures are. The service does supply the very strong need of some people who suffer from sexual doubts or problems, the need to get advice without the risk of exposure. If done properly, it could be helpful; however, it can also postpone the time that people will reach out for needed help. Also, lay people exposed to easy access and bad practices cloaked in professional claims may later doubt the ability of any professionals to give help.

Introduction services and party lines, unless they serve minors, have very little potential for damage. They mainly give an opportunity for people to create relationships at a safe distance with as many defenses as they wish. It also allows people some safety measures prior to creating nonmediated interactions.

The sex talk, fantasy-activated lines operate on a different level, something that many people are unaware of. These services allow people to act out their fantasies in a partial manner, while interacting with a supposedly real person at a distance, allowing the imagination to add the missing elements of reality. For some people, especially sexually distressed ones, this could erode the line between fantasy and reality, creating a few features of virtual reality that may increase the distress instead of alleviating it. Another problematic feature is that commercial considerations demand that the service providers play the stereotypical roles, many of them demeaning and degrading ones, in order to please the customers. Whether these act as cathartic experiences or add themselves into a positive feedback loop is still a question.

Commercial sexual services ignore their potential for harm. They claim they sell a service that no one is forced to buy, and therefore should not be regulated in the name of freedom of speech. It is possible that serious studies undertaken jointly by the service providers and sexuality researchers, followed by self-regulation, will provide an optimal solution. Strong demands are being made by many organizations to limit the access to these services to customers who explicitly request it. Legal efforts are currently being challenged by the industry in courts on the basis of their rights to free speech.

9. Contraception, Abortion, and Fertility Planning

A. Contraception

Modern contraceptives are easily accessible through several outlets within the health system: mainly the Mother and Child Primary Health Care (MCH) and ob/gyn clinics of the sick funds, including outpatient clinics in obstetrics departments. There is no legal restriction on the use of contraceptives.

Adolescents

Despite the availability of contraceptives several studies have found that the rate of their use by adolescents at first intercourse, and in general, is very low. One found that only half of the sexually active boys and a third of the girls were using contraceptives regularly. Another reported that only 40 percent of sexually active adolescents have ever used contraceptives. The level of knowledge, as measured in these studies, was not a limiting condition, as it was much higher than the rate of use.

A frequent characteristic of those with early sexarche is that they either use no contraception or rely on the traditional methods of withdrawal or rhythm, and that they are also lower contraceptors later on. Not only do they start without contraceptives, but they also take longer to achieve adequate protection. Whether there is any causal relationship at all between the two phenomena, and in which direction, is a very important research topic, but it seems to be consistent with the view that many of those initiating intercourse at a younger age do so as acting out or under personal and social pressures, and are therefore more prone to conflicts and their sequels. The fact that kibbutz youth with more egalitarian and permissive attitudes are also better contraceptors adds support to these interpretations; see Section 14 under Kibbutz for details.

Married Women

Use of contraceptives among married Israeli Jewish women is given in Table 2 and demonstrates some of our arguments.

Sterilization is frowned on in the Jewish tradition. While more than two thirds of married Jewish women use medically prescribed contraceptives, the use of both male and female sterilization is less than 1 percent, very low compared to other industrial countries with comparable health systems. The demand for sterilization is low because of the importance of childbearing and other issues. But even when requested, there are many barriers a man or woman needs to overcome to achieve their desire. The reasons given by physicians are the irreversibility of the process and distrust of the ability of people to make irreversible decisions without later regrets.

Professional Control

The licensing, sale, and fitting of contraceptives are controlled through medical and medicopharmaceutical regulations. This highlights another issue, the power struggle between professions over controlling the availability and use of contraception. While in several Western industrial countries, IUDs and diaphragms are fitted by paramedical professionals, in Israel this is still the absolute prerogative of physicians. Insertion of IUDs is the only invasive procedure that is restricted by regulation to one type of physician, a gynecologist. Thirty years ago, the practice in most clinics was that before being fitted for an IUD, a woman had to have three or four children; later the number came down to two and even to one. Today, most clinics still refuse to fit an IUD to nulliparous women, especially unmarried ones, on the basis of good medical practice and the wish not to endanger their fertility.

Other social restrictions are also exerted mainly through the medical/health system. A more subtle aspect of the professional power play is the disagreement about the role of psychosocial counseling in the fitting of contraceptives and the success/failure of their use.

Table 2

Current Contraceptive Use Among Married Israeli Jewish Women (Aged 22-44 Years, Exposed Women Only[1], 1988)

Method of Contraception	Number of Women (*n*)	Percent of Exposed	Percent of Total
Effective methods	**794**	**59**	**47**
Pill	259	19	15
IUD	519	39	31
Sterilization (male and female)	16	1	1
Less-effective methods	**138**	**10**	**8**
Condom	66	5	4
Diaphragm	65	5	4
Spermicidesonly	7	0	0
Traditional methods	**260**	**19**	**15**
Withdrawal	175	13	10
Rhythm	71	5	4
Others	14	1	1
No method	**152**	**11**	**9**
Sub-Total (exposed)	**1344**	**99**	**80**
Nonexposed	**346**		**21**
Grand Total	**1680**		**101**

[1] Exposure to contraception was determined by three independent variables: not-pregnant, not trying to become pregnant, and currently engaging in sexual intercourse.

Family Planning

Fertility and family size are mainly a personal and familial decision shaped by normative forces, but also part of the public domain, and strongly dependent on policy decision, laws and regulations, authorizations, and financial support or constraints. Family planning and contraception in Israel can be viewed as part of a multidimensional domain built of several axes, of which the most important ones are: modernity, nationalism, and religiosity. While some people view religiosity as belonging to the axis of modernity, this is not always the case in Israel. While among Moslem women, high fertility is inversely associated mainly with modernity (women's education being a major component), in the Jewish population it is mainly associated with religiosity. Among Jewish women, one finds a defined group of highly educated, professional women, who espouse a combination of religiosity with nationalistic ideology and pride themselves on having more than five or six children.

It is important to note here that while the commandment to "be fruitful and multiply" is taken almost literally, Jewish *Halachah*, which strongly opposes family planning, allows the use of contraceptives on the basis of individual need within the rather wide Halachic formulation of *Pikuach Nefesh* ("danger to the soul"). Moreover, some features of Jewish religious law create unique situations. The fact that many commandments, including "do not spill your semen in vain," bind men only, and allow women to use contraceptives, provided there is no direct damage to the men's sperm. Thus while vasectomy, withdrawal, condoms, and spermicides are almost universally forbidden, pills, IUDs, and even diaphragms can be used within boundaries.

Apart from the personal position and family decision making, the public stand of Jewish orthodoxy has always been against organized family planning and the development of fertility control and contraceptive services.

Public Policy and the Family Planning Movement

The movement for birth control or birth planning, and the utilization of modern contraceptives as an integral part of it, are relatively recent in Israel. The Israeli Family Planning Association (IFPA) was founded in 1966. Mother and Child Primary Health Care clinics (MCH), the mainstay of public health in Israel, received an official mandate to deal with birth control issues only in 1972.

The predominant approach to birth control and family planning in the late 1960s and 1970s was a mixture of demographic and health approaches with social/ethnic ideology. The main features concerned the national melting-pot ideology regarding immigrant groups, and the wish to better the situation of the groups with a low socioeconomic status through the control of their family size. From today's perspective, the latter component was not only flawed in its premises, but also parentalistic in its nature (Ronny A. Shtarkshall has coined the term parentalistic, as opposed to paternalistic, because of its less-sexist connotations). This approach was in conflict with two other important axes that strongly influenced family planning—the religious and nationalistic, both of which were pronatalist. Nevertheless, the strong medicalized approach to health in general and pride in medical professionalism resulted in one of the first field studies that heralded introduction of IUDs for worldwide use.

Professionals in several disciplines, including health professionals, were dissatisfied with the medical/demographic framework and favored adoption of a human/family-rights approach. Implementation of this new approach has minimized the authority of the professionals, and focused on enabling the clients to take charge of their own needs and on adapting the counseling process to the need of specific groups. However, responses to recent immigrants from the former USSR and Ethiopia have shown that old habits die very slowly and can be resurrected easily when some service providers decide that they "know better" and intervene without appropriate preparation and adequate concern for sociocultural factors.

Client-Oriented Services

The initiation of special counseling services for youth by the IFPA was also a step toward developing services adapted to the clients' needs. These are not only more accessible services that meet the unique needs of this population, but also a declaration that the sexual experiences of youth are not intrinsically negative. The informal approach, the environment, and the mode of counseling in these advisory centers aim at minimizing the feelings of adult social control of youth sexual behavior. Currently, many municipal services, sick funds, and other NGOs have established such services, so that the IFPA is phasing out direct service to youth and going into an advisory training role for developing such services.

Groups at Risk for Unplanned Pregnancies

Some service providers and organizations view the 19 percent of the couples who want to postpone or terminate fertility, but use traditional, inefficient methods, as one of the main targets for family planning education. Several studies have shown that most of the married couples belonging to this group really want more effective contraception, but are hindered from using it by lack of knowledge, suspicion, fear, and subjective difficulties in accessing services.

Unmarried adolescents and young adults, including soldiers in the service, students, and recent immigrants from the former USSR, are also the foci of family planning efforts, because of underuse or misuse of contraceptives and the high rate of unwanted pregnancies. (See Section 14 for issues of family planning and contraception among Moslem women and couples, and among Russian and Ethiopian immigrants.)

As much as the contribution of the family planning services is appreciated, it cannot be ignored that the convergence of fertility rates among the second-generation immigrants was largely achieved, not through their action, but rather through intermarriages of Jews of different ethnic origin, the action of a universal, largely egalitarian, educational system, the unifying force of the IDF, and entry of women into the paid workforce.

B. Unmarried Motherhood

Looking at the development of never-married mothers in the recent years, one concludes that, in Israel, for an increasing number of women, the drive toward childbearing is stronger than the convention that motherhood is only accepted within marriage.

The rate of live births per 1,000 never-married women aged 15 to 44 rose by 70 percent from 2.3 per 1,000 in the early 1970s to 3.9 per 1,000 in 1989. But the crude rates are not as informative as the age-specific rates: while the rate for the two younger age groups, 15 to 19 and 20 to 24, actually dropped (from 1.4 to 0.8, down 43 percent, and from 3.4 to 2.9, down 15 percent, respectively), the rates for the older aged groups increased significantly in the last two decades. In the two decades between 1970 and 1989, the rate has more than doubled for the 25 to 29 age group, from 4.1 to 9.1 per 1,000, tripled for the 30 to 34 group from 6.8 to 20.3 per 1,000, and more than quadrupled for the 35 to 39 group, 5.2 to 21.9 per 1,000.

The drop in the rate of birth of unmarried young women is probably the result of Article 2 in the abortion law that allows legal termination of pregnancy to unmarried women (see under Abortion below). Most abortions of unmarried women are concentrated in the 15 to 24 age group where a sizable proportion of the sexually active women are still not only unmarried, but also in unfavorable conditions to marry or give birth. Since abortion is also available to unwed older women, the lower rate of abortion and higher rate of unwed motherhood among older women reflects the need of older unmarried women to exercise their right to childbearing.

By Jewish law, a child born to an unwed mother is legal, and there is no stigma attached to his/her birthright. It is the mother who carries the burden of shame, according to the religious ruling and much popular belief, and not the child. Obviously, an increasing number of women are willing to pay the price or do not feel the stigma.

There is no available information on the proportion of unwed women who choose to become pregnant by sexual intercourse or artificial insemination. Some institutions perform artificial insemination by donors with no requirement that the recipient be married, but several court cases reveal that at least some of women prefer impregnation by intercourse.

The issue came into public attention when women sued the fathers, some of them public figures, for child support. Several such cases included signed contracts waiving child support as part of the agreement by the men to impregnate the women. These contracts were declared void by the courts because the court is bound to decide in the best interests of the child even if both parents agree otherwise. In several cases, there were claims that the women misrepresented either their fertility status or the fact that they were using a specific contraceptive. The courts declared this argument to be irrelevant because, even if proven true, it had no bearing on the interests or the legal status of the child.

Several such involved fathers have formed an organization, "Fathers Not by Choice," and now lobby for the rights of fathers. They contend that the prevailing situation, giving them no custody rights in such cases, and in many cases no other rights, constitutes sex discrimination.

C. Abortion

Several times in the short history of Israel, abortion has been a major public and political issue with highly emotional and ideological arguments that embody tensions between different segments of the society, and a discrepancy between public policy and private practices. While playing a prominent role, the element of women's rights to their bodies was not as dominant as in some other countries. This may be because the issue of abortion touches on other issues highly important to the Israeli public: relations between religion and state, national identity and aspirations, and the collective memory of the annihilation of more than half of the Jewish people of Europe in the Holocaust.

Jewish religious laws, the *Halachah,* give precedence to the life of the mother over the life of the embryo/fetus until that moment of delivery when the head is fully out. An abortion because of danger to the life of the mother can be accepted by religious authorities, but only after consulting a Halachic authority. All other abortions are perceived to be murder. Abortion is presented by its opponents as the ongoing denial of life of its future children to a society that had lost one third of its people, 1.5 million of whom were children, and continues to suffer loss of young life by warfare and terrorism.

It has not helped that the professional view of family planning efforts within certain organizations providing abortions was predominantly biomedical. As a result, women seeking abortions were sometimes looked down upon as ignorant or failing to use medically available contraceptives properly. There was a feeling that they should have known better. This view is encountered mainly toward young unmarried women, though in the past it included women of low socioeconomic status who had already had several children. Recently, this attitude was revived in public discussion by the increased demand for abortions from the former USSR immigrants.

It is also possible that some vested economic interests were involved in the opposition to legalizing abortions. Some professionals objected to providing abortions in public hospitals as a waste of public money, while they or their colleagues were performing them privately for a fee.

During the abortion debate, reproductive health data was frequently misused. Those who objected to abortions exaggerated the health risk of abortions—both mortality and the risk to future fertility—as an argument against it. This was mainly done by comparing the mortality and morbidity rates from induced abortions to the successful prevention of pregnancy by contraceptive use, instead of comparing abortion mortality and morbidity with the risk incurred by carrying the pregnancy to term and its delivery. This argument is also facetious because, despite the fact that Israel has a very low perinatal morbidity and mortality, these are still much higher than the risks of abortions performed according to accepted medical standards.

Legally, abortion is still defined as a felony in the criminal code. As with most laws in Israel, abortions continue to be regulated by British colonial laws. For almost thirty years, 1948 to 1978, the only legal reasons for the performance of legal abortions were purely medical. Nevertheless, illegal abortions were widespread. Oddly enough, almost all the illegal abortions were performed by licensed gynecologists or general surgeons under accepted medical standards. Extremely few cases were prosecuted, and these only in cases where a woman lost her life.

Since the mid-1960s, several organizations, mainly human rights activists, the Israeli Family Planning Association, the women's segment of the Histadrut, the labor union, the feminist caucus, and organizations seeking to decrease the political power of the religious over individuals, have united in uncoordinated efforts to change the law. The fact that there was a vast difference between the law and the practice, and that the main barrier to seeking abortion was economic, has played a psychological role in paving the way to the change.

In 1977, the Knesset changed the abortion law (enacted January 1978). The main change was the establishment of hospital committees that could allow the performance of induced abortions under five clauses: age (women under 17 or over 40); pregnancy resulting from out-of-wedlock, adulterous, or unlawful relationships; medical conditions relating to the embryo (genetic or developmental malformations); medical conditions endangering the mother physically and/or mentally; and social or economic hardship.

The law stated explicitly that parental consent is not a condition for performing an abortion on a minor and that seeking abortion is free of regional restrictions on the dispensation of medical services. On the other hand, no physician is required to perform an abortion, even a legally authorized one. The establishment of committees in public and private hospitals that were medically authorized to perform abortions was at the discretion of the hospital management. Several hospitals did not establish such committees because of religious or other ideological reasons. The fact that permission for abortion is granted by a hospital committee does not mean that the hospital is required to perform the abortion. The committees are autonomous in determining their procedures and regulating their activities, provided that each committee includes at least one gynecologist, one social/mental health professional, and one woman. In most committees, the woman was also the social worker, thus combining two functions in one person who also has lower status in medical institutions. Some committees demand that the petitioning woman appear before the committee in person and answer questions; others only review a file prepared by the social worker. Some committees convene only once a week, others meet daily; some are known to be "liberal," while others are "hard."

This differentiation became highly important in 1980, only two years after enactment of the new law, when religious parties succeeded in striking out Article 5 allowing abortions for social or economic hardship. Since then, because there are no regional administrative restrictions on where women can seek an abortion, women have preferred to approach the more liberal committees. Thus the demand for legal abortions among married women, and their performance, has not changed much in the years following abrogation of Article 5 (Table 3). Only the reasons for which these abortions were granted have shifted. There was a fourfold increase in granting abortions for physical or mental medical reasons (from 8 to 36 percent).

Table 3

Induced Terminations of Pregnancies Performed in Hospitals in Israel (1979-89)

Year	Total Number of Abortions	Rates per 1000 Women (Ages 15-49)	Rates per 1000 Live Births
1979	15,925	17.7	17.0
1980	14,708	18.0	15.6
1981	14,514	17.4	15.6
1982	16,829	19.8	17.4
1983	15,593	17.9	15.8
1984	18,984	19.1	19.2
1985	18,406	18.1	18.3
1986	17,110	16.8	17.2
1987	15,290	16.0	15.4
1988	15,255	15.6	15.2
1989	15,216	15.2	15.1
1990	15,509	14.9	15.0
1991	15,767	15.1	14.9

As of late 1994, privately performed, illegal abortions are still performed largely by physicians under medically accepted conditions. The latest estimate by knowledgeable sources is that their number is 5,000 to 7,000 annually, about 25 to 33 percent of the total number of abortions performed. This estimate is for the period prior to the arrival of the large 1990/91 immigrant wave from the former USSR (see Section 14 below).

In 1990, there was an attempt by religious parties to restrict abortions further by reducing the number of hospitals authorized to have committees and perform abortions, and to limit them to public hospitals only. Since the right-wing government at the time was favorable to this attempt for both ideological and political reasons, a coalition of family planning and health professional organizations, the feminist lobby, and human rights activists was needed to defeat this attempt.

Antiabortion organizations are active, especially among youth and among women seeking abortions. Their propaganda disregards the data and claims that every second or third pregnancy is willfully terminated, while the actual number is less than one in five, even if one counts the illegally performed abortions.

The IDF's attitude toward abortions is consistent with the wider tolerance toward premarital sex in late adolescence. In the past, a pregnant soldier was discharged whether she carried the pregnancy to term or terminated it. This caused many female soldiers who wished to continue their service to hide their pregnancy and have illegal abortions. This rule was changed, and currently a pregnant soldier can seek an abortion through the IDF and stay in the service. The rules still give the IDF an option to discharge a woman on the basis of incompatibility. As far as is known, this option is used only in the case of repeat aborters and if other adverse conditions exist.

As noted in Section 9B on unwed mothers, it seems that the decrease of unwed motherhood in the younger age groups is due mainly to the availability of legal abortions to unwed women. It would have been very interesting to be able to estimate how many "forced marriages" are avoided because of the availability of legal abortions to unmarried women. Research in Israel has shown that among marriages that suffer from abusive patterns, the rate of premarital conceptions is by far the strongest associated variable marking the difference between them and divorcing marriages that do not suffer from an abusive pattern.

A significant aspect of abortions in Israel is their cost. Prior to the 1978 law, abortions were very expensive, creating additional hardship for less-well-to-do women. Since 1978, the prices are between $250 and $600, between 40 to 100 percent of the minimal legal monthly wages. Only abortions performed for medical reasons in one of the public hospitals are covered by the sick funds; the foundation for children run by the Ministry of Welfare pays for abortions for women under 17; all abortions performed on soldiers are covered by the IDF. In all, an estimated 65 percent of all abortions are paid for by public funds.

Most abortions in Israel are first-trimester abortions by suction and curretage. Most hospitals use general anesthesia during induced abortion in order to minimize the psychological effects on the woman. Very few institutions perform second-trimester abortions (evacuation), mainly because of staff objections. Mortality and morbidity from induced abortions in Israel is very low.

The large immigration from the former USSR starting in 1989 and peaking in 1990/91 changed the demand for induced abortions and, possibly also, the conditions under which some abortions are performed. First, it is estimated that these immigrant Jews will increase the demand for abortions by about 10 percent (over their proportion in the overall population). Second, since most Russian women seeking abortion are married, and the cost of out-of-hospital abortions, privately performed by a licensed physician is rather high, there is both statistical and anecdotal evidence indicating these women seek abortions from USSR-immigrant physicians who are unlicensed to practice medicine or surgery in Israel. They charge less for abortions, are highly proficient in their performance, but sometimes perform them in medically problematic conditions.

D. Population Trends

Uniqueness of the Jewish Population

The Jewish population of Israel has the highest Total Fertility Rates (TFR, i.e., the average number of live children expected to be born to a woman during her lifetime as calculated from the age-specific fertilities) among the Western industrial countries—2.6 for 1991. This fertility is far above that of other major Jewish communities, including Eastern Europe and Latin America, even though both populations are descendants of survivors of the Holocaust (as is a large segment of the Israeli population). This is well above the replacement value and reflects the importance of children in the Israeli-Jewish lifestyle, including but not limited to the orthodox and ultra orthodox sectors. Among secular Jewish couples in Israel, it seems like the birth of the first two children is taken for granted and family planning considerations are usually reserved for timing and for additional children.

Also, the second generation of Jews immigrating from different parts of the world to Israel change markedly in less than a generation, so that their fertility patterns resemble the Jewish-Israeli pattern more than the patterns in their countries of origin.

Time Sequence of Fertility Changes

Despite the just-mentioned facts, the fertility patterns over the last three decades do show a general drop in fertility among all the national and most ethnic groups in Israel, concomitant with modernization and the rise in both economic and educational level (Table 4).

Closer analysis of the TFR in various Jewish ethnic groups reveals a more complete picture. While there is a consistent drop in the TFR for Jewish mothers born in Asia and Africa, for mothers born in Israel, and those born in Europe and America, there is a rise in the TFR until the first half of the 1970s and then a decline. The overall the rate of increase for both latter groups was similar, 0.3 to 0.4 child per mother. If these trends—the rise in age at first marriage, the delay of age at first birth, and the lowering of the desired number of children—continue, the result can be a continuous decrease of the TFR among Jews in Israel. It is hard to predict to what levels and what will be the forces acting to speed, slow, or reverse this trend. Whatever the situation, the TFR of orthodox and ultra orthodox Jews will be a factor.

Table 4

Total Fertility Rates of Jews and Non-Jews in Israel (1965-1989)

Period	1960-1964	1965-1969	1970-1974	1975-1979	1980-1984	1985-1989	1990	1991
Jews (total)	**3.39**	**3.36**	**3.28**	**3.00**	**2.80**	**2.79**	**2.69**	**2.58**
Mothers born in Israel	2.73	2.83	3.05	2.91	2.82	2.82	2.76	2.70
Moslems	**9.23**	**9.22**	**8.47**	**7.25**	**5.54**	**4.70**	**4.70**	**4.70**
Jews (mothers born in Asian and African countries)	4.79	4.35	3.92	3.40	3.09	3.14	3.09	3.27[1]
Christians	**4.68**	**4.26**	**3.65**	**3.12**	**2.41**	**2.49**	**2.57**	**2.26**
Jews (mothers born in Europe, America (N&S), Australia, and Southern Africa)	2.38	2.59	2.83	2.80	2.76	2.66	2.31	2.05[2]
Druze and others	**7.49**	**7.30**	**7.25**	**6.93**	**5.40**	**4.19**	**4.05**	**3.70**

The Total Fertility Rate (TFR) is the total number of live children born to a woman throughout her fertile period. It is based on the sum of age-specific fertilities for women between the ages of 14 to 49 and assumes that women of a specific group have the specific age fertility appropriate for their group when they are at that age.

[1] The rise in TFR among Jewish women born in African countries in 1991 is probably due to the wave of immigration of Jews from Ethiopia.

[2] The rather sharp drop in TFR in 1990 and 1991 among women born in Europe/America is probably due to the large wave of immigration from the former USSR where the TFR among Jewish women is below 2.

Factors Shaping Israeli Fertility

Forces shaping Israeli fertility changes in the last forty years include: modernity, mainly women's education; changes in economic status and perspectives; entrance of women into the labor force; a general downgrading of the collective/national elements within the prevailing ethos; and a concomitant rise in the individualistic achievement-orientation components. Immigration was also a factor: Jewish women from Ethiopia contributing to a TFR rise in 1991; Russian immigrants to a drop in 1990 where the TFR among Jewish women is below 2.

The pronatalist attitude prevalent in modern Israel explains the socialization toward marriage and parenthood that Israeli adults feel ill at ease to defy. Willed childlessness is not presented as a viable option and childless couples are considered to be in need of help.

Fertility Services

A direct consequence of this cultural climate is the demand for fertility services, and especially in vitro fertilization (IVF), as aids to married biological parenthood. In 1993, there were roughly one IVF clinic for every 30,000 Israelis, more than in any other country over the world, and lower by more than a factor of magnitude than the per capita rate in the U.S.A. The research in fertility, and especially in IVF, in Israel is disproportionately high and several improvements on the methods originated here. Other fertility services are also highly developed in Israel, but the focus is mainly on the biomedical service, with minimal resort to accompanying psychosocial interventions. Several attempts in the latter direction report a marked increase in success rates of the biomedical interventions if they are done in conjunction with the psychosocial ones. Surrogate motherhood is still very rare and complicated by unresolved legal issues.

Adoption

Married couples who go down the fertility road to its limits without success resort to adoption. In an effort to protect the rights of the adopted children, adoption procedures in Israel are slow and cumbersome. These efforts sometimes backfire as children drag for years through institutions, foster homes, and the courts without stable environment and the ability to form lasting attachments. The processes are somewhat easier when older children or physically or mentally challenged children are involved, but in these cases the adoption process can be much more difficult.

From the side of the petitioning couples, the waiting and procedures are sometimes intolerable, creating a large market in adoption of foreign children. Romania was a source until government corruption and news of HIV infection in orphanages blocked this option. In several South American countries, what was a legal if costly process turned into illegal trade in forged documents, kidnapping, and extortion.

10. Sexually Transmitted Diseases

The public awareness of STDs in Israel in low. Syphilis, chlamydia, gonorrhea, and herpes genitalis are reportable diseases, but this regulation is not strictly enforced and not fully observed. A structural reason for this may be that Israel does not have STD clinics, specializing in both care and prevention.

In the late 1960s, an apparent doubling in reported STDs, believed to be caused by the influx of volunteers after the "Six Days' War," caused the ministries of Health and Education to recommend the study of sexual knowledge, attitudes, and behavior. This study, carried out in the early

1970s, also recommended the introduction of a sex-education curriculum into the schools.

The current prevalence of STDs in Israel for 1993 in annual rates of preliminary notifications were 1.1, 0.0, and 0.3 per 100,000 for syphilis, genital chlamydia trachomatis, and gonorrhea respectively. This is believed by researchers to be below the actual rate. For example, some estimates of chlamydia infection are as high as 10 percent of the women of 15 to 49 (2 percent of the population). Estimates of the prevalence of herpes genitalis are also quite high.

In 1988 a Society for the Study and Prevention of STDs was formed under the auspices of the Israeli Family Planning Association, with the aims of joining biomedical and behavioral efforts, integrating prevention with proper early detection and care, and for increasing the awareness of STDs and their risk to health among health professionals. It holds professional orientation and awareness meetings and formulates guidelines for better detection and care of various STDs. Its educational and public activities are conducted within the general framework of the IFPA.

11. HIV/AIDS

A. Situation Report

Currently HIV/AIDS has a low prevalence/low incidence in Israel. The documented number of AIDS cases for May 1994 was 292—cumulative incidence of 56/million—69 of which, 24 percent, are currently alive in Israel. As of June 1994, there were 1,152 people reported as HIV-seropositive who are not ill with AIDS, a cumulative incidence of 256 per million or 0.026 percent. It is believed that the reporting of cases is accurate. Tables 5 and 6 summarize the published data about both AIDS and HIV in Israel for June 1993.

The authorities cite the fact that incidence of new AIDS cases within Israel is flat as a support for their claim that the situation is under control. They also claim that since half of the new AIDS cases are previously known as HIV cases, the actual number of HIV cases is probably twice the number of AIDS cases reported from all sources.

However, it may be that this perception is only the short-sightedness of politicians and policy makers who do not realize that this may be the lower flat part of an atypical hyperbolic curve, below the threshold of doubling. Several facts apparent in these tables can be a cause for concern. First, the progression from HIV to AIDS may represent the transmission situation in the past five to ten years. Second, 30 percent of the HIV cases are of unknown risk factor, and almost 10 percent of all the people identified as HIV-seropositive are also of unknown gender; among those of unknown risk factor, 25 percent are of unknown gender. Since HIV testing in Israel is mostly voluntary, and there is no summarized and/or analyzed data about

Table 5

Cumulative Adult (Age 15+) HIV+ Cases in Israel (June 1993) Presented by Transmission Category (After Slater P. Sutton's *Law and AIDS Prevention in Israel*)

Transmission Category[1]	Males		Females		Unknown		Total	
	N	%[2]	N	%[2]	N	%[2]	N	%[3]
1. Gay & Bisexual Men	153	100.0	—	—	—	—	153	16.6
2. IV Drug Users[4]	97	78.2	14	11.3	13	10.5	124	12.6
3. Homophiliacs	47	97.9	1	2.1	0	0.0	48	4.9
4. Transfusion Recipients	7	53.8	5	38.5	1	7.7	13	1.3
5. Heterosexuals	199	58.0	139	40.5	5	1.5	343	34.7
Subtotal (known risk group)	503	73.9	159	23.3	19	2.8	681	68.9
6. Unknown Transmission	173	56.3	58	18.9	76	24.8	307	31.1
Total	676	68.4	217	22.0	95	9.6	988	100.0

[1] RS would have preferred the use of risk practice or risk behavior to the use of transmission category or risk group. This would have changed the structure of this table. For example, the use of anal sex as risk practice (with subdivision for gay or heterosexual groups) could have clarified the relative role of this practice in heterosexual transmission in Israel, without loss of the ability to calculate the risk to encounter an HIV+ partner in sexual encounters within specific groups.

[2] % of the total number of cases in this specific category.

[3] % of this category in the total number of HIV+ in Israel at that date.

[4] Including drug users with additional risk factors.

the people who have been tested for HIV, there is no information about over- or undertesting in important subpopulations like age groups or genders. This results in a puzzle with more holes than picture.

B. Sociopolitical Issues

There are several troubling questions that relate to HIV/AIDS being a biopsychosocial construct, interlocking with sexuality and other social, political, and cultural issues.

The responsibility for dealing with all the aspects of AIDS has been allocated to the Ministry of Health with its mainly biomedical outlook. The decisions of the National AIDS Steering Committee, which is always headed by a physician, are only recommendations to the director general of the ministry. Thus, decisions to implement policies or actions that may have a strong psychosocial component can be taken up only from its biomedical end, resulting in a distinct bias with serious and unpredictable results.

A second issue is more pervasive. On the one hand, there is the perception that HIV/AIDS and infected persons are marginalized and stigmatized.

Table 6

Accumulative Adult (Age 15+) AIDS Cases in Israel (June 1993) Presented by Transmission Category (After Slater P. Sutton's *Law and AIDS Prevention in Israel*)

Transmission Category[1]	Males N	Males %[2]	Females N	Females %[2]	Total N	Total %[3]
1. Gay & Bisexual Men	110	100.0	—	—	110	45.6
2. IV Drug Users[4]	43	84.3	8	9.8	51	21.2
3. Homophiliacs	28	100.0	0	0.0	28	11.6
4. Transfusion Recipients	7	87.5	1	12.5	8	3.3
5. Heterosexuals	26	74.3	9	25.7	35	14.5
Subtotal (known risk group)	214	92.2	18	7.8	232	96.3
6. Unknown Transmission	9		0		9	3.7
Total	223		18		241	100.0

[1] RS would have preferred the use of risk practice or risk behavior to the use of transmission category or risk group. This would have changed the structure of this table. For example, the use of anal sex as risk practice (with subdivision for gay or heterosexual groups) could have clarified the relative role of this practice in heterosexual transmission in Israel, without loss of the ability to calculate the risk to encounter an HIV+ partner in sexual encounters within specific groups.

[2] % of the total number of cases in this specific category.

[3] % of this category in the total number of HIV+ in Israel at that date.

[4] Including drug users with additional risk factors.

This perception influences the ways in which people with AIDS or HIV and HIV/AIDS issues are treated. On the other hand, there is a proneness in the responsibility for public health to avoid discussing the fact that, in different situations and under different conditions, it may not only be responsible, but essential to undertake unpleasant or even restrictive measures. (In accordance with the traditional Judaic approach, the application is highly dependant on unique situations that need to be weighed from all sides and in relation to all those who are involved, even though the laws are general and cover everyone.) This chain of bias-guilt-avoidance is hardly suitable to deal with the sensitive issues of HIV/AIDS. It may also be responsible for the fact that Israel has yet to form a midrange plan to deal with the disease.

Another issue is the influence of organizational structures and vested interests on the nature of the efforts to stem the disease. Such phenomena affect the definition of prevention and the perception of appropriate behavioral interventions; they are also the source of the phenomenon that policies are formulated, and interventions designed and implemented, prior to ascertaining the behavioral patterns, psychological, social, and cultural determinants of behaviors involved in this disease.

Vested interests come into play, especially when dealing with allocation of budgets, human resources, control, and research opportunities. Thus, the AIDS centers that are located in eight hospitals, and that are treatment-oriented and medically controlled, strive to retain the overall responsibility for prevention, even of interventions that are community-oriented and those in which the behavioral, and even cultural components, are predominant.

Most of the HIV tests are done on these sites in which precounseling and postcounseling to the people who test seronegative is limited to printed brochures. The people who test seropositive receive a mixture of medical and social counseling with little organized support and few educational programs. Attempts to alleviate the situation, even with the help of volunteer services, meet with suspicion on the one hand, and financial constraints on the other.

C. Priority Groups for Preventive Interventions

The prioritization of groups, and development of educational interventions, have been done without prior behavioral and psychosocial studies or any organized decision-making process. Recently, the topic was discussed in an article with several published commentaries recommending the use of epidemiological data to determine priorities for interventions. This proposal would not be a step forward, because it does not give any consideration to behavioral patterns. It also does not distinguish between risk-group, at-risk group, and risk behavior. Thus, it did not consider hemophiliacs, the highest HIV-seroprevalent risk-group, and failed to notice that they are currently at a very low risk for passing on the infection, that most of them are under constant medical supervision and counseling for their primary disease, and that the at-risk group for infection are their sexual contacts.

The commentaries revealed deep differences between people who deal with AIDS, bordering on a communication gap. Thus, the head of the National AIDS Committee declared a commitment to implement a general AIDS education effort among adolescents in schools, while another commentator pointed out that there were still no behavioral data pointing towards that need, and suggesting that the existing epidemiological data, although scanty, favored the targeting of educational efforts to limited priority subgroups within youth.

The establishing of targeted priority groups is important not only because of the scarcity of financial and human resources, but also because of the need to target the educational messages to the specific needs and conditions of subgroups, if one is to expecting to make an impact (see below in AIDS Education Versus Sex Education). The general intervention efforts aim at the common denominators and, therefore, may be too diluted and unfocused.

The balance between targeting priority groups for interventions to lower the transmission within those groups, and support for those who are already HIV-seropositive, and stigmatizing these same groups, is very delicate, especially if the groups are marginalized or stigmatized to start with.

Recently, this issue raised its head when the educational and counseling efforts within an immigrant population suffering from high prevalence and incidence rates, and from a heterosexual pattern of transmission, were sensationalized in the media. The fear and shunning reactions of small segments of the population, combined with the sensitivity and shame within this traditional community, triggered reactions toward the professionals who were in close association with them, and set back some of the preventive efforts.

D. Contact Tracing and Educational/Counseling Programs

Epidemiological follow-up and notification, support for people who are HIV-seropositive, and counseling interventions could be highly effective, if implemented professionally, compassionately, and discreetly. This was possible in Israel as no anonymous testing is available, only confidential ones. Unfortunately, the system did not manage to make the essential accommodations to implement such policies.

In one case, when a whole group of immigrants from a country with a high prevalence of HIV was screened on entry, the recommendation for combined supportive and preventive interventions by case managers working within the community was postponed for more than two years. As transmission within the community continued, while people did not come in readily for voluntary testing, it is questionable whether the intervention can be as effective as if it had been implemented nearer to the screening date.

This immigrant community also posed the challenge of developing culturally appropriate educational programs and training personnel to deliver them. It also challenged the system with the necessity for cultural bridging, and the training of cultural mediators between professionals whose beliefs were embedded in biomedical models, and clients who used a combination of traditional lay beliefs and biomedical models.

This was achieved by creating an alliance between a group of professionals and a group of veteran immigrants who trained to become both educational agents and mediators while they also acted as cultural informants and consultants.

E. AIDS Education Versus Sex Education

This question, although general in nature, is especially relevant in Israel, a low-prevalence country in which adolescents can be defined by their moderate prevalence of heterosexual risk behaviors when compared to the

U.S.A. and European countries, and very low prevalence of individuals being at-future-risk for HIV infection and not at-immediate-risk.

While today's adolescents do not face the probability of HIV infection, they do face a much more tangible risk of pregnancy and STD infection. In this context, attempts to motivate youth by fear of the small risk of HIV/AIDS or by fear of the future may backfire.

On a more theoretical basis, it is questionable whether it is appropriate to introduce youth to the issues of sex through risks of either a deadly disease, other diseases, or a pregnancy. It is proposed that early sex education, focusing on communication and decision-making skills, on responsibility for one's actions and health and also for the health and welfare of one's partner, and on alternative, noncoital sexual expressions, would be both more appropriate for adolescents and, in the long run, more efficient in lowering the transmission rates.

It is also important to note that the differences between cultures are not limited to "esoteric" immigrants, but can also be between "similar" industrial countries. Thus the concept of "safer sex," which is embedded in the basic premises of a society that is highly individualistic and sometimes adversarial, may be insufficient or inappropriate in a culture that puts more emphasis on the sense of community and cooperation between individuals.

It is also questionable whether egoistic motivations, which are at the roots of safer sex, are sufficient in boundary conditions, where altruistic or secondary motivations are needed to augment the egoistic ones. Such considerations will call for alternative educational approaches. Dealing with issues of mutual protection and responsibility need a much more elaborate educational approach than focusing on barriers to condom use or on the mechanical skills of its use. These should be discussed in the wider scope of sex education.

The decision-making, communication, and protective skills learned in sex education are very similar and can be easily applied to protection against HIV/AIDS.

It is somewhat disappointing that the need for a comprehensive approach to sex education and the urgency of such implementation are wasted because the interests of some politicians meet with those of educational entrepreneurs. The latter promote the use of shelf programs aimed at the largest possible populations and designed to offend as few people as possible. They are thus focusing on "clinical," nonoffensive, and nonsexual aspects of HIV/AIDS, demand minimal training of the implementers, and minimal hours for delivery. The interest of educational and health politicians is in "magic bullet" interventions that can be put in place speedily and with minimal fuss and objections from vocal political minorities.

Such ready-made AIDS education programs allow them to shirk their responsibility, while pretending to fulfill it. It is only fair to say that some of these politicians do not know better and believe in what they are doing. The responsibility of the entrepreneurial professionals seems to be graver.

12. *Sexual Dysfunctions, Counseling, and Therapies*

A. Concepts of Sexual Dysfunction and Therapy

Despite the fact that several of the founders of modern sexology in Germany had either passed through or settled in Israel after the rise of the Nazi regime to power, sexology did not emerge in Israel as a discipline until the early and middle 1970s. Treatment for sexual dysfunctions was limited either to medically oriented interventions or to analytically oriented psychodynamic therapies, which were imported by members of Freud's Psychoanalytic Institute who immigrated to Israel and founded a similar institute with his blessings in the late 1930s.

The medical approach focused on functional symptoms alleviation as a means to solving the sexual dysfunctions, e.g., the use of dilators for vaginal spasms or numbing creams for early ejaculation. While the psychoanalytic approach recognizes dysfunctions and issues like orientation and gender confusion as separate diagnostic categories, and is interested in deep causes and their transformation, psychoanalysts did not treat them with the same methods and under similar basic assumptions as medical practitioners.

The development of sex therapy in Israel occurred mainly after Masters and Johnson and is, by and large, an import from the U.S.A. Most of the Israeli therapists are trained there rather than in Europe. Currently, there is a pluralism of approaches to the treatment of sexual dysfunctions, ranging from the purely medically oriented through the combined biopsychosocial approach, and couple-oriented systemic approach to the psychodynamic.

B. Availability of Diagnosis, Counseling, and Treatment

A World Health Organization (W.H.O.) report counted, at the end of 1988, thirteen centers offering sex therapy, across the country. This list was not exhaustive even for that date, and since then more services have opened up in different locations.

Most of the clinics are still located in public hospitals or specialists' clinics of the sick funds. Significantly, few of them have a free-standing status, and most are annexed to departments like Gynecology, Psychiatry, or Urology, depending on the medical training of the head of the clinic or on political considerations. These arrangements are typical of a situation in which sexology and sex therapy are still not considered a full-fledged, professional and/or academic enterprize.

The clinics, even those in the public hospitals and sick funds, are very heterogeneous. A few have several staff members from different disciplines working full- or part-time with a wide range of services. These can offer a full biomedical and psychosocial evaluation and a variety of therapies. Usually, they will also treat orientation- and gender-confusion issues, including evaluations for sex change, e.g., the sexual function clinics at the Hadassah Medical Organization in Jerusalem and the Sheba Medical center in Ramat-Gan. Most clinics focus on fewer aspects of the sexual functions or offer a smaller variety of services. Several sex-therapy clinics evolved in nonmedical family and marriage services. These offer mostly psychosocial evaluations and interventions. One of these clinics started in the early 1990s also offers surrogate therapy as part of its services. The male and female surrogates are selected and trained by the staff of that clinic.

Two centers specialize in rehabilitative sexology: Sheba and Beit-Lewin-stein Rehabilitative Center. These offer both posttrauma and postdisease treatment of sexual concerns and functions.

A relatively recent development is the appearance of specialized private-enterprize sex clinics that use aggressive publicity and cater mainly to men with erectile dysfunctions. These clinics offer mainly treatment by medication, mostly penile injections. There are several reports that they offer rather poor psychological and dyadic evaluations and interventions, and at least one of them is under investigation by the Ministry of Health.

A national association of sex therapists (ITAM) was formed in the late 1980s in expectation of the therapy-licensing regulations. This is a rather loose association that did not take a public initiative in dealing with defending potential clients against exaggerated publicity claims or misconduct.

13. Sexual Research and Advanced Education

A. Sexological Research and Advanced Education

There is not one academic department or academic program that focuses on sexual issues or sexology. All the research and training is done under the names of different "professions" with very little integration and/or interdisciplinary approach. One attempt to form an interdisciplinary group ended when the person who initiated it did not receive tenure and moved to Canada. Despite that, several studies concerning sexual function and dysfunction have been carried out in clinical and limited nonclinical populations. Other studies, in the educational, psychosocial, and health fields have included issues of sexuality, sexual behavior, and attitudes. The rise of interest in HIV/AIDS issues has focused some attention to what is defined as sexual risk behaviors.

Only one of the four medical schools includes a course on sexuality and sexual behavior in their regular curriculum. The other three do so only as an elective or intermittently. It is possible to be board licensed in gynecology and urology without any course or internship in the psychosocial and behavioral aspects of sexuality. The only specialization that includes some issues of sexuality in requirements for board certification is Family Practice.

As a result, at least one of the postgraduate courses in this specialty offers a thirty-two-hour unit on sexuality and sexual issues in the family practice and a sixteen-hour unit on family planning and contraception.

Several of the universities and colleges offer scattered academic courses on sexual issues within various faculties, schools, or departments. Such are the courses at the School of Social Work of the University of Tel-Aviv; sex education courses at the Kibbutzim teachers-training college, and others.

The Hebrew University of Jerusalem has several academic courses in Family Planning in various departments. One of them is an interdisciplinary course to train counselors in family planning, contraception, and sexuality-related issues. Although part of the MPH curriculum, this course is considered to be an intervention course in the School of Social Work, and a skills course in educational counseling and psychology. Other courses there are those focusing on the biological, social, and psychological bases of gender differences.

Several courses in sex education are offered within university schools of education. These are nonacademic, in-service training courses held in cooperation with the Unit of Family Life and Sex Education of the Israeli Ministry of Education and Culture. Nonacademic courses, mainly in sex education and family planning, are offered by the Ministry of Education and the Israeli Family Planning Association (IFPA). These take the form of annual courses or concentrated workshops on general issues, on specialized populations (e.g., immigrants and challenged youth), or special issues (e.g., dealing with rape and coercive sex in the educational system, new methods in sex education, and cross-cultural issues).

Recent developments may herald some changes. First, one of the courses in sex education, which is coheaded by Ronny A. Shtarkshall, is currently considered for inclusion in the master of arts degree program by the School of Education of the Hebrew University of Jerusalem. This is a 168-hour course for training facilitators for interactive experiential work in sex education. The 56-hour, theoretical-academic component of this course will give, if approved, four annual credits at the graduate level. Second, the IFPA has initiated within the Post-Graduate Training Program of the Sakler Faculty of Medicine of the University of Tel-Aviv an interdisciplinary program in population, family planning, sexual health, and counseling. Third, the IFPA board of directors and council approved criteria for the training and recognition of Sex Educators. These include academic studies, skills training, sensitization and desensitization to sexuality issues, and supervised experience. It is expected that these developments will create some change in the attitudes toward professionalism is sexual issues.

B. Sexological Organizations

Institute for Sex Therapy, Sheba Medical Center, Tel Hashomer, Israel; Phone: 972-3/530-3749; Fax: 972-3/535-2888

Israel Family Planning Association, 9, Rambam Street, Tel-Aviv, 65601, Israel; Phone: 972-3/5101511; Fax: 972-3/5102589

Ministry of Education & Culture, Psychological and Counseling Services, 2 Devorah Hanevia Street, Jerusalem, Israel; Phone: 972-02/293249; Fax: 972-02/293256

14. National, Religious, and Ethnic Minorities

A. The Moslems

Moslem Arabs, the large majority of Arab citizens in Israel, constitute 14 percent of the population of Israel. Their situation is unique: a minority within a Jewish state and culture that has been at continuous war with its neighboring Moslem countries since its founding.

Despite that, some sense of group autonomy that transcends individual rights is recognized by the state, as matters like marriages, divorce, and family law are in the jurisdiction of the Moslem religious courts.

While the national and political aspirations of Moslem Arabs in Israel may be at odds with the mainstream of Israeli society, it is interesting that both the Moslem establishment and the population approve of the Israeli system that allows the religious courts of each denomination to govern its own population.

The religious courts are bound by the civil code, which takes precedence in matters in which the religious courts are at odds with it, like the ban on polygamy and the legal age of consent for marriage. Only recently, the supreme court ruled that the religious courts cannot ignore the rulings concerning division of property between husband and wife, which give women more rights than under the religious canons.

This indigenous control also gives the traditional establishment power over younger "upstarts." If there is a movement striving to free the Moslem society from the strong hold of the religious establishment, it is much less visible than among the Jewish segment of the population, perhaps as a result of the value placed on a uniform stance as a minority.

There are several other factors that affect sexual, marital, and familial issues in which the Arab-Moslem society differs from the Jewish mainstream. The Jewish majority is largely urban with an industrial and service-based economy, with high measures of modernity including women's education and their participation in the workforce. The starting point of Arab-Moslem society is largely rural, its economy is based on farming, and the determinants of modernity are rather low. This is rapidly changing, but there is still a wide gap. In recent years, both academics and some small activist organizations have broken the unified front by publishing studies about marriage patterns, sexual violence, and other disputed issues, and waging public campaigns against phenomena like murder for the honor of the family. These reports provide a good background for discussion of such issues.

Marriage as a Public Transaction Between Families

The traditional view of marriage in the Arab, mainly Moslem, society is of marriage as a transaction between families, concerned mainly with strengthening the economic and political power of the extended family/tribe, the *Chamulah*. Love and sexual satisfaction have very little to do with marriage, but procreation is very important. This is typical of rural societies, depending on land for wealth and prestige and on unity for its preservation. Marriages are arranged between families, sometimes against the will of the bride or the groom.

Bride payment, *Mohar*, is paid according to the desirability of the bride and the purity of the name of the family daughters and the status of her family. The collection of appropriate *Mohar*, especially for a highly desirable bride from a prestigious family, is a very heavy burden on young men, if they do not have the support of their well-to-do families or if they are poor. Thus the practice of arranged marriages with high *Mohar* has acted not only to preserve the wealth, but to keep the younger men in line and preserve the social status quo. The payment of the *Mohar* has also represented symbolically the fact that the bride's family was losing a labor force, while the groom's family was gaining one as well as a potential mother of children. Therefore, the fertility of the bride's mother, her aunts, elder sisters, and cousins has been a factor in her desirability and her *Mohar*. This contributes to the fact that the pregnancies and childbearing of each woman in the *Chamulah* is the business of every other woman. Women move into the husband's extended family, but her family of origin is still responsible for her proper conduct.

Inbreeding

Several mechanisms exist to facilitate keeping the wealth, especially land ownership, within extended families. One is reciprocal marriages: families exchange two pairs of their offspring, one male and one female from each family. These male-female pairs are often a brother and sister or first cousins. This saves the dowry payments for both families, but also creates double-kinship lines. A second mechanism is the marriage of first cousins, second cousins, uncle and niece, or aunt and nephew, although this is not as common today as in the past. The result is that 45 percent of all marriages in the Arab society in Israel are between relatives; 25 percent are of first-degree kin.

This happens despite the decrease in arranged marriages and their transformation into ritual formalization of voluntary pair formation. This seeming paradox can be explained by the fact that, despite modernization, the Arab society is still a closed one with low mobility. The available choices for marriage are limited and usually come from the same village built around extended families.

The health implications of these phenomena can be dire. Several villages, which are socially or geographically isolated, suffer from an extremely high incidence of specific genetic defects. Efforts are being made to lower the rate of genetic defects, even among the married relatives, by appropriate genetic counseling.

One such defect within the domain of human sexuality is the existence of a large number of pseudohermaphrodites of the dihydrotestosterone (DHT) or 5-alpha reductase deficiency. First reported and studied in the Dominican Republic, this recessive gene mutation has been traced to one family that migrated from the Syrian mountains about 150 years ago and continued to intermarry. A brief attempt to study these people and their environment, while extending them medical help, was cut short by the realities of the Israeli-Arab conflict. It was ascertained that the extended family is aware of the situation and of the peculiarity of these children. Yet it was never clear whether this is an internal familial terminology or a public one. They almost invariably strive to become men because of the dominance of males in the Arab society. The very few individuals who live as females are servants within their own families.

Polygyny

Another aspect of marriage among Moslem Arabs in Israel is polygyny. The Islamic religion allows a man four wives and as many concubines as his household can support. In reality, it was very rare that a man had more than two or three wives. One of the customs was for the older and dominant wife to choose a younger one for the husband, usually one that she could dominate.

Polygamy is banned by Israeli law. This ban was enacted mainly as a measure affirming women's equality, as a reaction to the custom of Jews who immigrated from Islamic countries. Acceptance of the law by Moslem Arabs in Israel was almost universal until 1967 when it became possible for men to have another wife either from or in the West Bank or Gaza district. Despite this, most Moslem Arabs obey the law and there are very few prosecuted cases of polygamy.

Perceptions of Male and Female Sexuality

In Islamic cultures the sexuality of men and women is perceived as moving in different directions during a lifetime, a picture somewhat in accordance with some modern sexological descriptions of the early peaking of male and later peaking of female sexual prowess.

According to this Moslem view, men's sexuality is uncontrolled in their youth before they marry. This is the time to keep guard on them, but also to allow them to fool around with women of ill repute. This is also the time to go to war or to forage (where women are seen as the spoils of war). After marriage, as men grow older, their appetites, while undiminished, become more controlled because of their added wisdom. In men, wisdom, cunning, and cool control over situations is usually associated with age.

The sexuality of a women is believed to be low in her youth and she is perceived as innocent. It is only after losing her virginity that the sexuality of women will grow and may get out of control. Therefore, married women are to be guarded at all times. A man's inability to satisfy his woman or to keep her in line is a very bad reflection on the husband's manhood, in addition to bringing shame to the woman's family of origin.

Family Honor

Two concepts are strongly associated with family honor. The first is the public proof of intact female virginity at marriage; the second is punishment for its defilement. In a traditional wedding ceremony, the family of the bride, usually the mother and/or aunts, are expected to receive the sheet with the signs of hymen blood on it and exhibit it in public. Contrary to popular belief, this is not only a sign for the intactness of the bride's honor, but also proof of the groom's virility.

Sex therapists working with Arab populations encountered the male fear of slighting one's own manhood and family honor by failing to perform. On the other hand, there are reports that the literary description of shyness and reluctance, signifying a virginal nature, that are expected to be conquered by force are part of the construct of women's perception of the first intercourse. The emerging picture is that of a ritual choreography where each partner has to play his/her traditional role in order to bring it to its full destiny and honor both families.

Even in rural and highly guarded societies where marriages are arranged, young people find their ways to associate with each other. In recent years when schools became coeducational, when there is greater freedom of movement, and when Arab youth are attending universities together with a majority of Jewish students at the age of 18—they do not serve in the army—it is much harder to avoid romance and a certain amount of sexual play between youth. As already mentioned, family arrangements are many times a formalization of self-selection.

Despite this change, the symbolic meaning of virginity is still important. Two sexual practices help young people to keep the hymen intact while engaging in sex: interfemoral and anal intercourse. The first is more risky to the woman as she may become pregnant, and also the man may catch her off guard and penetrate the hymen. The second avoids both, but in the area of HIV/AIDS may be inadvisable. No research has been published on this subject among Israeli Moslems, although there is enough anecdotal information to say that both practices are prevalent.

"When the family honor is shamed, it has to be cleansed with blood." This is true not only of issues of honor relating to women, but also in other cases of honor, including blood feuds and ritual revenge. Both the annals of the courts and fiction are filled with such stories.

In case of sexual honor, there are some revealing features. First, when family honor is shamed in matters of sex and marriage, the women carries the main burden of punishment and men rarely are blamed. One possible reason for this is that killing a man will touch on another matter of honor and start a blood feud that may last for generations. Second, when a transgression is made public, it is the woman's family that carries the burden of cleansing it with blood and killing the alleged transgressor. It was found that in many instances, the women of the family either incite the men to action, or even actively participate in its preparations or the actual deed. This is understandable in the light of the fact that an unpunished transgression reflects mainly on the good name of the women of the family, thus reducing the chances of the unwed ones to marry or to receive a good *Mohar.*

In 1992, a group of Moslem women activists publicly agitated against this practice for the first time. They even demonstrated in public against it, an unprecedented action. It is still unclear whether Jewish female and male activists, by joining in this campaign, will strengthen or weaken it. There is certainly strong expressed sympathy from Jews toward this campaign.

Unlike the practice in some Islamic countries, the courts in Israel do not accept the honor of the family as a mitigating circumstance. On the contrary, they have expressed their lack of sympathy for such customs and followed it with the maximum punishment under Israeli law, which is a life sentence.

Fertility Patterns and Their Secular Trend

The Total Fertility Rates (TFR) of Moslem Arab women in Israel (4.65, 1993), is the highest among the national-religious groups composing its population. Still it has also undergone the most marked decline in the last three decades (see Table 4). The drop in TFR from 9.23 to 4.65 in thirty-five years is proportionally lower than that of the Christian Arab women (50 percent and 52 percent respectively), but in terms of absolute family size, it is much greater. Christian women are having, on the average, only 2.6 children less as compared to thirty-five years ago, and their TFR is the lowest among the studied groups (2.09, 1993), while Moslem women are having on the average 4.6 less children.

An attempt to study the contribution of different independent variables to this fertility change has revealed an interesting picture involving cumulation of seven independent variables. At the time of the study (1988), the independent variables that were the most strongly associated with both the desired and achieved number of children were the mother's age group, her education, and a traditional arranged marriage with payment of a

Mohar. Two other independent variables were associated with only one of the studied variables: Urban or rural locality was associated only with the desired number of children, while participation in the workforce was associated only with the achieved number of children.

Education seems to be the strongest of the associated variables, the difference in desired fertility between the two extreme educational categories being almost 2 children, and between the achieved fertility at a relatively young age (28.5) by one child. The type of marriage is variable showing the second strongest association. The differences in the desired and achieved fertility between the two types of marriages being 0.6 and 0.5 children respectively. The other variables, even when significant, showed much smaller differences. Prominent in their lack of association with either the desired or achieved fertility were religiosity and marital lifestyle (who gives up aspirations for the sake of the family).

The combination of the independent variables together show a better overall explanatory power for desired fertility than it did for the achieved fertility. One possible explanation of this discrepancy is the fact that the analysis was done with relatively young women who were still at an interim stage of achieving their fertility aspirations. Another explanation is that the study was dealing with cognitive conscious variables that associated with the verbal desired fertility, while achieved fertility is more associated with unconscious factors that are not available for this kind of analysis.

Contraceptive Use

Several studies have demonstrated that the availability and use of contraceptives, in themselves, were only weakly associated with the achieved fertility, the use of contraceptives, as an intermediate variable mediating between the desired fertility and the achieved one, being the behavioral means to space pregnancies or to terminate fertility. Table 7 compares the use of contraceptives among the Jewish population and Moslem Arabs. In order to get a better analysis, the study distinguished between women who do not use contraceptives because they are currently not exposed to additional pregnancies, and those who do not use them for other reasons. The former are pregnant women, women who try to conceive, infertile women, or those who do not practice sexual intercourse.

The first significant fact, in terms of fertility rates, is that the proportion of "nonexposed" women among the Moslems is much higher than among the Jewish women, 29.4 percent as compared to 20.6 percent of all the women respectively. The bulk of the "non-exposed" are pregnant women and those trying to conceive. This means that at any one time, roughly 40 percent more Moslem women were in the process of having children (Table 8).

The number of "nonusers" among the "exposed" is also very significant, 21.3 percent of the "exposed" Moslem women compared with 11.3 percent

Table 7

Comparison of the Use and Non-Use of Contraceptives Among Married Jewish and Moslem Israeli Women (Aged 22-44 Years, 1988)

	Number of Women	Percent of Total	Percent of Exposed
JEWISH WOMEN			
Users of contraceptives	1192	70.6	88.8
Non-users of contraceptives among exposed (non-use for reasons of fear, reluctance, principle, family opposition, no intercourse, or ill-defined)	152	9.0	11.3
Subtotal exposed	1344	(80.0)	100.1
Non-exposed non-users of contraceptives (non-use because pregnant, want to become pregnant, recently delivered, infecund, or no intercourse)	346	20.6	
Total non-users of contraceptives		29.6	
Total number of women	1680	100.2	
MOSLEM WOMEN			
Users of contraceptives	258	55.5	78.7
Non-users of contraceptives among exposed (non-use for reasons of fear, reluctance, principle, family opposition, no intercourse, or ill-defined)	70	16.1	21.3
Subtotal exposed	328	(70.6)	100.0
Non-users non-exposed (non-use because: pregnant, want to become pregnant, recently delivered, infecund, or no intercourse)	137	29.4	
Total number of women	465	100.0	

among the Jewish women—15.1 percent as compared to 9 percent of the total number of women respectively. This number is very important because it marks the percent of women among the "exposed" who do not want to conceive, but do not use means of protection from pregnancy. Therefore, these women may be a potential audience for family planning efforts. Another such group not shown here is the women who actually attempt to

Table 8

Use and Non-Use of Contraceptives Among Married Israeli Moslem Women According to Exposure/ Non-Exposure to Pregnancy and the Reason Given for the Exposure/Non-Exposure (Aged 22-44 Years, 1988)

	Number of Women	Percent of Total	Percent of Exposed
Users of contraceptives	258	65.5	78.7
Non-use on reasons of principle	25	5.4	7.6
Non-use because of reluctance, fear, ill-defined	45	9.7	13.7
Non-users of contraceptives among exposed (principles, opposition of family, reluctance, ill-defined)	70	15.1	21.3
Subtotal exposed	328	(70.6)	100.0
Fertility-targeted non-use (pregnant, want to become pregnant, or delivered recently)	115	24.7	
Infecund or no intercourse	22	4.7	
Non-users non-exposed	137	29.4	
Total number of women	465	100.0	

avoid conception, but who are using inefficient methods. Their percentage is also higher among the Moslem than Jewish women. The conclusion is that when looking only at the women who do not desire conception at a given moment, there is a strong need for family planning efforts among the Moslem Arabs in Israel in order to allow them to realize their desires.

Fundamentalist Islam and Women's Status

In the last ten years, the fundamentalist Islamic movement has gained power among the Moslem Arab population. The change is evident in both social phenomena and in the rise to power of the Islamic movement in the local elections. More women are seen wearing the traditional *chador* covering a woman from hair to toe at both high schools and universities. In previous years, such garb was limited to older rural women. Many mosques are being build in communities, boys and girls are separated in the schools, and there are overt attempts, some of them not so delicate, to bring women "back to their place," ban alcohol, permissive dresses, erotic films, etc. The Islamic fundamentalists, who are politically most antiIsraeli, are similar in several respect to some Jewish ultra orthodox groups.

Sexual Violence Against Women and Children: The Deep Silence

The issue of sexual exploitation, coercion, and violence against women and children in the Arab sector has only recently been discussed in public; a first study has been published on the matter and crisis centers have been opened.

Because several characteristics of Arab society, especially in the sexual arena, make it against the self-interest of women, children, and concerned caretakers to make public accusations or seek help in situations of abuse, crisis support is mainly provided by telephone hot lines that allow the caller complete anonymity. A virgin woman who loses her virginity, for whatever reason, has a lower value in marriage and a taint on the ability of the family to guard the virtue of its daughters (which may reflect on the marriage value of other female members of the family). If a married woman is raped, the perception of nonvirgin women as tempters may cause people to blame her for what happened and not the man (over whom women may have sexual powers). A raped boy or man may keep quiet in order not to raise doubts about his manhood, which is highly valued in that society, and therefore in his ability to marry. Thus, the rape crisis centers that have counseling, intervention, and hot line programs in Arabic report that their contacts in the Arab sector are predominantly by phone, and that fewer callers will agree to identify themselves, make contact, or press charges, as compared to the Jewish sectors.

B. Ultra Orthodox Jews

The ultra orthodox, or *Haredim*, have an ambivalent existence as non-Zionist Jews, recognizing only divine rules yet living within a Jewish state. In some sense, it is more difficult for them in Israel than in the diaspora, under the rule of non-Jews. Judaism, as a national as well as an individual religion, prescribes rules of conduct not only within the private domain, but also in the public one. These rules do not apply to non-Jews, so it is only among Jews of differing practice that many conflicts arise about public observance of certain rules.

Many of the ultra orthodox live within a defensive spiritual perimeter, trying to isolate themselves and their children from the encroaching influence of secular temptations. They have a separate educational system that, although financed by the government, is totally outside of its educational supervision. Most of their youth do not go to the army, a highly significant experience in the life of secular and orthodox Israeli youth, which has an impact on dyadic, gender, and sexual issues. They also often feel strongly that secular Jews do not understand the importance of their way of life and, being in conflict with them over their own needs, hate or ridicule them. They therefore shun strangers, even the ultra orthodox who belong to other sects or communities. As their communities are very closely knitted, their life revolving around the synagogue, the ritual bath, and other public functions, it is very difficult to penetrate into their life.

It is even more difficult to penetrate into issues of sex and marriage that are not discussed in public. A very few windows have been opened into these areas in both fiction and nonfiction written by people who were formerly ultra orthodox, in a study by a woman anthropologist among religious women, and in sexual counseling and therapy.

Arranged Marriages: Potential, Yichus, Health, and Money

Marriage in the orthodox tradition is one of the most revered institutions. Many if not most of the religious rituals are familial, and it is assigned a most important role in transmitting the Judaic values from one generation to another. Although Judaism allows divorces, they are highly stigmatizing; striving for the intactness of the family and keeping the peace within it are highly valued.

In the ultra orthodox tradition, marriages are arranged, either through marriage brokers, or through interested parties in large family circles, or among friends. Four factors are highly important in arranging marriages. They are not necessarily the same for men and women, but they interact in more than one way. First, and probably the most important factor for a man, is his potential in Halachic scholarship. As marriages are arranged around the age of 18 to 20 for men and 16 to 18 for women, a realized potential is rare. The heads of the religious academies or seminaries—the *yeshivas*—will be looking for a suitable match for their most promising students. These will be decided by the second and third qualities: *Yichus*, for which the nearest translation is lineage and financial security. The first *yichus* concern focuses on finding a woman who is herself from a family of Halachic scholars, and thus will not only literally support her husband in his struggle for scholastic excellence, but also increase the chances of bearing and raising children who will be such scholars. This set of *yichus* issues also includes all the qualities of the lineage, not only the hereditary ones, but also ones like the "name" of the family, past divorces of other family members, and other such factors. The second *yichus* concern looked for in women is the ability of her parents to support the continuing studies of the husband in the *yeshivah* for years to come. Such support is contracted for in marriages and may place a heavy burden on the parents, as they can last for three, five, ten, or even more years. During that time, the parents can expect to support not only the young couple, but between three to six children. The quality of *yichus* is also a determinant in the men's eligibility, but not the financial one, if they are scholars. The financial status is important in men who are not scholars and who are in business or in trade.

Another highly valued factor is health, that of the bride and groom, and the health of their families. Thus, families strive to hide any "problematic" health problems like mental health, developmental disabilities, genetic disorders, or subfertility. They may hide such a son/daughter, even to the point of denying full care because of denial mechanisms.

Many things can detract from the value of a person in marriage, even having a brother or sister who has become less religious. Thus, gossip can be very harmful, and whisper campaigns pernicious. The admonitions against disqualifying gossip about brides and grooms are severe, which attest to the importance of the issue.

Sons and daughters of the big rabbinical families usually marry only within "proven" lines. Sometimes three or four such families remarry for several generations. Such marriages acquire the proportions of almost royal events.

Thus, marriages are viewed mainly not as an issue of the heart, but rational arrangements whose main purpose is to establish a viable, socially, and financially secure unit with a good potential for reproduction, continuations, and excellence.

Rules of Conduct Regulating Intercourse

As stated before, in Judaic tradition, sex is an entity that intrinsically is neither good nor bad, but has a high potential for both. The nature of sex is dependent on its meaning, context, and practices.

For orthodox people, and certainly for the ultra orthodox, the context and practices are highly important and intermingled. The central role of intercourse is procreation in the spirit of the blessing "Procreate and multiply and fill the earth," although the Halachic basis for the rules and regulations covering the *mitzvah* to procreate are anchored elsewhere. On the other hand, it is important to note that sex is practiced as one of the marriage obligations of the husband, not only for procreation. Thus, contraception may be allowed either for spacing or for ending pregnancies, if one of several reasons recognized by the *Halachah* occur, even before the proscribed number of children is reached. During such periods, when procreation is not its reason, sex continues to be a *mitzvah*.

In terms of meaning, sex, as most other things, should be practiced for the glory of God and his creation. There are several degrees of elevation in practicing it, but if striving for a higher step disturbs one from fulfilling the *mitzvah* itself literally, then that person is really sinning and should change his or her ways. This sometimes has meaning in sex therapy, as the therapist encounters a phenomenon in which sexual dysfunction is explained by the need to strive for an elevation of the sexual act.

The context of practicing sex is restricted to the boundaries of marriage and to the prescribed period of the month that is determined by the woman's menstrual period (see below). The rules of conduct governing the actual act of intercourse are numerous, from the amount of light which is allowed into the room (only indirect), through the place of religious books during the act, through positions that are recommended and acts that are proscribed, to mention just a few. A most proscribed act is, of course, the spilling of semen in vain, which determines the fact that condoms and withdrawal are religiously banned. There is a discussion whether, if in the course of transgressing other laws, the use of condoms is allowed for protection against AIDS. Another rule of conduct that is perfectly natural and understandable to those practicing Judaism in its ultra orthodox variation is that women are prohibited from direct verbal initiation of intercourse, although they are allowed other means of initiation, including indirect verbal ones.

It is important to note that pleasure is considered an integral part of the act, and it is the duty of the husband to "please" his wife. This raises several interesting issues, some of which have a meaning in sexual counseling and therapy. First, what is the meaning of pleasing or pleasure in the differing minds of men and women? This will determine if at all, what, when, and how, they ask for something in practice. This also poses a problem for a nonorthodox therapist who may interpret pleasure either in a culturally nonappropriate manner, or neglect to include individual variations and needs within the stereotypical interpretation. A second question is what proportion of the couples practice intercourse strictly according to the rules, how prevalent are the private variations to the public norms and how far they go?

Purity Laws: Periodic Abstinence, the Public-Private Dualism of Sexual Intercourse, and the Social Control Over Fertility

Purity laws restrict the period in which a couple can practice intercourse to about half of the month. The cessation of not only intercourse, but any direct or indirect physical contact between husband and wife is determined by the onset of menstruation; this is called the *Nidah* period. Toward the end of her menstrual period, but not less than five days from its onset, the woman has to check with white cloth at the external opening of the cervix, whether she is still bleeding. When there are no signs of bleeding any more, she has to count seven "clean" days; at the evening of the last day, she has to cleanse herself in the "*mikveh*," literally a pool, which is the public ritual bath. On that same night, her husband is to approach her for intercourse.

This emphasis on purity and the high visibility of the dualism between impurity-purity in women's life, raise several issues that can be viewed from different aspects.

Writings by religious people directed mainly at nonobservant people argue in a mixture of apologetic and aggressive modes that these laws protect the health of women in the time when her body is most vulnerable to infections through sexual intercourse, that the periodic abstinence creates a healthy sexual tension between husband and wife, and not only increases the bond between them, but also puts some meaning into it. There are also claims that restriction on intercourse, and the timing of the first intercourse after the abstinence, act not only to increase fertility, but also to the lowering of birth defects. Little evidence has been compiled that will be accepted as supporting the biomedical claim, in fact, and some of the evidence is cited wrongly or out of context. As for the psychological and dyadic claims, this may be true for some couples, but may be totally the opposite for others. Ronny A. Shtarkshall observed in a biased population of help-seeking couples that the purity laws were sometimes the focus of strong suffering on the side of women and a cause for conflict. Some women, for example, complained that the ban of touching was unbearable, especially when in a low or depressed mood or when one is ill or suffering. This was also true when the husband or an adolescent child is suffering. Women also complained that intercourse at the end of the *Nidah* period had a "mechanical" aspect to it, which causes both individual and interpersonal difficulties. The fact that this mechanical aspect of the intercourse— fulfilling a *mitzvah*—may have been only perceived or partially true is unimportant here. The important aspect is that it could cause difficulties and that it has to be addressed.

A highly important point of view is the feminist discourse that includes these laws as one of the determinants of the status of women in the Jewish religious society. Despite the fact that this discourse totally ignores the fact that purity laws also apply to men and to sperm emission, in a highly elaborate way, they point to some very important issues.

First is the issue of fear of contact with a *Nidah* woman unknowingly, which governs the rules of conduct of many orthodox men who will refrain from any casual touch or shaking hands with women. Thus, every woman is suspected to be impure unless proven otherwise. This may be the explanation for grandmothers sometimes being more "touching" than mothers when boys are concerned, and the readiness of the adolescent boys to accept this physical contact.

Second is the heightened awareness of adolescent girls of their bodies, its potential for impurity, and the need to examine it regularly. On the other hand, adolescent boys are introduced to the female issues from a totally "impersonal" point of view, through learning about it in their Halachic studies. The fact that boys also become aware of their own bodies through the need to keep a constant watch over themselves as not to spend semen in vain (which include nocturnal emissions), and thus be in danger of defiling the religious scrolls, is not alleviating the potential harm that such awareness may impose on the development of girls.

It is important to emphasize that this discourse is mostly limited to nonreligious circles and to religious women of North American origin.

Writings about these issues from this point of view, or from related ones, by orthodox women are generally not available.

An important point that is raised by both religious men and women, sometimes from different perspectives, is the public nature of intercourse and of fertility that is dictated by the use of the *mikveh*. Some recent ethnographic/anthropologic literature describe the feelings of women who go back home after visiting the *mikveh*, feeling in the look of every person in the street, especially the men, the knowledge of the expected intercourse. Thus a very private act acquires a very public aspect. Both men and women in therapy for either lowered fertility or for sexual issues frequently comment on the fact that going to the *mikveh* is a public proclamation of the failure to conceive in a society where both internal familial and external pressures for procreation are very high, especially on young couples. Men and women commonly comment on the fact that it is public knowledge even before that, when people, especially parents and in-laws, can tell when they refrain from touching each other or making contact, even indirectly, through a dish. This may have several implications (see discussion of therapeutic issues below).

Fertility Patterns

Although the high number of children born to ultra orthodox families is obvious and an accepted fact which influences both perceptions and politics, there is little hard data on the fertility patterns of the ultra orthodox. This results from a combination of administrative restrictions and reasons embedded in the ultra orthodox culture. While the religion of the parents is noted on the birth certificates of newborns, there is no notation of religiosity on documents that are the basis for all the statistical calculations of birthrates, age specific birthrates, and TFRs. Thus secular, traditional, orthodox, and ultra orthodox Jews are in the same category. As the ultra orthodox tend to live in geographically cohesive communities, it is possible to get a handle on their fertility through statistical regions. The TFR for Jews in the city of Jerusalem, which has a high proportion of ultra orthodox (30 percent by municipal elections), is almost two children higher as compared to the TFR for Jews in the two other big urban centers—Tel-Aviv and Haifa—3.72 as compared to 1.86 and 1.91 respectively.

It is apparent even to naive observers that the fertility pattern is totally different both in spacing and in TFR, as it is common to encounter families with six to nine children and not uncommon to encounter families with ten to fourteen children. Young couples usually aim at having the first child as soon as possible, within the first year of marriage. Studies have shown that this is such a prevalent and internalized norm that couples rarely discuss this issue. As a woman's menstruation and pregnancy are public knowledge, loving and concerned pressure is brought to bear on couples early in the marriage. Parents and in-laws are sometimes unaware that such pressures can be devastating both to the fertility and to the sexual functioning of the young couple.

Even in a fertility survey, it was difficult to look at the ultra orthodox separately, because their women tended to avoid being interviewed and were therefore underrepresented. The reasons for refusal, especially when the interview touched on issues of children, fertility, and family planning, are perfectly understandable from inside their cultural environment. First and foremost, children and fertility are one of the most precious things in the life of women. In a society where the future and planning for the future are the prerogative of God, any tampering, even a verbal one can be construed as tempting fate or courting punishment. Second, there is the fear of being misunderstood and/or stigmatized by outsiders, especially nonreligious Jews. Third, there is the fear of the evil eye resulting from jealousy.

Contraception vs. Family Planning

Despite the strong emphasis on procreation, the Jewish *Halachah* allows contraception on the basis of individual needs and circumstances. As the principles of the *Halachah* do not recognize general rulings, each individual case has to be decided by a Halachic authority on the advice of medical opinion. On the other hand, there is a very strong public opposition to family-planning services. The delicate differentiation between family planning and the use of contraceptives lies in the realm of purpose. While family planning as such is a transgression, the use of contraceptives for religiously recognized purposes is allowed.

The religious rules govern not only the use of contraceptives, but also the types of contraceptives to be used. As already mentioned, two types of contraceptives are almost totally banned: male contraceptives and nonreversible contraception, whether male or female. Among temporary female contraceptives, currently the most acceptable ones are combined birth-control pills (for women with breakthrough bleeding), IUD, and diaphragm. Again there are personal variations and medical opinions are sought and listened to.

The public opinion against family planning and contraceptive services is such that ultra orthodox women, even those with strong need that will probably be acceptable to the Halachic authorities, refrain from seeking help. The tip of the iceberg was seen when women listeners started writing to a weekly radio program, "Not a Children's Game," devoted to reproductive health and family planning issues. A psychosocial analysis of the letters revealed that about half of the women writing in were from the ultra orthodox community. Half of those were vociferously and almost violently against the program as promoting promiscuity and being antinatal; the other half were women desperately seeking help in dire situations. Religious authorities consulted by the producers assured them that these women could and should receive help according the *Halachah*. It was also evident that these women will be able to accept help only if it will be within the religious tenets. They were confidentially referred to both medical and religious authorities in the relevant geographical area. This public-private dichotomy is sometimes typical of the religious community.

Transgressions

The fact that people adhere to many religious rules and live within a religious community does not mean that they do not transgress on any of its laws and rules. Transgressions on an individual basis are varied and should be only recognized and not discussed in such a paper. On the other hand, when cultural, ethnic, or other traditions within a religious community are in contrast with religious rules, or are in contradiction of the rules that these same people profess, these should be looked into.

One such example was mentioned above, when public and spousal pressure prevented women who probably deserved contraception within the *Halachah* from seeking and receiving help.

Another example that relates to contraception was noted in a study that examined the family-planning practices of a very orthodox community of immigrants from Yemen. While the women complained about unwanted pregnancies and the number of children, the husbands claimed that family-planning services should not be approached because of religious reasons. A study by family physicians revealed that the most prevalent family-planning practice in this community, one that the majority of couples used, was withdrawal—a grave sin according to the religious rules.

One can only conclude that, as strong as religion rules are among orthodox groups, cultural traditions sometimes modulate them in unexpected ways.

Issues in Sex Therapy

Nonobservant therapists working in areas with a concentration of ultra orthodox must resolve several therapeutic, ethical, and personal/professional issues.

First is the difference between the therapeutic paradigm and the basic tenets of the client(s) and their subculture. In essence, one can say that the place of sex in the worldview of the clients differs in some important points from that of the therapist and the therapeutic approach.

While the basic approach of sex therapy to sex is individual- and couple-oriented, hedonistic, and present-oriented, the approach of many of the clients is certainly different. While pleasure and fulfillment are not excluded from the constellation, they are certainly not at its center. The central themes of sex among the orthodox are its function in procreation and the preservation of the family; despite the strong shroud of secrecy and privacy, sex has several "public" aspects to it, especially within the extended families; through the centrality of procreation, sex acquires a strong future aspect to it.

In this domain, one can also include the egalitarian approach of sex therapy, implicit in many of its tenets and interventions. In the ultra orthodox point of view there is a strong asymmetry in terms of initiative, responsibility, and the duty of husbands for the sexual act and the fulfillment of their wives.

A second issue can be viewed as environmental. While one of the basic means of sex therapy is to lower the burden of performance from the partner who carries it and the introduction of nonperforming sex, among the ultra orthodox, who view procreation as a central aim of intercourse, there is not only an objective criterion for performance, but also a regular almost public viewing of it, at least to other women—the visits of the wife to the *mikveh.*

A third issue is a more individual one. The use of exploration, inventiveness, and flexibility is an important part in the therapeutic intervention. Here the therapist encounters various degrees of rigidity/flexibility as in any other population. The uniqueness is the connection that the clients are making with the religious rules of conduct, a very powerful barrier to possible change. An approach that is embedded in their belief system is that transgression is a matter of choice, and it is an individual choice between sins.

The resolution of these issues lies in the recognition by therapists that any therapy cannot buck the basic belief system of the client and that changes can mostly be affected within that system. In the case of working with ultra orthodox persons, the therapist must adhere to some self-imposed rules and restrictions. Some of these are harder than others. Such is the agreement to consult rabbinical authorities on issues within the therapy, when the client demands it, and to abide by their specific decision in working with the specific client for which the question was asked. This raises issues like divided or shared authority and the use of consultations as escape routes. Other issues are the specialized knowledge needed even to ask Halachic questions and the use of the therapist's own rabbinical authority in phrasing them.

The basic rule seems to be the ability to feel true respect from outside and to grasp meanings from inside of a culture that is basically alien to the therapist's worldview.

It is difficult and inadvisable to talk about prevalence of sexual problems, not only because there are no adequate statistics, but because the reasons for seeking help may be totally different from that of the general population. The main complaint is subfertility, which is later diagnosed as a primary sexual dysfunction or the wish to have more children in the case of secondary ones.

C. The Kibbutz Movement

The kibbutz movement comprises 2 to 3 percent of the Jewish population of Israel, a seemingly smallish part of the population to be dealt with separately. But this movement of collective communities, the first of which was founded eighty years ago, played an important role in the development of Israeli society. Several features of this subculture are highly important for the discussion of sexuality of youth, fertility patterns, and contraception. The first is that, even with the current changes in lifestyle, and the fact that most kibbutzes have changed sleeping arrangements so that children sleep at their parents' apartments instead of the children homes, kibbutz youth live a life much more independent of adult control in general, and parental control in particular, from early adolescence on than any other group of Israeli youth. Second, despite the fact that the kibbutz society is not as egalitarian as people used to think, it is apparently very much so in many aspects. Third, the kibbutz society emphasizes self-reliance and internal locus of control in many aspects of life by minimizing economic secondary motivations. It is therefore not surprising that people take charge of their life in many aspects, including sexual responsibility and sexual health.

On the other hand, in a seemingly contradictory vein, social pressures to conform are very high within the kibbutzes. It seems that the strongest effects occur when social pressures and the powers of the individual act in the same direction.

Intercourse During Adolescence and Young Adulthood

When comparing urban to kibbutz youth, it is apparent that beyond tenth grade (age 16) both kibbutz men and women report more premarital intercourse than others; they also start at a younger age. This difference is more pronounced for women than for men—the rate of reported intercourse for kibbutz men is either similar or slightly higher than that of urban young men. In contrast to urban youth, the ratio of kibbutz men and women reporting intercourse, among those who initiated it, was about 1:1 for all grades. Whether this is an egalitarian norm of reporting, or of initiating intercourse or both, needs further studies. These results have been verified in several independent studies over a period of about twenty-five years.

As reported earlier, it seems that since the mid-1960s, the age of sexarche in Israel is going down for those who practice premarital intercourse (see Figure 2). This is true for both youth in both social settings, and is especially marked for urban women. However, there is an interesting difference between urban and kibbutz women (Figure 4). In all three cohorts of urban women, there is a break in the curve and a rise in the slope between ages 16 to 17, and 18 to 19. Among kibbutz women, this is true only for the older cohort, those who reached age 16 between 1965 and 1969. The two younger cohorts of kibbutz women, who reached age 16 in 1970 through 1975 and 1976 through 1982, show a straight line between ages 14 to 15 to 18 to 19 (significant at the 0.01 level for all three cohorts).

Figure 4

Comparison of Sexarche Between Urban and Kibbutz Women Who Reached Age 16 at Different Time Periods

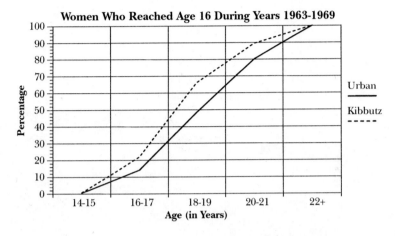

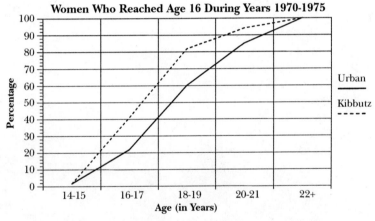

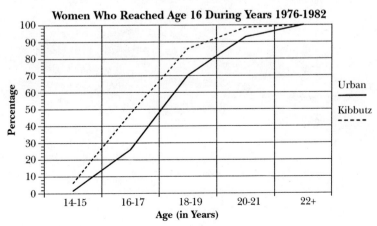

The "break" in the curve for urban women can be explained by the lowering of parental/social control for women who leave for the army at the end of twelfth grade. There are several possible explanations for the fact that for the kibbutz women the curve is straight: first, kibbutz women may be relying more on internal locus of control and, therefore, are less influenced by the parental/social controls; second, less parental control being exerted on kibbutz youth than on urban youth; and/or more accepting and egalitarian norms of sexuality among kibbutz youth that allow more women both to practice intercourse and to report it. Several indications in the data and in the general structure of kibbutz life indicate all of these factors may be acting together.

Fertility Patterns

A superficial analysis shows similarities between fertility patterns of urban and kibbutz women; closer analysis reveals a much more interesting picture. First, when comparing the TFR of kibbutz women to the segments of the population closer to them in composition, those of American-European origin, one finds that kibbutz women have more children. Second, when controlling for religion and comparing secular urban women with secular kibbutzes and religious (not ultra orthodox) urban women with religious kibbutzes (a small minority), one can see that in each sector, the kibbutz women have 0.5 more children. Third, the patterns of fertility are different. Kibbutz women marry older, give birth at a later age, and lag behind the urban women in number of children until about age 30, although they continue to have children until a later age.

Another difference is that the interval between giving birth is longer for kibbutz women, when controlled for religiosity, education, ethnic origin, age, stillbirth, and natural or induced abortion. Kibbutz women had intervals two months longer between the first and second child, and three months longer between the third and fourth child. The two latter differences point to a relatively high degree of planning and control of fertility.

When looking at the differences between various types of kibbutz ideologies and diverse lifestyles that emerged during recent years—like young children sleeping at home instead of at communal children's homes—it was found that the personal differences between women within kibbutzes contribute to the differences in TFR, much more than the differences between kibbutz movements.

Contraception

Does the fact that the kibbutz society supplies all the material needs of its members, including health needs; shows high prevalence of egalitarian attitudes to sexual behavior of men and women; and puts a high value on planning and control, in fact lowers some of the barriers to family planning and to efficient contraception that are so prevalent among many other groups? If this is the case, then the use of contraceptives among kibbutz women, married and unmarried alike, should be consistently higher than for urban women across all other variables like religiosity, educational level, ethnic origin, and birth order of the children.

As early as first intercourse, kibbutz women show a different pattern from urban youth: 43 percent of secular kibbutz youth used some kind of contraceptive at sexarche, about half of them—21 percent of all the women practicing premarital intercourse—used the pill on first intercourse. This number is much higher than the rate for secular urban youth: 27 percent and 13 percent respectively. The significance of this difference becomes more pronounced if one notes that it was already demonstrated that kibbutz women reach sexarche at a younger age than urban youth, and that age at first intercourse is a strong determinant of the ability of youths to protect themselves.

When comparing nonorthodox kibbutz women and urban women during their married life, it is clear that kibbutz women are more efficient and more consistent contraceptors. Only 15 percent of kibbutz women did not use any contraceptive prior to the first pregnancy, compared to 40 percent of the urban ones. During that period, only 12 percent of the kibbutz women relied on withdrawal as compared to 19 percent of the urban ones. The rates of pill use are reversed, 50 percent compared to 26 percent respectively.

After first pregnancy, the differences are even more pronounced: 90 percent of kibbutz women contracept and only 8 percent use withdrawal or rhythm, compared to 28 percent noncontraceptors and 26 percent withdrawal or rhythm contraceptors among urban women. These differences remain pronounced in higher birth order intervals. Among variables that might explain differences in contraceptive use prior to first pregnancy within the kibbutzes, the only ones with significance were the birth cohort—older cohorts using less contraceptives and less-effective ones prior to the first pregnancy, and ethnic origin—women of Asian-African origin using less effective contraceptives.

When comparing contraceptive use in 1987-88, kibbutz women progress from 79 percent efficient contraceptors prior to the first pregnancy, through 81 percent after the first and second pregnancy, to 89 percent after the third pregnancy. Urban women progress from 24 percent through 62 percent to 64 percent respectively. Not only is there a difference, but the pattern is different. It seems that urban women contact agencies that help them use efficient contraceptives only after giving birth to the first child, while the majority of kibbutz women do so prior to the first pregnancy.

Juxtaposing the patterns of contraceptive use with the patterns of fertility, and taking into account that kibbutz women who start having children at a later age and with longer birth intervals end up with more children over a longer fertile period, it seems that the group is very close to that of the ideal contraceptors—women who use contraceptives effectively to have as many children as they want at the time that they choose. This is also supported by information about much fewer reported unplanned pregnancies, most of which seem to be while using very safe methods.

15. Immigrants and Immigration

Israel is, as indicated, an immigrant society, albeit with some strong internal and external cohesive forces. There are some indicators that demonstrate that these forces are acting toward creation of a common meeting ground, in which some unique characteristics develop.

Nevertheless, two groups of recent immigrants give us the opportunity to look at issues and processes that both immigrants and the host society undergo when faced with the phenomenon of people from an alien culture transplanted into an established one.

One can claim that the immigrants from the former Soviet Union (USSR) and those from Ethiopia have nothing in common. The Ethiopian immigrant group is small even by Israeli standards, the recent wave arriving since 1991 being 20,000 people and the whole community numbering 50,000. More than half a million immigrants, 10 percent of the total population of Israel, have arrived from the USSR since 1989. The "Russians" came from a midindustrial, European country with a high literacy rate, mainly from urban areas, having a high rate of academic professionalization and with many family ties with the established old-timers' society. As a matter of fact, the Mayflower founding parents of the Israeli society and state immigrated from Tzarist Russia and its environments at the end of the last century and the beginning of this one. The immigrants from Ethiopia came from a country with a rich but isolated culture, nonindustrialized, with low literacy rates, mainly from rural-agricultural areas with low mobility, an extended family structure, and very little family ties with the old-timers' establishment.

On the other hand, both groups had undergone, through the dual process of emigration/immigration, being uprooted from one's original culture and transplanted into a new alien one. But the similarities may even go deeper. Both groups came from societies that had very strong external social controls. While among Jews in Ethiopia, the controls were mainly familial and "tribal"—the forces of tradition within a small, isolated, and sometimes persecuted group—those of the USSR were political and institutional. Also, at the time of their immigration, both original societies were undergoing some very strong processes of disruptive transitions. So one is faced with a unique chance of looking at two groups of immigrants undergoing a very similar process, but with somewhat different starting points and cultural contents.

Interest in the immigrants from Ethiopia and the former USSR is not one of explorers observing exotic cultures with mixed emotions, nor of amateurish anthropologists whose hidden aggenda is asserting their own cultural superiority. We are involved and vested participant-observers, with a strong interest in ameliorating the difficult process of immigration and acculturation. Ronny A. Shtarkshall is already an intervener-observer involved in the study and development of integrating interventions.

Because these immigrations are quite recent, the initial processes of cultural integration, some of which are very painful, are still going on. Sensitivities are high and the potential for stigmatization is frightening. Hence one cannot do more at this time than indicate that careful and sensitive work with these immigrant groups may well in the future provide a rich source for major new insights into the principles and functioning of a cross-cultural sex education program.

Glossary

Some Hebrew and Arabic words that are frequently used in the text, mainly for lack of an appropriately equivalent term in English (Some of these terms are italicized throughout the text).

Halachah: The accumulated body of religious laws, discussions, rules of conduct, interpretations, judicial decisions, and precedents that govern the life of an orthodox religious Jew. Generally the *Halachah* covers all the aspects of life of a religious Jew from birth to death, religious and secular, public and private. The more orthodox a person is, the more strict is the adherence to the Halachic rules and the more involved are the interpretations.

Haredim: A general name given to ultra orthodox communities by secular people. Most people who use this name do not distinguish even between the major variations of ultra orthodox Judaism.

Mikveh: Literally a place were flowing water will collect, the name of the ritual bath that serves for ritual purification of both women and men when this is required according to religious regulations. It is mostly discussed, especially by the secular population, in relation to the purification of women at the end of their impure period—*Nidah.* It should be noted that men should also purify themselves if they spill semen, and that many religious rituals require that men purify themselves in the *mikveh.*

Mitzvah: A combination of a religious law, personal obligation, and a privilege. The Hebrew name for the religious rules. The original biblical ones numbered 613 (not a small number in itself), but their development and interpretation in the Talmud increased their numbers several folds.

Mohar: Bride payment. Traditionally paid by Moslem grooms to the bride's father. *Mohar* can be paid in money or cattle. It is almost never paid with land.

Nidah: A period determined by the menstrual period and seven days after it, during which women are impure and untouchable. The root of the word also means ban or banishment.

Shabbat: The seventh day. Among orthodox and ultra orthodox, it is strictly kept. Not only no work is allowed, but things like lighting a fire or an electric instrument, driving or riding in a car, picking a flower, writing or tearing paper are banned. Although very holy and strictly observed, one is allowed to do most of the things if the purpose is to save lives. One of the things that is not only allowed but recommended on Shabbat night is intercourse.

Yeshivah: A high religious academy or a seminary.

Yichus: lineage.

References and Suggested Readings

Antonovsky, H. 1980. *Adolescent Sexuality*. Lexington, Massachusetts: Lexington Books.

Arieli, Y. 1992. "Being a Secular Jew in Israel." In Arieli Y. *History and Politics*. Tel Aviv: Am-Oved

Birenbaum, M. 1993. *Survey of Sex Education in General National Education Schools, 1991-1992*. Jerusalem: Unit of Family Life and Sex Education, Ministry of Education and Culture. (Hebrew).

Central Bureau of Statistics. 1993. *Statistical Almanac, 1992*. Jerusalem: Governmentís Press (Hebrew & English).

Herz, Fredda M., and Elliott J. Rosen. 1982. "Jewish Families." In M. McGoldrick, J. K. Pearce, and J. Giordano, eds. *Ethnicity and Family Therapy*. New York: Guilford Press.

Keysar, A. 1990. *Demographic Processes in the Kibbutzes of Israel*. A doctoral dissertation. Hebrew Univesity of Jerusalem.

Nathan, M., and A. Schnabel. 1975. "Changes in the Attitudes of Kibbutz Children Toward Friendship and Sexual Relations." *Studies in Education (Iunim Bechinuch)*. 6:117-32 (Hebrew).

Peritz, E., and M. Baras, eds. 1992. *Studies in the Fertility of Israel*. Jerusalem: The Hebrew University of Jerusalem.

Sabatallo, E. 1992. "Estimates of Demand for Abortion Among Soviet Immigrants in Israel." *Studies in Family Planning*, 23(4):268-73.

Sabatallo, E. 1993. "The Impact of Induced Abortion on Fertility in Israel." *Social Science in Medicine*, 36(5):703-07.

Sabatallo, E. 1993. *Continuity and Short Term Changes in Patterns of Fertility and Abortions Among Immigrant from the Former USSR*. Jerusalem: Social Security. (in press; Hebrew).

Shtarkshall R. A. 1990. "Formen und Trends im Sexualverhalten Israelischer Jugendlischer." In W. Melzer, W. Ferchhoff and G. Neubauer, eds. *Jugend in Israel und in der Bundesrepublik*. Weinheim un Munchen: Juventa Verlag.

Shuval, J. T. 1992. *Social Dimensions of Health: The Israeli Experience*. Westport, Connecticutt: Praeger.

Sketchley, J. M. 1991. *Psychosexual Services in Selected European Countries*. Copenhagen: World Health Organization, European Region.

NOTE: A more extensive list of references that were utilized in the preparation of this article can be obtained by writing to the first author: Ronny A. Shtarkshall, Ph.D., 15 Yasmin Street (Box 1116), Mevasseret-Zion, Israel 90805.

Japan
(*Nippon*)

Yoshiro Hatano, Ph.D., and Tsuguo Shimazaki*

Contents

Demographics and a Historical Perspective

A. Demographics

It was Marco Polo, a man from Venice, Italy, in the latter half of the thirteenth century, who wrote a book entitled *Le Merveilles du Monde*, in which he introduced the country of Japan to the Western world as *Jipang*, "the land of gold." His book was actually a collection of his experiences and information about his journey through central Asia and China.

---

*Note. The *Encyclopedia* editor is grateful to the authors for their effort to complete this chapter in time for inclusion in the first three volumes despite their concurrent responsibilities in coordinating the 12th World Congress of Sexology in Yokohama. The editor also acknowledges the invaluable assistance of Yoshimi Kaji, M.Ed., his former New York University graduate student, for her additional comments, for checking his editorial additions, and for helping to bring this important chapter to completion. Her comments have been integrated in the text in brackets with her name (Kaji) at the end of each comment.

Japan is an island country, located to the east of the Asian continent in the northwestern part of the Pacific Ocean. The islands face the Pacific on the east and south sides, the Sea of Japan and East China Sea on the west side, and the Sea of Okhotsk on the north side. The islands form a bow-shaped string stretching from the northeast to the southwest. In addition to five major islands, i.e., from the north Hokkaido, Honshu, or Main Island, Shikoku, Kyushu, and Okinawa, there are some 320 small islands over a square kilometer each, totaling 372,000 square kilometers. Japan is slightly larger than the land of Germany and smaller than Spain.

A relatively mild climate prevails, due to the location of most of Japan's islands in the Temperate Zone. With four distinctive seasons, there are variations due to longitudinal distribution of the islands. Due to the mild climatic characteristics, natural features of the islands, and religious philosophy, the Japanese people have developed a sensitive and cooperative attitude to the relationship between nature and humankind, in contrast to the Western culture, which is independent, and often exploitive or in opposition. Such views of nature and humankind may be regarded as characteristic of the Orient.

The land mass of Japan is rather small and approximately 87 percent of the land is mountainous. As a consequence, fields and basins of rather small scale are divided by mountain ranges. From the beginning, this geographic circumstance has isolated local communities—which in the early days were independent countries—producing different cultures, customs, and religious events in different areas. This situation persisted into this century. Since the Meiji Era (1868-1912), the influence of Western cultures, along with economic growth and the development and popularization of the mass media system in recent years, has promoted an increasingly shared (common) education and culture, resulting in the current unification of the Japanese culture. Cultures imported from China and Korea since the fifth century, and from the Western world since the Meiji Era, have been well absorbed by the Japanese people. The Japanese always kept a flexible attitude in accepting foreign influences to amalgamate traditional and imported cultures, forming their own specific culture.

In early 1996, the population of Japan was close to 126 million, equivalent to one half the population of the United States, or to the combined populations of France and Germany. The population in 1925 was approximately 60 million and it took nearly seventy years to double to our current size. Approximately 77 percent of the total population live in urban areas and less than 23 percent, 28 million, in towns and villages, clearly indicating an extreme urban-centered construction. Japan's cities have grown into metropolises as the focus of work. At the same time, the number of core (nuclear) families with a small number of children is increasing. As a result, the local community as the basis for human network activities and a humane life is often lost.

According to the report by the Ministry of Public Health and Welfare, the average life expectancy of the Japanese is 77 and 82 years for men and women respectively. The longevity of the Japanese is steadily increasing. On the other hand, the Japanese birthrate is 39.2 per 1,000 female population, in comparison to 51.8 in 1980, 63.6 in 1960, and 110.4 in 1950, only forty-five years ago. In 1992, the Japanese had 1.53 children per woman. The trend of longevity extension and decreased birthrate obviously is creating serious problems for Japanese society for future days. Japan has a high-aged society that represents a heavy concentration of aged people in contrast to the working population. The current ratio is somewhere around one retiree for every four workers.

The *1996 World Almanac* gives Japan's birth rate as 11 per 1,000 population and the death rate at seven per 1,000, giving a natural annual increase of 0.3 percent. Japan had an infant mortality rate of 4 per 1,000 live births in 1995, one hospital bed per 74 persons and one physician per 570 persons. Literacy in 1992 was listed at 100 percent with nine years of compulsory education, although most Japanese children attend at least 12 years of school. The per capita gross domestic product in 1993 was $20,400.

Japanese is the only language officially used throughout the nation. Nevertheless, in the Constitution of Japan, there is no statement about the language to be used. Regardless of the situation, almost 100 percent of those who hold the Japanese citizenship speak and write the Japanese language in daily communication and in carrying on their social life. Regarding racial problems, which have been the cause of turmoil in many countries in recent times, there are no current serious arguments to endanger the national unity. One needs to pay attention, though, to the possible problem with minority races, such as Ryukyu (Okinawa) and Ainos, and the forced immigrants from the Korean Peninsula during World War II. At this moment, administrative policies and responsive movements of adherence and preservation of the respective cultures are effectively carried out. These minority people speak and write the Japanese language officially, as well as in daily life.

B. A Brief Historical Perspective

According to Japanese legend, the empire was founded by Emperor Jimmu in 660 B.C.E.. However, the earliest records of a unified Japan date from a thousand years later, about 400 of the Common Era. Chinese influences played an important role in the formation of the Japanese civilization, with Buddhism being introduced to the islands before the sixth century C.E.

A feudal system dominated Japan between 1192 and 1867, with locally powerful noble families and their *samurai* warrior retainers controlling local government, and a succession of military dictators, or *shoguns*, holding the central power, This ended when Emperor Meiji assumed power in 1868. The Portuguese and Dutch developed some minor trade with Japan in the sixteenth and seventeenth centuries. United States Commodore Perry opened American trade with Japan in an 1854 treaty. Japan gained Taiwan and other concessions following an 1894-1895 war with China, gained the south half of Sakhalin from a 1904-1905 war with Russia, and annexed Korea in 1910. During World War I, Japan ousted the Germans from Shantung and took over the Pacific islands controlled by Germany. In 1931, Japan took over Manchuria, starting a war with China in 1932. World War II started with Japan's attack on Pearl Harbor, Hawaii, and ended with two atomic bombs being dropped on Hiroshima and Nagasaki in August 1945.

In 1947, Japan adopted a new constitution that reduced the Emperor to a state figurehead and left all the governing power with a Diet. In a few decades, Japan quickly moved to become a major world power and leader in economics, industry, technology, and politics.

1. Basic Sexological Premises

A. Gender Roles

In Japan, a strict hierarchy of social classes and clearly defined traditional gender roles have their roots in over two thousand years of cultural history. In terms of social classes, merchants or *chyonin* were beneath the farmers and artisans. *Samurai*, the social elite, were retainers in the service of the *shogun* and the *daimio*. The *samurai*, who represented the superior male, constituted a bureaucratic and conservative hereditary group. The *samurai* and his sword was more a class symbol than the fierce warrior pictured in American television mythology.

As for gender roles, Karel Van Wolferen (1989) gives a terse picture of the traditional/modern female gender role in *The Enigma of Japanese Power*:

> Although in reality Japanese tradition has never frowned on working women, and today the majority of working married women are obliged to help make ends meet in their families, the officially sponsored portrait of "wholesome" family life invariably shows that the proper place for women is at home. In a country where stereotypes are treasured, emphasis on the established proper roles of women is especially noticeable. It extends to demurely polite deportment, a studied innocent cuteness, a "gentle" voice one octave above the natural voice and always a nurturing, motherly disposition. The modern woman in the world of the salaryman [white collar workers] is a cross between Florence Nightingale and the minister of finance (as women are always totally responsible for household finances). Superior intelligence is a liability for girls and women, and must be disguised.

In early 1989, the Welfare Ministry launched a poster campaign to stress that the only difference between males and females is biological. The posters showed two romping, mud-splattered toddlers with the caption *Tamatama otokonoko, tamatama onnanoko:* "He just happens to be a boy; she just happens to be a girl." This notion gained little support from government ministries more closely allied to business and industry, who joined the politicians in upholding traditional gender role values as a means of continually exploiting the diligence of the people (Bornoff 1991, 452).

In a 1982 opinion poll conducted by the Prime Minister's Office, 70 percent of the Japanese surveyed agreed with the statement that "Japanese women still believe a woman's place is in the home and that little girls should be brought up to be 'ladylike.'" In a 1989 multinational survey by the same agency on the theme "Men should work and women should stay home," 71 percent of the Japanese women either completely or somewhat agreed with the premise (see also discussion of Figure 36 in Section 5B). Critics suggest that respondents to government surveys may be inclined to give answers they believe the authorities want to hear, so it is important to balance these government survey results with similar surveys in the private sector. In one such survey conducted by a noted cosmetics firm, four fifths of the women found working women admirable, and 70 percent rejected the notion that a woman should quit her job after marriage (Bornoff 1991, 453). Still, the argument that traditional sex roles are strongly valued in Japan is persuasive when one considers that only 20 percent of Japanese firms offer female employees a year's maternity leave, in most cases without pay, and that day-care facilities are woefully inadequate. (One should recall, however, that the record of American corporations is not much different on these issues, and certainly lags far behind the policies in some European countries.)

Gender roles are clearly defined, although they are also being challenged in modern Japan.

> At the two extremes of female and male in popular culture, one finds the geisha and the sumo wrestler: the dainty living doll standing for femininity and the mountainous icon of macho flesh with the little porcine eyes. Between the two bookends plenty of scope lies in a nebulous heaven of make-believe far from the constrictions of daily routine. Segregating the sexes during childhood and defining the contexts and nature of their encounters later on, Japanese society defines gender roles with adamantine rules. In the realm of the imaginary, the strict roles encapsulating male and female are broken, being transgressed in fantasies which can be singly and variously violent, sadistic, maudlin, sentimental or comical. Transcending the laws of society, authority and even gender, these fantasies reach apotheosis in the popular imagination with ethereal creatures as blessedly sexless as occidental angels. (Bornoff 1991, 437)

Gender definitions in Japan can transcend the anatomical; masculine and feminine attributes can fade or fuse through conventions. This is most clearly seen in public rituals, for instance, when the emperor becomes a female incarnation of the sun goddess Amaterasu during the *daijosai* enthronement ceremony (See Bornoff 1991, 15-16, for the legend of Amaterasu and Ama-no-Uzume, the Heavenly Alarming Female). Gender reversal is also common in both traditional theater and modern cinema. After centuries of evolution, *kabuki* became a sophisticated form of theater in which the all-male cast plays all roles. Kabuki theater has long found a female equivalent in certain geisha theatricals comprising dances and playlets in which some of the female cast adopt male roles. In Nobuhiko Obayashi's film *Tenkosei* ("Transfer Students"), a 1983 offbeat youth comedy hit about junior-high-school lovers who undergo a kind of Kafka-like metamorphosis when the girl's soul enters the boy's body, and vice versa, and are forced to confront their awakening sexuality, the characters adopt the physical and social gender roles of the other. Similarly, the famed Takarazuka Young Girls Opera, founded in 1914, embraces many older male-role superstars with female actors performing in braided pantomime in military uniforms, tuxedos, cowboy garb, and *samurai* armor, blue cheeks, and mustaches. The Takarazuka Opera is part of a virtuous theme park called Family Land, "a florid world of Tinseltown baroque in pink, a feminine Disneyland with rose-colored bridges spanning artificial water courses." In 1987, when Takarazuka unsuccessfully pushed for recognition as a traditional art form to gain tax exemption, male traditionalists were quick to point out that *geisha* theater provided the proper traditional female counterpoint to male *kabuki* (see also Section 7 on cross-dressing, gender-crossing, and transsexualism; Bornoff 1991, 436-439).

[In ancient times, Japanese women wielded considerable authority. Until the eleventh century, it was common for Japanese girls to inherit their parent's house. The rise of Confucianism and a conservative moral movement that preached the inferiority of women in the early eighteenth century significantly reduced women's role. In some respects, Japanese women today have less power in society than they did a thousand years ago. Fewer than one in ten Japanese managers is female; women in less-industrialized nations, like Mexico and Zimbawee, are twice as likely to be managers. Only 2.3 percent of Japan's key legislative body are women, compared with 10.9 percent in the U.S. House of Representatives. In this regard, Japan ranks 145 in a list of 161 countries, according to the Inter-Parliamentary Union.

[The public gender roles, however, are reversed when one steps inside the Japanese home. Typically, the wife handles and completely controls the household finances. She gives her husband a monthly allowance and has total control over the rest of the family income. Half of the husbands in one survey reported they were dissatisfied with the size of their allowance, but could do little if anything about it. While the husband and wife may have a joint bank account and automatic teller machines are available, wives often do not share access to these with their husbands (Kristoff 1996b). (Editor)]

[In recent years, a new phenomenon has appeared in Japan's vibrant big city night life that may echo other signals noted in this chapter suggesting that traditional Japanese gender roles are changing. A 1996 *New York Times* report by Miki Tanikawa focused on *New Ai* ("New Love"), the largest of Tokyo's estimated 200 "host clubs." The host clubs are a variation of the ubiquitous clubs where businessmen regularly unwind in the company of charming young women, except that the traditional gender roles are reversed and sex is not part of the host club scene. In the host clubs, it is the women who are flattered and flirted with by attractive men of their choice. The clientele are usually the wives of wealthy men or hostesses at the businessmen's clubs where they spend their working hours pampering male clients. On a busy night, *New Ai* entertains more than 300 customers in its rooms elaborately decorated with rococo-style furniture, statues, and chandeliers. A band provides music ranging from standard jazz numbers to Japanese love songs. Unlike their male counterparts, the host clubs are strictly for companionship and nonsexual entertainment. Still, an evening of flattery, chatting, drinking, and dancing is not cheap. An evening may cost the equivalent of five hundred American dollars or more. Regular clients may run up monthly bills of three or four thousand dollars.

[Traditional values are nevertheless evident in the absence of sexual activity and in the secrecy women are expected to exercise in their visit to a host club. Japanese men can have an open night life, including visits to the sexual hot spots known as soaplands. Japanese women do not have this freedom (see discussion of soaplands in Section 8B). Despite their efforts to defy social conventions, clients of the host clubs often choose a host and remain devoted to him for years, sometimes showering him with expensive gifts to express their affection (Tanikawa 1996). (Editor)]

B. Sociolegal Status of Males and Females

An important insight into the status of women and men in the realities of everyday life and legal statutes can be found in the workplace. Female employees who pass the *tekireiki*, or marriage age, without getting married often encounter discrimination, despite the enactment in 1986 of an Equal Employment Opportunity (E.E.O.) Act. While firing such a female employee is against the law, the atmosphere may become so strained because of inquiries from supervisors and colleagues that the unmarried female may decide to leave the company. Women who remain employees and unmarried after *tekireiki* must be compensated as they climb, however unwelcomed, the corporate ladder. *Onna dakara* ("Because I am a woman") is a line often heard in the perennially popular and unabashedly sentimental Enka folk songs. Indeed, in a conservative country in which Confucian *samurai* ethics were resuscitated in the 1880s and fomented lucratively ever since in industrial disguise, being a woman can be difficult. Obligatory marriage and motherhood, and subservience to her husband and his family, would seem to have no place in a technopolitan economic supergiant in which half of the work force is female (Bornoff 1991, 452).

The E.E.O. law has been largely ineffectual because large corporations have a strong standing with the government, making enforcement of any measures against sexual discrimination unlikely. From the largest international firms to the smallest businesses, the widespread view is that sexual discrimination is unethical only according to concepts adopted in recent years, concepts which, to some, are quite foreign. The law entitles women to complain, but this more often than not results in "counseling" rather than action, and so few women complain. Even if filing a complaint could theoretically win a woman higher wages and guard her from dismissal, the action of filing a complaint would be viewed as a complete lack of loyalty to the firm and only earn her complete ostracism by her colleagues. Nevertheless, some major firms, including several banks, have recently moved to put ability before traditional stereotypes and hierarchical promotion, and stress greater sexual equality in the workplace. However, even when management gives female employees equality with males, the male business associates the women have to deal with are often uncomfortable or unwilling to deal with a woman as an equal (Bornoff 1991, 452).

C. General Concepts of Sexuality and Love

The Shinto religion recognizes neither good nor evil, so the concept of sin and personal guilt so commonly associated with sex in Western cultures does not exist in the Japanese tradition. The persistence of fertility festivals echoes the acceptance of sex and romance as a natural component of everyday life. Rooted in folk religions and primitive animism, these festivals are celebrated by revelers wearing traditional masks representing the more frankly sexual and comical denizens of Shinto myth and carrying oversized papier-mâché phalli and vulva through the streets (Bornoff 1991, 14-15, 89-90).

Apart from the persistent traditional culture of Japanese sexuality, it is true that Japan has also experienced a rapid modernization, especially in the 1950s and 1960s. As in other societies, modernization in Japan has brought a series of changes in the daily life and lifestyles and hence in human behavior. Table 1 provides a summary of such changes as a model of trends, problems, and issues in lifestyles and human life that are the result of a variety of primary and secondary changes (Hatano 1972).

In general, technological development has resulted in a significant decrease in the amount of physical labor and inconvenient living circumstances. Development of scientific knowledge, along with popularization of education, brought more literacy and freer communications among the common people. The power of the patriarchal structure that originally gave an eccentric, unbalanced character to the family organization decreases as modernization proceeds. In this manner, communication within the family

Table 1

Trends, Problems, and Issues in Lifestyles as the Result of Primary and Secondary Changes in Societal Modernization

Primary Changes ⟶	Secondary Changes ⟶	Trends, Problems, and Issues
		More leisure hours
		Conformism
		Impersonal society
		Leaving hometown
		Extinction of the fireside
		Happy family circle
		Money first philosophy
	Mass media development	Longer adolescence
	Freer commuting	Lessened family concentric force
Technological development	Less concentric force in family	Less community activities
Industrial development	Less physical labor	Children leaving parents
Universal education	More work outside of the home	Nuclear family
Decline of agricultural economy	Materialism	Less social restrictions
Decline of patrimonial succession	Longer school life	Lack of self-realization
	Emphasis on human rights	Lack of sincerity
	More vocational and career opportunities for women	Lonely crowd
		Lack of communication
		Less emphasis on individuality
		Aimless life
		Generation gap
		Lowered moral code
		Family members not supporting each other
		Insufficient child care

is being ignored. Modern Japanese family life has come to the point where many parents are not taking care of the children and the children are not establishing their self-identity. On the other hand, with only one or two children, parents, and particularly mothers, may be overly protective to the point of rendering their offspring indecisive and inadequate in their interpersonal relationships.

Such changes also cause significant shifts in the way human sexuality is experienced in modern Japan, including the sexual consciousness and sexual behaviors among the people (Hatano 1991b, 1991c; see also Table 2). The impact of the scientific development invited marked progress in the knowledge of biology and genetics. This in turn stimulated the development of sexology. For example, much of the mystery in childbirth, especially the superstitions that there are certain relationships between the behavior of the parents in the past and the physical nature of the newborn,

Table 2

**The Development of Sexology Promoted More
Demand for New Sexuality Education**

Events	Contents
Development of science and sexology	Biology and genetics
Broadening perspectives on sexual behavior	Family planning, separation of reproduction and sex, liberation from traditional sex roles, freer sexual activities
More demand for new sexuality education	Transmission of accurate sexual knowledge and information, value judgment education as standard of behavior judgment, education for life planning

has gradually disappeared. The promotion of science education in public schools has helped this tendency.

The next event in this line was the development of sexology and knowledge about sexuality, such as the separation of reproduction and other sexual behaviors, family planning, emancipation from traditional sex roles, and subsequently a more liberal attitude regarding sexual activities. Promotion of family planning after the war years played a decisive role in decreasing the yoke of the women in Japan. At some times, abortion was the most frequently used method of family planning, resulting in certain aftereffects on women's health. In these societal trends, religion no longer played a strong role in controlling the code of ethics, because of the allergic reaction to the national control of religion during the dark days of World War II. However, at the same time, modern Japanese have often lost self-identity in terms of development of moral judgment and values.

The premodern Japanese had no choice but to accept and follow the lifestyles, behavior patterns, and basic philosophy of life of their parents or leaders in the society. Role models and lifestyle patterns were rather easily found among the family members, as long as one did not attempt to find something new in life. Modern Japanese people, confronted with an explosively large amount of information pouring into their brains, have had to learn how to sort and select this information before they can apply it to actual daily living. It is quite true that during the economic postwar prosperity period, Japan's economic growth almost became the standard of values for society, inviting severe criticism from people in other parts of the world.

Education in information selection systems or value systems—moral education, particularly in relation to sexual activities—has become a major necessity in formal and informal education. Likewise, education in sexual behavior, not in terms of instruction in a behavioral code but in terms of providing understanding of the stages of psychosexual development, will benefit the development of each individual's sexuality. Likewise, sexuality education is expected to enhance education for parenting. All of these needs share a common base as consequences of modernization. The current national Course of Study of the Ministry of Education does not include education for either value systems or for establishment of self- and sexual identity. Perhaps these aspects of education belong to the realm of family education. Unfortunately, in contemporary Japan, the national administration of public education is so well developed that the general public has almost forgotten the responsibility of family education. This is causing some serious social problems, particularly when parents expect the public schools to assume complete responsibility for teaching all the code of ethics, including sexual behaviors.

2. Religious and Ethnic Factors Affecting Sexuality

A. Source and Character of Religious Values

According to the latest statistics from the Japanese Ministry of Education, 96.25 million Japanese believe in Buddhism, 109 million in Shintoism, and 10.5 million in other indigenous Japanese religions. A total of 1.46 million are members of various Christian churches. The sum of these statistics exceeds by 75 percent the total population of Japan. The explanation lies in a characteristic of the Japanese people's attitudes toward religion, which may not be easily understandable for the non-Japanese. The logic of this seemingly illogical trait of Japanese life may be explained in a typical example of Japanese parents who have a custom of visiting a local Shinto shrine to pray to all the 8 million Gods of Shintoism for the healthy growth and well-being of a newborn baby. In the same family, the same parents may have held their wedding ceremony at a Christian church and prayed there for happiness of their newly formed family. The same couple may read the holy scriptures in the Buddhism temple when a family member dies, praying for the dead one to be accepted in the heavenly world safely. Such inconsistency is widely accepted among the Japanese without much friction. Indeed, "three *different* bells ring in the valley," instead of "three bells ring in the valley." Having a mix of various religions in one's daily life is a common way of the Japanese lifestyle. In addition to these well-organized religions, nature worship, which is closely related to Shintoism, is another prevalent religious belief.

Regardless of the mix of religions practiced, which heavily influences the Japanese consciousness on culture, sex, and sexuality, one needs to understand the substantial connection between religion in Japan and the culture, value system, and attitudes toward sexuality. This understanding requires a brief sketch of the history of religion in Japan.

The results of archaeological studies in Japan indicate a common practice of burying the dead with certain religious services and rituals during the Jomon and Yayoi culture periods, which ended somewhere around the third or fourth century C.E. During the Jomon period, which lasted several centuries, especially in the eastern part of Japan, remains indicate the special attention the ancestors of the Japanese people then paid to sex and procreation. This is well demonstrated in the artificial designs of the earthed works that are frequently excavated. Throughout the Jomon period, people lived by hunting and gathering, and there was little evidence of any power struggles or the existence of social classes. The Yayoi period arose after the Jomon, around 100 B.C.E., mostly in the western part of Japan. This culture introduced rice crops and ironware from the Korean peninsula and Chinese continent. With these new cultural influences came a disparity of wealth and social classes, which gradually spread throughout the society. (See Bornoff 1991, 7-16, for a helpful discussion of the sexual and coital implications of Japanese creation myths.)

Later, in the middle of the sixth century of the Common Era, Buddhism and Confucianism were introduced to Japan from Kudara in the Korean Peninsula. These religions rapidly spread nationwide, combining with the gradual permeation of a central government power ruled by the Emperor's family. Popularization of the new philosophy and new administration proceeded along with the preservation policy of these value systems by the central government. In adopting this new religion and culture, Japan followed a path distinctively different from that pursued in other countries. In most cultures, a religious war has been necessary before a newly introduced religion could gain acceptance. In Japan's case, the local religious practices and customs of the preceding culture were not abandoned; rather both old and new cultures and religions seemed to have coexisted quite peacefully.

From the early years until the end of the sixteenth century, the prevailing religion in Japan was an amalgamation of Buddhism, Shintoism, which is close to nature worshiping, and local religions. During the Muromachi Era in the fourteenth to sixteenth centuries, the Catholic form of Christianity was introduced and propagated to some extent by the Portuguese until 1590, when Toyotomi Hideyoshi issued a national policy prohibiting Christianity. In the next three centuries, during the Tokugawa (Edo) Era, the circumstances surrounding religion in Japan returned to the amalgamation of Buddhism, Shintoism, and local religions as before the Muromachi Era.

In 1868 when the Tokugawa Shogunate collapsed, the Meiji Era began with restoration of the emperor who held power within a new political system that promoted a policy of nationalism and who strengthened the nation's military force so that modern Japan could compete on even terms with other already modernized nations. As the spiritual basis of this strong Japan, the government pronounced that Shintoism would be the national religion. The emperor's family tree, it was claimed, could be traced back some 120 generations through more than two thousand years of history. Whether or not the historical facts were twisted to some extent, the government goal was to integrate all the religions in Japan into one by national decree. This idea was pursued until the end of World War II in 1945. Aside from the intention of national power, among the common people the concept of traditional Buddhism and citizen's beliefs were substantially followed. This is another proof of the variability of the religion of the Japanese.

In the newly adopted Constitution of Japan after World War II, freedom of faith was promised, and thus the religious control of the national government was abandoned. At the same time, the chaotic coexistence of various religions leaves the religious thoughts of today's Japanese more or less ambiguous, when compared with strict and clear-cut moral codes of behavior like that of Christianity.

B. Source and Character of Japanese Ethnic Values Affecting Sexuality

While culture has been variously defined by different researchers, the concept is used here to indicate the complex of phenomena, ideologies, religion, and literature which provide the fundamental orientation for all sorts of behavior patterns of the Japanese people. As was mentioned earlier, deep in the Japanese mind, the structure of cultural consciousness includes a tendency to nature worship and local religions. This may be due to the roots of the Japanese consciousness in an agrarian culture that has been uniquely molded by archeological and historical processes. It can be said that the general belief among the Japanese that children are the natural gift from the Gods is an expression of the sexuality of the Japanese people. In the ancient days of the Nara and Heian periods, the *Man'yoshu*, a late eighth-century collection of ten thousand Waka poems, many of which are love songs, and the eleventh-century *Romances of Genji*, fifty-four volumes of love stories by the woman novelist Murasaki Shikibu, strongly conveyed the attitude and message that love and sexuality were an important part of human thought and everyday behavior as a natural expression of human nature. In other words, sexuality was openly accepted among the early Japanese people.

In Japan's history, an aristocratic culture dominated in the Nara (710-794), Heian (794-1336), and Muromachi (1336-1573) Eras. In the Sengoku (Turbulence) Period, many warlords competed with each other until the Tokugawa Shogunate was established and national integration begun in 1603. Various groups of the military commanders maintained control of the culture and the behavior of the Japanese people during the Sengoku and Tokugawa Eras. Therefore, the cultural construction and sexuality of the Japanese people operated in a double-layer system. More specifically, extremely strict moral ethics and control of behavior were enforced on children and adults in the families of the *Samurai* class (soldiers and the commanders), who were influenced by the Confucianism originally intro-duced to Japan in the sixth century from China. In the feudal value system, as well as its family system, there was no room for any free expression of human passions and natural desires. Thus not only romantic love, but also immoral and adulterous behavior of any kind were strictly prohibited, and severe penalties, including capital punishment, were instituted for any case that came to light.

While the *Samurai* community kept to a strict behavior code of ethics, the commoners and the townspeople did not, except for the upper class commoners who closely followed the *Samurai* code of ethics. Romantic love was freely allowed among the commoners, and often an illegitimate child—a single mother and her child in today's sense—was accepted and reared without any prejudices in the community or tenement commune (Bornoff 1991, 83-149).

All of the *Ukiyoe* and *Shunga* (pornographic paintings) by Utamaro, Hokusai, and Kunisada were produced from the commoners' culture. Yoshiwara, the sexual amusement quarter in the city of Edo, painted by Oiran, a prostitute and social entertainer of the highest class, for example, prospered in the middle and later Edo Era. Few examples of erotica in the world tell us as much about the cultures that produced them as the *Shunga* tell us about the practices and fantasies of the Japanese. Among the more striking features of *Shunga* is the common presence of children, indicating just how very uninhibited and frank the Japanese were about sex (Bornoff 1991, 184-86).

These examples of a dual-layered social and cultural construction during the *Samurai* ruling periods produced a double standard of code ethics, each code composed of its own logical but superficial principles and real intention. These two codes are still actively practiced in contemporary Japanese society, making the understanding of the Japanese culture confusing and difficult.

It was during the very last stage of the Edo Era—in fact only 130-some years ago—when the country of Japan abandoned its three-century-old policy of national isolation, that free trading and cultural exchanges began with the other countries of the world. As has been already discussed earlier, the modernization process of the nation at such an extremely rapid pace produced certain distorted periods in the history of modern Japan. These periods of turmoil and confusion include the collapse of the Tokugawa Shogunate political system, the restoration of the Imperial ruling system in the Meiji Era, the rise of nationalism in the Taisho Era, and the dominance of the militarism that collapsed at the end of World War II in the middle of the Showa Era.

During the Meiji Era, in order for the country of Japan to be able to compete evenly with the other nations in the world, Japan took a policy of economic enrichment based on development of heavy industry, strengthening of the military power, and placing the Imperial family in the sacred order. The value of each individual in this social system was extremely neglected, resulting in the idea that a man is to serve the nation and a woman is to bear children. Any consciousness of sexual equality was thoroughly repressed, and sexual discrimination—the ideas that higher education is not necessary for women or that childless women deserve to be divorced—were commonly expressed and adhered to. Under such circumstances, a very patriarchal sexual culture emerged in which specific male-centered sexual behavior was accepted without any argument. The proxy engagement system, in which it is mandatory for parents to choose the marriage partner of their child, and in which the match-making ceremony takes place only after the parents have chosen the marriage partner (distinctively different from the match-making practice seen in the modern times in which the young couple has the right to choose to proceed or not), were typical of such practices.

The cultural structure in the Taisho Era is often called Taisho Liberalism. As a temporal reaction of the Imperial-family-centered social structure of the Meiji Era, some opinion leaders advanced distinctly liberal ideas during this era. This was particularly evident in literary works, as some women writers and cultural leaders proposed the very first expression of the feminist movement in Japan. Others followed by advocating communism and the birth-control movement. The case of Senji Yamamoto, the first sexologist in Japan, was certainly an example of this liberalization trend. Yamamoto had spent some time in America while young and had been influenced by its culture. He was assassinated in 1902, at age 40 years, by an ultra-right-wing terrorist opposed to Yamamoto's promotion of birth control, labor liberalization, proletarian theory, and the anti-Law of Public Peace Maintenance. The national leaders of that time regarded a person like Yamamoto, who recognized the sexual rights of each individual, worked hard against poverty, and had a strong anti-power attitude, as dangerous.

The Taisho Era, which lasted only fifteen years, was followed by the militaristic age of Showa, in which Japanese militarists initiated a series of wars, including the invasion of China and military actions in southeast Asian countries and the Pacific area, leading up to World War II.

In the historical process of Meiji, Taisho, and Showa, Japan's primary national policy consistently focused on economic enrichment and strengthening of the military power. Within this societal atmosphere, children were regarded as a national treasure, and thus they were reared comparatively freely. In contrast with contemporary urban life, adolescents in the agricultural community life that dominated the Meiji and Taisho Eras, learned most of the manners and rules that were necessary to spend a normal life in the adult community by spending time together with peers in the local community. A good example of this peer learning was the *Shuku* or "dwelling-together practice."

This *Shuku* community group is roughly classified as either *Wakamono-shuku* for young males and *Musume-shuku* for young females. Within the local community, it was mandatory for each youth to join the *shuku* of their respective sex at a specified age. In the *shuku*, they worked together for the village in the daytime and learned the traditional codes of behavior of the community in the evening. Sexuality education in today's sense was definitely included in this community education system. Within the local community, the freedom of love was widely accepted, as those who fell in love with each other were usually allowed to get married. Children of the ruling-class families, such as village master and landowner, however, were not allowed to enjoy this freedom during their adolescent and youthful days.

In 1945, after World War II, the Japanese people were granted the right to experience democratic and liberal lifestyles because of the cultural influences of the Allied Western countries. The Japanese people have enjoyed this freedom in the subsequent fifty years, and yet, at the same time, the traditional Japanese consciousness of the societal system, moral codes, and fundamental attitude toward life and sex formed throughout the centuries still regulate their thoughts and behaviors today. The highly successful experience of fifty years of newly available pro-Western ways of life visible on the surface of Japanese culture today is definitely overpowered by the centuries-old value systems and views toward sex, human beings, religion, and society at the conscious level and deep in the mind. The sexuality of the modern Japanese is therefore formed in a double-layered manner that, in effect, defies clear description or understanding by outsiders. The world has become smaller as the consequence of the vast development in the transportation and media systems. At the same time, however, it is often pointed out that deep in the mind of the modern Japanese people, the national isolation policy is still alive.

3. Sexual Knowledge and Education

A. Historical Perspectives

There are various opinions among the historians regarding the time of the establishment of Japan as a nation, but at least many agree that it was after the sixth century when the political system had gradually formed into a certain style, not in the modern sense, but in a way that was based on and facilitated by organized education run by Buddhist priests from their temples. With the coming of Buddhism in 538 or 552 C.E. (depending on the source cited), numbers of Buddhist priests came from Kudara on the Korean Peninsula. In addition, a likely larger number of Japanese priests went abroad to Korea and China to study. In these temples, education in Buddhist scripts and political administration was provided for the priests and the children of the national administrators.

It is commonly recognized that the first schools in Japan's history were the *Daigakuryo*, or College Dormitories, established in the nation's capital, and the *Kokugaku* or, National Schools, which were established in each major city, in accordance with the *Taihorituryo*, or Great Treasure Laws enacted in 701 C.E.

Subsequently, various educational systems were established to provide education exclusively for the ruling class, i.e., aristocrats, *Samurai*, and priests. Even though the political systems and/or power structure changed from time to time, these educational systems persisted because the schools were established by the ruling *Daimyo* (feudal lords or landlords) or *samurai* families. Education for the townsfolk and commoners, though not yet institutionalized, was initiated in the thirteenth and fourteenth centuries and continued afterwards in the Buddhist temples. During the Edo era (1603-1886), such private schools for elementary education became quite popular and were known as *Terakoya* or temple houses.

Education for women was not available in the rulers' schools, but was available to some extent in the "commoners' schools." Then, in the early 1700s, in the middle of the Edo Era, a unique educational organization developed as a function of the village and town community, for the education of the immature youths for daily life, including education in sexual behavior. These organizations were known as the *Wakamono-gumi*, or young men's activity group, and the *Musume-gumi*, or daughters' activity group. This system of community education was disbanded in the middle of the Meiji Era around 1890 in favor of promoting newly established public school systems.

In 1868, as the Shogunate political system collapsed, Japan made its first step into the modern world when Emperor Meiji transferred the capital from Kyoto—formerly Edo where the Shogunate was located—to Tokyo. In 1872, the new government announced a law known as *Gakusei*, or School System, based on the French school system, and launched a nationwide education-for-all. This educational law, intended to promote industrial development and the universal conscription system, was ultimately linked with the national policy of enriching the country and strengthening its armament. One may observe in this historic transition the germination of the Japan's militarism in this century.

The Law of Education, enacted in 1879, took a liberal direction in using the American school system as its base. This was quickly amended the following year by the "Revised Law of Education," which put the emphasis on Confucianism morals as the fundamental spirit. This traditional vision was obviously necessary because of strong opposition within the government against Western liberalism. "Catching up with the already modernized nations in the world" was indeed the priority motto of the Meiji government, but in terms of practical education, the goal of producing guns and battleships outranked the education of humans. In 1903, the government took over supervision and authorization of textbooks in order to develop uniformity in people's thoughts and minds. As a result, Japan's education was overwhelmed by the moral and behavior codes of Confucianism ethics based on the emperor system and nationalism.

A short-lived liberal trend developed between 1912 and 1926, when Emperor Taisho was on the throne. This liberal movement, however, was not strong enough to change the government's educational policy, and in the long term, the militarists regained power.

The militarism, and later fascism, grew stronger and matured in the Showa Era beginning in 1926 and climaxing in education's dark period during World War II (1941-45). After the 1945 defeat, Japanese education was completely transfigured with the adoption of a 6-3-3-4 year sequence, the first 9 years being mandatory (6 years of elementary school and 3 years of junior high school). This newly implemented system also brought to Japan substantially equal opportunity of education for boys and girls and all social classes.

The outstanding economic growth of Japan throughout the postwar years is regarded as a contemporary marvel. Along with it, education in Japan also made great progress quantitatively as well as qualitatively. Much of its content will be introduced in the following section. It should, however, be explained here that the Showa Era was closed in 1989 upon the passing of Emperor Showa, and now it is the era of Heisei.

B. Sexuality Education in Contemporary Japan

The Background Education System

As of 1994, Japan has a total of 65,000 schools of all kinds for its total population of 124.3 million. This includes approximately 25,000 elementary schools (grades one to six), 12,000 junior high schools (grades seven through nine), 5,500 senior high schools (grades ten through twelve), 1,100 colleges and universities (including two-year junior colleges), 6,700 vocational colleges (mostly two-year), 15,000 kindergartens, and 1,000 special schools for handicapped children. The rate of actual participation in required education has been as high as 99.9 percent since around 1910, although the length of mandatory education was much shorter before 1945. These statistics exclude some 1,200 heavily handicapped children and an estimated 100,000 prolonged absentees due to illness and unwillingness to participate.

The great majority of those who complete the required education of nine years by age 12 go on to three-year senior high school, specifically 94.3 percent of the boys and 96.4 percent of the girls. Advancement to colleges and universities is 36.3 percent for men and 39.2 percent for women. This trend to high academic achievement orientation has created stress and mental pressure in the "entrance examination war" all Japanese youths experience. Because of overemphasis on the entrance examination, many recognize the necessity of *Juku*, extracurricular schools in the evenings and on holidays, tutors, and/or correspondence courses to prepare for the examinations. Such practices are common in Japan these days, perhaps more so than in other countries, suggesting the need to discuss the effects and consequences of the *Juku* for the social life of Japanese adolescents and young adults.

The detailed curriculum in each school level, the general objectives of each subject, and aims and contents of each school year for each subject are precisely controlled by the *National Course of Study*. It may seem that the national government limits and controls the contents of education and its teaching methods; however, the *Course of Study* only presents the frame structure of the teaching and the classroom teacher has the liberty of the details presented. The *Course of Study* is revised once every decade or so.

As in some other countries, the Ministry of Education provides a list of approved textbooks from which teachers select those to be used in their classes. It is true that sometimes court cases have arisen about the suitability of the national policy on textbooks, questioning whether the government is interfering with education, whether the examination/approval system conflicts with the Constitution, or whether the system infringes on the freedom of expression. However, so far the system is functioning well with individual schools and teachers free to choose classroom content and presentations aside from government approval of texts and teaching materials.

Sexuality Education

There is no distinct sexuality or family-life education course included in the subjects to be taught in the Japanese school system. The *Course of Study* does not require anything to be taught about sexuality, nor does the national government determine any objectives or the content of sexuality education wherever a local school or teacher decides to deal with this topic at any grade or school level. The official statement provided by the Ministry of Education states that "The contents of education regarding sex (and sexuality) are distributed in various respective subjects (relevant to biology, sociology and health, etc.) and sex (and sexuality education) is certainly expected to be integrated in all these subject matters at each school." Therefore, the promoters of sex (and sexuality) education, such as those involved in the Japanese Association for Sex Education (J.A.S.E.), have been advocating school instructional programs by developing and publishing *Sex Education Guidelines* for various school levels and various grades. J.A.S.E. was established and was officially approved by the Ministry of Education in 1972, and has since been the leading nonprofit organization in the field of sex education.

On the other hand, improvement in education for HIV and AIDS is increasing in Japan's schools because of the rapid spread of HIV and AIDS throughout the world since the late 1980s. This in turn has strengthened the importance of sex education in the Japanese schools.

Since 1992, as a result of revisions in the elementary school *Course of Study*, childbirth has been introduced into the science textbook, and physical and psychological changes of adolescence into the health education textbook, indicating that some changes can be made in the *Course of Study*. Any changes in the *Course of Study* automatically means definite changes in the instructional contents at every school. At present, all upper grade elementary school children are expected to be exposed to the physiological and psychological aspects of human sexuality. However, so far no textbook describes any aspects of sexual intercourse, which has prompted some criticism from classroom teachers about the incomplete vision and unrealistic attitude of the Ministry of Education.

In the junior high school level, certain topics in sex education are dealt with in health education, science (biology), social studies, and domestic science. However, these are handled less candidly and actively than in elementary schools in the same system or district. The case is similar as well in the senior high schools; the reason perhaps being that classroom instruction is regarded much less as an education for human living than as a preparation for the next entrance examination, i.e., senior high school for the junior high students, and colleges and universities in the case of senior high school students.

"Education indeed is the greatest prevention" is the standpoint of the Ministry of Education regarding HIV and AIDS prevention. Because of this view point, elementary school faculty are strongly encouraged to teach that HIV and AIDS are not transmitted by mosquito bites or by shaking hands with others, and that no person with HIV or AIDS should be discriminated against. It is greatly regretted by many educators and members of J.A.S.E. that sex education in Japanese schools currently needs to be improved so much and that teaching the fact that HIV can be transmitted through sexual intercourse is still not well accepted among the school children. This impacts also on a number of cases in which hemophiliac patients have become HIV-positive because of contaminated blood transfusions. [By 1985, about 40 percent of all Japanese hemophiliac patients, more than 2,000 people, had contracted HIV through contaminated imported blood products. As of 1995, hemophiliac patients accounted for 60 percent of Japanese people with HIV. See Section 11 on HIV/AIDS. (Kaji)] Even these patients are hesitant, because of public ignorance, to admit they are HIV-positive. As a matter of fact, voluntary admission of HIV-positive status is almost nonexistent in Japanese society. This is because, for most Japanese people, admitting to being HIV-positive is viewed as a kind of social suicide and societal discrimination is definitely expected.

Because of centuries of a national isolation policy that rejected anything that might endanger cultural and religious harmony, a person with any unusual handicap or disease like HIV was commonly treated as an enemy of society, or at least rejected. It is therefore difficult to judge whether appropriate HIV-related education would produce any effects in changing the attitudes of children of any age to HIV-positive persons. [An added problem is the great reluctance, especially among elementary school teachers, to mention, let alone discuss, sexuality in their classrooms (Kaji)]. Even in junior and senior high schools, where one might expect teachers to be more open in dealing with sexual issues, and students to be more open to education about discrimination prevention, the effectiveness of education in reducing discrimination against persons with HIV is unclear.

The content of the sex education actually received by students was studied in 1981 and 1987 surveys; Figure 1 shows a breakdown in the content of sexuality education by subject (J.A.S.E. 1988). When these subjects are clustered into three general categories, (1) physiobiological, (2) psychological, and (3) social, the youth surveyed reported that 29.4 percent—three out of every ten—had received no sexual education at all (type 0) while an identical figure of 29.4 percent received an education that covered all three general categories (type III). A little over 20 percent had sexuality education that covered only the physiological and biological aspects (type I), while 13.5 percent and 12.8 percent had instruction that covered the physiological-biological and social (type IIA), or psychological-biological and psychological (type IIB) respectively. In Figure 1, the heavy concentration of responses on the top six items, which cover the physiological/biological background of sexuality, supports the conclusion that when Japanese children do receive sex education, it is more often limited to the facts of physiology and biology.

Figure 2 presents the percentage of each type of sex education actually given to students of different school levels (J.A.S.E. 1988). Naturally, the amount of education, particularly that of type III, increases as the level of schooling advances. In addition, it is shown that in junior high school, the psychological aspects of sexuality are emphasized. This may be an understandable trend since the biological and psychological aspects of pubescent events occur just before or in the early stages of adolescence.

As mentioned earlier, the contents of sex education in Japanese school systems are more or less centered around physiological aspects and are therefore cognitive-oriented rather than attitudinal-behavior-oriented. In order for sex education in Japanese schools to become the comprehensive sexuality education it needs to be, more consideration must be given to the psychological and sociological aspects of sexuality. HIV and AIDS education and prevention needs to be incorporated in this framework as a well-balanced education within the national *Course of Study*.

C. Informal Sources of Sex Education

Teen sex magazines are popular and widely read by Japanese youth. They are noticeably different from their adult counterparts, comparatively wholesome, or at least harmless or insipid. Instead of the violent, sadistic, and degrading content common in adult pornography, teen sex magazines are

Figure 1

Subjects That Were Taught in Sex Education

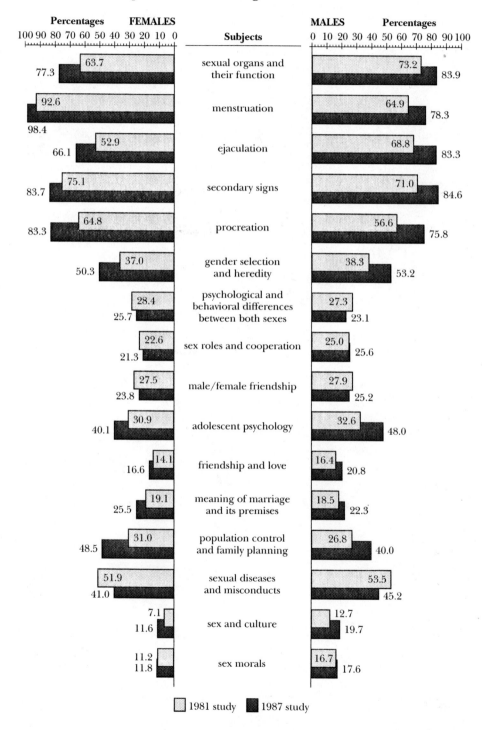

| | | 1981 study | | 1987 study |

Figure 2

Types of Actually Given Sex Education
Among Various School-Age Groups

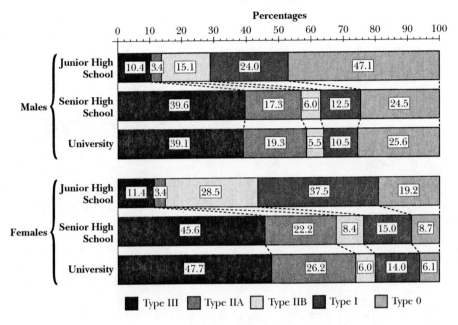

filled with frivolous, inane, and unabashed boys' club talk and candid cheerleader squat-shots and near-nudist pictorials. Since true sexuality education is absent from Japanese education, and parents and the community no longer communicate this essential information to youths, these magazines do perform an important function, providing limited but basic information about sexual anatomy. Unfortunately, their popularity depends on adolescent titillation that ignores the need to provide information on STD prevention and contraception. Japanese television is also a major informal source of limited sexual information, particularly in the early evening television cartoon programs that cater to adolescent male curiosities about female anatomy (Bornoff 1991, 71). (See Section 8C for comments on the *Roricon* or "Lolita complex" that is so widespread in Japanese sex magazines and can be said to constitute a national characteristic.)

4. Autoerotic Behaviors and Patterns

There are clear gender differences in terms of the masturbation fantasies and concrete activity that Japanese boys and girls pursue in their adolescent behavioral development. In reality, the great majority of the senior high school boys practice masturbation, while the majority of girls of ages 20 and 21 years still ignore masturbation after experiencing their first intercourse (Figure 3; J.A.S.E. 1994). The median 22-year-old female has not engaged in masturbation. This may indicate a difference in the degree of sexual drive between the two sexes. But another possible reason that females are not eager to engage in masturbation is the social pressure against the female's self-motivated sexual activities that are unrelated to procreation, although this belief is steadily becoming weaker. The majority of young Japanese women perhaps do not give serious consideration to autoeroticism because of the subconscious expectation that a good Japanese woman should always be modest in any sexual activity. [This may be changing as young Japanese women increasingly reject traditional female roles. (See Section 5C Marriage and Divorce below) (Kaji)]. According to the 1981 survey results, females discover and first experience masturbation as a result of "incidental touching of the genital organ by something" and/or "reading erotic articles." For males, there is an indication that being "taught by some friend" is the more common inspiration.

Figure 3

**Cumulative Frequencies of Masturbation Experiences
Among Japanese Youths in the 1987 and 1993 Surveys**

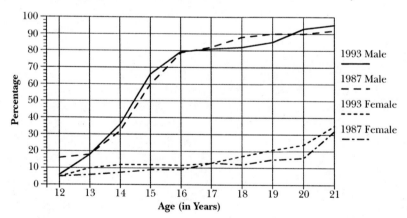

The teen sex magazines mentioned above in Sections 3C and 8C, which are used primarily by young males as a masturbatory stimulant, pose many societal and cultural questions. [The sex magazines and comics targeted to young females are also popular and raise many controversial questions. (Kaji)]. Apart from their relatively healthy content in terms of normal psychosexual development, one controversy centers on the degree to which the staggering amount of these magazines produced and their extensive use by teenagers and older males for masturbation is all that wholesome. Do these magazines promote normal psychosexual development, or do they support and promote an unhealthy, introverted social isolation? Is the plethora of teen sex magazines an unhealthy substitute for many young men who have not developed the interpersonal skills they need relate to women on a mature and intimate adult level? (Bornoff 1991, 71).

5. Interpersonal Heterosexual Behaviors

A. Childhood Play and Sexual Behaviors

The Threat of a New Subspecies

Since education in sexuality and education for parenting share a common basis, it may be helpful to sketch the possible role and position these two aspects of education hold in the natural developmental sequences of play and sexual behaviors children pass through as they mature (see Figure 4) (Hatano 1991b, 1991c). Throughout his or her growth and development, the child is expected to experience certain events and to develop certain skills, so that development of a mature consciousness and behavior will be promoted. Regular mother-child behavior like breast feeding during infancy is believed to stimulate mental activity of the baby and to enhance a trustworthy relationship between parent and child. Based on this sort of relationship, the time spent in play and fun experiences between the two would promote a sense of playful exploration and form the basis of interpersonal relationships, as well as emotional security. This in turn enhances the ability of a child to play with other children and successfully join in peer-group activities.

Peer-group activities, especially involving play activities among young children, is believed to develop the social aspect of personality. It seems that social development of an individual includes acquisition of communication skills with others, procedures to maneuver human relations, leadership development within a group, and coping skills between boys and girls, between elders and the young, and between the strong and the weak. As a person grows and becomes ready to engage in heterosexual relationships and sexual behavior, these human relationship skills will become necessary to cope with the opposite sex. Likewise, the above skills are needed when a person becomes a parent.

Together with increasing urbanization and modernization, Japan, especially in recent years, is witnessing the emergence of a new type of young person—what may be termed *Neo Homo Sapiens*—who often does not accept traditional institutional human relationships and prefers living exclusively at the keyboard of a computer, communicating via networks, and avoiding

Figure 4

Human Developmental Stages and Assignments of Play and Sexual Behavior and Positions of Sex Education and Education for Parenting

Developmental Stage	Events and Activities	Resultant Effects
Infant	Breast feeding (Kinship) ⟶	Stimulation of mental activity Parent-child reliance
	Parent-child play ⟶	Emotional stability and development
Preschool child	Peer group play and activity (Experience of pain, group control) ⟶	Cooperation, adjustments, and durability
Childhood	Human interpersonal relationships (Social behavior development)	Methods of communication Human relationship techniques Group leadership/discipline Male/female relations Coping with handicapped children
Puberty	Communication with opposite sex ⟵	Sex Education—biological and socio-psychological Education for parenting
Adolescence	Sexual behavior and interactions	
Adulthood	Family life ⟵	Family relations Parent-child Relationships

direct human relations with the others. These young people are often cruel, lacking in interpersonal relationship skills in the sense of human relationships with the others, and unskilled in heterosexual or homosexual relations in later adolescent life. This is evidenced in the increase in older bachelors and in the increasing frequency of *Narita divorce*—divorce upon returning to Narita New Tokyo International Airport from a honeymoon trip outside of Japan—indicating the lack of patience, human relationship maneuvering skills, and inability to maintain a married relationship.

> What usually happens [in a Narita divorce] is that newlyweds take a honeymoon in a place like Australia or Hawaii, and the husband is so intimidated by overseas travel that he scarcely wants to leave his hotel room.

The wife, on the other hand, has already taken several foreign trips with girlfriends and is much more comfortable with the idea of being abroad. She wants to spend her days scuba diving and her nights bopping in the disco, and she finds her husband a dreadful bore. So she dumps him at the end of the honeymoon, and they say a final good-bye at Narita (Kristof 1996a).

The need for sexuality and parenting education is expected to increase as technology continues to transform Japanese society

The Past and Present Contrasted

According to the latest national statistics, the average married Japanese couple has 1.6 children, definitely one of the lowest rates in the modern world. This tendency to a small number of children is a reflection of urbanization and a high-economic, growth-centered family life with the wife being a highly educated career woman. [This tendency for Japanese couples to have fewer children may also reflect the lack of sufficient social welfare and public child-care systems, which pressures mothers to stay home and take care of their children. Many Japanese women are reluctant to have more children because of inflexible working hours required by Japanese companies, long-distance commuting to work, the high cost of housing, and the lack of child-care facilities. (Kaji)] Apart from the need and preference of each individual family, this trend is not necessarily a healthy phenomenon for society in general, particularly because of the consequences of impediments the individual single child encounters in his or her development (see the third column in Figure 4).

In the past, the Japanese family was often situated in a large, family-tree system where several families related by kinship lived together on the same land but in different houses. This arrangement sometimes accommodated different families of three or four different generations. The children learned many important matters from the members of the various families, as well as from their own immediate brothers and sisters. With many children in each family, each child enjoyed excellent educational opportunities within the family community. Indeed, everyday life in the community functioned as the community education. The advent of modernization brought an urban life that forced the extended family and neighborhood community to abandon its educational function. In addition, the daily human exchanges and the network system with the neighbors were lost.

In the premodern community, children of similar ages formed peer groups and played together near their farm homes, in a backyard, an open field, or in the barn. The children often obtained interesting and helpful information related to sex from observing the farm animals; in this manner, sexuality education went on in an informal manner. The "doctor/nurse play" they often enjoyed within their peer group in a secret space provided sexual information and fantasy, which in turn helped them form a healthy sexual identity of their own.

Children in contemporary Japan, first of all, now have fewer brothers and sisters in their family so they seldom have opportunities to cope with a small baby, with a younger child, or with an older and stronger child. Some young children of 3 start special training in preparation for the entrance examination for kindergarten. In addition to public school, almost all elementary school children today attend *Juku*, or special training school, for entrance examination for some junior high school, that may provide a better opportunity for future school advancement. In addition, training in piano, ballet, and swimming, for example, is becoming a common practice among children of all ages. As a result, the children have very little time for spontaneous activities such as playing and spending time together with the children of the peer group. One's ability to live socially and peacefully with other people of different types and capabilities is usually cultivated in these childhood circumstances; however, contemporary Japanese children are not in the position to experience such education. It may not be surprising then to find young grownups today who lack the usual skills of living, playing, and communicating with young people of the same and/or other sex. Human relations require skills in sexuality-related behaviors, such as talking with and obtaining trust from the peers of the other sex, and these are skills that may not be attained by merely reading books or watching television programs.

Contemporary children, who are busy with *Juku* and extracurricular training programs, must watch television programs, play television/computer games, and read comic books during the precious free activity hours, perhaps an hour or so in the late evening, after finishing all the previously scheduled programs. While there is much information related to sex and sexual behaviors on television and in comic books, exposure to this information is not sufficient when they have to use it on their own, cognitively and affectively. They need to perceive this information in the context of actual human relations and experiences. In actuality, most contemporary Japanese children build their knowledge pertaining to sex in a passive manner that results in distortion and inflexibility. The sex-related knowledge should be actively acquired by each individual with a positive attitude in order for one to handle sexuality in later life constructively and with enjoyment. The reality in Japan today seems to be quite different from what it should be.

This is not to imply or suggest that today's children will grow up to become sexual deviants or criminals. However, it is obvious that attention needs to be paid to the fact that in Japan today, the psychosexual developmental processes of the infants and children are experienced in abstract textbooks rather than in actual experience-oriented activities.

B. The Sexuality of Adolescents

The Results of Four National Surveys

The office of the Prime Minister sponsored nationwide surveys of sexual development and sexual behaviors of Japanese youths in 1974, 1981, 1987, and 1993. The surveys, conducted by the Japanese Association for Sex Education (J.A.S.E.), mobilized nearly 30,000 youths of ages between 12 and 22 years each time. The reports provide a substantial picture of the sexuality of Japanese youth. The full reports were published in Japanese by J.A.S.E. (1975, 1983, 1988, and 1994) and summarized for the international community on several occasions by Yoshiro Hatano (1988, 1991ab, 1993).

According to the 1993 survey report, the majority—50 percentile ranked, median)—of 12-year-old girls have already experienced their first menstruation, and 14-year-old boys their first ejaculation (Figure 5; J.A.S.E. 1994). That girls start their adolescence one year or more before the boys is evident in Figure 6 (Shimazaki 1994-95). The majority of boys and girls admitted to having an "interest in sex" by age 14 (Figure 7; J.A.S.E. 1994). The majority of 14-year-old boys indicated an "interest in approaching a member of the opposite sex" (Figure 8; J.A.S.E. 1994). The same trend was seen in the "desire of physical contact with the opposite sex" (Figure 9; J.A.S.E. 1994). There is a clear difference between an interest in approaching a member of the other sex and the desire for physical contact, in that the boys are strongly interested in direct physical contact with the other sex while the girls are only interested in becoming closer with the other sex.

Figure 5

Cumulative Frequencies of Menstruation (Female) and Ejaculation (Male) Events Among the Japanese Youths in the 1987 and 1993 Surveys

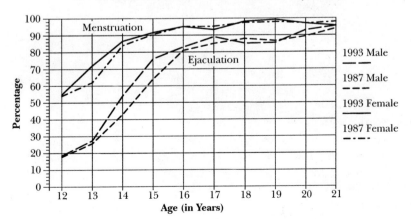

Figure 6

Comparison of Ages of First Experience of Menstruation and Ejaculation Among the Japanese Youths in the 1987 and 1993 Surveys

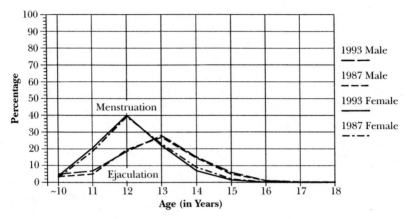

Figure 7

Cumulative Frequencies of Development of "Interest in Sex" Among the Japanese Youths in the 1987 and 1993 Surveys

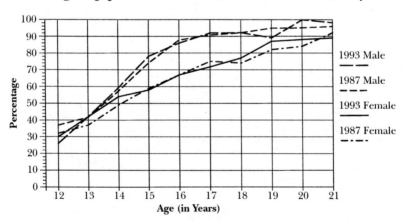

Although these young people, both male and female, seem to start their adolescence with these heterosexual "interests" by age 13 or 14, this interest does not have a concrete outcome in social activity, namely dating, for some years. Actually, a remarkable growth in the dating activities among the girls was observed in the 1993 survey as shown in Figures 10 (J.A.S.E. 1994) and 11 (Shimazaki 1994). Further analysis of these statistics suggests that the girls do not necessarily pursue real love-seeking activities, but prefer spending some time with a friend of the opposite sex. As a matter of fact, they

Figure 8

**Cumulative Frequencies of "Interest in Approaching the
Opposite Sex" Among the Japanese Youths in
the 1987 and 1993 Surveys**

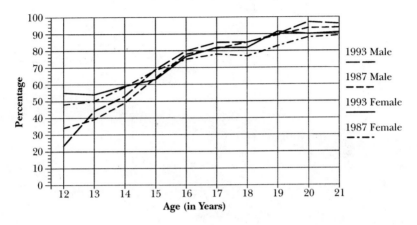

Figure 9

**Cumulative Frequencies of "Desire of Physical Contact
with the Opposite Sex" Among the Japanese
Youths in the 1987 and 1993 Surveys**

are slow in becoming involved in sexual arousal experiences (Figure 12
and Table 3; J.A.S.E 1994), while their male counterparts demonstrate a
different developmental trend: sexual arousal comes ahead of dating for
males and after dating for the females (Figure 13; Shimazaki 1994-95).

An examination of cumulative frequencies for kissing and touching the
body of the other sex indicates that for boys kissing and touching the body

Figure 10

Cumulative Frequencies of Dating Experiences Among the Japanese Youths in the 1987 and 1993 Surveys

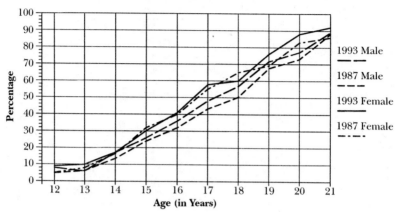

Figure 11

Age of First Dating Among the Japanese Youths in the 1993 Survey

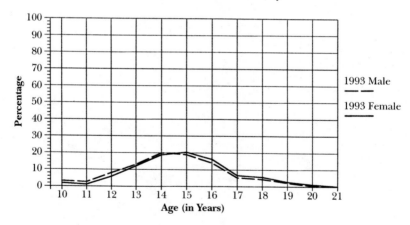

of the other sex occurs at the same age level, very probably with the two activities occurring as part of the same encounter. In the meantime, the girls are again slower in the physical contact behaviors, and they perhaps consider kissing itself and their first kissing experience very seriously (Figures 14 and 15; J.A.S.E. 1994).

Japanese youths, both male and female, show a remarkably slow development in sexual behaviors in comparison to other societies. There is no clear antisexual activity policies existent in the nation, nor any discourage-

Figure 12

**Cumulative Frequencies of "Experience of Sexual Arousal"
Among the Japanese Youths in the 1987 and 1993 Surveys**

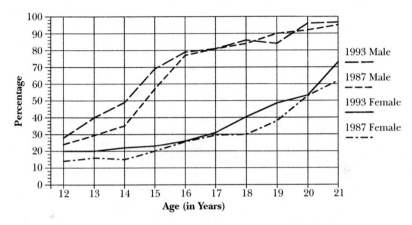

Table 3

**Rate of Desire to Touch Body of Opposite Sex and Sexual Arousal
Experiences by School Classification (in Percentages)**

	Junior High		Senior High		College	
	Male	**Female**	**Male**	**Female**	**Male**	**Female**
Desire to touch body of opposite sex	43.8	13.2	81.0	32.3	93.9	53.9
Sexual arousal	47.5	21.2	81.1	30.4	92.5	54.7

Figure 13

**Ages of First Experience of Sexual Arousal and Dating
Among the Japanese Youths in the 1993 Survey**

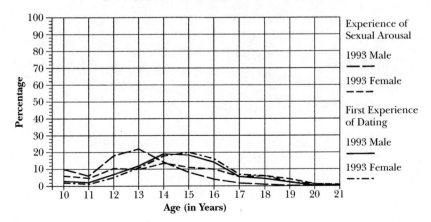

Figure 14

Cumulative Frequencies of First Kissing Experience Among the Japanese Youths in the 1987 and 1993 Surveys

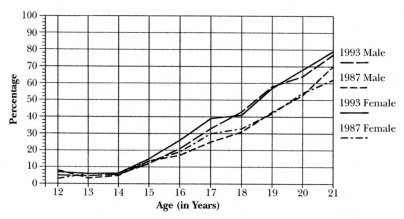

Figure 15

Cumulative Frequencies of "Experience of Touching the Body of the Opposite Sex" Among the Japanese Youths in the 1987 and 1993 Surveys

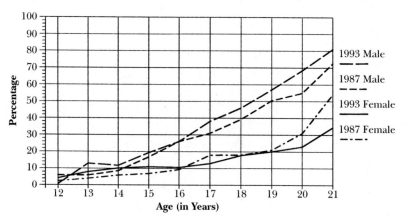

ment of male-female relations in the nation's limited sexuality education. The most probable reasons behind the slow psychosexual development lie in the traditional societal attitude toward the free sexual activities, particularly when they involve educated, upper-class women, and the society's strong respect for education, which results in suppression of sexual behaviors among the youths. The cumulative frequencies of petting and intercourse experiences by age progression are shown in Figures 16 and 17

Figure 16

Cumulative Frequencies of Petting Experiences Among the Japanese Youths in the 1987 and 1993 Surveys

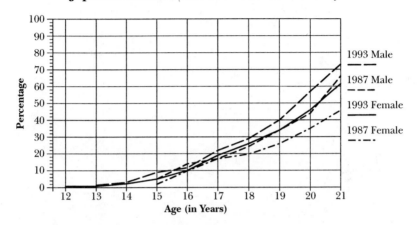

Figure 17

Cumulative Frequencies of Intercourse Experiences Among the Japanese Youths in the 1987 and 1993 Surveys

(J.A.S.E. 1994). Figures 18 and 19 compare the cumulative frequencies of kissing, petting, and intercourse experiences for males and females respectively (Shimazaki 1994-95). Table 4 provides survey data on the total number of coital partners classified by sex and school levels (Shimazaki 1994-95). As with previously cited results, these data indicate more active behavior for males than for females. Psychologically, the girls seem to develop their interest in the other sex earlier in adolescence; by 12 years of age, 50 percent of the girls already demonstrate a

Figure 18

**Cumulative Frequencies of Kissing, Petting, and Intercourse
Experiences Among the Japanese Males in
the 1987 and 1993 Surveys**

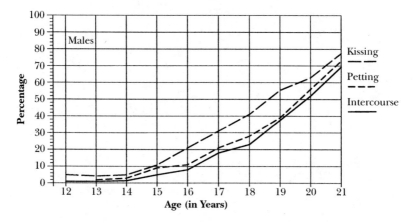

Figure 19

**Cumulative Frequencies of Kissing, Petting, and Intercourse
Experiences Among the Japanese Females in
the 1987 and 1993 Surveys**

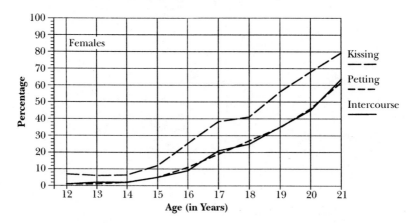

general interest in boys, as opposed to the 14-year-old median boy. But
such interest in the other sex among the girls is more mental and fantasy-
based, and not necessarily accompanied by actual physical activities, such
as physical contact, in which the boys are four years ahead of the girls,
and sexual arousal, in which boys are five years ahead of the girls (see
Figure 9).

Table 4

Total Number of Partners Engaged with Intercourse Experiences (in Percentages)

Number of Partners	Junior High Male	Junior High Female	Senior High Male	Senior High Female	University Male	University Female	Total Male	Total Female
1	52.6	43.3	49.7	48.7	31.3	50.0	38.8	49.0
2	5.3	16.7	15.9	19.6	18.1	17.9	16.7	18.5
3	5.3	13.3	10.3	8.9	14.0	8.0	12.3	8.8
4	0.0	0.0	2.1	2.5	6.6	8.5	4.7	5.5
5	5.3	0.0	4.1	3.8	6.2	4.2	5.4	3.8
6+	21.1	6.7	9.0	6.3	16.0	5.2	13.8	5.8
Don't Know	10.5	20.0	9.0	10.1	7.8	6.1	8.4	8.8
Total %	100.0	100.0	100.0	100.0	100.0	100.0	100.0	100.0
Responses	19	30	145	158	243	212	407	400

The sexual difference in the cumulative experience rate of dating in the age progression does not seem to be very great, but the women's special activeness, far surpassing men's activeness, has been consistently noticed in all of the four surveys. The similarity between the sexes on this behavior very probably occurs because males and females of roughly the same age level are generally dating each other. On the other hand, the increased dating activity of females 15 years and older may have come about because older males start proposing dates to younger females who became more accepting than in earlier times.

In terms of actual heterosexual behaviors, the age differences between the sexes were rather small or nonexistent: dating (boys one year ahead), kissing (the same age), petting (boys one year ahead—Figure 13), intercourse (boys one year ahead), and dating (girls one year ahead—Figure 10).

The 1987 data were used to construct a developmental sequence model of sexual events and experiences of the Japanese youths (Figure 20; Hatano 1991). For the median male, experience of ejaculation and sexual curiosity occur within the same developmental year, and related experiences like masturbation and interest in the opposite sex occur in the next year. Indeed, for males, a series of physical and psychological pubescent events suddenly occur within a short two-year period. On the other hand, the social events of adolescence seem to need a certain time to mature, as it took three years after the stormy coming of these pubescent events for these boys to reach the first dating experience. Then three more years are spent before the first petting experience. The time between first petting and first intercourse is usually quite brief; sometimes the two experiences occur simultaneously, in which case both occur with the same partner.

Figure 20

Sequential Developmental Model of Various Sexual Events and Experiences of the Average Japanese Youth as Seen in the Age of the Median Person for Respective Events (as of the 1988 Survey)

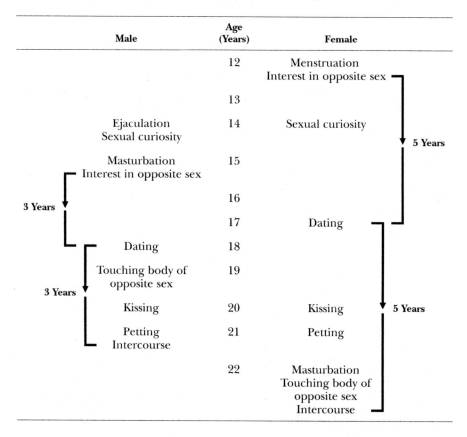

Male	Age (Years)	Female
	12	Menstruation Interest in opposite sex
	13	
Ejaculation Sexual curiosity	14	Sexual curiosity
Masturbation Interest in opposite sex	15	
	16	
	17	Dating
Dating	18	
Touching body of opposite sex	19	
Kissing	20	Kissing
Petting Intercourse	21	Petting
	22	Masturbation Touching body of opposite sex Intercourse

For the median female, the first menstruation is a clear sign of puberty; however, other psychological and behavioral pubescent events are not as concentrated as they are with the male. A Japanese median girl takes about five years after menarche to reach the first dating experience, and another five years before the first experiences of petting and intercourse. In other words, the adolescent time of a boy is three years shorter than that of a girl.

In the case of a boy, sexual curiosity arises together with the ejaculation experience and quickly leads to masturbation. The pubescent male is thus mono-sex-organ-oriented (phallocentric). In the case of a girl, menarche occurs a good two years earlier than the first sexual development event of boys (i. e., ejaculation), but it does not lead to sexual curiosity for about two years on average, nor does it quickly move to masturbation, which comes towards the very end of female sexual development.

For a boy, the onset of dating leads to a sequence of heterosexual physical behaviors, such as touching the body of a member of the opposite sex, kissing, petting, and intercourse, within the short span of three years after the first date. Girls experience these events in the last three years of the five-year time span that starts with the onset of dating, two years after the average male.

Perhaps because girls traditionally do not initiate dates but rely on the male to take the initiative, and because it occurs one year earlier than in boys, there is a difference between them. At the same time, considering the data, the boy would have to date a different, slightly more mature girl after his first date partner in order for this hypothesis to be supported.

It should be noted that for girls, physical behavior, such as masturbation and touching a boy's body, occurs during the same last stage of development along with intercourse, whereas for a boy it is actually the key mechanism for the progression of subsequent development and is distributed over much earlier stages. The male experiences the series of physical changes and psychological developments in a shorter time span than the female, perhaps because of a strong sexual drive provided by male hormonal secretions. Male maturation is thus centered around more physical and concrete behaviors, and one event hurriedly leads to the next step. For the male, a sexual behavior means a direct phallic-oriented concrete activity, whether monosexual, such as sexual arousal and masturbation, or heterosexual, such as touching the body of a member of the opposite sex, petting, and intercourse.

Female masturbation, which occurs later than the male, seems to be more possible in relation to the aggressive behaviors of the male. A girl's maturation process is thus centered around vague, romantic loving; it is more psychological and, in the beginning and for some time, devoid of any concrete physical activities. Then, in its later stages, actual loving activities, such as kissing, petting, and intercourse, gradually proceed passively, along with concrete approaches made by the male.

The passiveness of the female in various heterosexual activities is demonstrated by the fact that the physical satisfaction/performance of the sexual activities, such as masturbation and touching the body of a male partner, is experienced at the same developmental time with intercourse and preceded by kissing and petting, which are only possible with a partner. This suggests that the sexually active male should change partners from one stage to the next, because the length of time devoted to the practice of one event varies between the male and female. Consequently, the male tends to seek a more permissive female as he moves rapidly along the developmental sequence. Thus, the typical Japanese male starts by dating a female a year younger than he, experiences the first kissing with a same-aged female, and experiences his first intercourse with third female, who is at least a year older than he is.

Acceleration/Deceleration Trends in the Sexual Development Sequence

Changes in the timing of various sexual events and experiences for the average Japanese male and female in these four surveys are shown in Figures 21 (male) and 22 (female) (Hatano 1991), and in Tables 5 and 6 (Shimazaki 1994-95). In the seven year intervals between one survey and the next, certain changes in developmental ages are observed, although the primary sequential order does not change. In particular, there was a slight acceleration tendency in the latter half portion of adolescence between 1987 and 1993. The steady and noticeable increase in the rate of actual sexual behaviors, like kissing, petting, and intercourse, especially among the college-level students, both male and female youths, is particularly noticeable. This "emancipation" tendency may be a sign of the modernization and Westernization of this age group. At the same time, one needs to consider the possible danger in the spread of STDs and AIDS, even though the latter was not really perceived as a threat in Japan as of mid-1995. (However, comments on the present and future of AIDS must be made with the utmost caution. The results of Table 4 on the number of sexual partners, for example, already indicate that more than 60 percent of male and more than 40 percent of female college students admitted to having multiple intercourse partners.)

Accelerated physical growth is often observed when more favorable circumstances are provided, a good example being nutritional improvement. Japanese Ministry of Education statistics, summarized in Figures 23, suggest a sharp acceleration in physical growth between 1950 and 1980, whereas Figure 24 suggests that this acceleration stopped by 1980 (Hatano 1991b, 1991c). Apparently, the Japanese postwar growth acceleration due to greatly improved nutrition reached saturation around 1980. More specifically, little growth acceleration was observed in males and females after 1960. Since the changes in the biological phase of sexual maturation ended over three decades ago, the recent accelerating changes in sexual behavior patterns must be due to social changes and new pressures. Likewise, since there was was no particular biological deceleration phenomenon during the past fifty years, decelerating behavioral changes can only be explained in terms of changes in social control.

Contemporary Japanese society is enjoying fully its freedom of creeds and beliefs, and rather radical liberal thoughts have been prevalent. As the scientific understanding of human sexuality spreads, people prefer more freedom in sex-related behaviors, as noted earlier in Figure 2. This tendency involves college- and university-level students since they are treated as "adults" in Japanese society, and experience little social restriction on their behavior. Under the circumstances, it may be rather natural to find an

Figure 21

**Sequential Changes in the Developmental Model of Various
Sexual Events and Experiences of the Average Japanese
Male in These Four Surveys as Seen in the Age of
the Median Person for Respective Events**

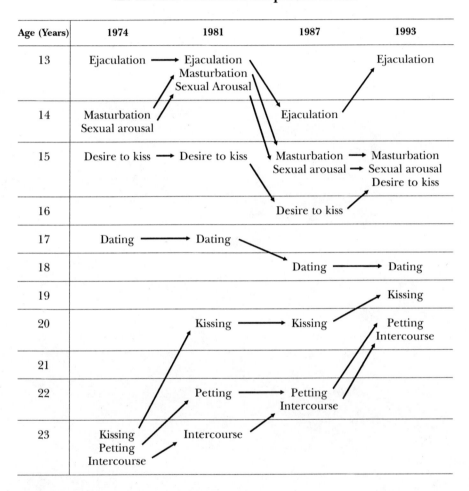

on-going behavioral acceleration among the youth of this age level. Changes in the rate of experiences of certain sexual events among university students in these four surveys are shown in Table 1.

Contemporary Japan is an overly matured society, and thus certain pathological phenomena may be observed in relation with child rearing and the educational systems. One example is the over-controlling of children by parents, particularly by mothers who overly emphasize academic achievement and sacrifice spontaneous play of the children. Hence children do not demonstrate autonomous development in their decision-

Figure 22

Sequential Changes in the Developmental Model of Various Sexual Events and Experiences of the Average Japanese Female in These Four Surveys as Seen in the Age of the Median Person for Respective Events

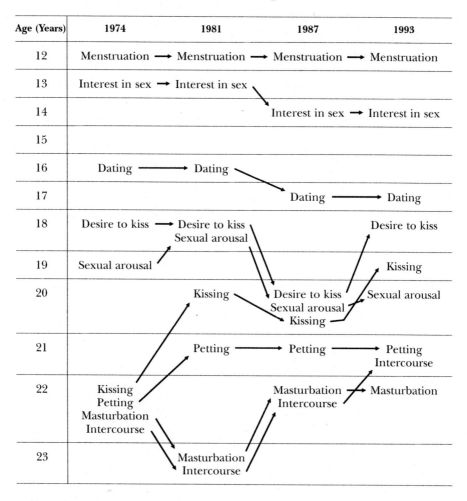

making abilities or their interpersonal human relations. Some observers are increasingly anxious about the possible lack of developments in interpersonal human relations and decision-making abilities among contemporary Japanese children. It would not be a surprise if these children were to show deceleration tendencies in their sexual behaviors because self-realization and individual independence are so important in the development of sexuality, and hence in the orderly development of sexual behavior.

Table 5

Comparison of Various Sexual Experience Rates Among the Japanese Youths in Four Surveys

Experiences	School Level*	Male				Female			
		1974	1981	1987	1993	1974	1981	1987	1993
Menstruation	JHS			37.8	46.7			75.0	80.3
(in females)	SHS		87.1	83.8	86.0		97.2	95.5	95.1
and Ejaculation (in males)	Univ.		95.4	92.0	91.5		98.4	98.4	98.0
Interest in Sex	JHS			52.5	53.9			45.5	48.6
	SHS		92.8	69.6	89.9		75.0	71.4	70.5
	Univ.		98.2	95.6	96.7		89.0	84.5	87.9
Dating	JHS			11.1	14.4			15.0	16.3
	SHS	53.6	47.1	39.7	43.5	57.5	51.5	49.7	50.3
	Univ.	73.4	77.2	77.7	81.1	74.4	78.4	78.8	81.4
Masturbation	JHS			30.0	33.3			6.9	10.1
	SHS	84.1	77.1	81.2	80.7	21.6	17.2	10.0	12.6
	Univ.	90.4	93.2	92.2	91.5	26.1	28.6	21.1	25.8
Kissing	JHS			5.6	6.4			6.6	7.6
	SHS	26.0	24.5	23.1	28.3	21.8	26.3	25.5	32.3
	Univ.	45.2	53.2	59.4	68.4	38.9	48.6	49.7	63.1
Petting	JHS				3.9				2.6
	SHS	13.9	13.1	17.8	18.2	9.6	15.9	14.7	16.5
	Univ.	45.2	40.3	53.3	60.6	17.9	29.9	34.8	42.8
Intercourse	JHS			2.2	1.9			1.8	3.0
	SHS	10.2	7.9	11.5	14.4	5.5	8.8	8.7	15.7
	Univ.	23.1	32.6	46.5	57.3	11.0	18.5	26.1	43.4

*(JHS = Junior High School Students; SHS = Senior High School Students; Univ. = University Students)

Another example is the unnecessarily tight pressure of university entrance examinations. Since admission to a university of rank is often considered to be the decisive factor for the whole life of a Japanese, senior high school students are particularly repressed in their sexual behaviors in lieu of preparatory studies. Based on the same logic, parents, and perhaps classroom teachers too, are eager to require that the children concentrate only on school work, and definitely discourage the sexual activity of the children. As a result, the onset of the pubescent developmental sequence, and the adolescent behavioral developmental sequence in general, are being decelerated at certain

Table 6

Changes in Rate of Experiences of Various Sexual Events Among University Students in Four Surveys (20 Year-Olds; Junior College Students Included in the Data) (in Percentages)

		1974	1981	1987	1993
Kissing	Male	45.2	53.2	59.4	63.4
	Female	38.9	48.6	49.7	68.5
Petting	Male	29.7	40.3	53.3	57.0
	Female	17.9	29.9	34.1	45.7
Intercourse	Male	23.1	32.6	46.5	52.7
	Female	11.0	18.5	26.1	44.9

Figure 23

Changes in Yearly Growth Rate in Postwar Years Among Japanese Boys

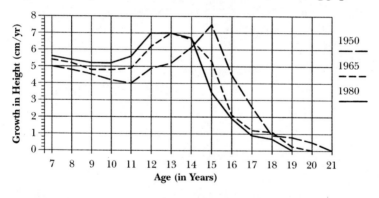

Figure 24

Changes in Yearly Growth Rate in the Past Decade Among Japanese Boys

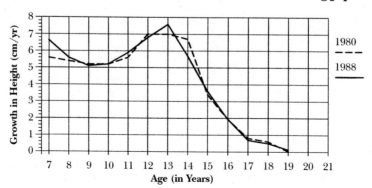

times. At the same time, due to the freer mode of sexual behaviors, particularly among post-senior high school youth, the last portion of the sexual development sequence is condensed to a shorter period of time.

How Japanese youth can cope with the shorter time span for adolescence and for sexual maturation and more liberal sexual behavior patterns is an issue of concern for both society and for sex educators and sexologists.

Thoughts and Attitudes Behind the Sexual Behavior of Youth

Certain data in the 1987 and 1993 national surveys suggest changes in the sociopsychological background of various sexual behaviors.

Figure 25 shows the survey results about the primary initiator of the dating and intercourse behaviors among the Japanese youths in the 1993 survey (J.A.S.E 1994). Between 40 and 49 percent of the male and female respondents reported that dating and intercourse were jointly initiated. In the remaining cases, 46 percent of the males and 35 percent of the women saw their male partner as the initiator of dating, while 44 percent of the men and 60 percent of the women saw their male partner as the initiator of intercourse. Often it is assumed that a female wants to pretend that she was forced to follow the male partner in certain sexual behaviors, even though such an attitude relieving the female of responsibility for her sexual behavior may be a reflection of a prevailing lack of self-identity in Japanese women. The ability to make one's own decisions in many important life events is one of the goals of sexuality education, and therefore, the situation is still quite challenging for sex educators.

Circumstances for the first sexual arousal experience in the 1987 survey are shown in Figure 26 (J.A.S.E 1988). The main source of sexual arousal

Figure 25

The Primary Initiator of the Dating and Intercourse Behaviors Among the Japanese Youth in 1993 Survey

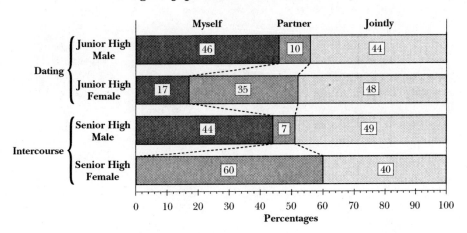

Figure 26

Circumstances for the First Sexual Arousal Experience

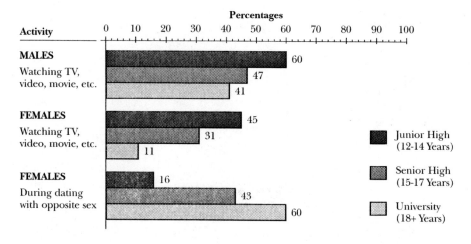

for junior high school boys, ages 12 to 14, and to a lesser extent, girls of the same age, is watching sexual material on television and the cinema, 60 percent versus 45 percent respectively. Among university students, on the other hand, 60 percent reported being sexually aroused—and only 11 percent by watching erotic visual material; 41 percent of university men reported being sexually aroused by watching erotic visual material.

The main rationales for the first kissing experience are shown in Figure 27 (J.A.S.E. 1988). Close to two thirds of both males and females found their justification for a first kiss in "liking the person." One in two males reported love or curiosity as their main motive, while significant numbers of women listed love, curiosity, being forced by the male partner, or no reason as their motive.

In terms of the partner's age at first intercourse, roughly equal numbers of university males reported their partner was older than, the same age as, or younger than they were, while more junior and senior high school boys indicated that their partners were either the same age as or older than they were (Figure 28; J.A.S.E 1988). Regardless of education, about two thirds of the females reported their first sexual partner was older than they. The use of contraceptive devices by both sexes in their first intercourse increased with the level of schooling, reaching 73 percent and 85 percent for university males and females, considerably higher than in the United States (Figure 29; J.A.S.E. 1988).

Among the reasons cited for the first coital experience, overall roughly half of the males cited "sexual arousal" and "liking the person," and a third reported "curiosity" or "loving the person." Six out of ten females cited "liking the person" and 38 percent "loving the person," while 18 percent were moti-

Figure 27

Major Rationales for the First Kissing Experience

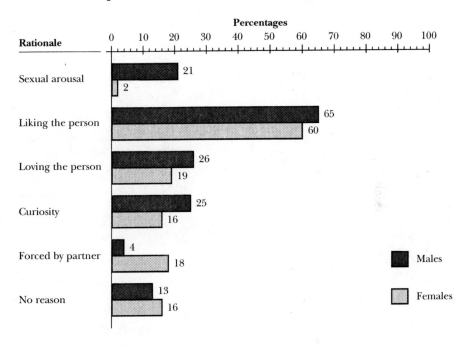

Figure 28

Partner's Age Classified by Age at First Experience of Intercourse

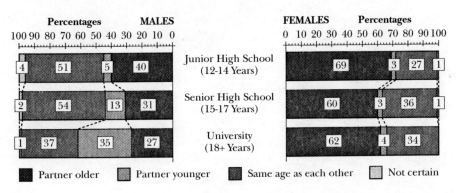

vated by "curiosity," 15 percent by "sport," and 13 percent by "coercion" (Figure 30; J.A.S.E. 1988). In breaking down these motives according to education, six out of ten senior high school and university males cited "liking the person," while junior high school girls mention coercion by the male partner more often than university females do (Figure 31; J.A.S.E.

Figure 29

Rate of Contraceptive Devices Used Classified by the Time of First Experience of Intercourse

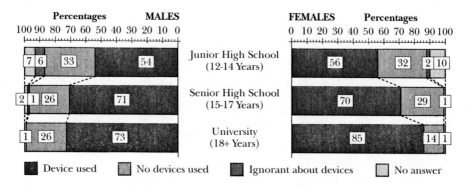

Figure 30

Rationales for the First Experience of Intercourse

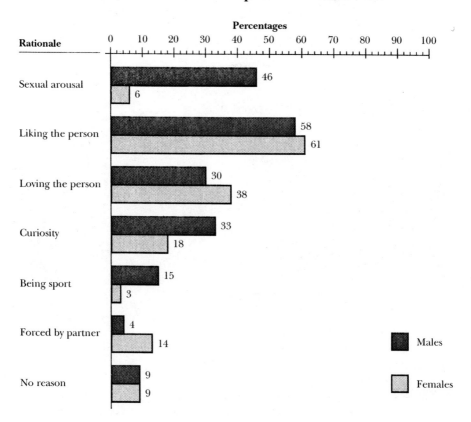

Figure 31

Rationales for the First Experience of Intercourse

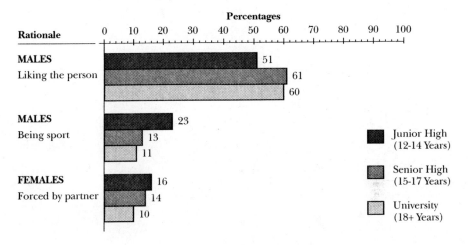

1988). Table 7 clearly shows that more females than males think they love their first intercourse partner, and a great many more males than females have intercourse because they were sexually aroused or more curious about the event.

Table 7

Rationales of First Sexual Intercourse Event by School Level of Occurrence (in Percentage; Includes Multiple Answers)

MALES	Time of Event*			FEMALES	Time of Event*		
Rationales	JHS	SHS	Univ.	Rationales	JHS	SHS	Univ.
Liking	52.2	61.9	62.1	Liking	56.6	66.0	61.7
Loving	34.1	28.4	32.9	Loving	39.5	31.0	53.0
Aroused	45.6	48.1	48.6	Aroused	6.6	7.6	6.1
Curiosity	37.9	32.2	34.3	Curiosity	18.4	21.8	13.0
Being sport	23.6	13.5	11.4	Being sport	10.5	3.0	0.9
No reason	14.3	8.7	5.0	No reason	14.5	10.7	5.2
Forced	11.5	2.4	0.7	Forced	17.1	14.2	10.4
Got drunk	8.8	8.0	5.7	Got drunk	10.5	5.6	2.6
Number used	182	289	140	Number used	76	197	115

*(JHS = Junior High School Students; SHS = Senior High School Students; Univ. = University Students)

In terms of attitudes regarding premarital intercourse and its connection with anticipation of marriage, the largest number of female university students in the 1987 survey believed that premarital sex is acceptable when there are certain agreements between the partners; the second largest group found it acceptable when based on love (Table 8).

Table 8

Relationship Between Attitudes on Marriage and Premarital Intercourse Among University Female Students

Attitude on Marriage	Attitude on Premarital Intercourse				Total N	Total Percent
	Unacceptable	Marriage Premise	Love Premise	Agreement Premise		
Earlier the better	11.1	25.8	31.7	36.1	208	100
When time comes	9.5	19.3	29.4	41.7	558	100
No desire	14.8	11.1	37.0	37.0	27	100
No idea	13.5	14.9	20.3	51.4	74	100
Total (percent)	10.5	19.0	29.4	41.1	757	100

Figure 32 indicates the degree of concern about pregnancy and STD/AIDS reported by sexually active senior high school and university males and females in the 1993 survey (J.A.S.E 1994). While both males and females expressed strong concern about pregnancy, 51 percent and 61 percent respectively, and 42 percent and 34 percent were "somewhat concerned," their strong concern about the risk of STDs and AIDS was significantly less. This might suggest that the threat of STD/AIDS is not as high in Japan as in other countries, or that the youth are not aware of their actual risk.

Throughout the four national surveys in these twenty years, sexually active Japanese youth showed a steadily increasing trend in their use of contraceptives (Figure 33; J.A.S.E 1994). Along with attaining "behavior emancipation," Japanese youths appear to be taking responsibility for protecting their own health and that of their sexual partners.

Across the education spectrum, Japanese males are more likely than not to agree that a man's role and place is to work outside of the home and a woman's role is to take care of the family. The split is more obvious among university students, with close to 60 percent agreeing and 40 percent disagreeing, indicating a conservative trend for more-educated males (Figure 34). Females were significantly more likely than males to disagree with this statement of roles, but university females also showed a clear conservative or traditional trend in their belief on this issue.

Figure 32

Degree of Concern While Engaged in Intercourse Among the Japanese Youths in the 1993 Survey

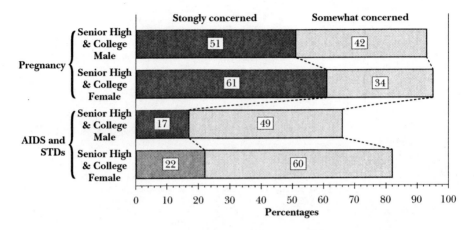

Figure 33

Rate of Contraceptive-Device Usage When Engaged in Intercourse Among the Japanese Youths in Four Surveys, 1974, 1981, 1987, and 1993

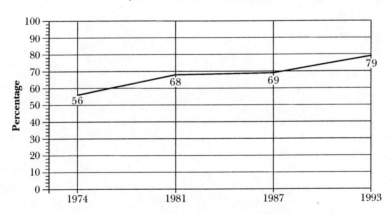

Traditionally Japanese married by age 25, but this expectation is clearly waning. Regarding their future plans of marriage, Japanese youth keenly reflect the current social trend toward later marriage. About one half of the young people indicated that they want to marry eventually, but are not concerned about the age at which they might marry. Only one in five wanted to marry soon (Table 9).

Figure 34

Attitudes about the Hypothesis "Man's Role Is to Work Outside the Home and Woman's Role Is to Take Care of the Family"

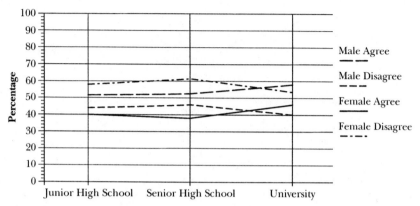

Table 9

Opinions about Marriage (in Percentages)

Opinions	Junior High Male	Junior High Female	Senior High Male	Senior High Female	University Male	University Female	Total Male	Total Female
Want to marry soon	20.3	22.3	17.6	23.1	19.6	27.9	19.1	23.7
Want to marry eventually, regardless of age	45.9	45.4	59.7	50.9	58.5	53.6	53.9	49.3
No preference to marry or not	14.3	18.7	13.1	17.7	15.6	14.1	14.0	17.4
Will remain unmarried	2.4	3.0	1.6	3.1	1.2	2.3	1.8	2.9
Other	1.2	0.7	1.1	1.1	0.9	0.8	1.1	0.9
Cannot answer	11.7	8.5	5.4	3.6	3.3	0.6	7.6	5.0
Don't know; Not answered	4.2	1.4	1.5	0.5	0.9	0.4	2.5	0.8
Total (percentage)	100.0	100.0	100.0	100.0	100.0	100.0	100.0	100.0
Total (persons)	1,008	1,008	1,008	1,008	424	488	2,440	2,504

C. Sex and Sexuality of Japanese Adults

Marital Sex

The Japanese ethical and cultural views of sex could probably be summed up in a few words as something repressed, embarrassing, and simply not talked about. Thus, statistics representing the Japanese concerning frequency of sexual intercourse, sexual positions, and level of satisfaction are still not reported today. Similarly, statistics on oral and anal sex in Japan are not available. One could probably conjecture, however, that the number of Japanese practicing such forms of sex has increased over the past decade or two, due to the influence of more-open conceptions about sex or of adult-oriented comics and magazines.

In November 1990, *The Weekly Post*, which boasts the largest readership for a magazine in Japan, published the results of a survey in which a random sampling of 2,000 readers took part. Of those surveyed, 33.6 percent of the men and 23.0 percent of the women gave complete, valid responses. The average ages of these men and women were 44 and 41 years old, respectively. According to the survey results, which may or may not be relevant to our discussion, 85 percent of the men indicated having had sexual intercourse in the past month. Among these, 55 percent had had sexual intercourse in the past week. Of all respondents, 15 percent had not had sexual intercourse in the past month.

Among the men who indicated having sexual intercourse in the past week, 51 percent had had it once, 31 percent twice, and 13 percent three times, making the average number for the previous week 1.7 times.

In other survey responses, 51 percent of the men indicated that they practice oral sex, and 8 percent replied that they practice anal sex. Twenty-nine percent of the women said that they always experience orgasm when having sexual intercourse, 30 percent replied frequently, 24 percent replied occasionally, and 8 percent said almost never or never.

While this survey cannot be said to represent the average Japanese, it does provide a general picture of their sexual practices. The results of this survey, when compared to a similar survey conducted by the Kyodo Press in 1982, show an increased percentage in every category, which clearly indicates that sexuality in Japan is becoming increasingly more open.

Marriage and Divorce

Dramatic improvement of women's status in society in the fifty years since World War II has resulted in great changes in the consciousness and attitude of the Japanese people toward marriage and family. Some obvious examples of such improvements are a steady increase in the number of women attending higher education institutions, a remarkable growth of professional and social activities by educated and enlightened women like Nora in Henrik Ibsen's 1879 *Et Dukkehjem* (A Doll's House), and development of a self-sustaining economic strength and expansion of independent life with individual decision making. The daughters of the traditional Japanese families, i.e., the Japanese female dolls wearing pretty kimonos, who used to be educated how to serve and follow the man (husband) and how not to express their own ego, desires, and needs are now nonexistent, having become a part of fairy tales. [An additional factor, mentioned in Section 4, may be the slow-fading expectation that a good Japanese woman should always be modest and not initiate any sexual activity. (Kaji)]

The consciousness and attitude of the men regarding marriage and family life have also been forced to change greatly throughout the time of high economic growth and the current economic stagnation and collapse of the "economic bubble." The unbalanced economic life between consumer life and insufficient income, and extremely poor housing conditions that come from living in highly concentrated dense metropolitan communities, are major examples of the forces that have caused changes in attitudes about marriage and family life. In 1950, the average age of first marriage of Japanese adults was 25.9 years for men and 23.0 years for women; by 1990, this was 28.4 and 25.8 years of age respectively. This rather high age of marriage is not expected to drop in the near future.

In 1946, divorce laws eliminated the old three-line letter whereby a man could dismiss his wife. Before World War II, Japan had one of the highest divorce rates in the world; that high rate is echoed in recent years, following after an all-time postwar low, with the difference that most divorces now are sought by women. Laws still leave alimony rather skimpy, but child-custody now favors the mother instead of the mandatory custody by the husband's family that prevailed before 1945.

According to a recent report from a survey of young adults' attitudes about marriage, the rate of those who indicated "marriage is not a must unless one needs to," and/or "living independently is more important than marriage," was 41 and 32.8 percent of women in their 20s and 30s respectively, and 32.9 and 37.1 percent of men in their 20s and 30s respectively.

The youth in older generations used to be concerned with a "get married to have sex and propagate" philosophy that was reflected in the statistical data. [Ten years ago, in a survey conducted by the Ministry of Public Welfare in 1987, 91.8 percent of the males and 92.9 percent of the females aged 18 to 34 indicated that they wanted to get married. A 1986 survey of university students reported that their cohabitation rate was only 0.3 percent for males and 0.8 percent for females (Kaji)]. However, the authors of this chapter believe that there is a trend among today's youths to move away from the traditional form of family life and marriage to accept cohabitation as a natural form of living in the male/female cooperation,. The majority simply hope that when all the conditions are fulfilled, it is not a bad idea to get married. [Surveys need to be conducted to support or disprove this interesting hypothesis. (Kaji)]

The traditional matchmaking system as a prelude to marriage is well known. The system was developed under the feudalistic atmosphere and warriors' society in which the preservation of the family was of priority importance. The so-called "middleman in honor" was asked by the parents of the young man or woman to find their child a proper partner in terms of the social level and position of the family. Traditionally, age was not a consideration.

This system is still widely practiced today, although the social status of the family and the respective person is increasingly becoming less important. In the 1960s, a survey analysis reported that 40.7 percent of all marriages were arranged in the manner mentioned above, and 57.0 percent were a freely made decision or love-oriented marriage. The rate of arranged marriage in a 1980s survey dropped to 22.8 percent for arranged marriages and rose to 71.8 percent for love-oriented marriages, leaving about a quarter of all marriages still arranged by a matchmaker. The newest trend in this system is an increase in the requests for arranged marriages among men over age 30, a reflection perhaps that these older bachelors tend to avoid the rather uneasy attempts to build a love-oriented heterosexual relationship. Marriage is not an easy life event for the young and middle-aged Japanese men in these days, particularly considering a 1991 poll by the Asahi Shimbund that reported 60 percent of Japanese women consider Japanese men "unreliable" (Itoi and Powell 1992). (See also the discussion of the "Narita divorce" phenomenon in Section 5A above.)

The attitude of the Japanese people toward divorce has changed as much as their attitude toward marriage. Historically, the divorce rate in the Meiji Era (1868-1912) was higher than the current figure, very probably because men could divorce wives easily, since the social status and human rights of women were regarded as light as a feather. No statistics are available regarding marriage and divorce before Meiji (1868).

Like many other democratic practices, the principle of male/female equality was first established throughout the legal structure of modern Japanese society in 1945. The Japanese people used to believe that ending a marriage in divorce for whatever reasons involved a loss of face and honor. Many, particularly among the older generations, still hold to this belief. In this respect, maintaining the marital structure, even when the husband/wife relations are practically broken, is socially acceptable and often the rationale for not divorcing. Considering this background, the divorce rate remained low during the 1950s and 1960s, less than 1.0 per 1,000. By the 1980s, the divorce rate had grown slightly to 1.5 per 1,000. The more recent rate is not much different from the 1980s rate. There are important differences in these general statistics. The divorce rate for couples in their early 20s was 17.0 per 1,000 in 1985, more than ten times the overall average. For couples in their 40s, the rate was 3.6 per 1,000, twice the overall rate. [There are about 24 divorces for every 100 Japanese marriages, compared with 32 per 100 in France, 42 per 100 in England, and 55 per 100 in the United States (Kristoff 1996a). (Editor)]

The increased rate of divorce among the young people may come from their immaturity in the social perseverance quality, while the rate among middle-aged people may be the result of changes in the male/female social strength relations. For the latter, factors to be considered include a rebellion of the women against the men-centered social structure, expansion of the economic independence of the housewives, and more promotion of women's emancipation. This, in turn, provides the starting point for a discussion about the husband/wife roles in the family life in the modern and future Japanese society.

[In a recent survey conducted by the Dentsu Research Institute and Leisure Development Center in Japan, married men and their wives in thirty-seven countries were asked how they felt about politics, sex, religion, ethics, and social issues. Japanese couples ranked dead last, by a significant margin, in the compatibility of their views. In another survey, only about a third of the Japanese said they would marry the same person if they could do it over. However, this incompatibility might not matter as much because Japanese husbands and wives traditionally spend little time talking to each other. This is not unexpected given the primacy most Japanese men place on their work, the disparate social positions and power of men and women in traditional Japanese society, and the suppression of emotions and feeling. The reality in many marriages is the "7-11 husband," so-called because he leaves home at 7 A.M. and returns home after 11 P.M., often after going out for an after-work drink or *mah-jongg* session with buddies. A national survey found that 30 percent of the fathers spend less that 15 minutes a day on weekdays talking with or playing with their children. Fifty-one percent of the eighth grade students reported they never spoke with their fathers on weekdays. In reality, then, the figures for single-parent Japanese families are deceptive, with the father in dual-parent families more often than not a theoretical presence (Kristof 1996a).

[Two major factors in Japanese culture have kept the divorce rate very low despite the lack of couple compatibility, communications, and emotional satisfaction. On the male side, shame is still a powerful social and financial sanction, especially in the workplace where many companies are reluctant to promote employees who have divorced or have major problems at home. A divorce is always a negative factor in the employment world. Women also face serious financial consequences from divorce. While child custody goes to the mother in three quarters of all divorces, most Japanese mothers do not have a career or much in the way of financial resources. Only about 15 percent of divorced fathers pay child support (Kristof 1996a). (Editor)]

Sexuality and Older Persons

Recently, surveys in Japan have enthusiastically taken up the topic of sexuality among the middle-aged and aged population. In 1979, Hideko Daikuhara, a public health nurse in Tokyo, conducted Japan's first-ever research on the actual condition of sexual activity among aged persons. Later, Yoshiaki Kumamoto and others at the Sapporo Medical School firmly established research on gerontology—in Japan gerontology is a branch of andrology. Kumamoto reported the results of a survey on the relationship between sexual activity and aging that was conducted as a part of his research. The survey revealed that 14.2 percent of men in their early 60s were no longer sexually active. For men in their late 60s, the percentage of inactive males was 22.8, with 32.0 percent in their early 60s, 50.3 percent in their late 70, and 62.6 percent of men aged 80 or older were no longer sexually active. Of those who indicated being sexually active, 60 percent in their 60s, 40 to 55 percent in their 70, and 30 percent 80 or older said they had sex once or twice a month.

Kumamoto's survey was given to 5,500 men. Although it would be difficult to say his survey is representative of middle-aged and aged men in Japan, it is sufficient reference for the trend of sexual activity in these age groups. "Human beings do not lose their sexual drive until they die," has been an expression heard among the common populace of Japan for many years. This is evidence that the Japanese have had sufficient knowledge of the sexual activity made evident in Kumamoto's survey. On the other side of the coin, the popular expression regarding men who are "forever chasing after women, in spite of their age" offers proof that Japanese have a both an official and a private stance when it comes to sexuality.

[*Extramarital Relationships*

[Traditionally, the Japanese male has always had much more freedom for extramarital affairs than the women. In Japanese culture, there is no sin in sex. It is treated as a natural part of life by the Japanese, even more so than in European cultures. Few Frenchmen were upset when the widow and the former mistress of President Mitterand stood side by side at his funeral, because the whole affair was handled with proper decorum. Unlike the United States, Japanese culture has been even more accepting of the private extramarital affairs of high-ranking Japanese politicians, business executives, and ordinary husbands. Extramarital affairs traditionally posed no problem unless the man either allowed this side of his private life to interfere with his duties, or he lost face by not maintaining proper social decorum. One loses face and shames one's family by making public something that should be private (Bornoff 1991, 262-300).

[While no data are available on the incidence of extramarital sex and affairs, the incidence of such behavior is undoubtedly affected by several factors in the changing scene of Japanese male-female relations. While husbands have many avenues for extramarital sex available with *geishas*, soap ladies, and the sex workers who ply their trade via telephone clubs, pink leaflets, mobile van services (*Pinkku Shiataru*), lover's banks, massage parlors, date coffee shops (*deeto kissa*), or on the street, the number of Japanese wives who seek a lover as a way of spicing up their lives with a bit of romance seems to be increasing. In the 1983 *More Report on Female Sexuality*, 70 percent of the women ages 13 to 60 surveyed reported being sexually unsatisfied. Add to this the fact that Japanese wives control the household finances and have considerably more leisure time than their husbands. Many of the part-time sex workers in Soaplands are female students and frustrated housewives who control their own work schedules and can use the extra money easily available in this work. A 1986 survey conducted by the Prime Minister's Office found that 10 percent of the 680 women sex workers arrested by the police were housewives (Bornoff 1991, 334). (See also Section 8B.) (Editor)]

6. Homoerotic, Homosexual, and Ambisexual Behaviors

[A. Homosexuality in Pre-Modern Japan

[Masculinity and virility were exalted in the ancient nature religions and in Shinto precepts and rituals that prepared the ground for the warrior culture. In the Shinto winter ritual of *hadaka matsuri*, males of all ages purified themselves with an icy dip in a mountain spring or waterfall, liberally consumed purifying *saki*, and then piled on top one another within the confines of the shrine in a seething mass exaltation of manhood. Masculinity was also exalted by the *samurai* and *shoguns* who kept legions of pretty young pages in attendance. Even among the Buddhist priesthood, where the injunction of chastity forbade all sexual contact of monks with women, homosexuality was considered an acceptable substitute, as it was elsewhere in Buddhist monasteries throughout the Far East. Each novice pledged himself to an older monk for a number of years. In exchange for tuition, the mentor provided his pupil with instruction in the sacred texts and the spiritual quest. The novice embraced the status of "sworn friend," serving his master, body and soul.

[During the long civil wars, violence and the warrior ethic reigned supreme and women were nothing more than a necessary incubator for progeny. Homosexuality was the *ne plus ultra* of virility and masculinity. In the stoic way of the warrior and the code of the *samurai, nanshoku* (male passion) was not a perversion but a lofty ideal. Strict conventions limited the passive female role of recipient to youths and boys, while the older male played the active male role of insertor.

[For centuries, the traditional Japanese theater, another male preserve, also had an established current of homosexuality flowing through it. As soon as the female precursors of *kabuki* were banished from the stage in the early 1600s, the overwhelming majority of their male replacements were beauteous catamites and followers of Shudo, "the way of the youth" (Bornoff 1991, 422-33). (Editor)]

[Yanagihashi (1995) has identified four main characteristics evident in pre-modern Japanese homosexual traditions, namely:

1. The relationships are typically between an adult man and a minor;
2. The relationships tend to exist in contexts where contact with the other sex is limited;
3. Female homosexuality seems to be entirely non-existent; and

4. The relationships were formed exclusively among members of the privileged classes.

According to Yanagihashi, homosexuality was understood as a substitute or supplement to heterosexuality in a fundamentally heterosexual and male-dominated society. (Kaji)]

B. Male Homosexuality Today

[Although Japanese culture has in its history a tradition of sexual love between men, and tolerates the expression of affection for the same sex at most levels of society, the contemporary Japanese attitude toward homosexuality is in general very negative. However, the issue has yet to be discussed as a social issue. For example, according to a nationwide survey of 188 university professors who are teaching subjects related to human sexuality, only 30 (15.8 percent) have ever addressed the issue of homosexuality in their curriculum (National Survey of Sexology and College Education, 1995). Though many lesbians and gay men are suffering from the prejudice and insensitivity of Japanese society, most heterosexual Japanese people may be unaware of the negative feelings that drive such prejudice and insensitivity. (Kaji)]

None of the larger urban entertainment districts in Japan is without its quota of gay bars and clubs. The laws against prostitution are fairly nebulous, but especially so when applied to homosexual prostitution. When a gay bar or club comes to grief from the law, it is usually because it employed boys under the legal age of consent or hired exotic youths from other lands who violate the provisions of their visa by working.

Until the specter of AIDS arose in the mid-1980s, many foreign homosexual men found Japan, with its very long, colorful, and venerable gay history, to be a paradise. The fear of AIDS and a touch of xenophobia have closed most gay facilities to foreigners. Exclusion of foreign gays from Japanese gay facilities provides the reassurance of freedom from the risk of AIDS if Japanese homosexuals associate only with other Japanese gays.

[Japanese male homosexuals are called *okama* (august pots), a derogatory colloquial metaphor equating the common cooking pot with the human buttocks. Increasingly popular is the "Japlish" *gei*, or gay. In a 1981 survey, about 6 percent of male college students reported being active homosexuals; a third of high school boys surveyed reported latent homosexual inclinations. In a similar 1987 survey, both figures declined to 4.5 and 20 percent respectively, with a proportionate increase in heterosexual activity.

[Apart from one gay support group with an overwhelming foreign membership, there are no gay activist groups uniting Japanese in coming out of the closet and political advocacy. Gay magazines, such as the famous *Bara Zoku* (The Rose Tribe) and gay comics are sold everywhere, but like the many heterosexual erotic publications, their emphasis is more on titillation than information, and certainly not on sociopolitical activism. Gay liberation parties on the political fringe do occasionally surface, especially at elections, but most Japanese gays would rather continue living their erotic lives contentedly in the closet, perusing their gay magazines, and attending gay bars or clubs when they can, rather than become involved in the risky business of political activism (Bornoff 1991). (Editor)]

[This situation began to change in 1991 with the filing of the first court case pertaining to gay issues, The Association for Lesbian and Gay Movement vs. Tokyo Municipal Government. In this case, also known as the Fucyu Youth Activity Center Case, the Tokyo District Court reversed a decision by the Tokyo Metropolitan Government Board of Education that refused to allow homosexual groups to use a youth activity center. Beginning in 1994, the Annual Lesbian and Gay Pride Parade has been held in Tokyo. In 1995, about two thousand people attended this event, which was co-sponsored by twenty-eight groups with predominantly Japanese membership. Also, in 1995, gay professional organizations, such as the Association of Gay Professionals in Counseling and Allied Medical Fields, were founded. (Kaji)]

[C. Lesbianism

[In ancient times, the neglected ladies of the *o-oku*, the *shogun*'s harem, were well known for taking consolation in lesbian relationships. Unlike the celebration of male homosexuality among the warriors and their pages, however, Japanese culture has preferred to ignore—neither condemning nor celebrating—lesbian relations. *Shunga* with a lesbian theme are relatively rare. There are *resubian sho* (lesbian shows) which are a staple in the modern striptease parlor frequented by heterosexual males, but more as a foreign import than indigenous expression. For a brief time in the early 1980s, Tokyo had a single lesbian bar, but given the contentedness of gay men in the closet and the pervasiveness of female submissiveness, there are even fewer lesbians anxious to come out in public. While most gay bars exclude all women, some are known to cater to lesbians on certain days, and then only for a couple of hours. In modern Japan, lesbianism is shrouded in comparative obscurity (Bornoff 1991, 433-47). (Editor)]

[In Japan, as in most other cultures around the world, lesbians have been doubly stigmatized as homosexuals and as women. Lesbians have been typically viewed by Japanese society as a common element in the pornography targeted to men or as "gender-bending" and anti-social. A variety of colloquial terms are used for Japanese lesbians, all of them more or less derogatory. (Kaji)] Lesbians are sometimes known as *onabe* (stew-pot) in contrast with the male *okama*, or august pot, or more commonly by the "Japlish" *resz. Rezubian* (lesbian) is the most commonly used term. The *otachi*, or butch, the actress playing male roles, and the *nenne* or *neko* (cat), *Çnue*, or femme, mark the two ends of the lesbian spectrum.

[One uniquely Japanese custom of gender bending is found in the *joshi-puro* (women professional wrestlers). Elsewhere in the world, women wrestlers are shapely Amazons in bikinis intently watched by males. In Japan, women wrestlers mimic their male *sumo* counterparts, with some interesting twists. *Joshi-puro* stars, such as Chigusa, with a boyish hairstyle and tacky, gaudy leotards, serenades her audience of teenage and preteen girls with popular songs before climbing into the ring to attack, gouge, pummel, and drag her mountainous opponent around the rings. Commenting on the adulation Japanese girls show for their heroes in the All-Japan Women's Pro Wrestling Association, the director of AJWPWA has suggested that young girls see women pro wrestlers as very strong, ideal men, a substitute for boyfriends. They feel safe getting close to them because they are female. They provide vicarious thrills for the young girls, and models of aggressive champions of self-assertiveness (Bornoff 1991, 433-444). (Editor)]

7. Gender Conflicted Persons

Except for the practices of certain ethnic groups in the world, cross-dressing, transvestism, gender-crossing, and transsexualism were, until about fifty years ago, generally considered "diseases" that either required medical treatment or were simply not practiced out in the open.

Reaction in Japan was similar, although there were some exceptions. *Kabuki*, Japan's traditional theatrical art, is one. All parts in a *Kabuki* play are played by male actors. Thus, cross-dressing and transvestism, at least in the theater, has long existed in *Kabuki* roles. One can easily imagine that the actor's psychological state, or mental makeup, walks a fine line between masculinity and femininity, as the actor tries to immerse himself in his role. Actors responsible for female roles were, from their early childhood, compelled to experience first-hand the everyday life, customs, and etiquette of the women they played. Although this extreme practice is not seen in the modern *Kabuki* world, it cannot be denied that an aesthetic sensibility exists in the mental makeup of Japanese in which importance is placed on the beauty of men acting in female roles. As a counterpart to *Kabuki*, Takarazuka Young Girls Opera, which began in 1914, has provided a stage for only female actors and continues to enchant many women today.

These phenomena may provide a clue when considering gender-crossing, transvestism, and cross-dressing in Japan. That is, the roles in both *Kabuki* and Takarazuka Opera have come to be viewed as a performance, something one sees only on the stage. Accordingly, occurrences in these fictitious worlds are not always so easily tolerated in the real world. A "drag queen" appearing on television, for example, lives in "television land," a world from which most people feel detached.

Gender-crossers and transsexuals have not yet been accepted into Japanese society. This is because the majority of people have a dualistic gender bias, believing that a man's role is to impregnate a woman and a woman's role is to bear children, while only a minority advocate a society where people are free to choose their gender.

In recent years, gatherings and study meetings on transsexualism and transvestism as a human issue rather than a moral issue have been provided in Japan, as well. Saitama Medical School created a stir in July 1996, when its ethics committee approved female-to-male sex-change operations. There is no legal precedent for this in Japanese law and many problems remain concerning how society will accept those people who undergo a sex-change operation.

8. Significant Unconventional Sexual Behaviors

A. Coercive Sexual Behaviors

Rape

Rape, according to Japanese law, is described as having sexual intercourse with a woman through force or against the woman's will, but there is no clear legal definition for rape. According to Article 177 of the Criminal Code, "if a girl of 13 years or more is forced to have sexual intercourse by means of a violent act or threats . . . or if sexual intercourse is performed with a girl not yet 13 years of age, regardless of the method or whether there was mutual consent," the offender will be punished. However, the victim or her parent or legal guardian must file a complaint in order for the rape to be recognized as a criminal act.

In 1994, when victims of rape were required to go through this vague and complicated procedure, 1,616 cases of rape were reported. The number of cases actually dropped between 1980 (1,800 cases) and 1990 (1,500 cases), but recent years have seen a slight increasing trend. In Japan, many feel that, because rape is an offense subject to prosecution only upon complaint, few cases come to light. The actual number of cases is sometimes said to be five to ten times the number reported. This is really the problem we should be concentrating on in our discussions, while striving to settle on a clear legal definition of rape. Although sexual crimes, such as indecent assault, sexual abuse, and sexual harassment, were not until recently taken up as social problems, we can at least say that surveys and case studies on these topics are being performed, and that the formation of a nationwide study network is anticipated for the future.

Sexual Harassment

In 1986, Japan passed an equal-opportunity law for women that was purely advisory and only asked companies to make "an effort" to prevent discrimination against women. The 1986 law provided no penalties for companies that discriminated; it did not even mention the term "sexual harassment." In December 1996, a Labor Ministry panel recommended putting teeth into the 1986 law by publicizing the names of violators and specifically barring sexual harassment. The panel said that the revised law should expressly forbid gender discrimination instead of simply recommending efforts against it and should ban advertising that describe jobs as "open only to women." Despite these efforts, protection against sexual harassment in Japan lags far behind American and European standards.

Incest

According to Japanese myth, Izanami and Izanagi, the god and goddess couple credited with creating the islands that make up Japan, were in fact siblings who then married. Also, many stories have been handed down from the fourth and fifth centuries concerning consanguineous marriages (incest) in Japan's Ruling Family (thought by some to be the ancestors of today's Imperial Family, but this is uncertain). However, since that time, incest has been taboo and avoided in Japan, as in the Christian spheres of America and Europe.

Yet, reports of incest between a mother and son have become a phenomenon in the last few decades. Such reports have come mostly from volunteer groups that provide counseling over the telephone. Frequent situations in the reports include: 1) a mother who sees her son masturbating in his bedroom and begins helping him, which leads to sexual intercourse; and 2) a boy in a stupor or irritated from studying for exams who is embraced by his mother, who feels sorry for him, leading to sexual intercourse. Many psychologists hypothesize that the anonymous nature of the telephone counseling may result in calls that provide an outlet for the expression of fantasies peculiar to young people. However, there is no reason to totally discount the findings from this counseling method. We look forward with great anticipation to future surveys and studies.

[B. Prostitution

[Prior to 1948 and the enactment of the Law for the Regulation of Businesses Affecting Public Morals, prostitution was not a criminal offense. The 1956 Prostitution Prevention Law granted the country's red-light districts a year's grace, after which the estimated 260,000 sex workers in the 50,000 hitherto licensed brothels would have to find other means of earning a living. The 1956 law also banned sexual slavery and the practice of selling daughters into the brothel trade. New revisions of the public morals were added in 1984.

[While the commercial sex industry has undergone many changes, it has retained much of its vitality and varied character.

> Both before and after the new law, however, the operation of sex-oriented businesses was, and is subject to obtaining "prior permission" from the police and local authorities. This at once casts doubt upon how illegal such things actually are and just what kind of arrangements

operators are expected to make in order to open shop. The fact is that bars, cabarets and other concerns employing hostesses are free to operate, provided their services abide by officialdom's favorite old (and sometimes highly coercive) chestnut of "voluntary restraint." "Most of the sex industry is illegal, yet it goes on just the same," the editor of a Tokyo magazine focusing on the *mizu shobai* recently affirmed. "As in the strip theaters, people usually know when the police are coming to raid them. In businesses like these, there's a lot of money changing hands under the table." (Bornoff 1991, 332)

[According to the 1984 *More Report of Male Sexuality*, the majority of men over 30 had their first sexual intercourse experience with a prostitute, whereas those in their 20s tended to have their first encounters with a girlfriend.

[*Soaplands*

[It is still quietly accepted and understood that a Japanese husband may join business associates or friends for a visit to a "Soapland" red-light district. The "Soapland" districts in Japanese cities are not an ordinary European or American red-light district. Like the fantasy land of the "love hotels" which provide much-needed romantic privacy for young couples living with parents or with their children in tiny living quarters with no privacy, a "Soapland," like Kobe's venerable Fukuhara district,

> leaves nothing to be desired in terms of local color, and works up a merry throng on Saturday nights (the streets are nearly deserted on weekday nights). In Fukuhara's unimaginably gaudy streets, the pre-dominant bordello architecture would put even the most fanciful love hotels to shame. The usual shoguns' castles are dwarfed by edifices with stucco baroque façades arrayed with colorful *son et lumière*, and the odd rickety little old Japanese brothel is eclipsed by adjacent chrome-and-smoked glass pleasure domes and sci-fantasy ferroconcrete extravagan-zas from some Babylonian lunatic fringe. Here and there touts in proper *yakuza* uniform lunge in front of the doorways, all short-cropped frizzy hair and neon lights winking kaleidoscopically in their dark glasses. Otherwise pandering seems undertaken entirely by the descendants of the old *yarite*, aging women sitting on chairs and hailing passers-by.
> Fukuhara's Soapland foyer interiors have to be seen to be believed. Sprayed fluorescent pink, statuary modeled after Botticelli's Venus rising from the waves stand blushing outlandishly beneath a red roof evoking a Shinto shrine; traditional Japanese cranes in chromium wing their way across a back lit diorama of the Château de Chenonceaux. . . . In the interests of mandatory discretion, the showy façades com-pletely conceal the executrixes within. Upon crossing the threshold, it becomes apparent that Soapland ladies join the employees of cabarets

and pink salons in a great variety of fancy dress: old-time courtesans in florid kimono, nurses, airline flight attendants, bunny girls, Suzy Wongs in high-necked mini cheongsams slit up the sides, SM leather goddesses and Buddhist and Catholic nuns (Bornoff 1991, 271, 263-264)

[The leisurely ritual of a Soapland visit starts with a ceremonial undressing, followed by a relaxing sudsy sponge bath and gentle massage, a rinse, and a lather dance (*awa-odori*) or body-body massage in which the *Toruko-jo* (female) or *Sopu-reedi* (Soap-Lady) massages every part of her client's body with every part of her body on a king size inflated rubber mattress. Another rinse and a skillful *shakuhachi*, in which the Soap-Lady displays her charms, lead into an artistic performance of sexual arousal that culminates in intercourse. All this occurs with a curious single-minded determination and absolutely no pretense of emotional involvement.

[The old-style, leisurely coital sex play with *geishas* and Soap Ladies, however, is declining in favor of quick, cheaper (and hence more frequently affordable) masturbation, oral sex, and voyeurism. The equivalents of "fast food," non-coital sexual release for males, now account for nearly half of the commercial sex trade. *Herusu massagi* and *fashon massagi*, health and fashion massage, are increasing in popularity. Independent women work in the video game halls, discos, date coffee shops (*deeto kissa*), mobile van services (*Pinkku Shiataru*), lovers' banks (telephone date clubs), nude photo studios (popular in the 1970s and in decline since), or wait for calls responding to the pink leaflets (*pinkku bira*) they post in appropriate public places or drop in private mail boxes (see Section 8D in the chapter on the United Kingdom for a British parallel to *pinkku bira*). One factor in this shift is the high-pressure life and lack of leisure in the male business world; most white-collar workers (salary men) do not have a lot of leisure time or spare money to spend on the traditional commercial sex. Another factor, of course, is a recent growing awareness and concern about AIDS (Bornoff 1991, 282-300).

[According to a 1981 survey, younger prostitutes remained in the trade for three to four years; another small survey of sex workers in the Senzoku-Yoshiwara area in 1988 showed the average age was 26 and careers lasting about sixteen months. In the 1986 survey conducted by the Prime Minister's Office, nearly 10 percent were housewives, another 10 percent office employees, and 4 percent students. More than half cited "making a living" as the motivation, 14 percent were doing it "for the sake of the family," 11 percent were doing it to pay off debts, while others cited money for clothes, travel, and leisure (Bornoff 1991, 273, 334). (Editor)]

C. Pornography and Erotica

Arguments over the definition of pornography in Japan tend to converge on the issue of what is obscene. The Japanese courts define obscenity as that which "excites or stimulates sexual desire to no purpose, causes harm to a normal person's sense of sexual shame, or goes contrary to a good sense of sexual morality." However, it would be reasonable to say that an interpretation of this correlates with social and cultural changes of the times. In fact, when D. H. Lawrence's novel, *Lady Chatterley's Lover,* was translated into Japanese and published in 1957, it was deemed obscene and banned. Now, in 1996, the same fully translated book is published without problem. In addition, until just a few years ago, photogravures of nude models in which the pubic hair can be seen were never printed in magazines. Now, however, seeing the pubic hair of nude models in Japan's weekly magazines that target adult readers is no longer a novelty.

When discussing pornography in the context of Japanese culture, one cannot leave out the *shunga* genre of the Edo period (1603-1867). *Shunga* is an art form that enjoyed high regard among the people of its time, but at the same time was kept secret. That is telling of the great artistic impact *shunga* had on society and, consequently, the ambivalent state of people's sense of shame, which was attacked by this shocking art form. Even Japanese today are most likely divided in their opinions of whether or not *shunga* is pornographic or obscene.

Turning our attention to modern times, Japanese who live in the big cities frequently come across shops that specialize in "adult goods," similar to what one might see in Europe or America. These adult shops house rows and rows of magazines and videos for the purpose of showing explicit sexual activity, although the sexual organs have been painted black or obscured. The reality is that even a junior high school student, albeit one big for his age, could enter such a store and make a purchase. Thus, one could say that Japan is completely open to pornography.

Japanese are often described as ambiguous, neither black nor white, but in a nebulous state of indecisive gray. They do not denounce the adult stores nor do they speak of them in good terms. They merely let the situation stand in a state of ambiguity. Once a year or once every few years, the police crack down on these stores, at which time the media raises a fuss over the issue for a short time, and then once again the problem is forgotten.

Recently, some mothers' and women's groups began a campaign to banish pornography from the viewpoint that it is degrading to women. How to effect a change in the male consciousness in order for such grassroots activities to take root is now a major topic, albeit one which is only being discussed among women.

Sexually Violent Fantasies in Comic Books

A contribution to a local newspaper in the summer of 1990 complaining that the contents of comic books had become grossly obscene sparked debate between freedom of expression in Japanese comic books and the negative influence these magazines have on young people. This debate has grown into a major social issue. It is certainly true that a great many scenes in the comic books read by young boys and girls would trouble sensible adults. It should be noted that the authors or publishers of these comics have exercised self-imposed control concerning sexually explicit matter. However, there has been apparently no control from either party in limiting scenes containing violence.

This tolerance of violence is due to the norms of Japan's male-dominated society and to its long history in which violence was condoned as a symbol of manliness. As a result, the sexual content of comic books aimed at young people has been curbed, whereas the authors and publishers have been given free rein in depicting violence (Bornoff 1991, 69-71). The past few years, however, have seen an active increase in movements, spurred on largely by women's groups, to denounce sexual violence in the media. As a result, major enterprises, publishers, and television stations have revised their presentations of sexual violence. However, there are always people, in any society, eager to make a profit through work in the underground. It is an undeniable fact that comic books depicting sexual violence can be found in Japan today. Now, many people are crying out that urgent attention be given to sex education, in order to confront the sexism, gender bias, and sexual depravity found in such people as the authors and editors of these comic books.

[*"Ladies Comic Books"*

[One type of popular Japanese erotic comics (*ero-manga*) is the "ladies comic books" that seem to glorify sexual violence and rape. These are not a tiny fringe phenomenon—*Amour*, the leading such comic, has been published for six years and claims a sales circulation of 400,000. *Amour, Taboo, Cute, Scandal, Love*, and other similar *ero-manga* have a greater impact than their substantial sales would indicate, because copies are often passed around among friends. Even so, these magazines are also not standard fare for the average Japanese woman.

[The paradox of these "ladies comic books" lies in the fact that, although their readers are overwhelmingly women, mostly in their 20s and 30s, the cartoon stories glorify sexually passive women, sexual violence, and rape. Ninety of the 316 pages in the December 1995 issue of *Amour*, for example, contained rape scenes. Despite the growing independence of Japanese women, these comics portray passive women being brutalized rather than assertive women who control their own lives. When interviewed by a *New York Times* reporter, Masafumi Mizuno, editor of *Amour*, admitted that "Sometimes we carry stories where the woman takes the initiative, and those kinds of stories have their fans. But most readers seem to prefer when the women are in a passive position." Mariko Mitsui, a former politician and active feminist, finds it puzzling that many young Japanese women really do not want to be liberated. "They want to escape independence, and so for them to be raped seems better" than negotiating their own sexual encounters.

[Another popular comics theme, particularly in those aimed at teenage girls, deals with romances between gay men. These are less graphic and more sentimental than stories of heterosexual romances. They are also erotically engaging without being personally threatening for teenagers who are just discovering their sexuality (Kristof 1995). (Editor)]

D. Sadism and Masochism

It is well-known that sadism and masochism (S&M) have been taken up in Japan's literature and paintings. A number of works by Seiu Ito on the subject of *shibari* (bondage) are famous examples. One depicts a woman being tortured while a drooling jailer looks on in delight. Another shows a naked woman suspended upside down, while under her an old man is enjoying a drink of *saki*. These are typical of Seiu Ito's works. Of course, works such as these are not part of Japan's mainstream literature or paintings, but rather are learned of only in the quiet mania of the back streets.

It is uncertain how many people are interested in this type of sadism and masochism today, but their numbers are not few. Roughly ten thousand magazines dealing in S&M are thought to be sold each month, by which one could estimate the number of interested people to be perhaps two or three times that number.

On the other hand, in the Japanese media's typical fashion of trying to stimulate the reader's interest, some minor weekly magazines print photographs or articles that depict situations with a sadistic mistress and a masochistic man. Naturally, most of these depictions are contrived, as people who really practice S&M do so in secret, hidden from public view. Both Tokyo and Osaka have nightclubs in their busiest night spots that make money off of S&M. Still, experts say that the people who go to such places probably realize it is all just an act.

9. Contraception, Abortion, and Population Planning

A. Contraception

Various contraceptive devices became available in the democratic days after the war, including use of the pessary (diaphragm), contraceptive jelly and foams, etc. Nearly 80 percent of Japanese people still choose the condom as their most favorable contraceptive device. This choice, however, is conditioned by the government's near-total ban on the oral contraceptive pill. [As of January 1997, only a medium-strength form of the pill was available in Japan for medical (non-contraceptive) purposes. However, some women were using it as a substitute for the low-dose contraceptive pill normally taken by American and European women. Originally, the Ministry of Health and Welfare cited the possible link between the hormonal pill (OCP) and cardiovascular disease, weakened immunity, cervical cancer, and thrombosis as its reason for not approving distribution of the pill in Japan. In 1996, new research studies undermined this objection, and the Ministry of Health and Welfare gave signs that it might remove its over three-decade-old ban on the OCP, perhaps even by the end of 1997. The Ministry admitted to some continuing concerns about removing the ban. There is a fear that, with the birthrate at 1.4 live births per woman, pushing the OCP might drop the birthrate even lower. More realistic is the fear that use of the OCP rather than the condom would increase the spread of AIDS among those who use the pill. More basic to the cultural values of Japanese men and women is the fear that Government approval of the OCP may send a signal of promiscuity and upset the delicate dynamics in male-female relationships. Even married women tend not to discuss contraceptives openly with their husbands. Traditionally, Japanese men are accustomed to taking the lead in relationships, especially when it comes to sex. Japanese women frequently express their awe at the independence of American women who make their own decision to use the pill. Nevertheless, after decades of public and national administration debate, approval of the OCP may be expected in the near future (WuDunn 1996). (Editor)]

Japanese contraceptive practices naturally reflect this limitation. According to the latest statistics, 77.7 percent of contracepting Japanese use a condom; one in five, 21 percent, use the Ogino method/rhythm method/BBT method; 7.1 percent use withdrawal (coitus interruptus), 7 percent rely on surgical sterilization, and 3.7 percent on the intrauterine device. The rather high popularity of condom usage among the Japanese people is due to the strong policy of the Imperial Army Administration throughout the militarist period, when it was consistently used to prevent various venereal diseases.

Margaret Sanger (1883-1966), the American nurse who eventually organized the International Federation of Birth Control, visited Japan early in the Showa Era, the late 1920s, to promote the birth control movement in Japan. At the time, the national administration disliked this idea because of its own policy of promoting childbirth for national security reasons. Thus, the government publicly opposed the birth control movement. Nevertheless, because the military widely promoted use of the condom for prevention of venereal diseases, it eventually was firmly accepted by the common people in Japan as an effective method of birth control. Later, in the post-World War II years, this positive attitude of the Japanese people toward the condom functioned effectively in promoting the family planning movement.

Condoms are often sold to housewives by door-to-door "skin ladies." In 1990, moralists were disturbed when, after a marked increase in teen abortions, a condom company targeted the teenage market with condom packets bearing pictures of two cute little pigs or other cartoon animals and names like "Bubu Friend" (Bornoff 1991, 337).

The greatest obstacle in Japan to contraception is the national control of the contraceptive pill (OCP). In the 1970s, the promoters of feminism were openly against induced abortion and thus started a movement to make the OCP available. However, when they recognized that high-dosage OCPs had side effects, they changed their position and strongly opposed its free use. As is widely known now, the majority of current low-dosage OCPs pose little danger. Consequently, some of the current feminist promoters in Japan are not against expansion of choices by making low-dosage OCPs widely available. Nevertheless, the great majority of Japanese feminists still maintain their skepticism about the use of OCPs.

[B. Unwed Teenage Pregnancy

[Japan has consistently maintained one of the world's lowest incidence of out-of-wedlock births, well below 5 percent (Lewin 1995). A 1995 study by the Population Council, an international nonprofit New York-based group, reported that only 1.1 percent of Japanese births are to unwed mothers, a figure that has been virtually unchanged for twenty-five years. In the United States, this figure is 30.1 percent and rising rapidly (Kristof, 1996a). (Editor)]

C. Abortion

As has been mentioned earlier, the national policy of Japan after the Meiji Era, when Japan's modern national structure emerged, was to strengthen the nation. Thus children were considered to be the treasure of the nation, and abortion was naturally deemed illegal.

With the rebounding of the post-World War II social order, the Eugenic Protection Law was implemented in 1948, and induced abortion became a fully legal and allowed method of birth control in Japan. The law set out certain premises to be satisfied for abortion to be permitted, but many accepted it quite readily. Thus induced abortion became the most popular method of family planning in Japan in the mid-1950s, with 1.2 million abortions a year, an extremely high rate of 50.2 per 1,000 women annually. Later, the rate and the number of the induced abortions declined rapidly, dropping from 1.1 million cases in 1960, to 730,000 cases in 1970, and 457,000 cases in 1990. By 1990, the abortion rate was 14.9 per 1,000 women a year, less than a third of the rate of forty years ago. This significant and important change came about because of the special effort of advocates of a sound family planning movement and the increased use of condoms. It should be noted that this reduction in abortion and the popularization of family planning were achieved despite the unavailability of the oral contraceptive pill and a quite low IUD usage rate.

Even though the current rate of induced abortion is becoming acceptably low, there are still disturbing elements in the statistics, mainly a gradual increase of abortion among teenage youths. In the 1970s, the total number of abortions for teenage pregnancy was approximately 13,000. This number increased to 14,300 in 1970, 19,000 in 1980, and 29,700 in 1990. The rates of abortion among women under 20 years of age increased as follows: 3.2 per 1,000 in 1960 and 1970, 4.7 per 1,000 in 1980, and 6.6 per 1,000 in 1990. Keeping in mind that the sexual activity of young people in this nation is increasing, it is apparent that more efficient education of the youth for pregnancy prevention is strongly needed. For one thing, sex education within the public education system is far from being well developed in this country. The traditional value systems about sex and sexuality, such as the theory of purity education that prohibits and condemns premarital sexual activities as a crime, for example, creates burdens for the young people, even though two thirds of them accept premarital relations. Such beliefs often affect the sexual behavior of the young and interfere with their acquisition of knowledge and skills about pregnancy prevention.

[Japan has no debate over the morality of abortion, and no politicians taking political stands for or against abortion In fact, virtually everyone believes that abortion is each woman's own private business. Despite this wide acceptance of abortion, there is an ambivalence about abortion among many Japanese women and men that reflects the dualism one finds throughout Japanese sexual attitudes. At Buddhist temples around the country, one finds galleries of hundreds, even thousands of tiny memorial statues dedicated to aborted fetuses, miscarried and stillborn babies, and those who died as infants. These *mizuko jizo* are dressed and visited regularly, sometimes monthly, by Japanese women who have had an abortion or lost a baby, and feel a need to atone for their loss. Japanese women, and sometimes men, visit their *mizuko jizo* to express their grief, fears, confusions, and hopes of forgiveness for ending a human life so early, however rational and necessary that decision may have been.

[The concept of the *mizuko jizo* did not develop until after World War II and has since been linked more and more with abortion rather than miscarriages, stillbirths, or infant deaths. Even some gynecologists who perform abortions regularly visit the temples to purify themselves in a special Buddhist ritual. In former times, fetuses and even newborns were not believed to be fully human or have a spirit or soul until the newborn was ritually accepted into its family and linked with its ancestors, so abortion and even infanticide was accepted matter of factly. The recent tradition of the *mizuko jizo* appears to satisfy many of the emotions and feeling traditional suppressed in the acceptance of abortion (WuDunn 1996). (Editor)]

D. Population Control

From ancient times, population control, particularly in each village community, has been maintained publicly perhaps as part of the wisdom of the public welfare. In premodern days, the actual method often involved certain techniques related to primitive religions and/or incantations "turning childbirth changing into stillbirth." What in Western culture is termed infanticide was not necessarily considered illegal or unreasonable according to the faith and/or ethics of that era. According to authentic ancient belief and practice, the baby belongs to God until the very moment of its first cry. Therefore, suffocating the newborn before it cried, before it was "really born," and returning the incipient life to God was not considered wrong. Western culture would consider this culpable infanticide, but such was not the case in ancient Japanese beliefs; see the discussion of abortion and *mizuko jizo* in the preceding paragraph. [Similarly, in many regions of China, a newborn infant is not considered "fully born" and human until the whole family gathers three days after the infant's birth to celebrate its "social birth" and official recognition by the family's patriarch and, through him, by the whole family and their ancestors. (Editor)]

By 1995 the Japanese government had become so concerned about its plunging birthrate—1.53 per woman and declining—that the Institute of Population Problems, a part of Tokyo's Health and Welfare Ministry, sent out questionnaires to 13,000 single Japanese citizens asking them what they thought about marriage, families, and children. In view of the plunging birthrate and a heating up of the war of the sexes, Japan is facing a demographic time bomb. As the population ages and the birthrate shrinks, the tax burden on the Japanese work force will rise. Economists also suggest that Japan's famously high rate of savings will increasingly have to support its retired population, and not factories and other productive investments (Itoi and Powell 1992).

[With its birthrate plunging to 1.4 in 1996—Tokyo's birthrate was 1.1—Government projections suggested that within a hundred years, by 2100, Japan's population will tumble to 55 million, from 125 million today. That would be the same population Japan had in 1920. At 55 million, Japan would have a population density five times that of the United States today, but its position as a global power would certainly be reduced, when in 2050 Japan's population drops to just one quarter of America's projected population. By the year 3000, it could drop to 45,000, according to a weekly magazine projection. To counteract this trend, many Japanese cities are paying women residents a bonus, up to $5,000, when they have a fourth baby. Among the other incentives being considered are: cash upon marriage, cut-rate land for child-bearing couples, importing Philippine women of marriageable age, and cash grants to parents when their children turn 3, 5, and 7, which are all auspicious birthdays in Japan. Because of the discouraging cost of childrearing, some have recommended an annual financial bonus. In 1995, when Prime Minister Hashimoto was Finance Minister, he suggested a novel way of encouraging fertility: discourage women from going to college.

[In 1996, the average Japanese woman marries at 27. Seventeen percent of women in their early 30s are still unmarried. One of the reasons cited by women who chose not to marry was a common negative view of the Japanese male as a desirable mate (Kristoff 1996c). (Editor)]

10. Sexually Transmitted Diseases

Japan's Venereal Disease Prevention Law has remained unchanged since it went into effect in 1958. However, venereal diseases (VDs) common at the time this law was established, along with genital herpes, chlamydia, trichomoniasis, and HIV/AIDS, have come to be called sexually transmitted diseases (STDs) in Japan, as well.

Of these STDs, HIV/AIDS excluded, typical VDs of the past, such as syphilis and gonorrhea, have followed a steady decline year after year. The number of gonorrhea cases, for example, reported to the Ministry of Health and Welfare, in line with the Venereal Disease Prevention Law, declined from its peak of 178,000 cases in 1950 to 4,000 in 1964. Slight peaks in the number of cases reported were seen thereafter, with 12,000 in 1967 and 13,500 in 1984, but between 1970 and 1980, the number hovered between 5,000 and 7,000 cases. As concern for HIV/AIDS began to intensify in Japan in the 1990s, the number of gonorrhea cases showed a steady decline from 3,465 cases in 1992 to 1,724 cases in 1993 and 1,448 cases in 1994. As for the number of syphilis cases reported to the Ministry, a steady decrease can be seen from 6,138 cases in 1970 to 3,635 in 1975, 2,081 in 1980, 1,904 in 1985, 1,877 in 1990, and only 804 cases in 1993.

On the other hand, the actual number of herpes, chlamydia, and trichomoniasis cases is unclear since reporting of these diseases is not required. However, the Ministry of Health and Welfare began collecting data in the late 1980s from selected hospitals, with reports gathered from about 600 hospitals throughout Japan. This data suggests the following trends: trichomoniasis and condyloma acuminatum have shown a decrease, albeit slight, but the same cannot necessarily be said for chlamydia and herpes. Reports indicate that the number of infections among people in their teens or 20s has become particularly striking. Such reports cannot be said to be unrelated to the increase in sexual activity among Japan's youth. Since sexual activity among these youths is expected to become even more prevalent in the future, it is obviously desirable that we tackle countermeasures for these STDs in earnest.

11. HIV/AIDS

Japan has not been quick to respond to the HIV/AIDS problem in its own country. Patients showing signs of Kaposi's sarcoma and *pneumocystis carinii pneumonia* for which no cause could be found began to appear in America in 1981. The following year, the United States Centers for Disease Control and Prevention (CDC) began calling the syndrome AIDS. In 1983, it became known to the world that a virus, named HIV, was the cause.

At last, Japan's Ministry of Health and Welfare was moved to action, forming an AIDS research task force, which began surveillance for occurrences of AIDS in Japan. The first AIDS patient that the surveillance committee found was a homosexual returning briefly from America in March 1985. In May of the same year, they announced that AIDS patients contracting the disease through blood transfusions had been confirmed. In 1996, the country became embroiled in an extremely serious debate, in which the government or several committee members of the AIDS research task force and pharmaceutical companies were suspected of a secret pact to cover up the outbreak of "the real first" AIDS patients who had contracted the disease through unheated blood products. This problem was resolved in July of 1996 when the government and the pharmaceutical companies apologized to these victims and paid them an out-of-court settlement. However, not everyone feels that the agreement reached is a complete solution to the problem.

Turning to the situation of HIV/AIDS in Japan, current as of the end of May 1996, 3,642 people had been infected with HIV (including those with AIDS symptoms), of which 1,806 contracted the disease through unheated blood products. Although these numbers are extremely low compared to those of other countries, one cannot discount that the HIV/AIDS problem in Japan is a large one. For example, only 13,703 people underwent examinations for HIV in 1995, just one third of the 37,774 tested in 1992, when the number of people taking the examination reached its peak. In Japan, the number of people taking the test has declined over the past three years, from which one could assume Japanese feel the danger of contracting HIV/AIDS is becoming more and more remote.

For those unlucky enough to contract AIDS in Japan, there are 203 AIDS-authorized hospitals throughout the country where one can receive treatment. However, the names of nearly half of these hospitals are currently not being made public. Furthermore, some hospitals, even some of the AIDS-authorized hospitals, refuse treatment to AIDS patients, as reported by the Osaka Plaintiffs in AIDS Litigation Organization.

Of course, not everything about the HIV/AIDS problem in Japan is negative. For instance, until recently, major newspapers and other companies serving the public, such as NHK Television, had not directly taken up sexual problems. However, with the current situation, including the HIV/AIDS problem, even the most strait-laced newspapers and television stations have begun to use such words as condom, homosexuality, and anal sex. Such a trend has engendered the makings of informative reports on human sexuality. This issue is not felt in the media alone; it is also having a great impact on Japan's educational system. HIV/AIDS is clearly introduced in junior high school textbooks on health as an infectious disease. Thus, all children in Japan are now learning about HIV/AIDS.

Furthermore, teachers of social studies, home economics, and home room classes are actively educating students about HIV/AIDS in order to dispel any prejudices and discriminations the students may have. Naturally, this education is not only aimed at HIV/AIDS discrimination, but is related to sexual discrimination, as well. Although sex education in Japan is not sufficient in its current state, this education aimed at HIV/AIDS and discrimination may be the breakthrough Japan needs, and perhaps a golden opportunity to firmly establish sex education in the schools. This can certainly be viewed as a positive influence.

[The incidence of AIDS in Japan is still very low, although some suggest that the official figures underplay the actual incidence and danger. Only 15 deaths from AIDS were reported in 1986 for a population of 120,000,000. By mid-1988, the death toll had risen to 46 with an additional 34 confirmed in hospitals, and 1,038 persons who tested seropositive.

[As of August 1995, the reported number of AIDS-related deaths was 626. The cumulative number of reported cases of HIV infection was 3,423 among Japanese persons and 881 among non-Japanese (see Table 10). Among this number were 1,803 hemophiliac patients who contracted HIV as a consequence of the use of contaminated blood products in their daily treatment.

[The initial response of the Japanese gay community to the AIDS epidemic in the early 1980s was misguided. Because the number of Japanese gay men infected with HIV had been comparatively low, many Japanese gay

Table 10

Reported Accumulative Cases of Persons with HIV and Persons with AIDS

Source of Infection	Male		Female		Totals	
	Japanese	Non-Japanese	Japanese	Non-Japanese	Japanese	Non-Japanese
Heterosexual Contact	334	82	477	365	811	447
Homosexual Contact	328	55	0	0	328	55
IV Drug Use	10	8	0	0	10	0
Mother to child	2	1	6	3	8	4
Contaminated blood	1,782	—	21	—	1,803	—
Other	18	6	18	1	36	7
Unknown etiology	132	76	295	285	427	361
Totals	2,606	227	817	654	3,423	881

Source: Ministry of Public Welfare, as of August 31, 1995.

men, like the rest of the Japanese people, found it easier to view AIDS as an exclusively foreign phenomenon. Discrimination against foreign, especially Western, gay men by Japanese gay men was widespread. One consequence of the fear of AIDS is that homosexuals visiting Japan report that many former gay paradises, particularly the no-holds-barred male sauna, are now closed to non-Japanese. (Kaji)]

12. Sexual Dysfunctions, Counseling, and Therapies

Unfortunately, no compiled information is currently available on sexual dysfunctions in Japan. However, by drawing inferences from many researchers on the subject, certain facts come to light. The most common dysfunction, accounting for about half of all informally reported sexual disorders, is erectile dysfunction. Other common dysfunctions include sexual phobias, sexual avoidance, decreased sexual desire, dyspareunia (painful intercourse), female orgasmic disorder, vaginismus (painful vaginal spasms), homosexuality, and gender identity disorder.

One dysfunction that has become an issue of late is that of sexual inactivity among couples. Dr. Teruo Abe, a psychiatrist who studied under the American Helen Singer Kaplan, defines the term sexually inactive couples as "couples who do not engage in consensual sexual intercourse or sexual contact for a period of one month or longer, despite the lack of special circumstances, and who can be expected to remain sexually inactive for a long period after that." Abe reports that the number of such sexually inactive couples during the period from 1991 to 1994 increased by 2 to 4 times the number between 1985 and 1990. Yet, over a ten-year period, only 303 patients with this dysfunction came to seek Abe's assistance. Assuming that there are about 50 institutions in Japan that treat this sexual disorder, estimating generously, then only about 12,000 to 15,000 people have visited doctors for this sexual disorder over the past ten years. While there are probably many opinions on whether this number is large or not, the number reflects the current state of the disorder in Japan.

There are no types of sexual dysfunctions peculiar to the Japanese. The most common dysfunctions are treated by such specialists as gynecologists, urologists, and psychiatrists, or clinical therapists and counselors. Unfortunately, these fields of medicine remain too isolated from one another in Japan. It would be desirable, therefore, for the medical institutes themselves to gain an understanding of all aspects of human sexuality.

In 1976, the Japanese Red Cross Medical Center was the first public medical institution in Japan to establish a sexual counseling center. Although before that time, sexual treatment was carried out in the gynecology, urology, and psychiatry departments of private and university hospitals, such treatment was mainly for functional disorders. It was very rare for these hospitals to provide treatment from the perspective of total human sexuality.

Japanese doctors, counselors, psychologists, and sociologists who first became aware of the importance of sexual counseling and treatment met and formed the Japanese Association for Sex Counselors and Therapists (JASCT) in July 1979. The Association welcomed Patricia Schiller, founder of the American Association of Sex Educators, Counselors, and Therapists (AASECT), as honorable chairman and adopted the ideology of her organization. The JASCT proceeded to take charge of sexual counseling and therapy in Japan and continues to do so today. JASCT's objective is to carry out surveys and research with the help of sex counselors and doctors who treat sexual disorders. They do not issue licenses in recognition of qualifications.

From what limited information is available, it certainly seems that Japan is very active in the treatment of sexual dysfunctions, but unfortunately the reality is that a lot more problems remain unsolved. Underlying those problems in Japan is the popular notion that sex is not something you talk about, and the belief that, except in cases of extreme pain, as long as you can tolerate the problem, it will heal in time and you will not have to bother others about it. Recently, however, an increasing number of people in their 40s or younger, who have been exposed to a more sexually open society in their youth, are moving away from this tendency and seeking sexual counseling and treatment

13. Research and Advanced Education

A. Research and Advanced Education

With the exception of such scientific subjects as reproduction and birth taught in the fields of biology or medicine, Japan's institutions of advanced education have only made sex a direct topic of research in the past two or three decades. Traditionally, sex has not been made a subject of learning in Japan's academic world. Thus, on the rare occasion that someone has pursued the study of human sexuality, that person has been seen as an outcast, and, at times, ostracized, as was the case with Senji Yamamoto, who taught in the Biology Department of Doshisha University and early in this century was Japan's first sexologist.

Although Japan became a democratic society in 1945 allowing for the freedom to study human sexuality, even in institutions of advanced education, a wall remained standing in the academic world inhibiting such freedom, and the wall was high and thick. No reason exists for the academic world to be separated from society. It has become gradually understood that sex education is necessary in higher education in order to address the various problems in Japanese society, such as sexual problems among youth, information on sex provided by the media, the issue of STDs and HIV/AIDS, and the phenomenon of more couples opting to rear fewer children.

Universities for training teachers and departments of education were the first to show an interest in teaching sex education at the university level. Regardless of its quality, sex education in Japan's elementary and junior high schools and institutes of advanced education is usually taken up in the health and science curricula. Therefore, it was natural for sex education to be first taught to those interested in teaching. Recently, an increasing number of departments of human science have been established in Japanese universities, wherein study of basic human sexuality has become abundant.

Still, sex education in universities and other institutions of advanced education cannot be said to be functioning sufficiently. Take, for example, the estimate that only about 5 percent of Japan's 1,150 universities and junior colleges provide lectures on human sexuality. One can assume that developing more programs on sex education in universities and other institutions of advanced education will become a major issue in Japan's educational system.

B. Sexological Organizations and Publications

Until mid-1996, the authors of this chapter, Yoshiro Hatano, PhD, served as Director, and Tsuguo Shimazaki as Secretary of the Japanese Association for Sex Education (J.A.S.E).

Japanese Association for Sex Education. Address: J.A.S.E., Miyata Building, 2F, 1-3 Kanda Jinbo-cho, Chiyoda-ku, Tokyo, 101 Japan. Telephone: +81-3-3291-7726; Fax: +81-3-3291-6238. J.A.S.E publishes, *Sex Education Today*, a monthly journal.

In mid-1996, Tsuguo Shimazaki established the Nikon Information Center for Sexology (NICS). Address: N.I.C.S., Hobunkan Building, 6F, 3-11-4 Kanda-Jinbo-cho, Chiyoda-ku, Tokyo 101 Japan. Telephone: +81-3-3288-5900; Fax: +81-3-3288-5387. N.I.C.S. publishes *Sexology Updater* (ten times a year).

Other Japanese sexological organizations and publications include:

Japanese Association of Sex Educators, Counselors, and Therapists (JASECT), JASE Clinic, 3F Shin-Aoyama Bldg (West), -1 Minami- Aoyama, 1-chome Minato-ku, Tokyo 107 Japan

The Japan Family Planning Association, Inc. (JFPA). Address: Hokenkai-kan Bekkann, 1-2, Ichigaya Sadohara-cho, Shinjuku-ku, Tokyo 162 Japan. Telephone: +81-3-3269-4041; Fax: +81-3-3267-2658. JFPA publishes the journal *Family Planning and Family Health* (monthly).

Japan Federation of Sexology (JFS). Address: c/o Nikon Information Center for Sexology (NICS), Hobunkan Building, 6F, 3-11-4, Kanda-Jinbo-cho, Chiyoda-ku, Tokyo 101 Japan. Telephone: +81-3-3288-5200; Fax: +81-3-3288-5387

Japan Institute for Research in Education, 4-3-6-702 Kozimachi Chiyodaku, Tokyo 7102 Japan. Phone: 03-5295-0856; Fax: 03-5295-0856

Japanese Organization for International Cooperation in Family Planning, Inc. (JOICFP), 1-1, Ichigaya Sadohara-cho, Shhijuku-ku, Tokyo 162 Japan. Phone: 81-3/3268-5875; Fax: 81-3/3235-7090

Japan Society of Adolescentology (JSA). Address: c/o Japan Family Planning Association, Hokenkaikan Bekkann, 1-2, Ichigaya Sadohara-cho, Shinjuku-ku, Tokyo 162 Japan. Telephone: +81-3-3269-4738. JSA publishes the journal *Adolescentology* (four times a year).

The Japanese Society for Impotence Research (JSIR). Address: c/o First Department of Urology, Toho University School of Medicine, 6-11-1, Omori-nishi, Ota-ku, Tokyo 143 Japan. Telephone: +81-3-3762-4151, extension 3605 or 3600. Fax: +81-3-3768-8817. JSIR publishes the *Journal of the Japanese Society for Impotence Research.*

Japanese Society of Sexual Science (JSSS). Address: c/o Hase Clinic, Shin-Aoyama Building, Nishikan 3F, 1-1-1, Minami-Aoyama Minota-ku, Tokyo 107 Japan. Telephone: +81-3-3475-1789. Fax: +81-3-3475-1789. JSSS publishes the journal *Japanese Journal of Sexology* (semiannually).

References and Suggested Readings

Asayama, Shinichi. 1979. "Sexuality of the Japanese Youth: Its Current Status and the Future Prospects." *Sex Education Today*, 36, 8-16 (in Japanese).

Benedict, Ruth. 1954. *The Chrysanthemum and the Sword—Patterns of Japanese Culture.* Charles E. Tuttle Co.

Bornoff, Nicholas. 1991. *Pink Samurai: Love, Marriage and Sex in Contemporary Japan.* New York: Pocket Books.

Earhart, H. Byron. 1984. *Religions of Japan.* New York: Harper and Row.

Hatano, Yoshiro. 1972. "L. A. Kirkendall: His Platform for Sex Education and Its Background." *Bulletin of Tokyo Gakugei University*, 24(5), 164-77 (in Japanese).

Hatano, Yoshiro. 1988. "Sexualerziehung von Kindern und Jugendlichen in Japan." In N. Eicher, et al., eds. *Praktische Sexual Medizin*, Verlag Medical Tribune. pp. 34-42. (in German)

Hatano, Yoshiro. 1991a. "Changes in the Sexual Activities of Japanese Youth." *Journal of Sex Education and Therapy*, 17(1), 1-14.

Hatano, Yoshiro. 1991b. "Education for Parenting Viewed from Education of Sexuality." In: Japanese Ministry of Education, ed., *National Women's Education Center.*

Hatano, Yoshiro. 1991c. "Child-Socialization and 'Parenting' Education." In: *International Seminar on Family Education Proceedings*, pp. 272-92.

Hatano, Yoshiro. 1993. "Sexual Activities of Japanese Youth. *Journal of Sex Education and Therapy*, 19(2), 131-44.

Hatano, Yoshiro, and R. Fujita. 1976. "Sexual Behavior of Selected College and Vocational School Students in Tokyo." *Bulletin of Tokyo Gakugei University*, 28(5), 262-72 (in Japanese).

Itoi, Kay, and Bill Powell. 1992 (August 10). "Take a Hike, Hiroshi." *Newsweek.* 38-39.

Japanese Association for Sex Education (J.A.S.E.), ed. 1975. *Sexual Behavior of Japanese Youth.* Tokyo: Shogakukan Press (in Japanese).

Japanese Association for Sex Education (J.A.S.E.), ed. 1983. *Sexual Behavior of Japanese Youth.* Tokyo: Shogakukan Press (in Japanese).

Japanese Association for Sex Education (J.A.S.E.), ed. 1988. *Sexual Behavior of Junior High School, Senior High School and University Students in Japan.* Tokyo: Shogakukan Press (in Japanese).

Japanese Association for Sex Education (J.A.S.E.), ed. 1994. *Sexual Behavior of Junior High School, Senior High School and University Students in Japan.* Tokyo: Shogakukan Press (in Japanese).

Kristof, Nicholas D. 1995 (November 5). "In Japan, Brutal Comics for Women." *The New York Times,* Section 4, pp. 1 and 6.

Kristof, Nicholas D. 1996a (February 11). "Who Needs Love? In Japan, Many Couples Don't." *The New York Times,* pp. 1 and 12.

Kristof, Nicholas D. 1996b (June 19). "Japan Is a Woman's World Once the Front Door Is Shut." *The New York Times,* pp. A1 and A8.

Kristof, Nicholas D. 1996c (October 6). "Baby May Make Three, but in Japan That's Not Enough." *The New York Times,* p. 3.

Lester, Robert C. 1987. *Buddhism.* New York: Harper and Row.

Lewin, Tamar. 1995 (May 30). "Family Decay Global, Study Says." *The New York Times.* p. A5.

More Report on Female Sexuality. 1983. Tokyo: Shueisha.

More Report on Male Sexuality. 1984. Tokyo: Shueisha.

National Survey of Sexology and College Education. 1995. *Sexual Science,* 4(1):27-68.

Shimazaki, T. 1994-95. Upon Completing the Fourth Youth Sexual Behavior Investigation. *Monthly Report Sex Education Today,* 1994, 12, 9-12, and 1995, 13, 1-3. Tokyo: The Japanese Association for Sex Education (in Japanese).

Tanikawa, Miki. 1996 (September 8). "Clubs Where, for a Price, Japanese Men Are Nice to Women," *The New York Times,* Styles Section, p. 49.

Wolferen, Karel Van. 1989. *The Enigma of Japanese Power.* New York: Macmillan.

WuDunn, S. 1996 (November 27). "Japan May Approve the Pill, but Women May Not." *The New York Times,* p. A1, A10.

WuDunn, S. 1996 (January 25). "At Japanese Temples, a Mourning Ritual for Abortions. *The New York Times,* p. A1 and A8.

Yanagihashi, Akitoshi. 1995. "Traditional Homosexuality in Japan." *OCCUR (Association for the Lesbian and Gay Movement).* A paper submitted to the 12th World Congress of Sexology, Yokohama, Japan.

Kenya
(*Jamhuri ya Kenya*)

Norbert Brockman, Ph.D.*

Contents

Demographics and a Historical Perspective

A. Demographics

Most African nations, being political artifacts of colonialism, are multiethnic and multilinguistic. Patterns of sexual behavior are therefore quite varied, the result being complexity rather than uniformity. Nowhere is this more clearly demonstrated than in Kenya, a nation slightly smaller than the state of Texas.

One in four Kenyans lives in modern urban areas, notably the capital Nairobi. which has become a melting pot for all Kenyan cultures, and Mombasa, a tourist mecca on the Indian Ocean. Kenya is the leading Black African tourist destination, with splendid coastal areas, highly developed

---

*Additional comments provided by Paul Mwangi Kariuki are given in brackets with his name in parentheses are the end of the comment.

wildlife-viewing opportunities, and an infrastructure that has been very safe, comfortable, and competently run.

[Nairobi, the capital and center of industrialization, has a population of more than one million. Mombasa, Nakuru, Eldoret, Kisumu, Nyeri, Embu, Meru, and Thika are other large cities with a diversity and employment opportunities that attract many people from the rural areas, creating the usual urban problems. Recent unrest with political tribal clashes have occurred primarily in the Rift Valley region from which the president hails. Kenya has, since independence, had only one political party. The advent of multiparty politics in 1992 was decried by the president as a Western idea that would divide the people along tribal lines and plunge the country into lawlessness and anarchy. At the same time, legislators from the Rift Valley started preaching and demanding publically a change from the "Majimboism" (federal) system. Many tribes have co-existed peacefully in the Rift Valley for many years. These legislators asked the indigenous people, the people who originally owned the land before it was sold to others, to drive out these other people. With strong backing from the government, this effort resulted in a deadly, indiscriminate massacre of defenseless citizens, loss of property, and increased poverty, since a good percentage of the country's corn and pyrethrum is grown in this area. The children lost out on educational opportunities when the schools were closed and no teachers were willing to work in these areas. Most of the people found refuge in church buildings, but in recent times the government has driven them out. Nevertheless, the current situation is calm, and the churches and opposition parties have kept up their significant work for peace, restoration and reconciliation. (Kariuki)]

Kenya's population at the end of 1995 was close to 29 million. The age distribution was 48 percent, age 14 or younger; 49 percent between ages 15 and 64; and 3 percent age 65 and older. Life expectancy at birth in 1995 was 51 for males and 54 for females. The 1995 birthrate was 42 per 1,000 population; the death rate 12 per 1,000, for an annual natural increase of 3 percent. Kenya had one physician per 7,410 persons and one hospital bed per 737 persons. Infant mortality rate in 1995 was 73 per 1,000 live births. Half of the population are literate, with 86 percent attending primary school. The 1995 per capita gross domestic product was $1,200.

Economic and social factors that impact upon sexual patterns, therefore, include traditional cultures (initiation, courtship, and marriage customs), colonial imports (Christian and Islamic values, and education), and contemporary Western influences (consumerism, and the media).

B. A Brief Historical Perspective

When the vast Bantu migration of the late medieval period—perhaps the largest human movement in history—turned south at Lake Victoria, it found small groups of well-entrenched Hamitic tribes and a few bushmen.

The Bantus also encountered large Nilotic tribes that had arrived from the north, and these racially diverse nations settled into an uneasy relationship around the Lake region. Their descendents number about twenty-five million in Kenya, which straddles the equator on the east coast of Africa. Arab colonies exported slaves and spices from the coast of today's Kenya from the 700s on. Britain took over the country in the nineteenth century. In 1959, the Mau Mau uprising swept the country. British colonialism brought half a million East Asians and about a quarter million Caucasians in the early 1930s, both settler families and short-term expatriates connected with commercial, missionary, and international organizations.

[The agenda of the Mau Mau organization was to gain independence from the British, win control of their land, and self-rule, and obtain the release of Jomo Kenyatta, then in British detention. Violence was widespread as the Mau Mau forces in the forests fighting the British were supported by a nationwide network involving the majority of Kenyas, both men and women. Defectors, traitors, and those who collaborated with the British were killed.

[For two decades, following Kenya's independence in 1963, the country was politically stable and prosperous, with a steady growth in its industry and agriculture, under Presidents Jomo Kenyatta (1963-78) and Daniel arap Moi (1978-), under a modified private-enterprise systems. In 1982, the military Air Force attempted to overthrow the government. Since then, government corruption, top-level scandals, the employment of unqualified people in upper-level positions, serious inflation, and the collapse of government services and systems have resulted in low morale throughout the work force and an unstable economy. Recent years have seen increased challenges to Moi's authoritarian rule, however, and only divisions among his opponents allowed Moi to triumph in the country's first multiparty elections in 1992. The lead-in to the elections included significant social turmoil and violence, often along tribal lines. The rigging of elections and a partisan electoral commission that set electoral boundaries favored Moi's victory. Representation in the Parliament gave the ruling party one seat for 19,000 votes while the opposition seats required 43,000 votes, giving the Moi party a three-to-one advantage. (Kariuki)]

1. Basic Sexological Premises

A. Character of Gender Roles

Social reinforcement maintains clear gender roles in all Kenyan societies. Western education has produced a small female professional class, but expansion of women into new spheres of activity occurs only in Western roles that were unknown in traditional society, Western medicine, education, and bureaucracy. The Kenyan government has given strong support to educated women, appointing government officials, diplomats, and leaders from among them.

B. Sociolegal Status of Males and Females

Among all Kenyans, there is strong belief in the existence of ancestral spirits. The ancestors assume functions of social control and must be placated when offended. There is a bond between the worlds of the living and the dead, and a mutual interdependence. It is important, therefore, to maintain a balance in populations between the two worlds by having children. The "living dead" need descendants to perform rites in their honor. Add to this the economic incentive of having large numbers of children in order to provide for old age, and the cultural resistance to population control becomes apparent. In the African family, children are received with delight and treasured. The firstborn is especially important in the family. The orphaned are taken in by their extended families. Institutional orphanages are almost unknown.

Infanticide was practiced in traditional culture, but is now illegal, and practiced rarely and surreptitiously. A baby may be killed if it is the result of an incestuous union or, in different ethnic groups, if an albino, triplets, or born feet first. The newborn of an uncircumcized Nandi girl is exposed to die if no one adopts it.

Life from childhood is organized around progress through age sets within a kinship system, each with its own preparation and responsibilities. These stages vary from tribe to tribe, but always include childhood, an initiation period leading to junior adulthood, marriage, family building, and the status of elder.

C. General Concepts of Sexuality and Love

Sexuality is always a part of the kinship system, controlled within it, and subject to its purposes. Love is recognized and accepted as part of personal relationships. One may choose a marriage partner because of personal attraction, even though arranged marriages continue. Nevertheless, love is not a high value in itself. In polygamous marriages, junior wives will often be chosen by the first wife to meet work needs.

A great deal of sexual freedom for both sexes is allowed within these social controls. Unmarried boys and girls slept communally in many Kenyan societies, and several provide youth huts. [In a number of tribes, the Kikuyus, for instance, young men and women are allowed to dance, play, and even sleep together at certain organized times (*guiko*, among the Kikuyus), but no sexual activity is allowed although it may occur in these situations. Generally, premarital pregnancy disgraces a girl. Love, as an emotionally expressed feeling, was never valued in the tribal tradition. Today, it is treated as a Western idea and viewed with a lot of suspicion especially by the older people. However, love as an act of the will has always existed. (Kariuki)]

2. Religious and Ethnic Factors Affecting Sexuality

A. Source and Character of Religious Values

For Africans, religion is a natural, present, and pervading influence, deeply interwoven with culture. Everyday life is nowhere secularized as in the West, and religion as a personal and private activity is quite foreign to African sensibility. This is indicated by the presence of a mere 0.1 percent atheists and nonreligious persons in the country (see Table 1). The importance of religion for sexuality, therefore, is far beyond the issues of moral behavior so dominant in Western thinking.

Table 1

Estimated Religious Distribution in Kenya

Religion	Percentage of Population
Roman Catholics	29
Protestants and Anglicans	27.4
African independent churches	21
Orthodox	2.6
Christian Total	80
Traditional animists	12
Moslems	6
East Asian religions	2

Both Catholic and Protestant churches are very conservative theologically and morally, the former because of dependence upon expatriate (Irish/Italian) missionaries, and the latter due to a mass evangelical movement that has dominated Protestantism for several generations. Kenya is a center for the independent church movement, with over five hundred groups ranging from African denominations to prophetic cults. Many allow polygamy and permit women prophetic figures, but are intolerant of abortion, contraception, sex education, and social equality for women. President Daniel arap Moi is a member of an evangelical Kenyan denomination, the African Inland Church.

Many Kenyan Moslems are East Asian disciples of the Aga Khan. African Moslems, primarily Swahilis on the coast, follow a moderate, relaxed form of Islam, and their numbers are declining.

B. Source and Character of Ethnic Values

The ethnic distribution in Kenya in 1995 was: Kikuyu 21 percent, Luhya 14 percent, Luo 13 percent, Kalenjin 12 percent, Kamba 11 percent, and the remainder divided among Europeans, Asians, and Arabs.

There are essentially two layers of cultural influences in every Kenyan. The first is the traditional tribal value system, and the second consists of Western influences. Sexual values, traditions, and behavior arise from the matrix of these influences, which vary among individuals. One family may speak a tribal mother tongue, continue traditional practices of initiation, bride wealth, and taboos, while another may speak Swahili or English predominantly, take many values from Christianity and the media, and feel free of tribal tradition. Several factors influence these differences: degree of urbanization, tribal intermarriage, religion, and level of education.

Moral strictures within Kenyan societies tend to be based on shame rather than on guilt. Disapproved sexual behaviors cast shame upon one's age group, clan, or tribe, rather than produce feelings of personal unworthiness through guilt. There is a strong social element to all ethical norms, including sexual norms. Sexual behavior in Kenyan societies is significant only in terms of the social realities of childbearing and family alliances. Consequently, where ethnic influence breaks down, as when a Kenyan moves to an urban area outside the tribal milieu, the inhibition of shame may be removed, resulting in behavior that by Western standards seems promiscuous and irresponsible.

There are contrasts in sexual norms among different ethnic groups. In some groups such as the Luo, women who give birth before marriage are disgraced, while in other groups this is seen as a valuable sign of fertility. Virginity in women is highly prized in some groups such as the Somali, Maragoli, and Luo, and regarded as unimportant in others, among the Kisii, Kikuyu, and Nandi. Among the Kikuyu, an infertile or impotent husband may provide another sex partner for his wife. Among the Nandi, a married woman can continue to have sex with her former lover or other members of her husband's age set. In contrast, the Maragoli regard extramarital sex as adultery. Therefore, the sexual culture shock in urban areas comes not only from contact with Western ideas and media, but also from interaction with diverse traditional value systems.

3. Sexual Knowledge and Education

A. Government Policies and Programs for Sex Education

Sex education is treated with great ambivalence in Kenya. School curricula are nationalized, and there is no curriculum for sex education. Nevertheless, the idea is endorsed, and units of Family Life Education (FLE) are integrated into various curricula. These have been designed by nongovernmental organizations (NGOs), particularly the National Christian Council of Kenya, the Kenya Family Planning Association, the YMCA, the Kenya Catholic Secretariat, and the National Women's Federation (Maendaleo wa Wanawake). All of these organizations also provide various training programs for sex education teachers.

When tested in 1991 on six topics—menstruation, wet dreams, pregnancy, contraception, STDs, and AIDS—80 percent of the adolescents had received instruction on at least one topic between the ages of 12 and 15. Further testing on specific issues, however, showed that only 23 to 37 percent had practical knowledge on specific topics.

The government attempted to use television for sex education in the late 1980s, developing a popular soap opera series in Swahili. After several episodes, President Moi ordered the program stopped, endorsing instead traditional sex education by tribal elders. The fact that today, fewer youths live in rural areas or undergo traditional initiation, was never broached. Media such as television and comic books are used well in AIDS education, but this is the only topic systematically dealt with.

[The issue of sex education has become a major issue in Kenya. As mentioned, the government has made some efforts to introduce it in the schools, but this has met with considerable resistance from religious groups, particularly the Muslims and the Catholic Church. The Boy Scout movement, with the help of pathfinder funds, published a book on family life education for their members. This book discussed topical issues on sex education, human anatomy, and abortion. Subsequently, the government used this book as the basis for a sex education syllabus to be taught in the schools. Following much resistance and criticism from the religious groups and parents, the President ordered the book's withdrawal from all bookshops and stores in 1985.

[The issue of AIDS, which is alarming, has complicated the issue of sex education for several reasons. For one thing, the people do not take the AIDS threat seriously. Neither the government nor the churches consider AIDS a priority. The problem is with the level of information given, coupled with and complicated by the prevention methods advocated. The people in the churches who could be most effective in communicating the needed information believe the information about condom use as a way to reduce the spread of AIDS is scientifically false and that the people are not being told the truth. They are also aware of the economic factors in the sale of condoms: the manufacturers are out to make money with ineffective condoms while the users continue to die as AIDS spreads. There is a widespread belief that the whole issue is linked with a eugenics movement whose aim is to produce a "thoroughbred" race through genetic engineering. Africans are aware that some have classified them as a lower race. This belief in a eugenics-oriented link is supported by the requirement of the World Bank and the International Monetary Fund that 20 percent of every loaned dollar go to the provision of contraceptives and abortifacients. Government hospitals and clinics like the Maria Stopes clinics are flooded with these drugs, while there are absolutely no other drugs available to treat other ailments. The government preaches ensuring good health for everyone as a national goal. But when the only drugs the people find available are for AIDS and pregnancy prevention, they question the credibility of the government and its policies, and lose faith in anything it tries to advance.

[As a result, the main religious groups organize protest marches through the major towns, where thousands of people young and old attend. These marches are climaxed with the burning of condoms and sex education books. These people call for telling the truth about the effectiveness of condoms. They advocate that sex education be left to parents, and that parents be involved in any decision that would affect their children. They also advocate AIDS prevention through abstinence and chastity. For married couples, they call for "zero grazing," strict marital faithfulness. (Kariuki)]

B. Informal Sources of Sexual Knowledge

Traditionally, sex education was undertaken as part of the initiation process. It began, however, much earlier in the extended family and social structures of particular ethnic groups.

Sex instruction does not often come from parents. In the presence of their children, they are expected to avoid any words, acts, or gestures of a sexual nature. The rules of shame might allow openness about sexual matters with a grandparent, however, and among the Kisii a grandmother could be the confidant of her grandchildren on their sexual experiences.

A small child will remain with its mother until about age 7. At this point, in some tribes, boys move in with their father or older boys. In other groups (Maragoli and Luo) both boys and girls go into separate huts with older children or into the homes of an elderly couple. These village dormitories provide socialization, sex education, and opportunities for sexual experimentation. The last is conducted in secret, although girls often "fail to notice" a youth visiting in the girls' dormitory. Two lovers might also go into the bush. A father and older sons might build a private hut for a son who reached puberty, especially since initiation ceremonies might be held only every few years. Under these circumstances, young men have free rein to engage in sexual activities. In slang, these huts are sometimes referred to as "the office," and "going to the office" means having a girl over for sex.

These patterns of sex education have continued into present-day society, where studies show that parents are a negligible source of information, while 31 percent of girls and 38 percent of boys indicate teachers as the most important source. This does not reflect organized sex education in the schools, but the influence of proctors and teachers in boarding-school settings.

4. Autoerotic Behaviors and Patterns

In Kenyan tradition, self-pleasuring is unacceptable among girls, and was part of the motive for clitoridectomy. For uninitiated (uncircumcized) boys, however, self-pleasuring is considered a proper preparation for a mature sex life. Boys in the same age group may engage in self-pleasuring together without shame, but all such activities are to be given up with initiation.

Adult male self-pleasuring is regarded as immature and childish after initiation, even for the unmarried. It is therefore surrounded with taboos. A man who has been circumcized is regarded as unready to assume adult responsibilities if he engages in self-pleasuring.

5. Interpersonal Heterosexual Behaviors

A. Children

Living in the unmarried men's hut, a boy has ample opportunity to listen to sexual conversations and observe older boys with their sweethearts. The degree to which an older boy may "play sex," as youth slang puts it, depends upon social custom. An uncircumcized Nandi boy rarely has an opportunity for intercourse, due to the strict controls of the warrior age set. Maragoli girls often participate in sex play with boys, although intercourse does not take place until after puberty. The Kisii tolerate extensive sex play among smaller children, although shame taboos require that after about age 7, such activities are not to be seen by parents.

Western influences have rendered many of these customs invalid. Many children are sent to boarding schools, where socialization is controlled by older children with little supervision. Nocturnal visits that are manageable in a traditional setting often turn into rape under these circumstances. Older youths who are not part of a tribal social system often feel little responsibility for younger children, and certainly not for female students who include no sisters or members of tabooed clan groups.

The urban family must dispense with age-set socialization entirely and keep their children in the home. Grandparents are seldom available for counseling or instruction. Other children and youths come from differing cultures, so that peer influences rarely reinforce traditional values.

B. Adolescents

The sexual world of the Kenyan adolescent is extremely complex, combining traditional initiation rites, Western values and ideas, and a changing set of social expectations.

In traditional society, adolescents were initiated in a clearly defined period and by a series of events. In all cultures, these included instruction in male/female roles within the tribe, marriage customs, morality, and acceptable sexual behavior. Bantu cultures included circumcision for men, and usually for women. The Luo are the largest group not practicing circumcision. Among the Maasai and Samburu, after initiation, the new warrior could take a mistress from among the unmarried girls.

Initiation was done by age sets that were given distinctive names and provided a strong sense of bonding. While there were differences among ethnic groups, the pattern was essentially the same. Age sets went through various stages of adulthood together and shared a common responsibility for one another. In a few cases (Nandi and Maasai), it was not regarded as adultery if a women slept with an age mate of her husband. Elsewhere, the opposite is the case—adultery within the husband's age set would be incestuous, and there are taboos against the marriage of a son or daughter to one of another age-set member. However different cultures interpreted it, the age-set bond defines sexual and marital relations.

Male circumcision is an important sign of adulthood, responsibility, and bravery. When performed as a part of an initiation ritual, the boys are expected to receive the surgery without flinching, lest they disgrace their families. It is preceded by a cold dip in a river to deaden the senses. Circumcision is such a public symbol, it is not unusual to hear a man say "I have been to the river," to mean "I know what I am talking about." Because of the social significance, youths who do not undergo initiation, either because the family lives away from the tribal area or they are in school, will arrange for private circumcision from a doctor or clinician. After his teens, an uncircumcized male is the butt of ridicule, and at considerable disadvantage in finding sex partners. A youth who cries out during the surgery is disgraced for life, and will be able to find a wife only among the handicapped, elderly, or those with illegitimate children.

Female circumcision will be discussed under Section 8D, Unconventional Sexual Behaviors.

Although custom severely restricts adolescent intercourse, in reality a certain amount of sexual activity takes place. This is most marked in mixed situations (e.g., in cities and boarding schools), but it is also the case in traditional settings. In several cultures, elaborate sex play is institutionalized. Neither penetration nor touching of the genitals is allowed to either partner. Among the Kikuyu, the girl wears a leather apron during this activity, which is conducted in a special hut set aside to provide privacy to young people. Breast fondling is the main stimulant, as well as frottage. The Luo use a method of interfemoral intercourse. Where intercourse is tolerated, the main technique of avoiding pregnancy seems to have been withdrawal.

Detribalized youths experience considerable social pressure to become sexually active, without balancing social support that might make sexual abstinance a viable option.

Two 1987 studies reported age at first sexual intercourse to be 14 in the cities, and 13.7 for boys and 14.8 for girls in the rural areas. By age 20, 42 percent of rural females and 76 percent of rural males had had intercourse. Almost all of these involved multiple partners. Forty-one percent of rural girls have had intercourse with more than one partner, 17 percent with three or more. The figures for boys are 72 percent and 51 percent respectively. A 1991 cross-cultural study of in-school adolescents reported 48 percent of primary school males, 69 percent of secondary, and 77 percent of vocational to be sexually experienced. The comparable figures for young women are 17, 27, and 67 percent. No studies record preferred sex partners, but the widespread prevalence of prostitution is not to be discounted for the disparity between males and females in comparable settings.

Correlates of sexual activity among adolescents are peer influence (males with sexually active peers are seven times more likely to be active themselves); weak religious commitment; risk-taking behaviors (smoking, disco attendance, and alcohol use); dysfunctional family situations (for females); attending boarding school (for males); and attending a rural school.

Only 5 percent of the general adolescent population use any form of contraception. In striking contrast, the figure for students is slightly less than 15 percent who use contraception regularly, indicating that birth-control use is strongly influenced by educational status. It must be remembered that somewhere around 90 percent (statistics are imprecise) of youths terminate schooling after Standard Eight, at about age 14 to 15. Correlates of contraceptive use among school girls are high academic achievement and upper socioeconomic status—each of these triples the likelihood of contraceptive use. There is only one correlate for boys, a sexual relationship with a girl supportive of contraception, which doubles the likelihood of contraception.

C. Adults

Premarital Courtship, Dating, and Relationships

Traditionally, premarital sex activity was circumscribed and controlled. A youth who impregnated a girl was liable for brideprice to her father, and might be punished in addition. While a few nomadic peoples like the Maasai institutionalized mistress relationships for unmarried warriors, this was the exception. Those practicing female circumcision usually demanded proof of virginity at marriage.

Courtship is dominated by brideprice. All marriages involve brideprice or bride wealth, regardless of whether they are traditional or among the educated elites. The origins of this payment to the father's family is recompense for the lost economic services of the daughter. Brideprice was paid originally in cattle and goats, but today usually involves money. Negotiations are often protracted, and various members of the extended family receive gifts over a period of time which corresponds to the Western engagement period. One Kenyan manufacturer uses a television ad showing the suitability of its blankets for brideprice gifts. A woman with education or skills is highly prized, while someone of low status—a housemaid, single mother, or orphan—might bring only a small bride wealth, and be viewed as appropriate only as a second or third wife.

[The payment of the brideprice has several functions beyond compensating the family of the bride for their investment and loss of the daughter's economic services. Part of the ceremony is to announce to all the intention of the couple to marry. After the traditional goats and bananas are offered, the clan members of the man and woman meet to negotiate issues like who the daughter is, what her skills are, her level of education, and the general duties she will undertake in her new home. The purpose here is to give the visitors, the man's relatives, a general overview of the woman's family, their status, and prosperous attitude as reflected in the daughter. This gives them a better reason to offer something substantial to compensate for the work done by the family on their daughter.

[The brideprice agreed to is always on the high side. This insures that the ties between the two families will never end. A Kikuyu aphorism states that the brideprice never ends. This underlines the purpose of the brideprice in maintaining the clan/family bond. Other ceremonies, involving a goat slaughter, sharing of the meat, and a traditional liquor between the clans, reinforce this bonding. While the brideprice ceremonies differ from one tribe to another, the principle and purpose remain the same. Among the social elite, the primary function may be the economic benefit, but for most Kenyans this is secondary. (Kariuki)]

If a marriage is not successful, the bride wealth is to be returned. Kenyan men marry at a later age than women, in part because of the burden of bride wealth. In Kenya, however, difficulties in acquiring bride wealth do not prevent marriage, as it has in neighboring Uganda, and the Kenyan government continues to support the practice. Brideprice is a further indication that marriage is primarily seen as the alliance of families rather than an interpersonal commitment based on love. Marriage is cemented by the bride wealth, giving a large number of the bride's family a material stake in the perseverance of the marriage, a form of marital insurance.

Sexual Behavior and Relationships of Single Adults

This area of life has undergone great change. In traditional society, male youths became warriors after initiation, protecting the tribe and its herds. With this function lost, unmarried youths have no clear position in the kinship system. Those fortunate enough to pass rigorous examinations usually attend boarding schools, separated from the influence of their extended families. This has had disastrous results for identity, producing alarming rates of promiscuity, premarital pregnancy, and AIDS. Substantial numbers of women in the university and professional schools drop out because of pregnancy, a tremendous economic loss for the country and a major force holding back the advancement of women. A 1988 government study estimated that 400 to 500 women drop out of normal schools each year due to pregnancy. Pregnancy screening is now a condition for admission to teachers' colleges, and random screening is conducted among students after admission.

Working-class youths suffer similar dislocation. About 90 percent of young people terminate schooling by the end of Standard Eight, around age 14. [While the 90 percent figure just cited seems high to me, it is clear that the average age of terminating education varies from region to region. Today, the higher percentage of young people end their education by the end of form four (high school) and fewer by the end of Standard Eight (grade or elementary school). In the central region where I worked as education secretary for seven years, the majority ended their education with the completion of high school. (Karuki)]

Where traditional initiation has lapsed, circumcision of boys takes place in a clinic or by bribing a clinic worker to perform the surgery at home. Girls' circumcision is becoming less common. The sexual information imparted at initiation is not given, and sex education is dominated by peers. Youths have evolved an argot of Kiswahili known as "Sheng," a street language seldom understood by adults. Kiswahili has a very restricted, even prudish, sexual vocabulary, but Sheng is rich in sexual slang.

Huge populations live in massive slum areas surrounding Nairobi and a few other major towns, and these have become breeding grounds for prostitution, venereal disease, and sexual abuse. Radically altered social conditions have shattered traditional mores in the cities, while providing no alternative social controls.

Marriage and Family

Most Kenyan societies are patrilinear, meaning that descent is reckoned in the father's line and authority over children rests with the father. In matrilinear societies, children are in the descent group of their mothers, but under the headship of the males in that line. The only significant implication of this presently is in marriage. In matrilinear societies, males are limited in their search for a wife, since they will bear responsibility for children in their sisters' families.

Matrilinear groups usually also practice levirate marriage, in which a man must take his brother's widow and children as his own. If the dead man has left no children, the brother may father children in the dead man's name. This aspect of African traditional law has been accepted into Kenyan jurisprudence in a contentious case involving a deceased Luo lawyer whose widow, from a prominent Kikuyu family, refused to accept Luo traditional law. When she lost the case, the brother's family seized the body to bury it in traditional fashion. By refusing to attend this ceremony, or to accept her brother-in-law as her new husband, she was regarded as divorced, and the deceased was buried as an unmarried man.

Of the five recognized forms of marriage in Kenyan law, three are monogamous—Christian, civil, and Hindu marriages. Islamic marriages are potentially polygynous, and African customary marriages are poly-gynous. Although the precise word for marriages of single husband/mul-tiple wives is "polygyny," Africans use the broader term "polygamy," and it will be so used here.

A man may take junior wives only if he is able to support them, which limits polygamy. Bride wealth alone inhibits polygamy, but the increasing cost of educating children is equally daunting. A man may take a second wife as a display of wealth or prominence, to provide an assistant in farm work for the first wife, or to begin another family. Each wife has to have living quarters for herself and her children. In practice, men arrange a small plot of land that the wife works to support the children.

A polygynous husband is expected to be sexually active with all his wives. In some groups, she is entitled to a visit between each menstrual period. More commonly in the rural areas, a man will sleep with his wives in rotation, several weeks at a time.

In contemporary society, the husband may take a job in the city, and visit his wife or wives from time to time. It is not uncommon today for a man to live apart from his legal wives for many years in this way.

In some cases, one or more wives may live on the *shamba*, or garden plot, while another stays in the city, caring for her husband. In addition, many men will take a "city wife," a form of concubinage in which the man supports the woman in the city while not having a legal relationship with her. Many wives, living on the *shamba*, prefer this to another legal wife or the prob-ability of her husband's resorting to prostitutes. Children born to a "city wife" are the father's, and are raised by his wife.

Polygamous marriages were never in the majority, and today are declin-ing under economic pressures. At the same time, other, less formal arrange-ments have become common. These include the phenomenon of the "city wife" and polyandrous mistresses. This latter arrangement involves several urban men who jointly support a woman. None of them live with her, but she shares a sexual relationship with each. In one case known to the author, one man paid the woman's rent, another her food bills, and a third paid for her clothing. Her arrangement was known to her peers since she held a professional position, and she was not regarded as a prostitute. Any children born of such arrangements are regarded as fatherless. [I am not aware of this polyandrous relationship involving a wife openly maintaining a sexual relationship with two or more men. However, a wife or mistress may have sexual relationships with more than one man, for the purpose of obtaining money from each. When the men eventually learn about the multiple relationships, the result is a breakup that may escalate with a thorough beating of the woman or fighting between the men involved. (Kariuki)]

In the tradition, a marriage must be fruitful. The advanced stages of elderhood are marked by fathering children, having them come to the age of initiation, and having grandchildren. Among the Kisii, an impotent husband could recruit an *omosoi nyomba*, literally "warmer of the house," to impregnate his wife. He was preferably chosen from descendents of the same grandfather, and any children are the husband's heirs, not the biological father's. A childless widow could also make the same arrangement.

Since childbearing is such a central condition of sexuality, female orgasm is not sought in itself. Nevertheless, it is approved and acceptable. Male orgasm, however, is a sign of potency, and men will seek sexual relief even when abstaining from intercourse. Abstinence is observed from the time pregnancy is obvious until some time after birth, and during menstruation. During this period, if a man has only one wife, he may engage in other forms of sex, including fellatio. Kikuyu men, conditioned to breast stimulation, often center on this activity.

An interesting birth practice is found among the Luo, who are Nilotic and not Bantu. Several days after parturition, when a woman is to leave the birth hut with the newborn, her husband must have intercourse with her. Before this act, she may have no contact with anyone who has had intercourse, including midwives or relatives. To do otherwise would afflict the child with *chira*, a spiritual curse resulting in the child's death or the parents' sterility.

Sexuality and the Disabled and Aged

The Kenyan government estimates that 5 percent of the population is physically disabled, mostly with deformed limbs and eye afflictions resulting from poor birth-delivery conditions. No studies of the sexual adaptations of this group have been reported, but the disabled can be observed in all types of relationships, married and otherwise.

Since childbearing so defines a married woman's importance, later sex is not spoken of. In at least one tribe, parental sex was supposed to stop when the first child was married. A wealthy man might take a young junior wife when his first wife reaches menopause, causing him to cease having sex with her.

Incidence of Oral and Anal Sex

Vaginal intercourse is the norm for marital sexual activity, with little foreplay. Anal sex is associated with homosexual rape, not unknown during civil strife, and both anal and oral sex are culturally abhorrent, though fellatio is acceptable in a few cultures during periods of abstinence, such as the lactation period.

6. Homoerotic, Homosexual, and Ambisexual Behaviors

A. Children and Adolescents

Certain types of same-sex activity were tolerated in tribal tradition, but only as childish behaviors unworthy of an initiate. In tribes where initiation involves long periods of separation from female contact along with power-ful emphasis on male group bonding (Maasai), situational homosexuality is not uncommon. When limited to mutual self-pleasuring, it is regarded as merely unmanly. Oral or anal intercourse can, however, result in expul-sion from the age set, severe beatings, and disgrace. One finds some nonpenetrative homosexual behavior among Maasai *askaris* (guards) who have migrated to Nairobi or the coast.

Urban poverty has created an underclass of abandoned street youth, almost all male, ranging in age from 7 to late teens. These "parking boys" survive by protecting parking spots, begging, petty crime, and scrounging for garbage. Though the older protect the younger, situational homosexu-ality is normative.

B. Adults

Self-identified gay Africans hardly exist in Kenya, although homosexual activity is not unknown. There are no homosexual gender roles, such as the *berdache* in Native American societies, or the effeminate *gà'tuhy* of Thailand. Because homosexuality profoundly violates the traditional social pattern, it has been tabooed to the point that subcultural social norms have never developed.

Kenya has retained many aspects of the colonial British penal code, and homosexuality continues to be illegal as a "crime against nature." It is regarded with disdain and disgust by the majority of the population, and persons arrested for homosexual activity are treated harshly by the police. In some traditions (e.g., Kikuyu), homosexuality could be punished by death.

Kenyans discriminate against same-sex behaviors. Self-pleasuring with a partner or spouse present is regarded as childish, but relatively harmless, particularly between friends. While socially and legally tabooed, playing the inserter role in same-sex acts does not define a man as homosexual. Accept-ing insertion, especially in anal intercourse, is regarded with extreme disgust.

There are no gay venues nor any overt gay presence in Kenya. A small white, predominantly British, homosexual society exists in Nairobi. Most expatriate white homosexuals avoid African partners because of the drastic consequences, and confine themselves to sexual activity on trips to Europe.

Male prostitutes are readily available on the streets of Nairobi and Mombasa, usually catering to tourists. They are well dressed in order to be able to enter international hotels. Male prostitution serving an African clientele does not seem to exist. The prostitutes themselves are probably bisexual, many having girlfriends or wives, and considering themselves heterosexual. All religious groups abhor homosexuality and condone its complete suppression. There are no gay activist or support groups in Kenya, nor any gay publications. Foreign gay publications are proscribed.

Lesbian and bisexual relationships are either so rare or so hidden as to be unnoticeable. The "woman-to-woman" marriage discussed in Section 8 should not be confused with lesbianism, even if an occasional sexual exchange may occur.

Homosexuality is often ascribed to the coastal Swahili, Arabs, and Moslems generally as a racist slur, and the few Africans involved are said to be exploited by these groups. The sexual act in these accounts is always sodomy, which as an image of rape and political dominance effectively excludes mutuality in same-sex relationships. Male homosexuality is politically interpreted in terms of racist, anti-black exploitation by whites (former colonial masters) and Arabs (former slavers).

This pattern, both expatriate and African, is typical of sub-Saharan Africa except for the Republic of South Africa. Although the dramatic AIDS pandemic has generated interest in research on same-sex behavior, almost no such research has been done in Africa. A 1995 study indicated that such research is almost unknown in sub-Saharan Africa. In Kenya, all survey research designs must be approved by the Office of the President, a sufficient damper on any same-sex studies. The National AIDS Programme has no literature or outreach to homosexuals in Kenya.

The imposition of Western social notions of homosexual/gay patterns tends to obscure any true picture of same-sex activities in Africa. To say that there is no organized gay community in Kenya does not mean that there is no homosexual activity. There are cliques of men who are predominantly or exclusively homosexual, but who limit their sexual activities to their acquaintaince group. In this sense, in urban concentrations such as Nairobi and Mombasa, these serve as homosexual analogs to age-set groups. Occasionally, one finds a group organized as a brotherhood or fraternity, a form of homosexual support group providing casual, although not promiscuous, pairings. A 1995 survey indicated that violent assault was either likely or possible for homosexuals in Africa—at 69 percent, the highest in the Third World. This helps to explain the closed nature of homosexual society in Kenya and other African countries.

7. Gender Conflicted Persons

Gender conflicted persons are regarded as homosexuals, and treated as criminals. Suppression is so complete as to make such persons, to the extent that they exist, invisible.

Kenyan traditional societies did not provide for special gender roles. During the independence movement, sodomy was practiced by some in the Mau Mau society, with the sole intent of making the participants ritually unclean and thus unable to participate in normal society. This is the only ritual use of homosexual behavior known.

8. Significant Unconventional Sexual Behaviors

A. Coercive Sex

Sexual Abuse

Child sexual abuse seems to be increasing, and is part of a generalized child abuse resulting from pressures of social change and loss of the holding power of traditional taboos. An alarming new development, however, has appeared with the rise of AIDS. This is the exploitation of pubescent girls by older men, hoping to find inexperienced partners who are unlikely to be infected. The image of the prosperous "sugar daddy" is a stock figure in Kenyan humor, accompanied by his *dogo-dogo* (literally, "little-little").

Incest

Incest is as socially condemned in Kenya as in the West, and seems to be rare. The Kisii sometimes excuse it due to drunkenness, but in other societies it would be severely punished by mob justice. In some cases, children conceived incestuously would be killed.

Pedophilia

True pedophila, involving sexual contact between adults and prepubescent children, is rare in Kenya, scorned and severely punished. Girls between 12 and 14 are often objects of older men's attentions, however, even though this is socially disapproved. Peasant fathers may accept bride wealth from men seeking a young wife, and this is not regarded as selling one's daughter. The government has campaigned against the practice, but has not been able to eradicate it in rural areas. In one district in 1988, only one girl completed Standard Eight, all the rest of her class having been married before completing elementary school.

Sexual Harassment

The forms of sexual harassment found in Western society are probably as common among the professional class of Kenyans as elsewhere. There is also a serious problem of sexual exploitation of schoolgirls by male teachers.

Poverty forces many rural girls, as young as 10, to be employed as housemaids and child minders in middle-class homes. Besides the economic exploitation they endure, sexual harassment by males in the household is common. Being from rural areas, often speaking only a tribal language, these girls have no power to resist sexual advances. If they become pregnant, they are cast out and often forced into prostitution.

Rape

Reports of rape have been increasing in Kenya, although exact statistics do not exist. Practically speaking, only violent stranger rape is acknowledged as criminal. Neither Kenyan law nor general attitudes accept the concept of marital rape. Rape of such subordinate women as prostitutes or house-maids is regarded very lightly.

Sexual exploitation of girls in boarding schools and universities is common. A young woman who enters into a social relationship with a male student is expected to be available sexually. Because women have been conditioned to serve men and accept their orders from childhood, refusal of sexual overtures is difficult. In 1991, incidents involving mass rapes in secondary schools, in one case leading to several deaths, brought international publicity leading to government attempts at reform.

B. Prostitution

Female prostitution is widespread, and patronized by both tourists and Kenyans. Technically illegal, it is tolerated by the authorities. Prostitutes tend to come from the less-educated class of women, including single mothers, junior wives driven out of their homes by first wives, abandoned girls, and economically distressed women. A working-class prostitute earns the equivalent of one U.S. dollar per encounter, less in the poorer slums. Under these conditions, by 1990, almost 85 percent of Nairobi prostitutes tested positive for HIV. With weak economic inducement for remaining in prostitution, however, church programs such as Maria House in Nairobi teach cottage-industry and market skills that make it possible for women to earn a comparable living outside the sex trade.

Despite Kenyan government disapproval, sex tourism is promoted by German operators, including a "Sun and Sex Safari" that includes an antibiotic injection on return! Sex tourism in Kenya has never approached the exploitive level found in Thailand and the Philippines, but it is an ever-present element.

Male prostitution is a phenomenon of sex tourism, and is found mostly in coastal resort areas, such as Mombasa and Malindi.

C. Pornography

All forms of erotica and sexually oriented publications are illegal in Kenya, and not available for sale. This includes publications featuring nudity, which is culturally offensive.

D. Female Circumcision

Female circumcision is practiced by Nilotic and some Bantu peoples. It still continues widely among the Somali and Turkhana, and surreptitiously among others. Its purpose is to reduce female sexual pleasure, and make women docile to their husbands and less likely to engage in adultery. Women not circumcised are referred to by traditionalists as "unclean" or as "prostitutes." As a Kikuyu girls' circumcision song concludes, "Now we can make love, for our sex is clean."

The Kikuyu, Maasai, and Meru only removed the clitoris (clitoridectomy) during initiation, at puberty. The Turkhana and Somali practice pharaonic circumcision, removing the clitoris and the labia minora. The wound is then sutured (infibulation), leaving a tiny hole for menstrual flow. This is often inspected at betrothal as a sign of virginity. Pharaonic circumcision is performed on girls between the ages of 3 and 7.

The Anglican Church strongly opposed female circumcision, and it has been illegal since the colonial period. The campaign reached a crisis in 1929 when the Church of Scotland Mission made opposition a condition of employment and school entry. This politicized the question and gave rise to the Kikuyu resistance, and the independent church and school movements. In 1930, an elderly female missionary died after rape, forced circumcision, and mutilation. Jomo Kenyatta, the Father of Kenya, made resistance a cornerstone of liberation, declaring that female circumcision "symbolizes the unification of the whole tribal organization."

After independence, Kenyatta permitted female circumcision, but President Moi again outlawed it in 1982 after the deaths of fourteen girls. He reaffirmed this in 1990 after a widely publicized tribal ceremony. There are indications that the practice is waning.

E. Woman-to-Woman Marriage

Some thirty Bantu societies provide for marriage between two women, including a dozen Kenyan ethnic groups. Among these are several large tribes—the Kisii, Nandi, Wakamba, and Kikuyu. In other parts of Africa, this was characteristic of status women, such as royals or political leaders, but in East Africa, it ordinarily represents a surrogate female husband who replaces a male kinsman as jural "father." The wife may bear children for her husband, in whose clan line they then belong. In other cases, women marry women to achieve economic independence, and brideprice is paid. These autonomous female husbands are accepted as men in male economic roles. This dual-female marriage is economic, and illustrates the separation of sex and gender in African societies.

There is no evidence of lesbianism in any of these marriages, and the wife is often provided with a male sexual partner to raise the children. She is not permitted to refuse him when he visits the household for this purpose. The husband figure is henceforth forbidden to have sex with a man, because this would constitute homosexuality due to her legally male status. She may become an elder, and among the Nandi, may attend circumcisions, forbidden for females.

Although Westernization has made female marriages embarrassing, they were confirmed in customary law by the Kenyan courts in 1986, and are subject to divorce legislation.

F. Bestiality

Among pastoral groups and nomads, occasional instances of bestiality take place. When they involve uncircumcised youth, they are punished with a beating. Initiated males are treated more harshly. They are so disgraced after the public judgment of the elders that they would most likely go to a city. For a married man, bestiality is sometimes punished by death by mob justice.

9. Contraception, Abortion, and Population Planning

A. Contraception

Foreign birth-control agencies cooperate with the government population-control program. Condoms are distributed at hospitals and clinics, supplied in large numbers by the U.S. Agency for International Development (USAID) and by such nongovernmental organizations (NGOs) as the United Kingdom's Marie Stopes Institute. The government has forbidden their distribution in schools, and school contraceptive education is severely limited. Condom use runs counter to the common taboo forbidding a wife to touch her husband's penis with her hand.

Because of cultural resistance to condom use, Natural Family Planning (NFP), using the Billings Method, has had some modest acceptance by combining NFP with traditional periods of abstinence, such as during lactation. Operating throughout the country in both mother tongues and Kiswahili, NFP has promotion and training teams made up of unmarried youth and married couples practicing NFP.

Contraceptive methods requiring medical intervention, IUDs, and the pill, are beyond the means of most Kenyans, and limited to the elites and expatriates.

B. Teenage Unmarried Pregnancies

Having a baby outside marriage is unacceptable in much of Kenyan society, where tribal customs are very strong. Teenage pregancies reported among schoolgirls between 1985 and 1990 ranged from 6,633 to over 11,000. These rough figures of only a small segment of the adolescent population indicate a serious problem.

C. Abortion

Abortion is illegal, unless the mother's life is at risk or unless two doctors certify that the pregnant woman is mentally unstable and incapable of caring for a child. It is likely to remain so in the foreseeable future. President Moi strongly disapproves of abortion, and no religious tradition accepts it. Under the law, anyone convicted of assisting in an abortion or killing of an unborn child can face 14 years in prison.

With abortion illegal and the widespread practical ignorance about contraception—and cultural prescriptions that prohibit its use—thousands of Kenyan young women and teenagers are forced every year to turn to illegal and unsafe abortions, which are a lucrative underground business, especially in the sprawling squatter slums of Nairobi.

Statistics are unavailable, but Nairobi's Kenyatta National Hospital with 2,000 beds treats forty cases of incomplete abortion daily. About 50 percent of its gynecological admissions are due to complications from induced and incomplete abortions. Dr. Khama Rogo, a gynecologist at the private Agha Khan Hospital, has estimated that at least 187,500 illegal abortions were performed in Kenya in 1993. One third of Kenya's maternal deaths are due to unsafe abortions. With an extensive hospital and clinic system throughout Kenya, this represents only a tiny fraction of botched abortions. [Kenya has both government-run and church-managed nursing schools. While the church-run schools do not permit abortion, the state schools require that nurses record and document how many abortifacients they have inserted in patients to pass their licensing examination. In one state school I visited, the principal informed me that if the student nurses do not do this, irrespective of what they believe, they fail the examination. In the same school, a number of back-door abortions were carried out by the students for money. (Kariuki)]

The Marie Stopes Center, a grassroots organization with 10 clinics, is one of the few to provide counseling and abortion under the mental health provisions. These clinics also provide family planning and medical care (Lorch 1995).

D. Population Control Efforts

Kenya's population growth rate is among the highest in the world, currently between 3.8 and 4 percent annually, at the current rate doubling every seventeen years. With only 13 percent of its land arable, there is considerable population pressure. The government endorses population control as a national goal, and foreign-aid donors commonly demand active population-control programs as a condition for full assistance.

Kenya has succeeded in increasing contraceptive use to 27 percent of married couples, as compared with 10 percent throughout sub-Saharan Africa. Lifetime number of births per woman went from 7.7 in 1984 to 6.7 in 1989, but this still remains higher than the 6.4 figure for sub-Saharan Africa generally.

[The idea of population control has been unpopular among Kenyans for several reasons. Traditionally, children are embraced as a great blessing: they continue the family and clan lineage and also take care of the aged. The majority of Kenyans are firm in their Muslim or Christian faith, and all the religious sects have worked very hard to decry the Western methods of population control, which are viewed with great suspicion. Most Kenyans view the arguments for population control as overstretched and many times exaggerated. Most of the land is underutilized, and the real solution to the country's economic ills is not to reduce the population growth, but to provide good political governance and a sound economic system. With proper government and economy, Kenya can support its current growth rate. (Kariuki)]

10. Sexually Transmitted Diseases

Syphilis and gonorrhea are widespread among certain ethnic groups (e.g., the Maasai). Nomadic tribes are heavily infected, as are urban prostitutes, street youth living rough, and the residents of the most degraded squatter slums in Nairobi. Antibiotic treatment is available at all hospitals and clinics, and mobile clinics treat nomadic peoples, who are especially at risk.

11. HIV/AIDS

Because it borders Uganda and Tanzania, two countries with an extremely high incidence of AIDS, Kenya is vulnerable to AIDS. Since tourism is the greatest hard-currency earner, however, the government downplays the incidence of the disease. The first AIDS case was diagnosed in 1984, but the first death ascribed to AIDS was listed in 1984. In 1992, a powerful party leader argued in parliament that "it is not in the national interest to release alarming AIDS figures." The Director of Medical Services in the Ministry of Health was dismissed for revealing that 700,000 Kenyans were diagnosed HIV-positive, with 40,000 confirmed AIDS cases, in an estimated population of 28 million. Current (1994) estimates are 800,000 HIV-positive Kenyans, including 30,000 children; an estimated 100,000 have AIDS. Dr. Frank Plummer of the University of Manitoba, who has done fieldwork in Nairobi for several years, calculates the infection rate among urban youth at 12 percent (see also Section 3). The numbers are about equally divided between males and females, and heterosexual contact is the primary source of infection.

In Kenya, AIDS programs are based on a threefold attitude toward the significance of the disease. It is seen simultaneously as a health problem, a threat to the tourist industry, and as a insult to national pride.

Traditional initiation customs encouraged safe-sex practices among youths and limited intercourse outside marriage. With Westernization and urbanization, these controls have lapsed, however, and promiscuity is widespread. Condoms are readily available in the urban areas, but most traditions do not accept them. Christian and Islamic groups both disapprove, and in 1991, a prominent Moslem leader was disgraced when a condom was found in his luggage during a search by militant Islamic youth. The influence of religious groups is high, especially as President Moi is an evangelical Christian. When attempts have been made to use television for safe-sex promotion, he has personally stopped them.

Despite political misgivings, the Ministry of Health has embarked on an extensive AIDS-education program since 1990. Devised by a national committee that has been relatively free of political pressure, it has centered on educating basic health providers and community leaders. This includes professionals such as physicians and nurses, but also herbalists, midwives, ritual circumcisers, and "market mamas," the influential local traders. Consequently, grassroots understanding of the causes of AIDS is high. For the future elites, use is made of the national service period, which is a condition for admission to higher education. Sex and AIDS education (with condom distribution) is included, and given in mother tongues. Studies done by the Marie Stopes Institute have shown that even university-educated youth respond to safer-sex education when it is given in their mother tongue, even though they may be fluent in English and Swahili.

Blood supplies have been screened for HIV since 1985. Despite this, as a further reassurance for the skittish tourist industry, special safari insurance was introduced, providing for air evacuation of injured tourists to Europe if necessary.

The implications of AIDS are very serious for the tourist industry. In 1987, the United Kingdom Ministry of Defense banned holiday use of recreational facilities on the Kenya coast to British troops. Resultant publicity in Europe caused extensive cancellations at resort areas, with loss of 20 to 50 percent of all bookings that season. Because of the catastrophic effect of this on the economy, the AIDS question is a delicate political issue.

Kenya, like many African countries, has been deeply offended by speculative Western theories that AIDS originated in Africa. This is ascribed to racism and colonialism, and has prompted denial and a defensive attitude towards AIDS and AIDS research. Conversely, it has spurred support for research leading to an "African solution." The government has strongly supported the work of Dr. Davy Koech of the Kenya Medical Research Institute (KEMRI) on oral alpha interferon (Kemron). Unfortunately, when Kemron was tested by the World Health Organization (WHO) and a Canadian NGO, Dr. Koech's positive results could not be replicated.

U.S. Agency for International Development (USAID) projections in 1993 show Kenya with 1.2 million cases of HIV/AIDS by 1995, 1.7 million by 2000, and 2 million by 2005. The government has acknowledged the problem and admitted that its educational program has not brought about behavioral changes. What seems to have created the crisis mentality in the government is the realization that HIV/AIDS is disproportionately high (and rising) among the best-paid workers, the base of the middle class. This includes urban business and long-haul truck drivers.

The Kenyan government health-care budget for 1993 was $60 million in a falling economy, with 20 percent earmarked for AIDS prevention. Of this, Kenya contributed only $77,000, the rest coming from foreign donors. The United States doubled its $2 million contribution in 1994, but Western pressures to reduce foreign assistance make this source an unreliable one for the future.

There has been a recent shift in attitudes in the national leadership. Both President Moi and his vice president now regularly address AIDS prevention, although they do not speak out with the candidness of President Yoweri Museveni of neighboring Uganda, who openly endorses condom use. Although condoms are available in clinics, the government has not yet allowed them to be distributed to the young in schools. Since the great majority of high school and university students live in dormitories, this effectively removes the largest at-risk group from condom education.

According to a July 1996 report at the eleventh International Conference on AIDS, Kenya ranked fifth in the world with 1.1 million people infected with HIV.

12. Sexual Dysfunctions, Counseling, and Therapies

Professional therapy is a serious lack in Kenya. The University of Nairobi has a post-M.D. psychiatric training program, but it includes very little preparation for dealing with sexual dysfunctions, and has only a few graduates. The services of psychiatrists are also beyond the means of all but the wealthy.

Kenyan cultures exalt the dominant virile male. Erectile dysfunctions are therefore considered serious and deeply shameful. Impotence is often a symptom of the pressures on men from traditional backgrounds who attempt to succeed in a competitive, capitalist, and urban milieu. Successful Western therapies that involve progressive levels of sensate and sexual exploration are seldom successful, since men rarely admit impotence to their wives. Male dominance allows them to assert that they have an outside "girlfriend" and thus no further interest in their wives. The average Kenyan wife would not challenge this. The level of marital communication is very low.

Male self-pleasuring is regarded as a dysfunction after initiation, but an acceptable release before. It is seen as a symptom of immaturity and sexual failure, and is rarely admitted by adult men.

An American Catholic missionary group has established the Amani Counseling Center in Nairobi, where a wide spectrum of services is available on a sliding-fee scale. The most commonly reported presenting issues of a sexual nature are male impotence, sexual abuse of subordinate women (e.g., maids and students), male self-pleasuring, and fear of homosexuality.

Amani also sponsors a weekly newspaper column from letters received from around the country.

The Kenyatta National Hospital has operated a sex therapy clinic one afternoon a week since 1981, treating about thirty patients a year. Presenting problems are: erectile failure, 46 percent; ejaculatory problems, 25 percent; and reduced libido, 29 percent.

With no licensing requirements for therapists, charlatans abound. While witchcraft is illegal and vigorously suppressed, traditional healers and herbalists advertise cures for impotence, AIDS, and homosexuality, and are eagerly sought out.

13. Research and Advanced Education

Research on sexual matters is conducted either through the Ministry of Health or the Kenyatta National Hospital. Quality surveys of adolescent sexual behavior have been done, and statistics are kept on AIDS. There are no centers engaged in sex research on a regular basis, and there are no courses at the university level on human sexuality.

Research by expatriates must be approved in advance by State House, the office of the president. This is regardless of topic, and a condition of getting an entry visa. In addition, the results of all approved research may be released only with government approval. Approval for sex research has been rare, and only when of benefit to national policy. A Canadian medical group has been allowed to study the incidence of AIDS among prostitutes.

There are graduate-level programs in counseling (United States International University—Africa, and Catholic University of East Africa), pastoral counselling (Amani Center), and psychiatry (University of Nairobi). All include courses in sexuality or marital therapy, but there is no program devoted to sexuality.

There is no professional association for sexologists, and there are no journals on sexuality in East Africa. However, a related organization, the Family Planning Private Sector Programme, is a possible source of information; address: Fifth Floor, Longonot Place, Kijabe Street, P.O. Box 46042, Nairobi, Kenya. (Phone: 254-2/224646; Fax: 254-2/230392).

References and Suggested Readings

Lorch, Donatella. 1995 (June 4). "Unsafe Abortions Become a Big Problem in Kenya." *The New York Times*. p. 3.

Molnos, Angela. 1972-73. *Cultural Source Materials for Population Planning in East Africa.* Nairobi: University of Nairobi Press. (This four-volume study contains comparative studies of sixteen Kenyan ethnic groups on sex life, marriage, and pregnancy.)

Mexico
(*Estados Unidos Mexicanos*)

Eusebio Rubio, Ph.D.

Contents

Demographics and a Historical Perspective

A. Demographics

Mexico, with the official name of United Mexican States, is a country of 756,065 square miles located in North America, bordered by the United States to the north, and Guatemala and Belize to the south. Mexico is bordered on the east by the Gulf of Mexico and on the west by the Pacific Ocean. It is the third-largest country in Latin America, three times the size of the state of Texas, and a republic formed by thirty-one states and one Federal District. Sandwiched between the Sierra Madre Oriental Mountains on the west coast and the Sierra Madre Occidental Mountains on the Gulf coast is a high, dry, temperate central plateau. The coastal lowlands are tropical. About 45 percent of the land is arid.

In 1995, 72 percent of Mexico's 94 million people lived in cities. Twenty million people live in metropolitan Mexico City, making it the most populous city in the world. The nation's sex ratio is slightly unbalanced with 49.1 percent males and 50.9 percent females. Life expectancy at birth in 1991 was 70 for males and 77 for females. The 1995 birth rate was 27 per 1,000 and the death rate 5 per 1,000, with an annual natural increase of 2.2 percent. Mexico had one hospital bed per 1,367 persons, one physician per 885 persons, and an infant mortality rate of 29 per 1,000 live births. The 1995 age distribution was 36 percent for those under age 14; 15 to 59, 60 percent; and 65 and over, 4 percent. Literacy is 87.1 percent, with ten years of compulsory schooling (INEGI 1992). Among most of Mexico's rural population and urban poor who constitute by all measures a majority of the population, the standard of living is close to subsistence. In 1990, 63.2 percent of adult Mexicans reported a monthly income below the minimum wage, a measure of income that in 1993 corresponds to a yearly income of approximately $3,000 (INEGI 1992). The gross per capita domestic product in 1995 was $7,800.

B. A Brief Historical Perspective

Mexico was the early site of advanced indigenous civilizations, starting with the Olmecs (1500 B.C.E. to 300 B.C.E.) and the Mayas, who also began as early as 1500 B.C.E. As they moved north from the Yucatan to Mexico, the Mayas brought with them their advanced agriculture. They built immense stone pyramids and invented a very accurate calendar. Classic Mayan civilization collapsed between 790 and 900 C.E. The Aztecs, who overcame and replaced the Toltecs, built their capital city, Tenoochtitian, in 1325 on the site of present-day Mexico City. The Aztec civilization collapsed following its first encounter with Spanish conquistadors under Hernando Cortes, between 1519 and 1521.

After three centuries of Spanish rule, the people rebelled under the leadership of two priests and a general, the latter declaring himself Emperor Augustin I in 1821. A republic was declared in 1823. At the time, Mexico's territory extended into the American southwest and California. In 1836, Texas revolted and declared itself a republic. After the Mexican-American War (1846-1848), Mexico gave up all claim to lands north of the Rio Grande River. French support helped put an Austrian archduke on the throne of Mexico as Maximillian 1 (1864-1867), but American pressure forced the French to withdraw. Porfirio Diaz headed a dictatorship between 1877 and 1880 and again between 1884 and 1911.

In 1917, rival forces agreed to social reform and a new constitution. Since then, Mexico has developed large-scale social programs of social security, labor protection, and school improvement, although many segments of the population, including the indigenous natives, barely manage to subsist.

1. Basic Sexological Premises

A. Character of Gender Roles

Gender roles are changing. Some fifty years ago, gender roles in Mexico could be easily described as the traditional separation, magnification, and stereotyping of male and female differences. Women were dichotomized into the two double-moral-standard subtypes of the princess and prostitute, and men were instructed to be the impenetrable and insensitive provider who exercised his power over women.

Today this is changing. In a sample of 10,142 high school students representative of the whole country, the National Population Council conducted a national survey on various aspects of sexuality (CONAPO 1988). In 1988, 83.1 percent of the respondents thought men and women had equal legal rights (as they do), 69.7 percent thought that authority at home should be shared by men and women, and only 13.2 percent thought housework to be the exclusive responsibility of the woman. In another survey among 2,983 male and female 15 to 24 years olds, Morris et al. (1987) found that only 6.6 percent of females and 13.7 percent of males thought that a woman who works outside the home is deceiving her husband and not fulfilling her obligations as a wife. In 1984, Rubio et al. (1988) found in a sample of 521 first-year medical students that only 17.7 percent agreed with the statement that women are naturally passive and 91.3 percent thought it is equally important for men and women to pursue professional educations.

The process of recognizing the equality of women and men has clearly begun, although it is also true that, in practice, women have more disadvantages than men. Women are overrepresented in the lower-income levels and underrepresented in the higher levels. Only 19.6 percent of Mexican women are engaged in paid work compared to 68 percent for males (INEGI-2 1992). It is also a fact that most working women have, in fact, two jobs: the paid one and the housework.

B. Sociolegal Status of Males and Females

The fourth Article of the Constitution explicitly recognizes the equality of men and women. In 1974, a revision of all legislation was effected to eliminate any gender discrimination, and there are several other laws and a national program aimed at evaluating and promoting the integration of woman in the nation's development. Despite these efforts, there are a number of areas where women are at a disadvantage. The expansion of industrial labor has benefited males more than women. Inequality also shows in other areas of work: 74.1 percent of professionals are men, 80.6 percent of the executive positions in the government belong to men, and only 3.4 percent of those who work in domestic jobs are men (INEGI-2 1992).

Technically, male and female children and adolescents enjoy equal benefits as far as education, health care, and social significance go within society and the family. However, gender-dimorphic training begins early. In general, lower-socioeconomic-level families tend to transmit the older values. As the social class and education level of the parents increase, one observes a tendency toward transmitting an egalitarian ideology.

C. General Concepts of Sexuality and Love

There have been attempts at picturing empirically the constructs people have of sexuality and love. In general, it can be said that both sexuality and love are seen as positive and desirable aspects of life both for men and women, but ambivalent feelings on sexuality are often encountered. Díaz Loving's (1988) nonrandom sample of 300 individuals in Mexico City found that love, although seen positively, has many interpretations. Romantic love is seen as an idealization, passionate love as being vulnerable. Furthermore, there are important differences in how males and females perceive love: females tend to see love more positively, while men tend to think of it as genital and sexual; men more often than women see it as an unattainable utopian dream.

In the CONAPO (1988) survey the participating students thought that the aims of sex were: intimate communication 63 percent, mutual pleasure and satisfaction 37 percent, and having children 15.5 percent. In another survey effected in Mexico City with 613 individuals randomly selected from households, De la Peña and Toledo (1991a) found that respondents mentioned the following objectives for sex: enjoyment 48 percent, physical outlet 29 percent, and having children 18 percent. In a subsequent report (1991c), the same authors reported that, of the sexually active respondents, only 3 percent of males and 6 percent of females think of sexual intercourse as something unpleasant or have an indifferent attitude towards it. A survey of medical students found that the majority, 69 percent, disagree with the statement that procreation is the most important goal of sex (Rubio et al. 1988).

2. Religious and Ethnic Factors Affecting Sexuality

A. Source and Character of Religious Values

There are two sources of religious values in Mexico: European Hispanic Catholicism and the indigenous religions that dominated the area prior to the arrival of the Europeans. Both have blended in the course of almost 500 years of interaction. Religiosity has followed the same pattern of other cultural phenomena in the history of Mexico. Rather than one system giving up in favor of the other, a complex mixture of both cultures has generated a new and unique culture. In 1990, 90 percent of the population was Catholic, but the Catholicism practiced is different from the Catholicism of other countries. As with the ethnic blending, religiosity has gone through a process of syncretism. The best example of this is the cult to the Virgin of Guadalupe, which quickly gained popularity because it could be integrated with preexisting cults of Aztec gods.

To complicate the picture, the prehispanic source was not a single one. There were at least four major cultures with important religious differences: Olmec, Toltec, Mayan, and Aztec. The Aztecs dominated much of the land that is now Mexico when the Spaniards arrived, but they were the dominant political power and empire, not the only culture.

The Aztec religion was characterized by a view of the universe where a constant fight for cosmic order took place between the forces of the sun and the forces of the moon and the night. Light, endurance, sobriety, and sexual self-constraint were on the sun's side; cowardice, drunkenness, and sexual incontinence worked for the moon, the night, and the evil forces (Wolf 1975). Sex was seen as something to be controlled, but its value in procreation and as a source of pleasure in both men and women was also recognized. Polygamy was common among the wealthy and divorce rare but regulated.

An interesting aspect in the Aztec religion is the place that childbirth held in the culture. Childbirth was seen as a combat in which the woman was the warrior. A woman who died in childbirth received war honors at burial.

Moderation on every aspect of life, including sexuality, was central in the ideology of the education (Morgan 1982). In other aspects, religion and society were highly repressive: homosexuality was severely punished, although practiced; the official penalty was death (Lumsden 1991).

The other religious components in this synergistic interaction were the beliefs and behavior patterns brought to Mexico by the Catholic Hispanic conquistadors. Historical documents clearly indicate that the Church teachings were not the norm of behavior among the people. The Council of Trent (1545-63), a response to Protestantism, served as a basis for the teachings of the clergy in charge of indoctrinating the indigenous population. A document from the seventeenth century written by Fray Gabino Carta, summarizes the Church's sexual teachings: there were seven ways in which lust could appear, all conducive to mortal sin: (1) simple fornication (intercourse out of wedlock), (2) adultery, (3) incest, (4) ravishment (forcing a woman to participate in sex), (5) abduction of a woman, (6) sins against nature (masturbation, sodomy, which usually meant homosexuality, but sometimes applied also to "unnatural" heterosexual coital sexual positions—different from men above women lying on her back and, bestiality), and (7) sacrilege (Lavrin 1991).

B. Source and Character of Ethnic Values

The ethnic composition of Mexico is complex. The majority of the population, 55 percent, is *mestizo* or *mestee*, a mixture of the European, mainly

Spanish, with the indigenes that populated the area before the arrival of the Spaniards. Creoles, descendents of persons born in the New World from parents born in Europe, still constitute an important segment of the population, 37.5 percent. Being European in origin and not racially mixed, they can be considered Caucasian. A third group consists of a very heterogeneous minority called Indians. These indigenes are composed by fifty-six linguistically differentiated groups. In 1990, the indigenous population was 5,282,347, that is 7.5 percent of the total Mexican population (CNP 1989).

It is difficult to pick out a single overriding characteristic in the ethnic values in Mexico. In the background, we have the original cultural sources that still can be observed today in many aspects. However, what is Mexico today only began to constitute itself some hundred years ago. There are many traces of the conquered culture. The resulting culture, best described by Octavio Paz (1950), is hermetic, inscrutable, full of resentment, and searching for refuge and finding it in the Virgin Mother María de Guadalupe-Tonantzin. According to Paz, Mexican culture is also hiding, always behind masquerades like the macho role where men attempt to calm their fears of being penetrated in a sexual way. Yes, but more importantly, Mexicans also hide in their inner self, behind a very sophisticated strategy of simulation and lies. Almost every foreigner soon learns when dealing with people of low social level that words and promises do not mean what they normally mean. When Mexicans lie or simulate they feel protected and safe. The cult of the Virgin of Guadalupe, the macho attitude, the propensity to simulate and to lie are the results of a process lived by a culture that, instead of being eliminated, was dominated.

[*Note:* In addition to the value of *machismo* mentioned above, Mexican sexual attitudes and behaviors are strongly influenced by three other values—*marianismo, ediquetta,* and *pronatalism*—which are commonly shared with some minor variations across the Latino world of South and Central America. To avoid duplication in several chapters, these four basic values are described in detail in Section 1A, Basic Sexological Premises, in the chapter on Puerto Rico. The reader is referred to this material in Volume 2 of this *Encyclopedia.* (Editor)]

But the Mexico of 1995 is by no means well depicted by the above comments. The process of the last two decades has exerted a profound impact on the character of Mexican culture. Proximity to American culture is a major factor. The American dream is at the same time desired, hated, and feared, but the shaking of economic structures during the 1980s has led to a new identity search that is currently in the process of being delineated. This is evident in the sexual attitudes and behavior of people, as can be seen below.

3. Sexual Knowledge and Education

A. Government Policies and Programs for Sex Education

In the last five to ten years, the need for sex education has been recognized and accepted by most sectors of the population. There are, however, differences about what this education should include and how it should be effected, depending on the ideology of the subsector of the population one considers. Both the government and the Catholic Church have stated that there is a specific need to pay attention to the educative process of sexuality.

Education in Mexico is centralized. The Ministry of Education is in charge of developing programs for all basic school levels—the first ten years of education. This it implements with free schooling in an extensive system of public schools. Official textbooks are provided for these schools and their use is compulsory. Private schooling does exist, but their programs have to cover the official program material.

This situation has facilitated the inclusion of sex education themes. Since 1974, when the official population policy changed from a pro-procreative to a policy promoting low population growth, sex education has been seen as an important element of this policy. A National Population Council was established to pursue actions necessary to implement the new policy. One of the early programs undertaken was the National Program for Sex Education. As a result of this program, the content of the official programs and textbooks began to include sex education themes.

Initially the sexual contents were limited to basic biological information. This raised considerable opposition, but after almost twenty years the general public has come to accept the need for sex education and to demand more completeness in the program.

Most adolescents, especially females, now have access to information about puberty through the school system. The contents of sexual education programs now include psychological, family, and community considerations of sexual development. Meanwhile, sex education has been integrated into a more general framework of population education (Saavedra Arredondo 1986). The major shortcoming is the lack of adequate training for the teachers who apply these programs.

B. Informal Sources of Sexual Knowledge

In the last ten years, an increase in the role of parents as reliable informants has being observed. Friends, popular literature in the form of comics with stories, and television and radio constitute the alternative sources of information. Popular literature deserves a special comment because it is probably the material more frequently read by Mexicans. Unfortunately, it is one of the means of perpetuating sexual myths and ambivalence towards sexuality. In the last four years, there has being a growing interest in the mass media to include sexuality themes in their broadcasts. In general, this has become a new source of scientific information for most people.

4. Autoerotic Behaviors and Patterns

A. Children and Adolescents

Children frequently engage in self-pleasuring, but it still causes anxiety in many parents. The exploratory activities of children are well recognized and tolerated, but more explicit practices of sexual arousal are repressed. There are no figures of the incidence of this phenomenon.

Adolescent self-pleasuring is also very common. Reactions to it vary with the social context. In 1984, in a survey of single university students non-randomly selected for a comparative study with American single students (mean age in both groups 20), Rubio (1989) found an incidence of 50.8 percent that, interestingly, was not different from the American incidence. In another study among younger students (17 to 19 years of age), Rubio et al. (1988) found a rate of 65 percent with an important gender difference: 88 percent for males and 39 percent for females. In a more recent study among 728 students 17 to 26 years of age, Ordiozola-Urbina and Ibañez (1992) found similar numbers: 83 percent of males and 22 percent of females.

Attitudes towards self-pleasuring are not clearly oriented towards accepting or denouncing it, but a tendency to view it as a natural act and not a sick one is clear. Morris et al. (1987) found that 46 percent of adolescent females and 75 percent of males said that autoeroticism was OK once in a while, but 34.5 percent of the females and 49 percent of the males said that self-pleasuring was bad for the health. Rubio et al. (1988) found less restrictive attitudes, but the respondents were medical students: only 29 percent agreed that self-pleasuring is not a healthy practice.

B. Adults

There is less systematic information on adult autoeroticism and attitudes about it. Among Mexico City adults, De la Peña and Toledo (1991b) found that 75 percent of males and 20 percent of the participating females said they had engaged in self-pleasuring. Interestingly, more than half of those who were currently engaging in this sexual outlet at the time of the study said they liked it very little or not at all. My own personal experience with the mass media on this issue indicates that self-pleasuring is still one of the most anxiety provoking of all sexual issues.

5. Interpersonal Hetereosexual Behaviors

A. Children

Sexual exploration and sex rehearsal play occurs very often in children. There are forms, like doctor's play, which are tolerated and understood. More explicit sex play is not tolerated and is usually repressed by parents and other caretakers, such as teachers.

B. Adolescents

Puberty Rituals

There are no widespread rituals of initiation to puberty.

Premarital Sexual Activities and Relationships

During early adolescence, 11 to 15 years of age, most adolescents begin to explore in a form of ritualized relationship called *noviazgo*, formally a relationship period prior to marriage. However, during early adolescence, *noviazgos* are commonly established without marriage as a goal. For young adolescents, it is a social way to regulate interpersonal relationships. It appears that the major part of early dyadic sexual exploration takes place in this form, though no formal data exist. At this early age, *noviazgos* are usually of short duration. Once an adolescent has had his or her first *noviazgo*, it is not difficult for either a male or female to continue with subsequent *noviazgo* relationships. Intercourse is usually deferred to a later age.

The possibility of having had the first intercourse increases after 15 years of age: the CONAPO (1988) survey found that the typical age for first intercourse is 14 to 17 years of age for males and 16 to 19 years for females, but only 23 percent of participants had had sexual intercourse. Figures from other studies are higher: in a 1984 group of unmarried students, Rubio (1989) found a figure of 40 percent. Also in 1984, among medical students (17 to 19 years of age), Rubio et al. (1988) found 46 percent had had intercourse (59 percent of males and 31 percent of females).

The last decade may have seen an increase in early sexual intercourse, especially in the big cities. In their Mexico City study, Morris et al (1987) collected information from 2,983 youngsters in 1985 and found among the group of 15 to 19 years: 13.4 percent of the females and 44 percent of males had had intercourse, with 39 percent and 85 percent respectively for the 20- to 24-years-of-age group. More recently Ordizola and Ibañez (1992) found among 728 university students that 31 percent and 74 percent of males had had sexual intercourse.

C. Adults

Premarital Courtship, Dating, and Relationships

De la Peña and Toledo (1991c) studied adults in Mexico City and found that 76.3 percent of their respondents had had premarital intercourse. In another study by the same authors on adults living in the state of Baja California bordering the United States, the figure for premarital intercourse was 93 percent for males and 54 percent for females.

Those who will marry follow a clear set of rules for courtship, with a formal *noviazgo* that includes several assumptions: mutual exclusivity of sexual interaction, regular scheduling of dates, and, when the decision to marry has being taken, many activities to prepare the couple for the common life. Sexual intercourse is common in these adult relationships as the institution of *noviazgo* has gained autonomy in the past thirty to forty years, and surveillance by an older woman in the family, the *duana*, has declined. In the larger cities, the *noviazgo* often has much less restrictive rules than it did in the past. Economic difficulties may delay or make the marriage plans impractical. One result is that a significant number of persons elect a single life as the style of life, either never marrying or after one or more marriages. These individuals may establish *noviazgos* where marriage in fact is not considered for the future.

Although not prevalent, there are some forms of courtship and premarital sexuality that deserve mention. In many communities, some close to Mexico City, a man and woman may decide to live together, but the man is said to "steal" the woman from her family. Depending on the economic possibilities, the woman goes to live with the man's family or the couple establishes a home of their own. After some years, and some children, the couple may decide to marry, and a wedding takes place, usually with a long series of festivities that may extend to several days. In some communities of the state of Oaxaca, the tradition of arranged marriages persists, many times in a less definitive form because the opinions of the man and woman are considered. In other instances, the man or the woman may spend some time, usually months, living with the family of the spouse-to-be to gain approval of the family to proceed to marriage.

Marriage and the Family

Two types of marriage exist in Mexico: civil and religious, and, since one type does not have validity in the other domain, people tend to have both types. The 1990 data of the census indicate 45.8 percent of those 12 years or older are married, 7.4 percent live together but are not married, 40.6 percent are single, 1.9 percent are divorced or separated, and 3.6 percent are widows (INEGI 1992).

Mexican families have varied structures, with the extended and nuclear family patterns dominant. Extended families include father, mother, and children with the addition of some other relatives such as grandparents, uncles, aunts, or others. One form of extended family, characterized as "unstable" because some of its members, aunts and cousins, spend only a limited time with the family, is also very common. López-Juárez (1982) describes this family style as typical. The extended family functions as a social-support mechanism, substituting for other forms of social support that are nonexistant, or exist on a very low scale, in Mexico (e.g., unemployment insurance and care for the elderly). The extended family used to be the norm, but the frequency of nuclear families, groupings limited to father, mother, and children, increases as social class rises higher and urban living spreads. The mean number of household members dropped from 5.8 in 1970 to 5.0 in 1990 (INEGI 1992).

As indicated above, cohabitation is frequent but not the norm. Monogamy is the rule and bigamy is penalized with jail. Although some individuals do in fact have two or more concurrent marriages, discovery entitles the concerned ones to send the guilty party to jail, and there are cases of this. While there are no recognized forms of plural marriage, it is important to note that this refers to formal marriage. Informal liaisons that include sexual interaction and forms of economic support, and cohabitation where one or both of the concerned have other concurrent liaisons, are not infrequent.

Divorce and Remarriage

There are two forms of civil divorce: an administrative divorce, where the couple agrees, and the necessary divorce, where one of the spouses has incurred a legally recognized cause of divorce. Divorce statistics are not reliable, but a general feeling is that it is becoming more frequent than it used to be some fifty years ago. The fate of the divorcee appears to differ according to gender: males tend to remarry more than females. A trend observed in my own clinical practice is that the stigma and social barriers associated with divorce have decreased in the last ten to twenty years.

Extramarital Sexual Relations

Marital sexuality, surprisingly, is not the most frequent form of sexuality, at least in Mexico City. De la Peña and Toledo (1991c) found that, of their respondents who had had sex in the month previous to the survey, only 45 percent were married. In another report (1991d), the same authors found that among the 613 adult respondents in Mexico City, extramarital behavior was reported by 29.7 percent (50 percent of males and 10 percent of females). In a report on the state of Baja California (de la Peña and Toledo 1992b), the figure was 40 percent of males and 15 percent of females.

[A form of concurrent liaison that used to be common occurs between a married man and his female lover who, after some time, acquires a higher status than a simple love affair and establishes herself in a separate household, usually helped or totally paid for by the man who has a kind of second family with her. This relationship may include children and practically all the elements of a family, except for the legality of marriage and for the daily cohabitation, because the previous marriage is maintained. This phenomenon is known as *la casa chica*, literally, "the small home"—the term is also used to refer to the paramour. In January 1997, a prominent Mexico City politician, president of the Democratic Revolutionary Party, may have witnessed a change in public attitude when he called on his fellow politicians to abandon their widely known, and renown, custom of maintaining several *casa chicas* and commit themselves to marital fidelity.

[Deterioration of economic standards of living seen in the last two decades appears to have made this pattern of liaison less common today than in the past. Mexico's economy shrank by 6 percent in 1995 when inflation was expected to top 50 percent, banks were charging an astronomical 70 percent interest on credit cards, and corporate benefits and largess for executives and middle managers dried up, leaving males unable to support their usual number of *casa chicas* and paramours.

[Although this custom is widely practiced and has a long standing in Mexican culture, such relationships usually leave the woman totally unprotected by the law when it comes to inheritance and separation rights (food, pension, alimony, etc.). While most Mexican wives would likely be happy to see the mistresses out of work, economists are greatly troubled by estimates that tens of thousands of single women who have relied on the *casa chica* tradition for much of their livelihood will be added to the swelling unemployment lines. Most of these women have few if any marketable skills. The paramours are taking steps to cope, forming support groups, sometimes called *Las Numero Dos*, to help rebuild their lives and find jobs. Although Mexico's economy remained seriously depressed into 1997 and many middle class and wealthy males were obliged to reduce the number of paramours they supported in separate houses, the resilience of the tradition and the adaptability of Mexican males is evident in the booming popularity of "pass-through hotels," which charge couples by the hour. However, Carlos Welti, a demographer who has been studying Mexican sexuality for twenty years, reports that the decline of the *casa chica* has been part of an evolution in sexual mores that has followed fundamental changes in the condition of women, including increased education and growth in the number of women working outside the home. Also, because of easy access to birth control, the average Mexican woman today bears about three children instead of the 6.8 average that prevailed in 1976 (Padgett 1995; Dillon 1997). (Editor)]

Sexuality and the Physically Disabled and the Aged

The prevailing attitude is that disabled and older persons are nonsexual and have no need for sexual intimacy. Only recently, and then in very small ways, has this public attitude begun to change with a slowly growing awareness of these special population's needs.

The Incidence of Oral and Anal Sex

De la Peña and Toledo (1991a, 1992a) have provided some information on attitudes toward oral and anal sex: 44 percent of Mexico City respondents think oral sex is an acceptable practice, 41.2 percent think anal sex is acceptable. In the Baja California study (1992b), the corresponding figures were 33.3 and 22.2 percent.

Behavioral information gives similar rates: de la Peña and Toledo (1991ab) report 45.3 percent of respondents as practicing oral sex: more than 50 percent of males but only one third of women in the Mexico City study, and 42 percent of males and 40 percent of females in the Baja California study. Among Mexico City students, Ordiozola and Ibañez (1992) found that active oral sex was practiced by 21 percent of females and 51 percent of males, while 22 percent of females and 52 percent of males had engaged in passive oral sex. In a study of younger single university students, I found a figure of 28 percent (Rubio 1989).

Anal sex is slightly less common than oral sex: 32 percent of males and 26 percent of females (de la Peña and Toledo 1992b); 7.4 percent of female university students and 13.8 percent of males (Ordiozola and Ibañez 1992); and 18.5 percent of participants in my study of university single students (Rubio 1989).

There are no legal restrictions to practice oral or anal sex.

6. Homoerotic, Homosexual, and Ambisexual Behaviors

A. Children and Adolescents

The values of mainstream Mexican culture are highly homophobic, as would be expected in a culture derived form two homophobic precursors, the Hispanic European and Precolombian cultures. There is little evidence of the incidence of homoerotic or homosexual behavior during childhood and adolescence, but it is my clinical impression that these behaviors occur in an important number of people during development, especially during adolescence when identity formation is helped by closeness to same-sex friends in both males and females.

B. Adults

Homosexual behaviors are infrequently studied by Mexican sexual researchers. The studies of de la Peña and Toledo (1991ab) report homosexual behavior in 3.3 percent of the respondents: 5 percent of males and 2 percent of females for the Mexico City study, and 9 percent of males and

5 percent of females for the Baja California study. I found a percentage of 6.2 percent of single students with some form of homosexual behavior (Rubio 1989).

Attitudinal information is also scarce. A tendency toward tolerating the homosexual person seems to be emerging, but few people think this is an acceptable form of sexual behavior. Only 9.9 percent of males and 9.7 percent of females in the de la Peña and Toledo (1992) study thought homosexuality was correct. While I found that 58.7 percent of medical students do not think legal measures should be taken against homosexuals, 40.3 percent nevertheless think homosexuality is a degeneration. Still, 58.2 percent of female and 56.1 percent of male adolescents in the Morris et al. (1987) study thought it was no problem to have a homosexual friend.

According to my clinical and professional experience there are no fixed patterns of selection of one of the traditional gender roles in male and female homosexual persons. Lumsden (1991) notes that Mexican homosexuals do not suffer the degree of loneliness typically experienced by American and Canadian homosexuals, because friends and families stay close to the individual.

The courtship patterns in the homosexual individuals have adopted an American pattern: organizing support groups, well-established spots in the cities, specialized bars, and gathering sites. An important number of homosexual and bisexual individuals, however, suffer from the restrictions of a society that is highly homophobic and undergo a long period of isolation before integrating themselves in the homosexual social network. There are no legal restrictions for homosexual behavior, although lower-level authorities, i.e., local police, sometimes exert repression against the homosexual individuals, a manifestation more of internalized homophobia than institutionalized persecution.

During the past fifteen years, homosexual persons have organized a variety of support groups. There are homosexual groups in almost every city of size. These groups work for the recognition of the legal and human rights of homosexual persons, and with AIDS prevention, education, and support.

7. Gender Conflicted Persons

A. Transvestites, Transsexuals, and Transgenderists

There is no systematic information on the incidence of transvestism, transsexualism, and transgenderism. The three situations do occur and the number of people who have these conflicts is not small. The following comments reflect my impressions.

Transvestism occurs in four distinct forms. First, the fetishistic transvestite, who is generally a heterosexual who cross-dresses to achieve sexual arousal, usually with complicated rituals forming part of the arousal process. When this situation generates conflict with the partner, the individual may seek treatment, usually on an individual basis with a private professional. One private institution offers help at low-cost rates for these and other sexual problems (see Section 13 below). Second, the professional transvestite, who may be heterosexual or homosexual, who impersonates females working in transvestite shows. Third, the homosexual who sometimes likes to cross-dress as a means of expression of his sexual preference. Some of these individuals find in prostitution a way of living; other male prostitutes just cross-dress in order to gain more customers. The fourth type is the truly gender-conflicted person who finds relief for an internal craving to express his gender identity/role by cross-dressing for variable amounts of time during his daily life. Psychological adjustment of this last subtype varies. These people usually go through a period of high satisfaction cross-dressing and then suffer from various forms of anxiety that make them seek help from a mental health practitioner.

Transsexuals in Mexico suffer from a lack of systematic attention and knowledge on the part of most health professionals. They are often mistakenly diagnosed as homosexuals in conflict; the usual response from the medical profession is rejection. I have participated in the psychotherapeutic treatment of some transsexual individuals but, until very recently, I was without any resource in the official health system to offer any help beyond psychological and behavioral counseling. In 1993, one public hospital agreed to pursue the medical and surgical treatment of transsexuals in collaboration with psychotherapeutic supervision by staff at Asociacion Mexicana para la Salud Sexual A.C. (AMSSAC). There are major needs in this area still uncovered by official health policy.

B. Specially Gendered Persons

Mexican mainstream cultural expectations are very dichotomized in considering individuals either male or female. This is reflected in the difficulties encountered by gender-dysphoric patients described above, and by the lack of any kind of third gender or sex as found in some cultures.

I have one verbal report from a student some fifteen years ago that in a region of Oaxaca near the Tehuantepec Isthmus, there are communities where a third gender is considered, with social norms ascribing to the effeminate man activities in the household and prohibiting him from pursuing more-typical male activities. I have not had the opportunity to corroborate this information.

8. Significant Unconventional Sexual Behaviors

A. Coercive Sex

Sexual Abuse and Incest

All sexual behavior of an adult with a preadolescent (prepubertal) child is considered a crime. Around 1985, the government of Mexico City established special police offices dedicated to working with victims of sexual crimes and to legally prosecuting the perpetrator. Before this change, regular police handled these crimes and many victims avoided contact with the police fearing further mistreatment. Some other states have adopted this new policy.

Recent information suggests the level of child sexual abuse, although underreporting can be assumed. During three months in 1991 in the Mexico Federal District, 122 cases of sexual crimes where the victim was under 12 years of age were investigated: in 53 percent, the crime was rape, and in 91 percent, the aggressor was known previously by the victim (the father was the aggressor in 12 percent of the cases) (Muñoz Gonzalez 1992).

Incest is a taboo for most of Mexican society. Among some low-level socioeconomic-class communities, it is evident only when the daughter delivers a child fathered by her own father, and this is acknowledged by the neighborhood as one more of the facts of life. Scientific knowledge of this phenomena is very limited and far from satisfactory.

Among some isolated ethnic groups that have conserved their purity of race by not mixing with outsiders, incest may be an acceptable way of organizing and perpetuating society. This is the case, at least, among the Huicholes, a group of some 8,000-9,000 people living in West-Central Mexico. According to Palafox Vargas (1985), various forms of incest are practiced and accepted in the community.

Sexual Harassment

Sexual harassment is considered a crime only in modifications to the law effected in 1990 after intense participation of feminist leaders. Sexual harassment, both in labor and academic settings, seems to be common, but it has been difficult to document cases. Penalties are possible for sexual harassment, but there is very little experience in applying the law.

Rape

Rape, forced sexual intercourse with a man or a woman, has long been considered a crime. Recently, the penalty for rape was increased to seven years in jail, which prevents early freedom for convicted perpetrators. Still the crime is not adequately or sufficiently prosecuted. In Mexico City between January 1992 and November 1993, 1,645 rapes were reported to authorities (Casorla, in press). This figure of about 900 reported rapes annually in Mexico City is far below the estimates of authorities there of a yearly figure of reported and unreported rapes between 15,000 to 20,000. The figure for the whole country is difficult to estimate, but some authors put the figure at about 60,000 rapes per year (Ruiz Harrel 1979).

B. Prostitution

Prostitution is a common practice in Mexico. There are no legal penalties for the prostitute, but there are for anyone who exploits her or him. The pattern of prostitute activities has varied with changing policies of the governments. Some fifty years ago, there were zones in the cities where open prostitution was accepted and regulated by authorities. This still is the case for several cities, but in Mexico City, the law now prohibits open acceptance zones. This policy has generated a lack of control of where and when prostitution is practiced.

There are many levels of prostitutes, from the street girl or boy to the sophisticated call girl, and even some specialized services where the contact is established by phone and arrangements made beforehand. Since these more sophisticated and organized forms of prostitution are illegal, it is difficult to find any information on the extent of the business.

In recent years, prostitutes working independently in the streets have organized themselves in groups to fight for their rights. Claudia Colimoro, the leader, now has a full program being pursued in the political arena. She estimates the number of street prostitutes in Mexico City at about 15,000 (Colimoro 1993).

C. Pornography and Erotica

There are vague legal restrictions to the commercialization of pornographic material, vague because the material has to be considered obscene to be forbidden, and there are no clear criteria for this. Despite restrictions, soft-core pornography circulates openly and legally, and hard-core is widely available. Soft-core publications are produced in Mexico mainly through joint ventures with large American companies such as Playboy and Penthouse. Hard-core is not produced in Mexico, although American, and sometimes European, videotapes are illegally copied and distributed very efficiently to street markets, making them very easy to obtain. The dimension of this illegal business is unknown to anyone not inside it, but it is certainly a profitable and large business. In the last year, the Playboy subsidiary began mail distribution of legally authorized hard-core videotapes produced in the United States, but for the first time with translations in subtitles.

9. Contraception, Abortion, and Population Planning

A. Contraception

Contraceptives are easily obtained by anyone seeking them. They are offered free of charge through the official health care system and can be purchased at any drugstore with few restrictions. This fact speaks about the informal values of Mexican society and the nominally Catholic people: the Catholic Church officially opposes the use of contraceptives, but this opposition is not reflected in the usage rates of the Catholic population. The Morris et al. 1987 study of a representative sample of adolescents in two sections of Mexico City clearly shows that the attitudes of youngsters do not correspond to Church positions: only 22.3 percent of females and 15.5 percent of males thought God should decide the number of children to be procreated by the couple. The CONAPO survey documented that a majority of youngsters who have had sex actually use contraception: 64.6 percent of young males and 58.2 percent of young females, with condoms used by 38.8 percent and oral contraceptives by 23.8 percent. Women reported 23.9 percent using condoms, 23.3 percent rhythm, and coitus interruptus 21.5 percent.

Adult use of contraceptives is common. According to the information from the National Survey of Health and Fertility, the percentage of women in a marriage, cohabitation, or other sexually active relationship who use contraceptives is 52.7 percent, up from 30.2 percent ten years ago (Secretaría de Salud 1990).

B. Teenage Unmarried Pregnancies

Adolescent pregnancy occurs frequently. An annual rate of 56 births for each 1,000 women in the 15- to 19-years-of-age group is reported (Urbina-Fuentes 1992). The fate of these pregnancies is not clear. Eskala et al. (1992) followed 189 pregnant unmarried adolescents at one of the main centers of high-risk pregnancy care in Mexico City, reporting that most unwed mothers decided to live with the father of the child. This option was much less popular for mothers with high education expectations. Since abortion is illegal, there is no reliable information on what percentage of pregnant adolescents terminate their pregnancy and what percentage carry through to birth.

C. Abortion

Voluntary (on request) abortion is not legal in Mexico. The law permits abortion in cases of rape or when the health of the mother is at risk. However, the legal procedure is so complex that in practice it is almost impossible. Illegal abortions are, nevertheless, widely practiced. A source of the Mexican Social Security Institute, a huge social medicine system that provides medical care to everyone who has a formal job, estimated there were about two million during 1989 (IMSS 1990). According to some not very systematic reports, abortion is the fourth cause of death, although this does not show up in the official statistics because cause of death is recorded under another category such as generalized infection (Abasolo 1990). This same source estimated that for each 100,000 babies born, 5.7 women, most of them adolescents, die from abortion complications. De la Peña and Toledo (1991d) reported that a third of their female respondents said they had had an abortion. The National Survey of Health and Fertility reported that 14.3 percent of Mexican women had had an abortion (Secretaría de Salud 1987).

Abortion is one of the most controversial issues in Mexico. Among the Mexico City respondents of de la Peña and Toledo (1991a), 30.3 percent approved abortion if there was a medical reason and 28.9 percent if a woman wishes it for social reasons; 17.1 percent said they would never accept it. Givaudán and Pick de Weiss (1992a) interviewed 500 persons in two groups in Mexico City and found that most respondents approve the decriminalization of abortion, 60 percent think abortion is a decision of the woman only, 62 percent think public hospitals should offer abortions, and 76.2 percent think legalization would reduce maternal deaths. The opinions of men and women in these studies did not differ significantly. In a second study, Givaudán and Pick de Weiss (1992b) interviewed 300 people representative of the two most important cities in the state of Chiapas where in 1990 abortion was legalized briefly. After some days, the local congress reversed its position and suspended the new law. While the opinions reported were more divided than in the Mexico City survey, half of the respondents think abortion is a woman's decision and that the Catholic Church should change its point of view. Half of the respondents also think abortion services should be provided by public hospitals; slightly more than half think depenalizing abortion would reduce maternal deaths.

D. Population Control Efforts

Official policy is clearly oriented towards reduction of population growth. The policy changed twenty-one years ago from a progrowth policy. In 1974, the government recognized that a low population growth would be favorable for national development. As a result, there has been a major campaign to achieve the new goal, and there are many indications that the efforts have been conducive to concrete results. The current population growth rate is 2.6, down from 3.2 between 1950 and 1970. Efforts include actions at many levels: free family planning at public hospitals, education and information programs at many levels, programs for women looking for an increase in the quality of life, and actions to promote a better distribution of population and many others.

10. Sexually Transmitted Diseases

Evaluation of the available data on the incidence of sexually transmitted diseases is difficult because not all the cases are reported. The data reported by the health care system include the following figures for 1991: gonococcal infections: 15,681 cases (18 per 100,000 habitants), genital herpes: 3,480 (4 per 100,000), and syphilis: 3,282 (3.8 per 100,000) (Secretaría de Salud 1992). There are no statistics for the other sexually transmitted diseases, except AIDS. Despite the problem of underreporting, investigators have come to some interesting conclusions: the rate for gonorrhea has been declining, from 230 cases per 100,000 inhabitants in 1941 to the current rate of 18 per 100,000. Researchers who have attempted to document prevalence among these diseases consistently report higher figures, suggesting that the problem is much more frequent than the levels reported by official statistics (Del Rio, in press). STDs are more frequently a problem for males between 20 and 24 years of age and women between ages 18 and 24.

11. HIV/AIDS

AIDS (SIDA) was first diagnosed in 1983 when seventeen cases were identified. Since then, the increase in diagnosed cases can be divided into three phases: from 1983 to 1986, the growth was moderate; from 1987 to 1989, a rapid growth period was observed where cases doubled in only a few months with an exponential increase in identified cases; and from 1989 to the present, when there has being a slower, yet still exponential, growth in the number of cases. As of December 31, 1993, the total number of cases reported to the Health Ministry was 17,387 cases. However, estimates of the real number of cases, correcting for late reporting and underreporting, takes the figure to 27,000 cases (Del Rio, in press).

Another alarming point in these statistics is a doubling of the number of cases in women from 7.9 percent of all the cases in 1987 to a current 14.8 percent of all cases. The current male/female case ratio is 6:1 (INDRE 1994). (Table 1 shows the numbers of reported cases from 1983 to 1993.)

Most of the cases are due to sexual transmission. Thus, it is clear that education is the only preventive measure available. The severity of the AIDS epidemic has not escaped officials, but the effectiveness of preventive measures remains under discussion. Early in the epidemic, the government set up a special office to deal with the problem: The Consejo Nacional para el Control y Prevención del SIDA (CONASIDA). This agency has launched several campaigns in the mass media to increase the awareness of the general public of the risk posed by AIDS, but the campaigns have being criticized by both those who say they are offensive to the moral conscience of people and those who argue the contents of the messages are not clear enough. There has been an upsurge in the number of independent nongovernmental organizations (ONGs) that devote themselves to preventive and educative work, but their efforts are restricted by financial limitations. In the beginning, these organizations focused their work on the gay community, which was the hardest hit in the early stages of the epidemic. In the recent years, many of these ONGs have included actions to reach all the sexual orientations.

Public attention to the problem has increased considerably in the last three years, and the mass media has both responded and been responsible

Table 1

New Cases Of AIDS per Notification Year and Sex 1983 to 1993

Year	Cases per 1,000,000	Incidence	Rate Male:Female	Percentage of Cases in Women
1983	6	0.07	6:0	0.0
1984	6	0.07	6:0	0.0
1985	29	0.3	14:1	6.9
1986	246	2.9	30:1	3.2
1987	518	6.6	12:1	7.9
1988	905	10.6	6:1	13.5
1989	1,607	18.3	6:1	15.2
1990	2,588	31.8	5:1	16.2
1991	3,167	37.9	5:1	15.4
1992	3,220	37.5	6:1	15.2
1993	5,095	58.5	6:1	14.8
Cummulative Data from 1983-1993	17,387	200.00	6:1	14.8

Source: INDRE. Boletín Mensual SIDA/ETS (México) 8, 1:2576-2593. January 1994.

for these. It is common for radio stations, television, and the print media to devote space to discussions and informative programs on AIDS.

12. Sexual Dysfunctions, Counseling, and Therapies

A. Concepts of Sexual Dysfunction

The concept of sexual dysfunction as a health problem is only recently gaining acceptance in Mexico. The traditional approach ignored the quality of sexual interaction of people. If one interprets the decisions of the official health system on health-care policies, attention to these problems was considered either unnecessary or a luxury. The assumptions were that problems of sexual dysfunction were always in the realm of psychoanalysis and traditionally outside the realm of possibilities available to the majority of Mexicans due to the high cost of treatment. Also, emotions of shame and undue guilt prevailed among those who had such problems, preventing any search for help. This panorama has changed in the last fifteen to twenty years. I have had the experience of people who at 50 years of age ask for help for problems they have been aware of for thirty or more years, and who express their relief at the change they experienced in society. It is now easier to admit that one has a sexual problem and to seek help. The resources to provide effective help are still limited to a few private organizations with limited resources. I have been in the forefront of this change, because the institution (AMSSAC) where I work devotes its efforts specifically to the treatment of sexual dysfunction among economically restricted individuals, and to providing formal training in sex therapy to professionals.

In the mind of lay people, the concept of sexual dysfunction is still very vague. Most people immediately identify terms such as impotence and frigidity with the lack of ability to complete intercourse and to experience pleasure and orgasm. In more-professional settings, increasing attention is being paid to sexual dysfunction. Medical associations and medical schools are beginning to include themes on sexual functioning in their curricula and in their programs for congresses and professional meetings.

As a frame for clinical treatment and research, the following concept of sexual dysfunction has been proposed: a series of syndromes where the erotic processes of the sexual response occur recurrently and persistently in a way that results undesirably for the individual or the social group (Rubio and Díaz, in press). There is no information on the incidence and prevalence of these problems among the general population, but there are a number of indirect indicators that show the problems to be very common. In six years, the sexual dysfunction clinic set up at AMSSAC has been used by close to 700 individuals, around 30 percent of whom seek help as a couple. This number is surely much lower than the total number of people seeking help at AMSSAC, because patients requesting treatment are requested to wait a long time before their treatment can begin. The data in Table 2, reported by González in 1993 and based on 195 initial-intake diagnostic interviews during an 8-month period, give an idea of the relative frequency of the sexual problems encountered at AMSSAC. Generalization, however, is difficult, because the center is a specialized center in Mexico City. Comparative information from other regions of the country is not available.

B. Availability of Counseling, Diagnosis, and Treatment

Specialized treatment for sexual dysfunctions is available, but the few trained professionals and treatment centers severely limit this. This is particularly true in the smaller cities and rural areas. In the big cities such as Mexico City, Guadalajara, and Monterrey, individual professionals who have obtained specialized training both in Mexico and aboard—mainly the United States—offer sexual therapy privately. However, this is far from sufficient for the size of the population. The situation in more critical in the official health system where sex counseling and therapy is not offered in any systematic way. Some professionals working for the official health system have been trained in sexual counseling, and they do provide this service, but with no organized structure.

As mentioned above, AMSSAC is involved in the training of sex therapists, and some already trained professionals offer their services within the

Table 2

Frequencies of Diagnosis of Sexual Disfunction in 195 Diagnostic Interviews at the Sexual Dysfunction Clinic, Asociacion Mexicana para la Salud Sexual, A.C. (AMSSAC)

Diagnosis	Males (138)		Females (57)	
	n	%	*n*	%
Hypoactive desire	67	26.07	7	29.13
Hyperactive desire	2	0.78	0	0.00
Inhibited excitation	86	33.46	36	28.35
Anorgasmia	10	3.89	38	29.92
Pain syndromes	9	3.50	5	3.94
Premature ejaculation	77	29.96	0	0.00
Sexual phobia	6	2.33	7	5.51
Vaginismus	0	0.00	4	3.15

Source: González, 1993. Patients may have more than one diagnosis.

sexual dysfunction clinic at AMSSAC. This clinic, although privately run, serves only patients whose economic situation prevents them from seeking help in a private clinic. Much work is needed before it can be said that the Mexican population has the ability to solve its sexual dysfunctions via professional treatment. Unfortunately, one result of the above situation is the proliferation of street therapists and fraudulent remedies to which many people still look for help.

13. Research and Advanced Education

Sexual research is conducted as a formal activity by very few researchers. However, their work is beginning to give a panorama of what goes on in the country. This has reduced the need for constantly referring to foreign research and literature.

There are researchers working now at every level of the sciences that deal with aspects of sexuality. Basic physiological research in animals is conducted following state-of-the-art methodologies in highly specialized centers. Psychological research, conducted basically by a group in the Universidad Nacional Autónoma de México, has produced interesting information on the sexual behavior of young people, some of which is reviewed in this article. Anthropology researchers have also produced original work on gender issues in both the Universidad Nacional Autónoma de México and in El Colegio de México. Clinical research on sexual problems is just starting, but some information is beginning to appear. The systematization of these efforts into a body of sexual science, however, is far from being realized. Sexology, as a formal discipline, is only recently being considered, and this with considerable reticence.

Advanced education in sexology has been offered by private institutions for some twenty-five years, but these efforts have been concentrated in Mexico City. Recently, a number of private and public universities have opened up the possibility of short programs on sexology, focusing on sex-education issues. The list below reflects the efforts and achievements of the main groups that have participated in the construction of the human sexuality body of professionals.

The Asociación Mexicana de Educación Sexual (AMES), a private non-profit organization, was the first to offer systematic training in sex education, with good foundations in sexology. This organization has offered courses for professionals—usually professionals trained in other disciplines, such as education, psychology, and medicine—courses of approximately 180 hours, since 1974. Other institutions, such as the Instituto Mexicano de Sexología, followed this pattern, although with modifications in length and format of the courses offered.

Then, organizations with a focus on special problems, such as adolescent contraception, and family planning followed. Among the latter, the Fundación Mexicana para la Planificación Familiar (MEXFAM) has distinguished itself in systematizing the training in sexuality via postgraduate courses in sex education and sex counseling. This organization has promoted the institutionalization of training in public universities in other cities in addition to Mexico City, in what has become known as the Diplomats in Sexuality.

Training in sex therapy has being available since 1987 in our institution Asociación Mexicana para la Salud Sexual (AMSSAC). Training includes clinical experience and formal lectures and readings over two years, with 650 hours of instruction.

Official institutions have included courses on sexology in the medical and psychological curricula, but no formal graduate courses are offered, with the exception of the aforementioned Diplomats in Sexuality. No formal degrees in sexology are offered.

References and Suggested Readings

Abasolo, Guillermo, Director of Social Communication of the Medical Services of the México City Government. June 19, 1990. Quoted in a newspaper note: *Uno Más Uno.*
Casorla, Gloria. (In press). "Conductas Sexuales Delictivas: Violacion, Incesto, Abuso Sexual, Hostigamiento Sexual y Lenocinio." In Consejo Nacional de Poblacion, ed. *Antologia de la Sexualidad Humana.* México.
CNP—Consejo Nacional de Población. 1989. *Programa Nacional de Población 1989-1994.* México City: Secretaria de Gobernacion.
Colimoro, Claudia. June 1993. Personal Communication. México City.

CONAPO—Consejo Nacional de Población. 1988. *Encuesta Nacional sobre Sexualidad y Familia en Jóvenes de Educación Media Superior, 1988*. Consejo Nacional de Población, México.

De la Peña, Ricardo, and Rosario Toledo. May 26, 1991a. "El Sexo en México" (Part 1). *El Nacional Dominical.*

De la Peña, Ricardo, and Rosario Toledo. June 2, 1991b. "El Sexo en México Segunda de Cuatro Partes: Debutantes y Solitarios." (Part 2). *El Nacional Dominical.*

De la Peña, Ricardo, and Rosario Toledo. June 9, 1991c. "Vida ¿en Pareja? El Sexo en México. Primer Informe" (Part 3). *El Nacional Dominical.*

De la Peña, Ricardo, and Rosario Toledo. June 16, 1991d. "El Sexo en México. Primer Informe." (Part 4). Cuerpos y Susurros. *El Nacional Dominical.*

De la Peña, Ricardo, and Rosario Toledo. March 1, 1992a. "Primer Informe Sobre Sexualidad en Baja California." (Part 1). *El Nacional Dominical.*

De la Peña, Ricardo, and Rosario Toledo. March 8, 1992b. "Primer Informe Sobre Sexualidad en Baja California." (Part 2). *El Nacional Dominical.*

Del Rio, Carlos. (In press). "Enfermedades de Transmisión por Contacto Sexual." In: Consejo Nacional de Poblacion, ed. *Antologia de la Sexualidad Humana*. México.

Díaz Loving, Rolando. 1988. "Desenredando la Semántica del Amor." *In La Psicología Social de México: 1988*. México: Proceedings of the Congess of Social Psicology.

Dillon, S. 1997 (January 22). "How to Scandalize a Politician: Bare a Love Affair." *The New York Times*, p. A4.

Eskala, Emilia, et al. 1992. "La Adolescente Embarazada y Su Relación de Pareja." Psicología Social de México III. *Proceedings of the Congess of Social Psicology*. México.

Falicov, Celia Jaes. 1982. "Mexican Families." In M. McGoldrick, J. K. Pearce, and J. Giordano, eds. *Ethnicity and Family Therapy*. New York: Guilford Press.

Givaudán, Martha, & Susan Pick de Weiss. 1992. "Encuesta de Opinión Sobre el Aborto Inducido y su Despenalización en el Estado de Chiapas." *Psicología Social de México III. Proceedings of the Congress of Social Psicology*. México.

Givaudán, Martha, & Susan Pick de Weiss. 1992. "Encuesta de Opinión Sobre el Aborto Inducido y su Despenalización en la Ciudad de México." *Psicología Social de México III. Proceedings of the Congress of Social Psicology*. México.

González, Guillermo. 1993. "Panorama Sociodemográfico del Servicio de Preconsulta de la Clínica de Salud Sexual AMSSAC." *Gaceta Amssac*, 1(1):2-5.

IMSS—Instituto Mexicano del Seguro Social. 1990. *Síntesis IMSS*. México.

INDRE—Instituto Nacionál de Diagnónstico y Referencia Epidemiológicos. January 1994. *Boletín Mensual SIDA/ETS* (México), 8, 1:2576-93.

INEGI—Instituto Nacional de Estadistica Geografia e Informatica. 1992. *Estados Unidos Mexicanos: Perfil Sociodemografico XI Censo General de Poblacion y Vicienda, 1990*. México City: INEGI.

INEGI-2—Instituto Nacional de Estadistica Geografia e Informatica. 1992. *Estados Unidos Mexicanos. Resumen General XI Censo General de Población y Vivienda, 1990*. México City: Instituto Nacional de Estadística Geografía e Informática.

Lavrin, Asuncion. 1991. "La Sexualidad en el México Colonial: Un Dilema para la Iglesia." In A. Lavrin, ed. *Sexualidad y Matrimonio en la America Hispana: Siglos XVI-XVIII*. México D. F.: Grijalbo.

López Juarez, Alfonso. 1982. "Familia y Sexualidad en México." In Consejo Nacional de Población (CONAPO), ed. *La Educación de la Sexualidad Humana. Familia y Sexualidad*. México City: CONAPO.

Lumsden, Ian. 1991. *Homosexualidad, Socedad y Estado en México*. México: Solediciones Canadian Gay Archives.

Morgan, Maria Isabel. 1982. "La Sexualidad en la Sociedad en la Sociedad Azteca." In H. Carrizo, ed. *La Educacion de la Sexualidad Humana: Sociedad y Sexualidad.* México City: Consejo Nacional de Poblacion.

Morris, L., et al. 1987. *Young Adult Reproductive Health Survey in Two Delegations of Mexico City.* México City: Centro de Orientación Para Adolescentes.

Muñoz Gonzalez, Lilia. October 1992. "Departamento de Atención an Victimas: Procuraduría de Justicia del Distrito Federal." Personal communication.

Ordiozola-Urbina, Alberto & Berenice Ibañes-Brambila. 1992. "Actitudes y Conducta Sexual en Estudiantes Universitarios." *Psicologia Social de México III.* México: Proceedings of the Congress of Social Psicology.

Padgett, T. September 18, 1995. "The End of the Affair: Mexico's Threat to an Institution—Mistresses." *Newsweek,* p. 59.

Palafox Vargas, Miguel. 1985. *Violencia, Droga y Sexo Entre los Huicholes.* México: Instituto Nacional de Antropología e Historia.

Paz, Octavio. 1950. *El Laberinto de la Soledad.* México: Fondo de Cultura Economica.

Rubio, Eusebio. 1989. *A Cross-Cultural Investigation of Sexual Behavior, Religiosity and Familism Among American and Mexican Urban Single College Students.* Doctoral dissertation. New York, NY: New York University.

Rubio, Eusebio, et al. March 1988. "Caracterización de las Opiniones y Experiencias Sexuales de los Alumnos de Primer Ingreso a la Carrera de Médico Cirujano." *Salud Mental,* 11(1):25-34.

Ruiz Harrel, Rafael. 1979. Personal Communication. México City.

Saavedra Arredondo, Guillermo, ed. 1986. *La Educación en Población: Marco de Referencia.* México: Consejo Nacional de Población.

Secretaría de Salud. 1987. *Dirección General de Planificación Familiar.* México: Encuesta Nacional Sobre Fecundidad y Salud.

Secretaría de Salud. 1990. *La Salud de la Mujer en México. Cifras Comentadas. Dirección General de Salud Materno Infantil.* México: Programa Nacional "Mujer Salud y Desarrollo."

Secretaría de Salud. 1992. *Compendio de Estadísticas de Morbilidad 1991.* México: Dirección General de Epidemiología.

Urbina Fuentes, Manuel. 1992. "Jóvenes Reproductores." In H. Bellinghausen, ed. *El Nuevo Arte de Amar.* México: Cal y Arena.

Wolf, Eric. 1975. *Pueblos y Culturas de Mesoamerica* (3rd ed.). México City: Biblioteca Era.

Netherlands and the
Autonomous Dutch Antilles
(*Koninkrijk der Nederlanden*)

Jelto J. Drenth, Ph.D., and A. Koos Slob, Ph.D.*

Contents

Demographics, a Historical Perspective, and Dutch Sexology

A. Demographics

Located in northwest Europe on the North Sea, the Netherlands' 15,770 square miles are roughly the size of the states of Massachusetts, Connecticut, and Rhode Island combined. Belgium borders the Netherlands on the south, Germany on the east, and the English Channel and the United Kingdom on the west. The Kingdom of the Netherlands includes the Dutch

*This chapter draws extensively from the 1991 Special English Issue of the *Tijdschrift voor Seksuologie,* published on the occasion of the Tenth World Congress for Sexology, Amsterdam, June 18-22, 1991. We gratefully acknowledge the authors of this volume and the editors for their kind permission.

Antilles, the autonomous Caribbean islands of the West Indies. Curacao, Aruba, and Bonaire are near the South American coast; St. Eustatius, Saba, and the southern part of St. Maarten are southeast of Puerto Rico. (The northern two thirds of St. Maarten island belongs to French Guadaloupe). Combined, the six islands have an area of 385 square miles.

Over 88 percent of the 15.4 million Dutch live in cities. Life expectancy at birth in 1995 was 75 for males and 81 for females. The 1995 birthrate was 12 per 1,000 and the death rate 8 per 1,000, with an annual natural increase of 0.4 percent. The infant mortality rate was 6 per 1,000 live births. Age distribution is 18 percent for those under the age of 14; 15 to 64, 69 percent; and 65 and over, 13 percent. The Netherlands has one hospital bed per 172 persons and one physician for 400 persons. The per capital domestic product in 1995 was $17,200.

B. A Brief Historical Perspective

In 55 B.C.E., Julius Caesar conquered the Celtic and Germanic tribes that inhabited the region that is now the Netherlands. After Charlamagne's empire fell apart in the mid-800s, the Netherlands, then what is today Holland, Belgium, and Flanders, was divided among dukes, counts, and bishops. Holland soon passed through the Duke of Burgundy to King Charles V of Spain. In the later 1500s, as the area drifted toward political freedom and Protestantism, William the Silent, prince of Orange, led a confederation of the northern provinces that declared independence from Spain in 1581. The United Dutch Republic's rise to naval, economic, and artistic eminence came in the 17th century, only to end in 1795 when Napoleon made his brother Louis king of Holland. Napoleon annexed the country in 1810, but the French were expelled in 1813 and the kingdom of the Netherlands, including Belgium, established. The Belgians seceded and formed a separate kingdom in 1830.

The Netherlands remained neutral in World War I, but was invaded and brutally occupied by the Germans between 1940 and 1945. After several years of fighting, Indonesia gained its independence in 1949; West New Guinea was turned over to Indonesia in 1963. The independence of former Dutch colonies was followed by mass emigrations to the Netherlands.

C. Dutch Sexology

To understand Dutch sexology, one needs to keep in mind five general characteristics of our society that crystallized in the latter half of the nineteenth and first half of the twentieth centuries:

1. The role of the family and the position of men and women is central in Dutch society. Excluded from the labor process, women were supposed to derive their task, fulfillment, and satisfaction from marriage and

family. Together with Ireland and Sicily, the Netherlands has the lowest rate of working wives and economically independent women. Even today, many politicians support this inequality of social roles. In recent decades, however, the position of the housewife has gradually declined, a factor that may impact on sexual problems for women and men.

2. Since the origin of the Netherlands in the seventeenth century, there has been a strong segregation between Catholicism and Protestantism, with many subdivisions among the latter. In the nineteenth century, humanism, socialism, and liberalism were influential. As a result, the Netherlands now has a very strong compartmentalization or "denominational segregation." Some forty different organizations and over twenty-five political parties have access to television broadcasting and the elections. Due to different, sometimes very powerful religious influences, extreme contrasts in social and sexual behavior exist between various groups. For instance, one fundamentalist Protestant political party still discriminates against women in membership and office eligibility, although over half of those voting for this party are women. On the positive side, this compartmentalization has resulted in a willingness to cope with differences in opinion and a rather liberal attitude towards varying social groups and lifestyles. The pedophile movement, for example, openly expresses its views on child-adult sexual relations. Our homosexual movement is widely respected, and our national organization for homosexuals even received royal assent. The Protestant University of Amsterdam houses the world's only chair of transsexology.

3. Holland, in the west, was rich and industrialized with extensive colonial ventures; the east was less prosperous and mainly agrarian. The west is the focus of political, economic, cultural, and social development, including a large group of sexologists. This geographic separation also influences differences between groups in Dutch society.

4. When the Dutch East Indies became independent Indonesia in 1949, several hundred thousand people came from this culture to the Netherlands. A similar immigration occurred in 1975 when Dutch Guiana became independent Suriname. The Netherlands has also received its share of labor from the Mediterranean. A second and third generation of Turkish and Moroccan origins, most born in the Netherlands, still struggle with the problem of being rooted in two cultures. Political refugees are the latest contribution to our multi-ethnic society. Some 7 percent of our population was born in other countries. The result is a profoundly multiracial society in which sexual rules and values sometimes differ greatly, presenting a major challenge for sexological research and treatment.

5. Sociosexological research in the Netherlands has been quite extensive since the 1960s. Initial research focused on problems resulting from a restrictive sexual morality. During the 1970s, attention shifted to the

rapid process of sexual liberalization and its practical consequences, such as the need for family planning education and services. The past decade has been dominated by research on sexual abuse and the spread of STDs and AIDS. Published mostly in the Dutch language, this research has not had a significant impact outside Holland, despite the fact that open and permissive sexual attitudes give Dutch sexology a unique position, not just in terms of attitudes and behavior, but also in terms of research possibilities. More international comparative and collaborative research would benefit all.

Research on sexual behavior, attitudes and related subjects began in 1968, when the largest women's weekly, *Margriet,* commissioned a national *Seks in Nederland* (SIN) survey using a representative sample of 1,284 men and women, ages 21 to 65, and 809 youngsters ages 16 to 20 (Noordhoff et al. 1969). This study was repeated in a modified and extended way in 1974 (with teenagers only) and in 1981 and 1989. These surveys present a fairly accurate description of major social and demographic correlates of sexual attitudes and behavior, and the changes in these variables over time.

While strongly inspired by the 1948/1953 Kinsey studies, the 1968 Dutch study reflected the main interests and concerns of Dutch society at that time, namely self-pleasuring, premarital and extramarital sexual contacts, sexual desires, prostitution, homosexuality, contraception, and (illegal) induced abortion.

Kooy (1975) analyzed the 1968 SIN-survey, putting the data in a theoretical perspective of changing family relationships, declining moral influence of religion, and growing social equality between the sexes. The second SIN-survey (in 1981) had the character of a trend report (Kooy et al., 1983). The main trends observed were growing tolerance towards different kinds of sexual behavior and more equality between partners in heterosexual relationships. Secularization seemed to be the most important background factor in these changes. The 1989 survey was strongly influenced by fear of AIDS and a need for knowledge to underpin prevention programs.

In part, the study of adolescent sexuality parallels the adult studies, including sexual development, relationship development, sexual education, prevention of unwanted pregnancy, and induced abortion, and recently STD and AIDS prevention. In 1974, the first SIN-survey was repeated for adolescents only. De Haas (1975) interpreted and reported the data from an educational view point; Kooy (1976) used a sociological perspective. The 1981 adolescent data were not analyzed before they were used in the framework of the much larger 1989 study (Vogels and van der Vliet 1990). The 1974 and 1981 studies included 600 and 800 youngsters, ages 15 to 19, while the 1989 study included 11,500 youngsters and 11- to 14-year-olds. Finally, both the 1989 adolescent and 1989 SIN adult surveys were motivated by the fear of the HIV epidemic.

1. Basic Sexological Premises

A. Character of Gender Roles

It is difficult to generalize on gender roles in the Netherlands. Dutch society has become so diverse that, at any given moment, different groups will be influenced differently. Yet, in all but the most isolated groups, an awareness of the variation in social and sexual role responsibilities must have led to a rise in tolerance for less-conventional behaviors.

The classic Western role separation, men being providers and women housekeepers and care givers has been criticized intensively. Some feminist principles have found almost universal support. Holland is subject to Europe's legislation against sex discrimination, and today it is hard to find examples of sex discrimination in the workplace. Government policy includes a "positive action" plan: in some segments of paid labor, women will be favored in the job-application process to bring down the underrepresentation of women in these professions. The government has funded a mass-media campaign intended to raise girls' awareness of preparing for financial independence.

Countering these conscious efforts, mass-media influences, such as soap operas and commercials, are often extremely conservative in their depiction of role ideals. The impact of this on the general public's role awareness is hard to estimate.

B. Sociolegal Status of Males and Females

In recent years, legislation reforms have tended to equalize legal rights for men and women, homosexuals and heterosexuals. For instance, a 1991 reform of rape laws encompassed male and female rape. Children under age 12 are protected against all sexual contacts; for 12- to 16-year-olds, sexual contacts are legal offenses only if the adolescent, his/her parents(s) or guardian, or the Child Welfare Court files a complaint. Existence of a dependency relation between the adult partner and the adolescent is an exception to this. The law's intention is that the child's own judgment outweighs the parent's.

In the Netherlands, bypasses are available for teenagers to obtain oral contraceptives and abortions without parental permission.

C. General Concepts of Sexuality and Love

As oral contraception has uncoupled sexuality and procreation, so the possibility of uncoupling sexuality and love has also been recognized. Large groups of Dutch men and women sympathize with the need for sexual gratification of people who are not in steady relationships. Self-pleasuring and "recreational" sex are no longer taboo. Virginity is disappearing as an ideal. Self-pleasuring as a variation within a steady relationship is also no longer universally scorned.

Yet love is still probably the most-valued principle in Holland. Almost all Dutch men and women believe that steady relations must be built on love, and that sexuality with love is more satisfying that without it.

2. Religious and Ethnic Factors Affecting Sexuality

A. Source and Character of Religious Values

Denominational segregation, 34 percent Roman Catholic and 25 percent Dutch Reformed, has not played an important role in Dutch sexuality. The Dutch Society for Sexual Reform (NVSH) found its Protestant counterpart in the Protestant Society for Responsible Family Planning (PSVG) and a Catholic Bureau for Sexuality and Relations. But these religiously inspired organizations are small and limited to providing written information and educational materials. NVSH has separated into a lay persons' organization for political action and education, and a professional organization, the Rutgers Foundation, for medical and psychological help. The Dutch government funds the foundation's counseling centers and participation of foundation administrators and staff in international organizations, such as the International Planned Parenthood Federation.

Religious motivations have played an important role in our legal reform. The Dutch abortion law adopted in 1985 permits abortion on request with the sole restriction of a five-day waiting period. Opposition from fundamentalist Catholics has little support. Moreover, the Pope's regulations on contraception is almost universally ignored by Dutch Catholics, as are restrictions on homosexual behavior and the sexuality of the handicapped. Catholic and Protestant groups have played important roles in the acceptance of gays and lesbians, with some churches celebrating ceremonies of gay and lesbian unions. (Legal marriage is not available for homosexual couples in Holland.)

B. Source and Character of Ethnic Values

Most Muslims in the Netherlands came from Turkey or Morocco as "guest laborers" in the booming economy, women and children following the men after they settled in. The Netherlands now has a second generation and a third on its way. Tension between Muslim traditions and the Western way of life is common. Islamic traditions emphasize family honor, with specific restrictions on sexual behavior and distinct social roles for men and women.

Arranged marriages are common and the confrontation of two cultures sometimes leads to conflicts between parents and children who, raised in the Western world, want to choose their own spouse. Muslim tradition includes the ultimate measure of kidnapping to force a marriage. Incidents of this, and of Muslim girls running away from home to avoid an arranged marriage, are common, leading to the establishment of a shelter home for Muslim girls only. Muslim honor sometimes conflicts with the Dutch legal system, leading to tragic misunderstandings in the law courts. Helping professionals are only slowly learning how to handle such problems without trespassing on Muslim taboos. Relevant for sexological practice are the following:

- A male doctor will not be allowed to perform a physical examination of a Muslima in the absence of her husband;
- A male patient will often be embarrassed if asked about his sexual problems by a female doctor;
- Self-pleasuring is an almost-absolute taboo and should not be advised as a therapeutic modality;
- Prostitution is much less forbidden for Muslim men; and
- Direct communications are uncommon—a metaphorical presentation of the most distressing problems, infertility and erectile failure, is the rule.

Comparative research data on the influence of religious background on sexual topics include:

- Muslim adolescent boys commonly initiate all types of sexual activity earlier than their Christian and nonreligious male and female peers; Muslim girls are considerably less experienced;
- Christian and nonreligious adolescents tend to prefer sex in steady relationships, Muslim adolescents tend to have more casual sexual experiences and less steady relationships;
- Attitudes toward premarital sex in steady relationships are more accepting in Christian and nonreligious adolescents (80 percent) and less so in Muslim adolescents (40 percent). Muslima are very restricted.
- Muslim adolescents tend to advocate abstinence as the best way to avoid HIV infection, and are less willing to use condoms for this purpose (Sandfort and van Zessen 1991).

While incidence figures for induced abortion are generally low in the Netherlands, some ethnic groups have a higher risk of unwanted pregnancy and abortion (see Section 9). Among autochtonous* women, unwanted pregnancy is mostly due to contraceptive method failure; among Carib-

---

Note: In Dutch sociology, "autochtonous" means "of Dutch descent," including Dutch nationality, Caucasian, and raised in Western traditions. "Allochtonous" includes immigrants and their next generations from former Dutch colonies, immigrants from Mediterranean countries who came to Holland seeking work in the 1960s and 1970s, and political refugees from all over the world.

bean, Mediterranean, and refugee women, nonuse or inconsistent use of contraceptives is the more likely cause. A 1990 study of unwanted pregnancy among Caribbean women (Lamur et al.) identifies three groups with distinguishing attitudes towards contraception:

- Among women born in the six Caribbean islands, the strongest influence on sexual attitudes and practices is the Roman Catholic Church. Information on sexuality is extremely scarce. Strong negative moral and practical feelings toward contraception are common. The pill and IUD are often seen as severe health hazards; when used, physical complaints are common.
- Creole women from Suriname (formerly Dutch Guiana) also have little access to sexual information, but this is changing for Creole women born after 1960. In this younger group, middle-class women from stable families are mostly highly career-oriented and very concerned about unwanted pregnancy. Lower-class women are often familiar with a pattern of single women having children with fathers who are more or less distant. Among middle-class Creole families in the Netherlands, sexual information is more adequate and attitudes towards sex and protection less taboo-burdened. Yet these women are less constant in their choice of contraceptive methods and tend to have more physical complaints when using the pill. For all Creole women, abortion is not an easy solution for unwanted pregnancy. Despite a high abortion rate in this group, moral restraints are strong and abortion is definitely not seen as a normal contraceptive method.
- Hindustani women of Suriname descent have very strict family rules, and honor (*Izzat*) is a leading principle. Premarital sex is an absolute taboo. Education is highly valued and often considered part of a girl's dowry. In recent years, information on sexuality and contraception is provided to Hindustani girls, but effective premarital contraceptive use is rare. A sex taboo seems to prevent information from being absorbed adequately for practical use.

The problems of political refugees have not yet been researched. Dutch Amnesty International workers have some experience with the atrocious problems of sexual torture and humiliation some refugees have experienced.

A particular problem causing some public discussion is clitorectomy. A modified form of clitorectomy, incision of clitoral prepuce, has been under consideration as a result of requests mainly from Somalian women. The Dutch government recently prohibited all forms of clitoral mutilation. Incidentally, Islamic and Hindustani women commonly consult Dutch gynecologists for hymen reconstruction, as part of preparation for marriage.

3. Sexual Knowledge and Education

A. Government Policies and Programs for Sex Education

The Netherlands has the lowest rate of unwanted teenage pregnancies of all the industrialized nations. Some attribute this to a relatively effective use of contraceptives, especially the pill, among teenagers. This effective use is explained, at least in part, by a pragmatic and liberal attitude towards sex education, the high quality of information and education on sex and contraception in secondary schools and the mass media, and the wide availability of confidential and low-cost contraceptive services.

These results, however, are no reason for self-satisfaction or complacency. For one thing, contraceptive behavior among ethnic minorities and young adolescents is still ineffective, and the abortion rate among adolescents is still about 45 per 100 pregnancies. In terms of AIDS, about half of the sexually active teenagers appear to engage in risky behavior.

The Dutch government finances a number of sexuality organizations, including the Netherlands Institute for Social Sexological Research (NISSO), the Rutgers Foundation for contraceptive information, sexological education, and STD prevention, and the Foundation for the Study of STD. Recently, the government policy has tried to integrate these special service organizations into the general health institutions. The Rutgers Foundation, which has for decades provided the easiest access for teenagers to contraceptive information, has been forced to concentrate its services in seven offices in large cities and start a training program to share the foundation's specific knowledge and skills with physicians, mental-health workers, and educators.

In recent years, the government has strongly encouraged and promoted prevention programs. Health promotion is now obligatory in secondary schools, even though traditionally Dutch schools have formed their own curricula. Numerous educational courses and an amalgam of materials on sex and AIDS have been developed by several local and national organizations. Special materials have been developed for Catholic, Protestant, and nonreligious schools. Despite underlying philosophical differences, most of these programs are very similar in terms of goals, methods, and materials.

On a national level, knowledge of the proportion of schools providing sex and AIDS education, what teachers teach, and what methods and materials they use is limited. A late 1980s survey suggests that some sex and AIDS education was provided by about 85 percent of the Dutch secondary schools, generally by hygiene or biology teachers. The major topics covered were biological-physiological aspects of puberty and unwanted pregnancy. Topics such as intercourse and sexual desire received lowest attention. As for AIDS education, practical guidelines for reducing risk were the main topics covered, along with attitudes towards homosexuality. The way teachers covered these topics, however, varied widely, depending on the teacher's area of expertise and teaching methods. Biology-hygiene teachers seemed to focus on transmission of knowledge of biological and physiological aspects. Sociology teachers and counselors seemed to emphasize relational aspects, such as gender-role patterns, cohabitation patterns, friendship, sexual orientations, and being in love.

Eighty percent of Dutch secondary schools offer a mean of four to five hours of AIDS education. Forty percent use one of four AIDS courses developed for national use on AIDS, though often not according to the specific methodological guidelines. More time is devoted to knowledge transfer than to training in social skills. Teachers were not sufficiently trained or supported to implement these courses, and the materials are not tailored to normal school practices.

Criticism of teachers' training in providing sex and AIDS education is widespread. Yet there was for some years in the mid-1980s, a three-day in-service postgraduate course for secondary school teachers, during which about 500 participants were trained (Schraag 1989). A unique feature of this course was that teachers and pupils worked together to express their underlying convictions and wishes about sex education in school and to develop a program for sexual education. The course program and contribution of the trainers have been evaluated on many occasions, leading to continuous adjustments and corrections.

Although it is frequently argued that health education should be a systematic process, most sex-education courses and materials have not been developed in a systematic way. Very few consider behavioral determinants, and little is known about the effectiveness of the various courses and materials. Besides, only two of the evaluative surveys on sex and AIDS-education classes have used an adequate experimental design. Both surveys concluded that the courses under scrutiny produced only an increase in knowledge and minor changes in some attitudes, results similar to evaluations of United States sex education programs and the more general results of health education. Besides knowledge transfer, health education should offer students the opportunity to involve their social environment and develop skills necessary for an adequate performance of the desired behavior. In the 1990s, organizations responsible for implementing educational innovations in health and sex education were encouraged to cooperate with groups responsible for development of educational programs (Kok and Green 1990). Future research should clarify how interventions based on behavioral-science theories can improve diffusion and adoption of health education programs.

Government-financed mass media campaigns are an important means of educating the public. In 1987, the first campaign to alter social norms of condom use focused on a number of Dutch celebrities who use condoms themselves. In 1988, a second campaign focused on "Safe Sex for Holidays," followed in 1989 by ironically confronting 18- to 24-year-olds with irrational beliefs and popular excuses for risky behavior. "Sleep well" was the final comment on each poster and the campaign's title. A pretest/posttest evaluation proved that the majority of respondents had noticed the poster campaign and understood its irony. Those who had noticed the campaign differed from the pretest group by better acknowledgment of the personal risks they took and a lower endorsement of three popular excuses. Condom use in this group rose slightly. Yet, only half of the group ever used condoms, and a quarter were inconsistent in their use.

A 1992 addition to government involvement in sex education and prevention is a mass-media campaign directed at child sexual abuse. This campaign, "There Are Secrets You Should Talk About," is designed to reach children in abusive situations and make the public aware of the reality of child sexual abuse. A second mass-media campaign, "Sex Is Natural, But Never Self-Evident," addresses boys and men on the topic of coercion in sex. Evaluative data on these campaigns are not yet available.

B. Informal Sources of Sexual Knowledge

Veronica, a Dutch broadcasting company, has had a Sunday-afternoon, three-hour phone-in radio program on sex and related subjects since 1985. Themes discussed on program "Radio Romantica" range from light-hearted to serious, including sexual fantasies, falling in love, rape, incest, sexual abuse, safe-sex techniques, coping with AIDS, unwanted pregnancies, homosexuality, bisexuality, and pedophilia. A professional sexologist hosts the program with a liaison officer and a team of students and graduates trained in psychology and social work. The program draws about 250,000 listeners.

In a less systematic way, almost all Dutch broadcasting companies have programs dealing with sex and AIDS. Since the sexual revolution of the 1960s and 1970s, sexuality has provided prime topics for radio, television, and magazines. Books on sex education, for adults and adolescents, are numerous, and vary widely in quality. Pornography is easily available, although the information and messages propagated in these magazines is a matter of concern for many educators. The impact of pornography as an educational source has not been evaluated. (Section 11 deals with numerous mass-media campaigns on AIDS and safe sex.)

4. Autoerotic Behaviors and Patterns

A. Children and Adolescents

Research on child sexuality is relatively underdeveloped. In 1990, readers of the magazine *Ouders va Nu* (*Parents Today*) responded to a questionnaire about their children's sexual behavior and their own attitudes concerning sexual education (Cohen-Kettenis and Sanford 1991). The children's ages ranged from 0 to 7. The results of this survey on child autoeroticism are shown in Table 1.

Table 1

Childhood Self-Pleasuring Behavior (in Percentages)

Behavior	Boys	Girls
Touches genitals with the hand	96	94
Self-pleasures by hand	58	39
Self-pleasures using an object	13	21

In the 1989 adolescent study, 88 percent of 12- to 13-year-old boys and 77 percent of the girls reported at least one sexual fantasy. Frequency of sexual fantasy correlated strongly with self-pleasuring experience. Self-pleasuring according to age is shown in Figure 1.

Figure 1

Percentages of Boys and Girls Engaging in Self-Pleasuring

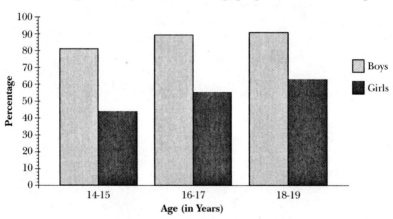

Source: Vogels and van Vliet (1990), Figure 3.2, p. 37.

B. Adults

In the 1989 research (Sandfort and Van Zessen 1991), questions on personal habits disclosed a distinct sex difference of several issues.

- 55 percent of the women and 23 percent of the men had never read sexually explicit books or magazines;
- 71 percent of the women and 47 percent of men had never watched sexually explicit videos or movies;
- 30 percent of the women and 5 percent of the men never looked at an attractive man with sexual intent, 26 percent of the men reported this behavior "often";

- 77 percent of the women and 90 percent of the men were familiar with sexual fantasies. Men tend to fantasize more often and have a more positive view of fantasies. Fantasies featuring power balance and violence were uncommon.
- 92 percent of respondents reported a positive attitude toward self-pleasuring; only 16 percent opposed self-pleasuring in a steady relationship. Autoerotic behavior was related to sex, age, and current relationship status. (See Figures 2, 3, and 4.)

Figure 2

Percentage Frequencies of Self-Pleasuring According to Sex

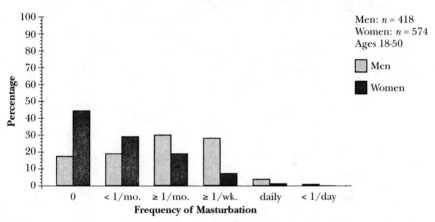

Source: Sandfort and van Zessen (1991), Table 4.10, p. 129.

Figure 3

Percentage Frequencies of Self-Pleasuring According to Age

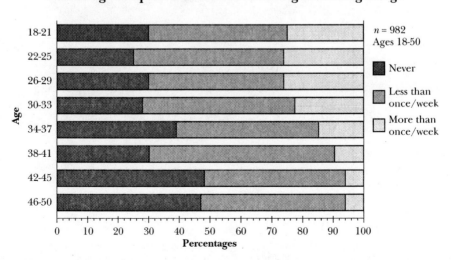

Figure 4

Percentage Frequencies of Self-Pleasuring
According to Relationship Status

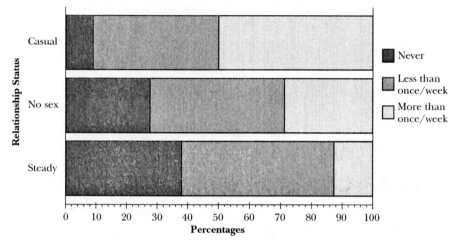

(*n* = 982; steady relationships, 75%; casual relationships, 13%; no sexual contact
in past year, 12%). *Source*: Sandfort and van Zessen (1991), Table 4.6, p. 129.

5. Interpersonal Heterosexual Behaviors

A. Children

In the *Parents Today* study (Section 4A), many questions referred to childhood sexual behavior. Table 2 gives a selection of the data. In this study,
Dutch parents reported considerably more sexual behavior than United
States parents in similar studies, so U.S. data are not useful as criteria in
diagnosing child sexual abuse in Dutch children.

Table 2

Childhood Heterosexual Behavior (in Percentages)

Behavior	Girls	Boys
Interested in the opposite sex	63	63
Plays doctor-and-nurses games	44	43
Tries to see nude people	44	43
Touches genitals of others	39	32
Tries to undress other people	30	22
Shows genitals to adults	15	25
Shows genitals to children	16	24
Kisses with tongue out of mouth	13	16

B. Adolescents

Puberty Rituals

There are no common puberty rituals among autochtonous Dutch groups, although as a result of the more open attitude towards sexual development in some progressive families, young girls will have their menarche greeted by some festive, yet intimate, parental or family attention.

It has been argued that in modern Western society, parallel to individualization tendencies, rituals have disappeared, leading to loss of emotional anchors. In psychotherapy, the use of individually tailored rituals is quite often recommended.

Premarital Sexual Activities and Relationships

The 1989 survey of children ages 11 to 19 involved more aspects than previous studies, and the presentation of many subjects that were put into longitudinal perspective. Data suggested an expanding "sexual moratorium," a period in which the adolescent is sexually active, but not in a steady relationship open to procreation. In recent years, it has been increasingly common for young adults to go through a period in which they have a number of sexual partners, in more or less steady relationships (Figure 5).

Survey responses revealed a common pattern of four years between the first French kiss and sexual intercourse. The sequence of steps in this personal development is remarkably uniform, and showed no sex difference (Figure 6).

Figure 5

Age at First Menstruation, First Sexual Intercourse, and Marriage or Cohabitation by Year of Birth

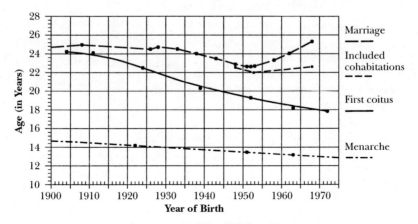

Source: van der Vliet (1990), p. 54.

Figure 6

Sexual Development: Age at Which Half of the Respondents Had Experienced Some Behaviors (*n* = 11,500)

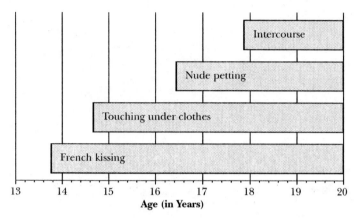

Source: Vogels and van Vliet (1990), Figure 3.3, p. 39.

In earlier studies, the concept of a "stepwise interaction career" was developed by Straver and coworkers (1986), based on Glaser and Straus's (1980) elaboration of symbolic interactionist theory and Simon and Gagnon's (1980) approach to psychosexual development. This approach emphasizes the active role of youngsters in shaping their own sexual identity and their sexual relationships. Rademakers (1992) later used this theoretical framework in her study of the causes of ineffective contraceptive behavior at initial sexual contact among adolescents (see Section 9).

Going out to bars or discotheques is a major factor affecting sexual experiences, increasing sexual experiences at all ages and in all aspects. Young people with lower educational levels showed less permissiveness and less experience in communication, but experienced sexual intercourse at an earlier age than adolescents with more education.

Responses to the question "Do you ask your partner what he/she likes in love making?" suggest that boys take responsibility for their partners' satisfaction more often, especially at an earlier age (Figure 7). Assessing personal limits is another competence aspect; girls more than boys seem to consider this to be their task at all ages (Figure 8).

Sexual contacts between children and adults have been examined in several Dutch studies. Unlike most such research data, these contacts were not considered abusive by definition. Sandfort (1982) studied the experience of twenty-five boys, ages 10 to 16, involved in sexual relationships with adult men. Almost all the respondents indicated the sexual contact was predominantly positive and did not have a negative influence on their general sense of well-being. The friendships also fulfilled several of the boys' personal needs. Although these results do not have

Figure 7

**Percentage of Respondents Who Ask Partner What He/She
Likes While Making Love Always or Most of the Time,
According to Age and Sex**

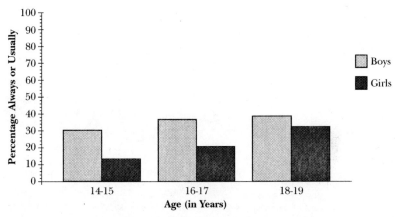

Source: Vogels and van Vliet (1990), Figure 3.9, p. 45.

Figure 8

**Percentages of Respondents Who See to It That Lovemaking
Does Not Get Out of Hand Always or Most of the Time,
According to Age and Sex**

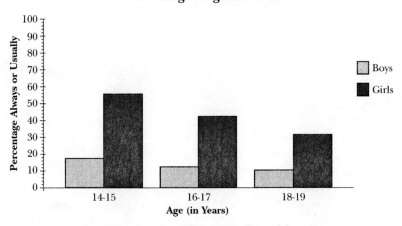

Source: Vogels and van Vliet (1990), Figure 3.9, p. 45.

general applicability, they counterbalance the predominant notion that
all adult-child sexual involvement is abusive. In a later study, Sandfort
(1991) used a much broader design to study the possible influences of
voluntary, as well as nonconsensual, sexual experiences before age 16 in
a random sample of 283 male and female subjects, aged 18 to 23 years,

who had had sexual experiences with adults. Controlling for other factors, these sexual experiences seemed to have positively influenced sexual desire, arousal, and anxiety irrespective of the partner's age. Nonconsensual experiences seemed to have caused sexual problems in later life, as well as more general psychosomatic complaints. The more severe these experiences, the stronger were the negative effects. Nonconsensual contacts with peers seemed, on average, to be less severe than nonconsensual experiences with adults. Using the same data, Goddijn and Sandfort (1988) showed the importance of the opportunity to express one's feelings about traumatic experiences in order to diminish the psychosocial complaints in later life. Studies on involuntary sexual contacts are dealt with in Section 9A.

C. Adults

Some Demographic Outlines

Remarkable changes in the popularity of marriage have occurred in the Netherlands in recent decades (Beets et al. 1991). Before the end of World War II, the Dutch tended to marry at a relatively late age. In the years of rapidly expanding economic possibilities in the 1970s, more men and women married at a younger age. In 1945, only 18.5 percent of 20- to 24-year-olds was or had ever been married; in 1974, the figure was 41.8 percent. Since 1974, marriage has again declined in popularity, especially for the young, as cohabitation became more popular. The mean age of first marriage was 22.8 in 1970; in 1990, it was 28.2 for men and 25.9 for women. Data on cohabitation are scarce, but what data are available provide some insights:

- Around 1985, almost half of all 20- to 24-year-olds who were living together were not (yet) married, in the 25 to 34 age group, 20 percent were not married;
- 70 percent of the unmarried said their living together would be long term; 40 percent of a cohort were still in the same relationship at a three-year follow-up;
- Cohabiting couples have fewer children than married couples; the wish for children is often the motive for marriage.
- Until 1975, only 2 percent of the children born annually were born out of wedlock. Since then, the figure has risen to 10.6 percent. "Extramarital birth" today can have several meanings: a child of cohabiting parents (about two thirds of all extramarital births); a child in a Living Apart Together (LAT) arrangement, a lesbian couple's child, or a homosexual or heterosexual unwed mother who intends to raise the child alone. By 1989, 10 percent of unwed mothers were single women and lesbian couples who were artificially inseminated with

donor semen (AID). In the past decade, self-insemination has gained in popularity, probably equaling physician-managed AID today.
· The classic unwed mother who had an unwanted pregnancy is almost extinct in Holland, forcing the Dutch organization for the support of unwed mothers to reorganize with new goals to support one-parent households and the victims of sexual violence (and their mothers).

Combining cohabiting and married couples, there is a recent slight decrease in the number of Dutch men and women living in two-person households. Divorce rates have gone up fast since 1968, from 11 percent of marriages in 1970 to 28 percent in 1988. One out of six children in the 1970s marriage cohort will experience their parents' divorce before age 21. One-parent families are also increasing. Ten years ago, 19 percent of Dutch mothers were raising their child(ren) alone. Divorcees outnumbered widows and never-wed mothers in this group, with most single mothers holding full-time employment outside the home.

Divorced persons are increasingly postponing a second marriage. In 1990, the mean age for males entering a second marriage was 42.7; for women, 38.8 years. In 1990, 77 percent of all marriages were first marriages for both partners. In 23 percent, one or both partners were divorced; in 10 percent, one or both were widowers.

Fertility rates have been decreasing, from 3.2 in 1964 to stabilize at just over 1.5 since 1976. In 1988, 4 percent of all 20-year-olds had one or more children, 32 percent of the 25-year-olds, 67 percent by age 30, and 87 percent by age 40. Government policy aims at zero population growth, a goal that seems feasible even though it will bring a considerable increase in the proportion of senior citizens. In 1990, 13 percent of the total population was over 65, compared with only 8 percent in 1950.

Single Adults

Prompted by a need for data and insights useful in AIDS prevention, the 1989 SIN adult study was the first to pay specific attention to sexual behavior of singles.

In this survey, 13 percent of male respondents ($n = 421$) and 11 percent of females ($n = 580$) reported no sexual contacts in the year before the interview. Some 40 percent were sexually inexperienced. Part of this group could be adequately characterized as "late starters," but at age 30, 8 percent of males and 4 percent of females were inexperienced in heterosexual intercourse. The higher percentage of male homosexuals in the sample may only partly explain the high figure of inexperienced males, because half of the male respondents who labeled themselves as homosexuals had in fact had sexual intercourse. Men tended to be more dissatisfied than women with being single, 70 percent versus 57 percent preferring to have a relationship. In the larger cities, the proportion of respondents with no sexual relationships is slightly lower. In their solo-sex experiences, this group differs only slightly from couples: 18 percent never fantasize sexually, and only 19 percent more than once a week; 28 percent never engage in self-pleasuring and 26 percent do so more than once a week.

In the 1989 study, "singles with sexual contacts" were defined as: no steady relationships of at least one year at the time of interview; one or more casual or short sexual contacts. By definition, this group must include a certain number of persons with new relationships that will eventually turn out to be long term: 10 percent of women and 18 percent of the men fell into this category. Respondents under 25 contributed most to this group, with respondents 33 to 50 rarely in this group. Singles with sexual partnerships tended to live in larger cities. Like the group with no sexual experiences in the last year, they, too, tended not to be politically involved. One-night stands were uncommon: only 13 percent had casual sex (defined as once or twice); 50 percent of men and 25 percent of women had casual sex besides one or more longer partnerships (the latter with a mean of twenty-five sexual encounters). Males reported a higher number of partners in the past year (mean 2.4 versus 1.8 for women; maximum of ten for men and five for women). Vaginal intercourse was the most popular technique for men (96 percent), but women preferred manual stimulation to vaginal intercourse, 95 percent to 86 percent. Anal intercourse was quite unpopular. Men used condoms in only 31 percent of their coital acts; women scored even lower with 21 percent.

Adults in Dyadic Relations

In 1989, mean coital frequency for men and women in stable relations was seven times a month, higher than in 1968 and 1981, but respondents in the earlier surveys were aged 20 to 65, while the 1989 sample was 18 to 50 years old (Table 3, Figure 9). Length of the relationship is more important than age for coital frequency (Tables 4 and 5, Figure 10). In all groups, women tended to be content with their current frequency and men more likely to want more. Men were more affirmative in thinking their sex could be better. Women were more likely to admit to making love without the desire to do so and engaging in sexual acts they did not really like. Other satisfaction-related statements on which men and women gave similar responses included: general satisfaction with sex, conflicts about sex, admitting gender differences in sexual desire, admitting being pressured to engage in sexual contact, and communications on sexual preferences. On a one-to-ten scale, the mean rating of men for their satisfaction with their own sex life was 7.3; for women 7.5.

Abstinence in these stable relations is nonexistent, when defined as refraining from all sensual body contact (hugging, kissing, and cuddling). When sexual contact is defined as genital contact, 0.5 percent of these

Table 3

Duration of Living Arrangement in 751 Stable Relationships

Age Group (in Years)	Mean Duration of Relationship (Years)	Married (%)	Cohabiting (%)	Living Apart (%)
18-25	4.0	24	33	43
26-33	8.8	73	20	7
34-41	14.1	86	5	9
42-50	22.4	97	1	2

Men: $n = 276$; Women: $n = 452$

Source: Sandfort and van Zessen (1991), Table 3.3, p. 65

Figure 9

Percentage Frequencies of Making Love in 751 Stable Relationships

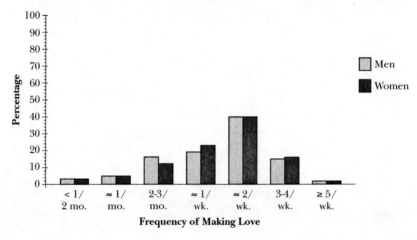

relationships were abstinent; when defined as vaginal intercourse, 4 percent were abstinent during the past year (Figure 11).

"Extramarital" Sex

Marriage was the only form of stable relationship studied in 1968 and 1981. In the 1989 study, questions regarding sex with more than one partner were edited differently to include cohabitation and stable Living-Apart-Together (LAT) relations. Moreover, the 1968 and 1981 studies focused on 21- to 65-year-olds, whereas the 1989 study dealt with 18- to 50-year-olds. Longitudinal comparisons must therefore be done with some caution.

Table 4

Mean Frequency of Sexual Contact in Steady Relationships, by Age

Age Group (in Years)	Mean Frequency of Sexual Contact, per Month
18-25	7.4
26-33	7.0
34-41	6.9
42-50	6.8

Table 5

Mean Frequency of Sexual Contact by Duration of Relationship

Duration of Steady Relationship (in Years)	Mean Frequency of Sexual Contact, per Month
1-2	8.5
2-5	7.5
Over 5	6.8

Source: Sandfort and van Zessen (1991), Table 3.4, p. 66

Figure 10

Satisfaction with Frequency of Making Love, by Sex and by Three Groups of Frequency

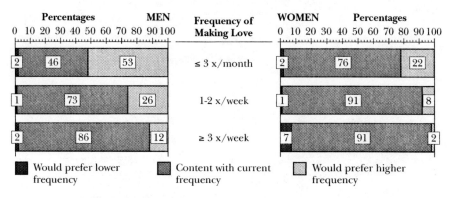

Source: Sandfort and van Zessen (1991), Figure 4.2, p. 107.

In 1968 and 1981, men were more tolerant than women on extramarital sex, with a shift for both genders toward more tolerance. In 1981, 13 percent of the men and 6 percent of the women had no objections at all, with 48 percent of the men and 39 percent of the women accepting extramarital

Figure 11

Sexual Behaviors in Stable Heterosexual Relationships, According to Sex

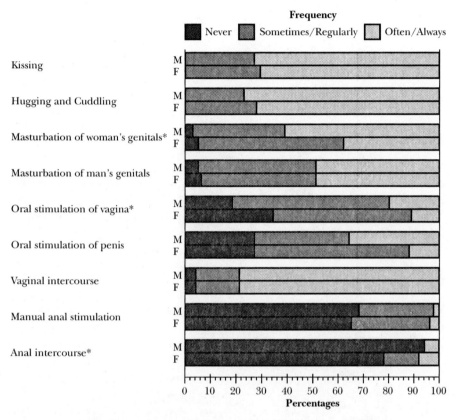

Men: *n* = 276; Women: *n* = 452. An * indicates a significant sex difference.
Source: Sandfort and van Zessen (1991), Figure 3.2, p. 67.

sex in certain situations. In 1989, more questions were included on this topic. Seven percent of the men and 5 percent of the women agreed that partners in a stable relationship should allow each other to have sex with a third party; 82 percent of men and 88 percent of women firmly opposed this (Table 6).

Since extramarital sex is taboo more than other behaviors, underreporting cannot be ignored. In 1989, the fear of AIDS seemed to be a more potent motive for denying extramarital sex than moral restraints in general. Marriage is the type of stable relationship that contributes most to monogamy: In the total group of respondents in a stable relationship for over one year, 14.6 percent of the men and 9.2 the percent of women reported sexual contact with more than one partner. In the year preceding the interview,

Table 6

Extramarital Sexual Contacts in 1968, 1981, and 1989, in Percentages

Frequency	1968		1981		1989	
	Male	Female	Male	Female	Male	Female
Occurred often	1	0	3	2	—	—
Occasionally	10	2	11	7	12	7
Never	78	86	80	86	88	93
Not Answered	11	12	7	5	0	0

Source: Sandfort and van Zessen (1991), Table 3.10, p. 751

6.4 percent of the men and 2.8 percent of the women had engaged in sex with a second partner; 2.1 percent of the men and 3.7 percent of the women were aware of their partner's extramarital relations. Three quarters of the men keep their extramarital sex a secret; three quarters of the women informed their partners of their affair. "Extramarital sex" was casual in 50 percent of the cases; long-standing affairs were limited to one out of six. Prostitution and sexual contacts abroad were only a small proportion of the reported extramarital-sex contacts.

Sexuality and the Disabled and Chronically Ill

In the early 1970s, when Heslinga gained national and international notoriety with his plea for better information and sex education for the handicapped with his book *Not Made of Stone: Sexuality of the Handicapped People,* these services are not routinely provided by doctors, and empirical research was also scarce. Today, close to a hundred organizations provide support and written information on the sexual consequences of such conditions as adrenogenital syndrome, anorexia nervosa, breast cancer and mastopathy, depression, diabetes, gynecological cancer, incontinence, ostomy, multiple sclerosis, premenstrual syndrome, postmenopause, posthysterectomy, and schizophrenia patients and their families.

Direct sexual services for the handicapped are available through the National Foundation for Alternative Partnership Mediation. In one ongoing research project, the Rotterdam sexology department and the department for industrial design at Delft Technical University developed a water-driven self-pleasuring aid for manually disabled men and women to be used in the bath or under the shower.

Mental-health institutions have also gained some awareness of their residents' sexual problems and the tension between controlling and understanding patients' sexual needs. Professionals in homes for the mentally handicapped seem more eager to take additional courses in sexual education. Awareness of the high figures for past sexual abuse among patients is growing rapidly, and competence in addressing these problems is probably also expanding.

In the past decade, Dutch sexologists have carried out longitudinal research on sexual rehabilitation of (1) women with ovarian, cervical, endometrial, and vulvar cancers, (2) men with testicular cancer and Peyronie's disease, and (3) men and women with diabetes, various ostomies, chronic kidney disease, and skin diseases. Because of the uniqueness of these studies, a summary of their findings follows.

(1) *Cancer of the Female Genitals* (Main sources: Leiden and Groningen University Gynecology Departments). The Dutch Cancer Foundation has funded a steady series of research programs on treatment for female genital cancers. Bos-Branolte used a semistructured interview and questionnaire to evaluate psychosexual functioning of sixty-nine women treated for ovarian (twenty-nine), cervical (twenty-four), endometrial (twelve), and vulvar (four) cancers. Posttreatment follow-up ranged from six months to seven years. Results showed a decrease in sexual activity (59 percent) and intimacy (22 percent) with an increase in need for intimacy (19 percent), emotional support (30 percent), and open communication (23 percent). In addition, 33 percent reported a negative change in their partner's sexual activity. Many women had the impression that, although their partners needed emotional support during their illness, they did not receive this help. Intimacy, emotional support, and open communications seemed to contribute more to a positive relationship than sexual expressions.

In 1984, Weijmar Schultz and Van de Wiel started a series of research projects with a pilot study of ten women treated for vulvar cancer. A self-report questionnaire evaluated sexual functioning some two years after treatment. Despite many problems, eight of the ten couples resumed sexual contacts, with or without restrictions. Sufficient information, coping, and communications did not guarantee complete sexual rehabilitation. Motivation for sexual expression and mutual affection might be more important than any physical restriction imposed by surgery. A small-scale prospective longitudinal study of the sexual functioning of women treated for vulvar cancer tested this observation. Ten couples and an age-matched control group were interviewed and filled out questionnaires at admission and at six, twelve, and twenty-four months posttreatment. Only at six months could an increase in sexual dissatisfaction be detected. Over the remaining period, in spite of persisting poor perception of genital symptoms of sexual arousal, the women's satisfaction did not differ from pretreatment satisfaction and control group ratings. Satisfaction with sexual interaction under these circumstances appears to be more dependent on intimate aspects than on physiological arousal, suggesting information and counseling as the most promising focus for intervention.

A more detailed assessment of seven of these women at twelve months posttreatment confirmed that, although in the patients' own opinion cancer and its treatment had caused rather dramatic changes in their sexual life, comparison with the age-matched group revealed only minor differences in sexual satisfaction, behavior, and motivation. The only significant differences were in experienced sexual arousal and orgasm. The authors hypothesized that sexual rehabilitation itself is guided on a higher level by a more general striving for balance in the relationship. Interventions to prevent or reduce sexual problems after treatment for cancer of the female genitalia should be directed toward both the patient and partner.

A similar design was used for thirteen couples with wives treated by simple hysterectomy for benign gynecological disease and thirteen age-matched control couples. At a one-year follow-up, all patients reported some disruption in the sexual response cycle, whereas current behavior and motivation for sexual interaction were within the normal range. The women clearly expressed general satisfaction with their sexual functioning and little relational dissatisfaction. Here too, arousal experience is found not to be the sole reason for sexual motivation and satisfaction. The authors stress that post-treatment counseling should not be limited to hysterectomy patients with a cancer diagnosis. A more-detailed examination of eleven cervical cancer patients at six months posttreatment revealed that sexual interaction was valued significantly less than control subjects, while no changes in overt behavior occurred. The most important psychosexual variables underlying this reduced sexual valuation were found to be a considerable decrease in the self-image of oneself as a sexual partner. Apparently women try to cope by conforming to the sexual demands of their partner and to prevailing norms. Cervical carcinoma treatment appears to have a strong negative effect on the sexuality of the patients, and often amplifies an already existing ambivalence toward sexual interaction common in many women.

Sixteen partners of patients treated for female genital cancer were interviewed one year posttreatment on two general themes: involvement and support, and sexuality and relationship. Many men reported experiencing the process of providing support as stressful, and had serious doubts about the efficacy of their efforts. Furthermore, these men appeared to have extensive sexual problems, which could not be adequately solved. It was hypothesized that the disease and its treatment also poses a crisis for the partner, which leads to a regression towards a more rigid, male-stereotypical way of coping. Consequently, while treating the patient, the partner and their communication patterns should be the focus of attention too.

Finally, data on seven vulvar cancer patients and twenty-five cervical cancer patients were analyzed for prognostic variables for future sexual adjustment. The small sample size allowed only a few cautious conclusions. Overt sexual behavior after treatment can be predicted quite accurately by past sexual experience. Satisfaction, motivation, and sexual response are less predictable. This outcome supports the conclusion from the comparative study on cervical cancer treatment and simple hysterectomy, that psychological variables are more decisive than physical ones in predicting future sexual rehabilitation.

(2) *Testicular Cancer Treatment* (Source: Groningen University Urology Department). Nijman et al. studied sexual functioning of 101 patients following bilateral retroperitoneal lymph node dissection for stages I and II nonseminomatous testicular cancer. All patients were without evidence of disease after at least four years' follow-up. Twelve men experienced antegrade ejaculation, while eighty-nine experienced retrograde ejaculation ("dry" orgasm). In seventy-five of the 101 men, urine analysis after intercourse or self-pleasuring showed retrograde ejaculation in fifty-five men, and lack of ejaculatory emission into the urethra in twenty patients.

Seventeen patients had diminished sexual desire (especially after radiotherapy), twelve experienced difficulty reaching orgasm, and six complained of erectile dysfunction. A second study of fifty-six men with nonseminomatous testicular cancer stages II and III, before and after treatment (surgery and chemotherapy). Two years after completing therapy, 54 percent experienced sexual dysfunctions. Greatly reduced or absent antegrade ejaculation was reported by twenty-six patients; eighteen of them had undergone retroperitoneal lymph-node dissection in varying degrees of extensiveness, whereas eight had not. Chemotherapy may have caused ejaculatory disorders in 30 percent of the patients. Only two reported a change in quality of erections; seven experienced a markedly reduced libido, and five reported their orgasms had changed in a negative way. The remaining testis showed signs of atrophy in twenty-one patients.

(3) *Diabetes Mellitus* (Source: Rotterdam University Sexology Department). Slob et al. recorded subjective and objective psychophysiological responses to erotic visual stimulation for twenty-four women with diabetes mellitus type I and ten control women. No significant differences in subjective response (general sexual arousal and genital arousal) was reported. The objective response (thermistor readings from one minor labium) varied with the height of the initial temperature. Since the initial temperature was significantly higher in the patient group, the subsequent rise during erotic visual stimulation was less in diabetic women than in controls. When samples of the two groups were matched for initial temperature, the difference in increase of labial temperature was no longer significant. When women with high initial temperatures (37° C) were excluded, there was in both groups a significant correlation between the degree of subjective arousal and the rise in labial temperature. Patients with serious neuropathy and/or angiopathy did not participate in this study.

(4) *Peyronie's Disease* (Source: Groningen University Urology Department). Van Driel studied surgical treament, compared with the natural course, in thirty-two patients with Peyronie's disease and twelve with a congenital

penile curvature. Subjective symptoms were recorded by check list, objective symptoms by means of Polaroid photography during erection at home. Patients were seen at three-month intervals until a steady state was reached. In twenty-three patients, spontaneous recovery was sufficient. When pain persisted longer than one year, a Nesbitt operation (surgical shortening of the contralateral side) was performed; twenty-one patients were treated this way. All were satisfied with the functional and cosmetic outcome, although a completely straight penis was not accomplished in four. No complications were met. Conservative management in cases of bent penis seems preferable; however surgery is a good and safe alternative when complaints and dysfunctions persist.

(5) *Ostomy* (Source: Groningen University Sexology Department). The first step in Dutch research on sexological sequelae of ostomy operations was a study in which readers of a stoma patients' monthly were asked to complete a questionnaire: 995 men and 512 women gave a retrospective account of changes in their sexual life following ostomy. Results confirmed that men are more hampered in their sexual functioning by ostomy than women, and that colostomy had a stronger negative effect than ileostomy. Results suggest the most serious impact on sexual functioning is found with urostomy, especially in men. Prospective confirmation is needed.

(6) *Chronic Kidney Disease* (Source: NISSO). Van Son-Schoones used a semistructured interview and psychometric questionaires to evaluate psychosexual functioning in seventy men and forty-seven women with chronic kidney disease; thirty-four male partners and forty-seven female partners were included. Evaluation included the effect of treatment method (hemodialysis, continued ambulatory peritoneal dialysis, or transplantation) on sexual functioning, personal well-being, and coping with the disease, as well as the quality of information and counseling. Few differences were found between the three treatment modalities. Organic sexual dysfunctions, psychosocial problems, and acceptance problems were most frequently found in the hemodialysis group. Partners, irrespective of treatment, did have more sexual problems and were less satisfied with the sexual relationship. The quality of information and counseling appeared to be insufficient.

(7) *Skin Disease* (Source: Leiden University Dermatology Department). In 1990, a research study was initiated to quantify the well-known sexual problems of patients with psoriasis and constitutional eczematous rash: fifty-two psoriasis patients (twenty-eight men, twenty-four women, mean age 37) and twenty-five eczema patients (nine men and sixteen women, mean age 28) completed extensive anonymous questionnaires: 10 percent had no partner, 3 percent only incidental partners. Men felt most ashamed in social situations of partial nudity, women were more ashamed in sexual

situations. Sexual motivation was lower than average, and women scored lower than men. On sexual satisfaction, only women scored below average. Facial skin symptoms were most embarrassing. One third had difficulties initiating contacts and entering a sexual relationship, and felt shame in an intimate relation. Psoriasis patients felt more inhibited than eczema patients. Many expressed the conviction that a good sexual relationship is beneficial for the skin disease.

The authors advocate more discussion of sexuality in the care for skin-disease patients, especially when young and inexperienced in sexual relations. Women, psoriasis patients, and patients with facial symptoms are most in need of counseling.

Incidence of Oral and Anal Sex

Growing concern about HIV transmission and recognition that anal intercourse is high-risk behavior have attracted researchers' attention to anal sex. In 1989, 12 percent of women and 6 percent of men in steady heterosexual relationships reported being more or less experienced in anal intercourse. Anal sex seemed to be nonexistent in casual and extramarital heterosexual relations.

In the Amsterdam large-scale longitudinal cohort research project on homosexual behavior and seroconversion, the proportion of men who engaged in anal intercourse slowly declined from 88.6 percent in 1984-85 to 62.4 percent in 1987-88.

There are no legal restrictions on anal sex in Holland; social attitudes towards this form of eroticism probably shows wide variation. The idea that anal sex is not an exclusively homosexual variation, but can be part of heterosexual lovemaking as well, is gradually being acknowledged in the general public.

In 1989, experience with fellatio and cunnilingus was the rule for both men and women (see Figure 11).

6. Homoerotic, Homosexual, and Ambisexual Behaviors

In the United States, the Kinsey-scale differentiation between exclusive homosexuality and exclusive heterosexuality based on combined sexual behavior and erotic experiences dominates most orientations theory and research. Historical, sociological, and psychological studies of homosexuality in the Netherlands leans toward a different paradigm in which homosexuality is seen as a design for living in which erotic and sexual attraction is embedded in a wider context. Dutch study of homosexuality thus focuses on gender and gender development, family studies, and lifestyle and lifestyle management. Changing social attitudes to homosexuality made this paradigmatic change possible.

A. Children and Adolescents

The large-scale 1968 and 1974 studies of adolescent sexuality paid only limited attention to homosexual behavior and feelings. Tolerance towards homosexuals had grown considerably: In 1968, 55.3 percent believed that homosexuals should be free to lead their own lives; in 1974, 84.9 percent held this position. In 1968, 18.6 percent of male respondents said they had at least one self-pleasuring experience with peers; in 1974, this was 16.1 percent. In 1968, 5.5 percent reported being mostly or exclusively attracted to the same sex; in 1974, 1.8 percent. Some attraction was indicated by 10 percent in both surveys.

Information useful in AIDS prevention was a major objective of the 1989 study of 11,431 12- to 19-year-old boys and girls. On self-definition, 47 percent of the 12- to 13-year-olds reported not knowing the meaning of "homosexuality" and "bisexuality"; 6 percent of 18- to 19-year-olds were ignorant on this subject. Slightly less than 1 percent of boys and girls defined themselves as exclusively or predominantly homosexual; 1.3 percent of boys and 0.8 percent of girls defined themselves as bisexual; 8 percent of boys and 15 percent of girls reported fantasies of a homosexual nature. Such fantasies produced uncertainty on self-definition in only a minority; the youngest age group is most often uncertain on the subject of self-definition (60 percent of 12- to 13-year-olds did not know how to self-label).

Percentages of respondents experienced in homosexual behavior were low: boys 1.5 percent, girls 1 percent. Anal intercourse was practiced by half of these boys—among heterosexual 14- to 19-year-olds, 7 percent had at least one experience with anal intercourse. Bisexual experience was reported by 64 percent of the boys and 70 percent of the girls.

In the 1980s, several studies of homosexualities examined the process that homosexuals go through in self-definition. A large difference was found between males and females. More than 50 percent of men called themselves homosexual by age 17, 50 percent of women self-identified around age 23. Half of the boys experienced their first same-gender attraction by age 8; girls by age 14. In the process of sexual-identity formation, behavioral, psychic, erotic, and sexual responses appear more important for self-definition for boys. For girls, relational factors are characteristic, with identity formation and identity management centered on social, instead of sociosexual aspects. Defining oneself as a homosexual for boys means the coding of erotic and sexual responses, and for girls the coding of feelings of intimacy, bonding, and togetherness. These are relative differences and one could predict that, as soon as gender differences in development become less important, the gap between a gay and lesbian development of the self will disappear. This accounts for intergenerational differences and the positive influence of a warm and permissive climate at home on identity development. In a theoretical perspective, in families without polarized sex roles, not only do male-female differences become less important, but also the distinction between homosexual and heterosexual differences. What counts is the capacity for management of social interactions.

Of special interest are Dutch studies on the construction of intergenerational male intimacy. Sandfort (1987) described how this developed in the gay movement and how concepts of male homosexuality and male homosexual pedophilia changed between 1946 and 1981. In a monumental two-volume work, *Loving Boys* (1988, 1990), Brongersma maintained that intergenerational male intimacy has a biological as well as a sociological foundation. At the beginning of puberty, boys tend not to interact sexually with girls. In this period the sexual drive is high, so boys enter into sexual contact with peers and with older men. This view of man-boy relationships uses a theoretical framework that relies heavily on historical and anthropological material. These relations are seen as a *rite de passage*, emotionally loaded by images of becoming male, not homosexual. Another sociohistorical illustration was presented by Maassen, who described the work and life of Gustav Wyneken, an influential pedagogue of pre-Nazi Germany, accused of having had sexual relations with some of his pupils.

In a 1992 special women's issue of *Paidika*, the journal of pedophilia, some Dutch authors described woman-child intimate relations, of which the majority was homosexual and in some way pedagogic. While woman-girl relationships appear rare in Holland, Wekker describes a special kind of woman-girl relationship in Suriname Creole working-class women (*mati*) who are self-supporting and have children by men with whom they are in more or less steady relationships. They become familiar with homosexual contact in their teens, are mostly initiated by older women, and large age differences are common at all ages in this cultural group. One wonders whether the subject of adult-child sexuality is changing under the influence of coeducation, the development of youth cultures, and the acceptance of sexual relationships in early adolescence. Nowadays, adolescents can have sexual contacts with peers of both sexes, so the motivation for erotic commitments with adults may decline or disappear.

B. Adults

Gender Roles and Relationship Patterns

Tielman's *Homosexuality in the Netherlands* (1982) describes the Dutch Gay Emancipation Movement between 1911 and 1982. Warmerdam and Koenders (1987) described the homosexual organization COC between 1946 and 1966. Detailed oral histories of the discrimination against homosexuals and their emancipation are available. There are numerous impressions, accounts, and photographs available, and a lot is analyzed in *Homologie*, a scientific and cultural bimonthly. Still missing, however, is a broad and thorough study of the homosexual and lesbian subcultures in these periods from a nonpolitical perspective.

Hekma (1987) analyzed how during the nineteenth century, Dutch physicians and psychiatrists, influenced mainly by German and French ideas, constructed a homosexual identity with specific bodily and mental characteristics. This widely accepted image of gay and lesbian identity was disputed by Muller (1990), who showed that most German physicians relied heavily on personal statements of their clients, who in their self-confessions constructed homosexuality themselves. The theoretical issue is, as in other psychiatric cases of alcoholism and anorexia, who has the power in the discourse, who "invents" the images, the categories, the definitions of the self? It seems that in the nineteenth century, the "making of the homosexual" was mainly an interaction of physicians and their patients. In the twentieth century, homosexuals discovered themselves as a community.

Dutch research on gay and lesbian relationships took root in our tradition of research on alternative relationships. Instead of focusing on differences between marriage and alternatives, Dutch researchers try to understand the dynamics of different forms of relationships. Straver (1981) found that among unmarried couples—heterosexual, homosexual, and lesbian—some couples structure their relationship in a traditional, strong role differentiation, while others accentuate complete togetherness with a tendency towards independence. Still others emphasize self-development. Living together is no longer an essential condition in forming a relationship. Straver does not present a correlation between these models and sexual orientation.

Schreurs (1990) compared lesbian, cohabiting women (above average in education, income, and professional activity, and mainly in their 20s and 40s) with a similar group of heterosexual couples. Analysis produced Stravers types of relationships, except for the strong role-differentiation type. Relations characterized by togetherness led to the highest scores for relationship satisfaction; couples in autonomy relations expressed satisfaction with autonomy as well as with togetherness. A group characterized by distance scored identical on autonomy, but lower on togetherness. In comparison with heterosexual couples, only emotional and recreational bonding scored lower in heterosexual couples, and men scored lower on satisfaction with emotional bonding.

Schreurs criticizes current theories in which lesbian relations are considered a risk for symbiosis (i.e., high bonding with loss of autonomy). In lesbian relationships, a high degree of emotional bonding obviously is possible without loss of autonomy, an important consideration for therapists working with lesbian couples.

In a similar study, Deenen (1991) analyzed 320 men in steady homosexual relationships: 69 percent lived together; mean relationship duration 8.2 years (10-39 months: $n = 88$ with mean age 30; 40-199 months: $n = 138$ with mean age 36; 120-446 months: $n = 93$ with mean age 45. He found no support for the phasic developmental model of McWhirter and Mattison

(1984), who hold that sexual and emotional satisfaction depend on the time of a relationship between two men. Deenen found differences between short- and long-lasting relationships, and a difference between men younger than thirty years and older men. Both variables, relationship duration and partner's age, predicted relationship satisfaction and sexual satisfaction better than the phasic developmental model.

For women and men in homosexual relationships, emotional intimacy is the best predictor for relationship satisfaction. Sexual contact seems more important for men, but this difference may disappear if one relies on a less-strict definition of sexual contact and replaces it by affectionate bodily contact. One can go even further, seeing the whole erotic and sexual attraction embedded in the more general context of living, a line of reasoning also found in Dutch studies of sexual identity and identity development.

Social Status; Legal and Religious Restrictions

In the late 1960s, Dutch research on homosexuality was characterized by a social-scientific perspective in which the changing of social attitudes towards homosexuality was a primary objective. In 1968, 36 percent of Dutch adults believed that homosexuals should be restricted in leading their own way of life. In 1980-87, this figure stabilized around 6 to 7 percent.

Until 1971, the legal age of consent for homosexual acts was 21 years of age; for heterosexual acts, 16. This statute was abolished in 1971, mainly on the argument that scientific research showed that people did not become homosexual by seduction at puberty or in adolescence. The new law and general tolerance had a great impact on the counseling of people with problems of homosexuality. Gradually, the image of homosexuality as a psychiatric symptom disappeared completely. In the 1980s, newly established departments of gay and lesbian studies at the Universities of Utrecht and Amsterdam triggered a diversity of studies on homosexuality. Studies of genetic, hormonal, and neural factors are insignificant, the emphasis being placed instead on history, sociology, and social psychology.

While tolerance certainly has increased, this does not exclude all sorts of gross and subtle discrimination, including violence. For decades, youth gangs have beat up gay men in cruising areas. It took the homosexual movement a long time to persuade the gay victims (often men seeking anonymous sexual contacts while they were still "in the closet") to accuse their assaulters in court and to convince police officials that this form of violence should be taken seriously.

Two legal topics are currently under discussion, legislation against discrimination and legal recognition of gay unions. Legislation against discrimination on grounds of race, sex, sexual lifestyle, etc., has taken more than a decade. During these years, religiously inspired parties have tried successfully to introduce exceptions based on conflicting interests. The central issue is always whether Christian schools will dismiss or refuse to hire homosexual teachers.

Although Dutch civil laws do not specify the heterosexual essence of marriage, no gay or lesbian couple has been able to enter a legally recognized marriage. Two recent efforts to gain this recognition have been turned down by the high court with the suggestion that the matter should be studied by the government and a law reform prepared. All political parties support this opinion.

Discrimination and homophobia are expected in macho cultures such as the military. Since 1971 and the abolition of the penalty for homosexual acts after age 16, homosexuality has been tolerated in the military. A 1992 NISSO study of homosexuality in the military concluded that:

- Drafted men did not differ from the general population in homosexual feelings and experience;
- Male professionals less often reported homosexual feelings and experience;
- Female professionals more often reported homosexual feelings and experiences—women are not drafted for military service in Holland.
- In all branches and at all levels, respondents were aware that discrimination was not tolerated; female soldiers were more tolerant than their male colleagues. Yet, distancing and isolation in some form was a common reaction, and unconditional support was often withheld from homosexuals. When open about their sexual orientation, homosexuals were excluded from the comrade culture. Homosexuals tend to be isolated much more than allochtonous soldiers.
- Excesses, from abusive language to physical attacks, are not uncommon in the army.
- Homosexuals tend to mask their orientation while in service. In their immediate environment, homosexuals have little support—the Foundation Homosexuality and the Armed Forces functions only on a national level.

This 1992 NISSO research marked a milestone in the development of attitudes towards homosexuality in the military. COC, the national organization of homosexuals, gave the Dutch Minister of Defense and the Foundation Homosexuality and the Armed Forces its annual reward. In 1993, a national confidential counselor on homosexuality in the military was instituted.

There is not much information on homosexuality in other organizations, e.g., prisons. Coercive homosexual contact in institutions, as is known from reports in the United States, are reported incidentally, but these acts are definitely not prison routine. Homosexual rape is seldom reported to the Dutch police. A few cases of male pedophilic or incestuous offenses are brought to trial each year, but cases involving adult victims are rare.

Prevailing Patterns in Sexual Behaviors

The 1989 survey showed that homosexual and bisexual people tend to be the most permissive on the subject of sex in general (Table 7 gives results for 421 male and 580 female respondents).

Table 7

Homosexual Experiences

Experience	Male		Female	
	Number	Percent	Number	Percent
Ever felt physical attraction	54	13	59	10
Ever been in love	25	5	18	3
Ever has thought to be homosexual	33	8	19	3
Ever had sex with a person of the same sex	50	12	25	4
More than incidentally had sex with a person of the same sex	24	6	13	2
Same-sex attraction is currently present	24	6	19	3
Feels to be (primarily) homosexual	17	4	2	0.4

Source: Sandfort and van Zessen (1991), Table 2.3, p. 4

Physical attraction for same-sex partners was felt at a mean age of 14 for male and 19 for female respondents. This difference was smaller in the younger age groups. Respondents reporting attraction to same-sex partners generally were confused and worried by these feelings. After a mean duration of three years, these feelings subsided in about half of the men and two thirds of the women. Men who are attracted to men tend to have had some form of sexual contact at least once; in women, attraction led to sexual behavior in only a minority. The time from first sexual attraction to sexual contact was shorter for men than women (Table 8).

Homosexual and bisexual men had a much larger number of sex partners; for women, total numbers were too small to form conclusions. For homosexual men, the mean number of partners in the past year was 9.1; in the past five years, 48.6, and in their whole life, 270.3. In comparison, heterosexual men reported means of 1.1, 1.4, and 3.9 for the same periods. Bisexuals reported numbers between these two extremes.

Long-term relationships (mean duration six years) were reported by two thirds of the homosexual respondents. Of the men, half of this group had an open relationship with incidental contacts tolerated. The mean for such incidental contacts was twelve, which is not different from the mean of homosexual men not engaged in a steady relationship. In steady relations, anal intercourse was common (82 percent) and condom use was extremely rare. In incidental homosexual encounters, anal intercourse is practiced

Table 8

Current Sexual Orientation, by Self-Labeling and Behaviors, in Percentages

Criteria	Males	Females
Self-labeling		
Exclusively heterosexual	89.5	92.9
Almost exclusively heterosexual	4.5	4.1
Mainly heterosexual	1.9	2.1
Equally homosexual and heterosexual	0.0	0.5
Mainly homosexual	0.7	0.9
Almost exclusively homosexual	1.9	0.2
Exclusively homosexual	1.4	0.2
Behavioral		
Exclusively heterosexual	81.7	88.4
Bisexual	1.9	0.5
Exclusively homosexual	3.6	0.3
Never had sexual relations	12.8	10.7

by a quarter of the men with condom use uncommon. Gay bars and cafes, saunas and Turkish baths, some well-known highway parking places, and parks were the main sites for incidental contacts. All sorts of subculture variations are available, especially in Amsterdam, including leather and S-M, piercing, and tattooing.

In Deenen's 1991 gay-couples research, high frequency of sexual contact correlates with short duration of the relationship (but not very strongly) and with younger age (especially in longer standing relationships) (Table 9). A positive evaluation of the sexual interaction correlates with higher frequency, but less so in beginning relations. Dominance as a self-reported trait correlates with high frequency of sexual contact. No correlations were concluded for: emotional distance, intimacy in the family of origin, or positive self-image.

Bisexual respondents in the 1989 study are relatively young. They tend to self-label as heterosexual and their behavior pattern is similar to heterosexuals with short-term relations. Anal intercourse is rare and, when practiced, condoms will be used, contrary to vaginal intercourse in which condom use is rare.

It is remarkable that there has never been a research study on homo(bi)sexuality in marriage in Holland. The 1968 and 1981 studies showed that 2.3 percent and 3.3 percent respectively of male respondents with predominant or exclusive homosexual attraction were, or had been married. Married homosexuals sometimes will seek help from profession-

Table 9

Frequency of Sexual Contact in Steady Relationships

Frequency	Percentage
None	4.1
Once in a while	6.9
1-3 times a month	17.3
1-2 times a week	43.1
2-5 times a week	25.2
6 or more times a week	2.2

Source: Deenen, 1991

als, but the only organization for marriage and homosexuality is the self-help group Orpheus.

7. Gender Conflicted Persons

The first and most important clinic specializing in gender dysphoria is the Academic Hospital of the Free University of Amsterdam. The Dutch Gender Foundation was established in 1972. After several years of informal contact with the Free University Hospital, the ethics committee gave its approval to the medical treatment of transsexuals. The clinic started in 1976, mainly with hormonal treatment and a small number of surgical corrections. In 1982, a multidisciplinary team was formed, following the guidelines of the Harry Benjamin International Gender Dysphoria Association. Medical treatment is covered by health insurance. Support and peer-group contact are provided in some large cities by the Dutch Society for Sexual Reform (NVSH) and the Organization for Humanistic Help. Self-help groups often include transvestites. Special groups for parents and other family members have been organized recently. The most recent, and tragic, expansion of self-help for transsexuals is a group of persons treated with sex-reassignment surgery who regret the operation.

There are few legal barriers to the sex change after a legal reform that took place in 1985. A transsexual's sex may be corrected on the birth certificate if a medical declaration states that the person is irreversibly bodily corrected to the other sex and is permanently infertile. Married transsexuals must divorce before the birth certificate can be changed. At the same time (or sometimes earlier), a person's given name may be changed.

Thus far, some 1,500 transsexuals have been assessed by the Amsterdam gender team; approximately 150 sex-reversal surgeries (SRS) have been performed. In 1988, the Free University founded a chair for transsexology, which was awarded to Louis Gooren. Utrecht professor Peggy Cohen-Kettenis, whose chair (installed in 1992) is dedicated to gender development and psychopathology, works in close collaboration with the Amsterdam team. In some adolescent cases, treatment began before the patient's pubertal maturation process was fully completed; some twenty patients completed their SRS before or shortly after age 18. These teams also carry out training and research activities. Two smaller gender teams are active in Groningen and Arnhem, unfortunately not active in research.

The incidence of male-female transsexuality has been estimated at 1:12,900; and for female-male 1:30,400. Scientific attention to further diagnostic specification is expanding, especially for the concept of primary (aware since early childhood) versus secondary (awareness developing later in life) transsexuality.

Kuiper (1991) has provided the most extensive evaluation of the Amsterdam SRS treatment approach, reporting on 105 male-to-female and 36 female-to-male transsexuals, all at least in the phase of hormonal treatment. In a long-term follow-up, 50 percent of male-to-female and 75 percent of female-to-male transsexuals participated, with mean duration since the start of hormonal treatment being over ten years. The main conclusion is that there is no reason to doubt that SRS is effective in ameliorating the patient's gender-related distress. Other personal and social problems were much less influenced by SRS, and female-to-male transsexuals were found to be better adjusted socially (criteria: relations, work, sexual satisfaction, and loneliness). Psychic functioning was characterized by high scores on negativism, shyness, and psychopathology (delusional, paranoid, and bizarre thoughts), and this did not change after SRS. For male-to-female transsexuals, SRS proved to be a major health risk: in a group (mean age 37), 11 out of 105 had died at eight-year follow-up, with myocardial infarction as the most common cause. There is a great need for psychological help on nongender issues such as loneliness and shyness.

Verschoor (1990), a founder of the Amsterdam gender team, reported on a comparison of biographic questionnaires from SRS clients, transvestite members of the NVSH self-help groups, members of the homosexual organization COC, and controls. The youth of the transvestites appeared less conflicted than those of the transsexuals and homosexuals. Two thirds of the transvestites are married, often with resulting major problems in the relationship. Cross-dressing is sexually arousing for most transvestites. Progression towards transsexual wishes is uncommon—the transvestites in this group are certainly a selected group. For some transvestites, there is a link with S-M.

In 1984, Slijper studied female Congenital Adrenal Hyperplasia (CAH) patients (aged 6 to 16), comparing them with type I diabetes patients and controls. Diminished sex dimorphism in behavior correlated with severity of health problems (e.g., more pronounced in the salt-losing variant of CAH) and with the degree of their parents concern with the illness, especially the gender-confusion aspect. Genital virilization itself does not correlate with degree of tomboyism. In 1992, ten patients aged 16 to 33, were reevaluated on sexual and relationship experience and sexual anatomy. Self-pleasuring was frequent in seven. While gender-role behavior had been masculine throughout primary and secondary school, self-expressed sexual orientation was heterosexual in all. Yet, falling in love and sexual experience with partners was very rare. Only three women menstruated regularly. In contrast with the patients' conviction that their genitalia were normal, adequate functional anatomy was found in only four.

8. Significant Unconventional Behaviors

A. Coercive Sex

Child Abuse, Incest, and Pedophilia

Years of feminist activities directed at sexual violence resulted in 1982 in a large-scale government-organized conference to develop policies for future years. Since then, sexual violence has been high on the political agenda. Research flourished, volunteer movements were supported financially, the concept of expertise through personal experience was widely acknowledged, public attention was raised by mass-media campaigns, a network of confidential doctors for the anonymous reporting of child abuse was set up, and education for helping professionals was made available all over the country. In psychiatric hospitals, a more profound interest in the patient's sexual-abuse history is growing. Knowledge of the more complicated reaction patterns of childhood abuse, such as dissociative disorders, is expanding. More incest cases were brought to court, and perpetrators were sentenced to heavier penalties—the legal maximum being six years. A modest attempt with outpatient psychological help for perpetrators of sexual abuse was started, as an adjunct to the already existing residential compulsory programs for mentally disturbed violent sex offenders. A systems approach was introduced, in which all family members are supported by their own therapist, who work together to integrate the therapeutic process.

In the mid-1980s, Draijer (1990) carried out a nationwide representative study of female child sexual victimization by family members with in-depth interviews of 1,054 women, ages 20 to 40. This was 50 percent of all women approached. Intrafamily sexual abuse before age 16 was reported by 15.6 percent. For 25 percent, this study was their first discussion of these events. On a severity scale, 55.6 percent were found to be mild or not severe; 44.4 percent were classified as severe or very severe. (Step)fathers were the most inclined to commit more-intrusive forms of abuse. The level of education, level of professional occupation, religion, and geographical isolation were insignificant predictors. Family backgrounds that correlated significantly with incest included: conservatism in male-female roles, restricted sexual norms, child emotional neglect, lack of physical warmth in child rearing, discontinuity in family life, physical aggression, illness, depression, emotional instability of the parents, and the father's possessiveness and controlling tendency. Sexual victimization correlates with problems in later life in a much higher degree than all other negative family dynamics. Only 13 percent had no negative effects whatsoever.

Child sexual abuse outside the family has gained less attention (see Section 5B). In the 1970s, because of society's greater tolerance for all sexual expressions, pedophilia was for some years less tabooed. A public discussion about adult-child sexual contact on a nonexploitative base was then possible. Since the legal reform of 1991, adult sexual contacts with boys aged 12 to 16 are felonies only if the boy or his legal representative wants prosecution: maximum penalty is six years. Gender equalization of pubertal sexual rights was also part of this reform.

Following a low in child sexual-abuse cases reported in 1983, there has been a steady increase in both reported cases and the percentage of cases prosecuted. In 1989, cases of child sexual abuse by nonfamily members or authority figures was 1.9 per 100,000 inhabitants.

Male victims of childhood sexual abuse come out of the closet much later than females. The double taboo on homosexuality and powerlessness results in massive shame and repression. Volunteer and professional help for male victims is more difficult to find. Some child-abuse cases attract a lot of the general public's attention, especially the difficulties in truth finding, e.g., the use of interviews with the so-called anatomically correct dolls.

B. Sexual Harassment

Since the 1982 government conference on sexual abuse, sexual harassment has been recognized as a major problem in all sorts of organizations, including schools and business organizations. It has certainly become easier for workers to lodge complaints. Confidential counselors have been introduced in schools, and training of personnel managers and administrators on this issue is available all over the country. Verbal and physical misconduct on gender-related issues is extinct, but the general public's recognition of the intolerability of such behavior is widely acknowledged.

One special type of sexual abuse requires mention: the sexual contacts between (para)medical professionals and their patients or clients. It has been found that women abused in childhood were often revictimized during therapy. Recently, extra attention has also be given to the mentally and physically handicapped. In the 1980s, ethical codes on this particular type of misconduct were formulated. In the 1991 law reform, medical and social work professionals were included with civil servants, teachers, youth leaders, and prison wardens in those faced with a maximum penalty of six years for abuse of authority.

C. Rape

Rape was an early target for the feminist movement in the 1970s. It took some years to convince police and the courts that rape cases deserved much more attention, and rape victims much more sensitivity during interrogation. Some rape characteristics shocked the general public, for instance, the almost universally denied fact that date/acquaintance rape is more common than stranger rape. A government-financed mass-media campaign in 1992 addressed young men on sexual coercion: "Sex is natural, but never self-evident." Until 1991, Dutch law did not allow prosecution for marital rape. Sexual assault, meaning all other forced sexual acts except vaginal intercourse, is a criminal offense between husband and wife. This law reform has been a major target for emancipation action. Rape victims have also profited from the victim movement's help initiatives and its achievements in training professional social and psychotherapeutic workers.

Maximum penalty in rape cases is eight years. The number of rape cases brought to the police is steadily rising. In 1991, 1,333 accusations (9 per 100,000 inhabitants) resulted in 858 rape cases (65 percent), 746 suspects, being cleared, a rather stable percentage over the years. For sexual assault, 2,427 accusations (16 per 100,000) resulted in 1,060 cases (43.7 percent) and 632 suspects being brought to court by the police.

D. Prostitution

Studies on prostitution are numerous, but almost all data are nonrepresentative. In Holland, prostituting oneself is not illegal, but creating the opportunity for prostitution, e.g., profiting from a brothel, is. In 1993, a legal reform lowered the sanctions and allowed local governments to formulate their own policies. Prostitute activists are dissatisfied with this reform, arguing that the new situation will not improve the prostitute's legal position. In the last decade, a movement to abolish exploitation and improve working conditions (safety, hygiene, and privacy) was initiated. Prostitutes fear that the new legal situation will lead to registration and taxing (including a Value Added Tax [VAT]), which will again force the weaker group members into evading the law. Today's urgent problems include the trade in women from Third World nations, exploitation, illegal immigration, and fraudulent parental claims by Antilles men for South and Central American girls intended to legalize their working for Dutch brothels, and violence.

The total number of prostitutes in the Netherlands has been estimated at 15,000 to 20,000, the vast majority being women. Some 10 percent are supposed to be streetwalkers, 30 percent in window prostitution, 30 percent working in a sex club, 15 percent in an escort service, and 15 percent work in their private residence. Drug addicts, including drug tourists, are nu-

merous in the streetwalker group. Window and club prostitution are dominated by Caribbean, South-American, African, and Asian women. In recent
years, condom use among these groups has been promoted by means of
audiotaped messages. It is generally believed that today most prostitution
intercourse is protected, with drug-addicted streetwalkers as the most likely
exception.

In 1968, more than half of all single men and 12 percent of husbands
refused to answer questions about paid sexual encounters. In both groups,
12 percent admitted to having visited a prostitute at least once. In 1981,
refusal was almost nil and 11 percent admitted to having visited a prostitute
at least once. Moreover, 19 percent of the married group, especially the
younger-age group, had visited a sex club at least once. In 1989, 13.5 percent
of the male respondents reported having paid for sex at least once; 2.6
percent had had at least one paid sex experience in the past year.

In the 1989 study, visiting prostitutes seemed to be motivated more by
the desire to maintain independence than by social inadequacy. For men
in steady relationships, common motives are variation or a strong desire
for special forms of sex their partner refuses them. Condom use seems
almost to have doubled as a result of the safe-sex campaigns.

Male heterosexual prostitution is extremely rare in Holland, but one
study of escort boys was published in 1989. In recent years, male strippers
("Chippendales") have made a remarkable appearance in the entertainment world.

Male homosexual prostitution is estimated to count some 1,300 men, of
which a large group must be relatively young. Some consider themselves
true professionals, with a professional pride in working according to their
own standards. Others are motivated largely by drug addiction and home-
lessness. Sexual orientation is problematic: most boys consider themselves
to be heterosexual, which suggests limits on the behaviors they consider
acceptable or not. Fortunately, these restrictions result in a rather low
prevalence of unsafe sex; homosexual prostitution seems to be a minor risk
factor in the AIDS epidemic. Unfortunately, this discrepancy between
self-perceived sexual orientation and behavior can lead to resentment and
violent outbursts. A boy who feels trapped, especially when a man wants to
perform anal penetration, will sometimes commit violent acts against his
customer, as this behavior is most threatening to his masculinity. In ten
years, eighteen murder cases with this dynamic were reported in Amsterdam. Moroccan boys were overrepresented, and this may reflect high
vulnerability for threats to their masculinity as a result of their Islamic
culture.

E. Pornography

Pornography as a subject of public decency laws has almost completely
disappeared from the legislative discourse since the 1960s sexual revolution

movement. Feminist criticism of the misogyny obvious in a lot of pornography has been heard throughout the nation, but this did not influence legislation to any substantial degree. In the latest reform, the protection of children and women in the pornography-producing business has gained more impetus than the decency aspect. Penalties up to three months can still be given for public exposure of indecent materials, exposure to children under 16, and selling child pornography. Child-abuse laws are often applied in cases of the production of child pornography; maximum penalty: six years.

Child pornography has been under scrutiny as a result of allegations from the U.S.A., implying that enormous amounts of these materials were being imported from the Netherlands. It cannot be denied that in the mid-1980s, Holland produced and exported child pornography, some of which, especially heterosexual material, clearly qualified as hard-core. Yet, the American interest in Dutch pornography has all the characteristics of a witch hunt, exaggerating the numbers of victims. In 1989, six child pornography cases led to convictions.

The use of pornography is quite common. In the 1989 study, only 23 percent of the men and 55 percent of the women had no experience at all with erotic magazines or books, while 54 percent of the men and 12 percent of the women had watched pornographic movies or videos. The "new kids on the block" are erotic pay-phone lines (06-numbers); 12 percent of the men and 4 percent of the women reported having phoned a sex line. This erotic option has become an addiction for some Dutchmen. Recently alcohol-and-drug services have begun treating some of their patients for 06-phoning problems.

F. Other Unconventional Behaviors

Some paraphilic behaviors are well embedded in society. Transvestites, for instance, have formed groups, often with transsexuals, for mutual support and opportunities to cross-dress without the risk of ridicule or violent reactions. People interested in sadomasochistic sexual contacts have formed two national organizations, and numerous sex clubs offer opportunities for expression. Gay and lesbian S-M groups are also active, and one occasionally sees some very aesthetic expressions of the S-M preference, especially in photography.

Indecent exposure is the most common sex crime; in 1990, 1.8 percent of all women were confronted with an act of exhibitionism. The number of reported cases shows a slow decline: 3,840 in 1991 (26 per 10,000). Only 30.5 percent were brought to court by the police. Exhibitionism complaints often result in a warning, and when brought to court, suggestions for some sort of therapy will often be the judge's sentence. Unfortunately, no studies of results of court-ordered out-patient treatment of exhibitionists are published.

9. Contraception, Abortion, and Population Planning

A. History

Contraceptive advice in Holland started in the 1880s. The inspiration for a Neo-Malthusian League was imported from the United Kingdom by Alette Jacobs (1854-1929). This remarkable woman, the first Dutch woman ever to enter secondary school, the university, and become a medical doctor, was strongly influenced by feminist ideals and a heartfelt concern for the poor. The League, founded by Jacobs and two other doctors, found little support and more often violent opposition in medical circles.

After Mensinga invented the diaphragm in 1881, this became the main weapon in the struggle against large, poor families. Free clinics started in Amsterdam in 1882, and soon afterwards in Rotterdam and Groningen. The Neo-Malthusian League produced leaflets and books in enormous numbers. Some midwives joined the clinics, and from the 1890s on, lay women were trained in instructing and prescribing the diaphragm. The clinic network expanded rapidly, as condom quality improved and more precise information on the Ogino-Knaus method of periodic abstinence became available.

In 1939, the Neo-Malthusian League performed Holland's first socio-sexological research, distributing 26,010 questionnaires to its members; 7,788 were returned and analyzed (Nabrink 1978); see Table 10 for some results of this survey.

Table 10

Contraceptive Use and Failures in 1939 (n = 7,788)

Method	Females			Males		
	n	Failures	%	n	Failures	%
Coitus interruptus	155	29	18.7	165	46	27.9
Diaphragm	1,484	75	5	1,409	44	3.2
Condom	1,105	67	6	1,036	79	6.7
Cervical cap	95	19	20	91	12	13.2
Patentex jelly	56	20	35.7	61	20	32.7
Periodic abstinence	56	12	21.4	53	17	32

When the Germans occupied the Netherlands, the Neo-Malthusian League was abolished. After World War II, a new organization replaced it, the Dutch Society for Sexual Reform (NVSH). Again a chain of consultation bureaus was established and education for the general public gradually became more accepted. The ideals of the NVSH became more political, and the sexual revolution further radicalized the movement.

Following the introduction of the oral contraceptive in 1962, general practitioners and gynecologists were initially reluctant to prescribe the pill, sometimes for reasons blatantly moralistic. The NVSH consultation bureaus soon became a well-known alternative for teenagers, unmarried couples, married couples who wanted to postpone procreation, widows, and divorcees. Professional expertise in the NVSH bureaus was also on a higher level in those pioneering years. In 1969, the society separated into a professional organization for the management of the consultation bureaus, the Rutgers Foundation, and a layman's organization for political action, education, and discussion and self-help.

Since the mid-1970s, contraceptive advice has become part of the regular physician's routine; gynecologists play a minor part in contraception in Holland. The Rutgers Foundation still was a useful alternative for girls and women who sought extreme discretion (e.g., young girls and women in extramarital relations whose spouses had vasectomies) and for more specialized questions on contraception and "second opinions." Since 1992, the Rutgers Foundation has concentrated its services in seven large cities, and guides its efforts more to educating the regular providers of contraceptive and sexological services.

From the mid-1960s on, contraceptive use and attitudes have been major research issues. Unwanted pregnancy and induced abortion caused major social, medical, and political concern. Accordingly, in the past two decades, questions about contraceptive use and the prevalence of unwanted pregnancy were almost always included in surveys, particularly those for adolescents.

Several studies directly addressed the issue of family planning. Initially, research was mainly done by general practitioners and family-planning doctors. Social scientists entered the field a few years later. A 1974-75 representative study, involving 1,200 men and women, revealed that modern methods of family planning had been rapidly accepted, irrespective of social status or religion. NISSO did several studies in close collaboration with Stimezo-Nederland, the national abortion federation, which began its own research program in 1974. The role of induced abortion in society was studied as it related to changing patterns of family formation, sexual behavior after the "sexual revolution," and emerging modern contraceptive behavior. An international comparative investigation of the consequences of legal changes regarding abortion in Western Europe and the U.S.A. was followed by a study of contraceptive behavior throughout Western Europe (Ketting 1990).

In 1986, NISSO started a new research program on family planning, concentrating on specific groups. Studies published prior to 1993 include:

- Anthropologically inspired in-depth interviews on sexual and contraceptive behavior of Turkish immigrants;
- A similar study on Caribbean immigrants;

- An in-depth study of the social and psychological mechanisms underlying the effectiveness of contraceptive behavior of young girls at the
start of their sexual careers;
- A study on the rather new phenomenon of women's ambivalence
towards child bearing; and
- A representative study of the experiences of 1,200 women with, and
attitudes towards, oral contraception.

B. Some Data

Vogel and van der Vliet's 1990 study on adolescent sexuality gave a lot of
information on contraceptive use and the various motives for the use of
condoms. They concentrated on contraceptive motives, although this distinction is not always possible.

Mean age for first coitus in this survey was 17.5. In this first coital
experience, 57 percent used a condom. The earlier first coitus occurred,
the higher the proportion of condom users. Allochtonous youngsters
scored lower especially when not born in the Netherlands. In the older age
groups, as relations become steady, oral-contraceptive use is the rule, and
condom use for STD/AIDS prevention loses most of its impetus.

Many girls are using oral contraceptives before their first coitus. One in
five girls are taking the pill by the time they start petting naked. (A
prescription for medical reasons, e.g., menstrual discomfort, may account
for a proportion of this number.) Two thirds of all girls with some coital
experience have at some time used the pill; 60 percent were using oral
contraception when interviewed. When first intercourse was experienced
at an early age (11 to 13), the percentage was lower (just over 10 percent);
in the oldest group, almost three quarters were current users.

In keeping with the Dutch slogan, "If you take care of the condoms, I'll
take care of the pill," combined use of the pill and condom was practiced
by 13 percent of respondents (boys: 18 percent, girls: 9 percent) in their
last intercourse experience. The 14 to 15 age group is most conscientious
in this regard, 22 percent. The use of no contraception at all is rare; only
11 percent of 16- to 19-year-olds used no contraception in their last sexual
intercourse (see Table 11).

Adults

Van Delft and Ketting (1992) have reported the most recent number data
from 1988: Of the 18- to 37-year-old women, 43 percent used an oral or
injectable contraceptive, 22 percent no contraceptive, 7 percent each for
the condom or vasectomy, 5 percent each for vasectomy and IUD, and 3
percent tubal ligation. Only 13 percent of the married women, 5 percent
of the cohabiting women, and 14 percent of the women in steady relationships used no contraceptive (Tables 12 and 13).

Table 11

Pregnancies per 1,000 Unmarried Women, Grouped According to Consequences, 1980-1988

Year	"Forced" Marriage	Birth Out of Wedlock	Abortion	Total
1980	2.8	2.4	5.3	10.5
1981	2.9	1.9	5.3	10.1
1982	2.5	2.1	5.1	9.7
1983	2.3	2.2	5.3	10.0
1984	2.1	2.0	4.4	8.5
1985	1.9	2.0	4.4	8.4
1986	1.9	2.1	4.1	8.1
1987	1.6	2.3	3.8	7.7
1988	1.6	2.3	3.8	7.7

Source: Van Delft and Ketting (1992), Table 22, p. 61

Table 12

Current Contraceptive Method, by Age, in Percentages (1988)

Contraceptive Method	Age of Women (in Years)					Total 18-37
	18-19	20-24	25-29	30-34	35-37	
Oral-injectable	45	59	48	31	22	43
IUD	1	2	5	9	6	5
Tubal ligation	0	0	1	6	11	3
Vasectomy	0	0	3	12	23	7
Condom	5	5	9	9	8	7
Other methods	4	6	4	5	3	5
No contraceptive	45	24	19	16	15	22
Pregnant	0	3	9	6	2	5
Infertile	0	1	2	6	9	3

Source: van Delft and Ketting (1992), Table 1, p. 10

No Dutch data are available on contraceptive failures for different methods. While a number of unplanned pregnancies are accepted after discovery, it is known from various sources that over 90 percent of all children born in the years 1981-88 were planned. A comparison of Dutch failure data with U.S.A. figures reveals that each method, except for periodic abstinence, is more reliable in Holland and the difference is enormous. Three sources of confusion are mentioned by van Delft and Ketting:

Table 13

Current Contraceptive Use, by Relationship Status, in Percentages (1988; Ages 18-37)

Contraceptive Method	Married	Cohabiting	Steady Relationship	No Male Partner
Oral-injectable	35	68	67	28
IUD	7	7	3	1
Tubal ligation	5	2	2	1
Vasectomy	13	3	1	—
Condom	9	6	6	4
Other methods	4	5	6	4
No contraception	13	5	14	58
Pregnant	9	4	1	0
Infertile	5	1	1	3

- American data often report method failure in the first year of use. Most methods gain in reliability in time;
- The "morning after pill" is easily available in Holland and is used by women who are aware something has gone wrong with their usual method;
- Some American data may be distorted by including users who deliberately stopped using the method.

It is generally acknowledged that U.S.A. data on method failure cannot be used for Dutch educational materials (Table 14).

Estrogen dose-dependent side effects, especially cardiovascular ones, led to the introduction of the so-called sub-50s in 1975. In five years, they became the leading oral contraceptive. Today, most physicians prescribe sub-50s. This seems to work reasonably well: abortion data show that women on 50s and sub-50s have comparable risks of unwanted pregnancy.

Concern over the pill's side effects around 1980 led to a short but sharp decline in pill use. Introduction of sub-50s largely removed this concern. Today, most women are aware of positive side effects. Nevertheless, total oral-contraceptive use once again showed a slight decrease in 1990. Condom use for STD and AIDS prevention may have led some women to stop or postpone oral contraception. The decline in popularity of hormonal contraception led to a short increase in IUD use (Table 15).

Gynecologists and the Rutgers Foundation were the early providers for IUDs. From 1983 to 1987, the Dutch industry producing the most popular IUD ran educational workshops for physicians, increasing the use of IUDs. Early on, there was an awareness of negative side effects, menstrual discomfort, and a rising number of extrauterine pregnancies.

Table 14

Distribution of Hormonal Contraceptive Use by Type of Method, 1980-1989, in Percentages

Year	Sub-50 Combination	Tri-phasic	50(-plus)	Injectable	Others
1980	41.9	0.1	46.7	4.3	7.0
1981	47.5	5.6	36.5	4.8	5.6
1982	55.6	10.1	25.3	4.7	4.3
1983	57.2	14.8	20.4	3.9	3.7
1984	58.7	18.8	16.6	2.8	3.1
1985	69.7	20.8	14.5	2.4	2.6
1986	61.0	22.1	12.5	2.2	2.2
1987	61.4	23.8	11.2	1.8	1.8
1988	61.7	25.2	8.2	1.6	2.0
1989	62.8	25.2	8.2	1.6	2.2

Source: van Delft and Ketting (1992), Table 11, p. 26

Table 15

Total Number of IUDs Sold in the Netherlands and Estimated Duration *in Situ*, 1980-1990

Year	Number Sold	Mean Years *in Situ*
1980	100,000	2.00
1981	97,000	2.25
1982	79,000	2.50
1983	78,000	2.75
1984	77,000	3.00
1985	67,000	3.25
1986	48,000	3.50
1987	45,000	3.75
1988	40,000	3.75
1989	39,000	3.75
1990	38,000	3.75

Because condom use has been so strongly motivated by disease prevention, it is discussed in Section 11.

The diaphragm was never very popular after World War II, being used predominantly by women in steady relationships and dissatisfied with alternatives. It has its place in a lifestyle characterized by conscious living with health risks. In small circles, modified and perfected forms of periodic abstinence are also used. We have no reason to suppose that Roman Catholics are a large proportion of abstinence users. In 1992, the woman's condom (Femidom) was introduced. Among 300 women, ages 21 to 40, who were regular users of oral contraception, IUD, or sterilization during the trial period, 155 women reporting using Femidom on at least three occasions. Both men and women appear reasonably satisfied with the Femidom.

Surgical sterilization peaked in 1979, when 132,000 men and women had vasectomies or tubal ligations. The proportion of men is growing steadily, because it is well known that sterilization is much easier in men. The operation is most often performed between ages 35 and 44. Since 1985, the percentages of sterilized men and women in each age group has been rather constant. In the 35 to 39 age group, 18 percent of women and 20 percent of men are sterilized; in the 40 to 45 age group, about 25 percent of women and men are sterilized; about 30 percent of men and women 45 to 49 have been sterilized. Forty percent of all couples aged 30 to 49 have one spouse sterilized.

In recent years, sterilization has decreased in the younger age group, most probably due to an ongoing tendency to postpone having a first child. Also, some couples are debating for a number of years whether or not they want to have children at all. This has led to an expanding group of last-chance mothers with considerable fertility problems caused by a more advanced age. This group of doubters, combined with a growing conviction that oral contraception is not a major health risk, will likely lead to a further decline in sterilizations.

Interception with the "morning after pill" (MAP) and the "morning after-IUD" (MA-IUD) along with abortion, is one of the adjuncts of planned contraception. The MAP is easily available for use after unprotected intercourse, as well as for backup for incidental failures with the regular method. The largest group using MAP is the 16- to 18-year-olds. Around 1980, when the negative attitude toward the pill peaked, use of MAP also peaked. The original MAP (5 x 5 mg ethinyl estradiol) has been replaced with the Yuzpe regime (100 mg EE plus 500 mg norgestrel repeated after 12 hours) introduced in 1982. By 1986, the Yuzpe MAP accounted for 85 percent of MAP prescriptions. In 1986 and again in 1992, some doubt was cast on the effectiveness of the Yuzpe regime, leaving the future of this method open to question.

C. Abortion

Just over 30,000 abortions are performed yearly in Holland, a quite stable number in recent years. More than 90 percent are done in abortion clinics, almost all under local anesthesia; the rest are done in gynecology departments, 80 percent under total anesthesia. Among women living in Holland,

69 percent have their abortions within six weeks after conception; 2.2 percent were pregnant longer than fifteen weeks in 1989-90. Large numbers of abortion patients (35 to 40 percent) visit our clinics from western Germany, Belgium, Spain (showing a sharp decline since 1988), and numerous other countries.

Separate data are available from women in Holland, Suriname, the Dutch Antilles, Turkey, and Morocco. Abortion rates in these groups show significant, but rather stable differences, with a slight increase for the Moroccan and a slight decrease for Suriname, Antilles, and Turkish women (Table 16). Moroccan women tend to be relatively young, primigravidae, and unmarried; it is supposed that the rising number for Moroccan women indicates some alienation from their traditional culture. For Turkish women, data suggest that abortion is used mostly to put an end to the expansion of the family. Allochtonous women have used abortion more often than autochtonous women, and it must be assumed that this implies more user failures. Moreover, one third of these women had used no contraception at all compared with 20 percent for Dutch women. For allochtonous women, some 25 percent, the abortion in 1989-90 was not their first. For Suriname and Antilles women, it is recognized that they show more fear for unhealthy side effects of oral contraceptives. This leads to an eagerness to stop taking the pill, for instance, when a relationship falls apart.

Table 16

Abortion Rates, per Ethnic Groups, Ages 15-44, per 1,000

Ethnic Group	Rate
Autochtonous	3.4
Surinam	28.8
Antillies	31.1
Turkey	17.8
Morocco	12.4

Source: Rademakers, 1992, Table 2.11, p. 20

Teenagers as a group are constant in their risk of abortion in recent years, around 4 per 1,000 girls aged 15 to 19. Teenagers have shown a slight increase in live birthrates in recent years.

As Dutch couples conceive later in life, the number of prenatal diagnostic tests for fetal malformation and disease will rise, and so will the decision for an abortion to resolve an unfavorable outcome. Precise numbers of such abortions are not available.

D. Government Policies on Contraception and Population

In 1970, the Dutch Parliament decided that medical contraception and the cost of medical contraceptive advice should be included under general health services. Condoms are the only contraceptives that are not covered. Even in AIDS-prevention campaigns, a recommendation to include condoms has been ignored. In the recent economic recession, with a growing need to reduce health expenses, hormonal contraception is quite often mentioned as one possibility to cut costs. Thus far, these suggestions have led to strong reactions, especially because risk groups, such as minors and allochtonous women, will be the first to suffer the consequences of unwanted pregnancy and abortion.

In 1979, the Dutch government endorsed its State Committee on Population Questions recommendation that all Dutch couples were free to decide their number of children and the time they wanted to have them. Since then, the government has supported effective contraceptive behavior by stimulating and financing research, general education, and low-level professional help. The effectiveness of Dutch contraceptive practice is based on the opportunity for almost all young people to get the pill. Today, most general practitioners are able to handle the delicacy of prescribing the pill to young girls, even if their parents are not informed. In coming years, it will be learned whether or not unwanted pregnancy will increase as a consequence of the Rutgers Foundation's concentration in seven cities.

Abortion was a criminal offense in the Netherlands until a long-awaited legal reform took place in 1982—1953 was the last time a physician was prosecuted for performing an abortion. In 1969, Stimezo, a national organization for medically qualified induced abortion, was formed. Stimezo standards of good advice and care have found their way into today's practice. On the insistence of the religious parties, the 1982 law includes one aspect contrary to the practice of that time, e.g., a waiting and reconsideration time of five days after the initial consultation with a doctor. Since that law passed, abortion has been free for all Dutch citizens. Minors living with their parents need their parents' consent, but a legal alternative is available.

Population planning is not an active concern of the Dutch government. Zero growth is accepted, and a changing population stratification (young groups shrinking, elderly groups growing) causes only moderate concern. Will the future active group be able to support a large retired population? In gynecological circles, some concern is growing about the tendency of couples to postpone having children until an age when fertility definitely is lower. A popular slogan, "A smart girl plans her pregnancy in time," is a variation of an earlier advertisement by the Institute for Idealistic Propaganda: "A smart girl is prepared for a future for herself."

10. Sexually Transmitted Diseases

A. Incidence, Patterns, and Trends

According to Mooij's (1990) history of STD, gonorrhea and syphilis were rare in the Netherlands in comparison with the surrounding countries—until 1942. During World War II, a rapid increase was reported, with a peak in 1947. In 1952, numbers were again as low as they were in the 1930s. A steady decline was observed until 1960, but since then, a second, and longer, epidemic has occurred, with rapid increases in the 1970s. Undoubtedly, these growing numbers were the result of a new enthusiasm for sexuality, the sexual revolution, supported by the general public's knowledge that STDs were now easily cured. Public education almost forgot primary prevention in these years.

The sexual revolution certainly changed the medical and health professionals' ideas on specific risk groups. Prostitutes were no longer the main source of concern; homosexuals, teenagers, foreigners, and Dutch tourists who had sex while vacationing abroad became new targets for information campaigns. It is remarkable that these predictions, based on information from abroad, were not confirmed by Dutch experience, except for homosexuals, and recently Turkish and Moroccan men.

The neglect of primary prevention gradually ended when hepatitis B and herpes, which are not curable by penicillin, appeared. Herpes caused considerable panic in heterosexual circles. Alarming data from the U.S.A. were uncritically transposed to Holland and connections with cervical cancer and neonatal disease exaggerated. The number of diagnoses peaked in 1985, perhaps biased by a more widespread availability of diagnostic services and an antiviral medication that might have prompted people in fear of herpes to be finally tested. In this peak year, the number of herpes cases at the Amsterdam free clinic was 25 percent of the number of gonorrhea cases. Today, herpes is infrequently diagnosed and the attention paid it by the general public and media is insignificant. However, it is reasonable that herpes promoted a growing concern for primary prevention in the 1980s, as the sharp decrease in STD diagnosis started some years before AIDS appeared.

Two STDs are among the infectious diseases for compulsory notification to the National Health Inspection: gonorrhea and syphilis. Unfortunately, only about 35 percent of all cases are reported. Free clinics have a more complete reporting, including data on location of the disease (urethral, rectal, and/or pharyngeal), ethnic background, sexual preference, prostitution, and earlier infections. Unfortunately, they have no information on the characteristics of groups using their services, and whether or not this group's composition is stable or changing.

National registration numbers for gonorrhea steadily decreased from 13,199 in 1983 to 3,024 in 1989. The peak year for men was 1981 (140 per 100,000 inhabitants); for women, 1984 (65 per 100,000). An increase in 1990 was followed by the lowest number ever in 1992. In free clinics, similar trends were observed. The fastest decreases were among male homosexual and bisexual men, since 1984. Female prostitutes showed a little slower decrease, and later—since 1985. For homosexual and bisexual men, 1989 already showed some increase, including more anorectal infections, and unfortunately this trend has continued into 1990 and 1991. Moreover, these patients tend to be slightly younger in recent years.

For the Amsterdam free clinics, repeaters are a growing population in the total numbers. Percentagewise, homosexuals are declining and prostitutes are increasing. In all years, the peak age for male infections is 25; for women, age 20.

The percentage of Penicillinase-Producing Neisseria Gonorrhoeae (PPNG) in Dutch patients is steadily increasing. The first cases of PPNG were reported in the Netherlands in 1976; in 1990, 29 percent of all gonococcal infections was caused by PPNG. Since 1985, a rapid increase in Tetracycline-Resistant Gonorrhea (TRG) has been observed. In 1989, 40 percent of PPNG cases also involved TRG.

Syphilis was still decreasing in 1992, with only 190 new infections reported. In Amsterdam free clinics, in 1987, an increase in syphilis incidence was reported in heterosexual men, and some increase in female prostitutes. In that year, heterosexuals for the first time outnumbered homosexuals. In 1989, homosexual men in Amsterdam also showed an increase in new cases of syphilis, similar to tendencies in gonorrhea and seroconversions, perhaps due to a decrease in safer-sex practices.

In Holland, since the early 1950s, all pregnant women are screened for syphilis in the first trimester. In the Amsterdam area, 1985-89, only 55 out of 3,520 blood samples were positive for both TPHA- and VDRL-tests. Only four cases of congenital syphilis were reported in 1990. However, screening is still cost-efficient in Amsterdam, and a second screening later in pregnancy should not be introduced as a routine restricted to women having many partners during pregnancy.

Chlamydia trachomatis probably is the most widespread STD today, but information is scanty on this subject since reporting it is not mandatory. The most thorough research took place in 1986-88. In a 1986-88 Amsterdam free clinic survey of 1,000 clients (65 percent male) at the free clinic, chlamydia was found more often than gonorrhea: 14.3 percent versus 11.5 percent in men, 19.2 percent versus 6.3 percent in women. Combined infections were found in 2 percent of men and 2.6 percent of women. Combination infections were low in homosexual men. In men, signs for urethritis were found in all but 1, with negative tests for gonorrhea and chlamydia in 41 percent of the cases. In the department of gynecology of a large Amsterdam hospital, 1985-89, the incidence of gonorrhea dropped from 1.1 percent to 0.4 percent, and chlamydia from 8.6 percent to 4.1 percent.

While chlamydia definitely is the most common STD in Holland, there are good grounds for concluding that the epidemic has peaked. However, the serious consequences for fertility justify further efforts to control the disease. In 1986, in the Tilburg Infertility Clinic, of seventy-seven women receiving their first treatment, tubal abnormality was thought to be the cause of infertility for sixty-nine; 54 percent had significant titers for chlamydia.

Data on condylomata acuminata are rarer, with indications that incidence is in the same range as herpes, increasing slightly up to 1985 and decreasing in recent years. Tropical STDs are rarely diagnosed in Holland, with occasional small epidemics of haemophilus ducrei.

Allochtonous men are a growing proportion of free clinic customers. Data suggest that Turkish and Moroccan men are six to ten times more at risk for contracting STDs. Turkish men have gonorrhea in a high proportion and a high proportion of PPNG. They also report prostitution as the source of their infection in a higher percentage. Suriname and Antillian men show a higher proportion of syphilis.

B. Government Policies Concerning STD

The Dutch government has recognized STDs as a special group of diseases, with associated shame and stigma calling for special forms of illness management. Alternatives for discreet and anonymous help have been financed. Local health services provide free clinics in all large cities; the Rutgers Foundation is another alternative for STD diagnosis and treatment. For syphilis and gonorrhea, a service is offered to assist patients anonymously in contacting the sexual partners they think they have infected or been infected by.

A national organization for STD control, the SOA Foundation, produces a scientific bimonthly and contributes to the discussions in medical and political circles, and to prevention programs. In the last decade, physicians' organizations have produced consensuses for standard medical care. More intensive health and STD education programs have been incorporated in a framework of sexuality and relationship management in schools. STDs other than AIDS have never been the target for specific primary prevention programs until recently. The SOA Foundation has applied for funding for a Chlamydia Public Information campaign, but this has not been forthcoming. Target groups other than teenagers in schools also have never been defined for prevention programs on STDs other than AIDS. Special attention to allochtonous groups can be justified by these groups' higher infection rates, and their higher proportion of PPNG.

11. HIV/AIDS

A. Incidence, Patterns, and Trends

Unlike syphilis and gonorrhea, notification of AIDS cases to the National Health Inspection is voluntary. While syphilis and gonorrhea cases are underreported, AIDS reporting tends to be almost complete because of the serious nature of the epidemic. Many intravenous drug users die of health risks inherent in their lifestyles before their HIV-positive status is detected. Starting with 5 new cases of AIDS in 1982, 437 cases were reported in 1991 and 419 in 1992. Only 10 cases of HIV-2 infection were reported. Homosexual men, followed by IV drug users (male and female), and heterosexual men and women, account for most AIDS cases, with the incidence remarkably stable through the years. Men ages 30 to 45 and women 25 to 35 are most at risk. Survival time has increased from nine months in 1982-85 to twenty-two months in 1989, because of earlier diagnosis and better treatment (Tables 17 and 18).

Table 17

Number of Newly Diagnosed AIDS Patients per Year

Year	New Patients
1982	5
1983	19
1984	31
1985	66
1986	136
1987	242
1988	321
1989	389
1990	413
1991	437
1992	419
TOTAL	2,478

Source: National Health Inspection, 1993

The number of HIV-positive persons in Holland is unknown. Individuals may be tested anonymously, in which case their status is not reported. Some data is available on segments of the population from research groups studying pregnant women, drug users (30 percent of whom are IV users), clients at the Amsterdam free STD clinic, Amsterdam prostitutes and their customers, and voluntary applicants for blood donation.

Table 18

Number of AIDS Patients, According to Risk Group and Sex

Risk Group	Male	Female
Homosexual-Bisexual	1,930	—
Intravenous Drug User	145	67
Homosexual-Bisexual + IVDU	26	—
Hemophilia	40	1
Blood Transfusion	20	15
Heterosexual	108	74
Mother-to-child	2	9
Rest/unknown	33	8
TOTAL	2,304	174

Source: National Health Inspection, 1993

In a national prospective research project on HIV-infection in pregnancy, testing is voluntary and the percentage of women choosing to be tested varies widely for different hospitals. Between September 1, 1985, and January 1, 1991, fifty-five women were found to be positive: 60 percent were not born in Holland. In 58 percent, intravenous drug abuse was the risk factor; in two of the twenty-two women supposed to be heterosexually infected, blood transfusion was also reported. Ten were born in an area where AIDS is endemic; seven had at-risk male partners. Of thirty-six women for whom test results were known before twenty weeks of gestation, two had spontaneous and ten induced abortions.

Among the estimated 2,500-plus hard-drug users in Holland, only 30 percent are IV users. IV use varies from practically zero among allochtonous groups to 70 percent for "heroin tourists." Combining results of a cohort survey amongst injectors in Amsterdam started in 1985 with reported AIDS numbers resulted in an estimation of 750 to 800 HIV-positive IV drug users in Amsterdam as of July 1, 1991. Even more rough is an estimate of HIV-positive IV drug users outside Amsterdam, ca. 500. Local differences are large and unexplained: Participants in a detox clinic in the Hague were all seronegative, while their injection behavior was no more risky than an Amsterdam group. Prevalence of seropositivity among all IVDUs is estimated at 25 to 27 percent. Specific preventive measures include a syringe-exchange program and condom promotion, especially for those active in prostitution (some 80 percent of all female IV drug addicts).

In an Amsterdam free STD clinic, during ten weeks in 1991, 90.5 percent of all the patients accepted testing: 22 percent of the homosexual men were positive, as were 12 percent of the male and 41 percent of the female IV drug users. Prevalence in heterosexuals without other risk factors was 0.5 percent (5 of 997) for men and 0.1 percent (1 of 771) for women.

When prostitutes and their customers were tested in Amsterdam in 1991, three (from Ghana, Nigeria, and the Dominican Republic) of 199 prostitutes were HIV-positive. One customer who admitted to homosexual contacts was HIV-positive.

Blood-donor volunteers in any HIV risk group are asked not to donate. In 1985, fifteen donors were found to be HIV-positive; in 1990, the new discouragement policy resulted in only five infected donors. This procedure does not totally exclude HIV transmission by blood transfusion, because of latency between infection and seropositivity. Blood products for hemophiliacs have been heat-treated since 1985, so this is no longer a risk group. Early in the epidemic, about 13 percent of hemophiliacs were infected.

B. Effectiveness of Prevention Education Programs

In a sample of 1,013 homosexual men in Amsterdam followed since 1984, an extensive change in behavior has been documented in two directions: a decrease in the number of sex partners and a lower prevalence of anogenital contact. These behavior changes resulted in a decline in seroconversions to almost zero in 1987. However, since the end of 1989, there is an increase in the incidence of HIV infection in the same cohort. Interviews with this group revealed that higher percentages of both seropositives and seronegatives had had anogenital sex without protection, especially in casual sexual relations.

In recent years, AIDS health promotion has changed its message from "avoid anal sex" to "avoid unprotected anal sex." The availability of special condoms for anal intercourse has been a major factor in this development. Recently, condom efficacy was studied among cohort members. Condom failures (torn, slipped) were seen more often when vaginal condoms were used or when no lubricants, or oil-based lubricants, were used. Personal efficacy prevents failure by slipping, but not by tearing the condom. In-depth interviews with men who seroconverted indicate the significant role of the use of alcohol and other drugs, as well as the divergent individual background of each seroconverter. Personality factors, like coping styles and health locus of control, seemed to be almost completely unrelated to behavioral change. Preceding sexual behavior seems to be the best predictor of actual behavior.

In a quasi-longitudinal telephone survey, changes in beliefs, attitudes, and behaviors related to AIDS were followed from early 1987 onwards. Knowledge regarding the use of condoms to prevent HIV transmission increased to a level that can be considered sufficient by the end of the 1980s. The general population seems to opt for monogamy and condom use as preventive measures. The use of condoms rose, especially among teenagers and persons in nonsteady relationships. These observations were confirmed by condom sales figures and STD incidence. However, there seems to remain a discrepancy between the inclination to use condoms and the actual use.

In the 1989 study, sexual behavior of 1,000 respondents is described in the context of HIV transmission as it relates to: potential risk, awareness, knowledge, and endorsement of misconceptions on transmission. Based on sexual behavior, 12 percent should be considered to have taken at least some risk in the year preceding the interview. Of these 124 subjects, 58 percent completely ruled out the chance that they might have been infected. In general, the level of knowledge is rather high. The knowledge of the subjects who have been at risk ironically is slightly greater than average. This might imply that more intensive prevention strategies should be directed at subgroups who are relatively more at risk.

In the 1989 teen study, sexual mores are found not to be changed by AIDS. To avoid HIV infection, teens prefer postponing sex till one has found the right partner or using condoms during intercourse. In general, however, in fact youngsters do not postpone their first sexual contact. Only a few of those who advise the postponing of sex have had unsafe sexual contacts. Half of those recommending the use of condoms do not stick to their own advice. Condoms are used especially in the beginning of affairs; but later on, many couples switch to oral contraceptives to avoid pregnancy. Moreover, a questionnaire survey among school children revealed that intentions of consistent condom use for HIV prevention decreases with the amount of actual intercourse experience. They seem to ignore the fact that their relationship career will most likely be characterized by serial monogamy. This research suggests more attention to efficacy aspects of condom use: buying them, raising the topic with a new partner, etc.

Based on a theory of sexual networks, 60 percent of the 18- to 19-year-olds seems to run no risk whatsoever of getting infected with HIV. This network analysis research is a promising new branch of sociosexual study. Other new approaches are studies on negotiations between male and female prostitutes and their customers to find out to what extent they could take health-promoting measures.

C. Treatment, Prevention Programs, and Government Policies

Since the onset of the AIDS epidemic, an elaborate system of care and prevention for homosexual men has been developed in the Netherlands. The gay community took the initiative for the first nationwide AIDS education campaign (1983) aimed mainly at homosexual and bisexual men. Also in 1983, an ambulatory venereal disease and AIDS clinic for homosexual men was started in Amsterdam, the Supplementary Services Foundation (StAD), supplementing regular services.

In 1984, as the AIDS epidemic spread among gay men, the StAD started a small-scale primary prevention course for gay men, aimed at altering sexual habits. This was modeled after an American example and was successful throughout the country. The foundation still organizes numerous prevention activities aimed at gay men, such as safe-sex workshops, video workshops, shows in gay bars, and activities in gay cruising areas (parks, public toilets). Postgraduate education programs and material on AIDS have been produced by StAD and a number of Amsterdam physicians who have many AIDS patients. Doctors employed by the StAD support some of the doctors in Amsterdam with the heaviest burden of AIDS patients by taking over office hours and home visits.

Another important gay health-care institute is the Schorer Foundation. In the AIDS field, the foundation has offered psychosocial care for gay men and their friends and families since 1984. It also initiated, and now coordinates, the "buddy" home-care projects all over the country. This project offers AIDS patients free volunteer support at home. The foundation also produces education programs and training courses for workers in psychosocial health care.

Although these gay organizations are important care providers, most gay men with AIDS make use of general health institutions such as general practitioners, district nurses, hospitals, psychiatrists, and social workers. Therefore gay (and other) lifestyle elements need to be included in postgraduate education for all caregivers, to prevent communication problems. After all, HIV has no precedent as an extremely serious health and culture problem in the gay community.

The total number of women infected is smaller, but the progression is faster in women. Attention to women and AIDS seems to be restricted to their role as infectors (prostitutes, IV users, and pregnant women). In December 1990, on World AIDS Day, which was dedicated to women, it was observed that women should be the target for more and better campaigns for the prevention of AIDS, and that care for women should be improved. For some years, the Rutgers Foundation has provided short-term support and education groups for HIV-infected women.

Care for HIV-positive IV drug users is often complicated by aggravated addiction behavior, which often makes these patients difficult to deal and make appointments with. Municipal health centers and general practitioners in the big cities, and local clinics for the addicted, monitor a substantial percentage of IV drug users. This includes health education, education on HIV prevention, assessment of physical condition, and often also the prescription of methadone, a heroin substitute. A needle/syringe exchange program is an important part of prevention. Education for hemophiliacs and support for those infected has been helped by the very active national haemophilia patient association.

Treatment for HIV is evaluated nationally. Recently a national consensus on early Zidovudine (AZT) treatment was published. In the early years, testing was thought to be of limited value because no health gain was to be expected, and for preventive measures, the individual's serostatus was supposed to be of no importance: safe sex should be practiced by seronegatives as well as seropositives. Today, early detection is expected to be effective, even if it does not change the patient's sexual habits. Testing is always on a voluntary basis, and if the patient wants to be tested anonymously, this is always possible.

A policy decision currently under discussion is the desirability of contact tracing and notification in heterosexually infected cases of HIV, as is common practice for gonorrhea and syphilis. Because of low heterosexual prevalence, this approach might be highly cost effective.

12. Sexual Dysfunctions, Counseling, and Therapies

A. General Views

Dutch clinical sexological practice follows the international framework of diagnosis and the DSM-III-R with some hesitance about the normative aspects of such procedures. Feminism and emancipatory trends have had an enormous impact on Dutch sexology. Health Care for Women projects have been substantially financed by the government with sexuality a major area of concern. In recent years, most of these projects have been integrated, sometimes unwillingly, into the general mental health-care institutions. Health Care for Women is situated methodologically between self-help and professionalism. Group approaches are highly valued and the group-therapy approach used more often than for men.

Another concern inherited from Health Care for Women is the power issue in heterosexuality. Since the early 1970s, there has been a passionate plea for better help for sexual-violence victims, stimulated by independent nonprofessional self-help organizations. Dutch sexologists have responded by initiating discussion on professional standards and ethical codes on therapist-client sexual contact. Current interests include: sexual abuse of the mentally and physically handicapped, and introduction of sexological diagnostic and treatment approaches as an adjunct to personality-oriented diagnosis.

Desire problems: There is a modest amount of literature on desire discrepancies. The interactional aspect, the incapacity for intimacy, has gained most attention, along with unrealistic expectations and the balance of power. There is no literature available comparing male higher-libido with female higher-libido.

Arousal problems: The medical-sexological approach used with many cases of male erectile dysfunction has resulted in numerous articles but no relevant quantitative data. While clinical criteria are set by the Dutch Society for Impotence Research, concern is growing about over-use of methods prompted by cost and patient acceptance. Psychophysiological methods and pharmacoDuplex scanning are the most widely used methods; neuro-urophysiological, hormonal, and invasive methods are restricted to specific indications. It is widely recognized today that psychological inhibition can prevent the reaction on intracavernous vasoactive drugs, and that an erotic atmosphere enhances the reaction. Regarding treatment, a preliminary, cautious conclusion might be: Dutch men seem to be rather reluctant to accept prosthesis as a solution for erectile failure; intracavernous injections are acceptable for a larger group with a high discontinuation rate; vacuum devices are used, but here, too, discontinuation is high.

There is no specific literature on arousal dysfunction in women, except for a study on diabetes.

Orgasm problems: In 1977, the Utrecht psychology group enriched sexological theory by contrasting the "interaction phase" with the "solo phase" and emphasizing surrendering to one's own feelings as essential during orgastic release. Lonnie Barbach's group treatment is widely used for primary female anorgasmia, but there are no outcome studies. For female secondary and/or situational orgasm difficulties, sex therapists tend to prefer couple therapy. After analyzing 1,112 respondent questionnaires, De Bruijn (1982) tried to describe backgrounds of female anorgasmia. Among her conclusions: to some women, orgasm is simply not important in lovemaking; those regularly having orgasms during partner interaction tend to use techniques similar to their self-pleasuring techniques; in interaction, some women simply do not get stimulation long enough to attain orgasm; and orgasm by following the male's movements in intercourse is the only stimulation technique in which orgasm is linked to feelings of love and intimacy. Her findings, published in a best-seller, have been widely acknowledged by both professionals and the general public. Ironically, the 1939 survey of NVSH members reported female respondents attributing differences in satisfaction found in men and women to the short duration of intercourse. *Plus ça change, plus c'est la même chose.*

Inhibited and premature male orgasm have received less attention. Premature ejaculation is common and treated by standard modalities, but no treatment results are published.

Coitus problems and genital phobias: Vaginismus, dyspareunia, unconsummated marriage, and phobic avoidance of vaginal penetration are subjects of intense interest, characterized by an increasing tolerance of the symptom's hidden meaning. As early as 1917, Treub concluded that fear is the main cause and refrained from incision of the perivaginal muscles; in the 1960s, Musaph stressed the usefulness of psychoanalytical interpretations. During the 1979 World Congress of Sexology in Mexico City, Dutch women sexologists vented their annoyance with sexology's neglect of sex-role bias. Cohen-Kettenis criticized medical and behavioral sexologists for having only one goal in the treatment for vaginismus: consummation. Bezemer was the first to report on group treatment for women suffering for vaginismus, together with other primary dysfunctions in one group. Moch (1987) broke the taboo on reporting relapse after successful treatment for vaginismus. Drenth (1988) pointed out that for some couples, vaginismus is a fertility problem and can be treated as such by artificial insemination. In 1989, Drenth also identified genital fears, phobias, and obsessions as the male counterpart of vaginismus, pointing out that phobic avoidance of genital play can result in pseudo-phymosis. In 1989, the Dutch Society for Sexology organized a symposium on Vaginismus and Dyspareunia: The Dutch View.

B. Availability of Diagnosis and Treatment

Historically, treatment for sexual problems in the Netherlands began in the Neo-Malthusian League. In the League's counseling centers, psychoanalytic treatment of sexual problems was strongly influenced by Van Emde Boas and Musaph, pioneers in the Sexual Reform movement, until the 1970s. In 1969, when the Rutgers Foundation separated from the Dutch Society for Sexual Reform (the League's postwar successor), treatment of sexual problems was very much still part of its activities. As demand increased, the foundation reorganized its staff in multidisciplinary teams.

Dutch gynecologists also played a major role, led by the internationally renowned Theodor van der Velde. His book, *The Perfect Marriage* (1925), was the first such work to find a large general public. Fertility studies led to the formation of the Society for Psychosomatic Obstetrics and Gynecology in 1979. All academic hospitals now have a sexological outpatient department. Unfortunately, these clinics are much too small, except for Amsterdam and Leiden. Since psychiatry departments pay little attention to sexual problems, a Society for Impotence Research (NVIO) was founded in 1986.

The work of Masters and Johnson opened the sexological territory for social scientists. Between 1975 and 1986, Utrecht trained psychology students in the practical applications of group and couple sex therapy. Since then, some psychologists and social workers in private practice provide treatment for couples with sexual problems. The sexological knowledge of helping professionals has certainly expanded in recent years. However, specialized sexological help is sometimes hard to find for many patients. The total number of sexologists is small and concentrated in certain areas. Health insurance will pay for sexological help if a physician refers. Clients almost always have to pay their own sliding-scale bills for treatment by psychologists and social workers in private practice and by Rutgers Foundation sexologists.

C. Therapist Training and Certification

Sexology is not a regulated profession in Holland, so full-time sexologists are rare and reliable sexologists and therapists will always have other basic training in medicine, psychology, psychiatry, or social work, perhaps with some postdoctoral education in sexology. Sexological education in Holland lacks cohesion and formal recognition. A very small number of professionals has been educated in the Flemish University of Leuven Sexology Department, where one can earn a doctorate in sexology.

Recently, the Dutch Society for Sexology (NVVS) started to regulate sexological training. Since 1992, an introductory course in sexology is provided by the NVVS and Erasmus University Rotterdam. Specialized curricula for medical-sexological workers, educators, prevention workers, and researchers will follow. An applications course for psychopathic rapists will be the next step in regulating sexological training. Recently, the Amsterdam Psychotherapy Training Institute included sexology in behavioral psychotherapy training. A register of trained members and establishment of set standards for the education of professional sexologists are short-term goals for NVVS.

13. Research and Advanced Education

A. Sexological Research

The Dutch Institute for Socio-Sexual Research (NISSO) has been the center of surveys on sexual behavior, sometimes in collaboration with other organizations. Considerable research has been done on contraception, abortion, sex and disabilities/illness, homosexuality in the armed forces, and prostitution. Other areas being explored are: the (in)adequacy of sexual help by different groups of helping professionals; an interview study on respondents of earlier surveys who reported exceptionally positive sex lives; child sexual development; forensic sexology; and construction of sexologically relevant psychometric scales.

The multidisciplinary nature of Dutch sexology is illustrated by the diverse backgrounds of the professors holding the six chairs dedicated to sexology in Dutch universities: endocrinology (Gooren, Amsterdam), psychiatry (Hengeveld, Utrecht), medicine (Van Dijk, Amsterdam), psychology (Frenken, Leiden), psychology (Cohen-Kettenis, Utrecht) and physiology/biology (Slob, Rotterdam).

The Psychology Department at Utrecht University has examined the therapeutic effect of different behavioristic treatment methods for sexual dysfunctions in individuals with different sexual orientations. The Utrecht University Gay and Lesbian Studies group has ongoing studies in: historical research on lesbian lives; various subjects on discrimination and homosexuality-related violence; homosexuality and education; and homosexuality in health care. The Amsterdam Psychology Department initiated Dutch psychophysiological research including the effects of sexual imagery on sexual arousal, women's reactions to male- and female-made pornography, the effect of mood induction on subsequent visual stimulation, and the effect of subliminal visual stimuli. In Rotterdam, psychophysiological research includes study of the effects and interaction of visual and vibrotactile penile stimulation; the effect of papaverin-induced tumescence on perceptual threshold of penile stimulation in sexually functional and dysfunctional men, and the effect of menstrual phase on sexual arousability in women. In Groningen, research has included vaginal sensitivity in nonerotic conditions. Almost all academic urology departments are in some way active in research on erectile failure.

Animal sexology, centered in the Utrecht Department of Comparative Physiology, is an important aspect of Dutch sexology. Research at Utrecht and Rotterdam has focused on mating strategies in natural and semi-natural conditions: wolves, plains zebras, chimpanzees, orangutans and long-tailed macaques, savanna baboons, and stump-tailed macaques. The Rotterdam and Amsterdam groups have studied female initiative and hormonal influences on proceptivity and receptivity in rats, reward and aversive components in female sexual experience (including homosexual versus heterosexual preference conditions), hormone-dependency of self-stimulation behavior in the medial preoptic area; brain and behavior gender differentiation, and the determination of the different influences of various steroids. The sexually dimorphic nucleus of the preoptic area is also being researched.

B. Postgraduate and Advanced Programs

Treatment of human sexuality in medical, psychological, and social work curricula is subject to considerable variation, with the personal interest of faculty determining the impetus sexuality will have in the programs. Precise requirements and interdisciplinary training are defined in psychiatry and gynecology. There are no university sexology programs in other areas such as education, prevention, or research. In 1992, the Dutch Society for Sexology (NVVS) started a post-graduate training program (see Section 12C).

Journals

Tijdschrift voor Seksuologie (*Journal of Sexology*). Faculty of Medicine, Erasmus University, P. O. Box 1738, 3000 DR Rotterdam, The Netherlands

SOA Bulletin (*Journal of STD*). P. O. Box 19061, 3501 DB Utrecht, The Netherlands

Sekstant (*Journal of the Dutch Society for Sexual Reform* [NVSH]). P. O. Box 64, 2501 CB Den Haag, The Netherlands

Sexuality in Society. International newsletter of the NISSO. NISSO, da Costakade 45, 3521 VS Utrecht, The Netherlands

Organizations

A. de Graaf Foundation. (Prostitution), Westermarkt 4, 1016 DK Amsterdam

Interfacultaire Werkgroep Homostudies (Department of Gay and Lesbian Studies), Utrecht University, Heidelberglaan 1, 3584 CS Utrecht, The Netherlands

Dutch Centre for Health Promotion & Health Education, P. O. Box 5104, 3502 JC Utrecht, The Netherlands. Phone: 31-70/35-56847; Fax: 31-70/35-59901

Jhr A. Schorer Foundation. (Consultation bureau for homosexuality), Nieuwendijk 17, 1017 LZ Amsterdam, The Netherlands

NISSO (Netherlands Institute for Social Sexological Research), da Costakade 45, 3521 VS Utrecht, The Netherlands

NVIO (Dutch Society for Impotence Research), Department of Psychology, University of Amsterdam, Weesperplein 8, 1018 XA Amsterdam, The Netherlands

NVVS (Dutch Society for Sexology), Zijdeweg 17, 2811 PC Reeuwijk, The Netherlands

Rutgers Foundation (Contraception information and sexuality education), Groothertoginnelaan 201, 2517 ES Den Haag, The Netherlands

Rutgers Stitching, Postbus 17430, Croot Hertoginnelaan 201, 2502 CKs Gravenhage, The Netherlands. Phone: 31-70/363-1750; Fax: 31-70/356-1049

Stimezo (National organization for induced abortion), Pieterstraat 11, 3512 JT Utrecht, The Netherlands

References and Suggested Readings

Note: The Special Issue of *Tijdschrift voor Seksuologie* issued for the Tenth World Congress for Sexology contains an exhaustive list of literature.

Beets, G., et al. 1991. *Population and Family in the Low Countries 1991*. Amsterdam/Lisse.

Brongersma, E. 1988, 1990. *Loving Boys, 1 & 2*. Elmhurst, New York, U.S.A.: Global Academic Publishers.

Cohen-Kettenis, P. T., & Th. G. M. Sandfort. 1991. "Sexual Behavior of Young Children: Observations of 665 Parents." Paper presented at the Tenth World Congress for Sexology, 1991, Amsterdam.

Deenen, A. A. V. M. 1991. *Intimacy and Sexuality in Gay Male Relationships*. Dissertation, Utrecht.

Draijer, P. J. 1990. *Seksuele Traumatisering in de Jeugd. Lange Termijn Gevolgen van Seksueel Misbruik van Meisjes Door Verwanten*. Amsterdam: SUA.

Gianotten, W. L. 1988. "Sexology in the Netherlands: The Past and the Present." *Nordisk Sexologi*, 6:202-09.

Glaser & Straus. 1980. Cited in C. Straver, *Jong Zijn en Contact Zoeken (Being Young and Seeking Contacts)*. Zeist: Nisso.

Heslinga, K., A. Verkuil, & A. M. C. M. Schellen. 1973. *Wij Zijn Niet van Steen (Not Made of Stone: Sexuality of the Handicapped People)*. Leiden: Noordhoff stafleu.

Ketting, E. 1990. *Contraception in Western Europe*. Carnforth: Parthenon.

Ketting, E., & K. Soesbeek, eds. 1992. *Homoseksualiteit en Krijgsmacht*. Delft: Eburon.

Kooy, G. A. 1975. *Seksualiteit, Huwelijk en Gezin in Nederland*. Deventer: Van Loghum Slaterus.

Kooy, G. A. 1976. *Jongeren en Seksualiteit*. Deventer: Van Loghum Slaterus.

Kooy, G. A. 1983. *Sex in Nederland*. Utrecht/Antwerpen: Spectrum.

Kuiper, A. J. 1991. *Transseksualiteit. Evaluatie van de Geslachtsaanpassende Behandeling.* Utrecht: Elinkwijk.

Lamur, H., et al. 1990. *Caraibische Vrouwen en Anticonceptie.* Delft: Eburon.

Mooij, A. 1991. "De Ziektes van de Revolutie." In G. Hekma, et al., eds. *Het Verlies van de Onschuld.* Groningen: Wolters-Noordhoff.

Nabrink, G. 1978. *Seksuele Hervorming in Nederland.* Nijmegen: SUN.

Noordhoff, J. D. et al. 1969. *Sex in Nederland.* Utrecht/Antwerpen: Spectrum.

Rademakers, J. 1992. *Abortus in Nederland 1989-1990.* Utrecht: Stimezo.

Sandfort, Th. G. M. 1987. "Pedophilia and the Gay Movement." *Journal of Homosexuality,* 13:89-111.

Sandfort, Th. G. M. 1991. "The Argument for Adult-Child Contact. A Critical Appraisal and New Data." In O'Donohue & Geer, eds. *The Sexual Abuse of Children: Theory, Research and Therapy.* Hillsdale, New Jersey, U.S.A.: Lawrence Erlbaum Associates.

Sandfort, Th. G. M., & G. van Zessen 1991. *Seks en AIDS in Nederland.* Den Haag: SDU.

Schraag, J. A. 1989. "Sexual Education in Schools: Concepts and Possibilities." *International Journal of Adolescent Medicine and Health,* 3&4:239-250.

Schreurs, K. 1990. *Vrouwen in Lesbische Relaties. Verbondenheid, Autonomie, en Seksualiteit.* Utrecht: Publikatiereeks Homostudies.

Simon & Gagnon. 1980. Cited in C. Straver, *Jong Zijn en Contact Zoeken (Being Young and Seeking Contacts).* Zeist: Nisso.

Slijper. F. M. E. 1992. "Evaluation of Psychosexual Development of Young Women with Congenital Adrenal Hyperplasia: A Pilot Study." *Journal of Sex Education and Therapy,* 18:200-07.

Straver et al. 1986. Stepwise Interaction Career: First elaborated in J. Rademakers and C. Straver, *Van Fascinatie naar Relatie (From Fascination to Relation).* Zeist: Nisso.

van Delft, M., & E. Ketting 1992. *Anticonceptiege-Bruik in Nederland.* Houten: Bohn Stafleu van Loghum.

van der Vliet, R. 1990. De Opkomst van het Seksuele Moratorium (The Rise of the Sexual Moratorium). In G. Hekma & B. van Stolk, eds., *Het Verlies van de Onschuld (The Loss of Innocence).* Groningen: Wolters-Noordhoff.

Verschoor, A. M. 1990. *Een Dubbel Bestaan: Travestieten en Hun Omgeving.* Amsterdam/Lisse: Swets en Zeitlinger.

Vogels, T., & R. van der Vliet. 1990. *Jeugd en Seks.* Den Haag: SDU.

Poland
(*Rzeczpospolita Polska*)

Anna Sierzpowska-Ketner, M.D., Ph.D.

Contents

Demographics and a Historical Perspective

A. Demographics

Poland borders on the Baltic Sea, Lithuania, Belorussia, Russia, Ukraine, the Czech and Slovak Republics, and Germany. The national frontiers contain an area of 120,725 square miles with a 1995 population of 38.7 million. The country is a mix of industrial and agricultural activities with about 62 percent of the population living in cities.

The 1995 age distribution was 24 percent under age 15; 15 to 64, 65 percent; and 65 plus, 11 percent. Life expectancy at birth in 1995 was 69 for males and 77 for females. The 1995 birthrate was 13 per 1,000 and the death rate 9 per 1,000, for a 0.4 percent annual natural increase. Infant mortality is 12 per 1,000 live births. Poland has one hospital bed for 177 persons and one physician per 459 persons. The literacy rate in 1995 was

99 percent, with 97 percent attendance during eight years of compulsory education. The per capita domestic product in 1995 was $4,680.

B. A Brief Historical Perspective

Local Slavic tribes converted to Christianity in the tenth century and Poland became a great power from the fourteenth to the seventeenth centuries. The country was partitioned among Prussia, Russia, and Austria in 1772, 1783, and 1795. After World War I, in which it was overrun by the Austro-German armies, it declared its independence in 1918. Large territories in the east were annexed after a 1921 war with Russia. In 1939, at the start of World War II, the country was invaded and divided by Germany and Russia. Some 6 million Polish citizens were killed by the Nazis, half of them Jews—practically all the Jewish population of the country. After Germany's defeat, Poland declared its independence and was recognized by the United States, while the Soviet Union pressed its claims. Following a 1947 election dominated by the Communists, Poland ceded 70,000 square miles to the Soviet Union and received in turn 40,000 square miles of German territory east of the Oder-Neisse, Silesia, Pomerania, West Prussia, and part of East Prussia.

After twelve years of rule by Stalinist Communists, workers in Poznan rioted to protest rising prices, nationalization of industries, collectivization of the farms, secularization of the schools, and imprisonment of Church leaders. A new, more independent Polish Communist government, which came to power in 1956, reversed some of these conditions. In 1970, new riots broke out in several cities, protesting new incentive wage rules and price rises. In 1980, after two months of labor turmoil crippled the country, the government met the demands of striking workers at the Lenin Shipyard in Gdansk. Following a nationwide referendum that favored establishing a non-Communist government, the government declared martial law and arrested the leaders of the opposition. An accord was reached in 1989, and a non-Communist government elected in 1990. A radical economic program, designed to introduce a free-market system, led to protests from the unions, farmers, and miners over inflation and unemployment. In 1993, former Communists and other leftists returned to power.

1. Basic Sexological Premises

A. The Character of Gender Roles

The pervasive presence of gender-role stereotypes, consensual expectations about the fashion in which males and females behave, is likely to have a strong and continuing impact on male/female behaviors and on feelings about that behavior in Polish society. Gender roles in Poland were evolving away from the traditional stereotypes after World War II because of the very common situation when women had to look for work outside their homes.

Women now comprise 45 percent of total number of employees and 52.6 percent of the unemployed. However, their part in the workforce creates a semblance of equality between the rights of men and women. The average pay for women is 30 percent lower than that of men. In Poland, one can observe a visible feminization of certain professions, mainly education and social welfare, because they are so poorly paid. Although the paychecks for men in these professions are the same as women's, men usually try to find better-paying jobs because of their traditional role as providers. During the Communist regime, women had a number of privileges that protected their professional situations. For example, they could retire five years earlier than men and could obtain a leave of absence to take care of a sick child. In the present transition to a market economy, these apparent privileges significantly reduce women's chances in the work market.

Women's efforts to find employment were clearly connected with economic pressures and did not reflect the real situation of women in Poland. The part played by women in the political and social life of the country is rather marginal. Women, for instance, comprise only 10 percent of the members of parliament. Feminist organizations are small and not particularly popular, playing an unimportant role in society.

B. Sociolegal Status of Males and Females

From the legal viewpoint, as children, adolescents, and adults, Polish men and women enjoy the same rights. Men and women have the same right to vote and equal rights for education and employment. Children and adolescents attend coed schools.

Current political changes in Poland have created a danger in favor of conservative understanding of social roles, especially for women. The recently propagated family model has a patriarchal character with the woman professionally inactive and playing only the role of mother. Very restrictive antiabortion legislation has produced a particularly heated discussion of women's rights that is assuming the form of a political campaign. [Election results in late 1995 shifted political power away from the Church-supported government and back to former Communist politicians, in part as a rejection of the Church's antiabortion and anticontraceptive stance. (Editor)]

C. General Concepts of Sexuality and Love

In Poland, one can find two models of sexuality and love: both restrictive Catholic and permissive European models. While the sexual attitudes of Poles vary depending on gender, age, region of residence, and religious attitude, these two models have existed separately for several decades and have collided occasionally. At present, with the increasing influence of religion and the Church on political and social life, they are the subject of acute confrontations.

The rural population and city dwellers of rural origin characteristically have strong links with Catholic religious ceremonies and the deep influence of the Catholic Church. This group is also characterized by a low level of education. This group is very numerous, because of the extermination of highly educated Poles during World War II and intensive migration from rural areas to the towns after the war. This group is the main standard bearer for the traditional model of sexuality in which sex and love can be fulfilled only in marriage. In this model, all premarital and extramarital sexual contacts are condemned, only the rhythm or so-called natural methods of family planning are accepted, and the use of other contraceptive methods, such as the hormonal pill and condom, are prohibited.

Among Poles with a higher level of education, one finds sex education based on publications, an acceptance of varied forms of petting and premarital sexual contacts, extramarital sex, liberal attitudes towards different sexual orientations and behaviors, the use of varied forms of contraception, and greater criticism of traditional sexual standards.

In comparing attitudes towards sexuality and love among Poles of different educational levels from different regions of the country, one seems to be dealing with two different societies, the first being attached to traditional attitudes and the second expressing permissive values and attitudes that are more and more popular in the West.

2. Religious and Ethnic Factors Affecting Sexuality

A. Religious and Political Factors

Since the end of World War II, the people of Poland have generally shared a single ethic, and one religion, Roman Catholicism. According to 1990 research data, 94 percent of Poles are Roman Catholics and 79 percent of adult Poles considered themselves religious or deeply religious.

The Catholic faith has been predominant among Poles since the recorded beginnings of the state in the eleventh century. The period of the Reformation did not change this situation, despite the proximity of German Lutheranism. The multiethnic Jagiellonian Poland of the fifteenth and sixteenth centuries, and the Commonwealth of the Two Nations, as the union of Poland and Lithuania was called until the seventeenth century, were comprised of at least one third ethnic minorities who, to a great degree, represented religions other than Roman Catholic. In the first half of the twentieth century and during World War II when eastern territories were lost and western lands added, one third of the country's population comprised Jews, Ukrainians, Germans, Byelorussians, and others. These ethnic minorities professed mainly the Jewish, Greek Catholic, Protestant, and Eastern Orthodox religions.

Catholicism has become one of the main elements of the national self-determination and self-image of Poles, possibly as a result of the historical destiny of Poland in the last few centuries, and especially since the nineteenth-century partitions. Religious ceremonies thus became the occasion for expressing national and political views, which were often of greater social and psychological importance than the pure religious feelings. Also in the 1980s, the Solidarity period, subversion of the totalitarian Communist regime and appointment of a Pole as Supreme Pontiff of the Church in Rome strengthened the political authority of the Church in Poland.

It should be stressed here that Poland is currently undergoing significant changes associated with the democratic processes common in countries of the late Communist regime. At this turning point in our history, the situation of sexology in Poland is determined by two opposing tendencies: the increasing influence of religion and the Church on Polish political and social life, and European tendencies, which are coupled with the reality-based social attitudes to sex and sexual behavior. These opposing influences mark the main line of controversy on moral and legal policy in Poland today. Although there is a visible divergence between sexual behaviors and the formal religious views of society, the restrictive attitude of the Catholic Church is more and more evident, affecting most legal and medical problems as well as sex education.

B. Ethnic Factors

According to unofficial data, ethnic minorities comprise about 5 percent of the population. Most of them are Byelorussians and Ukrainians. As a result of the invader's policy during World War II, and the change of borders after the war causing the loss of one fourth of the country's eastern territory, most ethnic minorities have disappeared. The remaining minorities, at present, do not demonstrate any particularly characteristic sexual attitudes or behaviors.

3. Sexual Knowledge and Education

It needs to be emphasized that sexual education has always been a kind of taboo in Poland. This was clearly reflected in the language used by the state in the past, referring to sexual education as "preparation for the life in a socialistic family." After 1989, sexual education was halted in the schools without any national debate about the relationship between the state and the Church, and the only textbook specially prepared by sexologists for school use was definitely forbidden. This was subsequently followed by introduction of religious instruction in all Polish schools.

Research in 1992 with a nationally representative sample revealed that friends were reported as the principle source of sex information with half of the men and one third of the women surveyed. The second source, reported most frequently by young people in large cities, was publications. Parents hardly ever wanted to provide input into sexual education, preferring to have their children obtain this information in school or from publications. Still, less than 10 percent of the respondents approved of school as a source of sex information.

4. Autoerotic Behaviors and Patterns

A. Children and Adolescents

Retrospective research on the autoerotic behaviors of Polish children and adolescents has been carried out on a few select groups. M. Beisert (1990) found that about 15 percent of the girls and 29 percent of the boys remembered touching and manipulating their genitals in a repeated manner during childhood to evoke some pleasant feelings. In most children, an intensification of autoerotic behaviors is observed at ages 5 to 6, during nursery school education. The main purpose of autoerotic behaviors is to awake some positive emotions in oneself. Up to 80 percent of all children who engage in self-pleasuring consider the pleasure obtained as an autonomous value, while about 12 percent treat that pleasure as a side effect of fulfilling the need connected with what is termed a stimulation deficit, the deprivation of the need of receiving new and attractive stimuli from the surroundings.

Research demonstrates that there are two types of autoerotic behaviors: one open, observed in children who are unaware of the common negative valuation of that behavior, and the other hidden and characteristic of children who are aware of the forbidden character of that behavior. An important source of information about the need to hide autoeroticism from parents is the child's peers. According to investigations, 80 percent of parents have never learned about the autoeroticism of children.

Polish literature dealing with sexual education presents two opposite views: an opinion that self-pleasuring is a normal stage of psychosexual development in human beings and the contrary view that self-pleasuring is a sin reflecting in a negative way on human development. These opinions lead to two contrary educational recommendations. Adolescents appear to be aware of these contradictory views and their implications. Survey data indicate that 90 percent of adolescent boys and 45 to 75 percent of girls engage in self-pleasuring. At the same time, 20 percent of girls and 32 percent of boys reported fears accompanying their self-pleasuring. Half of those investigated were afraid of parents, siblings, or other people learning about their self-pleasuring practices. The correlation of self-pleasuring and religiousness was not statistically significant in adolescents.

B. Adults

In a 1991 nationally representative survey, 28 percent of the women and 64 percent of the men reported engaging in autoerotic behaviors. In other research with university students, 99.1 percent of the men and 42 percent of the women reported autoerotic behavior.

5. Interpersonal Heterosexual Behaviors

A. Children

M. Beisert's 1990 investigation reveals an undulatory character in the child's interest in sex. The first inflow is observed before the end of 5 years of age with the next during the prepubertal period, about the age of 10 and 11.

Contacts with other children in nursery school are conducive to some exploratory activities. Up to 56 percent of investigated adults place their first discoveries connected with gender at that period. The most important source of knowledge are other children, particularly peers. The first discoveries are connected with playing together, bathing, and other hygienic activities. However, the awareness of a strict injunction not to stare at the naked bodies of others, and particularly their genitals, is passed down at a comparatively early age and is widely popularized. The division between erotic play and cognitive activities is a difficult one, especially since sexual curiosity is at the bottom of much of children's play. However, when children want to study their own bodies, they often do it openly and clearly state their interest. In approximately 2.8 percent of childhood sexual exploration, coercion is a factor.

The cognitive methods are a bit different in families with many children of both genders. When the children in a family are close in age, or when the age interval is larger but older children participate in taking care of the younger, sex differences are not particularly exciting nor do they offer any special discoveries. The situation is similar when a child has no siblings but is brought up in a family with liberal attitudes towards sex.

Many different children's games include an erotic element or produce specific pleasure connected with stimulation of the genitals. Nearly 70 percent of students surveyed remembered not only the fact of such games, but also all the details accompanying them. Gender was not a factor in such games. Considering all the functions fulfilled by erotic games, such as pleasure, learning, and stimulation, they were grouped separately from other forms of childhood activities. The essence of most games is to imitate a fragment of adult life. The most popular games imitate adult roles that create an opportunity of mutual touching, undressing, and body manipulation, playing doctor, hospital, nurse, mother and father, king and queen, convalescent home, masseur, or the theater, ballet and strip-tease. Among other inspirations for childhood games, direct observation of adult life takes place first, then movies, fairy tales, and stories told by others. Imitations of such adult activities that provide excuses for body contact are the most important children's games.

A particular, qualitatively different variety of games is among those designed for only two children. In such games, watching and touching meet the needs of demonstrating a mutual bond. Children embrace each other, kiss, and touch. Such pairs are accepted by their peers, and their range of behavior does not differ from the behavioral patterns of groups. Solitary play also provides an outlet for sexual curiosity and rehearsal, as when a child enacts erotic scenes using dolls, draws pictures of naked girls and boys, or plays scenes that evoke pleasurable excitement.

The second period of interest occurs during the prepubertal age. Up to 35 percent of children report gaining knowledge about gender differences at the age of 10 or 11 years. The interest is focused on details and confirmation of earlier knowledge and intuition. Watching and touching is limited mainly to the genitals, and the aim is to gain pleasure along with a clear understanding of gender differences. These games occur in pairs, and sometimes in groups of peers of the same and other gender. Boys, for instance, may compare penis length or compete in urination contests. Girls concentrate on bust observations or dressing as adult women. Often pair games are clearly directed at pleasure, and consist of genital exploration and touching without the pretext of playing doctor or hospital.

According to survey data, most Polish children are well aware of the forbidden nature of these erotic games. The punishing attitude of parents towards erotic games reaffirms the fear of childhood eroticism and the unfavorable attitude towards self-pleasuring. Parental dissuasion and limiting the child's time with peers are more mild forms of unfavorable reaction. However, two thirds of parents who catch their children in such games threaten them, punishing them verbally and/or physically for engaging in them. About 1 percent of parents do not adopt a punishing attitude, but quietly maintain their differing opinion of such games. Only 10 percent of parents treat these games as a normal stage in childhood development.

B. Adolescents

Puberty

The period of puberty involves three phases dominated by changes connected with biological, mental, and finally social maturity. In girls, signs of physical maturation generally appear at the age of 10 or 11. About a year earlier, mothers usually take some steps to prepare their daughters for their physical maturation and menarche. Research shows that nearly all unprepared girls react in a negative way to their maturation. Girls in this group usually start menstruating at an early age, around 10 years, and are easily distinguished from their peers by their physical maturity. Not knowing the purpose and course of the pubescence process, they exaggerate the significance of the physical changes, interpreting them as pathological symptoms.

The reactions of boys to the signs of maturation follow a different pattern. Only a small percentage of boys react negatively to the changes. Their negative reaction is usually conditioned by a lack of proper preparation. The male response to puberty shows greater uniformity, with a greater acceptance of manhood often compensating for some neglect in their sex education.

Research shows that the first menstruation in girls and the first nocturnal emission or conscious ejaculation in boys cause a strong emotional reaction. In these specific experiences, the reaction is unfortunately negative, irrespective of gender. Most often, the girls inform their mothers about their first menstruation. However, about 20 percent try to hide the fact. On the other hand, few boys inform their parents, preferring to boast about it among their peers.

The appearance of a new sexual behavior, namely petting, also marks the pubertal period. Up to 50 percent of Polish girls admit that an emotional bond with a boyfriend prompted them to start petting. Only an emotional involvement would make them agree to physical contact, although that agreement does not indicate a real need for relieving their sexual tension or taking the initiative to do so. Only a small percentage of girls admit their strong sexual tension and the need to relieve it. Among the reasons reported by girls, curiosity played only a small part in their decision. Much more important was the pressure exerted by the partner, although they did not consider the decision to start petting as being imposed on them. In their opinion, it was the natural consequence of their feelings towards their partners and not the consequence of sexual pressure. Boys more often explained the decision to start petting by their sexual tension. The need to relieve this tension resulted in less sensitivity in choosing their partner. Even a girl they scarcely knew would be acceptable. Polish boys try to start petting at the age of 16 and girls a year later.

Petting sets the stage for first sexual intercourse. According to data from a nationwide representative sample, 12.5 percent of the men and 6.6 percent of the women have sexual intercourse before age 16. By age 19, 54 percent of the men and 43 percent of the women have had coitus. Every fifth man and every third woman has first sexual intercourse after age 20. For 73 percent of the women, emotional involvement is the prime reason for initiation. Men most frequently cite emotion and love (41 percent), curiosity (35 percent), and the need to become an adult (16 percent). Only 40 percent of the women and 46 percent of the men rate their first sexual intercourse as a positive experience.

C. Adults

The first statistical investigations of sexual behavior were carried out in Poland at the end of the last century when Z. Kowalski examined the attitudes of Warsaw University students. More recent sexological studies were carried out in the 1960s and 1980s with selected groups of students, soldiers, and workers. In 1963, H. Malewska studied the sex life and its determinants in Polish women. The first research of sexual behavior using a nationally representative sample of 1,188 adults was carried out in 1991.

Premarital Relationships

According to 1991 data, 72 percent of unmarried adults admit to premarital relations. Among married people, premarital relations were acknowledged by 80 percent of the men but only 50 percent of the women. This reflects the attitude of women towards virginity. Contrary to men, women paradoxically more often reveal their belief in the need to preserve virginity until marriage.

Single Adults

Data on sexual behavior of single adults in Poland are limited, mainly because of the strong pressure on sex for reproduction within marriage. In 1988, 85 percent of Polish women aged 37 to 49 were married, 6 percent were singles who had never married, about 6 percent were divorced, and 3 percent were widows.

Marriage and Family

In the 1970 research of Trawinska on values in marriage, adolescent and adult respondents gave priority to fulfillment of emotional needs, love, sex, the chance for self-realization, and achievement of economic success. People who had been married for several years placed the relative lack of conflicts and stability of the union on a par with emotional ties, respect, love, and sex.

The courtship period is short, and up to 60 percent of marriages are contracted between ages 20 and 24. Despite early marriage, the time of reaching social and economic independence with a separate apartment is delayed. Since the prewar period of the 1930s, the stage of marital childlessness has become shorter. One fourth of all women are pregnant when they marry. As in most European countries, the model of a small family is becoming a standard. A family with two children is usual, less often three children. In a family of two children, procreation is over in three years; with three children it usually ends in five or six years.

Monogamy

In Poland, marriage is monogamic in character. In the 1991 survey, nearly half of the women and one fourth of the men had had only one sex partner. Monogamic behavior is more common among people from small towns with a primary or secondary school education and a strong religious affiliation. Eighty-five percent of wives and 56 percent of husbands reported no extramarital sexual experiences. Sporadic extramarital sex was acknow-ledged by 10 percent of men and women. Less than 1 percent of respon-dents had more than ten sexual partners during their marriage. Extramari-tal sexual relations are more frequent in respondents over age 40, living in large cities, with a higher education, and better economic status.

Data on attitudes to sex show that for over 85 percent of respondents, sex is an expression of love and bonding. Sex without any emotional ties is accepted by 14 percent of women and 35 percent of men. The frequency of marital intercourse for most respondents ranged from a few times a week to a few times a month.

Divorce

In 1991, Polish courts granted 34,000 divorces. A peak of 53,000 was reached in 1984. The most frequent reported causes for divorce are infidelity (30 percent), excessive drinking, and incompatibility of character. Usually it takes four to six months to obtain a divorce. Most often couples seek a divorce after five to ten years of marriage. Usually the divorcing couple has no children or only one child. In three out of four cases, the mother retains custody. About 1 percent of children in divorces are placed in children's homes or with foster families.

Incidence of Oral and Anal Sex

According to 1991 data, oral-genital sex, usually cunnilingus, is practiced by 30 percent of Polish men and women. Anal sex is acknowledged by 2.4 percent of respondents. There are no legal restrictions on fellatio, cunni-lingus, or anal sex in Polish law.

6. Homoerotic, Homosexual, and Ambisexual Behaviors

The Polish legal code of 1932, as well as the current code of 1969, are among the most progressive in respect to sexuality. Homosexuality was always legal in Poland. The current criminal legislation does not mention homosexuality or homosexual relations at all. As with heterosexual con-tacts, only the homosexual intercourse of an adult with a partner under 15 years of age, or forcing a person to have intercourse against his or her will are against the law and liable to penalty.

There is a divergence between liberal legislation and the degree to which homosexual persons openly take part in the social life. The first homosexual movement and organizations started in 1985. At that time, representatives from Warsaw and Wroclaw joined the International Lesbian and Gay Asso-ciation. Programs and discussions with homosexuals appeared on television and the radio. The press published articles about the problems encoun-tered by homosexual persons. The following years marked the appearance of official organizations and clubs for homosexuals in big cities in Poland. Also a homosexual section was organized to fight the spread of AIDS. Until this time, the public had little knowledge of homosexual issues.

In surveys, 4.4 percent of the women and 6 percent of the men acknowledged being homosexually active. So far, there has been no research in Poland investigating the character of homosexual relations, behaviors, and sexual patterns. A few publications on this subject have been based on West European and American research. Thus, the main source of information about homosexual issues and lifestyles is the gay press, which provides several local and national publications.

The Catholic Church in Poland maintains a restrictive attitude towards homosexuality. It is described as a "moral disorder," and homosexual activities are condemned as contradictory to the procreative purpose of sex. In the Church's opinion, sexual relations are morally right only in marriage. The Church also maintains that there are many ways to restrain a person from fulfilling his or her unnatural sexual desire.

7. Gender Conflicted Persons

An estimated 1,000 Poles are transgenderists or transsexuals. The research of J. Godlewski indicates there are one male-to-female transsexual for every seven female-to-male transsexuals. Five hundred persons have had hormone treatment and four hundred surgery. The development of therapy for transsexuals started in the 1980s. In Poland, there are about a hundred unions or cohabiting couples in which one partner is a transsexual and five where both partners are transsexuals. Two marriages were contracted legally.

Polish legislation, in principle, allows the change of gender, but no law regulates the surgical treatment of a transsexual. According to the Polish Criminal Code, it is comparatively easy to have one's sex/gender and name corrected in a birth certificate. A correction in the birth certificate is a necessary condition for further surgical treatment.

There are no legal restrictions on transvestites. However, transvestism is a marginal phenomenon in Poland.

8. Significant Unconventional Sexual Behaviors

A. Coercive Sex

Sexual Abuse, Incest, and Pedophilia

Child sexual abuse has only recently forced its way into the social consciousness and scientific research. Investigations in 1991 revealed that 5 percent of the girls and 2.5 percent of the boys under the age of 15 years had had sexual contacts with family members, and 7.5 percent of underage girls and 17 percent of boys with virtual strangers.

In Poland, sexual contacts (coitus and coital equivalents) between children and their siblings (including adopted sibs), parents, and grandparents are subject to legal punishment. The penalty for incest ranges from six months to five years imprisonment.

Polish criminal law forbids sexual contacts with minors under 15 years old. The terms "sexual contacts" includes coitus and coital equivalents, fellatio, cunnilingus, anal sex, and digital-vaginal/anal penetration. The penalty for such contact can be up to ten years imprisonment. However, sentences of six to twenty-four months are not uncommon.

In cases of sexual abuse of a minor, it is impossible to ascertain the incidence of pedophilia because this sexological category is not included in the diagnosis. In these cases, some perpetrators exhibited a pedophilic character. In other instances, the victim would not be considered a child, being a postpubertal adolescent.

Paraphilias

There are no statistics on cases or the incidence of paraphilias in Poland.

Sexual Harassment

As of 1995, Polish legislation did not distinguish this category of behavior. [By late 1996, however, the situation had changed somewhat as central European countries and corporations began to be influenced by publicity in the news media and by the policies of western European and American companies conducting business in eastern Europe. In 1996, Poland's main government television channel ran a prime-time docudrama about sexual harassment, followed by a discussion with a studio audience and telephone calls from viewers. Despite the message to women workers that if they took their case to court, they could win, Poland has weak labor and civil-rights laws that have been largely untested in court because so few sexual harassment cases have been filed. Only 5 percent of those responding to a 1996 Polish newspaper poll said they had encountered cases of sexual harassment at work. Adding to the reluctance of Polish women to report cases of sexual harassment is a heritage of 40 years of Communist rule in which they accepted and endured sexual harassment as the norm. Today's harsh economic circumstances also encourage women not to complain. "We have a long way to go in raising the consciousness of women and men and making them realize what is not appropriate," Ursuzula Nowakowska, director of Warsaw's Women's Rights Center, a pro-bono group of lawyers, has reported. In the summer of 1996, Ms. Nowakowska appealed to the visiting lawyer-wife of U.S. President Clinton, Hilary Rodham Clinton, to help by urging large Western corporations to drop what she called their "double standard." She was referring to the tokenism of many Western and American corporations which issue policies against sexual harassment for all their offices worldwide, but then seldom let the employees in western European branches hear of these policies and fail to enforce their policies when charges are brought (Perlez 1996). (Editor)]

Rape

In Polish law, rape refers to coitus or coital equivalents (fellatio, cunnilingus, anal sex, and digital-vaginal/anal penetration) using force, violence, threat, or taking advantage of someone's vulnerable situation. The penalty for rape is between one and ten years imprisonment. A person under the age of 15 years cannot give legal consent to sexual intercourse. The concept of statutory rape does not exist. Within the legal category of rape, two types of rape are singled out: rape involving qualified cruelty involving brutal injuries to the body or mind; and collective or gang rape. Application of the law prohibiting marital rape requires real evidence of the use of force or coercion.

The minimum penalty for convicted rapists is three years imprisonment. However, depending on the type of rape, the prison sentence can range from six months to over five years. According to the data collected by Polish sexological expert witnesses, the majority of convicted rapists were drunk when they committed the crime.

B. Prostitution

In Poland, neither heterosexual nor homosexual prostitution is subject to criminal penalty. However, in 1952, Poland signed the United Nations Convention, undertaking an obligation to abolish prostitution. Inducing or soliciting another person to prostitution or profiting from another person's prostituting him or herself are subject to legal penalties of one to ten years.

There has been a steady decline in the demand for prostitutes since 1987 because of the growing concern about AIDS. Statistics on the total number of prostitutes in Poland are not available. The police estimate that there are about 12,000 prostitutes working in Poland. There are no houses of prostitution, but there are call-girl agencies, massage parlors, and other avenues of contact.

C. Pornography and Erotica

The development of democratic liberties in Poland since 1989 has been accompanied by a growing access to pornography and an increasing number of pornographic publications on the market, even though the law prohibiting production and distribution of pornography is still in force. Despite legislation, both hard- and soft-core pornography are easily accessible in Poland today.

In recent discussions, there has been some pressure to extend the meaning of pornography to include erotica and introduce more rigid restrictions. The controversy is complicated by the lack of a clear definition of pornography. Some forensic experts, referring to the criterion of social harm, want to limit the meaning of pornography only to materials dealing with sexual relations with animals and children, and cruel or violent material. The dispute over pornography is part of the more general discussion about sexual liberalism or rigorism.

9. Contraception, Abortion, and Population Planning

A. Contraception

The lack of sexual education in recent decades has affected negatively contraceptive behavior. Data from a 1988 POLL survey with a nationally representative sample, from the Polish Family Planning Association, and other sources, revealed that the number of women who used oral contraceptives and intrauterine devices (IUDs) was not higher than 10 percent. About a third of those polled reported using coitus interruptus as their contraceptive method. Another third used a method based on the menstrual cycle, sometimes only the calendar method. A lack of information about contraceptive methods and prejudice against contraception has created favorable circumstances for acceptance of the so-called natural methods promoted by the Church. In a 1988 study by W. Wróblewska of a nationally representative same of 1,266 teenage mothers, about 90 percent had no knowledge whatsoever about contraceptive methods.

B. Teenage Unmarried Pregnancies

In the 1988 study of 1,266 teenage mothers, published by the Family Planning Association in 1992, W. Wróblewska reported the youngest mother was 13 years old and nearly 50 percent were age 19. At the time of childbirth, one fourth of the teenage mothers were unmarried. Polish law makes it difficult for girls to contract marriage at the age of 16 or 17. Girls who wish to marry at that age must obtain a special license. Girls who are not yet 16 cannot marry.

Prior to getting pregnant, a large group of these mothers, 41.2 percent, were professionally active. One third, 37.6 percent, were attending school. The research did not confirm the hypothesis that these mothers had poor relations with their parents and were using pregnancy as an excuse to leave home. Only 9 percent of the teen mothers described the atmosphere in their homes and family relations as not too good or even conflictive. Over 80 percent of the teenage mothers came from two-parent families and 80 percent of the parents of teenage mothers had at least an elementary education. Generally, the girls were brought up in large families and had many siblings. The mothers of most respondents had started their own procreation earlier than other women of their generation.

Nearly 40 percent of the teenage mothers did not anticipate the possibility of becoming pregnant, or even realize such a possibility, when they became sexually active between the ages of 11 and 19. Only 15 percent of the respondents knew anything about contraceptive methods. Only 10 percent mentioned the contraceptive pill, IUD, condom, and calendar method. They were totally unfamiliar with other contraceptive methods. Only a third of these teenage mothers had even the minimum knowledge of how to protect themselves against pregnancy when they first engaged in sexual intercourse. Books, publications, and magazines were the basic sources of information for 61 percent of the mothers. Friends and acquaintances provided information for a third of the respondents. Slightly under a third, 28.2 percent, learned about contraception in school. Sexual partners were the source of information more often than parents. Only one in ten teenagers reported parents as a source of knowledge. More rarely cited was a doctor or nurse.

C. Abortion

Under Communist rule, from the end of World War II to 1989-1990, abortion was legal and widely used by Polish women despite the opposition of the Catholic Church. A restrictive law, enacted in March 1993, was overturned in October 1996. The situation, however, remains volatile and unpredictable.

Between 1956 and March 1993, abortion was legal for medical indications, when the pregnancy resulted from a crime, mainly rape, and for social reasons, such as the difficult circumstances of the woman. This law allowed for abortion in the first twelve weeks of pregnancy.

According to official statistics, the incidence of abortion remained stable for fifteen years prior to 1993, with about 133,000 abortions per year, or 19 abortions per 100 live births. This statistic does not include abortions done in private clinics. Some sources estimated that an additional one million abortions were performed each year in private clinics, with about 30,000 of these being for women under the age of 18 years.

In 1992, pressure from the Catholic Church supporting a repeal of the liberal abortion law was evident in a new Ethical Code adopted for physicians. This code allowed abortion only when the mother's health or life was in danger, or when the pregnancy resulted from rape or incest. In practice, this code eliminated all prenatal fetal examinations and abortion of malformed fetuses. In addition, contraceptive information was to be given by the physician only when required by the patient or in special cases. The new Ethical Code was a real paradox because it was much stricter than the then-existing liberal law.

Also in 1992, the parliament rejected by majority vote a liberal proposal prepared by the Women's Parliamentary Group and instead accepted the antiabortion proposal of the Catholic Nationalist Part (ZChN), which forbade abortion. The sole exception was that of a danger to the pregnant woman's life. The proposal for a national referendum was not accepted by the parliament. Meanwhile, research revealed that 56 percent of Poles were definitely in favor of abortion rights for women, 24 percent approved of some such rights, and only 13 percent were definitely against abortion rights.

In March 1993, the increasing influence of the Roman Catholic Church on Polish social life was a major factor in parliamentary enactment of a new law that replaced the 1956 liberal abortion-rights law with the most restrictive abortion law of any Eastern European country. A year after enactment of the 1993 restrictive law on abortion, critics pointed out that the number of clandestine abortions had increased, with unscrupulous physicians offering to provide an abortion for any women able to pay the equivalent of U.S.A. $350 to $1,000. The average monthly income was only about $200, with half of the population earning below the poverty line, defined as $80 a month. Some travel agents offered "abortion trips" to the Ukraine at 8 million zloty or about $400.

The 1993 law permitted abortion only when the pregnancy threatened the life or "seriously threatened" the health of the mother, when there was "serious and irreversible malformation of the fetus," or when the pregnancy resulted from "criminal action" (i.e., rape or incest). These provisions were further limited by many restrictions. For example, in the case of danger to the mother's health, supporting statements were required from two physicians independent of the acting doctor. And while prenatal tests were required to prove that the fetus was malformed, another section of the law appeared to allow for extensive prenatal tests, such as amniocentesis, only when there was reason to suspect a serious problem, as when a pregnancy occurred in a family with a history of genetic illnesses.

In March 1995, Poland's strict antiabortion law faced a painful test in court when a 37-year-old divorced woman, who was already supporting a 10-year-old child, persuaded a doctor in private practice to terminate her pregnancy. The physician was brought into court to face charges of violating the 1993 abortion law. If convicted, he could have spent two years in prison and had his medical license suspended for up to ten years. The woman's lover, who could only contribute about $10 to the child's support but gave her the equivalent of $125 for the abortion, faced up to two years in prison. Like other incidents of illegal abortion, this case became a legal issue when the child's father reported the woman's abortion because she refused to have his child (Perlez 1995).

In August 1996, the lower house of Parliament moved to liberalize Poland's restrictive abortion law, despite strong opposition from the Roman Catholic Church and its political allies. The bill, backed by the former Communists who dominated the Parliament after the November 1995 elections and a leftist opposition party, would allow women to end pregnancies before the twelfth week if they could not afford to raise the child or had other personal problems. Early amendments, however, required counseling and a three-day waiting period for women seeking an abortion, and penalties of up to ten years in jail for aborting a woman against her will, or after the fetus can survive outside the womb. Opinion polls suggested that most people favored this liberalization, although 90 percent of those polled were nominally Catholic. (In 1993, President Lech Walesa, a devout Catholic, had vetoed a similar bill.)

In October 1996, despite a huge campaign against the bill including a silent march on Parliament by 30,000 Poles, the lower house overturned a veto of the new law by the Senate with a 228-to-195 vote and 16 abstentions; Aleksandr Kwasniewski, the president, had already promised to sign the new bill.

Under this legislation, women would again be able to end pregnancies before the twelfth week if they face financial or personal problems. However, abortion is available only after counseling and a three-day waiting period. The law also provides for sex education in the schools and less-expensive birth control. Despite enactment of the new law, polls suggested that antiabortion sentiment has been rising, and that Poles, about 90 percent of whom are at least nominally Roman Catholic, are almost equally divided on the question. The future of abortion legislation in Poland, thus, remains uncertain.

D. Population Control Efforts

The model of a small family is at present predominant in Poland. There are certain premises for the advisability of a pronatal population policy with a model of families with two, or to a lesser degree, three children. The opposite model of uncontrolled fertility is promoted by the Catholic Church and is related to the Church's campaign to limit contraception and sexual education and prohibit all abortion.

10. Sexually Transmitted Diseases

The epidemiological situation of STDs was investigated by H. Zielinski and A. Stapinski in 1992. In the first years after World War II, there was a significant increase in venereal diseases, especially syphilis which was epidemic. At the time, there were an estimated 100,000 to 150,000 cases of syphilis a year in a population of 23 million. The therapeutic program, the so-called Action W, which included education, prevention, and outpatient clinics in every city, produced positive results and the epidemic was controlled. By 1954, early symptomatic syphilis had decreased to about 2,200 cases annually, about 8 cases per 1,000 people.

Between 1963 and 1969, there was another rapid increase in syphilis to 52 per 1,000 people, and the incidence of early syphilis (symptomatic and asymptomatic syphilis stages 1 and 2) to 66.6 cases per 1,000 people. The incidence of gonorrhea, which reached a low level of 80 per 1,000, also increased, although not so rapidly, to exceed 153 cases per 1,000 in 1970.

A new program of syphilis and gonorrhea control produced positive results. In the 1980s, the incidence of syphilis decreased steadily until 1989. In 1989, the number of new cases diagnosed was 4.6 per 1,000; in 1990, it was 4.8. In 1990, new cases rose to 4.9 per 1,000, a 5 percent increase. The 1991 incidence of early symptomatic syphilis remained stable from 1990, 2.8 per 1,000. However, the 1991 incidence of early asymptomatic syphilis was 9 percent higher than in 1990, while the incidence of late syphilis decreased by 16 percent. Similarly, the 1991 incidence of diagnosed gonorrhea decreased by 34 percent from 1990, less than 10 percent of what it was in 1970. In 1991, nongonococcal infections of the urogenital tract was 14 percent less than it was in 1990.

Information about the incidence of condyloma and genital herpes are fragmentary and have been included in the statistics only since 1990.

11. HIV/AIDS

Serological examination for HIV status for people at risk was inaugurated in Poland in 1985. Of the 2,426 cases of HIV infection detected by November 1992, 1,776 were drug addicts. The real number of carriers is at least three times larger. Between 1985 and November 1992, 118 cases of AIDS were diagnosed. In this group, 58 percent were homosexual or bisexual, 30 percent heterosexual drug addicts, 10 percent heterosexual, and 2 percent unknown. Over half the 118 had died as of November 1992.

In 1989, A. Stapinski et al. published the data of the Institute of Venereology in Warsaw on the prevention of HIV infection in drug addicts. Noting "that the infection spreads rapidly in this population," the authors predicted "a further rapid spreading of this infection in this risk group," and recommended providing addicts with free syringes, needles, and condoms. They also recommended systematic intensive training of personnel in drug treatment and rehabilitation centers, as well as extensive informational education of all adults.

Also in 1989, D. Weyman-Rzucidlo et al. reported on the prevalence of HIV infection in a group of 1,297 homosexuals. In Poland, as in Western Europe and the United States, "homosexual and bisexual males are the group of high risk for HIV infection."

Dermatovenereological outpatient clinics provide HIV testing for anyone who wants to be tested and medical care for those needing it. Provincial clinics are also engaged in training health-service workers and providing health education in their own districts.

A program for AIDS prevention and control prepared by A. Stapinski in 1988 includes multidimensional activities: staff training, diagnostic facilities, research units, and prevention of infection by sexual contact, blood, needles, and syringes. Much attention was given to protecting health-service workers against infection, and to health education for at-risk groups and the general population, especially adolescents. Voluntary testing for HIV antibodies is encouraged, and stress is placed on preventing discrimination against persons who are HIV-positive and have AIDS.

12. Sexual Dysfunctions, Counseling, and Therapies

The diagnostic criteria developed by Masters and Johnson are accepted by some Polish sexologists, while others follow the DSM-III-R. Clinicians specializing in sexology require personality evaluation before sexological diagnosis. Sexual dysfunctions are viewed in the psychodynamic categories and diagnosis connected with the evaluation of neurotic mechanisms and personality disturbances.

There are two departments of sexology associated with the medical schools in Warsaw and Krakow. Outpatient clinics in all the larger cities and towns provide diagnosis and treatment for sexological patients. These clinics employ some seventy medical doctors with clinical specialization in sexology, and also some psychologists.

13. Research and Advanced Education

A. Institutes and Programs for Sexological Research

The following are organizations for sexological research in Poland:

The Polish Medical Association, Medical Center of Postgraduate Education, Department of Sexology and Pathology of Human Relations, Director: Kazimierz Imielinski, M.D., Ph.D. Address: ul. Fieldorfa 40, 004-158 Warsaw, Poland.

The Medical School of N. Copernicus, Department of Sexology, Director: Julian Godlewski, M.D., Ph.D. Address: ul. Sarego 16, 31-047 Kracow, Poland.

The Academy of Physical Education, Sexual Division of Rehabilitation Faculty, Director: Zbigniew Lew-Starowicz, M.D., Ph.D. Address: ul. Marymoncka 34, 01-813 Warsaw, Poland.

Polish Sexological Society, Sex Research Department, Director: Anna Sierzpowska-Ketner, M.D., Ph.D. Address: ul. Marymoncka 34. 01-813 Warsaw, Poland. Correspondence: ul. Londynska [n'] 12/13, 03-921 Warsaw, Poland. Programs are offered on sex offenders, sexual dysfunctions, transsexuals, and the handicapped and sexuality.

Postcollege, graduate programs and courses are provided for psychologists and medical doctors by the Medical Center of Postgraduate Education, Department of Sexology and Pathology of Human Relations. A medical specialization in sexology has been available since 1985 for psychiatrists and gynecologists. Training is also provided by the Polish Sexological Society, with certification of Clinical Sexologists since 1991.

B. Publications

The Polish Sexological Society publishes the quarterly *Sexology*. Correspondence: Londynska 12/13, 03-921 Warsaw, Poland.

References and Suggested Readings

Mondykowski, Sandra M. 1982. "Polish Families." In M. McGoldrick, J. K. Pearce, and J. Giordano, eds. *Ethnicity and Family Therapy.* New York: Guilford Press.

Perlez, J. 1995 (April 2). "A Painful Case Tests Poland's Abortion Ban." *The New York Times*, p. 11.

Perlez, J. 1996 (October 3). "Central Europe Learns about Sex Harassment." *The New York Times*, p. A3.

French Polynesia
(*Polynésie Française*)

Anne Bolin, Ph.D.

Contents

Demographics and a Historical Perspective

A. Demographics

French Polynesia encompasses five administrative areas representing five archipelagos with 130 islands and atolls in the South Pacific, approximately 5,000 miles east of Australia. The Society Islands, the Gambier Islands, the Austral Islands, and the Marquesas are primarily volcanic islands, while the majority of the Tuamotu Islands are atolls. Oceania is divided into three broad cultural groupings, with Melanesia and Micronesia to the west and Polynesia to the east. French Polynesia as a political entity is situated within the indigenous culture area of Polynesia, which includes all the islands in a "triangle" stretching from Easter Island in the east to the Hawaiian Islands in the north and New Zealand in the southwest. It incorporates diverse societies of Polynesian peoples colonized by the French and declared a

French Protectorate in 1842 (Stanley 1992). In 1957, this area became officially known as Polynésie Française. It is important to note that French Polynesia is not an indigenous or cultural subdivision, but is rather a modern political entity.

European culture has impacted the indigenous culture of French Polynesia in a number of ways for over two hundred years. This chapter presents an overview integrating historically situated accounts of the traditional culture with perspectives on the influence of colonization and missionary activity on the cultural expression, beliefs, and values related to Polynesian sexuality. When available, contemporary sexual data will be presented. The focus is specifically on the sexuality of the indigenous peoples of French Polynesia and does not address that of the Europeans or the other minorities unless otherwise stated.

The Society Islands consist of fourteen atolls and volcanic islands and include the Windward Islands of Tahiti, Moorea, Maiao, Tetiaroa and Mehetia; and the Leeward Islands of Huahine, Raiatea, Tahaa, Bora Bora, Maupiti, Tubai, Maupihaa/Mopelia, Manuae/Scilly, and Motu One/Bellingshausen. Tahiti has a mountainous interior surrounded by a fertile coastline where cane and coconut are grown. The Marquesas Islands, popularized by Melville in *Typee*, consist of eleven islands, six of which are inhabited. Gauguin is buried on Hiva Oa, the most populated of the Marquesas Islands. Other inhabited islands include Tahuata, Fatuiva, Ua Pou, Nuku Hiva, Ua Huka, and Hova Oa. The Tuamotu Archipelago, which means "cloud of islands," situated north and east of the Society Islands, spans an arc of eighty coral atolls covering 1,100 miles. Included among the seventy-eight atolls in this group are: Tepoto, Napuka, Pukarua, Takaroa, Manihi, Rangiroa, Raroia, Rotoava, Tatakoto, Hao, Reao, and Pukapuka, among others. Copra and mother-of-pearl are important exports. The Gambier Islands are southeast of the Tuamotus and include three inhabited islands of which Mangareva is best known (Suggs 1960). According to a 1987 report, it is estimated that only 1,600 speakers of Mangarevan remained on the inhabited islands, a result in part of heavy out-migration. Their livelihood consists of horticulture with crops such as coconuts, taro, and bananas along with fishing (HRAF 1991:172). The Austral Islands include five inhabited volcanic islands. One of these is Tubuai, and the group is sometimes called the Tubuai Islands. Islands include Rimatara, Rurutu, Ra'ivavae, and Rapa. The Rapanese cash crops are coffee and potatoes, which are exported, while farming and fishing are primary subsistence activities (Hanson 1991:274). The Austral Island peoples are well known for their indigenous arts and temples.

Over half of the indigenous French Polynesians live on the island of Tahiti, along with French, Chinese, and genetic intermixtures of these groups. The total population of French Polynesia is 188,814 (Stanley 1992). The most recent population figures available by island groups are from the 1988 census (Institut Territorial de la Statistique) and are presented in Table 1.

Table 1

1988 Population by Larger Islands and Groups of Islands

Island	Population
WINDWARD ISLANDS	140,341
Tahiti	131,309
Moorea	8,801
LEEWARD ISLANDS	22,232
Huahine	4,479
Raiatea	8,560
Tahaa	4,005
Bora Bora	4,225
Maupiti	96
AUSTRAL ISLANDS	6,509
Rurutu	1,953
Tubuai	1,846
TUAMOTU ISLANDS	7,547
Rangiroa	1,305
Manihi	429
GAMBIER ISLANDS	620
MARQUESAS ISLANDS	7,358
Nuku Hiva	2,100
Hiva Oa	1,671
TOTAL POPULATION	188,814

Ethnic divisions include 78 percent Eastern Polynesian (*Mā'ohi*), 12 percent Chinese, 6 percent local French, and 4 percent metropolitan French. This ethnic-identity breakdown has been critiqued and remains a major obstacle to interpretation of the data. It is difficult to ascertain the precolonial population of these five island groups, because European contact resulted in a massive population decline throughout French Polynesia, both indirectly through disease and directly through European attacks, e.g., in 1595, Mendana's crew was responsible for killing over 200 Marquesans. Thomas (1991:188) estimates that the population of the Marquesas declined from 35,000 to 2,000 between the eighteenth century and 1920s. By the mid-1980s, the population had increased to about 5,500. The Mangarevan population may have once been 8,000 people, but by 1824, it was only 1,275 (HRAF 1991:172). According to Hanson (1991:273), the island of Rapa at contact had a population of 1,500-2,000, but by 1867, it reached a low of 120. Today, there are only an estimated 400 remaining Rapan speakers. The population of the Tuamotu Islands was estimated at 6,588 in 1863, but declined by almost 2,200 by the 1920s. A report in 1987 establishes the Tuamotuan population at 14,400, with 7,000 of these in the Tuamotu, but most of the remainder living in Tahiti. The Raroian population declined from 260 in 1897 to 60 in 1926. It rose to 120 in 1950 (HRAF 1991:276). Tahiti's population is believed to have declined from a 1767 estimate of

35,000 to 16,050 in the first missionary census in 1797. By 1869, it had declined to 7,169 (Oliver 1974, 1989:67, 117).

The official languages of French Polynesia are French and Tahitian or *reo Mā'ohi.* The Tahitians refer to themselves as *Mā'ohi* or *Ta'ata Tahiti.* Indigenously Polynesian languages form two major divisions: Western and Eastern Polynesian. The current population has an annual growth rate of 2.3 percent. The annual birth rate is 28 births per 1,000 with a total fertility rate of 3.3 children (1988 data; Stanley 1992). The death rate is 5 deaths per 1000 in the population, with an infant mortality rate of 15 deaths per 1,000 live births. Life expectancy is 68 years for males and 73 years for females. The 1988 census claims about 87 percent literacy in French and 64 to 68 percent in one of the Polynesian languages. In 1986-87, educational institutions included 176 primary schools, 7 secondary schools, and 18 high schools; the Université Française du Pacifique was established in 1987. The curriculum in public and private church schools alike is a French one. Of the 64,000 persons counted in the 1988 census as "having employment" out of the total population of 188,814, two thirds of the employed were men and three out of four worked on the Windward Islands of Moorea and Tahiti. In the outer Leeward Islands, 80 percent of the women and no more than 73 percent of the men had jobs. Most employed *Mā'ohi* work either as civil servants or in the tourist industry. Most Tahitians, even in the rural areas, are involved to varying degrees in the market economy, either in independent enterprises such as craft production, periodic wage labor, and/or cash cropping (Hooper 1985:161; Elliston, 1996).

B. A Brief Historical Perspective

The beauty of these islands have been captured in the paintings of Paul Gauguin and the writings of Herman Melville, Robert Louis Stevenson, Jack London, and W. Somerset Maugham, among other notables. Early explorers, such as Captain James Cook (1769) and Captain Bligh of Bounty fame (1788-89), contributed to Tahiti's reputation as a sexual paradise. Indeed, the peoples of the area, particularly the Society Islands, became distinguished for their sex-positive attitudes and known by Europeans for taking a casual approach to sex. Although the Polynesian sexual mores varied greatly from those of the Europeans, they were not unregulated. Polynesians had clearly defined cultural rules structuring sexuality and marriage, including exogamy, hierarchy, chiefly structure, genealogy, and incest rules.

The Polynesians' ancestors arrived in the frontier areas of Fiji, then reached Tonga and Samoa about 3,300 to 5,000 years ago (Oliver 1974, 1989:67, 117). Eastern Polynesian occupation occurred by 200 B.C.E. The Tuamotu Archipelago was probably occupied by voyagers from the Society Islands by about the ninth century, as were the Austral Islands (Suggs 1960:140-141).

The 1,544 square miles of area became a French overseas territory under the French constitution in 1957 and is currently administered by a French High Commissioner assigned by France, and a 48-member Territorial Assembly, both in the capital city of Papeete on Tahiti, the largest of the Society Islands. The Territorial Assembly is composed of locally elected representatives from the Windward and Leeward Islands of the Society Islands, the Austral Islands, Tuamotu Islands, Gambier Islands, and the Marquesan Islands (Elliston, 1996). "The Territorial Assembly has been granted more powers over internal affairs over the past twenty years, as a result of Tahitian calls for more 'internal autonomy'; the French High Commissioner, however, retains the right to overrule or modify any Assembly decision" (quote from von Strokirch 1993; Henningham 1992; Elliston, 1996).

The islands that now constitute French Polynesia are linguistically of the Eastern division and originally included proto-Marquesan and proto-Tahitian. Dialects of Tahitian are spoken on the Austral, Tuamotu, Gambier, and Marquesas Islands. (Tahitian is part of the Austronesian language family that spread and diversified 6,000 years ago.) This linguistic division is also replicated in terms of two cultural groupings: Western and Eastern Polynesia, with the Marquesas and the Society Islands identified as the cultural epicenters of Eastern Polynesia (Goldman 1970:xxvii). Robert C. Suggs suggests that these two archipelagos were centers of population dispersion for the other islands in Eastern Polynesia (1960:107, 137).

1. Basic Sexological Premises

A. Character of Gender Roles

Because cultures operate as integrated systems, the basic sexological premises, such as gender roles, social status, general concepts, and constructs of sexuality and love, must be considered within the broader Polynesian cultural context. Research on the status of women in traditional Polynesian societies supports the view that their position was regarded as high (Howard and Kirkpatrick 1989:82-83). High status prevailed in the face of a *tapu* system in which women and men were segregated and women were regarded as less powerful. (See Section 2A for a discussion of the concepts of *tapu* and *mana*.) In addition, although there was a division of labor between Polynesian women and men, it was different from the traditional Western gender bifurcation of public/domestic or inside/outside. In traditional Tahiti, men hunted pigs and fished, engaged in warfare, and built temples, while women fished for shellfish, gardened, and produced mats and bark cloth (Oliver 1974). However, role flexibility was differentially enacted among the various Polynesian societies (Howard and Kirkpatrick 1989:82-83). To fully understand women's position in pre-colonial Polynesia, the context of the "chiefly structure" must be considered. Chiefly status could take precedence over gender, and consequently, women could also assume positions of power as chiefs (Elliston, 1996).

Levy's work among the Tahitians from 1962 to 1964 suggests a culture in which attention to gender distinctions continues the precolonial trajectory (1973:230-237). Evidence of this is found in the Tahitian language in which gender is linguistically underplayed. While gender-specific occupational divisions do occur, there is a great deal of role pliability and cross-over, e.g., although women do not hold office in the formal political sector, they have an important voice and interest in politics (Levy 1973:233). The high position of Tahitian women continues a pattern reported early on by explorers. The traditional descent system of reckoning through either matrilineal or patrilineal lines provided women access to powerful positions in the social order. Levy's research concluded that a blurring of gender boundaries continues as a contemporary pattern in rural Tahiti. However, he found that in the more urbanized and Westernized setting of Papeete, this pattern of gender equality and blending was becoming polarized by the wage-labor economy in which men are the breadwinners and women the homemakers (Levy 1973:232-237). Elliston (1996) suggests that this pattern has not come to fruition, but rather women's employability is increasing while men's is decreasing.

Some researchers have proposed that in traditional times, in Eastern Polynesia (including the Marquesas and Society Islands), women's status was considered low because they were *noa*: common, impure, and polluting in regard to *mana*. Shore's examination of the literature suggests this may be an oversimplification. He cites considerable evidence to the contrary (1989:146-147). For example, Hanson and Hanson argue that women's menstruation was not regarded as "simply polluting, but as inherently dangerous because it represents a heightened time of female activity as the conduit between the worlds of gods and human" (1983:93 in Shore 1989:147).

In-depth discussions of gender roles in recent times are presented in Douglas Oliver's *Two Tahitian Villages* (1981), Greg Dening's *Islands and Beachers* (1980), and Robert Levy's *Tahitians: Mind and Experience in the Society Islands* (1983), among others.

Thomas (1987) has discussed Polynesian gender roles in order to highlight the dramatic effect of colonization and missionization on contemporary Marquesan women and men. Depopulation has impacted the Marquesans, as has the introduction of wage labor, which, in some areas, continues today as a mixed economy with subsistence, occasional copra sales, and/or intermittent wage work. The work of Marquesan women is *haka ha'e propa*, which means "to make the house clean." This includes a variety of domestic chores, child care, clothes washing, and cooking. Men engage in agriculture and horticulture, fishing, cutting coconuts for copra sales, and/or paid manual work. The division of labor is flexible, and women may work in gardens or collect Tahitian chestnuts, while men may do some work in the house which consists primarily of cooking. Unlike Western practices, cooking, washing dishes, and clothes washing in the nonurban areas are done outside the home. Even if a family has a gas stove or washing machine, this is placed outside the home.

But this model of gender roles that continues in more rural areas is changing in the more central, Westernized, and urbanized island locales, where the presence of schools, hospitals, post offices, and other administrative services, as well as greater opportunities for continuous employment, affect traditional patterns. Women participate in the workforce in these areas to a high degree, particularly in clerical positions, while men are employed primarily in the highway department with road maintenance. Women's pattern of employment is typically one in which they quit work to have children, but may later return to part-time positions. In contrast, men have a more consistent pattern of long-term, wage-labor employment (Thomas 1987).

Thomas (1987) suggests that these gender-role patterns and the division of labor is more likely a result of colonialism than a traditional Polynesian cultural pattern. The traditional pattern of gender roles in the early contact period (1790-1830) was quite different according to Thomas. Like Polynesian societies generally, the *tapu* system was an important part of the social organization of the Marquesas, and it frequently involved segregation of the sexes.

Traditional activities for men included fishing from canoes, which continues today, while traditional women's activities included gardening, preparation of bark cloth, and making mats. Prior to missionization, women had other opportunities for enhancement of their status. Coexisting with a class of male chiefs and priests was a class of women shamans whose importance varied throughout Polynesia. In the Marquesas, these women priests occupied a privileged position in society as curers and diviners who received food or pigs as payment for their services. The old Marquesan role parameters provided women with opportunities and access to prestige and power.

The Western disparity in gender roles delineated by separate but unequal domains of the public and the domestic was not expressed in traditional Marquesan gender roles. The *tapu* system also mitigated against such a Western public/domestic split, since typically men ate meals with men, not with women. As Thomas (1987) has noted, today Marquesan gender roles reflect Western tradition and the imposed Christian gender polarization of men-public-provider and women-domestic-nurturer. The demise of the *tapu* system occurred unevenly, but seemed to have been eliminated by the 1880s, facilitated by French colonial rule in 1842, the political efforts of the Catholic and Protestant missions, and the decline of the indigenous population. Colonialism and missionization disrupted the hierarchical aspects of the social system and eroded the chiefly structure, along with the system of *tapu* and *mana* that sustained it (Elliston 1996). By the late nineteenth century, polyandry, which was probably only practiced by the highest ranking females, had become almost extinct (Thomas 1987).

Major changes in the political economy resulted in the replacement of traditional landholding units and mechanisms of redistribution by autonomous groups engaged in their own subsistence. Missionaries felt that the traditional Marquesan practice in which women gardened was improper and unseemly to their sex. According to Christian dictates, the women should be confined to their homes while the men should work as the cultivators. This was successfully imposed on the Marquesan peoples and others in French Polynesia. Lockwood reports a similar pattern in the division of labor, in which men are the farmers while women are responsible for the household and child care on Tubuai (1989:199).

The impact of Western missionization on gender roles was particularly effective in French Polynesia because of the large-scale disruption in the indigenous way of life. All these factors converged to influence indigenous gender roles. Yet, the continuity of women's precolonial status vis à vis men cannot be underestimated (Elliston, 1996). However, this does not now mean that women cannot surmount the Christian ideologies that place men at the head of the household. Lockwood observes that Tahitian women are "socially assertive and are frequently willing to challenge male authority when in a position to do so." Oliver's description of ancient Tahitian women as "anything but a passive, deferential, submissive lot; certainly not in domestic matters and often not in 'public' affairs either" (1974:604) could be applied equally to contemporary Tahitian peasant women (1989:207).

B. Sociolegal Status of Males and Females

The sociocultural status of Polynesians throughout the life course varies in terms of ages and expectations. Oliver's (1981) and Levy's (1973) work on Tahitian life stages is particularly valuable in this regard. The infant, an *'aiu* ("milk eater") gradually becomes a child (*tamāri'i*) between 1 and 3 or 4 years old (also *tamaroa*, boy child, or *tamāhine*, girl child). Childhood is followed by *taure'are'a*, the period of pleasure. This stage is ushered in by signs of approaching puberty. Between the mid-20s and early 30s, one becomes *ta'ata pa'ari* ("a wise or mature person"). Old age is *rū'au* (old) and/or if an individual becomes senile, he or she is *'aru'aru*, "weak and helpless" (Levy 1973:25), see also Oliver (1981:340-400).

Traditionally, the status of individuals in many areas of French Polynesia was defined by a hierarchical pattern of genealogical ranking sustained by the belief in *mana* and encountered through the *tapu* system of behavioral rules and restrictions. The Polynesian system of genealogical ranking was one in which the firstborn child was of higher status than his or her siblings. Those in such a position, regardless of their gender, were in a state of *mana* and, according to some reports, were therefore secluded for certain periods. The aura of *mana* also extended to a lesser extent to other siblings as well.

In traditional Polynesian societies prior to disruption of the *tapu* system, children were regarded as highly potent and potentially dangerous. As a result, they had to undergo certain rituals to prepare them to interact in the secular world. All upper- and lower-echelon children were apparently imbued with this divinity. The Polynesian cosmology regarded this sacredness as a highly charged force that required precautions lest harm could befall the unprotected individual.

Jane and James Ritchie (1983) noted that the precolonial pattern of early childhood indulgence, community concern, and an extended-family concept of parenting has continued, especially in the more traditional areas at the time of their research. Children learn to be autonomous and responsible for tasks and chores at an early age. This transition to responsibility and autonomy occurs when the child is around 2 to 3 years old. By the middle years of childhood, peers are accountable for most of the child care. Polynesian groups, and French Polynesia is no exception, were noted for a pattern of fluid child adoption. This pattern still occurs today. Adoption may occur informally through kin networks that may bypass the legal adoption process. (See discussion below of marriage and the family.)

Gender was also conceived as an integral part of generalized Polynesian hierarchy, genealogy, and the status of the individual as adolescent and adult. Thomas (1987) has described Marquesan men as traditionally having *mana*, while women were *me'ie* (common or free of *tapu* in relation to men). The term *noa* is used in other parts of Polynesia. However, there were numerous situations in which women could become subject to *tapu* prohibitions. This represents the contextual aspects of the *tapu* system described earlier. Such contexts required precautions as well as certain restrictions on the individual, his or her possessions, and tasks. Certain kinds of activities were segregated by sex and locale, e.g., women learning a new chant, men making a net, or a woman placing herself under *tapu* to conceive or prevent a miscarriage. This kind of *tapu* involved communal eating, sleeping, and prohibitions on sexual activity for a particular period of time, or until the project was completed.

Thomas (1987) has also pointed out that *tapu* and *me'ie* were relational constructs, and that in the Marquesas, a man who was *tapu* in relation to a particular woman might be *me'ie* in relation to other men who were in a *tapu* grade above him. This same man would be *me'ie* in relation to women of chiefly status.

In addition to the elites in the Polynesian hierarchy, there were people who were low-status servants of the elites, as well as those who were nonlandholding tenant farmers. It was the commoners in the Marquesas who were most affected by the *tapu* restrictions, e.g., common men could only eat what was produced by women. Persons at the lowest level of the hierarchy were not affected by the *tapu* on food, since they were the servants and produced food for not only themselves but for the elite they served. The elite were less affected, because they neither produced nor prepared the food they ate.

C. General Concepts of Sexuality and Love

While sailors on the early European exploring ships regarded Polynesia as a sexual paradise, the missionaries they brought viewed the same cultures as dens of debauchery. Oliver (1989) cites a 1778 report of J. Forster who stated: "The great plenty of good and nourishing food, together with fine climate, the beauty and unreserved behavior of their females, invite them powerfully to the enjoyments and pleasures of love. They begin early to abandon themselves to the most libidinous scenes." Tahitians specifically, and Polynesians generally, became known for their sex-positive attitudes and open valuing of sexuality, although the cultural structuring and tacit rules for sexual expressions were not apparent to the Europeans. Sexual experience and expression for many Polynesians began early and continued throughout the life course.

Needless to say, the various explorers and colonial ship crews visiting the islands misunderstood Polynesian sexuality. For example, in the Marquesas, young naked girls swam out to the ships to engage in sexual trysts with the sailors. While the sailors took advantage of the sexual liberation of these young girls, they experienced some ambiguity because their own Western sexual paradigm had no comparable framework or referent. While Polynesian girls were similar in some respects to the prostitutes or sex workers who typically greeted these sailors at other ports, they were also very different due to their youth, nakedness, and willingness to swim out to greet the boats. In addition, not all young women swam out to the boats or engaged in sex with the sailors. The young girls that came out to the ships were outside the *tapu* classes, so their relations with the visitors provided them access to status and wealth that they would not normally have. Foreign sailors and observers were not aware of the situational and contextual factors behind this behavior (Dening 1980).

Others who swam out to the ships were the Marquesan *Ka'ioi*. These were adolescents who were separated at puberty in order to be educated in the social conventions and skills necessary to become singers and dancers at *koina* (feasts). For girls, this was a period of intense sexual play and display. It involved learning songs and dances for the feasts as well as the art of beautification, which included the application of oils and bleaches. High-status girls were not educated as *Ka'ioi*, nor did they swim out to the ships. However, it was this behavior among the Marquesans that also contributed to the Western stereotype of Polynesian sexual license (Dening 1980).

In their massive cross-cultural review of the ethnographic literature, Ford and Beach (1951) classified the Mangarevans, the Marquesans, and the Pukapukans as "permissive societies," characterized by tolerant attitudes toward sexual expression in the lifespan of the individual. According to Gregersen (1983), Polynesia is known for "public copulation, erotic festivals, ceremonial orgies and sex expeditions," which had disappeared by modern times. It should be pointed out that this does not imply a sexual free-for-all by any means, as noted by Douglas Oliver's account in *Ancient Tahitian Society* (1974). While missionaries were immediately struck by the Polynesian variance from Western Christian standards of sexual morality, it should not be assumed that Polynesian sexuality was without cultural rules. Like sexuality everywhere, Polynesian sexuality was structured and bound by norms, regulations, and sanctions—although these were different from those of the explorers, missionaries, and colonials. It was primarily the young and unmarried people who had the greatest sexual freedom; married people and the elite class had much less.

Although Polynesian societies condoned premarital sexual expression, access to partners was strictly structured. Gregersen (1983), for example, reported that on the island of Raroia in the Tuamotu Archipelago, there were only 109 people in 1951. Such a small population meant that seven of the nine women of marriageable age were prohibited from having sexual partners because of incest regulations. In the neighboring atoll of Tepuka in the 1930s, the young people were all related and had to journey to other islands or await the arrival of visitors to find a partner.

Specific laws were enacted with French colonization. In 1863, for example, the French administrators banned much of the traditional cultural practices that involved *tapu*, the religion, traditional songs and dances, warfare, naked bathing, wearing of perfumed oils, polygyny, polyandry, and other practices at variance with Christian morality. These laws did much to repress the precolonial culture, but, as Elliston (1996) point out, "Polynesians found ways around both the Church teachings against sex-outside-marriage, and against French laws."

2. Religious and Ethnic Factors Affecting Sexuality

A. Source and Character of Religious Values

Polynesians today are primarily Christian with 54 percent Protestant, 30 percent Roman Catholic, and 16 percent other, including Mormon, animist (the indigenous system), and Buddhist. The impact of missionary activity in the Pacific is reflected in the high percentage of Christian religious affiliation. Depending on the particular historical situation, different denominations may predominate in an area, e.g., the Marquesas Islands are over 90 percent Catholic; Protestantism dominates the Austral Islands and the Leeward Islands, while the Tuamotu Islands are two-thirds Catholic and one-third Mormon. Although Thomas (1987) suggests that Catholicism's antagonism to contraceptive use has resulted in typically large families, large families are more probably a continuation of an earlier pattern that existed prior to depopulation, rather than as the consequence of Catholic religious attitudes.

It is important to remember that once the Europeans arrived in Polynesia, the traditional culture began to undergo major change and disruption. Archival and historical research can provide important clues in unraveling the traditional patterns that have persisted despite European colonialism and missionary activity. Broadly speaking, the various denominations of missionaries found the Polynesian sex-positive cultures repugnant. They were appalled by the Polynesian joy of sex, and repelled by the marital practices that allowed for polygyny and even polyandry.

In discussing religion, it is inappropriate to segregate the sacred aspects of indigenous Polynesian life from the wider culture, since these societies are unlike the West where there is a clear division between the sacred and the secular. In contrast, the sacred and secular are interwoven in an integrated fashion within Polynesian cultures. An attitude in which sex was highly valued was reproduced as part of the synthesis of the social and the sacred in Polynesian life. Sacred aspects of sexuality incorporated beliefs about reproduction, fertility, and fecundity that were symbolically expressed through ceremonial sex. Marshall (1961) reports evidence of public sex associated with sacred temples on the Island of Ra'ivavae. This was also recorded for Tahiti. Among Tahitians, the sacred temples, or *marae*, served as the center of daily life. The religious system was based on beliefs in spirits and gods. Humans and gods were in a relationship that permeated all aspects of the Tahitian's daily life. Even the gods were regarded as joyous and sexually playful in concert with the positive-sex ethos of the culture.

The *tapu* (taboo) system regulated social behavior. It was based upon an important religious element, *mana*, a fundamental principal of divinity and sacredness, that has been likened to electricity, prevalent among some Polynesian societies. *Mana* provided a relational and contextual structure, as well as demarcated sacred boundaries around class, time, events, space, and people. "Theoretically mana is an inherited potential, transmitted genealogically, with greater proportions going to firstborn children. It is therefore a matter of degree—a gradient ideally coincident with kinship seniority. Ultimately it stems from the gods" (Howard and Kirkpatrick 1989:614). *Mana*, however, must be demonstrated through acts and activities of an individual. Success demonstrated the strength of one's *mana*, while failure signified weak *mana* (Howard and Kirkpatrick 1989:64). *Mana* was also associated with fertility, fecundity, and abundance—both reproductive and agricultural, according to Shore (1989:142).

Shore suggests that this aspect of *mana* may account for the traditional Polynesian emphasis on the genitals of the chief. In the *mana*, relational and contextual construct power was somatically embodied in the head and the genitals, which were regarded as sacred. For the Marquesans, these were the bodily sites for the protection of the self (Dening 1980). Linton reports that in traditional times, "there was constant mention of the genital organs of the chief, which were given names indicating their vigor and size" (Linton 1939:159 in Shore 1989:142). The Marquesan concepts of sacred personhood and the autonomy of the individual apparently also transcended class and gender in some respects. All individuals were credited with an inherent divinity that granted them inalienable social respect. However, in terms of ranking, the chiefly group held a higher position because it was believed that their personal *mana* far exceeded others. Nevertheless, regardless of rank or status, the individual was endangered if the *tapu* regions around the head and groin were violated.

Bradd Shore (1989:137-173) has described *tapu* in depth. *Tapu* is a difficult concept for Westerners to understand. It is not directly translatable into our concept of taboo. *Tapu* has multiple referents. According to Shore,

> First, the term has two quite distinct usages, one active, the other passive. As an active quality, tapu suggests a contained potency of some thing, place, or person. In its passive usage, it means forbidden or dangerous for someone who is noa [not divine, common]. Moreover, it seems to combine contradictory properties, suggesting on the one hand sacredness, reverence, and distinctiveness and, on the other, danger, dread, and pollution. (1989:144)

When people were engulfed by *tapu,* they were in sacred states, and consequently, restrictions and prohibitions were placed on their behavior as well as their person. *Tapu* was the system that structured behavior in relation to *mana.* For example, according to Nicholas Thomas (1987), females were considered *me'ie,* common or free of *tapu* in relation to men. This classification, however, did not mean that women could not have a high status or could not enter *mana* states. However, *mana* was a fundamental spiritual rationalization for segregation of the sexes that resulted in *tapu,* or restrictions on the interaction between the genders in certain domains.

Marquesan women were also regarded as potentially dangerous when menstruating, which provided them with certain kinds of power. For example, a woman could curse an object by naming it for her genitals or by placing the object beneath her buttocks. Similarly, *tapu* could be assigned to an object by naming it for one's head or placing the item above one's head. Among the Marquesans, who believed women were potentially dangerous, sexual restrictions were also placed on intercourse at various times. According to Thomas (1990:67) "some aspects of femaleness seem to be at the center of the tapu system." This was not, however, a universal pattern in French Polynesia.

The religious aspects of indigenous sexuality were also evident in the Tahitian *arioi* cult (discussed later in greater detail and described by Oliver (1974).) Members of the *arioi* society, an organization of traveling Tahitian entertainers, dancers, and athletes, were permitted unrestricted sexuality. Their roles as entertainers included sexual titillation and celebration for the public. The sexual element of this cult was permeated by the religious, as the *arioi* were dedicated to the Tahitian god, 'Oro (Oliver, 1974).

B. Source and Character of Ethnic Values

The peoples of French Polynesia are part of the larger culture area of Polynesia, sharing linguistic and many other cultural characteristics (Burrows 1968:179). However, in precontact times, there was much cultural variation and diversity among the five island groups making up French Polynesia. Today, unification by the French has provided "the Polynesians living in these different archipelagos and islands . . . new grounds for relating to one another, including the use of French and Tahitian languages (Elliston 1996). However, it should not be assumed that variation has been lost. For example, Oliver's study in 1954-55 of two Tahitian villages, one on Huahine and the other on Mo'orea, led him to state: "I came to recognize that there were almost as many subspecific varieties of Tahitian societal cultures as there were communities" (1981:xii). In Elliston's (1996) words, "Polynesians throughout the archipelagos continue to have a very strong sense of their own locally-based identities by which I mean that their contemporary identities are strikingly based on their islands and archipelagos of origin." Elliston explains this as "in part because Polynesians associate different characters, economic practices, even different cultures with different islands and archipelagos; where one is from encodes a great deal of information in the local signifying systems," noting that Polynesians themselves generally see a great deal of diversity in the islands.

Oliver spearheaded a research project in which the social organization of eight Tahitian communities were studied, two each by Douglas Oliver, Ben Finney, Antony Hooper, and Paul Kay. The social organization of these island peoples varied, as did their methods of food production, as adaptive responses to different environmental riches. In Eastern Polynesia, as in Western Polynesia, social organization was a ranked system. The precolonial social system was a chiefly structure and within it variance occurred. Therefore, unlike Western Polynesia in which rank was graded, Eastern Polynesia was stratified by class (Burrows 1968:185). Four major kinds of socioeconomic ranking or "degrees of stratification" existed in the traditional chiefly structures of what is now constituted as French Polynesia.

Tahiti had a very complex ranking system that usually included hereditary statuses consisting of *ari'i* (aristocracy), *ra'atira* (gentry), *manahune* (commoners), *teuteu* (servant class), and a small nonhereditary slave class of *titi*, captured during warfare. The people of Mangareva had "two basic status levels with tendency to form a third," while the Marquesas had "two status levels," and the Pukapukans "two status levels; the upper containing very few members" (Sahlins 1967; Stanley 1992; Ferdon 1991). While class stratification continues in modern times, the traditional categories have been abandoned (Oliver 1981:37).

These hierarchical aspects of Polynesian society were permeated with religious meaning since the chiefs and other elites were regarded as divine and rich in *mana*. *Tapu, mana*, the *arioi*, and a hierarchical chiefly structure were interconnected as aspects of the sexual system. For example, in Tahiti, as elsewhere, hierarchy was mandated by the gods and manifested in all levels of social organization. The kin-congregation or extended family had small *marae* to make offerings to spirits. Extended-family households were organized into neighborhoods that had larger *marae* with the chief's *marae*, which was the largest and most potent (Scupin and DeGorse 1992). It was believed that "the highest ranking chiefly family . . . was . . . descended from the first humans created by the creator god, Ta'aroa," and was therefore the most powerful spiritually (Scupin and DeCorse 1992:31).

The bilateral kinship system was one in which the chiefly status and sibling order (first-born siblings ranked in status above others) determined one's social position. This was not necessarily limited through the patri-lineage. Women, like men, could have access to chiefly positions. The practice of bilateral reckoning provided for flexibility in status and rank, facilitating affiliation through either the paternal or maternal line (Scupin and DeCorse 1992:313). As a result of colonialism and Christianization, the traditional social-political organization of inherited rank no longer exists (Hooper 1985:161).

3. Sexual Knowledge and Education

A. Government Policies and Programs for Sex Education

Because Tahiti contains over 70 percent of the population, public health efforts are focused in this area. Not currently available at the time of this writing is information from a sexual survey conducted in Tahiti in November 1993 under the auspices of La Direction de la Santé Publique.

B. Informal Sources of Sexual Knowledge

Informally, spatial organization and sleeping arrangements may contribute to sexuality education of the young. Ford and Beach (1951) reported that among the Pukapukans and Marquesans, families often slept in one room, thereby providing children an opportunity for sexuality education through clandestine observation. This, however, must be placed in cultural context. Parents were not putting on an open display for children; but, because families slept in close proximity, this provided children an opportunity to secretly observe their parents copulating. In these societies, discussions about sex with children were also very open and frank as part of a pattern of sex positiveness. For example, among the Ra'ivavaens studied by Marshall (1961:241), children were aware of orgasm, the role of the penis (*ure*) and the clitoris (*tira*) in sexual arousal.

Other avenues for sexuality education included practices around childbirth. Oliver (1989) recounts that on old Raroia in the Tuamotu Archipelago, childbirth was a social event in which the whole community attended, including children, and even male members who also assisted in childbirth. This custom of including males in childbirth as assistants is notable, for in many parts of Oceania, as elsewhere, men are prohibited from participating in childbirth.

Indigenous beliefs about conception in French Polynesia are part of the informal system of education. In a study of the Marquesas in the late 1970s, Kirkpatrick (1983) reported the then-current belief that, although babies were conceived through the copulation of males and females, this was not sufficient. Divine intervention was also a necessary component.

The Tahitian ethnotheory of conception asserted that the fetus received physical and divine characteristics from both parents. The infant's sacred attributes were regarded as cynosure of its birth. In old Tahiti, the genealogical system of ranking reckoned that the degree of divinity in each child was directly proportional to the degree of descent from his or her ancestral deities. The firstborn inherited more divinity or *mana* than the subsequent children, so that a genealogical line consisting of all firstborn children had more divinity than others. The amount of divinity was also synergistic, so that a firstborn of parents of equal divinity possessed more sacredness that either parent.

F. Allan Hanson (1970:1444-1446) has written on the "Rapan Theory of Conception." This analysis focuses on the Rapanese ethnotheory that conception is most likely to occur in the three to four days following menstruation when it is believed women are most fertile. In order to prevent pregnancy, Rapanese couples abstain from sex during this three- to four-day period. While this practice is not an effective method for limiting family size, it can be understood as articulating with Rapan theories of physiology and reproduction.

The Rapanese woman, based on Hanson's survey of 85 percent of the population, has an average of 6.3 births and raises about five children per woman. This is considered burdensome by the Rapanese who would like to reduce family size to ideally two to three children. The Rapanese say that:

> a fetus is formed when semen enters the uterus and coalesces with the blood harbored there. The existence of ovaries, Fallopian tubes, and ova is not recognized. Menustration ceases after conception, because all the blood goes to building the fetus. If conception has not occurred, the blood becomes stale after a month, is expelled in menstruation and is replaced with a fresh supply. The uterus opens and closes periodically, opening each month to allow the old blood to flow out . . . Semen cannot enter when the uterus is closed, so there is no possibility of conception during the greater part of the cycle. (Hanson 1970:1445)

This theory is also found in the Tuamotu archipelago on Pukapuka. In the Huahine and Mo'orea villages studied by Oliver (1981:334), as elsewhere in Tahiti, children were highly valued. Problems in conception were treated by a woman specialist who used an indigenous medication of hibiscus and green coconut.

4. Autoerotic Behaviors and Patterns

A. Children and Adolescents

Among the Pukapukans, Mangarevans, and the Marquesans, during indigenous times prior to Christianization, a tolerant attitude was taken toward childhood sexual expression. Among the Pukapukans, children masturbated in public with no opprobrium. The parents apparently ignored their behavior (Ford and Beach 1953). Levy's research among Tahitians from 1962-64, cites early explorer and missionary accounts of masturbation among adults and children (1973:113-116). His work among rural Tahitians indicates children masturbate, although the Tahitian term used to describe masturbation refers to males, since it includes the morpheme for uncircumcised penis. Levy notes that "the emphasis on prepubertal male masturbation is striking" (1973:115). It is considered a boy's activity outgrown with adolescence. However, adult censure of masturbation does occur and seems to be centered on the fear that the boy's foreskin might tear.

Masturbation by post-superincised males is criticized as an indication that he cannot attract a female.

B. Adults

According to William Davenport (1973), in traditional pre-Christian Tahiti, masturbation was sanctioned positively for young women and men.

5. Interpersonal Heterosexual Behaviors

It needs to be noted here that the three Euro-American developmental stages of childhood, adolescence, and adulthood may be of limited utility when encountering non-Western peoples. Adolescence is a fairly recent Western construct whose relevance and meaning cross-culturally will vary. For example, Kirkpatrick (1983) notes that the contemporary Marquesas islanders have an ethnotheory that encompasses four stages of human development: infancy, childhood, youth, and age.

A. Children

During the traditional times, the Pukapukans, Mangarevans, and Marquesans permitted children open sex play (Ford and Beach 1953). The cultural practices of Marquesans and Pukapukans not only allowed open sex play among children but, as mentioned earlier, provided children clandestine opportunities to observe adult sexual behavior due to sleeping arrangements. According to Oliver (1974) on Tahiti, coital simulation became actual penetration as soon as young boys were physiologically able. The Tahitians found children's imitation of copulation humorous. Other evidence suggests that young girls may have engaged in copulation before age 10 (Gregersen 1983).

Kirkpatrick's research (1983), based on twenty-five months of fieldwork in the Marquesas (primarily on Ua Pou and Tahiti during the late 1970s) provides much information on the life cycle, gender identities, and the integration of traditional patterns with new cultural influences. According to John Kirkpatrick, babies are massaged with oils and herbal lotions to make their skin smooth, and baby girls are given vaginal astringents to make the genital area sweet smelling. Such treatments for girls continue through puberty and include menstrual preparations as well. The application of fragrant oils, and the concern with cleanliness and personal hygiene, is tied into a wider Polynesian valuing of beauty and the body embedded in the traditional precontact culture. Suggs (1966:25) comments that in traditional Marquesan society, girls may have had their first coital experience by age 10, and boys were circumcised between 7 and 12 years old.

Oliver's (1981) ethnography includes in-depth discussion of infancy, childhood, and other life-course stages in Tahiti (see the chapter on "Passing Through Life," pp. 342-400). In this regard, he notes that children played in mixed-gender groups until 13 or 14 years old. The Tahitian attitudes to children playing at copulation was one of amusement (1981:366). However, as children approached the age of 11, adult parental attitudes shifted in regard to young females but not males. Oliver points out that parents objected to girls engaging in sex prior to marriage, an ideal that coexisted with an open and sex-positive attitude. Given Atean and Fatatan flexible definitions of marriage and the cohabitation of young people as a kind of trial marriage, the ideal of chastity in veiled-bride weddings accounted for only 8.9 percent of Atean and 22.5 percent of Fatatan weddings.

B. Adolescents

In discussing adolescents, it is especially important to avoid ethnocentrism. Adolescence is a Western construct with specific age and social concomitants that is of limited use cross-culturally. A more culturally relevant approach for a discussion of Polynesian sexuality is marital status and hierarchy rather than age.

Rites of Passage

Puberty rituals were practiced in traditional times among the Polynesians, including ceremonies in which male genitals were altered surgically, and females and males were both tattooed. These rituals defined the individual as having reached the age of procreation. Traditionally, superincision, along with tattooing, occurred some time after childhood, but before adulthood in the Society Islands.

Superincision continues to be part of contemporary Polynesian practices among some societies. One of the functions of the superincision is to make the penis hygienic and clean, just as vaginal astringents are used for cleanliness in young girls. This is part of the continuing traditional Polynesian cultural emphasis on beauty and cleanliness. It is believed that clean and sweet-smelling genitals make one more attractive as a partner (Kirkpatrick 1983).

However, the puberty ceremonies were and continue to be much more than male genital surgery. They are markers of a process of social-identity transformation as the youth approaches competence and adulthood. Kirkpatrick (1987) discusses Marquesan superincision as a "freeing or enabling event. It results in emergence into the world, rather than the incorporation of the subject into a new group or status" (1987:389). Young Marquesan males take pride in being superincised for these reasons. Additionally, it is not considered proper for an unsuperincised male to have intercourse. In the old Society Islands, Oliver (1974) notes that sex was allowed prior to the completion of the tattooing or superincision.

The superincision was traditionally done in the Marquesas by a local indigenous specialist. In the Old Marquesas, the superincision was performed after puberty, although Kirkpatrick (1983) found that in the late 1970s, the age of superincision was expanded to include 11- to 18-year-old boys. Frequently, a boy or group of boys would request that a superincision be performed.

Levy (1973) describes Tahitian superincision in very similar terms. Superincision among Tahitians is part of a boy's entré into *taure'are'a* ("the time or period of pleasure"). Levy points out that this precontact pattern continues in modern times because of its association with Christian circumcision. Peer pressure, such as teasing about smegma, is the reason boys gave when asked why they pursued superincision. Reinforcing this is a belief that superincision enhances sexual pleasure. Linguistic evidence includes an indigenous term for "skin orgasm," which describes the unsuperincised male's orgasm as quick and unsatisfying (Levy 1973:118-119).

In superincision, the foreskin is cut, various preparations may be applied on the wound, and then the penis is exposed to heat and salt water to heal. Young men will go to rock pools in the sea and expose their penis to the heat from sun-warmed rocks and then alternately bathe in the sea. When the incision is healed, the boys may return to their daily activities and wear shorts. This pattern is similar to the Tahitian regimen that has changed very little from traditional times. A group of boys gets together and asks a man known for his ability to operate on them. Parents are not told beforehand of the boys' plan to do this. A razor blade is now used to cut the skin, followed by bathing in the sea and application of herbal medicines. A fire is made with leaves and the boys heat the penis from the vapors and then bandage it (Levy 1973:118-119).

Marshall (1961, see below) reports that superincision, practiced among the ancient Ra'ivavaens, included sexuality education by a priest, as well as a training component in which the superincision scab was removed by copulation with an experienced woman. A boy cannot become a man, even among contemporary Ra'ivavaens, without the supercision. While specialists performed the superincision traditionally, any male with knowledge of the procedure may do so today. However, traditional elements persist in the technique, as well as in the removal of the scab through intercourse with the older experienced woman (Marshall 1961:248).

Superincision is a characteristic Polynesian practice. Although the foreskin is only slit, the outcome of exposing the boy's penis is the same as in circumcision, according to Davenport (1977:115-163). Although Davenport maintains that the dramatic ritual aspects of superincision have been lost, the genital operation continued at the time of his writing in 1976 in Polynesia.

Generally speaking, in the Polynesian area, women were not rigidly isolated when menstruating as in Melanesian groups. Like female puberty rituals throughout the world, the Marquesan girl's rite of passage is more continuous and less dramatic than the boys. Reproduction readiness was recognized by the growth of pubic hair. Kirkpatrick (1983) notes that if a menstruating female climbs a breadfruit tree, it is believed that the fruit will have blotched skin. In the old Society Islands, there was no ritual around menstruation, although at puberty, girls did receive tattoos on the buttocks. Menstruating women were not to enter gardens or touch plants. Levy reports in his early 1960s research that some traditional beliefs persist regarding menstruation among Tahitians. Apparently, young women who were menustrating were told to avoid getting chilled or eating cold foods, as this could result in *ma'i fa'a'i* (the filled sickness). It is believed that if a girl does not menstruate, and/or if she remains a virgin, the blood will fill her body and head and make her crazy, also leading to *ma'i fa'a'i*. One act of intercourse was believed necessary to ensure good menstruation (Levy 1973:124-126).

Premarital Sexual Activities and Relationships

Among traditional French Polynesian societies, and for Polynesia generally, there were two standards for premarital sex that varied by status and rank, according to Davenport (1976). For example, among the Tahitians, first-born daughters in lineages of firstborns were very sacred. As a consequence, their virginity was valued and protected until a marriage with a partner of suitably high status was arranged. Among these elite daughters, virginity was demonstrated, for example, by the display of a stained white bark cloth following coitus. Subsequent to the birth of their firstborn child, females of high rank were permitted to establish extramarital liaisons. On Pukapuka, according to Marshall Sahlins (1967), the chief kept a sacred virgin in his retinue as a symbol of his spiritual power.

Among the Margarevans and Marquesans, the only apparent restrictions on adolescent sexuality were incest, exogamy regulations, and/or the upper-class status of certain females. Premarital virginity was required for a chief's daughters but not for other youths. This pattern, according to Kirkpatrick (1983), continues even today, where concern for rules of exogamy and relatedness still persist among Marquesans. However, Marquesan youths may not be aware of their degree of relatedness to a potential partner when they begin a relationship, a source of concern to their elders.

Marshall's study of Ra'ivavae (1961), based on reports from the archives of ethnographer J. Frank Stimson, his own ethnographic research with elderly consultants, archaeological, and linguistic analysis, presents a picture of a highly eroticized Tahitian culture that has been largely dismantled by colonialism and Christianity.

The clitoris, among ancient Ra'ivavaens, received a great deal of cultural attention. Marshall reports that the clitoris was elongated by the child's mother through oral techniques as well as tying it with an hibiscus cord. An elongated clitoris was considered a mark of beauty. According to Marshall's research, the king would inspect a girl's clitoris to see if it was sufficiently elongated for her to marry. The girls who were ready for marriage would display their genital attributes at a sacred *marae* (Marshall 1961:272-273). Both cunnilingus and fellatio were practiced among traditional Marquesan youth and adults (Gregersen 1994:272; Marshall 1961).

Suggs (1966:71-73) describes contemporary Marquesan sex as including virtually no foreplay and lasting five or less minutes.

For the indigenous population of French Polynesia, the *taure'are'a* period in the life cycle is demarcated as a special status. *Taure'are'a* is part of a traditional pattern that continues today primarily in rural areas. In the Marquesas, adolescence includes a category known as *taure'are'a* that operates as a transitional period between childhood, *to'iki* (kid), and adulthood *'enana motua* (parent person). Kirkpatrick describes it as "errant youth" (1987:383-385). *Taure'are'a* are characterized by their sexual adventures and same-gender peer orientation. *Taure'are'a* are known for brief sexual liaisons in contrast to adult sexuality, which is integrated within the larger context of domesticity. As a period in the life cycle, *taure'are'a* is characterized by its pleasure-seeking goal and is looked back upon fondly by adults (Kirkpatrick 1987:387). *Taure'are'a* is regarded as a temporary status that gradually evolves into adulthood. It has one in which brief sexual encounters are replaced by relations and cohabitation with their partners (Levy 1973:123). It has also been argued that *taure'are'a* is a time of "testing relationships" through cohabitation with one or more partners serially (Elliston 1996).

According to Kirkpatrick (1983), peers are very important for the Marquesan youth, especially the finding of a confidant with whom one can share secrets, including sexual ones. Of apparent equal interest is the establishment of heterosexual relationships. These sexual liaisons must remain secret due to the rigid Christian sexual prohibition against premarital sex. For example, if pregnancy were to occur, the girl would be either forced into marriage or her relationship would be ended, although this is not true of Tahiti or other areas of French Polynesia. Peer relations are not severed with marriage, although one's behavior is expected to mature. Sexual gossip is considered normal for youths but not for adults. There is some expectation of a double standard for youthful males and females. Youthful females are expected to act more coy than their male counterparts. In the Marquesas of the late 1970s, males were the sexual initiators, while it was considered inappropriate for girls to take the lead. However, it is a cultural value that both partners should desire and enjoy sex.

Levy also reports on the *taure'are'a* period among rural Tahitians. *Taure'are'a* for Tahitians during the 1960s was very similar to that described for the Marquesans. For girls, *taure'are'a* status converged with menstruation and the development of secondary sexual characteristics. According to Levy, the girls' *taure'are'a* period is less distinctive than the boys in terms of role contrast with childhood norms (Levy 1973:117-122). For boys, *taure'are'a* status does not begin with superincision, but occurs gradually over the next year or two following it.

In Piri (a pseudonym), Levy notes that most youngsters had sexual intercourse between 13 and 16 years of age. Virginity was regarded as unusual for *taure'are'a* males and females, although shifting demographics, with the migration of *taure'are'a* girls to Papeete, seems to be having an impact on the prevalence of virginity. At the time of Levy's research

(1962-64), the *taure'are'a* male was the initiator in terms of making the arrangements for a sexual encounter (Levy 1973:122-124).

Douglas Oliver's *Two Tahitian Villages* (1981), historically situated in 1954-1955, offers a detailed enthnography of social life, life stages, sexual behavior, courtship, marriage, and relationships in two rural villages on Huahine and Mo'orea. Oliver's male Tahitian consultants began having intercourse between the ages of 12- and 15-years old. According to Oliver, the standard position was male on top. Male foreplay, which typically lasted from five minutes to half an hour, included: "breast fondling and kissing, clitoral manipulation, and cunnilingus; mutual orgasms were expected and . . . nearly always achieved" (1981:274).

Night crawling/creeping is a traditional practice that continues even today in various forms throughout Polynesia. It is known as *moe totolo* among Samoans and *motoro* among Mangaians and Tahitians. There is some controversy among anthropologists as to the function and meaning of this institution. Oliver (1989) regards night crawling/creeping as resulting from sleeping arrangements in which family members shared the same sleeping quarters. It seems to be embedded in the *taure'are'a* pattern for adventure by both females and males.

Night crawling is characterized by the efforts of a young man to sneak into the house of a sleeping young woman and copulate with her without her parents finding out. Apparently, this could be accomplished either with collusion from the young female or without her prior consent. In the latter case, the belief was that the suitor would penetrate the young female while she was asleep; and, if she awoke, she would enjoy it so much she would not want to scream and alert her parents. Oliver (1989) offers a different explanation, suggesting that the parents may have abetted the situation if their daughter was without suitors by making arrangements for a young man to sneak into their home, and then deliberately catching the couple and forcing them to get married. Levy reported that *motoro* continued among Tahitians in Piri at the time of his research, but that the pattern was on the decline (1973:123).

C. Adults

Cohabitation, Marriage, Family, and Sex

Adult interpersonal heterosexual behaviors, like other aspects of French Polynesian sexuality, must be placed within its cultural context. Oliver (1974, 1981, 1989) has reported that the traditional Tahitians, both premaritally and maritally, experienced sexuality with great joy and gusto, and that this value was expressed in the wider culture through styles of interaction and verbal banter, religion, entertainments, mythology, etc. This ties in with William Davenport's analysis of the "erotic codes" of Polynesia, defined as those symbolic aspects of culture that "both arouse sexuality and enhance its expression" (1977:127). Davenport's 1977 essay on "Sex in Cross-Cultural Perspective" is very useful in summarizing this cultural framework and describing intracultural variations.

Marriage was traditionally restricted between individuals by status in the chiefly structure and lineage. Upper ranks were not permitted to marry lower ranks. Formal marriages were relegated to the upper and perhaps middle echelons (Oliver 1989b). Although couples of disparate status were not usually permitted to marry, they could cohabit, although they were dissuaded from having children (Oliver 1974). Divorce was traditionally handled flexibly with the couple returning to her or his own family. They were then free to remarry. There was no formal legal divorce in premodern Polynesia, according to Weckler (1943).

Beauty and sex were closely linked in Polynesia, although in Old Tahiti it was most pronounced. In Tahiti, because large size was a symbol of beauty, higher ranked boys and girls were secluded, overfed, and prevented from exercise so that they could put on weight. Subsequently, they were displayed in all their pale and fat beauty so as to attract a potential spouse. According to Ford and Beach (1951), Pukapukans also liked plump builds on men and women. Apparently, the Tahitian's value on beauty was reiterated in the belief that a baby could have several biological fathers who would contribute their respective physical traits. Since extramarital, as well as premarital sex was accepted, women would select attractive and athletic young men as sexual partners. In the traditional Marquesas, Ford and Beach (1951) noted that elongated labia majora were considered attractive. Levy has uncovered an ethnotheory of relationships that suggests couples must have a physical compatibility. This is in contrast to one-night trysts in which one person may be as good as another (1973:129).

In the mid-1950s Aeta and Fatata, Tahitian attractiveness norms favored physical types that were neither too thin nor too fat. Aside from the veiled-bride weddings in which chastity, or at least evidence of strong parental control over the daughter's social behavior, was a prerequisite, previous sexual experience was not unexpected (Oliver 1981:291-292). See below for Oliver's (1981) typology of Tahitian weddings.

The sexual practices of indigenous French Polynesians include cultural-religious institutions. Gregersen's (1983) review of Oceanic sexual practices makes note of the *arioi* cult. This was an organization of Tahitian men and women divided into sects, located throughout the Society Islands, who traveled within the archipelago as singers, dancers, athletes, and sexual exhibitionists. Eroticism pervaded the Tahitian songs and dances of the *arioi* entertainers. The *arioi* members were allowed free sexual expression on their journeys, but they were not allowed to marry or have children. This organization was embedded with religious meaning and has been interpreted as a fertility cult. The *arioi* practiced abortion and infanticide, because having children was not permitted for the member. Should an *arioi* become a parent, he or she was humiliated and their participation in the cult limited. The *arioi* were well known for their sexual pursuits with one another and with noncult members encountered on their journeys. Members were selected on the basis of physical beauty and talent that transcended chiefly boundaries to include commoners as well.

Sex and eroticism were made public in other ways as well. Linton's 1939 report of the Marquesans revealed that naked dancing, along with public group copulation, was practiced as part of feasting and festivals as a pre-Christian traditional pattern. Linton disclosed that women would pride themselves on the number of men they had sex with. In ancient times, Pukapukans of the Tuamotu Archipelago would reserve places called *ati*, where men and women could go for sex parties. These were organized by a person who also acted as a guard, to prevent conflict by angry ex-lovers and husbands (Gregerson 1983).

One of Marshall's (1961:273) Ra'ivavaen consultants contended that, in traditional times, public sex followed men's prayers in the sacred temples. According to this particular consultant, various positions were used, cunnilingus was practiced, and "sperm was smeared upon the face and in the hair as a kind of mono'i' (coconut oil)" (Marshall 1961:273; Elliston 1996). Ceremonial copulation was integrated within the spiritual ethos, which, according to Marshall, was saturated with eroticism as a central theme. The erotic was related to fertility, reproduction, and the sacred.

Polynesian societies have been distinguished by a position for coitus at variance from the Western "missionary" position, as the Polynesians refer to the male-prone-above-prone-female position. According to Oliver (1989b), the "Oceanic position" was traditionally far more popular than the missionary position. The "Oceanic position" is one in which the couple sat facing each other. Other positions included the man squatting or kneeling between the woman's legs and pulling her toward him, lying side-by-side facing one another, or with the woman's back to the man's front. In the Marquesas, a sitting position was reported where the woman sat astride the man's lap or assumed a side-to-side lying position. A variety of sexual positions were used, although the woman on top seems to have been the more-prevalent position related to the generalized Polynesian concern for the sexual pleasure of women. The most common position taken today seems to be the missionary position, which is undoubtedly a result of Christian missionary efforts (Gregersen 1983).

Delayed ejaculation for the man was considered a valued expertise in Old Polynesia because it facilitated the female partner's pleasure. Multiple orgasms were valued by both partners in traditional Polynesia as well. Although there was a lesser emphasis on foreplay and more concern with intercourse, the Marquesans were known for practicing cunnilingus and fellatio. Coitus interruptus was also reported among the Marquesans. According to Ford and Beach (1951), the Pukapukans had no preference for sex during the day or at night; each was just as likely.

Kissing among Polynesians is a Western custom. The traditional Tahi-tian/Polynesian kiss (*ho'i*) consisted of mutual sniffing and rubbing of noses on the face. According to Levy (1973:128),

> kissing on the mouth is still considered a mild perversion. Contempo-rary Tahitian foreplay according to younger male Pirians includes: "kissing, fondling the woman's breasts, and occasionally cunnilingus." Fellatio was considered a practice of "bad girls" in Papeete. (Levy 1973:123)

Intercourse among Pirian youth continues the traditional pattern that emphasizes the female orgasm. A man is humiliated by not bringing his partner to orgasm. The role of the clitoris in women's pleasure, as in traditional times, still is part of people's sexual knowledge. In Piri, it is referred to as *teo*. Linguistic evidence provided by the term *'ami'ami* suggests a precontact focus on eroticism. It is considered a unique capability of some women who can contract and relax the vaginal muscles during coitus (Levy 1973:128). Elliston (1996) notes that Sahlins makes reference to the Ha-waiian term *'amo'amo* in *Islands of History*, writing: "Girls were taught the *'amo'amo*[,] the 'wink-wink' of the vulva, and the other techniques that 'make the thighs rejoice'" (p. 10).

Surveys on the frequencies of sex for traditional indigenous French Polynesians at various points in history are sparse, although qualitative reports found in the ethnographic literature are available for some of this area. Suggs's 1956-58 study, *Marquesan Sexual Behavior* (1966), combines qualitative and quantitative data. Frequencies for Marquesan adolescents are sometimes said to be more than ten times in a single night. This may be compared to frequencies for older married couples that are reported of from five times a night to two to three times a week. Questions of accuracy and bias must be considered in evaluating this data. Levy's Pirian male consultants reported that sex occurred daily in the first year or two of a steady relationship, but dropped to about one to three times a week, declining after several years to once every two or three weeks or once a month. A sex-positive attitude is evident as there is no indication of sanc-tioning of sex among the elderly. Sex continues up to two to three weeks prior to childbirth and is resumed in one to two months. However, sex is prohibited during menstruation (Levy 1973:125-126).

Data on contemporary sexuality in French Polynesia are not abundant. A sexual survey was considered in Tahiti under Le Direction de la Santé Publique in 1993, but had not been initiated as of early 1997. Spiegel and colleagues (1991) have provided recent sexual data collected between October and December 1990 on seventy-four sexually active women be-tween the ages of 18 and 44 who were working in bars or nightclubs. It must be noted that this sample is not at all representative of the population at large. The median number of sexual partners among this group was 3 (range 1 to 200), and the median number of sexual encounters was 104 (range 12 to 1,095). This segment of the population is important because of their risk for contacting and spreading sexually transmitted diseases.

Marriage patterns in traditional French Polynesia included monogamy, serial monogamy, polygyny, and polyandry. For example, Oliver (1974) observes that elite chiefs were required to engage in monogamy; lower male chiefs could have two to three wives, although only one wife's children could inherit titles and property. The middle and lower classes of Tahiti were known to have been polygynous. The Marquesas were known for polyandry. An elite woman's household might include a primary as well as secondary husbands (*pekio*). The secondary husbands were subordinate to the primary husband and performed menial duties, although as members of elite households, they had privileges associated with the aristocracy (Goldman 1970:142). According to Thomas's 1987 review of gender in the Marquesas, polyandry is better understood as part of domestic relations rather than conjugal relations per se. However, Goldman asserts that an unequal sex ratio of 2.5 men to one woman may account for the pattern (1970:142). Commoners practiced cohabitation rather than the formalized marriages of the privileged classes.

The Marquesans traditionally engaged in a ritual in which the husband was required to have intercourse with his wife almost immediately after childbirth. Following expulsion of the afterbirth, the wife would bathe in a stream. It was believed that intercourse should then occur while the wife was in the stream in order to stifle the flow of the bleeding.

In contemporary French Polynesia, marriage is legitimized by the Church although most people are not formally married. The Protestant Marquesans must be married before membership in the Church is granted. The transition from the secret liaison to marriage signals a dramatic change from youth to adulthood (Kirkpatrick 1983). On Ra'ivavae, Marshall found that of thirty-one marriages, twenty-nine couples had cohabited (1961:275). This continues the traditional pattern of premarital sex despite a Christian overlay.

Nonlegalized adoption, a common pattern throughout Polynesia, must be interpreted in the context of the social organization of the family. Kirkpatrick (1983) has noted that the traditional Marquesans had a pattern of large multicouple households that included not only extended families, but also others not closely related. Such households may have been indicative of wealth. This pattern would also include children whose biological parents were unable to raise them for a variety of reasons. Although this kind of adoption or fosterage is not legal in colonial French Polynesia, it is socially instituted and informally practiced. It represents an old and more widespread Polynesian pattern of fluid adoption that may include close kin, more-distant kin, and even those not directly related.

The trend in the Marquesas in the late 1970s was toward nuclear conjugal family dwellings. This represents the influence of Catholicism as well as broader Western trends. However, the traditional pattern of foster parents and casual adoption still continues today. Kirkpatrick (1983) found that on Ua Pou, 19 percent of the individuals in the households were unrelated to the household head. Tahitians have a similar pattern of fosterage. Levy reports that 25 percent of the Tahitian children were not residing with their biological parents at the time of his research (1973:474-483).

Polynesian childrearing patterns have continued to persist despite the social disruption caused by exploitation, missionization, and colonialism. The Ritchie's (1983) have identified several common themes delineating traditional Polynesian childrearing. Among these are fosterage and adoption as part of a wider pattern of community investment in children. Because the community was traditionally composed of lineages of related people, parenting was a collective endeavor, unlike that in the West where it is exclusive to the nuclear family. Howard and Kirkpatrick note that adoption continues today to function as a mechanism to foster relationships between families at the community level and to create alliances at a more macro level (1989:87). There are economic and ecological implications as well. Adoption of children may help a family with domestic labor since children have certain tasks to do. As they mature, they become important economic contributors for a household. Adoption is also "a powerful adaptive mechanism for equitably distributing people relative to resources, including land, in island environments" (Howard and Kirkpatrick 1989). In addition, early indulgence of infants was followed by an expectation of autonomy for children beginning around 2 to 3 years of age. Peer socialization began with sibling care and responsibility for younger siblings, and included larger community groups of peers who spanned a broad age range from 2 to 20 years old.

Extramarital Sex

Extramarital sex was also part of precolonial French Polynesian cultures. The Pukapukans celebrated a successful fishing expedition with extramarital sex. Apparently, women would initiate sexual joking as the men returned with their catch. This was followed by trysts in the bush. Both single and married people participated in these extramarital opportunities with no opposition from their spouse, provided they respected class and incest prohibitions (Oliver 1989b). Among the Tahitians, restrictions on sexuality occurred for upper-class women, sometimes before as well as after marriage, although men and women of common status were free to participate in extramarital sex (Oliver 1989b; Davenport 1977).

There were, therefore, two standards in effect for traditional Tahitians—one for commoners and others, and one for the very elite. Firstborn children, in genealogical lines of firstborns, were regarded as very high ranking and sacred. Purity of the genealogical line was important and controlled through rules against premarital and extramarital sex until, at least, the woman gave birth to a successor. Then, she was permitted extramarital freedom. For example, Douglas Oliver notes that married *ari'i* women were notoriously promiscuous (Personal communication with Oliver 1994). Elite women were known to separate from their husbands and to establish their own residence and have lovers (Oliver 1974). Men and women of common status faced no restrictions on extramarital sex (Davenport 1976, Oliver 1989).

On Tahiti, according to Sahlins (1976), a male chief who produced an illegitimate heir practiced infanticide unless measures were taken to alter the status of the mother to be equal to that of the chief. On Mangareva, the chief's power was such that the rule of prohibition against marriage to a first cousin was often disregarded.

Extramarital sex was also institutionalized in the Society Islands in terms of sexual hospitality. Male *taiō* participated in a form of formal friendship relations where sexual intercourse was permitted with one's married *taiō*'s wife. *Taiō* of the opposite sex were not permitted intercourse because their relationship was a social siblinghood and prevented by the incest taboo (Oliver 1974; Ferdon 1981). Sexual hospitality is regarded by some researchers as a widespread Polynesian pattern (Gregerson 1983).

Among the Pukapukans, adultery was believed to cause delayed delivery, and women in such situations were expected to confess (Gregersen 1983:255). Kirkpatrick (1983) did not find extramarital affairs practiced on Ua Pou, although Suggs (1966) reported that extramarital affairs were common in the Marquesas during his sojourn there. However, according to Goldman (1970:585) precontact adultery could have dire consequences, resulting in murder by jealous husbands and possible suicide by the wife of an adulterous husband. Suggs (1966:119-120) reveals that at the time of his research, although adultery was condemned, it still occurred. However, it caused jealousy and hard feelings among both sexes if found out.

Although adultery was the primary cause of breakups and divorce in Aeta and Fatata in the mid-1950s, it was not reason enough by itself. Oliver's Tahitian consultants regarded adultery as something any Tahitian, given an opportunity, would be likely to do (1981:317). While church pastors in both villages declared adultery as a sin and cause for explusion, the Tahitian attitude was more relaxed, reflecting a double standard of greater tolerance of male adultery than female (p. 334).

6. Homoerotic, Homosexual, and Ambisexual Behaviors

A. Children and Adolescents

Some Tahitian upper-class men, according to Douglas Oliver, kept boys in their household for sex, although this was not a widespread practice. Suggs (1966:24) states that homosexual experiences among boys, and possibly girls, were common among Marquesan adolescents.

B. Adults

Since first colonial contact, the indigenous peoples of Polynesia have been engaged in culture change and transformation. Indigenous systems of homosexual options may be influenced, or even reinvigorated, by the advent of Western homosexual identities. For French Polynesia, it is necessary to point to this complexity in order to understand homosexuality/bisexuality from a cultural perspective that is not a Western-based psychological model.

There were two forms of homosexual behavior in ancient Tahiti. Some Tahitian *ari'i* men, according to Oliver (1989), kept boys in their household for sex. The other context for homosexual expression was associated with the *māhū* status. The *māhū* was a transvestic tradition that included homosexual practices with nontransvestic males. It is important to note that since the *māhū* is a transgendered category, the term homosexual is not really an appropriate descriptor for *māhū* sexuality. Swallowing semen was believed by Tahitians to foster masculine vigor (Gregersen 1994:274). The indigenous pattern of the *māhū* is not an equivalent to Western subcultural homosexuality or Western transvestism, but was an integrated part of the wider Tahitian culture. The homosexual aspects of the *māhū* status were not its most significant features, but rather it was the cross-gendered aspects of dress and behaviors that identified one as a *māhū*. The *māhū* is reported throughout Polynesia and was found among the Marquesans, where it was very similar to the Tahitian form, according to Oliver (1989). Ferdon (1981) found evidence that the *māhū* began dressing in women's attire while very young. (See Section 7 on gender variation for further discussion.)

Data on Western-type homosexuality in contemporary French Polynesia is sparse. Chanteau et al. (1986) distinguish the presence of a male homosexual community of Polynesian men that frequented hotels, bars, restaurants, and night clubs of Tahiti (presumably in Papeete). This population was considered at high risk for LAV/HTLV-III infection by Chanteau et al. who conducted a serological survey. (See discussion on HIV/AIDS below.) The population recruited for the serological survey consisted of fifty transvestite homosexuals known as *raerae*. Forty percent of this population had only one partner and frequency of intercourse was once a week. Eighty-five percent of this group had intercourse only once a month. Some of this population had had plastic surgery and female hormone therapy. It is difficult from this report to assess the character of this population, since there are a number of possible gendered identities.

Spiegel and colleagues (1991) collected data from 156 male homosexuals aged 13 to 54 between October and December 1990. The annual median number of sexual partners was 9.5 (range 1 to 600) and the median number of sexual encounters was 156 (range 2 to 5,810). Of this population, 56.4 percent were transvestites. Unfortunately, it is not possible to place the transvestites in the cultural milieu, as sampling information was not provided by the researchers. Nor is it possible to determine the social identity of the transvestites in terms of the *māhū*, Western gay transvestism, a modern synthesis of both patterns, or some other identity (Williams 1986:255-258). These transvestites are employed in bars, hotels, and nightclubs. Apparently a *raerae* subcultural expression is found in the Miss Tane and Miss Male beauty contests. It should be noted here that the Western term transvestite is not really appropriate in describing the complexity of transgendered identities and homosexualities of French Polynesia.

Levy also records the introduction of the term *raerae* to refer to homosexual and lesbian behavior. While Pirians maintained lesbian behavior (oral and mutual masturbation) did not occur on Piri, it was believed common in Papeete in the bar scene. It was not considered part of a lesbian orientation but rather context-specific. Women who engaged in lesbian encounters were not stigmatized, according to Levy 1973:139-141, but more recent research indicates that lesbian lifestyles are problematic in Tahiti (Elliston 1996).

7. Gender Conflicted Persons

In discussing transgendered individuals among indigenous populations, Western-based terminology, such as "transsexualism" or gender dysphoria, are inappropriate since they refer to twentieth-century Western psychiatrically derived categories. The expression of cross-gender or transgender roles needs to be understood in the sociocultural context and not viewed from the Western perspective as "deviant" behavior. Levy (1971, 1973) has provided some of the most significant research on this subject in his study of the *māhū* of Tahiti. The *māhū* was a transgendered role for males who dressed and took on the social and occupational roles of Tahitian women including taboos and restrictions. According to Levy, the *māhū* tradition has continued from precontact times, although attributes of the status have changed somewhat, so that today the *māhū* no longer cross-dresses, but still engages in work that is considered traditionally female, such as household activities. Levy considers the *māhū* a role variant for men. An interesting parameter of the *māhū* in rural Tahiti is that a man can be "*māhū*-ish" without being *māhū*. *Māhū* are regarded as being "natural," yet one does not have to remain *māhū* throughout the life course. There is a conception of effeminacy associated with *māhū*. *Māhū* are not stigmatized nor are their heterosexual male partners. According to Levy, "a *māhū* is seen as a substitute female" (1973:34). In Piri, the *māhū* are not believed to practice sodomy, but are fellators of other men.

As mentioned previously, this institution was widespread throughout Polynesia. The *māhū* engaged in fellatio with nontransvestite male partners, but these partners were not considered *māhū* or homosexual. *Māhū*s were also reported to have been sex partners of chiefs. This suggests that the Polynesian gender paradigm is one in which sex and gender are discrete categories and the *māhū* identity functioned to highlight gender differences. Levy suggests that the *māhū* may be analyzed as an embodied warning to other males on how to avoid nonmale behavior.

In Tahiti, the *māhū* continues to be regarded as a natural phenomenon. While various explanations are offered for its occurrence, the *māhū* is generally a nonstigmatized status and accepted within wider Tahitian society. According to Kirkpatrick (1983), the Ua Pou Marquesans note that there are no *māhū* in their area today because the *māhū* have migrated to Tahiti. Kirkpatrick describes the *māhū* as an ambiguously or disvalued status. The Marquesans also have a more recently introduced term, *raerae*, which is used interchangeably with *māhū*. The Marquesan *māhū* are not considered women, but rather men who want to act as women. The significant attributes for the Marquesan gender paradigm in terms of *māhū* status relate to occupation and appropriate peer relations, rather than homosexual behavior per se.

Kirkpatrick (1983) reports on the Marquesan *vehine mako*, or shark woman, which is a gender-variant identity for females. Unlike the *māhū*, the *vehine mako* is not based on relational or occupational criteria. Instead, the shark woman is characterized by an aggressive and vigorous sexuality. The defining feature of *vehine mako* woman is that she is a sexual initiator, an activity defined as masculine. Thus, both the *māhū* and *vehine mako* are defined in terms of the reversal of gender-role attributes. However, *vehine mako* is not a female equivalent of the *māhū*, or recognized as a form of female homosexuality. Levy regards the institution of the *māhū* as a boundary-maintenance mechanism that identifies the limits of what is considered conventional male and female gender behavior, i.e., masculinity and femininity. Whether this applies to the *vehine mako* must be determined by further research.

8. Significant Unconventional Sexual Behaviors

A. Coercive Sex

Douglas Oliver's (1974) intensive research could not find evidence of rape in the precolonial Society Islands and according to J. E. Weckler, "rape is practically unknown in (traditional) Polynesia" (1943:57). However, today, rape does occur. According to one anthropologist with a research background in Tahitian culture, first encounters with a young girl are often forced by the young man. Levy's consultants argued that *haree* (rape) may have occurred in the past on Piri, but it does not occur today. Levy found no reports of violent rape on the island of Huahine in which Piri is located (1973:124). More recently, Elliston (1996) reported rape and attempted rape on Huahine and in Papeete.

B. Prostitution

Oliver reports that prostitution, as defined in the West, was associated with European contact and exploitation of the Pacific. In Old Polynesia, there were opportunities for women in the royal courts to entertain visitors sexually. These positions were not stigmatized in the least. One consultant reports that today, in the Westernized and urbanized city of Papeete, prostitution is not uncommon, although statistics were not available at the time of this writing. Stanley also reported that today there is evidence of male prostitution among some transvestites (1992:34).

C. Pornography and Erotica

Information was not available at the time of this writing. The sexual survey of La Direction de la Santé Publique (1995: see address in Section 13B) is expected to address this.

D. Paraphilia

It is especially important here to specify the culture of derivation in discussing unconventional behaviors. What is unconventional from Western perspectives is not necessarily regarded so from the indigenous view. Generally, the Pacific peoples have a low incidence of Western categories of paraphilia. In fact, Gregersen's review of the literature of Oceania revealed only the two rather suspicious reports described below. Archival data on which these reports are based may be inaccurate and even fanciful. It is with caution that these are presented here.

According to Gregersen (1983; 1987:278), among the precolonial Pukapukans, a form of sexual contact with corpses was said to have occurred. In this group, a strong aversion to corpses was expressed in *tabu*. Contact with corpses was prohibited and friends were not even permitted to look at the dead. This *tabu* was mitigated in certain circumstances by the belief that the "grief of a cousin will be naturally so intense that the tabus will be broken—not only by looking at the corpse but even embracing it and sometimes having intercourse with it." This violation of the corpse *tabu* was referred to with a special term, *wakaavanga*. Although contact with corpses was *tabu*, such behavior was expected of cousins. Archival data on which this report is based may or may not be inaccurate and is subject to Western and historical bias.

Gregerson (1983) also notes that sexual contact with animals occurred among the Marquesans when partners were unavailable. Men were known to have sex with chickens, dogs, and even horses, while women were said to have lured dogs into performing cunnilingus on them. However, this account may also be in need of further investigation of its accuracy.

From the vantage of the indigenous peoples of French Polynesia, there was one behavior that was considered sexually deviant. The celibate role of the priest is considered at great variance with male Marquesan ways of being, according to Kirkpatrick (1983). This role is considered distinctive and deviant with the nature of Marquesan masculinity.

9. Contraception, Abortion, and Population Planning

A/B/C. Attitudes, Practices, Teenage Pregnancies, and Abortion

In precolonial Tahitian times of the latter 1700s, discussion of teen pregnancies must be situated within the cultural and historical context. The *taure'are'a* was a period of sexual freedom during adolescence, and this, combined with fosterage, testifies that teenage pregnancy was not problematic and should not be interpreted in terms of Western concerns over teenage pregnancy, where the cultural ideal is delayed pregnancy until young adulthood. It was not unusual among traditional indigenous societies for pregnancy to occur during the teenage years; in many cultures it was the norm. Today, according to one consultant with Tahitian cultural experience, grandparents may adopt the child, while teenage marriage is much rarer.

The precontact Tahitians practiced infanticide and abortion on occasion. The stratification by class was castelike and intermixing was strictly prohibited. The offspring of parents who were respectively from an upper- and lower-class status was strangled at birth. The *arioi* society members were prohibited from producing offspring, since children would be a hinderance to the many religious activities required by cult membership (Ferdon 1981). Abortion and infanticide were practiced not only by *arioi* members, but also in cases where *arioi* couples of two different class levels conceived. In these cases, infanticide had no connection with population control, but was practiced instead to counter a violation of interclass marriage. This was tied to the status system in which titles and positions were inherited through chiefly lineages. Infanticide was practiced in situations in which either a woman's child was conceived with a male of lower rank or in which a man's child was conceived with a woman of lower rank. Although, according to Goldman, male infanticide was more common on Tahiti, Marquesan female infanticide was prevalent enough to result in a ratio in which men far outnumbered women (1970:563).

In the villages of Aeta and Fatata, mixed attitudes were voiced on contraception, although few, if any, used contraceptives regularly. According to Oliver, only "some [from both villages] . . . knew of the existence of contraceptive devices, mainly condoms (1981:341).

While attitudes about abortion was varied in these two Tahitian villages, it was generally viewed as the concern of the individual. A folk abortificient, a blend of green pineapple and lemon juices, was available from older women specialists and believed to cause miscarriage within two months (Oliver 1981:34).

D. Population Control Efforts

Information could not be obtained by the author at the time of this publication. See La Direction de la Santé Publique "Sexual Survey" (1995: see address in Section 13B).

10. Sexually Transmitted Diseases

In Tahiti, testing for STDs is available at STD and maternity public clinics. There is a dearth of information on the epidemiological study of chlamydia in the Pacific Islands, with the exception of one study in New Caledonia. Chungue et al. (1988) have examined the rate of chlamydia trachomatis in three populations of at-risk individuals in order to illustrate the importance of specific diagnostic testing for monitoring of this infection. Chlamydia was found in 53 percent of fifty-three bar women (ages 15 to 45), 24 percent of seventy-five women attending a public maternity clinic for routine care (ages 14 to 40), and 37 percent of seventy-one men attending a sexually transmitted disease clinic with acute or subacute urethritis (ages 17 to 37).

Neisseria gonorrhoea infection was associated with chlamydia infection in 11.4 percent of the bar women and 18.3 percent of the men with urethritis. Of the chlamydia-positive women, 58.3 percent of the bar women and 23.2 percent of the women at the maternity clinic were without clinical complaints. Eight bar women (15 percent) were infected with trichomonas vaginalis. This study proves that chlamydia trachomatis is common in Tahiti and warns that asymptomatic women who are chlamydia-positive may be vectors for the spread of the disease. The authors have proposed routine testing for chlamydia trachomatis in STD or maternity clinics.

According to a 1984 public health report by John A. R. Miles, in 1971 three cases of syphilis were reported, but by 1977, the rate was 23 per 10,000. The rate of gonorrhea is 27 per 10,000.

11. HIV/AIDS

A. Incidence, Patterns, and Trends

Several important surveys have been conducted regarding HIV in the French Polynesian population. Chanteau et al. (1986) conducted a serological survey screening for anti-LAV/HTLV-III antibodies using Institut Pasteur and Abbot Laboratories immunoassay kits. Four populations considered high risk were tested. These included eighty homosexual and transvestite men of low-SES (socioeconomic status); thirty-seven homosexual/bisexual men of Polynesian, European, and Chinese ethnic background of middle- or upper-SES, thirty-five female prostitutes, and thirty-three blood transfusion patients. Four positive results were obtained from the group of thirty-seven homosexual/bisexual men; three Europeans and one Chinese were positive. This group was a highly traveled population that appears to be the source of the introduction of LAV/HTLV-III in French Polynesia. Nicholson and colleagues (1992) measured the prevalence of HTLV-I using the ELISA test and confirmation by Western Blot in 19,975 blood samples from Australia and the western Pacific. No antibody was detected in the 198 sera from the French Polynesian population. However, a 1989 study by Alandry et al., a 1991 report by Spiegel et al., and research by Gras et al. (1992) all report evidence of HIV and AIDS in French Polynesia.

These researchers suggest that HIV was introduced in French Polynesia as early as 1973. Factors contributing to the introduction and spread of HIV include blood transfusions prior to August 1985, tourism primarily from continental France and the United States, and certain groups of individuals whose behaviors put them at risk.

The Allandry (1991) report on HIV is based on data collected over three years. In June 1988, 27,000 HIV tests were given, including 16,881 blood donors. Of the 27,000, forty-five were seropositive; none of the blood donors were HIV-positive. While an additional two children not older than 18 months were HIV-positive, these were not included in the study per se. The age breakdowns for the HIV-positive individuals are: 18 months to 6 years, 1; 20 to 29 years old, 24; 30 to 39 years, 10; 40 to 49 years, 8; 50 years and over, 2.

Of the thirty-two HIV-positive men and thirteen HIV-positive women, twenty-two are of Polynesian ancestry, nineteen are European, and four are Asiatic. Twenty-two are homosexual or bisexual males (48.8 percent), twelve are polytransfusions recipients (26.6 percent), six are partners of HIV-positive people (13.3 percent), three are heterosexuals with multiple partners, and two are former drug users. Based on this data, the rate of HIV-positives is 2.4 per 10,000.

Only 1 (0.7 percent) of the 147 homosexuals screened by Spiegel et al (1991) showed a positive result. A subsequent screening of 156 male homosexuals, among whom 56.4 percent are transvestites working in hotels, night clubs, and restaurants, and seventy-four sexually active females working in bars, was conducted between October and December, 1990. Among the male homosexuals 13- to 54-years old, 3, (1.9 percent) are positive for HTLV-I. Among the seventy-four females 18- to 44-years old, 3 (4.1 percent) are positive. The median number of sexual partners was 9.5 and the median number of sexual encounters was 156 in male homosexuals, while for the female population, the median number of partners was 3 and the median number of sexual encounters was 104 for the period of October to December, 1990. Among the total population of 230 subjects, 2 are IV drug users, but both are HTLV-I negative. The authors concluded that the risk for HTLV-I infection among male homosexuals is increasing, and the infection is also present in a female population at risk.

Gras et al. (1992) reported on ninety-six cases of HIV-positive and AIDS-infected persons. Of these, 78 percent were between 21 and 40 years old, seventy-two of the ninety-six had acquired HIV through sexual contact, and 94 percent live in Tahiti. The sex ratio was 2.8 males/1 female. Fifty-five percent were Europeans, 38 percent Polynesians, and 7 percent Asiatic. Gras estimates the rate of new HIV infection at 20 new cases per year in a French Polynesian population of 200,000, with 150 cases of AIDS per 1 million inhabitants. The rate of prevalence of HIV-positive cases between 1987 and 1990 per 100,000 was a mean of 9.45, a median of 9.65, and the extremes of 7.2 and 11.4. As of June 21, 1993, thirty cases of AIDS were reported for French Polynesia, according to the regional office for the Western Pacific of the World Health Organization (1993:9). Twenty-two cases were reported for 1979-90, five AIDs cases for 1991 with a rate of 2.7, and three in 1992 for a rate of 1.6, with no cases reported as of July, 1993.

The ELISA test can be performed in only six laboratories on the Island of Tahiti. A Western Blot confirmation test is required for the HIV-positive cases. HIV-positive patients are provided sex education on condom use and follow-up of asymptomatic individuals continues for six months. Treatment may be either by a private physician or under the Chef du Service de Medecine du Centre Hospitalier Territorial. A medical exam for the occurrence of opportunistic diseases is also available. Individuals with AIDS may be treated with AZT and pentamidine.

B. Availability of Treatment and Prevention Programs

Government policies contribute to the tracking of HIV through readily available testing at hospitals and public health centers. Testing may be done at the following centers: Le Centre de Transfusion Sanguine, Le Centre Hospitalier Territorial, L'Institut Territorial de Recherches Medicale Louis Malarde (Centre des Maladies Sexuellement Transmissibles, Centre de Lutte contre la Tuberculose). La Direction de la Santé Publique en Polynésie Française has been mandated by the Bureau d'Education to teach safe sex practices. A December 1985 law requires testing of blood donors. In 1986, a consulting commission for HIV was formed along with efforts at follow-up. Since 1987, condoms may be imported tax-free. In 1990, free and anonymous testing was made available to the public. In monitoring HIV, the French Polynesian Public Health Service and health authorities have implemented HIV-serum surveillance following World Health Organization guidelines. Twenty thousand screening tests for both HIV I and HIV II are done on a population of less than 200,000. Thus far, only HIV I has been found.

12. Sexual Dysfunction, Counseling, and Therapies

A. Concepts of Sexual Dysfunction

Sexual dysfunction must be considered within the cultural context. For example, sexual dreams with orgasm among Levy's rural Tahitians were thought to be the work of spirits and were regarded as "dangerous" (Levy 1973:129). The concept of "dangerous" is not translatable as a sexual dysfunction, but neither is it considered desirable.

Hooper (1985:158-198) collected ethnomedical data in two rural Tahitian communities on the Iles Sou-le-Vent, a group of islands northwest of

Tahiti in the 1960s. Indigenous folk medicine continues despite the cultural disruption caused by missionization and colonialism and the introduction of Western medicine. Hooper describes a form of "ghost sickness" with sexual implications. Ghost sickness, *mai tūpapa'u*, is a special category of illness that is believed to be caused by *tūpapa'u*. Such illnesses are characterized by their "bizarre" aspects and can only be cured by an indigenous healer, a *tahu'a*. *Tūpapa'u* is an incorporal aspect of the self, distinct yet coexisting along with the Christian notion of the soul. Each person has a *tūpapa'u* that can travel during one's dreams. When an individual dies, his *tūpapa'u* continues to remain in the vicinity watching over his kin. The *tūpapa'u* is regarded as having a personality and can be protective, but also vengeful and playful.

One form of ghost sickness entails visitations from *tūpapa'u* of the opposite sex. While erotic dreams are regarded as encounters with *tūpapa'u* of the opposite sex (no mention of same sex was made) and are therefore not really dreams at all, these are not regarded as problematic if they are occasional and the partners are varied. However, illness can occur if an individual becomes obsessed with a particular visiting *tūpapa'u*. In such a case of ghost sickness, the individual may lose weight, refuse sex with his or her spouse, and may be seen chatting and laughing with invisible *tūpapa'u*. Hooper describes the case of B, who refused sex with her husband. "She would bathe in the evenings, put on scented oil and special clothes, and lie on a separate bed, talking and laughing with a *tūpapa'u tāne* (male ghost)." A healer was called in who "commanded the *tūpapa'u* to leave and never return. B slept soundly for the rest of the night and had no more dealings with the male ghost again. According to . . . the healer . . . the ghost was 'ripped up' by his familiar" (Hooper 1985:178).

Levy's Pirian consultants reported that frigidity and impotence did not occur. The only conditions acknowledged as leading to impotence were illness or getting chilled. The Tahitian theory of sexual attraction may explain this, and clearly points to the importance of a relativistic perspective when regarding Western categories of sexual dysfunction. A Tahitian man who does not have an erection with a woman in an intimate situation, assumes that he must not want to have intercourse (Levy 1973:128-129).

13. Sexual Research and Advanced Education

A. Sexological Research

Sexual research concerning indigenous peoples of the area of French Polynesia includes the work of Richard Levy, as well as Douglas Oliver (1989a and 1989b, 1974), I. Goldman (1970), W. H. Davenport (1977), R. Linton (1939), and R. C. Suggs (1966) among others. In addition, contemporary sex research with a focus on HIV and at-risk sexual behaviors has been conducted by G. Alandry et al. (1989), C. Gras et al. (1992), and

Spiegel et al. (1991). La Direction de la Santé Publique conducted a sexual survey in November, 1993. The results were to be available in 1995, but were not published at the time of this writing. The interested reader is encouraged to write for the survey. There is no organized advanced education in sexuality in French Polynesia.

B. Major Sexological Surveys, Journals, and Organizations

Journals and periodicals in which sexological information, research, and reports on French Polynesia may be found include:

La Direction de la Santé Publique "Sexual Survey," Epistat CMRS Laure Yen, BP 611, Papeete-Tahiti, Polynésie Française

Counseil Economique Social et Cultural, Avenue Bruat, BP 1657, Papeete, Tahiti, Polynésie Française

Ministry of Social Affairs, P. O. Box 2551, Papeete, Tahiti, Polynésie Française

Institut Territorial de la Statistique, BP 395, Papeete, Tahiti, Polynésie Française

Service d'Information et de Documentation, BP 255, Papeete, Tahiti, Polynésie Française

Institut Territorial de Recherches Medicales, Louis Malarde, BP 30, Papeete, Tahiti, Polynésie Française

The Medical Journal of Australia, Australasian Medical Publishing Company, 1-5 Commercial Road, P. O. Box 410, Kingsgrove, New South Wales, 2208 Australia

Medecine Tropicale, Institut de Medecine Tropicale, Marseille Armee, France

Oceania University of Sydney, Oceania Publishing, Mackie Building, Sydney, New South Wales, 2006 Australia

Bernice P. Bishop Museum Bulletins, 1525 Bernice Street, Box 19000-A, Honolulu, HI 96817-0916, U.S.A.

Journal of the Polynesian Society, University of Auckland, Anthropology Department, Polynesian Society, Private Bag, Auckland, New Zealand

Journal de la Sociétédes Océanistes, The Association for Social Anthropology in Oceania.

The Journal of Pacific History
Pacific Studies
Australian and New Zealand Journal of Sociology

Acknowledgments

I am deeply indebted to Dr. Douglas Oliver who gave generously of his time in reading and commenting on this manuscript. His expertise and many works have been an invaluable source of knowledge and inspiration to me.

I would also like to thank Dr. Victoria Lockwood and Dr. Paul Shankman for their helpful suggestions for researching this subject. Dr. Deborah A. Elliston provided an extremely detailed commentary on this paper. Her research among the Tahitians has been critical in this review, as she provided thoughtful and up-to-date feedback. I am grateful to Linda Martindale for manuscript preparation, editing, computer magic, and reference research.

References and Suggested Readings

Alandry, G., et al. 1989. "Infection par le Virus de l'Immunodeficience Humaine (VIH) en Polynésie Française." *Medecine Tropicale*, 49(1):71-72.

Blackwood, E. 1986. "Breaking the Mirror: The Construction of Lesbianism and the Anthropological Discourse on Homosexuality." *Journal of Homosexuality*, 11(3-4):1-17.

Burrows, E. G. 1968. "Polynesia: Culture Areas in Polynesia." In A. P. Vayda, ed., *Peoples and Cultures of the Pacific*, (pp. 179-191). Garden City, NY: The Natural History Press.

Chanteau, S., F. Flye Sainte, M. E. Chungue, R. Roux, & J. M. Bonnardot. 1986. "A Serological Survey of AIDS in a High Risk Population in French Polynesia." *The Medical Journal of Australia*, 145(2):113.

Chungue, E., et al. 1988. "Chlamydia Trachomatis Genital Infections in Tahiti." *European Journal of Clinical Microbiology & Infectious Diseases*, 7(5):635-638.

Davenport, W. H. 1977. "Sex in Cross-Cultural Perspective." In F. A. Beach, ed., *Human Sexuality in Four Perspectives* (pp. 115-163). Baltimore, MD: Johns Hopkins University Press.

Dening, G. 1980. *Islands and Beaches*. Honolulu, HI: University of Hawaii Press.

Elliston, D. 1996 (January 15). "Comments re Bolin, Anne, 'The Polynesian Islands: French Polynesia.'" Unpublished comments.

Ferdon, E. N. 1981. *Early Tahiti: As the Explorers Saw It 1767-1797*. Tuscon, AZ: University of Arizona Press.

Ferdon, E. N. 1991. "Tahiti." In T. E. Hayes, ed., *Encyclopedia of World Cultures. Volume II: Oceania* (pp. 305-307). Boston: G. K. Hall & Company.

Ford, C. S., & F. A. Beach. 1951. *Patterns of Sexual Behavior*. New York: Harper & Row.

Goldman, I. 1970. *Ancient Polynesian Society*. Chicago: University of Chicago Press.

Gras, C., et al. 1992. "Surveillance Epidemiologique de l'Infection par le Virus de l'Immunodeficience Humaine (VIH) et du Syndrome d'Immunodeficience Acquise (SIDA) en Polynésie Française en 1991." *Medecine Tropicale*, 52(1):51-56.

Gregersen, E. 1983. *Sexual Practices: The Story of Human Sexuality*. New York: Franklin Watts.

Gregersen, E. 1994. *The World of Human Sexuality: Behaviors, Customs, and Beliefs*. New York: Irvington Publishers, Inc.

Grosvenor, M. B., ed. 1963. *National Geographic Atlas of the World*. Washington, DC: National Geographic Society.

Hanson, F. A. 1970. "The Rapan Theory of Conception." *American Anthropologist*, 72(6):1444-1446.

Hanson, F. A. 1991. "Rapú." In T. E. Hayes, ed., *Encyclopedia of World Cultures, Volume II: Oceania* (pp. 273-276). Boston: G. K. Hall & Company.

Hays, T. E., ed. 1991. *Encyclopedia of World Cultures. Volume II: Oceania*. Boston: G. K. Hall & Co.

Henningham, S. 1992. *France and the South Pacific: A Contemporary History.* Honolulu: University of Hawaii Press.

Hooper, A. 1966. *Marriage and Household in Two Tahitian Communities.* Cambridge, MA: Harvard University, an unpublished Ph.D. dissertation.

Hooper, A. 1985. "Tahitian Healing." In C. D. F. Parsons, ed., *Healing Practices in the South Pacific* (pp. 158-98). Honolulu, HI: The Institute for Polynesian Studies.

Howard, A., & J. Kirkpatrick. 1989. "Social Organization." In A. Howard & R. Borofsky, eds., *Developments in Polynesian Ethnology* (pp. 47-94). Honolulu, HI: University of Hawaii Press.

Howard, M. C. 1989. *Contemporary Cultural Anthropology.* New York: Harper/Collins.

Human Relations Area Files. 1991. "Mangareva." In T. E. Hayes, ed., *Encyclopedia of World Cultures. Volume II: Oceania* (p. 172). Boston: G. K. Hall & Company.

Human Relations Area Files. 1991. "Raroia." In T. E. Hayes, ed., *Encyclopedia of World Cultures. Volume II: Oceania*(pp. 276-277). Boston: G. K. Hall & Company.

Institut Territorial de la Statistique, Polynésie Française. *Résultats du Recensement Général de la Population de la Polynésie Française du 6 Septembre 1988.*

Kay, P. 1963. *Aspects of Social Structure in Manuho'e.* Cambridge, MA: Harvard University, an unpublished Ph.D. dissertation.

Kirkpatrick, J. T. 1985. "Some Marquesan Understandings of Action and Identity." In G. M. White & J. T. Kirkpatrick, eds., *Person, Self, and Experience: Exploring Pacific Ethnopsychologies* (pp. 80-120). Berkeley, CA: University of California Press.

Kirkpatrick, J. T. 1983. *The Marquesan Notion of the Person.* Ann Arbor: UMI-University of Michigan Research Press.

Kirkpatrick, J. T. 1987. "Taure'are'a: A Liminal Category and Passage to Marquesan Adulthood." *Ethos*, 15(4):382-405.

Levy, R. 1971. "The Community Function of Tahitian Male Transvestism: A Hypothesis." *Anthropological Quarterly*, 44:12-21.

Levy, R. 1973. *Tahitians: Mind and Experience in the Society Islands.* Chicago: University of Chicago Press.

Linton, R. 1939. "Marquesan Culture." In A. Kardiner, ed., *The Individual and His Society* (pp. 138-196). New York: Columbia University Press.

Lockwood, V. S. 1989. "Tubuai: Women Potato Planters and the Political Economy of Intra-Household Gender Relations." In R. R. Wilk, ed., *The Household Economy* (pp. 197-220). Boulder, CO: Westview Press.

Mann, J. M., D. J. M. Tarantola, & T. W. Netter. 1992. *AIDs in the World: The Global AIDs Policy Coalition.* Cambridge, MA: Harvard University Press.

Marshall, D. 1961. *Ra'ivavae.* Garden City, NY: Doubleday & Co., Inc.

Miles, J. A. R. 1984. "Public Health Progress in Polynesia." In J. A. R. Miles, ed., *Public Health in the Pacific* (pp. 157-173). Helmstedt, Germany: Geo Wissenschaftliche Gesellschaft.

Moorehead, A. 1966. *The Fatal Impact: An Account of the Invasion of the South Pacific 1767-1840* (Part I. Tahiti, chapters 1-6, pp. 3-86). New York: Harper & Row.

Nicholson, S., et al. 1992. "HTLV-I Infection in Selected Populations in Australia and the Western Pacific Region." *Medical Journal of Australia*, 156(12):878-880.

Oliver, D. L. 1974. *Ancient Tahitian Society.* Honolulu, HI: University of Hawaii Press.

Oliver, D. L. 1981. *Two Tahitian Villages: A Study in Comparisons.* Provo, UT: Brigham Young University Press.

Oliver, D. L. 1989a. *Oceania: The Native Cultures of Australia and the Pacific Islands* (Volume I, Part 1. Background and Part 2. Activities). Honolulu, HI: University of Hawaii Press.

Oliver, D. L. 1989b. *Oceania: The Native Cultures of Australia and the Pacific Islands* (Volume II, Part 3. Social Relations). Honolulu, HI: University of Hawaii Press.

Ritchie, J., & J. Ritchie. 1983. "Polynesian Childrearing: An Alternative Model." *Alternate Lifestyles,* 5(3):126-141.

Sahlins, M. 1967. *Social Stratification in Polynesia.* Seattle, WA: University of Washington Press.

Scupin, R., & C. R. DeCorse. 1992. *Anthropology: A Global Perspective.* Englewood Cliffs, NJ: Prentice-Hall.

Shore, B. 1989. "Mana and Tapu." In A. Howard & R. Borofsky, eds., *Developments in Polynesian Ethology* (pp. 137-174). Honolulu, HI: University of Hawaii Press.

Spiegel, A., et al. 1991. "HTLV-I in French Polynesia: A Serological Survey in Sexually Exposed Groups." *Medical Journal of Australia,* 155(11):718.

Stanley, D. 1992. *Tahiti-Polynesia Handbook.* Chico, CA: Moon Publications.

Suggs, R. C. 1960. *The Island Civilizations of Polynesia.* New York: The New American Library.

Suggs, R. C. 1966. *Marquesan Sexual Behavior.* New York: Harcourt, Brace and World.

Thomas, N. 1987. "Complementarity and History: Misrecognizing Gender in the Pacific." *Oceania,* 57(4):261-270.

Thomas, N. 1990. *Marquesan Societies: Inequality and Political Transformation in Eastern Polynesia.* Oxford, England: Clarendon Press.

Thomas, N. 1991. "Marquesas Islands." In T. E. Hays, ed., *Encyclopedia of World Cultures. Volume II: Oceania* (pp. 188-191). Boston: G. K. Hall & Company.

Vayda, A. P., ed. 1968. *Peoples and Cultures of the Pacific.* Garden City, NY: The Natural History Press.

von Strokirch, K. 1993. *Tahitian Autonomy: Illusion or Reality?* Doctoral dissertation. Bundoora, Victoria, Australia: Department of Politics, La Trobe University.

Weckler, J. E. 1943. *Polynesian Explorers of the Pacific* (Smithsonian Institution War Background Studies. Number 6). Washington, DC: Smithsonian Institution.

Williams, W. L. 1986. *The Spirit and the Flesh: Sexual Diversity in American Indian Culture.* Boston: Beacon Press.

World Health Organization. 1993. "The Current Global Situations of the HIV/AIDs Pandemic." *Global Programme on AIDS.* Geneva: WHO.

Worldmark Encyclopedia of Nations. 1988. New York: World Press, Ltd.

Puerto Rico
(*Estrado Libre Asociado de Puerto Rico*)

Luis Montesinos, Ph.D., and Juan Preciado, Ph.D.

Contents

*Demographics and a Historical Perspective**

A. Demographics

Puerto Rico is the easternmost island of the West Indies archipelago known as the Greater Antilles. Cuba, Hispaniola (Haiti and the Dominican Republic), and Jamaica are larger islands in this group. This island commonwealth of 3,435 square miles has the Atlantic Ocean to the north and the Caribbean sea to the south. Three quarters of the island are mountainous, forcing most of the people to live in a broken coastal plain.

---

*The reader is encouraged to check the other chapters in this *Encyclopedia* which provide different perspectives on the varieties of Latino culture that complement that provided here. Of specific interest are the chapters on Argentina, Brazil, and Mexico, and the brief discussion of Latinos on the mainland of the U.S.A. in Section 2 of the chapter on that country.

Sixty-seven percent of Puerto Rico's 3.8 million people (1994 estimate) live in the island's urban areas. Life expectancy at birth in 1994 was 71.5 years for males and 78.4 years for females. The sex ratio favors females by 51 percent to 49 percent. Most of the population is young with a median age of 26.8 years of age, with 11.1 percent under the age of 5 and about 4.7 percent age 65 and over (Castro-Alvarez and Ramirez de Arellano 1992). The 1995 per capita domestic product was $6,360.

An additional estimated 2.7 million Puerto Ricans live on the United States mainland, mainly to the New York metropolitan area. Major migration to the mainland occurred in the 1950s and 1960s. Since 1974, there has been a reverse migration flow back to the island. The present report will focus on the sexual behavior and beliefs of people living in the island commonwealth. It could be pointed out, however, that the so-called yo-yo migration between the island and the mainland is a significant factor in the incidence and prevalence of the AIDS (SIDA) epidemic in Puerto Rico (Castro-Alvarez and Ramirez de Arellano 1991). Puerto Ricans have constant contact with residents of eastern U.S. cities where the HIV-infection rate is high (Robles et al. 1990).

The birthrate in 1994 was 19 per 1,000 and the death rate 8 per 1,000. The infant mortality rate was 14.3 per 1,000 live births. The total fertility rate was 2.4 in 1988. The literacy rate was 89 percent and 8.2 percent of the gross national product is committed to education.

B. A Brief Historical Perspective

The island now named Puerto Rico was first visited by Columbus on his second voyage in November 1493. Puerto Rico was originally named Borinquen after the indigenous Arawak Indian name Boriquen. Fifteen years later, Spanish colonists arrived, and the Arawak natives were quickly killed off.

Sugarcane was introduced to Puerto Rico in 1515, and slaves were imported three years later to work the cane harvest. The Spaniards fought off a series of British and Dutch attempts to take over. Slavery was abolished in 1873.

In 1898, the territory was ceded by the Spaniards to the United States after the Spanish-American War, and since then, Puerto Rico has been an island commonwealth of the West Indies associated with the United States. In 1952, its inhabitants became United States citizens, and travel between the island and the continent has increased dramatically since then. Thus, in addition to the influence of the Spanish colonial times, being part of the United States has also had an impact in the life and sexuality of Puerto Rico's society.

In the late 1940s, Puerto Rico began its famous "Operation Bootstrap" to change its status as "The Poorhouse of the Caribbean" to an area with the highest per capita income in Latin America. Although manufacturing and tourism are very successful, the per capital income is low compared with that of the mainland United States. In 1991, an 89-year bilingual policy in which English and Spanish served as joint official languages ended, when Spanish became the only official and legal language of the island.

1. Basic Sexological Premises

A. Character of Gender Roles

In describing the sexological premises commonly ascribed to by Puerto Ricans, it should be noted at the onset that major differences exist within the society, where most of the low-income population agree with the more-traditional values, and more-educated single females, and to a lesser extent males, tend not to fit the stereotypical feminine role.

Puerto Rican culture, like other Latino societies, stresses a very strong gender difference from birth on that is reflected in every aspect of sexual expression and male-female interaction. The predominant value of *machismo* sees males as superior and females as sexual objects whose aims are to fulfill men's desires and needs (Burgos and Diaz-Perez 1985). Outside the Latino cultures, the terms *macho* and *machismo* carry a common pejorative implication of a chauvinistic, tyrannical male domination. However, in Spanish, the terms refer to male pride. *Machismo* has been defined as the set of attitudes and beliefs that sees males as physically, intellectually, culturally, and sexually superior to females (Pico 1989). Puerto Rican boys are indoctrinated in the importance of being macho from a very early age.

> One way the male child is socialized and reminded of his maleness [in the rural cultures of Puerto Rico and the Dominican Republic] is by his parents and other adults admiring and fondling the baby's penis. Little boys are valued for being male from the moment they are born into the family; even if there are older sisters, the male sibling is the dominant figure, both in the eyes of the parents and in sibling interactions. Mothers train their daughters early on to play "little women" to their fathers, brothers, and husbands; and train their sons to be dominant and independent in relationships with their wives as well as other women (Medina 1987).

Males express *machismo* by having sex with as many females as possible, and by emphasizing their capacity as procreator and willingness to have as many children as possible, preferably males (Mejias-Picart 1975). There is practically no societal control over male sexual behavior, while female sexuality is openly repressed. It is expected that the males assume the active role, initiate sexual activity, and be responsible for the satisfaction of the female.

The female equivalent of *machismo* is *etiqueta*, a complex value system that requires Latina women to be both feminine and pure, and at the same time very sensual and seductive. Little girls are taught to hide their genitals and not to focus much attention on their vagina. Yet, girls are valued for and taught to enhance their sexual appeal. From birth, girls are adorned with earrings, bracelets, and special spiritual amulets. Their very feminine dress makes Latina girls extremely seductive and even provocative. However, a woman's virginity is highly valued and families are careful to protect the virginity of their daughters. Because girls are taught to be sensual and seductive, chaperons have the responsibility of making certain that young women who are being courted do not stray.

Latina girls are constantly reminded of their inferiority and weakness, since a vital aspect of *etiqueta* is the concept of *marianismo*, the model of the obedient and docile female. (Maria is by far the most popular female name. It is not uncommon for several daughters in the same family to have the first name Maria and a different second given name, a reminder that all women should model themselves on the Virgin Mary, the mother of Jesus). Women are expected to sacrifice their own needs for the sake of their children and husband (Comas-Diaz 1985). A wife is not expected to enjoy sex herself or to seek it—she is there to please her husband. Females are expected to be passive, ready to respond to the male requirements and not to assume responsibility for their own pleasure. A good woman is always ready for her man, but she should never be comfortable with sexual issues or with sexual intercourse. To do otherwise suggests a lack of feminine virtue. In a recent survey, almost 80 percent of the husbands surveyed were found to initiate sexual activities almost all of the time, while 90 percent of household chores (cooking and cleaning) were carried out by the wives (Vasquez 1986).

A strong pronatalist value also underlies Puerto Rican culture. Large families with many children are preferred. The family is not structured as the American or European nuclear family tends to be. A girl who has a child out of wedlock is initially frowned on for violating *marianismo* and *etiqueta*, but she and her child will usually be quickly accepted by her whole family because of her child. The pronatalist value is supported by the anticontraception and antiabortion position of the Catholic Church. Nevertheless, both contraception and abortion are commonly used.

The Civil Rights Commission in 1973 concluded that discrimination against women outside and inside the home existed and subtle discriminatory practices occurred. In 1984, a study done by the Puerto Rican Senate found that the same pattern of discrimination continued to exist. Although there have been some changes in the recent past, oppression, control of women, male power, and heterosexuality continue as the dominant parameters of the Puerto Rican society (Zorrila et al. 1993).

Women themselves are in part liable for the preservation of this situation, since they continue to accept the sole responsible for child rearing and play an essentially domestic role. But this form of sexism is also "imprinted" in children who are socialized to accept the stereotypical roles from early childhood, where the main role of the female is to be mother, in spite of also working outside the home. Dependency, obedience, and submission are reinforced in daughters, while independence, aggression, and lack of emotion are reinforced in males (Burgos and Diaz-Perez 1985; Mock 1984). Females are socialized to be submissive, passive, attractive, compliant, obedient, and dependent, and they are expected to behave this way in their sexual interactions (Santos-Ortiz 1990).

During the school years, gender roles are reinforced by a biased curriculum. A study on the illustrations and contents of social sciences texts used in primary schools (Pico 1989) found that men were portrayed as relevant and superior while females were relegated to a secondary role, and when depicted appeared in more-traditional stereotypical roles. Men and boys appeared more frequently than girls and women, in spite of the fact that females constitute over half of the population. Women appeared frequently working in their home, engaged in passive activities such as reading, praying, playing with dolls, and were rarely depicted outside of it. This is epitomized by a page in a text under the title "What I most enjoy doing." There are pictures of sliding, swimming, bicycle riding, skating, and other activities—all of them performed by BOYS; not a single girl appears in those activities. Although this research was done in the early 1980s, there is no reason to think that the pervasiveness of the gender stereotype has changed at all.

It has been only recently that the Department of Education on the island has established a program to train its personnel and to develop curricula for sexual education in schools (Mock 1992). Before that, with very few exceptions, such programs did not exist.

B. Sociolegal Status of Males and Females

The number of common-law partnerships has increased consistently during the last few decades, in spite of the fact that they are not recognized and consequently do not have any of the entitlements of legally married couples. Children, however, are recognized as legitimate offspring of the parents and have the right to be supported by them until they are 21 years old. Legal custody of children is almost always awarded to the mother.

C. General Concepts of Sexuality and Love

The basic values of *machismo, marianismo,* and *etiqueta* are evident in various sexual behaviors. In a 1985 survey, 60 percent of working-class women and 50 percent of professional women reported faking orgasm in order to end intercourse soon or to avoid the husband's questioning about their achieving orgasm or not. While the great majority of women surveyed did not disapprove of self-pleasuring, very few women engage in autoeroticism, or admit to this in surveys (Burgos and Diaz-Perez 1985).

For Latino men, this uncomfortableness with sex is expressed in ridicule and rejection of anything that hints of homosexuality. Even in the Latino culture of Brazil, where boys are encouraged to explore everything sexual, all men—even those who in the United States would be considered bisexual or homosexual—see themselves as *homens*, men in the sense of always taking the active phallic sexual role (Medina 1987; Parker 1987).

As more women enter the workforce and pursue an education the traditional maternity role has changed and continues to change. This is evidenced by the large number of Puerto Rican women who postpone marriage and childbearing until their late 30s. As mentioned before, out-of-wedlock partnerships have increased in popularity, especially among white-collar workers and educated people.

2. Religious and Ethnic Factors Affecting Sexuality

A/B. Source and Character of Religious and Ethnic Values

The early inhabitants of Puerto Rico migrated either from Florida in the north or from the Orinoco River delta in Columbia, South America. When the Spaniards arrived in 1493, the island was inhabited by the peaceful Arawaks who were threatened by the neighboring Carib Indians. The island was finally invaded and conquered for Spain in 1509 by Ponce de Leon.

Introduction of sugarcane cultivation in 1515 was quickly followed by the importation of African slaves to work the cane fields. Although slavery was finally abolished in 1873, the impact of the forced African immigration can still be felt today in the Puerto Rican society. Indigenous, Spanish, and African elements permeate the Puerto Rican culture even today, with the Spanish influence dominant, since they occupied and controlled the island for nearly four hundred years.

In 1898, Spain ceded Puerto Rico to the United States as part of the treaty of Paris that ended the Spanish-American War. In 1952, the people voted for self-government as a Commonwealth of the United States.

It appears that in the island pre-Colombian societies, women had more power and were highly respected. Pre-Colombian women are also believed to have had an active sexual life. Men, especially those in the upper classes, were allowed to be polygamous.

Later on, the Spaniards introduced their patriarchal society with its values of *machismo*, *marianismo*, and *etiqueta*, which emphasize female virginity, and a pronatalist familism. The popular traditions and doctrines of Catholicism introduced by the Spanish have played a major role in the shaping of the society's sexual values and attitudes. However, this influence, as will be seen, is more formal than real when it comes to some private decisions. Even though 80 percent of Puerto Ricans today identify themselves as Catholic, most are not highly active in the Church (Burgos and Diaz-Perez 1985).

Although the culture seems sexually repressive, in reality Puerto Rican society is eroticist and exalts sexuality in pervasive and subtle ways. Sexual themes permeate Puerto Rican popular music and dances (*salsa*) as well as nonverbal communications. Perhaps because of this, there are very few written articles about sexuality in Puerto Rico, and very little is known about sexual behavior and attitudes of Puerto Ricans (Burgos and Diaz-Perez 1985; Cunningham 1991).

In keeping with its strong Christian roots, Puerto Rican males today hold a superior and dominant role, reflected in the saying "females are expected to have babies and males are expected to make history." The reproductive function of sexuality is seen as its natural goal, while its pleasurable aspects are viewed as a necessary incentive for accomplishment of this goal. All other sexual behaviors apart from penile-vaginal intercourse are generally seen as immature and undesirable (Mock 1984). Nevertheless, sexuality is commercialized and widely available in both pornography and prostitution (Mock 1984).

As stated before, although the influence of the Catholic Church is felt in all aspects of sexuality, studies indicated that Catholics have as many abortions as non-Catholics (Ortiz and Vazquez-Nuttall 1987), and that religious affiliation has no bearing on the use of contraceptive methods, including sterilization and the pill (Herold et al. 1989).

3. Sexual Knowledge and Education

A. Government Policies and Programs

As a result of *marianismo*, the Church's opposition, and the reluctance of society and families to acknowledge female sexuality openly, many girls experience their menarche with no formal education about it, and although males are expected to have their first sexual experience before marriage, they do not receive formal education either. Obviously, neither females nor males have any knowledge about the health implications of various sexual practices (Burgos and Diaz-Perez 1985).

There are no systems or district-wide sexuality education programs, such as exist in most, if not all the mainland States. A program to train sexuality education teachers has been proposed and was being developed in 1994. As in other places where formal programs have not been developed, individual teachers may take the initiative into their own hands and incorporate various aspects of sexuality education into their standard courses, such as biology and health.

B. Informal Sources of Sexual Knowledge

The media also play a role in perpetuating sexist stereotypes and prejudices against women. A study found that articles in the popular media usually portrayed women as submissive and presented acts of violence against women as normal (Maldonado 1990).

The same kind of sexual information portrayed in movies, television, and radio in the mainland United States is also available in the commonwealth island of Puerto Rico. The ready access to cable television and video tapes has permitted islanders to be exposed to the same kind of information that is available to individuals living on the mainland.

4. Autoerotic Behaviors and Patterns

When asked about self-pleasuring in a 1985 survey, a great majority of women do not disapprove of it. However, they reported not practicing it themselves. A survey of 191 adolescents found that 32 percent (61) of them engaged in self-pleasuring, 53 of them males and only 8 of them females (Burgos and Diaz-Perez 1985).

5. Interpersonal Heterosexual Behaviors

A. Children

Childhood sexual rehearsal play and sexual exploration no doubt occur in private as they do in many other cultures, but there are no statistics or information on their incidence or extent.

B. Adolescents

Puberty Rituals

There are no public rituals to mark menarche for girls or the onset of puberty for boys.

Premarital Sexual Activities and Relationships

Studies of adolescents in public schools have found that a good number of them are sexually active before the age of 15, and that most of them do not use contraceptives to prevent pregnancy and/or sexually transmitted diseases (Mock and Ramirez 1993).

As mentioned before, the fact that more females are postponing marriage, and that more couples are opting for common-law partnerships as opposed to legal marriage, has resulted in an increase of individuals engaging in premarital sex. It is estimated that almost 50 percent of young Puerto Ricans are sexually active (Cunningham 1991).

Premarital Courtship, Dating, and Relationships

Courtship and dating behavior is governed by strong and clear gender-dimorphic roles and rules. It is very difficult for young people, particularly young women with older brothers or male cousins, to escape the pervasive pressure and surveillance of family members that enforce the dual stardards of behavior expected of Puerto Rican males and females. The custom of a chaperone's accompanying a young woman disappeared long ago, since no one young or old recalls it.

Young Puerto Ricans attending colleges and universities are very similar to their student counterparts elsewhere in the world. However, some relevant differences are worth addressing here. Surveys done by Cunningham and collaborators (1991), with randomly selected students at the Universidad de Puerto Rico, show that almost half of them are sexually active, 70 percent of the males and 40 percent of the females. Of those sexually active, 80 percent had experienced vaginal intercourse, more than 50 percent had tried oral intercourse, and over a third had tried anal intercourse.

Eighty-five percent of those practicing vaginal intercourse and 84 percent of those practicing oral sex reported having only one partner during the three-month period antedating the study. With respect to the use of condoms, 55 percent of the sample declared they had used one at least once; only 16.8 percent of the males and 13.6 percent of the females declared they always used a condom (Cunningham and Rodriguez-Sanchez 1991).

C. Adults

Marriage and the Family

It used to be that the divorce rate was very low, probably due to the strong influence of the Catholic religion. However, there has been a dramatic increase in the rate of divorce during the past decade, as well as an increase in the number of households headed by women. In 1960, it was 18.7 percent; by 1980, the incidence was 25 percent (Vasquez-Calzada 1989). More recently, increasing numbers of single mothers have been noticed (20.9 percent in 1980 to 32.9 percent in 1989) (Castro-Alvarez and Ramirez de Arellano 1991). In 1988, the percentage of teen births was 17.4 percent, while those out of wedlock reached 32.8 percent.

Extramarital Sex, Cohabitation, and Single Mothers

As in any strongly patriarchal culture, the double moral standard allows males much more freedom than it does females. Macho men, but not women, are allowed and expected to have extramarital sexual relationships. However, as is happening in other cultures, the increasing incidence and recognition of cohabitation and single mothers is definitely weakening this pattern.

Sexuality and Disabled and Older Persons

There is little if any discussion, and no statistics, on the sexual needs or behaviors of physically and mentally challenged persons and older persons.

Incidence of Oral and Anal Sex

Unexpectedly, 35 percent of university students surveyed in 1989 and 37 percent of those surveyed in 1990 had participated in anal intercourse. Approximately 40 percent of the males who had engaged in this activity were homosexual. And although those who practice anal intercourse do it less frequently and tend to use condoms in higher percentages, they also tend to have more partners than those who practice other types of sexual activity. Results show that almost 36 percent of those who practice anal intercourse (22 percent of the females and 46.5 percent of the males) had two or more partners during the three months previous to answering the survey. The reasons for engaging in this practice were different for males and females: while the males reported they did it for pleasure, females reported that they did it mostly to satisfy their partners.

No data is available on the attitudes towards or the incidence of either anal or oral sex among nonuniversity-students, and single or married adults.

6. Homoerotic, Homosexual, and Ambisexual Behaviors

In Puerto Rico, as in most societies of the world, being openly gay carries a negative stigma, and in consequence most of the gay community remains "invisible." Thus, no reliable information about the percentage of the population with homosexual or bisexual orientation or experience is available (Cunningham and Cunningham 1991).

There is a strong rejection of homosexuality, especially male homosexuality. This negative attitude is present even in Puerto Rican males living in the New York area. In fact, law-enforcement officials tend to harass those who have sexual relationships with someone of their own gender or commit a crime "contrary to nature."

Due to the AIDS (SIDA) epidemic, homosexuals affected by the disease have organized support groups and started to acknowledge their sexual orientation publically. Within these groups, two distinct reactions have been observed: a group of individuals have reacted by increasing their sexual activity, while others have abstained almost completely from it (Ortiz-Colon 1991). However, in Puerto Rico, the main mode of transmission of HIV has been through intravenous drug use and, increasingly, through heterosexual contact.

There is a history of more than twenty years of gay and lesbian civil rights movements. The Comunidad de Orgullo Gay (Pride Gay Community) was founded in 1973; since then, other organizations have been established. The Coalicion Puertoriquena de Lesbianas y Homosexuales, created in 1991, publishes a bimonthly magazine dealing specifically with issues of discrimination, and encouraging support among lesbians and gays. Due to the AIDS epidemic, other groups that deal specifically with this issue have been established in different parts of the island.

7. Gender Conflicted Persons

As in other parts of the world, transvestites and transsexuals do exist in Puerto Rican society. However, scientific data on the extent of this population and its practices are unavailable.

8. Significant Unconventional Sexual Behaviors

A. Coercive Sex

Sexual Abuse and Incest

There are no reliable statistics about the incidence of family violence, including the sexual abuse of women and children, and incest, but centers to protect victims of family violence, Casa Protegida Julia de Burgos, reported almost 500 cases of spouse abuse in 1984, and the Department of Social Services reported over 5,000 cases of abuse and neglect of children in 1985. The Centro de Ayuda a Victimas de Violacion reported 181 cases of rape and 21 cases of incest for the period 1984-85 (Burgos and Diaz Perez 1985).

Sexual Harassment

This is a relatively new concept that has not been widely accepted in Puerto Rican society. Most people believe that these are the natural behavioral patterns in relationships between men and women (Alvarado 1987). Sexual innuendoes, jokes, and repeatedly asking for dates are all expected in male-female interactions (Martinez et al. 1988).

Recent studies have found harassment rates of 44 percent among women attending a conference on women in the work place, to as high as 73 percent for women working in the health-care sector (Alvarado 1987; Martinez et al. 1988). The great majority of these women had been harassed by supervisors (over 60 percent) or coworkers (almost 30 percent). Although more than 60 percent of the women confronted the harasser, only 13 percent reported the situation to their superiors (Alvarado 1987).

Although there is no specific law in Puerto Rico against sexual harassment in the workplace, there is a law that prohibits discrimination in any form at the workplace. Current efforts focus on raising the public's awareness of the nature, pervasiveness, and social unacceptability of sexual harassment in a culture where it has been universally accepted and expected as an important part of behavior of macho males.

Rape

Outside of the scattered and nonrepresentative statistics mentioned above on incest, child sexual abuse, and spouse abuse, no data exist on the incidence of rape.

B. Prostitution

As in other parts of the world, prostitution is tolerated or permitted in Puerto Rican society, although it is considered illegal and immoral. Males are encouraged to seek prostitutes as sexual outlets so as to maintain the purity of those whom they will eventually marry. This, however, is changing, as more and more young adults are engaging in premarital sexual relationships.

The recent increase in AIDS among heterosexuals has been in part attributed to the male contact with an infected prostitute (Mock and Ramirez 1993).

C. Pornography and Erotica

Erotic elements appear to be very common in writings (novels), and popular songs and dances. Pornography, however, is not as developed as it is on the mainland, although access to magazines and television channels, such as the Playboy Channel, is possible through cable TV. There is little if any indigenous pornographic material, since a variety of such material is easily brought home by Puerto Ricans traveling back and forth between the island and the mainland to visit family and relatives.

9. Contraception, Abortion, and Population Planning

A. Contraception

The first attempts to establish birth control services in Puerto Rico date to 1925, when a group of professionals, headed by Jose A. Lanauze Rolon, a physician, founded the Liga para el 'Control de la Natalidad (Birth Control League) in the city of Ponce. This venture paralleled Margaret Sanger's efforts on the mainland. In fact, Mrs. Sanger sent Dr. Lanauze the necessary forms and information for them to affiliate with the American Birth Control League. The goals were then the same: dissemination of information for women regarding safe and available contraceptives, and maintaining appropriate statistics and studies demonstrating the negative consequences of overpopulation. Consequently, the league was very active in pursuing public birth control services, arguing not only from the negative consequences of overpopulation, but from the positive outcome of reducing the high rate of abortion. However, due to strong opposition from the Church and the lack of funds, the clinic founded by the league, as well as two others founded in San Juan and in Mayaguez in the early 1930s, were closed.

Federal agencies established contraceptive services in the mid-1930s, but these were also closed during the later years of the Roosevelt Administration due to dissatisfaction with their results and the strong opposition of the Catholic Church.

Today, contraceptive use in Puerto Rico is widespread. It is estimated that three fourths of Puerto Rican women have used contraceptives at least once (Davila 1990). Despite the purported influence of the Catholic Church, religious affiliation has no bearing on contraceptive use. Data show that Catholics use contraceptives as often as non-Catholics. Furthermore, studies have found that contraceptive level of use is similar across socioeconomic classes, educational levels, and urban versus rural regions (Vazquez-Calzada 1988; Herold et al. 1989). It should be noted, however, that a significant number of university students were found to have little knowledge of contraception, especially regarding barrier methods, that may decrease the spread of STDs and AIDS (Irrizarry 1991). Overall, birth control usage reflects the prevalent belief that birth control is the main responsibility of women (Davila 1990).

The most widely used contraceptive by women who intend to have more children is the pill. Studies indicate that about half of the married women have used the pill at least once (Davila 1990). The pill is less popular nowadays, as usage decreased from 18.9 percent in 1968 to 11.9 percent in 1982 (Vazquez-Calzada 1988).

The IUD and the diaphragm are used significantly less than the pill (Robles et al. 1990). It has been reported that about one third of the women had used these methods once (Davila 1990). The rhythm method is used much less (18 percent). However, it should be noted that the popularity of the rhythm method has increased from 2.9 percent in 1968 to 7.7 percent in 1982 (Vazquez-Calzada 1988).

The use of condoms is not very high. About 6.6 percent of women reported that their partners used condoms as a means of birth control in 1968. About the same rate was reported in 1976 and again in 1982 (Vazquez-Calzada 1988). Researchers have suggested that religious beliefs and culture norms in Puerto Rico may be responsible for men's low usage of condoms and women's inability to demand the use of condoms from their partners (Menendez 1990).

B. Teenage Unmarried Pregnancies

Statistics for the year 1985 show that 17 percent of all pregnancies occurred among adolescents between the ages of 10 to 19 years (Mock and Ramirez 1993).

C. Abortion

It has been estimated that between 50,000 to 75,000 abortions are performed every year in Puerto Rico (Pacheco-Acosta 1990). Abortion is more common in single than in married mothers. Furthermore, studies have found no differences between Catholics and non-Catholics in abortion incidence (Herold et al. 1989). It has been suggested that Catholics may prefer abortions to contraceptives because the former involves only one violation or sin, and one confession, while the ongoing use of contraceptives requires repeated confessions in which absolution might be refused because of the lack of true repentance and the unwillingness to discontinue contraceptives. If the abortion can be kept secret, the person in question can continue to go to Church, whereas if the pregnancy is brought to term, everybody would know about it (Ortiz and Vazquez-Nuttall 1987).

D. Population Control Efforts

Population-control policies in conjunction with migration—almost a third of Puerto Ricans live outside their country—have been long-term basic tenets of economic development on the island. This has permitted constant experimentation with contraceptives among Puerto Rican women. They served as human "guinea pigs" for the first contraceptive hormonal pill that was later withdrawn from the market because of its severe negative side effects (Davila 1990).

During the 1940s and 1950s, family planning and population control were supported by the government, and sterilization became a common practice. By the 1970s, Puerto Rico had one of the highest rates of sterilization in the world, and it was estimated that at least 35 percent of the women of reproductive age were sterilized (Acosta-Belen 1986; Robles et al. 1988). Data from recent decades indicate that sterilization increased from 56.7 percent in 1968 to 58.3 percent in 1982 (Vazquez-Calzada 1988). Sterilization remains the most accepted method of family planning among Puerto Rican women, and the island continues having one of the highest rates in the world (Vasquez-Calzada et al. 1989; Robles et al. 1988). The same study showed that women who had Cesarean sections opted for sterilization. Despite the strong influence of the Catholic Church, sterilization is as prevalent among Catholics as it is among non-Catholics (Herold et al. 1989).

It has been suggested that the high incidence of female sterilization is another manifestation of *machismo/marianismo*: since women are not expected to enjoy sexuality, they are not expected to give much importance to their sexual organs (Burgos and Diaz-Perez 1985).

Vasectomy seems to be more common now than it was a few decades ago. There has been an increase from 2.4 percent in 1968 to 6.6 percent in 1982 (Vazquez-Calzada 1988). Vasectomy is more popular among educated males living in urban areas.

10. Sexually Transmitted Diseases

Only partial data on the incidence of sexually transmitted diseases is available. The rate for syphilis (all stages) was 25.4 per 100,000 in 1984, which was more than twice as high as that of the mainland for the same year (12.2 per 100,000) (Sexually Transmitted Diseases 1984). While rates are not available for the last three years, available data on the absolute number of cases show a decline from 2,551 cases in 1989 to 1,940 cases in 1991 (MMWR 1989; 1990; 1991).

The rate for gonorrhea in 1984 was 103.6 per 100,000 (Sexually Transmitted Diseases 1984). This rate is less than one third that of the United States for the same year (374.8 per 100,000). Once again, rates were unavailable for the last three years. However, the cumulative number of cases reported for the last three years show a dramatic decrease from 1,513 cases in 1989 to 668 case for 1992 (MMWR 1989; 1990; 1991).

The statistics also indicate that sexually transmitted diseases occur most frequently among adolescents and young adults. Adolescents and young single adults are a common high-risk group in most societies today, where barriers to adolescent sexual behavior are falling without society's recognition of the need for education in reducing the risks of sexually transmitted diseases (Mock and Ramirez 1993).

11. HIV/AIDS

A. Adolescent and Adult HIV/AIDS

The first case of AIDS in Puerto Rico was reported in 1982 and the vigilance/prevention program was started in 1983. Initially due to physicians' reluctance to report the cases they diagnosed as being HIV-positive or having AIDS, the reported rates were very likely serious underestimates of the true number of cases. By October 1991, a total of 6,732 cases had been reported, of which 4,336 (63 percent) had already died.

The most recent data on the reported number of AIDS cases per 100,000 population through June 1992 show that Puerto Rico has a 50.9 rate per 100,000, among the highest in the world. It was estimated that by 1993, the number of new cases would reach 11,000, due in part to the changing diagnostic criteria that added tuberculosis, cervical cancer, and recurrent pneumonia to the AIDS syndrome in January 1993.

The greater proportion of deaths from AIDS on the island occurred among people between 25 and 34 years of age, an age of great productivity and an active social and sexual life. In 1987, it was reported that AIDS was the primary cause of death for women between ages 25 and 29, and for males between 30 and 39 years of age (Cunningham 1991). In 1989, 3.7 percent of all deaths in Puerto Rico were due to AIDS. However, in comparison to those living on the island, Puerto Ricans living in New York

City have a five-times greater chance of dying from AIDS—this is true both for men and women (Menendez 1990).

In Puerto Rico, the use of intravenous drugs constitutes the most important risk factor in the development of AIDS (Marrero-Rodriguez et al. 1993). In fact, the largest concentration of IV drug users among AIDS cases in the United States is found in Puerto Rico (Colon, Robles, and Sahai 1991). It is estimated that more than 63 percent of AIDS patients on the island are addicted to intravenous drugs. Among males, 59 percent of AIDS cases are associated with the use of drugs, compared to only 19 percent for mainland United States. The relevance of this risk factor makes the epidemiology of AIDS different in Puerto Rico from what is encountered in other parts of the world. It is estimated that there are 100,000 drug addicts in Puerto Rico, 2.7 percent of the total population, 80 percent of whom are intravenous drug users (Rivera et al. 1990).

Most of the 100,000 drug users are young, heterosexual males, who continue being sexually active and practicing high-risk behaviors. Thus, one can expect that their partners would be infected through sexual contact. Epidemiological data show that IV drug users' male partners account for 84 percent of heterosexual transmission in women. It has been suggested that the geography of Puerto Rico, which is a relatively small island, creates an opportunity for knowing and contacting a lot of people, and thus facilitating the spread of the disease. Furthermore, given the high rate of sterilization among women, a significant number may find no incentives to use barrier methods that may decrease the risk for contracting AIDS and other STDs (Robles et al. 1990). An additional factor may be that men expect women to be responsible for birth control, and these may prefer the use of methods, particularly the pill, which in turn may decrease the possibility of men using condoms (Davila 1990).

The second most common mode of HIV transmission in Puerto Rico, and one that is on the rise, is heterosexual activity. The data show that heterosexual infection increased from 6 percent in 1988 to 10 percent in 1991. By 1993, heterosexual transmission had increased to 1,350 cases, 854 of whom were women. Heterosexual transmission in women is increasing at a much faster rate than in men. The problem of heterosexual transmission seems to be worsened by the existence of *machismo* and the subordinate role that women are expected to play in sexual matters. Within such cultural beliefs, women have little power to negotiate safer sexual behavior with their partners. Yet, women who become infected must care for and financially support their infected male partners, as well as their children (Santos-Ortiz 1991).

B. Pediatric AIDS (SIDA)

Unfortunately, Puerto Rico has one of the highest incidences of pediatric AIDS (SIDA), with a higher incidence in urban areas. The first pediatric AIDS case in Puerto Rico was reported in the San Juan Municipal Hospital in 1984. By November 1991, 190 cases had been reported. This figure clearly underestimates the magnitude of pediatric AIDS, because for every diagnosed case, there are between two and ten children who are infected but have not been diagnosed (Beauchamp et al. 1991).

The most comprehensive epidemiological picture of pediatric AIDS cases emerges from a study conducted in the San Juan Municipal Hospital (Quiroz et al. 1991). It has been estimated that 90 percent of the AIDS cases are acquired perinatally. Pediatric AIDS occurs more commonly in females than in males, with a ratio of three to two. The median age for onset of full AIDS symptoms is 5 years. The profile shows that more than 80 percent of the pediatric cases acquired the disease from their infected mothers. The main risk factor identified was being born to an intravenous drug-user mother (67.2 percent, born to an infected mother) or father (65 percent), and having a parent with multiple partners (27 percent). The marital profile revealed that most of these mothers were "not legally married" (42.4 percent), or were never married (33.3 percent), and only a small number were "legally married" (15.2 percent). Many of the mothers have completed 12 years of education (64.6 percent), with an average schooling of 11.39 years.

Interestingly, one study found that 40.3 percent of the HIV-infected children who lost their parents live with their extended family members—aunts, uncles, and grandparents (Beauchamp et al. 1991). Apparently, prior to their death, infected parents made private arrangements with extended family members to insure that their children would be taken care of. Legal custody was declared in approximately 14 percent of the cases, suggesting that most parents made private arrangements. The care of HIV-infected children is often burdensome to an extended family that may be overwhelmed by the extra services and care needed by them. Shelter care for HIV-infected children is often unavailable.

Pediatric cases among school-age children present an additional challenge in Puerto Rico. Schools need to know the serologic status of students in order to provide appropriate student services. In Puerto Rico, as on the mainland, prejudice and discrimination exist, so that some schools have tried to deny access to parents whose children have revealed that they are HIV-infected. Hence, parents are sometimes reluctant to disclose their children's serological status to school officials. Nonetheless, it should be noted that the Department of Education in Puerto Rico has an AIDS (SIDA) policy that adequately addresses the needs of HIV-infected children in the schools.

12. Sexual Dysfunctions, Counseling, and Therapies

A. Concepts of Sexual Dysfunction

The data on types of sexual dysfunction is limited to small nonrandom samples. A 1985 report by Mock states that the most common sexual dysfunction among males was erectile dysfunction, followed by lack of sexual desire and premature ejaculation. For females, the most common problem was inhibited female orgasm, relationship problems, and lack of sexual desire.

In Mock's opinion, the male dysfunctions are due in part to three main factors: the belief that it is the male's responsibility to satisfy his partner, masculinity as defined by the ability to obtain and sustain erection, and the fear of homosexuality. In the case of the female, issues such as inhibitions to express their sexuality freely and the fear of losing a partner seem to play important roles in sexual dysfunctions.

B. Availability of Counseling, Diagnosis, and Treatment

There are several private practitioners in Puerto Rico, most of whom have been trained in the United States and possess doctoral degrees, as well as certification as sex counselors and/or therapists. Most of them are members of professional organizations in the United States such as the Society for the Scientific Study of Sexuality (SSSS), the American Association for Sex Educators, Counselors, and Therapists (AASECT), and the Society for Sex Therapy and Research (SSTAR).

13. Sexual Research and Advanced Education

Human sexuality courses are part of the academic offerings in the colleges and universities in Puerto Rico. Major universties, such as the Universidad de Puerto Rico, conduct research in sexuality and AIDS (SIDA).

Due to the relevance of AIDS in Puerto Rico there are numerous organizations and centers providing services and conducting ongoing research in this area. Worth mentioning are two publications: *El SIDA en Puerto Rico*, edited by a group of scholars working at the Recinto de Rio Piedras of the Universidad de Puerto Rico (Cunningham et al. 1991), and the second one by Mock and Ramirez (1993) titled *SIDA: Crisis o Retor Transformador.*

The most important center for research on general aspects of sexuality is the Instituto Puertorriqueno de Salud Sexual Integral (Address: Center Building, Oficina 406, Avenida de Diego 312, Santurce, Puerto Rico 00909; telephone: 809-721-3578). There are also several centers and associations that deal with specific aspects of sexually transmitted diseases and AIDS (SIDA).

Final Comments

In summary, sexual behavior and attitudes in Puerto Rican society reflects the social, political, and economic conditions of the country. A model of economic development based on population control and immigration has resulted in high rates of sterilization and the use of its population, especially the female, as involuntary experimental subjects for contraceptives such as the pill. This same pattern has been reported with the use of hormones to feed poultry and livestock, which has also impacted on the health status of the inhabitants of the island.

The so-called yo-yo migration and high rates of intravenous drug use have resulted in a high incidence of AIDS (SIDA) with heterosexual transmission being more important than other means of contracting the virus.

The institutionalized inequality of women on the island contributes not only to high rates of AIDS (SIDA) among them and their newborn, but also to the repression of their sexuality and engagement in high-risk behaviors only to satisfy their partner or because of the fear of losing them.

References and Suggested Readings

Acosta-Belen, E. 1986. *The Puerto Rican Woman, Perspectives on Culture, History and Society.* Rio Piedras: Universidad de Puerto Rico.

Alvarado, M. R. 1987. "El Hostigamiento Sexual en el Empleo." *Homines,* 10:192-96.

Amato. A. 1993 (October 31). "Multiplying in Smaller Numbers." Santiago, W.: *The San Juan Star.*

Beauchaump, B., L. Flores, L. Lugo, L. Robles, and I. Salabarria. 1991. *SIDA Pediatrico: Experiencia en el Hospital Pediatrico Universitario. El SIDA en Puerto Rico Acercamientos Multidisciplinarios.* Rio Piedras: Universidad de Puerto Rico, Instituto de Estudios del Caribe.

Burgos, N. M., and Y. I. Diaz-Perez. 1985. *La Sexualidad: Analisis Exploratorio en la Cultura Puertoriquena.* Puerto Rico: Centro de Investigaciones Sociales.

Castro-Alvarez, V., and A. B. Ramirez de Arellano. 1991. "The Health Status of Puerto Rican Women in the United States and Puerto Rico." Paper presented at the Public Health Service Conference, "A Celebration of Hispanic Women's Issues," San Antonio, Texas.

Castro-Alvarez, V., and A. B. Ramirez de Arellano. 1992. "The Reproductive Health of Puerto Rican Women in the United States and Puerto Rico." *Journal Multi-Cultural Community Health,* 2:9-14.

Colon, H. M., R. Robles, and H. Sahai. 1991. "HIV Risk and Prior Drug Treatment Among Puerto Rican Intravenous Drug Users." *Puerto Rican Health Sciences Journal,* 10:83-87.

Comas-Diaz, L. 1985. "A Comparison of Content Themes in Therapy." *Hispanic Journal Behavioral Sciences,* 7:273-83.

Cunningham, I. 1991. "La Mujer y el SIDA: Una Vision Critica." *Puerto Rican Health Sciences Journal,* 9:47-50.

Cunningham, E., and I. Cunningham, I. 1991. "La Metafora del SIDA en Puerto Rico: El Reportaje de Una Epidemia." In Cunningham, Ramos-Bellido, and Ortiz-Colon, eds., *El SIDA en Puerto Rico Acercamientos Multidisciplinarios.* Rio Piedras: Universidad de Puerto Rico, Instituto de Estudios del Caribe.

Cunningham, I. and H. Rodriguez-Sanchez. 1991. "Practicas de Riesgo Relacionadas con la Transmision del Vih y Medidas de Prevencion Entre Estudiantes de la Universidad de Puerto Rico." In Cunningham, Ramos-Bellido, and Ortiz-Colon, eds., *El SIDA en Puerto Rico Acercamientos Multidisciplinarios.* Rio Piedras: Universidad de Puerto Rico, Instituto de Estudios del Caribe.

Davila, A. L. 1990. "Esterilizacion y Practica Anticonceptiva en Puerto Rico, 1982." *Puerto Rican Health Sciences Journal*, 9:61-67.

Garcia-Preto, Nydia. 1982. "Puerto Rican Families." In M. McGoldrick, J. K. Pearce, and J. Giordano, eds. *Ethnicity and Family Therapy*. New York: Guilford Press.

Herold, J. M., et al. 1989. "Catholicism and Fertility in Puerto Rico." *American Journal Public Health*, 79:1258-62.

Irrizarry, A. 1991. "Conociminetos, Creencias y Actitudes Hacia el SIDA en Jovenes Puertorriquenos." *Puerto Rican Health Sciences Journal*, 10:43-46.

Maldonado, M. A. 1990. "Violencia Contra la Mujer por ser Mujer." *Puerto Rican Health Sciences Journal*, 9:11-116.

Marrero-Rodriguez, et al. 1993. "HIV Risk Behavior and HIV Seropositivity Among Young Injection Drug Users." *Puerto Rican Health Sciences Journal*, 12:7-12.

Martinez, L., et al. 1988. *El Hostigamiento Sexual de las Trabajadoras en sus Centros de Empleo*. Universidad de Puerto Rico, Centro de Investigaciones Sociales, Facultad de Ciencias Sociales, Recinto de Rio Piedras.

Medina, C. 1987. "Latino Culture and Sex Education." *SIECUS Report*, 15(3):1-4.

Mejias-Picart, T. 1975. "Observaciones Sobre el Machismo en la America Latina." *Revista de Ciencias Sociales*, 19:353-64.

Menendez, B. S. 1990. "Mortalidad por SIDA en Mujeres Puertorriquenas en la Ciudad de Nueva York, 1981-1987." *Puerto Rican Health Sciences Journal*, 9:43-45.

Mock, G. 1984. "La Sexualidad Femenina: Reflexiones para Reflexionar." *Pensamiento Critico*, 16-20.

Mock, G. 1992. Personal Communication.

Mock, G., and M. Ramirez. 1993. *SIDA: Crisis o Reto Transformador*. Marrisonburg, VI: Editorial Cultural.

MMWR—Morbidity and Mortality Weekly Reports. 1989. Centers for Disease Control: Summary of Notifiable Diseases, 38(54):4-9.

MMWR—Morbidity and Mortality Weekly Reports. 1990. Centers for Disease Control: Summary of Notifiable Diseases, 39(53):4-8.

MMWR—Morbidity and Mortality Weekly Reports. 1991. Centers for Disease Control: Summary of Notifiable Diseases, 40(54):4-9.

Ortiz, C. G., and E. Vazquez-Nuttall. 1987. "Adolescent Pregnacy: Effects of Family Support, Education, and Religion on the Decision to Carry or Terminate Among Puerto Rican Teenagers." *Adolescence*, 22:897-917.

Ortiz-Colon, R. 1991. "Grupo de Apoyo con Hombres Homosexuales VIH Positivo: un Estudio de Caso en Puerto Rico." In Cunningham, Ramos-Bellido, and Ortiz-Colon, eds., *El SIDA en Puerto Rico: Acercamientos Multidisciplinarios*. Universidad de Puerto Rico.

Pacheco-Acosta, E. 1990. "El Aborto Inducido en Puerto Rico: 1985." *Puerto Rican Health Sciences Journal*, 9:75-78.

Parker, R. 1987. "Acquired Immunodeficiency Syndrome in Urban Brazil." *Medical Anthropology Quarterly*, n.s. 1(2):155-75.

Pico, I. 1989. *Machismo y Educacion*. Rio Piedras: Editorial Universidad de Puerto Rico.

Quiroz, J., et al. 1991. "Perfil Sociodemografico y Medidas del Crecimiento Fisicos en Pacientes Pediatricos con el Sindrome de Inmunodeficiencia Adquirida Seguidos en el Hospital Municipal de San Juan: 1986-1990." *Boletin de la Asociacion Medica de Puerto Rico*, 83:479-84.

Rivera, R., et al. 1990. "Social Relations and Empowerment of Sexual Partners of IV Drug Users." *Puerto Rican Health Sciences Journal*, 9:99-104.

Robles, R., et al. 1988. "Health Care Services and Sterilization Among Puerto Rican Women." *Puerto Rican Health Sciences Journal*, 7:7-13.

Robles, R., et al. 1990. "AIDS Risk Behavior Patterns Among Intravenous Drug Users in Puerto Rico and the United States." *Boletin de la Asociacion Medica de Puerto Rico,* 83:523-527.

Santos-Ortiz, M. C. 1990. Sexualidad Femenina Antes y Despues del SIDA. *Puerto Rican Health Sciences Journal,* 9:33-35.

Santos-Ortiz, M. C. 1991. "El SIDA y las Relaciones Heterosexuales." In Cunningham, Ramos-Bellido, and Ortiz- Colon, eds., *El SIDA en Puerto Rico: Acercamientos Multidisciplinarios.* Universidad de Puerto Rico.

Sexually Transmitted Diseases Statistics, 1984. Issue 134, U.S. Department of Health and Human Services. Washington, DC: Public Health Service, Center for Disease Control (U.S. Government Printing Office).

Vazquez-Calzada, J. 1988. *La Poblacion de Puerto Rico y su Trayectoria Historica. Rio Piedras: Escuela Graduada de Salud Publica.* Recinto de Ciencias Medicas, Universidad de Puerto Rico.

Vazquez-Calzada, J. 1989. "Variantes en la Estructura del Divorcio del Hogar Puertoriqueno." *Puerto Rican Health Sciences Journal,* 8:225-30.

Vazquez-Calzada, J., I. Parrilla, and L. E. Leon. 1989. "El Efecto de los Partos por Cesarea Sobre la Esterilizacion en Puerto Rico." *Puerto Rican Health Sciences Journal,* 8:215-25.

Vasquez, M. M. 1986. "The Effects of Role Expectations on the Marital Status of Urban Puerto Rican Women." In E. Acosta-Belen, ed., *The Puerto Rican Woman: Perspectives on Culture, History and Society.* Rio Piedras: Universidad de Puerto Rico.

Vasquez, S. M. 1985. "Homophobia Among College Students of Puerto Rican Descent as a Function of Residence and Acculturation Factors." Institute of Advanced Psychological Studies, Adelphi University.

Zorrilla, L. D., J. Romaguera, and C. Diaz. 1993. "Recomendaciones para el Manejo de Mujeres con Infeccion VIH." *Puerto Rican Health Sciences Journal,* 12:55-61.

Russia
(*Rossiyskaya Federatsiya*)

Igor S. Kon, Ph.D.

Contents

Demographics and a Historical Perspective

A. Demographics

Russia's 6.5 million square miles, over three quarters of the total area of the former Union of Soviet Socialist Republics, makes it the largest country in the world. Russia stretches from Finland, Poland, Norway, Latvia, Estonia, and Ukraine on the west, to the Pacific Ocean in the east, spanning ten time zones. Its southern neighbors include Georgia, Azerbaijan, Kazakhstan, China, Mongolia, and North Korea.

The 1995 population was 150 million, and very socially and culturally heterogeneous, with over a hundred distinct ethnic groups. Seventy-three percent of Russians live in urban areas, with Moscow close to 9 million, St. Petersburg, 5 million, and Samara and Nizhny Novgorod, 1.5 million each.

The rest of the people live in rural areas. In 1995, 22 percent of the population was under age 15, and 11 percent age 65 and older. Male life expectancy in 1995 was 64 and, female, 74. Life expectancy in Russia appears to be descreasing significantly and rapidly because of the deteriorating quality of the country's infastructure and economics. The birthrate, according to the *World Almanac,* was 13 per 1,000 in 1995, and declining rapidly in response to the economic situation; the death rate was 11 per 1,000, for a 0.1 percent annual increase. The infant mortality rate was 26 per 1,000 live births. Statistics from 1993 indicate a literacy rate of 98 percent, with most Russians receiving eleven years of schooling. Russia's health care system is in decline because of serious economic trouble since the break-up of the Communist system. Russia has one hospital bed per 74 persons and one physician per 225 persons. Many hospitals are poorly equipped and most are poorly supplied with necessary medicines. The *1996 World Almanac* gives Russia's per capita domestic product as $5,190 (U.S.A.).

B. A Brief Historical Perspective

Slavic tribes began migrating into Russia from the west in the fifth century of the Common Era. The first Russian state was founded in the ninth century with centers in Novgorod and Kiev. In the thirteenth century, Mongols overran the country. The grand dukes of Muscovy (Moscow) led the Russians in recovering their land; by 1480, the Mongols were expelled. Ivan the Terrible (1692-1725) was the first to be formally proclaimed Tsar. Peter the Great (1672-1725) extended the domain and founded the Russian Empire in 1721.

Under the aegis of Empress Catherine the Great (1729-1796), European culture was a dominant influence among the Russian aristocracy, particularly in the years prior to the destruction of the monarchy in the French Revolution. In the nineteenth and early twentieth centuries, Western ideas and the beginnings of modernization spread through the huge Russian empire. Political evolution, however, failed to keep pace.

Military reverses in the war with Japan (1905) and in World War I undermined the Tsarist regime. In 1917, sporadic strikes among factory workers coalesced into a revolution that deposed the Tsar, and established two brief-lived provisional governments in sequence. In brief order, a Communist coup placed Vladimir Ilyich Lenin in power. Lenin's death in 1924 led to a struggle from which Joseph Stalin emerged as the leader. Purges, mass executions, mass exiles, and even a famine engineered in the Ukraine marked Stalin's regime and resulted in millions of deaths, according to most estimates.

Although Russia and Germany signed a non-aggression pact in 1939, Germany launched a massive invasion of Russia in June 1941. Counterattacks during the brutal Russian winters of 1941-1942 and 1942-1943, coupled with the Nazi failure to take and hold Stalingrad, started the German retreat and eventual defeat. After Stalin's death in 1953, the "De-Stalinisation" of Russia began under Nikita Khrushchev. In 1987, Mikhail Gorbachev began a program of reform that included expanded freedoms and democratizing the political process. This openness (*glasnost*) and restructuring (*perestroika*) was opposed by some Eastern-bloc countries and hard-line Communists in the U.S.S.R. In August, Gorbachev resigned and recommended dissolution of the Communist Central Committee. By the end of 1991, seventy-four years of Communist government had ended with declarations of freedom from the Russian, Ukraine, and Kazakhstan republics, and the Union of Soviet Socialist Republics was dissolved. This opened the door for the many recent changes in the sexual lives of Russians detailed in this chapter.

1. Basic Sexological Premises

A. Character of Gender Roles

Soviet Russian general attitudes to gender roles and sex differences can be defined as a sexless sexism. On the one side, gender/sex differences have been theoretically disregarded and politically underestimated. The notions of sex and gender are conspicuously absent from encyclopedias, social-science and psychology dictionaries, and textbooks. On the other side, both public opinion and social practices have been extremely sexist, all empirical sex differences being taken as given by nature.

B. Sociolegal Status of Males and Females

A paramount slogan of the October 1917 Revolution was the liberation of women and the establishment of full legal and social gender equality. The Soviet regime revoked all forms of legal and political discrimination against women. A host of women was attracted into industrial labor, education, and public activities.

Like all other actions by the Bolsheviks, however, the program was naive and unrealistic. Gender equality was interpreted in a mechanical way, as a complete similarity. All historical, cultural, national, and religious-based gender differences were ignored, or viewed merely as "reactionary vestiges of the past," which could and had to be removed by political means (Kon 1995, 51-127).

Soviet propaganda boasted of the fact that women, for the first time in history, had been drawn into the country's sociopolitical and cultural life. By the time Soviet history reached its peak, women comprised 51 percent of the labor force. The percentage of women with university educations was even higher than that of men and, in such professions as teaching and medicine, women absolutely predominated.

Yet, it was not so much an equalization as a feminization of the lower levels of the vocational hierarchy. Women occupy the worst-paid and less-prestigious jobs and they are grossly underrepresented on the higher rungs of labor. Women's average salary was a third less than that of men. With the transition to a market economy and the overall economic collapse of recent years, the position of women has deteriorated sharply. Entrepreneurs simply do not want to take on pregnant women or mothers with large families.

Russian public life remains dominated and governed by men. Women remain socially dependent. Seventy-three percent of the unemployed population are women, and women receive only about 40 percent of men's salaries. Women are also underrepresented in political bodies (Kon 1995, 129-157).

In the family, the situation is more contradictory. About 40 percent of all Russian families may be considered largely egalitarian. Russian women, especially urban women, are more socially and financially independent of their husbands than at any time in the past. Very often, women bear the main responsibility for the family budget and for resolving the main issues of domestic life. Russian wives and mothers are frequently strong, dominant, and sure of themselves. On the other hand, their family load considerably exceeds that of the man and is sometimes absolutely unbearable. The length of the work week was the same for women as for men in the 1980s. Yet, women had to spend two or three times more hours than men on household work.

The fair distribution of household duties is a paramount factor in satisfaction with and the stability of marriage. Mutual recrimination and arguments about who is exploiting whom are a typical feature of Russian press comments going back many years. Women passionately and sorrowfully bemoan the lack of "real men," while men complain about the dying breed of women who show feminine tenderness and affection.

The overall trend in Soviet history has been towards the demasculinization of men. Given all the ethnic, religious, and historical variations, the traditional male lifestyle and stereotyped image has always emphasized such virtues as energy, initiative, and independence. These qualities are extremely important for male self-esteem. Yet, the economic inefficiency of the Soviet system, the political despotism, and bureaucracy left little room for individual initiative and autonomy. At any moment in his life, from the cradle to the grave, the Russian boy, adolescent, man felt socially and sexually dependent and frustrated.

This social dependency was intensified by the global feminization of all institutions and processes of socialization. As a result of the high level of undesired pregnancies and divorces, every fifth child in the U.S.S.R. was brought up without a father or, at least, a stepfather. In the mid-1980s, some 13,500,000 children were being raised in so-called single-mother families. Yet, even where the father was physically present, his influence and authority in the family and his role in bringing up the children were considerably less than those of the mother.

Thus, from the start of his life, the Russian boy is dependent on a loving but dominant mother. In the nursery and at school, the major authority figures are women; male teachers are extremely rare. In official children's and youth Communist organizations recognized by adults, the Pioneers and the Komsomol, it was also girls who set the tone. Junior and senior boys only found kindred spirits in informal street groups and gangs where the power and the symbols of power were exclusively male. As in the West, many of these male groups exhibit strong antifeminist tendencies.

When a young man marries, he has to deal with a solicitous, but often very dominating wife, much like his mother once was in his youth. The wife knows much better than he how to plan the family budget and what they need for the home and family. The husband ends up merely carrying out her instructions.

Finally, in public life, absolutely everything came under the control of the powerful maternal care of the Communist Party, which knew better than anyone what was best for its citizens and was ever ready to correct a citizen's mistakes by force if necessary.

This has produced three typical reactions: (1) Psychological compensation and overcompensation through the acquisition of a primitive image of a strong and aggressive male, affirming himself through drunkenness, fighting, and both social and sexual abuse; (2) The combination of humility and subservience in public life, with cruel tyranny in the home and family directed at the wife and children; and (3) Social passivity and learned helplessness, a flight from personal responsibility to the careless, play world of eternal boyhood.

All this is equally bad for both men and women. Aggressive sexism as a means of compensating for social helplessness gives rise to sexual violence. Many Russian women are obligated to withstand patiently the vulgarity, drunkenness, and even physical abuse of their husbands, thinking that it cannot be otherwise. Sometimes, they even see in that the manifestation of love, as it was in Ancient Rus: "A man who doesn't beat his wife doesn't love her." An intelligent and educated women frequently sacrifices her own professional and public career to maintain the family, but also because she is afraid of surpassing and thereby offending her husband.

As a result, opposition to the idea of gender equality has been mounting and widening since the 1970s. Men find it painful to lose their old privileges and accept the uncertainty of their social status. Women feel themselves deceived because they are under a double yoke. As a consequence, there is a mighty wave of conservative opinion dreaming of turning the clock back to times that were not only pre-Soviet, but prior to the industrial revolution and Peter the Great. Of course, a return to the premedieval (Domostroi) household rules is a conservative utopia. However tough life is for present-day Russian women, the overwhelming majority would never agree to reduce their social roles to being only a wife and mother. Younger and better educated men also have more egalitarian social views and take on a greater domestic, including fatherly, responsibility.

[The collapse of Soviet rule changed everything in Russia, except the relationship between the sexes, which has deteriorated significantly. Expectations in heterosexual relationships have been and are low, but divorce rates remain high, and the number of single mothers, either divorced or never married, keeps growing. In contrast with the United States where single mothers have become the hallmark of the poorest urban areas, Russian women from all walks of life, domestic and factory workers, college graduates, university professors, and professionals alike, have grown inured to raising their families without men, relying on a support network of mothers, sisters, and aunts in a kind of matriarchal society with a downward spiral of poverty and limited horizons. Paternal absence and neglect is a reality widely shared by Russian women, regardless of background, aspirations, or income.

[Even in Communist times, the unhappiness of Russian families was hard to hide. The divorce rate in the 1970s was 40 percent; now it is 51 percent. In the past, sociologists blamed Soviet life, its regimentation, oppression, and lack of individual freedom, for men's alcoholism and apathy to work and family. Today, the major factor appears to be an economic free fall that humiliates men who cannot provide for their families, to the point where they just walk away with little social censure. An estimated 15 to 20 percent of all Russian families are now headed by a single parent, 94 percent of whom are women. This number is not significantly higher than those in Western and Eastern Europe and far lower than in the United States, where sociologists estimate 27 percent of mothers are single.

[Some Russian sociologists suggest that single mothers are not much worse off than married mothers, because so many single mothers—31 percent—live with their mothers or relatives. Others point out that single mothers generally do not want to live with relatives, but have no other choice. In a study begun in 1991 comparing Russian single mothers with European single mothers, half of the single mothers in countries like Switzerland were living with boyfriends, whereas only 5 percent in Russia had found a new partner. In addition, Russian divorce law does not allow joint custody, and child-support payments, while required by law, are difficult to collect and increasing. Given the free-market economy, men are better off hiding their real income from tax collectors and ex-wives. Many single mothers in the larger cities do not have residency permits and cannot apply for state welfare help, minimal as that is. While parliament is drafting a new law aimed at providing absent fathers with more-flexible child-support payments, few expect the government to have much impact on this deeply rooted social problem (Stanley 1995). (Editor)]

C. General Concepts of Sexuality and Love

Contrary to an opinion widespread in the U.S.A., Russians are very attached to the ideal of romantic love, which is considered a necessary precondition of marriage and even sex. In a 1992 national public-opinion poll, 53 percent of the men and 49 percent of the women said that they have experienced "real love." "Sex without love" was approved as normal by only 15 percent of the respondents, while 57 percent strongly disapproved of it (Kon 1995, 19-25, 52-53, 158-175).

But such attitudes may be unrealistic and reflect the contradictions of a classical Russian excessive romanticism that was formulated in Chekhov's short story "Ariadna" (1895):

> We are not satisfied because we are idealists. We want the beings who give us birth and produce our children to be higher than us, higher than anything on earth. When we are young we romanticize and idolize those we fall in love with; love and happiness are synonyms with us. For us in Russia, loveless marriage is scorned, sensuality is mocked and induces revulsion, and those novels and stories where women are beautiful, poetic and elevated enjoy the most success. . . . But the trouble is as follows. Hardly do we marry or hit it off with a woman than, give or take a couple of years, and we feel we've been disappointed, let down; we try other women and again we find disillusion, again horror, and ultimately we convince ourselves that women are liars, petty, vain, unjust, uneducated, cruel—in a word, even immeasurably lower, not simply not higher, than us men.

According to 1990-92 research of Russian university students, they, especially women, have more-pragmatic and less-romantic attitudes about marriage, particularly a readiness to marry without love, than their American, German, and Japanese counterparts. Nevertheless, as everywhere in the world, their real sexual-erotic motivations are mixed, contradictory, and heterogeneous. Also, general developmental trends in Russia are more or less similar to those occurring in Western countries:

- Earlier maturation and sexual initiation of boys and girls;
- Growing, and more or less universal, social and moral acceptance of premarital sex and cohabitation;
- Weakening of the traditional double standard for men and women;
- Growing recognition of the importance of sexual satisfaction for individual happiness and for marital stability;
- Growing public interest in all kinds of erotica and a demand for sexual freedom;
- Growing generational gap in sexual values, attitudes, and behaviors—many things that were considered deviant, unacceptable, and even unmentionable for parents, are normal and desirable for their children (Kon 1995, 158-175).

As in any other large country, sexual values and attitudes are heterogeneous, depending on gender, age cohort, education level, social milieu (whether the person lives in a large city, a small town, or in the countryside, and where he or she spent childhood and adolescence), ethnic identity, and religious affiliation.

Younger and better-educated people are more prone now to accept sex for pleasure only, without relation to love and marriage. On the other hand, as a reaction to this new individualism, normative anomie, and the weakening of family ties, some conservative and religious writers and philosophers criticize not only hedonistic eroticism, but even classical romantic, passionate love, which, they claim, should be subjugated to the quiet, conjugal love and traditional family values.

Because of the economic collapse, the institution of marriage is in a deep crisis. In 1992, there were 20 percent to 30 percent fewer new marriages concluded in Russia than in 1990. In the same period, the number of divorces has risen by 15 percent. About half of all Russian men and women have at least one divorce during their lifetime. About a third of the divorced are young couples who live together less than five years.

2. Religious and Ethnic Factors Affecting Sexuality

A. Source and Character of Religious Values

Despite the seventy-four-year effort of communism to promote atheism, 25 percent of the people still adhere to Russian Orthodox Christianity. While approximately 60 percent of Russians were nonreligious when the communist regime fell, Christianity and Orthodoxy are experiencing a mild revival. Among the non-Russian populations, Islam and Buddhism are widespread.

Ancient Slav paganism was rich with sexual symbols and associations. Sexuality was believed to be a general cosmic force. There were numerous openly sexual rites and orgiastic festivals at which men and women bathed naked together, the men symbolically fertilizing the earth and the women exposing their genitals to heaven in order to invoke the rain. In spite of the Church's efforts to eradicate certain "devilish" pagan sex rituals, some of these survived among Northern Russia peasants until the end of the nineteenth century (Kon 1995, 11-49).

The Christianization of Russia, beginning in the ninth century, introduced a new philosophy of sexuality, but this influence has been slow and superficial. The Russian Orthodox Church, *volens nolens*, had to accommodate ancient sexual practices in numerous regional and ethnic diversities. On some issues like clerical celibacy, it was more lenient, or rather, more realistic, than the medieval Catholic Church. While complete abstinence from sexual relations, even in marriage, was officially classified as a "holy deed," in everyday life, sexual activity in marriage was fully accepted. While celibacy was obligatory for the monks from whom the highest Church leaders were chosen, ordinary priests were obligated to marry and to have children. Unable to eradicate certain ancient pagan customs, the Church concentrated more on matters of social representation and verbalization.

Hence, we have the persistent normative conflict between the naturalistic pagan attitudes to sexuality in the "low" everyday peasant culture and the extreme spiritualism and otherworldly asceticism of the official "high" culture. Everyday life was openly sensual, cruel, and carnal. Debauchery, drunkenness, sexual violence, and rape were quite common. Russian folk tales are filled with polygamous heroes. Various sexual exploits, such as the rape of a sleeping beauty, are sympathetically described. It was permissible and noble, for example, "to dishonor" or rape a virgin girl in just revenge for her refusal to marry the hero. There was no place for modesty and privacy in the lives of peasants, and the nude body was often unwillingly and deliberately (ritually) displayed. Russian communal bathhouses, where men and women often washed together, surprised and shocked more than a few foreign travelers in the sixteenth and seventeenth centuries.

At the same time, the limits on symbolic, artistic representation of the body were extremely narrow. In Western religious painting since the Renaissance and even in the late Middle Ages, the entire human body was represented as real, living flesh. Only the genitals were veiled. In the Russian icons, only the face is alive. The body is entirely covered or outlined in an emaciated and ascetic manner. Nothing similar to the paintings or sculpture of Michelangelo, da Vinci, or Raphael was permitted. Secular paintings of nudes did not appear until the end of the eighteenth century.

Sexually explicit art emerged in Russia only in the middle of the eighteenth century, under the direct influence of French "libertines." The Imperial Court of Catherine the Great (1729-1796) was highly eroticized. The first explicitly sexual Russian poetry by Ivan Barkov (1732-1768) was deliberately crude and arrogant. It lacked the elegance of French "libertine" literature and was never published legally. Russian nobility took lovers and read pornographic literature (mostly imported) (Kon 1995, 23-38).

In the West, the Church and clerical forces were a major foe of the erotic art and culture of pleasure. In Russia, the Church was particularly powerful because of its close relations with the state. Russian censorship was stricter and more pervasive than in Western countries.

B. Source and Character of Secular and Ethnic Values

Three facts are important for understanding the specific features of Russian eros.

First, the contrast between the official high culture and the low everyday culture of the common people was considerably greater in Russia than in the West. The official high culture was sanctified by the Church and antisexual by its very nature, while the low culture of the common people accorded sexuality a positive value common to all medieval European Christian cultures.

Second, refined, complex erotic art came into being and gained acceptance much later in Russia than in the West. And it is only through the medium of erotic art that sexuality could be included in high culture at all.

Third, the development of civilized forms of everyday social life was, in Russia, more closely associated with state power that with the civil society. Because new rules of propriety were often introduced by political authorities, there was more pressure towards uniformity of everyday conduct than towards individualization and diversification; and without some established and reasonably diverse subcultures, there can be no basis for normative pluralism, one manifestation of which is sexual tolerance.

These three factors are interconnected both historically and functionally.

In addition to the religious influence, one special factor has powerfully influenced sexuality in Russia: nineteenth-century, left-wing radical revolutionary-democratic literary criticism. Young aristocrats of the early nineteenth century received a good secular home education from early childhood. Whatever their moral and religious convictions, they tried to distance themselves from official bigotry and were not afraid of their own sexual feelings and experiences. The most revered Russian poet, Alexander Pushkin (1799-1837), wrote some elegant and witty erotic poetry.

For the next generation of Russian intellectuals, who came mainly from a clerical background and were often themselves former seminarists, such freedom was impossible. While breaking with some of their parent's principles and values, they were unable to overcome others. Constant inner battles against their own unconventional sexual practices and feelings, particularly self-pleasuring and homoeroticism, turned into a global moral and aesthetic rejection and denunciation of sexuality and hedonism as something vulgar, dangerous, and unworthy. Only broad social objectives, such as liberation of the poor and oppressed, were morally justified. Everything that was private or personal was considered secondary—and egotistical.

These antisexual, antihedonistic attitudes have become an integral part of a definite ideological trend in Russian culture. As in the West, it was a moral expression of the middle-class, bourgeoisie opposition to aristocratic individualism. In Russia, however, this opposition was more radical. While religious bigots condemned eroticism as godless and amoral, populists rejected it as politically incorrect, vulgar, and nonaesthetic.

Any artist or writer who dared to walk up that "slippery slope" came under immediate attack both from the right and from the left. This seriously hampered the birth and development of a lofty, refined erotic art and language, without which sexual discourse inevitably appears base, dirty, and squalid. Inhibitions against sexuality and sensuous pleasure are generally typical for Russian classical literature. Sex is presented as a tragedy or quasi-religious revelation, very rarely as a pleasure.

On the eve of the twentieth century, the Russian cultural climate began to change. Leo Tolstoy's *Kreutzer Sonata* (1891) stimulated a philosophical dispute about the nature and relationship of love, sex, marriage, and erotica, with prominent Russian writers like Anton Chekhov and philosophers like Vladimir Solovjev, Nikolai Berdjaev, and Vassilij Rozanov taking part. While this metaphysics of sexuality tried theoretically to rehabilitate eroticism, it had no place for real, everyday, routine sexual pleasure (Kon 1995, 39-49).

While sophisticated erotic art and literature did appear in Russia in the early twentieth century, the artists of that era were seeking more a legitimization of eroticism than portraying sexual enjoyment. Exceptions like the poet Mikhail Kuzmin and the painter Konstantin Somov only confirm this general pattern. Whatever its aesthetical and moral value, early-twentieth-century Russian erotic art was marginal both to the official and popular cultures. It was looked upon as decadent and was equally denounced with vehemence by the right and by the left.

In the early 1900s, the first sexual surveys were conducted among students at Moscow and other universities. Sexual concerns were raised within the disciplines of medicine, history, ethnography, and anthropology. The word "sexology" as a name for a special subdivision of science was suggested by Rosanov in 1909.

The October Revolution of 1917 liberated sexuality from its traditional religious, moral, and institutional restraints. No longer was sex a taboo subject. On the contrary, traditional sexual morality and marriage as a social institution were themselves suspect. Everywhere there were fierce discussions of "free love" and debates over whether the proletariat needed any sexual restrictions whatsoever. The first net result, however, was sexual anarchy, the growth of unwanted pregnancies and births, induced abortions, sexually transmitted diseases, rape, and prostitution (Kon 1995, 39-49).

"The sexual question" being politically important, the Soviet government in the 1920s sponsored some sociological, biomedical, and anthropological sex research, as well as elementary sex education. Yet, the elitist, individualistic, and "decadent" erotic art was absolutely incompatible with the new revolutionary mentality. Sexual pleasure was only a hindrance and distraction from the goals of the Socialist revolution. In the 1920s, a few liberal Communists, like Alexandra Kollontai, suggested "to make way for winged Eros," but that was against the mainstream.

Already in the 1920s, erotica was treated as morally and socially subversive. The only legitimate function of sexuality was reproduction. According to the influential party educator and sexologist, Aaron Zalkind, "sexual selection should proceed according to the line of a class revolutionary-proletarian consciousness. The elements of flirtation, courtship, and coquetry should not be introduced into love relationships" (1924). In the article on "Sexual Life" in the first edition of the *Great Soviet Encyclopedia* (1940), the emphasis is exclusively on social control: the dangers of "unhealthy sexual interest" are discussed and the aim of sex education is clearly described as the "rational transmission of sex drive into the sphere of labor and cultural interests."

Another historical factor that has affected the sexuality of the Russian people is their rather prudish approach to nudity and bodily functions.

Thirty years ago, there was controversy about wearing any kind of shorts in public, including at beach resorts. Now walking shorts are no longer prohibited in the western regions. The attitudes of Moslems in the eastern republics are even stricter. Body exposure by Moslem women is still strictly forbidden, and violating the taboo can lead to severe punishment. In these regions, shorts even on men are considered indecent.

Bodily functions are not openly acknowledged in Russian culture. Direct reference to the need for a toilet is considered impolite. Russians will just quietly disappear from a meeting or social gathering, or, at most, will simply refer to their intention to walk in a particular direction. Even young people who are dating and know each other well often make up artificial explanations before excusing themselves to find a toilet.

An additional contributor to the avoidance of overt discussion of bodily functions may be the sorry state of the country's plumbing. Part of the general breakdown of material goods and services in Russian society following the 1991 revolution includes the public restroom facilities, which are no longer free and often broken or dirty. Wash basins may stand idle, or may yield only a dribble of cold water. Toilet tissue is scarce; its substitutes include newspaper, magazine pages, used office papers, and even cardboard.

Despite the attention to cleanliness paid by many citizens, the combination of bodily inhibitions and inadequate material resources have combined to threaten their overall health, making personal hygiene difficult. Even the interest in improving physical fitness through better diet and exercise is only beginning, despite a long history of purported government commitment.

The Russian ambivalence toward nakedness, bodily functions, intimate hygiene, and sexuality combined with a history of heavy censorship and the contemporary lack of material resources to make the impact of these factors on everyday life and sexuality even greater.

Sexual enjoyment and freedom have been incompatible with totalitarian state control over personality. As George Orwell put it in *1984*:

> It was not merely that the sex instinct created a world of its own that was outside the Party's control and which therefore had to be destroyed if possible. What was more important was that sexual [de]privation induced hysteria, which was desirable because it could be transformed into war-fever and leader-worship. . . . For how could the fear, the hatred, and the lunatic credulity which the Party needed in its members be kept at the right pitch, except by bottling up some powerful instinct and using it as a driving force? The sex impulse was dangerous to the Party, and the Party had turned it to account.

The history of the Soviet regime was one of sexual repression. Only the means of legitimation and phraseology of this suppression was changeable. In the 1920s, sexuality had to be suppressed in the name of the higher interests of the working class and Socialist revolution. In the 1930s, self-discipline was advocated for the sake of the Soviet state and Communist Party. In the 1950s, state-administrative control was gradually transformed into moral-administrative regulations, this time for the sake of stability of marriage and the family. But with all these ideological differences, the practical message regarding sex remained the same: DON'T DO IT! The Communist image of sexuality was always negative, and the need for strict external social control was always emphasized. The elimination of sexuality was beyond the abilities of the Soviet regime. But the net result of this sexophobia was an extermination of all sorts of erotic culture and the prohibition of sexual discourse, whether in the area of sex research, erotic art, or medical information. No wonder that the breakdown of the Soviet regime in 1991, and ever earlier with the advent of *glasnost,* sexuality became one of the most important symbols of social and cultural liberation.

3. Sexual Knowledge and Education

A. Government Policies and Programs for Sex Education

As in the former U.S.S.R., Russia today still has virtually no systematic sex education, although some efforts have been made to develop school-based programs since the early 1980s. Table 1 shows the responses in a late-1989 national public-opinion poll to the question, "What channels of information on sexual life do you believe are the most acceptable and efficient?"

Table 1

Preferred Sources of Sexual Information (in Percentages)

Source of Information	Percentage
Special school course	46
Special educational literature	43
Special educational films or TV	29
Conversation with a physician	22
Conversation with parents	21
Personal experience	6
Discussion with peers	5
No need for sex education	3

Clearly, a majority of the Russian people favor organized sex education. But the Communist Soviet government did not want it, and the present Russian government has no money for anything. However, an experimental 12-hour sex-education course for adolescents, based on a program from the Netherlands, was to have begun in eight schools in 1995 (Kon 1995, 75-76, 95-100, 108-110, 117-118, 192-193).

B. Informal Sources of Sexual Knowledge

According to a 1992 national survey, only 13 percent of Russian parents talk with their children about sexuality. The main sources of sexual information for teenagers, therefore, are their peers and the mass media. For adults, some medical and psychological information services are available in the larger cities. Several popular Western books have been translated, and a few have been written by Russian authors, after 1987. Sexual issues are now often discussed on television and in the newspapers. But there is neither strategy nor money to do this effectively. The main source of sexual knowledge for many people are pornographic magazines and erotic newspapers. The monthly newspaper *SPID-info* (AIDS-information) has the second largest print run in the country, 4.5 million. It says little about AIDS, but gives popular information about sexuality and erotic topics.

4. Autoerotic Behaviors and Patterns

Children and adolescents normally have their first sexual experience through self-pleasuring. Boys generally start to engage in self-pleasuring at the age of 12 or 13, reaching a peak at age 15 to 16. Girls begin to self-pleasure at a later age and do it less frequently. According to a 1982 survey by V. V. Danilov, 22.5 percent of the girls had engaged in self-pleasuring by age 13.5, 37.4 percent by age 15.5, 50.2 percent by age 17.5, and 65.8 percent by age 18.5.

Until the late 1970s, official attitudes to self-pleasuring were completely negative. Children were told that it results in impotence, deterioration of the memory, and similar harmful consequences. As an antidote, there was a clandestine teen ditty: "Sun, fresh air, and onanism reinforce the organism." Nevertheless, many Russian teens and adults still have strong anxieties regarding it. Many sexual dysfunctions are attributed to self-pleasuring experiences, and adults are terribly ashamed of it (Kon 1995, 43-44, 189-199).

5. Interpersonal Heterosexual Behaviors

A/B. Children and Adolescents

Puberty

The overall trends in the psychosexual development of Russian children and adolescents are the same as in Western countries. Above all, there has been a substantial acceleration of sexual maturation. The average menarche age fell from 15.1 years to 13 among Muscovite girls over a period of thirty-five years, from 1935 to 1970. Similar trends are also typical for the boys.

Sexual maturation confronts the teenager with a host of bodily and psychosexual problems. Many boys are worried about delay in emergence of their secondary sexual attributes in relation to their peers—shortness of height or of the penis, gynecomastia (transitory female-breast development), etc. Girls are concerned about hirsuteness, being overweight, the shape of their breasts, etc. (Kon 1995, 194-209).

Premarital Sexual Activities and Relationships

There is clear evidence that sexual activity is beginning earlier for today's Russian adolescents than in past generations. The mean age for first coitus dropped in the last ten years from 19.2 to 18.4 for males, and from 21.8 to 20.6 for females. According to the only survey of teenagers ages 12 to 17 (Chervyakov, Kon, and Shapiro 1993), sexual experience was reported by 15 percent of the girls and by 22 percent of the boys. Among 16- to 17-year-olds 36 percent were sexually experienced; among 14- to 15-year-olds, 13 percent; and under 14 years, only 2 percent. Boys are generally more sexually experienced than girls, but the difference gradually disappears with age. Just as it was in the West in the late 1960s, early sexual experience is related to some form of deviant or counter-normative behavior: drinking, smoking, drug use, lower academic grades, poor school discipline, and closer association with peer group. Psychologically, sexually active 16-year-olds are more prone to be involved in different sorts of risky behavior, and some of them are from socially underprivileged families (Kon 1995, 62-63, 166-169).

The largest percentage of young people become sexually active between ages 16 and 18, with the incidence of intercourse reported in various studies ranging from 22 to 38 percent of the boys and 11 to 35 percent of the girls. "Love" is reported by many young people to be the primary motivator for sexual activity, about 30 percent of males and 45 percent of females. "Desire for enjoyment" or "pleasure" are reported by 20 percent of males and 10 percent of females. Many young people separate sexual motives from those involving marriage and engagement.

C. Adults

Premarital Courtship, Dating, and Relationships

The overall trend is towards a reduction in age and a rise in moral toleration of premarital sex and cohabitation. Among the university students surveyed by Golod in the 1978-79 academic year, four out of every five men and every second woman had had sexual experience by the time they were surveyed. A total of 3,741 students from eighteen colleges and universities were asked why they thought young men and women entered into sexual relations nowadays. The responses are shown in Table 2 (Golod 1984).

Table 2

Motivations for Sexual Relationships (in Percentages)

Motives	Men (*N* = 1,829)	Women (*N* = 1,892)
Mutual love	28.8	46.1
Enjoyable pursuit	20.2	11.4
Desire to obtain pleasure	18.1	9.2
Desire for emotional contact	10.6	7.7
Intended marriage	6.6	9.4
Self-affirmation	5.5	3.6
Prestige, fashion	4.1	4.8
Curiosity	4.9	5.6
Extending sense of freedom, independence	1.8	2.2

It is clear from these data that certain gender differences still persist in sexual behavior and motivation; men are more likely than women to justify sex merely for pleasure and to engage in premarital sex, not only with the beloved one, but also with some occasional partners. And, in fact, the men do have more sexual partners than the women (Kon 1995, 158-177).

Marriage and the Family

As in the West, individualization and intimization of the marital relationship have been taking place in Russia over recent decades. Sexual harmony is playing an increasingly important role here. According to Golod's (1984) surveys, sexual harmony invariably takes third place among factors contributing to perceived marital success and stability, after spiritual and psychological compatibility, among spouses who have been married for up to ten years, and after spiritual and domestic compatibility for those who have been living together for between ten and fifteen years. Sexual satisfaction and general satisfaction with the marriage are closely interrelated. Practically all couples maximally satisfied with their marriages believed they were sexually compatible, while only 63 percent were sexually compatible among the maritally dissatisfied (Kon 1995, 158-177).

Gender inequality and sexism manifest themselves in the marital bed as well (Kon 1995, 129-157). The natural and widespread disharmony of sexual-erotic needs and desires between wives and husbands, which should be the subject of exploration and discussion, is often seen by Russian spouses and those about them as a manifestation of an ineradicable organic sexual incompatibility; the only way out is divorce. Even in the professional literature, this problem is often discussed not in process terms—how the spouses adapt and grow accustomed to each other—but in essentialist terms—whether spouses and their individual traits are compatible to each other.

The woman is almost always the first to suffer from poor sexual adaptation. The lack of a common language and the sexological ignorance create a mass of communication difficulties among married couples. Instead of exploring their problems together or going to a doctor, the spouses run off to their same-sex friends.

Another major problem is the lack of privacy, the shortage of housing, and poor housing conditions. Millions of Russians spend many years, or their whole lifetime, living in dormitories or communal flats, sometimes several families in one room, where every movement is seen or heard by others. Among 140 Soviet immigrants living in the U.S.A. asked by Mark Popovsky in 1984, "What hindered your sexual life in the Soviet Union?" the absence of a separate apartment was mentioned by 126 (90 percent), the absence of a separate bedroom by 122 (87 percent), and the excessive attention from the neighbors living in the same apartment by 93 respondents (66 percent). The lack of privacy is an even worse problem for nonmarital sex. "Where?" is the desperately important and difficult question to answer. Lack of privacy is detrimental for the quality of sexual experience and produces anxieties and neuroses.

The divorce rate is very high; approximately one marriage of three ends in divorce. More than half of all divorces are initiated by the wife.

Cohabitation is more and more widespread among younger couples. Sometimes it is a first stage of marriage, until children are born, and sometimes an alternative form of marriage. Public opinion, especially among younger people, is gradually becoming more and more tolerant of cohabitation.

Extramarital sex, both casual and long-term, is quite common; according to S. Golod (1984), more than three quarters of the people surveyed had extramarital contacts in 1989, whereas in 1969, the figure was less than half. But public opinion is critical of extramarital sex. In the VCIOM 1992 survey directed by Professor Yurt Levada (Kon 1995, 275), only 23 percent agreed that it is okay to have a lover as well as a husband or wife, while 50 percent disagreed. Extramarital affairs seem to be morally more acceptable for men than for women (Kon 1995, 21, 45, 63, 166-167).

Sexuality and the Physically Disabled and Aged

Because of poverty and poor medical services, the sexuality of the physically disabled and the aged person has not so far attracted professional or public attention. Nothing is done to help these people.

Incidence of Oral and Anal Sex

Younger and better educated Russians often complain about the poverty of their sexual techniques. Anal and oral sex are legal and quite widespread, though some people believe these behaviors are sexual perversions. In some legal documents, both anal and oral sex are referred to as unnatural forms of sexual satisfaction.

6. Homoerotic, Homosexual, and Ambisexual Behaviors

Although the Russian Orthodox Church has always severely condemned sodomy and other forms of male and female homosexuality—especially when it threatened the monasteries—the state tended to turn a blind eye to such things in everyday life. In sixteenth- and seventeenth-century Russia, homosexuality was not an unmentionable subject; it was, in fact, often the subject of very frank discussion and ribald jokes.

The first state laws against *muzhelozhstve* (male lechery, buggery) appeared in military statutes drawn up on the Swedish model during the eighteenth-century reign of Peter the Great. The initial punishment of burning at the stake was changed to corporal punishment. The criminal code of 1832 based on the German model punished sodomy (buggery) with deprivation of all rights and exile to Siberia for four to five years. New criminal legislation adopted in 1903 reduced punishment to incarceration for no less than three months or, in aggravating circumstances, to three to eight years.

This legislation, however, was employed extremely rarely. Many Russian aristocrats, including members of the imperial family, as well as eminent artistic figures of the turn of the century openly led homosexual or bisexual lifestyles. A few lesbian couples were also quite well known at the time. Homoerotic poetry, literature, and painting began to appear. Same-sex love began to be debated seriously and sympathetically in philosophical, scientific, and artistic literature.

After the February 1917 Revolution and the demise of the old criminal code, the legal persecution of homosexuals ceased. In the Soviet Russian Criminal Codes of 1922 and 1926, homosexuality is not referred to at all, but in those parts of the old Russian Empire where it was most widespread—the Islamic republics of Azerbaijan, Turkmenia, and Uzbekistan, as well as in Christian Georgia—the legislation remained in force. In the 1920s, homosexuality was treated as a sickness rather than a crime.

Up to the 1930s, the situation of Soviet homosexuals, who frequently called themselves "blues," was reasonably bearable and many played a prominent part in Soviet culture. However, the opportunity for an open, philosophical and artistic discussion of the theme, which began at the turn of the century, gradually diminished.

In 1933, male homosexuality (*muzhelozhstve*) again became a criminal offense and literally an unmentionable, even in scientific literature, vice in the U.S.S.R. Conviction of this crime was punishable by deprivation of freedom for up to five years, or up to eight years if compulsion, violence, a minor, or abuse of a dependent was involved. This law (Article 121 of the RSFS Criminal Code) was frequently used up till the 1980s against dissidents and to extend terms in labor camps. Application of the law has always been selective. As long as they did not fall foul of the authorities, certain homosexual cultural and artistic celebrities enjoyed relative immunity. If they overstepped the mark, however, the law descended upon them with a vengeance.

Gay men in confinement have to endure absolutely unbearable conditions. A person who ended up in prison or labor camp under Article 121 usually became straightaway a "no-rights odd-bod" and recipient of constant taunts and persecution from other prisoners. Further, the rape of adolescents and young men is widespread in both prisons and labor camps; after such assaults, the victims forfeit all human rights, become "degraded," and have to act submissively to their violators. The status of the "degraded" is even worse than that of voluntarily passive homosexuals, who, to a certain degree, select their own partners and protectors (who perform an active, "male" sexual role that is not stigmatized and is even encouraged). The "degraded," on the other hand, are fair game for anyone. (Some Russian medical experts still make a "fundamental" division of homosexuals into "active" and "passive," depending on preferred sexual positions; moreover, they associate "passive" with "inborn" and "genuine," and "active" with "acquired" homosexuality.)'

In the 1980s, the AIDS epidemic worsened matters for homosexuals. When AIDS arrived in the U.S.S.R., health officials referred to morality and risk groups, especially gays, portraying them as carriers, not only of the dreaded virus, but of just about every other vice. This hypocritical moralizing and the search for scapegoats instead of a real sociohygienic policy helped to increase HIV infection already at a high level because of contaminated blood transfusions for hemophiliacs.

While the possibility of decriminalization of homosexuality has been debated by lawyers since 1973, these arguments have been secret and did not spill over into the newspapers until 1987. Since 1987, the popular press, particularly youth papers, radio, and TV, have discussed homosexuality: What is it? How should one relate to "blues"? Should they be treated as sick, criminal, or as victims of fate? From journalistic articles and letters from gay men and lesbians and their parents, ordinary Soviet people have, for the first time, come to recognize the scarred destinies, the police cruelty, the legal repression, the sexual violence in prison, labor camps, and armed forces and, finally, the tragic, inescapable loneliness experienced by people living in constant fear and unable to meet any of their own sort. Each publication has provoked a whole stream of contradictory responses that the newspaper editors have just not known how to handle.

After the breakup of the Soviet Union, some republics, beginning with Ukraine, Estonia, Latvia, Moldova, and Armenia, revoked their antihomosexual legislation. On April 29, 1993, Russian President Boris Yeltsin signed, and lawmakers approved, a decree repealing Article 121.1 dealing with consenting adult relations. Article 121.2 regarding minors and force remains in effect. The repeal did not address gay women since lesbianism was not acknowledged by previous Soviet governments (Kon 1995, 239-264). A new 1997 criminal code may well restore the former repression of gays.

Nevertheless, homosexuals remain the most hated and stigmatized social minority. In the VCIOM 1992 survey directed by Levada (Kon 1995, 275), the question "How ought we to act with homosexuals?" produced the following spread of answers: 33 percent favored exterminating homosexuals, 30 percent favored isolating them from society, and 10 percent said leave them alone. Only 6 percent favored helping homoscxuals.

The Communist, chauvinist, and fascist media methodically and consistently lumps together Zionism, democracy, and homosexuality. With few exceptions, Russian sexopathologists and psychiatrists still regard homosexuality as a disease, and repeat in their writings the negative stereotypes prevalent in the mass consciousness. Thus, parents are likely to be both worried and defensive when they confront behavior in one of their children that might lead to questions about homosexuality. If an adolescent appears to have a "crush" on a classmate or peer of the same gender, his or her parents may consult a physician or psychiatrist who is almost certain to discourage it directly, or attempt to eradicate the feelings and prevent any erotic activity.

Most gay and lesbian adults attempt to keep their orientation a secret from family, friends, and colleagues in the workplace. The risks of public scandal and humiliation, loss of a job, and other complications are too great. Gay men and lesbian women are often physically assaulted in the streets, beaten, and even murdered.

Nevertheless, the situation is rapidly changing. By 1989, after public discussions of homosexuality began in the mass media, on television and radio, sometimes quite sympathetic, gays and lesbians themselves initiated a struggle against discrimination. In 1990, the first openly gay and lesbian organization was formed in Moscow. As of mid-1994, there were several such organizations. In 1993, the National Union of Gays, Lesbians, and Bisexuals was formed. Gay activists take part in the AIDS-prevention work. Gay themes are now represented in the theater and movies. Several legally registered gay and lesbian newspapers (*Tema, Risk, 1/10,* and others) are published. In Moscow and St. Petersburg, there are gay discos, bars, and restaurants. Special consulting services are being organized. But all these effects suffer from the shortage of both money and professional personnel, as well as the lack of internal cooperation. Political activists quarrel among themselves and have little influence in the mainstream culture and mass media.

7. Gender Conflicted Persons

Among the native populations of Siberia and the Far East regions of Russia, the tradition of the *berdach,* a spiritual leader who is neither male nor female but a third gender, was widespread in the beginning of the twentieth century as an aspect of shaman behavior. The present situation of this custom is unknown.

In 1960, Professor Aron Belkin began biomedical (psychoendocrinological) research on transgenderists and transsexuals. However, the psychological and social factors of gender dysphoria are largely ignored. An Association of Transsexuals was formed in 1992 in Moscow to work for the human rights of transsexuals.

8. Significant Unconventional Sexual Behaviors

A. Coercive Sex

Child Sexual Abuse, Incest, and Pedophilia

Reports of child sexual abuse were extremely uncommon in the Soviet press. Officially, incest did not exist as a societal problem. Indeed, any kind of child abuse and violence in the family—and it is very widespread—is only beginning to come to the attention of authorities and the professional community (Kon 1995, 215-218).

Some health professionals and others have begun to uncover evidence of various kinds of sexual activity between adults and children, as well as between children of different ages in orphanages, youth camps, and even families. The data on sexual harassment, child abuse, and violence in Moscow and St. Petersburg are largely anecdotal and unreliable, but the problem is serious. In the 1993 adolescent sexuality survey conducted by Vladimir Shapiro and Valery Chervyakov of 1,615 students aged 12 to 17 years in Moscow and St. Petersburg, 24 percent of the teenage girls and 11 percent of the boys said they had experienced some sort of sexual pressure, someone pushing them to go further sexually than they themselves wanted to go. Six percent of those under the age of 14 years reported such pressure, as did more than 27 percent of the 16- to 17-year-olds. Sometimes the perpetrators are older youths, sometimes parents and other adults. Professional medical and psychological help for the victims is at its very beginnings (Kon 1995, 276).

[While sexism was admittedly common during the Communist regime, sexual harassment, defined as a boss demanding sexual favors from subordinates, was a crime; it was a seldom-prosecuted offense. The current lack of laws protecting employees from exploitation and harassment, coupled with the heady sense of permissiveness fed by pornographic videos, sexy advertising, nightclubs, casinos, beauty contests (Waters 1993), nude pin-ups, and open prostitution, have raised the level of sexual harassment to epidemic proportions, according to aggravated feminists. Some male observers counter that women simply view their bodies as a way of furthering their careers, while most Russian men, including husbands, dismiss the issue of sexual harassment as yet another silly Western hang-up. Most employers stress youth and sex appeal in advertizing for office help; some include as a prerequisite *bez kompleksov* or "without inhibitions" in their advertizements. Despite a few attempts to battle sexual harassment and initiate law suits in 1994, an unemployment rate for women three times higher than for men, and a decline in their wages from 75 percent of male salaries in 1991 to 40 percent in 1991 have provided fertile ground for sexual harassment (Stanley, 1994). (Editor)]

Rape

The number of rapes and attempted rapes is growing very fast. Since 1961, the increase in reported assaults has been 60 percent; since 1986, the increase has been 21.3 percent (Kon 1995, 207-222).

Most recorded rapes occur on the street or are gang rapes. Most date and marital rapes are not recorded in criminal statistics and remain unpunished. Of 333 persons who applied in 1992 to the St. Petersburg Helping Center for rape victims, only four also reported the crime to the police. The reasons for this unwillingness have been fear of the psychological trauma of investigation and trial; fear of information being spread in school and among acquaintances; doubts about the possibility of legal help; and fear of personal safety. All of these fears and doubts are quite justified. Even when the victims are children, the police are often unwilling to open a criminal investigation or even to initiate a medical examination.

According to criminal statistics—and these are unreliable—male youths between ages 14 and 17 commit 30 percent of all reported rapes; 37 percent of perpetrators are between ages 18 and 24; 19 percent between 25 and 29, and 15 percent over age 30. Two thirds of rapists are under age 22, with the most dangerous age being 16 to 17. Every fourth reported rape is a group or gang rape. The younger the rapists, the more often their assaults are carried out in a group. Some 40 percent of rapists have previous criminal records, and two thirds had been drinking prior to the attack.

The global socioeconomic, political, and spiritual crisis that Russia is now experiencing invariably causes a rise in violence and crime. Sexual violence is just one of its aspects, closely related also to the sexist psychology and cult of aggressive masculinity.

The psychological profiles of rapists are very similar to those provided by Western researchers. Sixty-one percent of convicted rapists are psychologically normal, but they perceive woman as hostile, aggressive, and dominating figures towards whom they experience an unwanted sense of passivity and dependence. Sexual aggression and rape are often a manifestation of "adolescent rebellion" against women in general.

Much of the male rape that occurs in correctional institutions is carried on to establish and maintain a social hierarchy. Coercive sexual activity is also widespread in the military, at schools, and in the arts.

At this time, Russian society is not equipped materially or attitudinally to confront these problems in a creative manner. Many Russian citizens simply lament the liberalization of traditional morality and blame the influence of "Western capitalism" and pornography. The current state of the Russian economy precludes economic or technical support for remedial services or preventive programs. The very first telephone "hotline" service for rape victims was established in 1992 in St. Petersburg. Specialized professional help focusing on sexuality is largely unavailable for sex offenders. The first registered rape recovery center and a crisis hotline for abused women opened in Moscow in 1994.

B. Prostitution

Until 1987, the existence of prostitution in the U.S.S.R. was often publically denied. Now, it is one of the most popular professions. It is highly stratified, beginning with those working exclusively with foreigners for hard currency, and ending at the very bottom of social life. Some prostitutes are professionals. For others, it means additional income for a family budget. Male prostitution is increasing. Prostitution is closely linked with organized crime. [Entrepreneurs have been quick to take advantage of the economic plight of young women in the former U.S.S.R., recruiting them to service the sexual needs and fantasies of middle- and upper-class males in some of the relatively affluent Middle Eastern countries. See parallel discussion in the chapter on Ukraine. (Editor)]

The legal status of prostitutes is unclear. Attempts to fight it with administrative measures have failed, but at least now, the issue can be discussed (Kon 1995, 42-43, 62-64, 222-229).

C. Pornography and Erotica

Stalinist sexophobia had practically exterminated all Russian erotic art. Now there are two trends: (1) the revival of genuine erotic art and literature, including translations of classical novels of D. H. Lawrence, Vladimir Nabokov, Henry Miller, and others, old Chinese and Hindu treatises, and erotic films from the West, and (2) a torrent of pornographic and semipornographic books, films, and videos. All of this is very new and unusual for the Russian people (Kon 1995, 113-116).

In the spring of 1991, the Communist Party tried to use this situation for its own political purposes, initiating a big antipornography crusade. In whipping up a moral panic in the country, the Communist Party pursued very clear political goals. The antipornography campaign was used to divert popular attention from the pressing political issues and to blunt awareness of the government's economic failures. In flagging its defense of morality and the family, the Party was deflecting blame from itself for the weakening and destruction of both morals and the family. On that basis, the Party leaders were able to cement the developing alliance between the Party and conservative organizations, including the Russian Orthodox Church and blatantly fascist groups. Antipornography slogans have been used by the Party to direct popular fury and frenzy against *glasnost* that was so hated by the Party *apparatchiks*, by branding the democratic mass media as being part of a Jewish-Masonic conspiracy intended to corrupt the morals of young people, destroy traditional values, etc. Under the pretext of concern for young people, the Party was endeavoring to restore its lost control over them.

This political campaign has failed. Public opinion polls show that the majority of Russians do not like pornography, but are positive about erotica. But to differentiate between the two is difficult, and there is a deep generation gap on this issue. Purely repressive police measures taken by some local authorities are ineffective. Instead of the former taboos on sexuality, it is now vulgarized, commercialized, and Americanized. The current Russian government is trying to bring the situation under control, but without much success.

9. Contraception, Abortion, and Population Planning

A. Contraception

One of the most disturbing consequences of the lack of sexual culture in Soviet society has been the exceedingly limited contraception culture, as a result of which induced abortion was, and remains today, the major method of birth control and family planning (Kon 1995, 61-62, 178-193).

Already in the early part of this century, Russian doctors officially recognized that the development of effective contraceptive methods was the only alternative to induced abortion with all its dangerous consequences. Soviet medicine also understood this. In 1920, induced abortion was legalized. Until the end of the 1920s, the U.S.S.R. was a leading world country in its family policies.

Nevertheless, in 1936, induced abortion was banned and no other means of birth control introduced. After the ban was lifted in 1955, induced abortion remained the principal form of birth control.

According to Andrei Popov (1992), Soviet family planning was distinguished by the following general traits right up to 1988:

- Although the right to family planning was formally proclaimed de jure in accordance with international conventions, this right was never de facto realized;
- Services were inaccessible or nonexistent owing to a total lack of information, an absence of qualified personnel and specialized medical services, and the unavailability of modern contraceptives;
- The only easily accessible method of family planning was and continues to be induced abortion; and
- Family planning behavior varies widely by region, according to the ethnographic, demographic, and socioeconomic realities within each region.

Without the necessary scientific information, modern contraceptives, and the ability to use them, the Soviet public was doomed to employ traditional and largely ineffective methods (see Table 3).

Until 1987, the Soviet Ministry of Health conducted a major propaganda campaign against oral contraceptives. Most Soviet citizens are relatively ignorant about the more sophisticated forms of contraception.

Table 3

Percentage of Users of Specific Contraceptive Methods
(Moscow Sample Surveys, 1965-1983)

Method	Year of Survey Publication			
	1965-1966	1978	1982	1983
Withdrawal	32	34	14	25
Rhythm (calendar)	—	18	28	27
Condom	46	42	22	24
Diaphragm	—	1	1	1
IUD	—	8	11	10
Oral contraceptives	—	4	4	2
Spermicides	1	—	3	3
Rhythm (temperature)	—	—	2	—
Douche	—	23	17	8
Combinations	12	—	—	12

Note: Respondents were allowed to indicate more than one method used.

Since 1987, the negative consequences of this situation have begun to be officially acknowledged, highlighting two obvious problems: the material shortage of modern hormonal, chemical, and barrier contraceptives, and the lack of information and psychological sophistication regarding sexual and reproductive practices.

In 1993, experts of the World Health Organization (WHO) found that both physicians and women in St. Petersburg were convinced that hormonal pills are terribly dangerous. And only 11 percent of Russian gynecologists recognized the right of teenagers to confidentiality, a condition sine qua non of the effective contraceptive services for teenagers.

The government survey in 1990 demonstrated that 30.5 percent of all girls under age 15 had no knowledge whatsoever about contraception. In the 16- to 17-year-old age group, this percentage was 24.6, and among 18 to 23 year olds, 11 percent. Over 96 percent of 16- to 17-year-old girls never used any contraceptives, Most teenage sex—and their sexual activity is growing—still goes unprotected.

B. Teenage Unmarried Pregnancies

As a consequence of the lack of contraceptives, the number of unplanned pregnancies and unwanted births is growing, despite the prevalence of abortion. According to national statistics, the rate of extramarital births was about 10 percent in 1987; in 1992, it was 17 percent. The rates are even higher in the largest cities. The rate of premarital conception of firstborn children among married couples in Leningrad rose from 27 percent in 1963 to 38 percent in 1978. Similarly, one study in the early 1980s found that, of 1,000 first pregnancies reported in a large Russian city, 272 were aborted, 140 births occurred out of wedlock, and 271 births took place in the first months of marriage—leaving only 317 children actually conceived within marriage (Kon 1995, 169, 181-182).

C. Abortion

The total annual number of abortions in the late 1980s, according to official data, amounted to 6 to 7 million. That was virtually a fifth or even a fourth of all abortions performed in the world. The number of "backstreet abortions" was estimated at 12 percent of the total, according to official estimates, but at 50 to 70 percent according to independent experts. Thus, the aggregate number of abortions in the U.S.S.R. came to 10 to 11 million a year. Even without these adjustments, the number of abortions per 1,000 women of reproductive age in 1985 surpassed by six to ten times the analogous figures for western Europe. On average, every woman in Russia has four to five abortions during her lifetime (Kon 1995, 61-62, 73-75, 178-193).

In 1989, a voluntary association, The Family and Health, was organized and affiliated with International Planned Parenthood World Federation to raise public awareness of family-planning options and improve the image of contraceptive methods other than abortion. Since 1991, it is supplemented by the Russian Family Planning Association. Mass media, particularly television, have begun to deal directly and positively with birth-control issues.

Unfortunately, but not surprisingly, this work is not very effective. According to the VCIOM 1992 survey, most women indicated that they had used some form of contraception during the last five years (Kon 1995, 275). Only 18 percent did not use any contraception. Most likely not to use contraception are women between the ages of 15 and 20 (40 percent), the unmarried (29 percent), the poorly educated (24 percent), and those living in rural areas (22 percent) (see Table 4).

Modern contraception tends to be popular largely with the younger (under age 25) and better-educated women, while the rest commonly employ traditional, less reliable, but more accessible methods. A 1990 survey of Soviet-German students (average age 25) showed that 15 percent of the female students had already had an abortion, 6 percent more than once. In 1992, 297,029 Russian teenage girls had an abortion; of these 16,320 were illegal.

The most-preferred contraceptive method was the IUD, most favored by half of the women and the second choice for 25 percent. The pill was less popular, favored by 18 percent as first choice and 25 percent as second choice. The pill is still believed to be unsafe and unreliable. The condom was the third-ranking first choice.

If the current plans of the government to make women pay for abortions, except when medically indicated, materialize, this situation will become

Table 4

Contraceptive Methods Used During the
Last Five Years (in Percentages)

	Frequency Used		
Method	Always	Sometimes	Not Used
IUD	37	11	52
Condom	18	51	31
Rhythm	17	31	52
Coitus interruptus	14	46	40
Vaginal douche	10	29	61
Pill	10	19	71
Spermicidal	2	14	84
Spermicidal + condom	1	4	95
Diaphragm	0	1	99

much worse. Even now, according to the St. Petersburg Yuventa Reproduction Center, in spite of the general availability of professional abortion services, 80 percent of women who contact the abortion clinics do so only after they have tried to do something, often dangerous, themselves.

10. Sexually Transmitted Diseases

The customary hypocrisy did not allow the Soviet people to talk openly about STDs. STDs have been consistently regarded throughout the century as shameful. This attitude has hampered health education, especially when new infections are confronted (Kon 1995, 229-231).

Nonetheless, free state medicine provided treatment in special dermatological and venereological clinics with mandatory official registration identifying the source of infection, and doctors assisted by police endeavored to follow the entire chain of dangerous contacts. Treatment was compulsory, and any infringement of that, or willful infecton of anyone with an STD, was punishable under the Russian Criminal Code. This policy enabled the state to confine the danger within certain limits.

In the early 1980s, physicians noted a substantial rise, especially among young people, in the so-called minor venereal diseases that often occur without symptoms. Russians had practically no knowledge of genital herpes or chlamydia until they encountered it in their own experience.

The demise of the Soviet system has acutely affected the epidemeological situation for the worse. Extensive sexual contacts with different partners, given the ignorance and lack of observance of elementary safety and hygiene rules, is dangerous in itself. State medicine is now debilitated, and in some areas collapsed, because of lack of funds, medicine, and equipment. Private medicine is not available to all, and, when available, it is less effective, especially when it comes to maladies requiring lengthy treatment with subsequent supervision. Administrative supervision is now worse, and official statistics have become even less reliable.

So there is an increase in sexually transmitted disease, particularly among young people. People are becoming infected at a younger age. A sharp increase in the incidence of syphylis began in 1988, followed by gonorrhea in 1991. In large cities, such as Moscow, these diseases have already reached epidemic proportions. Virtually half of that increase is accounted for by children and adolescents. According to the U.S.S.R. Health Ministry figures for 1985-87, the number of under-17 women infected by STDs increased by virtually a third throughout the country.

The overall STD picture is still not as bad as it is in many other countries. According to Russian statistics, the rate of syphilis infection is on the increase, with 9,873 cases in 1991 and 7,178 cases in the first six months of 1992. The gonorrhea rate has fallen slightly, from 180,883 in 1990, to 175,020 in 1991, and 87,724 in the first six months of 1992. These statistics do not take into account that many people use home treatment or seek help from a variety of private practitioners who are not part of the official statistical records.

A special epidemiological investigation by Olga Loseva shows that in 1991, the number of registered syphilis sufferers in Russia rose by almost 34 percent, in Moscow by 17 percent in 1991, and by another 50 percent in the first quarter of 1992 (Kon 1995, 277. This is due primarily to the rise in child and teenage prositution that often begins between ages 10 and 12 for girls and age 14 for boys. No less than half of the infected go to unregistered medics for treatment.

What is to be done? There are two competing strategies. The first demands more stringent administrative measures, namely enforcement of the law prohibiting private doctors from treating STDs. The second strategy would take the social and psychological reality into account. Patients should have the right to choose whether to go to a private doctor or use the state medical system. But the private doctor must report disease cases to the epidemeological services so the epidemeological situation can be correctly evaluated, trends forecast, and preparation made for future needs.

11. HIV/AIDS

Due to its relative social isolation in the past, the former Soviet Union, for a number of years, was spared the effects of the HIV-related diseases. Even now, the number of people infected and ill is much lower than in most Western countries (Kon 1995, 203-38, 261-62).

On April 1, 1994, the number of HIV-positive persons in the Russian Federation was 740, of whom 286 were children infected in hospitals and maternity homes. The number of AIDS sufferers was 124, of whom 96 were children.

However, this lead time on the HIV epidemic has been wasted by government authorities and medical professionals. Instead of preparing the country for the inevitable increase in infection rates, the Soviet Ministry of Health and government-sponsored mass media waged an ideological campaign in the early 1980s—even accusing the Pentagon and CIA of inventing the virus as a form of germ warfare! Next, the blame was put on homosexuals and drug addicts. Hopes for control of the disease were placed on the prisons (for homosexuals) and on moral exhortations in favor of monogamy (for the addicts and the remainder of the population). Unfortunately, this strategy continued even after the disease had claimed its first victims. As late as 1988, an appeal to explore the social and psychological aspects of the AIDS, including the dangers of an AIDS-induced public hysteria, brought violent attacks in the conservative media.

The major high-risk group in Russia turned out not to be gays, drug addicts, or prostitutes, but newborn children infected in maternity homes through lack of disposable syringes and the negligence of medical staff. Now the children and their families have become victims, not only of this terrible disease, but also of an AIDS-phobia. Medical personnel are scared of treating them, coworkers do not want to work with members of their families, and some schools are demanding their removal.

Since AIDS-prevention politics are completely in the hands of epidemiologists, millions of rubles are spent on diagnostics, HIV-tests—25 million were tested in 1993, and so on, but there is no money for prevention programs and sex education. Education and prevention programs are mainly in the hands of different voluntary organizations.

12. Sexual Dysfunctions, Counseling, and Therapies

The traditions of pre-1917 Russian sex research were completely lost in the 1930s and 1940s. Revival of medical sexology (sexopathology) as an area of clinical medicine that studies the functional (behavioral, personal, and social) aspects of sexual disorders began in the 1960s with a series of seminars under the leadership of Professor N. V. Ivanov in the city of Gorky (Nizhny Novgorod) and later in Moscow at the Sexopathology Department of the Moscow Psychiatry Research Institute. In 1973, this department gained the status of an All-Union Scientific Center on Sexopathology.

Initially, a monodisciplinary approach dominated Soviet sexopathology. Urologists, and to a lesser extent the gynecologists and endocrinologists, set the tone. Subsequently, however, when the neuropathologist Profesor Georgi Vasilchenko took charge of the center, the picture changed. Vasilchenko maintained that sexopathology should not take the "brigade" approach, where the urologist treats "his" pathology, the psychiatrist "his" and the endocrinomologist "his," while the sexopathologist operates as a transport controller. His approach viewed sexopathology as an independent, interdisciplinary clinical discipline. It was in this spirit that the first Russian handbooks for doctors were written under his editorship— *General Sexopathology* (1977) and *Special Sexopathology* (1983).

Professor Abram Svyadoshch set up the first Sexological Center in Leningrad. His book *Female Sexopathology* (1974) enjoyed three editions and became a genuine best-seller. The Leningrad psychiatrists Professor Dmitri Isayev and Dr. Victor Kagan began to study the formation of sexual identity and problems in juvenile and adolescent sexuality. They published the first Soviet guide for doctors *The Psycho-Hygiene of Sex Among Children* (1986).

Soviet sexological service was based on the principle of ambulatory assistance, preserving a normal living pattern, carrying on normal work, and sexual activity. The need for hospitalization arises only in cases of acute psychopathological disorder (where a patient will be placed in a neurosis unit or a daytime inpatient psychoneurological clinic), vascular insufficiency of the genitalia (admission to an angisurgical unit), acute urological illness (a urological unit), and specific endocrinopathy (an endocrinological unit). Inpatient treatment is normally followed by a period of ambulatory sexual readaptation by the partners.

Analysis of visits to sexological clinics reveals that the bulk (70-75 percent) of patients have sexual problems of a psychological nature. Women's visits to a sexopathlogist account for no more than 10 percent of the total number of patients. The percentage of patients who come because of misinformation or distorted knowledge about sex is fairly high, up to 10 or 15 percent.

In 1988, in the large cities, special family medical-psychological consultation units were introduced for:

- consultative-diagnostic selection of patients needing observation and treatment in the unit;
- comprehensive therapy of patients with sexual disorders through psychotherapy, physiotherapy, reflex-therapy, pharmacotherapy, and specialized procedures;
- psychological diagnosis and correction methods for family relationship disorders;
- hygiene-educative and psychotherapeutic work with the public and, first and foremost, with people just entering marriage and couples divorcing.

13. Research and Advanced Education

A. Russian Sexology

Historically, the professional training of sexopathologists was delayed in favor of other priorities. The first department of sexology was organized in the Leningrad (St. Petersburg) Institute for Advanced Medical Training only in 1989. Students at other medical colleges receive no sexological training at all.

The beginning of the 1990s saw extensive promotion of individual medical activity and group work. Numerous medical cooperatives and profit-making centers are increasingly advertising the services of sexopathologists. The development of this type of medical practice reflects the public's demand for it. The professional level of this practice is some-times problematic.

The Russian Sexological Association Health and Culture was established in February, 1991, to promote an interdisciplinary investigation of sexual behavior, sex education, and sex culture. But, like many other post-Soviet voluntary organizations, it exists only on paper and serves as a cover for private commercial activities like sex shops. Somewhat more efficient is the medically oriented Soviet Sexological Association.

B. Recent Soviet and Russian Sexual Surveys

Because not one Soviet or Russian sexual survey was ever published in the normal scientific way, with all tables, questionnaires, and methodological discussions, sexologists, such as the present author, are forced to rely on published papers and summaries, as well as whatever unpublished data, raw tables, and so on they can obtain from colleagues (Kon 1995, 275-277). Below is a short description of the most important recent Russian surveys.

1. The VCIOM "Culture" Poll of June, 1992, was conducted by *Vsesoyuznyi* (since 1992—*Vserossiiskii*) *Tsentr Izucheniya Obshchestvennovo Mnenia* (All-Union [since 1992—All-Russia] Center for Public Opinion Re-search) (VCIOM), with Professor Yun Levada as director.

   This poll involved a representative sample of about 3,500 persons in three different areas: Slav (Russia and Ukraine); Baltic (Estonia and Lithuania); and Asiatic (Uzbekistan and Tadzhikistan). In the Slav area, the population was surveyed without regard to ethnic origins or "nationality" (that is, not only ethnic Russians, but also Tatars, Jews, Germans, and others were questioned), while in the other two regions, only members of indigenous nationalities were surveyed (that is, in Estonia, Estonians but not Russians).

   Questionnaires were completed by the respondents in the pres-ence of a professional interviewer. Among many other questions, some were related to sexuality: Are people happy in love and family life? What are their family values, their attitudes to premarital and extra-marital sex, conjugal fidelity, erotica, sex education, and so on?

2. The VCIOM "The Fact" June 1993 Survey involved a representative sample for the Russian Federation, 1,665 persons. Demographics for this survey included 746 men and 909 women, aged from 16 to 84 (16-25 years, 285; 24-40 years, 546; 40-55 years, 383; and 55-84 years, 461), from thirteen different regions. The subjects' educational level

was: 235, university level; 803, high (secondary) school; and 616, fewer than 9 years of secondary school. The occupational demography was: nonworking pensioners, 409; manual workers, 330, professionals, 284; technicians, 136; other employees, 120; and students, 87. The subjects' place of residence included: capitals and regional cities, 604; towns, 614; and villages, 344. All standard procedures normally used in public-opinion polls were used.

Some of the questions concerned attitudes toward the following aspects of sexual behavior (on 5-point scales, from "It deserves censure" to "I don't see anything wrong in it"): masturbation, premarital sex, frequent change of sexual partners, marital infidelity, viewing of pornographic films, group sex, homosexual contacts, induced abortions, and so on. There were also a few questions about personal sexual experience, such as age at the first sexual contact, number of lifetime sexual partners, and present sexual activities. About 40 percent of respondents did not answer these personal questions.

3. The Adolescent Sexuality Survey published in 1993 and conducted by Vladimir Shapiro and Valery Chervyakov, Institute of Sociology, Russian Academy of Sciences, with Igor Kon as a consultant and Mana Gerasimova as the research organizer. This survey used an adapted version of American sociologist Stan Weed's questionnaire. The data were collected in late 1992 and early of 1993. The sample involved 1,615 students (50.4 percent boys and 49.6 percent girls) from sixteen high (secondary) schools and eight vocational schools in Moscow and St. Petersburg. The students' ages ranged from 12 to 17 years, and their grade levels from the seventh to eleventh grades.

The questionnaire contained 135 questions about aspects of sexual experience and attitudes: dating, going steady, age at, and the motives for, the first sexual intercourse, sources of sexual information, communications with parents and peers, moral and religious values, involvement in deviant behavior, and some personal psychological characteristics. The schools were selected to represent different social strata of the two cities' populations. Questionaires were completed in the classrooms, anonymously, voluntarily, and individually, in the presence of a professional interviewer. The permission of the school administration was obtained, but none of them had access to this confidential information. There were no refusals from students to take part in the research, but some respondents did not answer certain questions. Detailed statistical analysis may be available by the time this chapter is published; however, a general popular overview of the results was published by Igor Kon, Valery Chervyakov, and Vladimir Shapiro in 1994.

4. A second survey of adolescent sexual attitudes, representations, and practices was conducted by Igor Lunin (1994) of the St. Petersburg Crisis Prevention Service for Children and Adolescents between May

and September of 1993. The sample population for this survey was 370, (185 boys and 185 girls, secondary (high) school tenth graders and vocational school students from three socially and economically different districts of St. Petersburg). The average age was 15.9 years.

In this study, an anonymous questionnaire was preliminarily reviewed in teenage discussion groups. Participation, on the school premises, was individual and voluntary. Questions concerned sexual values and behavior, main sources of sexual and contraceptive information and the evaluation of its availability and reliability, sexual harassment, violence, and rape experience, and attitudes to condoms and to different forms of sex education. (In addition to Lunin (1994), see also Igor Lunin, Thomas L. Hall, Jeffrey S. Mandel, Julia Kay, and Norman Hearst, *Adolescent Sexuality in St. Petersburg: Russia in the Era of AIDS* (in press).) A detailed statistical analysis is also in progress.

5. A telephone survey was conducted by Dmitri. D. Isayev in St. Petersburg between September and December, 1993. The sample for this survey was 435 people, 16 to 55 years old; 155 men (average age, 35.4 years and 67.5 percent married), and 280 women (average age, 37.3 years with 67 percent married). Questions were asked about personal sexual experience and attitudes, number of partners, safe-sex practices, and AIDS-prevention measures.

6. An epidemiological study was conducted in 1991 by Olga Loseva, a Moscow venereologist. This unpublished dissertation summarized fifteen years of research of sexual behavior and sexual values of syphilitics. Loseva collected data on 3,273 heterosexual men and women at a venereological clinic in Moscow: 300 medical histories and about 3,000 questionnaires. The data came from 1,782 infected patients and 1,191 in a control group of persons without sexually transmitted diseases, plus 120 teenage girls. Sociologically, the samples were not representative, but a comparison of three control groups, divided by five-year intervals, is informative for the shifts in sexual attitudes and practices.

Conclusion

Sexuality is just beginning to be thought of as a subject worthy of consideration and study by Russian researchers. Clearly, sexual behavior is diverse in societies as large and heterogeneous as Russia and the other republics of the former Soviet Union. Although certain values are strong within and between these societies, there is no single standard of "normal" sexuality for family members. Marriage is valued as a primary arena for sexual expression; however, sex-related ideas, attitudes, and activities are extremely diverse. Citizens are exposed to sexual information and images from a variety of public sources. Naturally, their reactions to these differ, and the impact upon their behavior is varied. Parents seem concerned about the proper sexual development of their children. Yet, some of these same parents respond by suppressing expressions of sexuality in the family, others by obsessively explicating sexual guidelines, and still others by supporting social programs of sex education in schools and community institutions (Kon 1995, 265-272).

To develop effective public policies that encourage responsible sexual expression by citizens without reactionary negativism, and to accommodate pluralistic diversity without succumbing to crippling ambivalence—these will be the challenges common to our countries as they enter the twenty-first century.

An Update from Igor Kon

March 1997—Sexuality and sex education once again became a scapegoat in the anti-Western political rhetoric. The Russian Orthodox Church is rapidly assuming the Communist ideological mantle of sexual repression. Attacking all sex education in schools and any expression of sexuality as "satanic," Orthodox clergy have demanded a United Nations-sponsored sex education project be stopped immediately, because it is a Western conspiracy to depopulate Russia. Although a few medical efforts and the Russian Planned Parenthood helped reduce the abortion rate since 1991 considerably, teen syphilis rates increased thirty-fold, as teenage coital experience increased and began earlier. Orthodox clergy preach that they alone can provide proper sex education, and claim that Westerners are trying to exterminate Russian culture by reducing its birthrate with abortion, contraception, sexual excesses, masturbation, and homosexuality. Artistic and mass-media freedom is also threatened by the draft law's too broad and indiscriminate definitions of pornography and "products of a sexual nature."

References and Suggested Readings

Attwood, Lynne. 1990. *The New Soviet Man and Woman: Sex-Role Socialization in the U.S.S.R.* Bloomington, IN: University of Indiana Press.

Borisenko, K. K., and O. K. Loseva. 1994. "Zabolevaemost Molodyozhi Boleznyaimi, Peredavaemymi Polovym Putyom." *Planirovanie Semyi.* 4:20-22.

Chervyakov, Kon, and Shapiro. 1993. Full citation not available.

Engelstein, Laura. 1992. *The Keys to Happiness. Sex and the Search for Modernity in Fin-de-Siecle Russia.* Ithaca, NY: Cornell University Press.

Flegon, Alex. 1976. *Eroticism in Russian Art.* London: Flegon Press.

Gessen, Masha. 1994. *The Rights of Lesbians and Gay Men in the Russian Federation: An International Gay and Lesbian Human Rights Commission Report.* San Francisco: I.G.L.H.R.C.

Golod, S. I. 1984. *Stabilnost Semi: Sotsiologichesky i Demografichesky Aspekty.* Leningrad.

Karlinsky, Simon. 1989. "Russia's Gay Literature and Culture: The Impact of the October Revolution." In M. B. Duberman, M. Vicinus, and G. Chauncey, Jr., eds. *Hidden from History: Reclaiming the Gay and Lesbian Past.* New York: New American Library.

Kon, Igor S. 1989. *Vvedenie v Seksologiu (Introduction to Sexology).* Second enlarged edition. Moscow, Russia: Translations: Bulgarian (1990), Chinese (1990), Ukranian (1991).

Kon, Igor S. 1995. *The Sexual Revolution in Russia: From the Age of the Czars to Today.* New York: Free Press.

Kon, I., V. Chervyakov, and V. Shapiro. 1994. "Podrostki i Seks: Utrata Illuzii." *Ogonyok,* 2.

Kon, Igor S., and James Riordan, eds. 1993. *Sex and Russian Society.* Bloomington, IN: Indiana University Press. Includes chapters on "Sexuality and Culture," I. Kon; "Patterns of Birth Control," L. I. Remennick; "Sex and the Cinema," L. Attwood; "Sexual Minorities," I. Kon; "Soviet Beauty Contests," E. Waters; "Sex and Young People," S. Golod, and "Medical Sexology," L. Shcheglov.

Lenhert, Phillippe, Irina Pavlenko, Larissa Remennick, & Adrian Visser. 1992 (May). "Contraception in the Former USSR: Recent Survey Results on Women's Behavior and Attitudes." *Planned Parenthood in Europe,* 21(2):9-11.

Levin, Eve. 1989. *Sex and Society in the World of the Orthodox Slavs, 900-1700.* Ithaca, NY: Cornell University Press.

Loseva, O. K. 1991. "Seksualnoe Povedenie Bolnykh Sifilisom (Epidemiologicheskie I Mediko-Sotsialnye Problemy)," Avtoreferat Dissertatsii na Soiskanie Uchenoi Stepeni Doktora Meditsinskikh Nauk (Moscow: Tsentralnyi Nauchno-Issledovatelskii Kozhno-Venerologicheskii Institut, 1991)

Loseva, O. K., 1994. "Sotsialno-Meditsinskie Aspekty Boleznei, Peredavaemykh Polovym Putom, u Detei i Podroskov," Rossiyskaya Assotsiatsyia "Planirovanie Semyi," Pervaya Natsyonalnaya Konferentsya *"Problemy Planirovania Semyi v Rossii" (Materialy Konferetnsii. 7-9 Dekabrya 1993, Moskva,* Moscow "Kvartet," pp. 89-96.

Loseva, O. K., T. V. Chistyakova, A. V. Libin, and E. V. Livin. 1991. "Seksualnoe Povedenie Podrostkov, Bolnykh Sifilisom." *Vestnik Dermatologfi i Venerologii,* 2:45-49.

Lunin, I. I. 1994. "Seksualnoe Prosveshcheme Kak Faktor Profilaktiki Seksualnykh Posyagatelstv." *Problemy Planirovaniya Semyi v Rossii. Pervaya Natsionalnaya Konferentsia Rossiiskoi Assotsiatsii "Planirovanie Semyi"* (Moscow), pp. 96-105.

Lunin, I., T. L. Hall, J. S. Mandel, J. Kay, and N. Hearst, *Adolescent Sexuality in St. Petersburg: Russia in the Era of AIDS* (in press).

Maddock, James W., M. Janice Hogan, Anatolyi I. Antonov, & Mikhail S. Matskovsky, eds. 1994. *Families Before and After Peristroika: Russian and U.S. Perspectives.* New York/London: The Guilford Press.

Popov, A. 1992. "Induced Abortions in the U.S.S.R. at the End of the 1980s: Basis for the National Model of Family Planning." A paper for the Population Association of America 1992 Annual Meeting (Denver, Colorado, April 30-May 2, 1992).

Popov, Andrej, Adrian Visser, & Evert Ketting. 1993 (July/August). "Contraceptive Knowledge, Attitudes, and Practice in Russia During the 1980s." *Studies in Family Planning,* 24(4):227-35.

Stafford, Peter. 1967. *Sexual Behavior in the Communist World. An Eyewitness Report of Life, Love, and the Human Condition Behind the Iron Curtain.* New York: Julian Press.

Stanley, Alessandra. 1994 (April 17). "Sexual Harassment Thrives in the New Russia Climate." *The New York Times,* pp. 1 & 8.

Stanley, Alessandra. 1995 (October 21). "Russian Mothers, from All Walks, Walk Alone." *The New York Times,* pp. A1 and A5.

Waters, E. 1993. "Soviet Beauty Contests." In Igor S. Kon and James Riordan, eds. 1993. *Sex and Russian Society.* Bloomington, IN: Indiana University Press.

South Africa

Lionel John Nicholas, Ph.D., and
Priscilla Sandra Daniels, M.S. (Part 1)
Mervyn Bernard Hurwitz, M.D. (Part 2)

Contents

Demographics and a Historical Perspective

A. Demographics

The Republic of South Africa is situated at the southern tip of the African continent and extends over an area of 472,359 square miles (1,126,771 square kilometers), about twice the size of the state of Texas. The country surrounds the nation of Lesotho and is bordered on the north by Namibia, Botswana, and Zimbabwe, and by Mozambique and Swaziland on the east. The large interior plateau has few major lakes and rivers. Rainfall is sparse in the west and plentiful in the east.

In 1995, three quarters of the 45 million people of South Africa, roughly 30.7 million, were black Africans. The next largest racial group was whites, mostly Afrikaners (descendants of the original Dutch settlers), at 6.3 million or 14 percent, followed by 3.6 million or 8 percent coloreds, and 1.35 million or 3 percent Asian or Indian.

According to the 1995 census, 63 percent of the population was urbanized, with 90 percent of whites and coloreds, 95 percent of Asians, and over 60 percent of blacks living in urban areas. The age profiles of Africans, coloreds, and Indians are similar, with a large proportion of young people. The age profile for whites is more evenly spread across age categories. Half of the black population and a third of the white population are under 20 years of age. There are many more children between the ages of 5 and 9 than in any other age group. The white population is aging with 13 percent over the age of 60, whereas only 6 percent of the blacks fall into this age cohort.

In 1993, 18 million South Africans were living below the poverty datum line. Based on a minimum subsistence level of $90 per month, 13 million people were living below the subsistence level in 1991. In 1993, there were 105 colleges with 60,000 students, 21 universities with 337,120 students, 15 technical colleges with 130,000 students, and 128 technical colleges with 93,000 students (Cooper et al. 1994).

South Africa's first democratically elected government is currently grappling with unemployment, violence, illiteracy, and numerous other problems. It does, however, have tremendous natural resources, a well-developed industrial, educational, and transportation network, and enough skilled workers to start redressing the economic havoc apartheid has wreaked on South Africa. Many diverse ethnic, cultural, and religious groups make up the South African landscape, and these groups continue to influence one another, as they are in turn being influenced by the international community. Internal migration is a problem in South Africa, as socioeconomic and political factors force large segments of the population to leave rural areas and crowd into the cities.

General life expectancy at birth in 1995 was 63 for males and 68 for females, higher for whites and lower for blacks. The 1995 birthrate was 33 per 1,000 and the death rate 7 per 1,000, giving an annual natural increase of 2.6 percent. Infant mortality was 46 per 1,000 live births. There was one physician for every 1,264 persons and one hospital bed per 222 persons. The literacy rates are 99 percent for whites, 69 percent for Asians, 62 percent for coloreds, and 50 percent for Africans. Only 10 percent of blacks have a secondary high school education and only 6 percent have any education beyond high-school level. Unemployment is a major and ever-increasing problem. The current unemployment figure amongst the black population is conservatively estimated at 25 percent. The 1995 per capita domestic product was $4,000 U.S.

B. A Brief Historical Perspective

The roots of today's Republic of South Africa stretch back to the Dutch East India Company's arrival on the Cape of Good Hope in 1692. By the end of the eighteenth century, Boer or Afrikaner colonists numbered only about 15,000. Britain occupied the Cape colony in 1814 at the end of the Napoleonic wars, bringing another 5,000 settlers. Anglicization of the government and the freeing of black slaves drove about 12,000 Afrikaners to make the "great trek" northeast into African tribal territories where they established the republics of the Transvaal and the Orange Free State. The discovery of diamonds in 1867 and gold in 1876 brought an influx of "outlanders," whose presence spurred Cecil Rhodes to plot annexation of the British Cape and Natal colonies. A three-year war between the Boers and the British, 1899 to 1902, resulted in 1910 in the formation of the Union of South Africa, joining the two former republics and the two colonies.

South Africa became a charter member of the United Nations in 1945, but refused to sign the Universal Declaration of Human Rights. Apartheid—racial segregation—dominated domestic politics as the nationalists gained power and imposed greater restrictions on the Africans, coloreds, and Asians. In 1949, apartheid became national policy. Afrikaner opposition to South Africa's membership in the British Commonwealth ended on May 31, 1961, with the declaration of the Republic of South Africa and the severing of all ties with the Commonwealth. In 1963, South Africa established the Transkei, the first of four partially self-governing republics, territories or "homelands" for blacks. The Transkei consists of three discontinuous enclaves in the southeast. The seven areas of Bophuthatswana were joined in a northern Homeland in 1977. The Venda Homeland, with two discontinuous areas in the northeast, was established in 1979. In the southwest, Ciskei became a homeland republic in 1980. None of these territories has international recognition as a republic. In 1991, following negotiations between the government and the African National Congress, the parliament scrapped the country's apartheid laws that limited owner-ship of property, required registration of South Africans at birth by race, and supported minority rule.

[This unique history poses a different kind of challenge for sexologists. Fortunately, Mervyn Hurwitz, the only South African member of the Society for the Scientific Study of Sexuality, accepted the editor's invitation to prepare a chapter on his country. Equally fortunate—and unexpected—Ted McIlvenna, founder of the Institute for the Advanced Study of Human Sexuality, introduced the editor to Lionel Nicholas at the 1994 meeting of the Society in Miami, and Dr. Nicholas agreed to work with a woman colleague to provide a black perspective that complements the perspective provided by Dr. Hurwitz. The two parts of this chapter are two windows on sexuality in South Africa. (Editor)]

PART 1: A PERSPECTIVE ON THE PEOPLE OF COLOR

LIONEL JOHN NICHOLAS, PH.D., AND PRISCILLA SANDRA DANIELS, M.S.

1. Basic Sexological Premises

A/B. Gender Roles and the Sociolegal Status of Males and Females

South Africa is a strongly male-dominated society where violence against women is at a high level. Gender equality and freedom to express one's sexual orientation is enshrined in the new constitution of South Africa, but it is widely acknowledged that we have far to go before getting near to this ideal.

In general, women and men negotiate their lives differently, as well as express their sexual vulnerabilities differently. In a patriarchal society like South Africa, one may expect these differences to be more prevalent than reported in the relevant international literature. Sex counseling will have to take into account the differing sexual socialization experiences of women and men in societies that institutionally and structurally accept the domi-nance of men, and where many women and men may also have accepted sexist stereotypes (Nicholas 1994a, 6).

C. General Concepts and Constructs of Sexuality and Love

The concepts and constructs of sexuality and love differ markedly between urban and rural communities for all groups in South Africa. Much of this difference is influenced by the greater visibility of particular love or sexual behaviors and observable traditional practices in rural areas that are protected from new urban practices. The following example of peer pressure to have sexual intercourse is cited from Preston-Whyte and Zondi:

> They laugh at you and say you are old-fashioned not to sleep with a boy, and they tell you that you are not in the country now, with the peer group watching to see you only do ukusoma—that was 'external' intercourse. No mothers in town examine one to see if you are a virgin—just let them try! (Preston-Whyte and Zondi 1992, 235)

African and colored groups are likely to have developed a larger range of "nontraditional" sexual behaviors because of the massive efforts to destabilize these communities, including removing parental figures through an enforced migratory labor system and high mortality rates. White and Asian groups have had more-intact family and extended-family systems in both urban and rural settings, which increased the capacity of these groups to monitor and regulate sexual practices of their members. These groups do, however, experience the same challenge to the concepts and constructs of sexuality and love mainly informed by religious guidelines of chastity.

Loubser (1994) reported that Afrikaner junior high school pupils regularly watched pornographic videos and engaged in sexual intercourse, and many of those who were virgins anticipated that their status would change in the near future.

While all groups would consider the seduction of a young woman as a situation where reparation has to be made, the acceptable reparation would differ widely across groups, especially if a pregnancy has resulted from the seduction. The different African groups have elaborate formal negotiations involving family members on both sides. A go-between would also negotiate the amount of bridewealth on behalf of the man's family before marriage takes place.

2. Religious and Ethnic Factors Affecting Sexuality

A. Source and Character of Some Typical Religious Values

According to the 1991 census, 66 percent of the South Africans indicated they were Christians. This percentage would probably be larger if the 30 percent nonresponse to this question were accounted for. Hindu, Islamic, and Jewish traditions are also major influences in particular geographic areas. The most vociferous support for censorship has come from representatives of a range of religious denominations led by the Dutch Reformed Church. The religious-influenced taboos around sexuality are particularly strong in South Africa. Public discourse on sexuality has been severely restricted by legal, political, religious, and social norms. Stringent censorship has been a central and a bizarre feature of South African life. For example, in 1965, a film, *Debbie*, was initially banned because the chairman of the censor board believed that Afrikaner women do not get pregnant while unmarried.

Every month, bookshops and libraries throughout South Africa receive a list of banned books and objects that also contains recently unbanned materials and those undergoing review. The two main foci of censorship have been sex and politics. The work of sex counselors, and access to accurate sex information, have been most adversely affected by the draconian censorship on sexuality. Liberalization of the censorship laws was presented to parliament in 1995. The draft legislation advocates a ban on: (1) child pornography, defined as involving children younger than 16, (2) the depiction of extreme violence including rape, (3) depiction of bestiality, and (4) promotion of religious hatred (Swayer 1994).

The history of South Africa's only recently discarded miscegenation laws and prohibitions on a wide range of books on sexuality have effectively exacerbated the sex-related problems experienced, through the official encouragement of ignorance about sexuality. For example, in 1992, several books on sexuality, vibrators, and objects, such as a penis tip attached to a condom, were banned by the censor board.

Standard methods of intervention with sexual problems have not been available to sex counselors and their clients in South Africa. One cannot advise the use of a vibrator to assist in treating inhibited orgasm because it may be illegal to own a vibrator. Similarly, the range of informative books on sexuality easily available in other countries are not available in South Africa. Some films were restricted to those over 21 years of age; films that included birth scenes or sex education had to be shown to male or female audiences separately. Certain films were also limited to whites.

A censorship board, appointed by the President of South Africa, for example, made the decision that: "a massage instrument whose manufacturers obviously intend it to be used for purposes of masturbation does therefore not fall under the Act unless it is shaped for example like a male organ" (Van Rooyen 1987, 22). The implication here is that it is the duty of the censor board to disapprove of masturbation, but it will enforce its legal powers only if provoked.

The controversy around formal sex education is predicated on the erroneous belief that instruction about sexuality will increase premarital sexual behavior. It may in fact, however, make visible the sexuality that parents try to deny that children possess, and vice versa. When parents are considered as the ideal location for the dissemination of sex information, it is often overlooked that many children do not have both parents available to them, and that fathers have always had minimal involvement in the transmission of sex information in two-parent families.

Nicholas and Durrheim (1994) reported that negative attitudes towards homosexuality were significant, but only weakly associated with negative attitudes toward AIDS, high knowledge of AIDS, and high religiosity in a study of AIDS and knowledge, attitudes, beliefs, and practices of 1,817 black South African students. The sample was divided into those with high or low scores on Rohrbaugh and Jessor's (1975) religiosity scale (excluding virgins) by selecting individuals falling below the first quartile of the distribution of regliosity scores. The low scorers experienced their first sexual intercourse at a younger age (M= 15.92 years) than did the high scorers (M= 17.25 years). The high religious group was also less satisfied with their first sexual encounter, less likely to intend to be sexually active, less likely to make use of safe-sex practices, engaged in sexual intercourse with fewer partners during high school, and used condoms less frequently than the low religious group.

In a survey of 2,206 black South African students (Nicholas 1994a), 16.3 percent (361) of respondents indicated that they did not use condoms during sexual intercourse, because it was against their religion. While sexual stereotypes of the various ethnic groups in South Africa flourish, the paucity of research on sexuality in South Africa precludes any firm conclusions on various ethnic sexual practices. Black students who have consulted the first author have ascribed folk religious practices as being the cause of their sexual problems. It would not be uncommon to find a client consulting an indigenous healer for a sexual problem ascribed to witchcraft, in the belief that many approaches to the same problem would bring more-effective relief. These beliefs could be located within Christian faith healing, Islamic faith healing, or African herbal or psychic remedies.

B. Source and Character of Ethnic Values

The sociopolitical context of South African blacks, and South African black higher education students, renders them very vulnerable to sexuality-related problems. Most black schools provide very poor guidance to their pupils and sex education is the exception in schools. This lack of guidance and other resources is politically determined in that the bulk of the financing for these resources had been reserved for whites. Even in 1993, there still existed a disparity in the allocation of resources to blacks and whites at all educational levels. Political decisions have also ensured that blacks live in extremely crowded conditions by legally allowing blacks residential access to only 13 percent of the land of South Africa. These factors contribute significantly to sexual abuse, divorce, age-inappropriate exposure to sexual contact, and other high-profile sexuality problems prevalent in the black community (Nicholas 1994a, 4).

3. Sexual Knowledge and Education

A/B. Government Policies and Programs, and Informal Sources

Failure to use contraception is a critical problem on university campuses and schools. While sex counseling is being neglected at schools in South

Africa, it is likely to take up an increasing amount of resources elsewhere. For example, parents and religious leaders attacked the introduction of sex education in South African Indian schools as a pilot program in 1993, expressing fears that their children would be corrupted. Such programs had not been taught before in these schools (Chothia 1993). Cilliers (1989) found that all the school departments he consulted supported the idea of the school as a means for AIDS prevention, yet it is evident that sex education does not have similar support (Kagan 1989). Some sex and AIDS education programs have been initiated in the 1990s, but these are experiencing some opposition from parents and others (Gevisser, 1993). In 1992, service points at which family planning was provided numbered 65,182 (Cooper et al. 1994). As a result of these programs, 2,301,152 women were using contraceptives.

Intrafamial Communications

The following findings regarding intrafamilial communication about sex in South Africa were obtained in 1990 from 1,902 black first-year students at a South African university (Nicholas 1991).

Age at Which Sex Information Was Acquired. Table 1 shows how respondents to questions on age at which sex information was acquired reflect the small percentage of students who first learned certain concepts before the age of 10 years, and the relatively large percentage who learned about these sexual concepts when they were 16 years and older.

Statistically significant gender differences existed in the acquisition of sex information for the terms shown in Table 1, except for the acquisition

Table 1

Age at Which Sex Information Was Acquired (in Percentages)

Topic	Before Age of 10	After Age of 16
Sexual intercourse	17.6	1.8
Pregnancy	16.6	21.9
Abortion	1.8	36.6
Venereal disease	0.6	44.8
Menstruation	3.8	22.9
Female prostitution	4.7	32.4
Erection	12.9	32.5
Condoms	1.0	43.3
Male homosexuality	2.6	42.4
Female homosexuality	1.3	45.5
Fertilization	1.7	42.9

of information on pregnancy, female prostitution, and male and female homosexuality.

Manner in Which Sex Information Was Acquired. Males and females in this sample acquired their initial learning about these concepts from different sources (Table 2). Friends and the mass media are consistently ranked as the major source of initial sex information for this study, whereas school training showed severe limitations.

Table 2

Main Sources of Sexual Information (in Percentages) for 1,902 First-Year Black University Students

			Source			
			Friends		Mass	
Topic	Mothers	Schools	Same Sex	Other Sex	Media	Other
Intercourse			33.4	20.7		
Pregnancy	28.7			24.3		
Males	8.3					
Females	20.4					
Abortion		21.2		21.7	30.1	
STDs		28.5		17.1	27.2	
Menstruation	28.2		c. 33.0			
Erection				38.0		20.8
Female prostitution				27.3	37.0	
Male homosexuality				20.9	43.0	
Lesbianism				23.5	57.0	
AIDS				4.5	61.0	

Preferred Source of Information about Sexuality. The preferred source of sex information for this sample is school training, 27.5 percent; friends, 26.7 percent; and mother, 17.7 percent. Fathers were chosen as the preferred source only by 5.1 percent, 4.5 percent of male respondents and 0.6 percent of females. The high percentage of students with a preference for friends points to the potential value of peer counseling programs for sexuality-related issues.

Parental Provision of Sex Information. Thirty-eight percent of respondents indicated that they had received no sex information from their mothers; 8.2 percent of females and only 3.8 percent of males indicated that they received much information from mothers. As expected, 65.5 percent of respondents indicated that fathers had given no sex information; 4.5

percent, 3.1 percent of males and 1.4 percent of females, reported their fathers provided much sex information.

Provision of Sex Information at School. Sixty-two percent of respondents indicated that they received no sex information at primary school, whereas only 10.9 percent indicated that they received no sex information at high school. Guidance teachers seem to provide much of the sex information at school, with 30.3 percent of respondents indicating that they received much information from guidance teachers.

Approval for Sex Education. A large percentage of students are against the provision of sex education in kindergarten (69.5 percent). Almost a quarter of respondents (23.4 percent) are against provision of sex information in primary school, 1.8 percent are against sex education in high school, and 2.6 percent are against sex eduction at the university.

Attitudes Toward Premarital Intercourse. Forty-five percent of respondents disapprove of premarital intercourse (17 percent male and 28 percent female). As expected, males have significantly higher approval ratings for engaging in premarital intercourse than females.

Sex Myths. The endorsement of sex myths by male and female students were statistically significantly different for thirty of forty-nine myths included in the survey. Large percentages of students also indicated "don't know" to many of the questions, with females indicating "don't know" more frequently than male students for most of the questions. The "don't know" responses are consistent with the lack of sex-information resources, the inadequacy of sex education programs in the schools where they exist, and the writer's experience of counseling and teaching hundreds of university students who did not possess extremely basic sex information.

Summary. Because males and females do experience sexual socialization differently, it can be expected that females will endorse sex myths differently, or discuss sexuality differently, from men. Programs designed to intervene in problem behaviors stemming from beliefs in sex myths may have to target male and female students separately. A large percentage of students used the "don't know" option, indicating that hardly any discussion on those topics had taken place for those student within the family or school system, and that they may be genuinely uncertain.

South African students in this sample are less knowledgeable about sexuality and AIDS than North American students as indicated by North American research studies. South African students have less access to a range of sexuality resources that may better inform them, and researchers have to acknowledge that many students may simply not have been exposed to sex information in a number of areas related to sexuality.

Mosher (1979) contends that there may be more "heat" than "light" in the sex lives of university students in the U.S.A., making the point that the North American student may not be very knowledgeable about sexuality even with access to a variety of resources. It is clear from the results of this study that South African students are even less knowledgeable about sexuality than North American students.

Male students were more knowledgeable at the age of 9 or younger about all the terms listed than female students in this sample, except for menstruation. Very few students had acquired knowledge of these terms by age 10 compared to similar EuroAmerican studies. The percentage of knowledgeable students in this sample ranges from 0.6 percent for knowledge of venereal disease to 17.6 percent for knowledge about sexual intercourse.

It is generally assumed that children and young people are learning about sex at considerably younger ages than did their parents and grandparents. Gebhard (1977) verified this assumption, comparing unpublished data collected by the Kinsey Institute for Sex Research between 1938 and 1960 with data collected in the mid-1970s. No such earlier South African data exist to compare with the recent study, but comparison with the two samples in Gebhard (1977), called the "Kinsey Sample" and the "Recent Sample," illustrates the comparatively late acquisition of sex information of the 1990 South African sample on all items of sex knowledge acquisition. Initiatives are therefore necessary to establish the extent of late acquisition of sex knowledge and its implications for safer-sex practices and the development of sexuality-related problems, and they should enjoy high priority among research initiatives.

The implications of this study for research and education point to the potential usefulness of same-sex peer sexuality counseling as a primary method of prevention and intervention. Those who have not had access to sex resources may more readily accept advice in same-sex groups or present themselves for participation in such groups on sexuality.

This study confirms the fathers' lack of involvement in intrafamilial communication about sexuality, and emphasizes the need for research on South African fathers in this regard. Mothers are the most-preferred source of information about sexuality for female respondents, and school training is the most-preferred source for all respondents. The dynamics of mother-daughter communication about sexuality requires investigation in the South African context, as mothers may be a useful resource to school- and university-based sexuality programs, either by supporting such programs or through actively becoming part of campus-based extracurricular programs.

The overwhelming disapproval of the provision of sex education in kindergarten by 69.5 percent of respondents reflects the myth of the asexual child. A priority of sex education and sexuality courses should therefore be the acknowledgment of childhood sexuality. Myths that parents and teachers may hold in this regard also need to be investigated.

Forty-eight percent of respondents indicated experience in premarital sexual intercourse while only 30 percent approve thereof. It is likely that the number of first-year students who experience premarital sex will increase during their first year of study on campus. Counselors are required to prepare students for that probability and offer resources to facilitate decision making about engaging in premarital intercourse.

Of respondents, 75.6 percent consider abortion as an unacceptable means of terminating pregnancy. Yet a number of respondents will find themselves either pregnant or responsible for a pregnancy, given the high pregnancy statistics at the campus serving as a site for this study. Abortion is illegal in South Africa and counselors cannot therefore advocate this as an option, except in rare cases. Providing information and resources to promote safer sex should therefore be a high priority for campus counselors in South Africa.

These studies present findings of significant differences between male and female students in their experience of a range of sexuality-related problems. In South Africa, where sexuality programs are not well-established, counselors may be advised to structure intervention groups on a same-sex basis in the first stage of intervention for some sexuality problems.

The significant differences for gender that have been found for most sexuality-related concerns in this study require that a sex-counseling program includes a focus on particular gender-related needs of students. More emphasis may need to be placed on homophobia, prejudice, contraception, and belief in sex myths for male students, and emphasis on sex and AIDS knowledge acquisition, safety, and assertiveness for female students in such a program.

A 1994 study of 1,737 black South Africans in their first year attending a university conducted by the first author adds to the understanding of sexual education and the sources on sex information among black South Africans (Nicholas 1994a). The mean age of the subjects was 20.4 years with a range from 16 years old to 50 years old. Peers were reported as the overall primary first source of learning about sexual intercourse (Table 3). Male and female respondents received the information much more from opposite-sex friends, 35 percent and 25.2 percent respectively, than from same-sex friends, 18.2 percent and 19 percent respectively. Together with reading, this accounts for 73 percent of the sources of learning for this topic.

Although peers are still ranked as the preferred source of information about sexual intercourse, approximately only half of the respondents who indicated peers as their first source of knowledge also include it as their preferred source (Tables 4 and 5). The respondents indicated a much greater role for the school or guidance teacher (18.3 percent), mothers (18.2 percent), and fathers (5.1 percent). Peers are the preferred source of sex information for only a quarter of respondents. Peers are also supplanted by "reading" as the most important source of sexuality information. The father's current role in imparting important sexuality information is

Table 3

Sources of Learning About Sexuality (in Percentages): Most Important Source of Sexuality Information

Source	Male	Female	Total
Reading	33.0	27.2	30.3
Same-sex friend	17.0	14.0	15.5
Opposite-sex friend	14.1	12.7	13.5
School/Guidance teacher	17.0	19.4	18.1
Mother	4.8	13.4	8.9
Mass media	7.5	3.9	5.8
Other	2.6	0.4	4.4
Other relative	1.8	2.2	2.0
Father	2.2	0.7	1.5

Statistically significant gender differences: $\chi^2 = 37.34$; $df = 8$; $p = 0.0000$

Table 4

Preferred Source of Sexuality Information (in Percentages)

Source	Male	Female	Total
Same-sex friend	8.3	9.8	9.5
Opposite-sex friend	19.8	11.5	15.9
Reading	19.8	22.8	
School/Guidance teacher	21.1	17.2	19.3
Mother	8.4	29.2	18.2
Father	8.1	1.7	5.1
Mass media	6.6	2.5	4.6
Other	4.4	3.9	4.2
Other relative	2.4	1.5	2.0

Statistically significant gender differences: $\chi^2 = 89.63$; $df = 8$; $p = 0.0000$

negligible, but he is the preferred source for 8.1 percent of males, rivaling the same-sex peer that is the preferred source for 8.3 percent of male respondents.

4. Autoerotic Behaviors and Patterns

A survey of 1,896 black university students revealed that 34.2 percent, 348 males and 288 females, worried about the effect of masturbation (Nicholas 1993b). Of these students, 28.7 percent, 348 males and 190 females, also

Table 5

First Source of Information about Sexual Intercourse (in Percentages)

Source	Male	Female	Total
Same-sex friend	18.2	19.0	18.6
Opposite-sex friend	35.0	25.2	29.3
Reading	21.3	29.2	25.1
School/Guidance teacher	7.2	10.2	8.6
Mass media	9.0	3.7	6.5
Mother	2.7	6.7	4.6
Other	5.2	4.0	4.6
Other relative	3.4	1.2	2.4
Father	0.0	0.7	0.4

Statistically significant gender differences: $\chi^2 = 36.28$; $df = 8$; $p = 0.0000$

believed that women commonly insert foreign objects into the vagina. Over half, 51.9 percent, did not know whether or not masturbation causes pimples and acne, while 8.5 percent believed it does have these consequences. Fourteen percent of respondents believed that sexually fulfilled, mature adults do not masturbate, while 54.5 percent indicated "don't know." Similarly, 16.5 percent believed that most adults do not masturbate, and 58 percent indicated they did not know on this point.

5. Interpersonal Heterosexual Behaviors

A/B. Children and Adolescents

A 1995 survey of South African teenagers by a national newspaper revealed the following. Of respondents whose average age was 16 years,

- 41 percent considered sex before marriage as unacceptable,
- 54 percent accepted it only with someone they cared about,
- 5 percent said it is something to experience with as many people as possible,
- 81 percent considered contraception as both partners' responsibility,
- 80 percent considered gay-bashing unacceptable,
- 10 percent indicated that they had a gay experience, and
- 71 percent thought that they will make a better job of marriage than their parents.

Sixty-seven percent of the respondents were female, but the number of respondents was not indicated in this anonymous 1995 report.

A 1992 survey of 7,000 adolescents found that 17 percent had engaged in sexual intercourse, with a median age of 15 years at first intercourse (Cooper et al. 1994). (Dating customs, sexual activities, and relationships before college are described in the discussion of first intercourse experiences.)

Some insights into the sexual behavior of adolescent black South Africans can be drawn from a study of first intercourse and contraceptive experiences of 1,737 black South Africans conducted during their first year in a university (Nicholas 1994a). The mean age of the 754 females and 959 males was 20.4 years (with 24 missing cases). The age range was 16 years old to 50 years old. Of the sample, 37.7 percent spoke an African language, 28.1 percent spoke Afrikaans, 27 percent spoke English, and 7.2 percent indicated "other." Of respondents, 96.5 percent indicated that they were single. This discussion will focus on the 894 single students, 47.1 percent male and 52.9 percent female, who indicated that they had experienced sexual intercourse.

While females experienced first intercourse with a partner who was 2.5 years older, males reported experiencing first intercourse with a partner who was 1.0 year younger. Male respondents' mean age at first intercourse was 15.5 years and their partners' age was 14.5 years old. Female respondents' mean age was 17.8 years and their partners' mean age was 20.3 years old. Obviously, the first sexual partners of the female respondents were mainly outside the research group.

Most respondents indicated that they experienced their first intercourse with a steady friend. Males were, however, much more likely than females to have had their first intercourse experience with an unknown partner or casual acquaintance. It is a cause for concern that 4.1 percent of the sample indicated that first intercourse was experienced with a close relative (Table 6).

Males were more likely than females to have sexual intercourse again with their first partner (Table 7). Although most respondents had further sexual intercourse with their first partner, 35.5 percent of females reported no further intercourse with their first partner, as compared to only 20.6 percent of the male respondents. Almost 70 percent of respondents had sexual intercourse between 1 and 5 times with the first partner, which points to the short-lived nature of the sexual relationship with the first sexual partner for most respondents. First intercourse may have, therefore, influenced the relationships of the 60.6 percent of respondents who indicated "steady friend" as their first intercourse partner, because for at least half of this group, sexual intercourse occurred only 1 to 5 times during the "steady" relationship. Of respondents, 46.3 percent had had one sexual partner in high school and 20.8 percent had had the first intercourse experience after leaving high school, but before entering university (Table 8). Males reported significantly higher numbers of high school partners than females.

Table 6

Partner Relationship in First Sexual Intercourse (in Percentages)

Relationship of Partner	Male	Female	Total
Engaged partner	6.7	5.7	6.2
Steady friend	44.6	75.5	60.6
Casual acquaintance	24.0	5.7	14.5
Unknown Partner	8.4	2.6	5.4
Close Relative	5.3	3.1	4.1
Other	5.4	7.5	9.2

Statistically significant gender differences: χ^2 = 89.40; df = 9; p = 0.0000

Table 7

Times Intercourse Took Place with First Partner (in Percentages)

Number of Times	Male	Female	Total
Once	20.6	35.5	27.2
2-5 times	46.4	36.0	41.8
6-10 times	10.4	8.4	9.5
11-25 times	4.9	6.1	5.4
26 or more times	17.6	14.0	16.09

Statistically significant gender differences: χ^2 = 23.30; df = 4; p = 0.0001

Table 8

Number of High School Sexual Partners (in Percentages)

Number of Partners	Male	Female	Total
None	13.4	29.4	20.8
1 partner	37.6	56.3	46.3
2-5 partners	30.4	12.4	22.0
6-10 partners	8.5	0.7	4.9
11 or more partners	10.1	1.2	6.0

Statistically significant gender differences: χ^2 = 134.9; df = 4; p = 0.0000

Twice as many males as females indicated that they greatly enjoyed their first sexual intercourse experience (Table 9). A third of respondents disliked or greatly disliked their experience of first sexual intercourse, 14.4 percent of males and 56.9 percent of females.

Puberty rituals are described in Section 1.

Table 9

Characteristics of First Sexual Intercourse and High School Sexual Experience (in Percentages)

Satisfaction	Male	Female	Total
Greatly enjoyed	40.5	10.2	26.3
Enjoyed	45.1	33.0	39.4
Disliked	10.7	39.0	23.9
Greatly disliked	3.7	17.9	10.3

Statistically significant gender differences: $\chi^2 = 196.5$; $df = 3$; $p = 0.0000$

C. Adults

Sexual Behavior and Relationships of Single Adults

Very little published South African data are available on various interpersonal heterosexual behaviors. Much of the data currently cited, especially in anthropology texts, do not accurately reflect current sexual practices that have been tremendously influenced by modern Western practices. In ten years of sex counseling, the first author found that various sex practices, like anal sex, fellatio, and cunnilingus, were not uncommon. Approximately 40 percent of these clients had tribal affiliations.

Marriage and Family Structures

The migratory labor system has been undeniably destructive for the black African marriage and family structure. A consequence of introducing wage earners, forced to live in single-sex hostels in close proximity to impoverished communities with high levels of unemployment, is the inevitable bartering of sex and domestic chores for food and bed; similarly, with long-distance truck drivers and their "traveling wives."

In South African women's magazines, the problems of comarital and extramarital relationships, sexual satisfaction, and sexual outlets and techniques are openly and regularly discussed in advice columns. Among Muslims and Africans, polygamy is still being practiced.

Sexuality and the Disabled

The sexual needs of the disabled are still very much a neglected topic, and the sexual rights of the disabled are not very well served in South Africa (Nicholas 1994a).

Divorce

Divorces in South Africa, according to race in 1987, were 18,371 for whites, involving 24,673 children, for coloreds, 4,368 divorces involving 5,867 children, and for Indians, 1,046 divorces involving 1,405 children. In 1986, the illegitimacy rates for whites was 7.1 percent ($n = 5,172$), for coloreds, 55 percent ($n = 44,969$), and for Indians, 16.7 percent ($n = 3,265$), giving an average illegitimacy rate for these groups of 30.6 percent ($n = 53,406$). The idea that the typical family in South Africa is a two-parent, stable context for the transmission of sex information is therefore obviously fallacious.

6. Homoerotic, Homosexual, and Ambisexual Behaviors

Isaacs and McKendrick (1992, x) claim that an estimated one out of ten South Africans has a homosexual identity, even if this identity is disguised, denied, or suppressed. The formal gay movement, as represented by the Gay Association of South Africa (GASA), is now defunct as a result of political and social divisions. Splinter nonracial groups, such as the Gay and Lesbian Organization of the Witwatersrand (GLOW) and the Organization of Lesbian and Gay Activists (OLGA), attempt to address gay issues in parallel with human rights (Isaacs and McKendrick 1992, 158). *Link/Skakel*, the most widely read local newspaper published by GASA, ceased publication in 1985 (Isaac and McKendrik 1992, 157). David Moolman initiated the publication of a private gay newspaper *Exit*, which was criticized for its sexist, homoerotic, and political biases (Isaacs and McKendrick 1992, 157). A new column called "Outspeak" was introduced to expand coverage of the subject matter in *Exit*, and dealt more explicitly with issues of gay liberation and organization (Gevisser and Cameron 1994, 227).

There are only two formal organizations in South Africa that deal specifically with homosexual crises from the perspective of the crisis-intervention model. These are the Radio 702 Crisis Clinic and the GASA 60-10 Counseling Center in Cape Town (Isaacs and McKendrick 1992, 220) Homosexuals now feel safer about declaring their sexual preferences, and there have been gay-pride marches advocating gay and lesbian rights in the major cities of South Africa.

The first South African gay telephone directory was launched in Johannesburg recently, and the listing includes gay and gay-friendly businesses and services. The directory allows gay people to make use of the services of people who do not object to their lifestyle (Naidoo 1994).

There are not many referenced accounts of bisexual life in South Africa, but according to Zubeida, it is extremely difficult to be bisexual in a heterosexual society. The following excerpt from an interview with her illustrates her feelings:

> I guess I feel oppressed as a bisexual person. Most lesbian and gay organizations don't really cater for bisexuals—I think largely because bisexuals are even less visible than homosexuals. There is also so much distrust of bisexuals in the homosexual community. Sometimes we are

> seen as sitting on the fence and enjoying the best of both worlds; usually we are seen as being unable to come out of the closet. (Gevisser and Cameron 1994, 191)

Local university counselors are frequently confronted with ignorance about homosexuality in the campus environment, which may exacerbate the problems their homosexual clients present. A 1990 study of 1,902 first-year students at a black university revealed the following about homophobia and prejudice. Forty-three percent of the sample, 25.5 percent of the males and 17.9 percent of the females, believe that homosexuality is immoral. Twenty-seven percent of the sample, 13.7 percent of the males and 13 percent of the females, believe that a homosexual person cannot be a good religious person. Forty-six percent, 20.8 percent of the males and 19.4 percent of the females, believe that homosexual people could become heterosexual if they chose to. A quarter of the males and 21.8 percent of the females believe that homosexuality is not an acceptable orientation. A campus environment pervaded with highly homophobic beliefs such as these, is hardly one that provides support for homosexual clients or those struggling with their sexual identity (Nicholas 1994a, 73-74).

7. Gender Conflicted Persons

A survey of 2,209 black university students in 1994 revealed that 8.8 percent of respondents (*n* = 194) indicated a moderate need for help with issues of sexual identity, and 8.3 percent (*n* = 183) of respondents indicated a high need for help with sexual identity (Nicholas 1994b).

The Groot Schuur Hospital in Cape Town offers medical services for transsexuals who would like to undergo surgery to change their sex. The program includes an assessment by a psychiatrist who evaluates the candidate and makes a recommendation whether or not the surgery should be performed. After surgery, the patient continues counseling with a psychologist and social worker. Medical services for intersexual children are provided at the Red Cross Children's Hospital. The child's sexual orientation is assessed by a psychiatrist who makes a recommendation of the sex that would be most suitable for child. Again, postsurgery counseling and support are provided.

8. Significant Unconventional Sexual Behaviors

A. Sexual Coercion

In 1992, 15,333 cases of child abuse were reported to the Child Protection Unit. Of this number, 3,639 involved rape and 4,135 involved sexual abuse, including sodomy, incest, and other forms of sexual assault (Cooper et al.

1994). The rate of rape in South Africa in 1991 was 120 per 100,000 compared to 42 per 100,000 in the U.S.A. The inquiry into legislation on rape (Havenga 1985) was regarded as presenting resistance to genuine reform. This inquiry was launched in May, 1982, and was found to have certain inadequacies, mainly the emphasis on sexual aspects in the definition of rape (in contrast with the feminist emphasis on the violence aspects), the failure to make the definition of rape gender neutral, and the failure to include oral and anal sex and penetration by means of an object. The recommendation that the law stating that a man could not be found guilty of raping his wife be rescinded was qualified by the requirement that prosecution in such cases cannot proceed without permission from the attorney general. The previous sexual history of a rape victim/survivor can still be entered in evidence in camera.

The convictions for child sexual abuse for the years 1989-1992 were as follows: 1989, 1,086; 1990, 1,061; 1991, 1,345; and 1992, 1,124.

The Prevention of Family Violence Bill, tabled in 1993 in the parliament, made provision for a husband to be liable to prosecution for marital rape, and for failure to report that a child had been ill-treated, or suspicion thereof, to be regarded as an offense (Cooper et al. 1994).

South Africa does not as yet have sexual harassment legislation. Of the twelve universities and five technical colleges that responded to a request for information on their sexual harassment policies in 1991, only one, University of Cape Town, had a policy on sexual harassment. Educational institutions undoubtedly have an obligation to eliminate coercive sexuality on campus. However, the university's effectiveness in this regard is limited by several factors:

- South Africa as a patriarchal society;
- the underreporting of rape and sexual harassment;
- the desire to project the image of the university as a safe place and avoid publicity indicating the opposite;
- the lack of open discourse on sexuality in communities;
- the paucity of sex-education courses in educational institutions;
- the high level of violence in South African society, including sexual violence;
- the range of views on the appropriate expression of sexuality without the benefit of open discourse and education; and
- the lack of trained personnel in the area of sexuality (Nicholas 1994a, 105-106).

B. Prostitution

Prostitution is illegal in South Africa but has flourished in all major cities and townships for decades. In Cape Town, up to 200 prostitutes were allowed to work in the harbor area and were registered by the authorities as "port hostesses." They were recently banned from plying their trade, ostensibly because of safety concerns such as smoking on board ships carrying hazardous cargo (Underhill 1995). Daily newspapers have several columns devoted to advertisements for "escort services" that are fairly explicit offers of sexual services.

The socioeconomic status (SES) of black students has an influence on whether they are tempted to trade sexual favors for financial or educational gain. The difference in the SES between teachers and pupils led them to believe that they could have access to this perceived affluence through a sexual relationship. Pupils who trade sexual favors for financial gain are sworn to secrecy by allies and co-conspirators. In one case we are familiar with, Moses acknowledged that sex had taken place between a group of boys of whom he was one and their male teacher, but that they would "get" anyone who spoke out, as they were all "paid well."

Socioeconomic circumstances can lure pupils into prostitution, as in the case of five standard eight girls (age 15 to 16 years old) who were absent from school for three months and were subsequently found at a brothel. Female students also mentioned trading sex for grades. While these reports may not be completely accurate, it is sufficient for such allegations to gain currency in a school to damage seriously the confidence of pupils in the grading system. The lack of opportunities to discuss sexuality openly in school would, therefore, further exacerbate this serious problem (Nicholas 1994a, 4-5).

C. Pornography and Erotica

South Africa now has local versions of *Penthouse, Playboy,* and *Hustler.* The censor board keeps a vigilant eye on these and other similar publications and recently lost a case against *Hustler* under the new constitution's freedom-of-speech provision. A new swingers' magazine, *X Pose,* with graphic closeups of male genitals and female vulvas, was recently launched (Chapel 1995). Pornographic movies are not openly available, but have a wide underground distribution. See also comments in Section 1A/B above.

9. Contraception, Abortion, and Population Planning

A. Contraception

In a study of 1,737 first-year black South African students, first intercourse was primarily characterized by the lack of contraceptive use, with 35.7 percent of the males and 32.8 percent of the females indicating non-use of contraceptives, and 12.3 percent of the males and 7.1 percent of the females indicating "don't know" (Table 10). A further 6.2 percent reported using the unreliable withdrawal method (Nicholas 1994a, 88-94).

The major reasons given for not using a contraceptive were that the first sexual intercourse was unplanned (36.8 percent) and that no thought was

Table 10

Contraceptive Practices at First Sexual Intercourse (in Percentages)

Contraception Used	Male	Female	Total
No method	35.7	32.8	34.3
Pill	14.6	22.8	18.5
Condom	19.5	13.3	16.6
Withdrawal	7.4	4.8	6.2
Rhythm	1.1	0.5	0.8
Condom & Contraceptive	6.8	11.9	9.2
Other	2.7	6.9	4.7
Don't know	12.3	7.1	9.8

given to contraception at the time of the first intercourse act (38.1 percent) (Table 11). The belief that if one only has intercourse "a few times," contraception is not essential, was endorsed by 31.6 percent of respondents. The erroneous belief that having sexual intercourse only once or a few times protects one from the risks associated with unsafe sex, may significantly influence students to make the transition from virginity to nonvirginity without using contraceptives.

The opinion of significant others also influenced respondents' use of contraceptives. Male and female respondents almost equally were uncomfortable being too prepared (23.6 percent). Mothers' discovery of contraceptive use was cited by 18.8 percent of respondents, and fathers' displeasure was cited by 17.9 percent of respondents, as reasons that prevented contraceptive use. Of respondents, 18.1 percent indicated that contraceptive use was impractical when engaging in "many rounds of sex." Most safer-sex messages assume a single encounter requiring a single condom and neglect those who continue sexual activity after the first orgasm.

This study revealed that 54.2 percent of female respondents and 55.5 percent of male respondents had experienced sexual intercourse. Darling et al. (1992) cite relevant research indicating that, while males experience first sexual intercourse at a younger age than females, the average age for females is also declining to around 16 years of age. Further research is required to establish a trend towards gender convergence among South African students. Female respondents in this sample experienced first intercourse at 17.8 years old, compared to Darling et al.'s (1992) report of 17.7 years old. Male respondents initiated first intercourse at 15.5 years old, 2.3 years younger than the sample of Darling et al. (1992). No similar South African studies on first intercourse have been done to facilitate local comparisons.

Table 11

Factors Preventing Contraceptive Use During First Sexual Encounter: Response to Statement, "What Prevented the Use of a Contraceptive During Your First Sexual Encounter?" (Rank Ordered; in Percentages)

Reason Given	Male	Female	Total
I used a contraceptive	18.0	23.2	41.2
I did not think about it	21.6	16.5	38.1
I did not intend to have sex	14.8	22.0	36.8
I only did it a few times	18.0	13.6	31.6
I feared the side effects	12.6	11.8	24.2
I was uncomfortable being too prepared	11.6	12.0	23.6
There was none available	15.2	8.2	23.4
It is against my religion	9.8	9.8	19.6
I feared that my mother would discover my use of contraceptives	7.6	11.2	18.8
It is impractical for many rounds of sex	14.1	4.0	18.1
I feared my father would be displeased	8.1	9.8	17.9
It makes sex unpleasant	13.0	3.8	16.8
It is not my responsibility	6.5	8.2	14.7
I thought it was the wrong time of the month	2.9	5.4	8.3
It is too expensive	5.6	2.0	7.6
I thought I was sterile	4.0	2.7	6.7
I was drunk	3.6	0.3	3.9
I wanted to cause a pregnancy	2.4	1.3	3.7

This study found that many students do not use contraception during first intercourse. Similar to other studies, this reflects the unplanned nature of first sexual intercourse. Peers are reported as the primary first source of learning about sexual intercourse and are also considered the preferred source by respondents. "Reading," however, was indicated as the most important source of information about sexuality. More emphasis should be placed on the gender differences for peers' provision of sexuality information. This study found that opposite-sex friends are more likely to be the first source of sexuality information, as well as the preferred source of sexuality information. The same-sex friend was, however, considered the most important source of sexuality information. Peer sexuality programs could be guided by the preferred source of sexuality information in relation to gender.

The provision of information on safer sex has been found to be inadequate in facilitating desired behavior change (Keeling 1991). Those students who have not developed a pattern of risky sex practices may be more amenable to early intervention before high-risk patterns of sexual behavior set in. Students who have yet to make the transition to nonvirginity, as well as those who have had only a few sexual experiences, may be more open to establish patterns of safer-sex behaviors through early intervention by counselors.

Starting in 1990, the first author and several colleagues have conducted an annual survey of first-time entry, first-year university students enrolling at a predominantly black university (Nicholas 1994b, 1993a, 1993b, 1992, 1991, 1990; Nicholas and Orr 1994; Nicholas, Tredoux, and Daniels 1994; Nicholas and Durrheim 1994). All consenting first-year students who attended the orientation program completed a structured questionnaire on intrafamilial communication about contraception. In 1990, 1,986 students completed questionnaires that included 829 male students and 948 female students (18 missing cases). In 1991, 2,069 students completed questionnaires, 1,029 males and 1,040 females. In 1992, 1,558 students completed questionnaires that included 684 male and 834 female students (32 missing cases).

Forty-eight percent of the 1990 sample (885) indicated that they had had sexual intercourse. Fifty-four percent of the 1991 sample (1,115) indicated that they had had sexual intercourse. Fifty-three percent of the 1992 sample (793) indicated that they had had sexual intercourse. Less than 30 percent of the total sample indicated approval of premarital sexual intercourse, while more than 50 percent of the sample indicated nonvirgin status.

Approximately twice as many respondents felt that their mothers would be understanding about a problem concerning contraceptive matters, as opposed to fathers (Table 12). The percentage of students responding affirmatively about their mothers' understanding increased from 28.5 percent in 1990 to 38.3 percent in 1992. The percentage of respondents responding affirmatively about their fathers' understanding increased by only 4 percent from 1990 to 1992. Most students, therefore, do not consider their parents as understanding about a problem concerning contraception. Gender differences are significant at the probability level greater than .00001 ($p. > .00001$) level for respondents surveyed in all three years.

Over three quarters of respondents indicated that their fathers had not given them any information about contraception, compared to approximately 55 percent of respondents who indicated that their mothers had not provided such information (Table 13). There was no significant difference for gender in the 1991 and 1992 samples. For the 1990 sample, $p = .0004$. Slightly more males than females had received information about contraceptives from their fathers. On average, more than twice the respondents received this information from mothers than fathers. More males received information about contraception from mothers than fathers, emphasizing the lack of involvement of fathers in these discussions.

More students preferred that their fathers not know about their use of contraceptives than they did their mothers (Table 14). Twice as many female

Table 12

Response to Statement, "If I Had a Problem Concerning Contraceptive Matters I Could Count on My Mother/Father to Be Understanding"

	Sample Year					
	1990		1991		1992	
Response	Mother	Father	Mother	Father	Mother	Father
True	532	273	712	349	585	284
	(28.5%)	(14.7%)	(35.2%)	(17.5%)	(38.3%)	(18.8%)
False	736	977	698	991	545	803
	(39.4%)	(52.8%)	(34.5%)	(49.8%)	(35.7%)	(53.2%)
Don't know	600	601	615	650	396	423
	(32.1%)	(32.5%)	(30.4%)	(32.7%)	(26.0%)	(28.0%)
Column Totals	1,868	1,851	2,025	1,990	1,526	1,510
	(100%)	(100%)	(100%)	(100%)	(100%)	(100%)

Table 13

Response to Statement, "My Mother/Father Has Never Given Me Any Information about Contraceptives"

	Sample Year					
	1990		1991		1992	
Response	Mother	Father	Mother	Father	Mother	Father
True	1,060	1,424	1,123	1,563	835	1,160
	(56.5%)	(76.4%)	(55.3%)	(77.6%)	(54.6%)	(76.6%)
False	747	346	853	384	673	306
	(39.8%)	(18.6%)	(42.0%)	(19.1%)	(44.0%)	(20.2%)
Don't know	68	94	56	66	22	48
	(3.6%)	(5.0%)	(2.8%)	(3.3%)	(1.4%)	(3.2%)
Column Totals	1,875	1,864	2,032	2,013	1,530	1,514
	(100%)	(100%)	(100%)	(100%)	(100%)	(100%)

respondents disagreed with this statement than did male respondents. Gender differences are significant at the $p < .00001$ level for all three years.

Approximately three quarters of respondents indicated that they had not discussed contraception thoroughly with their mothers, and almost 90 percent of the respondents indicated this to be the case in relation to fathers (Table 15). Fathers were conspicuously absent as far as thorough discussion of contraception is concerned. Gender differences are significant at the $p < .00001$ level for all three years.

Table 14

Response to Statement, "If I Were to Use a Contraceptive, I Would Prefer That My Mother/Father Not Know about It"

| | Sample Year | | | | | |
| | 1990 | | 1991 | | 1992 | |
Response	Mother	Father	Mother	Father	Mother	Father
True	921	1,090	944	1,169	711	871
	(49.5%)	(58.8%)	(46.5%)	(58.5%)	(46.6%)	(57.5%)
False	666	404	826	477	628	376
	(35.8%)	(21.8%)	(40.7%)	(23.9%)	(41.2%)	(24.8%)
Don't know	275	359	258	352	186	268
	(14.8%)	(19.4%)	(12.7%)	(17.0%)	(12.2%)	(17.7%)
Column Totals	1,862	1,853	2,028	1,998	1,525	1,515
	(100%)	(100%)	(100%)	(100%)	(100%)	(100%)

Table 15

Response to Statement, "I Have Discussed My Contraceptive Use Thoroughly with My Mother/Father"

| | Sample Year | | | | | |
| | 1990 | | 1991 | | 1992 | |
Response	Mother	Father	Mother	Father	Mother	Father
True	302	84	377	118	302	86
	(16.3%)	(4.6%)	(18.9%)	(6.0%)	(20.0%)	(5.7%)
False	1,417	1,610	1,518	1,758	1,138	1,345
	(76.3%)	(87.7%)	(76.1%)	(89.1%)	(75.3%)	(89.7%)
Don't know	137	142	99	98	71	68
	(7.4%)	(7.7%)	(5.0%)	(5.0%)	(4.7%)	(4.5%)
Column Totals	1,856	1,836	1,994	1,974	1,511	1,499
	(100%)	(100%)	(100%)	(100%)	(100%)	(100%)

Approximately a third of respondents believed that their mother's estimation of them would not decrease if the mother knew they were using a contraceptive (Table 16). Approximately a quarter of respondents believed their father would not disapprove if he knew. Gender differences are significant at the $p < .0001$ level.

Three times as many respondents were encouraged to use contraceptives by mothers as by fathers (Table 17). Most students, however, have not been encouraged by parents to use contraceptives. Gender differences are significant at the $p < .00001$ level.

Table 16

Response to Statement, "If My Mother/Father Knew I Used a Contraceptive, Their Estimation of Me Would Go Down"

| | Sample Year | | | | | |
| | 1990 | | 1991 | | 1992 | |
Response	Mother	Father	Mother	Father	Mother	Father
True	576	638	566	643	487	543
	(31.0%)	(34.7%)	(28.6%)	(33.0%)	(31.9%)	(36.0%)
False	611	435	711	467	542	367
	(32.8%)	(23.6%)	(35.9%)	(24.0%)	(35.5%)	(24.3%)
Don't know	673	767	703	838	498	599
	(36.2%)	(41.7%)	(35.5%)	(43.0%)	(32.6%)	(39.7%)
Column Totals	1,860	1,840	1,980	1,948	1,527	1,509
	(100%)	(100%)	(100%)	(100%)	(100%)	(100%)

Table 17

Response to Statement, "My Mother/Father Has Encouraged Me to Use Contraceptives"

| | Sample Year | | | | | |
| | 1990 | | 1991 | | 1992 | |
Response	Mother	Father	Mother	Father	Mother	Father
True	301	113	380	116	327	109
	(16.2%)	(6.1%)	(19.2%)	(5.9%)	(21.5%)	(7.2%)
False	1,460	1,583	1,510	1,734	1,116	1,308
	(78.5%)	(85.6%)	(76.3%)	(88.9%)	(73.4%)	(86.8%)
Don't know	99	154	89	101	78	90
	(5.3%)	(8.3%)	(4.5%)	(5.2%)	(5.1%)	(6.0%)
Column Totals	1,860	1,850	1,979	1,951	1,521	1,507
	(100%)	(100%)	(100%)	(100%)	(100%)	(100%)

Few students indicated that they shared the same ideas and beliefs about contraceptives as their parents, with more of such sharing being evident in relation to mothers than fathers (Table 18). A large percentage of respondents also indicated "don't know," indicating the basic lack of communication between parents and children.

In a study to identify barriers to condom use among 700 high school students, Abdool Karim et al. (1992) found that the students were not using condoms to any significant degree, felt that condoms limited sexual pleasure, felt that condom use indicated a lack of trust in one's partner's faithfulness, challenged the male ego, and/or may indicate that

Table 18

Response to Statement, "I Think That My Mother's/Father's Ideas and Beliefs about Contraceptive Use Are Very Similar to My Own"

| | Sample Year | | | | | |
| | 1990 | | 1991 | | 1992 | |
Response	Mother	Father	Mother	Father	Mother	Father
True	735	507	716	473	617	417
	(39.5%)	(27.4%)	(36.3%)	(24.3%)	(40.6%)	(27.7%)
False	407	472	423	504	326	396
	(21.9%)	(25.2%)	(21.5%)	(25.8%)	(21.4%)	(26.3 %)
Don't know	718	871	832	969	578	692
	(38.6%)	(47.1%)	(42.2%)	(49.8%)	(38.0%)	(46.0%)
Column Totals	1,860	1,850	1,971	1,944	1,521	1,505
	(100%)	(100%)	(100%)	(100%)	(100%)	(100%)

one has an STD. Condom use was not well understood, and they were not accessible or available when required. Oral contraceptives cost about $30 per month and condoms $3 a piece. Both are available free at community clinics.

Implications for Counselors

Sex counseling as a discipline is not widely practiced in South Africa. The university's obligation to provide such a resource has been de-emphasized, influenced by the unresolved debate on the appropriate location of sex-counseling resources and the taboos around sexuality. The possibility that intrafamilial communication about contraception might make a major contribution towards eliminating unwanted pregnancy is slim, given the minimal involvement of parents in the provision of information about contraception, especially that of fathers. Schools are unlikely to make any major contribution to contraceptive education, and the thousands of university-bound students requiring guidance on contraception will become the responsibility of campus counselors.

The effective shouldering of this responsibility requires a knowledge of local circumstances and resources. For example, until 1996, abortion was illegal in South Africa, so counselors' efforts had to be largely focused on prevention. This would include facilitating programs that involve larger groups of students gaining access to contraceptive information, while still remaining accessible to individual clients. Knowledge of the incidence of sexual related problems at a particular university is crucial in making students aware of the risks of unprotected sexual intercourse that could directly affect them. The availability of postcoital contraception for use up to seventy-two hours after sexual intercourse should also be made widely known in the campus community.

Advice on condom usage by counselors has to be specific as to local availability and practices. Sidley (1991) found that choosing a brand of condoms in South Africa is bedeviled by a range of factors. Only one brand is produced locally, Crepe de Chine, and the rest are imported without being subjected to tests before being placed on the market. The twenty-four brands, which the South African Bureau of Standards (SABS) tested two years ago, failed. Up to 33 percent of the condoms tested by the Johannesburg City Health Department failed the trials.

The SABS tests for dimensions, mass, tensile strength, elongation, breaking point, aging, freedom from holes, and leakage, but does not make a standard mark compulsory. None of the imported brands bear the quality mark of their country. Three suppliers meet SABS specifications: Vulco, which is South African, F.T.C. Aircraft, manufactured in Thailand, and Freedom, made in Korea. One spermicide, Rendells, contains oil that can cause a rubber condom to blister and burst (Sidley 1991). Counseling clients with regard to condom usage, whether for prevention of pregnancy, STDs, or HIV transmission, has to take into account the many risks associated with condom usage (Masters and Johnson 1986). These include the care that has to be taken in avoiding having preejaculatory fluid spilling onto the labia, spillage of semen when the condom is removed or during detumescence, and the residue of semen on the penis that may come into contact with the vagina.

Effective contraceptive programs for university students must, however, not stop at providing accurate information about contraception. The acceptance of self and others as sexual beings, and of contraception as primarily a sexual rather than a reproductive decision, is essential for effective contraception programs among South African blacks.

B. Teenage (Unmarried) Pregnancies

In a survey at a local hospital, Sapire (1988) found that 75 percent of the pregnancies were unintended and 20 percent of the pregnant women were under 19 years of age. The seriousness of the problem is exemplified by requests for pregnancy tests and the morning-after pill at black universities (Nicholas 1994a, 63).

In Cape Town in 1987, of 2,800 teenage mothers, 2,300 were unmarried. The biggest increase in illegitimacy was among whites, where the percentage has doubled since 1982. In 1986, the percentage of white illegitmate births was 11.3 percent of all white births in Cape Town; in 1987, this increased to 17.2 percent. For coloreds, the number of illegitimate births increased from 6,700 in 1986 to 7,100. The percentage of illegitimate babies born to black, colored, and Asian women in Cape Town was 47.5 percent in 1987 (Stander 1988). A special clinic was instituted at a local hospital for pregnant teenages, 90 percent of whom were unmarried, so that that they would not have to attend with married women (Burman and Preston-Whyte, 1992). Ample evidence exists that a stigma is attached to teenage pregnancy while unmarried for both the mother and child in all sections of South African society. Pregnant pupils consequently conceal their pregnancy from parents who are often absent. Burman (1992, 31) quotes a nurse in this regard:

> Parent or teachers may discover when she gets labor pains that she is pregnant, and it is only then that she can be rushed to a hospital. Schoolgirls don't want to book in advance as this will require them to attend clinics on certain days, which will mean that they are absent [from school] . . . The focus will be on them and the classmates can guess their problem and will laugh at them. They don't want to be seen by neighbours frequenting the clinic as they will talk badly of them (Interview of November 23, 1988).

While stigma is attached to teenaged pregnancy, fertility also has a cultural value, as is illustrated in the following example of a 17-year-old African girl who became pregnant at 16:

> I knew I might get a baby, and the sister at school warned me also. But I had been going with my boyfriend for over a year and my girl friends were beginning to laugh at me. They whispered that I must be inyumba—that is, how you say, sterile. Even my boyfriend asked why I was not having a baby. Then, when I did get pregnant, my mother and father were very cross, but I was pleased as it showed everyone I can have a baby after all. (Preston-Whyte and Zondi 1992, 237)

C. Abortion

Further family instability may be caused by the inability to obtain a legal abortion, which is virtually impossible for the average South African woman. The Abortion and Sterilization Act No. 2 of 1975, which was the law until late 1996, allowed abortions only for instances of rape, incest, or when there is a danger to the physical health or life of the woman. The procedure for allowing a legal abortion was often so cumbersome that many who qualified opted for illegal abortion or went to another country where abortion is legal to have the operation performed.

In November 1996, a new abortion law passed its final legislative hurdle, clearing the way for President Nelson Mandela to replace one of the world's toughest abortion laws with one of the most liberal. The Choice of Termination of Pregnancy Bill was approved by a vote of 49 to 21 in the South African Senate. Twenty senators were absent when the vote was taken. The African National Congress insisted that members who could not support the new law absent themselves from the vote. The white-separatist Freedom Front, the National Party, and the Inkatha Freedom Party opposed the measure, as did Doctors for Life, which promised an immediate appeal to the Constitutional Court.

Under the new law, women and girls are entitled to a state-financed abortion on demand during the first twelve weeks of pregnancy if they have no private medical insurance. This support also applies between twelve and twenty weeks of pregnancy, subject to widely defined conditions. Physicians and midwives are required to advise a minor female to consult her parents, but the law specifically states that abortion cannot be denied if the minor refuses to inform her parents.

In 1986 and 1987 respectively, 770 and 810 legal abortions were performed in South Africa. During the same period, 26,062 and 35,882 operations for the removal of residues of a pregnancy were performed. These operations usually follow an illegal abortion and account for an unknown proportion of illegal abortions in South Africa. In 1992, 1,027 legal abortions had been performed in the first nine months, and eighty-two people were convicted between July 1988 and June 1991 of performing illegal abortions.

Of the 1,902 first-year students at a South African university, 75.6 percent were against abortion (35.8 percent male and 39.8 percent female). Only 15 percent of respondents felt that abortion is an acceptable way to terminate a pregnancy (8.6 percent male and 6.4 percent female).

10. Sexually Transmitted Diseases

In South Africa as elsewhere, sexually transmitted diseases (STDs) constitute a major public health problem. The annual caseload seen only at state/municipal clinics and in private practice is estimated at more than a million patients in a population of 40 million. Management of this endemic is worsened by the wide range of STDs encountered in South Africa, where the common Western STDs of syphilis, herpes, gonorrhea, and nongonococcal urethritis (NGU) coexist with tropical and sub-tropical entities like chancroid, lymphogranuloma venereum (LGV), and granuloma inguinale (Donovanosis). This poses a considerable number of diagnostic and therapeutic problems, especially among the people of color, the poor, and rural people.

In South Africa, considering the character of the primary health care and its context, where access to laboratory facilities is limited, diagnosis and treatment are based more on a clinical pathology grouping of ulcerative, discharge, lymphadenopathy, and pelvic inflammatory disease (abdominal pain and infection) than on laboratory tests for specific causative organisms. Diagnosis in South Africa is often by exclusion of other similar infections (gonorrhea) as laboratory facilities are often limited or inaccessible. Combination treatment of NGU and gonorrhea is usually cheaper than the laboratory costs.

Table 19 shows the results of research on STDs at a South African university for the years 1989 to 1991 (Nicholas 1994a).

Table 19

New Cases of Sexually Transmitted Diseases (First Infection by Year)

Disease	1989	1990	1991
Syphilis	47	46	31
Gonorrhea	337	325	312
NGU	67	79	107
Other	202	239	479
Total cases	653	687	929

Total student population: 13,000

Black secondary and post high-school students are at high risk of acquiring STDs because they are mostly single and the highest incidence of infection occurs in people between the ages of 15 and 24. Studies have shown, however, that the STD-infection rate decreases as education increases. Still, STD-infection rates for nonspecific urethritis, trichomoniasis, and herpes may be more common in college-educated people (Nicholas 1994a, 35).

A sample of general students surveyed reported a prevalence rate of STD of 18 percent. Studies at another South African university revealed an STD-prevalence rate of 19.9 percent to 23.8 percent for the years 1991 and 1992. For both years, the prevalence of STD was higher than the 13 percent reported by the nearby general local hospital.

In another study of 1,902 black first-year students at a South African university, 17 percent believed that only promiscuous people contract STDs; 11 percent did not believe that people are ethically bound to warn potential sexual partners if they have a sexually transmitted disease, 82 percent of students would not have a relationship with someone who had an STD, and 35 percent of students indicated that if they found out someone close to them had an STD, it would negatively affect their opinion of him or her (Nicholas 1994a).

11. HIV/AIDS

The total South African AIDS budget decreased from $6,076,337 in 1992/1993 to $6,045,556 in 1993/1994, a real decrease of 11 percent. According to the World Health Organization (WHO), South Africa should be spending $40 million a year on AIDS (Preston-Whyte 1995; Schoepf 1995).

Between April and September 1993, 488 cases of AIDS were reported in South Africa. Of these reported cases, 81 percent were African heterosexual men and women and 7 percent were infants. In nearly all the new cases of

AIDS, the virus had been transmitted by heterosexual intercourse, in comparison with the period 1982-1986, when 88 percent of cases of the virus had been transmitted by homosexual intercourse. The Department of National Health and Population Development has reported that 550 people in South Africa were being infected with HIV daily in 1993. About 7,000 people were expected to develop AIDS in 1993. In 1995, the rate of HIV infection was expected to rise to 2.8 percent for men and 4 percent for women (Cooper et al. 1994). Table 20 provides an overall picture of HIV infection and AIDS in South Africa.

Analyzing results of an anonymous structured questionnaire designed to obtain baseline data on knowledge and attitudes of first-year black university students about AIDS and their attitudes towards homosexuals in 1990, 1991, and 1992 (ns = 1,902, 2,113, and 1,558), it is obvious that the

Table 20

AIDS Cases According to Method of Transmission, Race, and Sex: 1982-1993 (Cooper et al., 1994)

	Homo- & Bisexual	Hetero-sexual	Hemo-philiac	Other Blood Transfusion	IV Drug Users	Pediatric	Total
African							
Male	3	313	3	4	1	99	423
Female	0	336	0	0	0	82	418
Unknown	0	6	0	0	0	4	10
Colored							
Male	21	13	1	1	0	0	36
Female	0	12	0	1	0	0	13
Indian							
Male	4	1	0	0	0	0	5
Female	0	0	0	0	0	0	0
White							
Male	61	14	13	12	1	0	401
Female	0	4	0	4	0	0	8
Unknown	0	1	0	1	0	0	2
Total							
Male	389	341	17	17	2	99	865
Female	0	352	0	5	0	82	439
Unknown	0	7	0	1	0	4	12
Grand Total	389	700	17	23	2	185	1,316

students' knowledge of AIDS was inadequate, and misconceptions about AIDS transmission abounded. Prejudiced and exclusionary beliefs about people with AIDS were also common. Little difference was evident on any of the scales over the three-year period (Nicholas et al. 1994).

An AIDS-knowledge survey of 2,209 black university students in 1994 revealed striking misinformation about the risk of contracting AIDS by giving blood (41.5 percent said yes, 10.5 percent were unsure), contracting AIDS from a toilet seat (6 percent said yes, 8.1 percent were unsure), by masturbating oneself (2.9 percent said yes, 26.2 percent were unsure), and a high risk through blood transfusion (57.4 percent said yes, 22.5 percent were unsure (Table 21).

In 1994, the newly appointed national AIDS director stated that previous AIDS-awareness programs only served to heighten fear and increase the stigma attached to AIDS, resulting in infected people's being reluctant to disclose their status. She promised to rebuild the AIDS program (St. Leger 1994). (See also Section 11, HIV/AIDS in Part 2 of this chapter.)

12. Sexual Dysfunctions, Counseling, and Therapies

As mentioned several times earlier, particularly in Section 1, the sexual denial and repression maintained by the South African government and its censorship policies have severely limited the development of the facilities and properly trained personnel necessary if the average citizen is to have access to the diagnosis of sexual problems and dysfunctions, sexual counseling, and therapy. Broad-ranging government censorship of all books on sexuality, coupled with bans on vibrators and other sexual objects, the lack of sexual-education programs, and the absence of public discussion of sexuality issues severely affects the provision of sexuality counseling and therapy.

Very little government support and public funds are available for research and education on sexuality issues. Without studies of sexuality among the indigenous populations of South Africa, sexual counseling and therapy is, of necessity, exercised by health professionals trained abroad using EuroAmerican models. Sexual counseling and therapy is available only to those who can pay private practitioners, or have access to the limited counseling available while they are attending the universities, colleges, technical colleges, and schools that currently fulfill only a peripheral role in primary prevention of the development of sexuality-related problems through research and consultancy services. Primary prevention services in the area of sexuality are meager, and campus sex counselors have to assume that hardly any students would be "unaffected" by sexuality-related problems. Only the degree to which students are affected by these problems will differ (Nicholas 1994a, 116-117).

Table 21

Responses to Knowledge of AIDS Scale Items

All items commence with "Do most experts say . . ."	Yes		No		Unsure	
	%	(n)	%	(n)	%	(n)
1. . . . there's a high chance of getting AIDS by kissing someone on the mouth who has AIDS?	7.1	156	84.3	1,851	8.6	189
2. . . . AIDS can be spread by sharing a needle with a drug user who has AIDS?	88.9	1,947	7.0	132	5.1	112
3. . . . you can get AIDS by giving blood?	41.5	907	48.0	1,049	10.5	229
4. . . . there's a high chance that AIDS can be spread by sharing a glass of water with someone who has AIDS?	3.6	78	89.9	1,969	6.5	143
5. . . . there's a high chance you can get AIDS from a toilet seat?	6.0	132	85.8	1,879	8.1	178
6. . . . AIDS can be spread is a man has sex with a woman who has AIDS?	97.6	2,137	1.4	31	1.0	21
7. . . . AIDS can be spread if a man has sex with another man who has AIDS?	84.6	1,855	3.0	65	12.4	273
8. . . . a pregnant woman with AIDS can give AIDS to her unborn baby?	96.4	2,116	1.7	37	1.9	41
9. . . . you can get AIDS by shaking hands with someone who has AIDS?	1.4	30	96.9	2,124	1.8	39
10. . . . a woman can get AIDS by having sex with a man who has AIDS?	96.6	2,116	2.8	62	0.6	13
11. . . . you can get AIDS when you masturbate yourself?	2.9	64	70.8	1,546	26.2	573
12. . . . using a condom (rubber) can lower your chance of getting AIDS?	92.4	2,020	3.7	80	4.0	87
13. . . . there's a high chance of getting AIDS if you get a blood transfusion?	57.4	1,255	20.1	440	22.5	491
14. . . . prostitutes have a higher chance of getting AIDS?	89.7	1,958	3.1	68	7.2	158
15. . . . eating healthy foods can keep you from getting AIDS?	7.2	158	77.0	1,684	15.8	345
16. . . . having sex with more than one partner can raise your chance of getting AIDS?	96.2	2,104	2.3	50	1.5	32

continued

Table 21 continued

All items commence with "Do most experts say . . ."	Yes		No		Unsure	
	%	(n)	%	(n)	%	(n)
17. . . . you can always tell if someone has AIDS by looking at them?	3.5	76	84.1	1,837	12.4	272
18. . . . people with AIDS will die from it?	86.8	1,898	7.9	173	5.3	115
19. . . . there is a cure for AIDS?	5.3	115	86.6	1,805	12.1	265
20. . . . you can have the AIDS virus without being sick from AIDS?	54.4	1,188	18.1	395	27.5	601
21. . . . you can have the AIDS virus and spread it without being sick from AIDS?	52.2	1,138	20.0	437	27.8	607
22. . . . if a man or woman has sex with someone who shoots up drugs, they raise their chance of getting AIDS?	55.9	1,218	12.9	282	31.2	679

Sample: 889 women; 1,318 men; Mean age: 20.6 years (sd = 4.2)

Mean Total Knowledge of AIDS Scale Score: 17.1 (sd = 3.3) N = 2,209

13. Research and Advanced Education

As mentioned in Section 1 and elsewhere, very little published research on the sexuality of South Africans is available, and hardly any sexuality research on black South Africans has been done. The sexual behavior of blacks has been misrepresented to such a degree that an objective discussion is very difficult. The paucity of sociological and psychological studies is striking, with even the landmark studies of Kinsey and Masters and Johnson paying scant attention to the sexuality of black Americans. An important, but still limited, remedy to this lack has been undertaken by the authors of this chapter at the University of the Western Cape and other black institutions in South Africa.

Our comments in Section 1 clearly indicate that the censorship policies and sexual repression of the South African government have severely limited sexuality research and advanced education in the country.

References and Suggested Readings

Abdool Karim, S. S., Q. Abdool Karim, E. Preston-Whyte, & N. Sakar. 1992. "Reasons for Lack of Condom Use Among High School Students." *South African Medical Journal*, 82:107-10.

Abler, R. M. & W. E. Sedlacek. 1989. "Freshman Sexual Attitudes and Behaviors Over a 15-Year Period." *Journal of College Student Development*, 30:201-9.

Anon. 1995. "Teens Have Their Feet on the Ground." *Sunday Times*, pp. 14, 16.

Bowers, D. W. & V. A. Christophersen. 1977. "University Student Cohabitation: A Regional Comparison of Selected Attitudes and Behaviour." *Journal of Marriage and the Family*, 39:447-52.

Burman, S. 1992. "The Category of the Illegitimate in South Africa." In: S. Burman and E. Preston-Whyte, eds. *Questionable Issue: Illegitimacy in South Africa*, pp. 21-35. Cape Town: Oxford University Press.

Burman, S., and E. Preston-Whyte, eds. 1992. *Questionable Issue: Illegitimacy in South Africa.* Cape Town: Oxford University Press.

Catlin, N., J. F., Keller, & J. W. Croake. 1976. "Sexual History and Behavior of Unmarried Cohabiting College Couples." *College Student Journal*, 10:253-59.

Chapel, D. 1995 (January 8). "Raunchy Mag for Swingers." *Sunday Times*, p. 12.

Chothia, F. 1993 (March 5). "Storm Over School Sex Education." *Weekly Main*, p. 5.

Cilliers, C. D. 1989. "The Role of the School in the Republic of South Africa in the Prevention of AIDS—A Situation Analysis." *South African Journal of Education*, 1:1-6.

Cooper, C., R. Hamilton, H. Mashabela, S. Mackay, E. Sidiropoulos, C. Gordon-Brown, S. Murphy, & J. Frielinghaus. 1994. *Race Relations Survey 1993/1994.* Johannesburg: South African Institute of Race Relations.

Darling, C. A., & J. K. Davidson Sr. 1986. "Coitally Active University Students: Sexual Behaviours, Concerns and Challenges." *Adolescence*, 21:403-19.

Darling, C. A., J. K. Davidson, & L. C. Passarello. 1992. "The Mystique of First Intercourse Among College Youth: The Role of Partners. Contraceptive Practices and Psychological Reactions." *Journal of Youth and Adolescence*, 21:97-117.

Daugherty, L. R., & J. M. Burger. 1984. "The Influence of Parents, Church, and Peers on the Sexual Attitudes and Behaviours of College Students." *Archives of Sexual Behaviour*, 13:351-58.

Gebhard, P. H. 1977. "The Acquisition of Basic Sex Information." *The Journal of Sex Research*, 13:13-21.

Gevisser, M. 1993 (April 8). "Sex in the Schoolroom—But It's Safer." *Weekly Mail Education Supplement*, p. 1.

Gevisser, M., & E. Cameron, eds. 1994. *Defiant Desire.* Johannesburg: Raven Press.

Hall, C. H. 1987. "Sexual Politics and Resistance to Law Reform: A Critique of the South African Law Commission Report on Women and Sexual Offenders in South Africa." Unpublished Master's thesis, University of Cape Town, Cape Town, South Africa.

Havenga, A. M. 1985. *Women and Sex Offenders in South Africa.* Pretoria: Government Printers.

Houston, L. N. 1981. "Romanticism and Eroticism Among Black and White College Students." *Adolescence*, 17:263-72.

Isaacs, G., & B. McKendrick. 1992. *Male Homosexuality in South Africa—Identity Formation, Culture, and Crisis.* Cape Town: Oxford University Press Southern Africa.

Kaats, G. R., & K. E. Davis. 1970. "The Dynamics of Sexual Behaviour of College Students." *Journal of Marriage and the Family*, 32:390-99.

Kagan, J. 1989. *An Investigation into the Sources of Sexual Information Among Pupils in Standard Nine and Ten in a Co-educational High School in Cape Town.* Unpublished Master's thesis, University of Cape Town, Cape Town.

Keeling, R. P. 1991. "Student Health in the 1990's." *Chronicle of Higher Education*, 37:B1 and B2.

Knox, D., & K. Wilson. 1981. "Dating Behaviours of University Students." *Family Relations*, 30:255-58.

Loubser, W. 1994 (May 19). "Seks en die Standerd Sesse." (Sex and the Standard Sixes). *Huisgenoot*, pp. 18-20.

Masters, W. H., & V. E. Johnson. 1986. *Human Sexual Response.* Toronto: Bantam.

Mosher, D. L. 1979. "Sex Guilt and Sex Myths in College Men and Women." *Journal of Sex Research,* 15:224-34.

Naidoo, C. 1994 (December 11). "Keeping It All in the Family." *Sunday Times,* p. 15.

Nicholas, L. J. 1990. "A Profile of 1,886 UWC First Year Students: Career Interests, Guidance Experiences, Knowledge and Attitudes Toward AIDS and Sexuality and Religiosity. An unpublished report: Centre for Student Counseling, University of the Western Cape.

Nicholas, L. J. 1991. "A Profile of 2,113 UWC First Year Students: Career Interests, Guidance Experiences, Knowledge and Attitudes Toward AIDS and Sexuality and Religiosity." An unpublished report: Centre for Student Counseling, University of the Western Cape.

Nicholas, L. J. 1992. "A Profile of 1,558 UWC First Year Students: Career Interests, Guidance Experiences, Knowledge and Attitudes Toward AIDS and Sexuality and Religiosity." An unpublished report: Centre for Student Counseling, University of the Western Cape.

Nicholas, L. J. 1993a. "Intrafamilial Communication about Contraception: A Survey of Black South African Freshmen." *International Journal for the Advancement of Counseling,* 16:291-300.

Nicholas, L. J. 1993b. "A Profile of 1,500 UWC First Year Students: Career Interest, Guidance Experiences, Knowledge and Attitudes towards AIDS and Sexuality and Religiosity." An unpublished report: Centre of Student Counseling, University of the Western Cape.

Nicholas, L. J. 1994a. *Sex Counseling in Educational Settings.* Braamfontein: Skotaville Publishers.

Nicholas, L. J. 1994b. "A Profile of 2,209 UWC First Year Students: Career Interests, Guidance Experiences, Knowledge and Attitudes towards AIDS and Sexuality and Religiosity." An unpublished report: Centre for Student Counseling, University of the Western Cape.

Nicholas, L. J., & K. Durrheim. 1994. "Religiosity, AIDS and Sexuality Knowledge, Attitudes, Beliefs and Practices of Black South African First-Year University Students." An unpublished report: Centre for Student Counseling, University of the Western Cape.

Nicholas, L. J. & Orr, N. (1994). "Reliability of Knowledge of AIDS Scales in a Sample of Black First-Year University Students." An unpublished report: Centre for Student Counseling, University of the Western Cape.

Nicholas, L., C. Tredoux, & P. Daniels. 1994. "AIDS Knowledge and Attitudes Towards Homosexuals of Black University Students: 1990-1992." *Psychological Reports,* 75:819-823.

Preston-Whyte, E. M. 1995. "Half-Way There: Anthropology and Intervention-Oriented AIDS Research in KwaZulu/Natal, South Africa." In: Han ten Brummelhuis and Gilbert Herdt, ed. *Culture and Sexual Risk: Anthropological Perspectives on AIDS.* Amsterdam: Gordon and Breach Science Publishers.

Preston-Whyte, E., & M. Zondi. 1992. "African Teenage Pregnancy: Whose Problem?" In S. Burman and E. Preston-Whyte, eds. *Questionable Issue: Illegitimacy in South Africa,* pp. 226-246. Cape Town: Oxford University Press.

Robinson, I. E., & D. Jedlicka. 1982. "Change in Sexual Attitudes and Behaviour of College Students from 1965 to 1980: A Research Note." *Journal of Marriage and the Family,* 44:237-41.

Rohrburg, J., & R. Jessor. 1975. "Religiosity in Youth: A Personal and Social Control Against Deviant Behaviour." *Journal of Personality,* 43:136-55.

St. Leger, C. 1994 (December 11). "New Boss to Revamp AIDS Campaigm." *Sunday Times,* p. 3.

Sapire, K. E. 1988. "Education in Sexuality." *Nursing R.S.A.,* 3:19, 21, & 41.

Schoepf, Brooke Grundfest. 1995. "Culture, Sex Research and AIDS Prevention in Africa." In: Han ten Brummelhuis and Gilbert Herdt, ed. *Culture and Sexual Risk: Anthropological Perspectives on AIDS.* Amsterdam: Gordon and Breach Science Publishers.

Sidley, P. 1991 (December 20). "Doing Detective Work on Condoms." *Weekly Mail,* p. 19.

Sorenson, R. C. 1973. *Adolescent Sexuality in Contemporary America.* New York: World Publishing.

Stander, K. 1988 (May 18). "City's Illegitimate Birth Rate 45 Percent—MOH Urges State Action." *The Argus,* p. 1.

Swayer, C. 1994 (December 7). "Censorship Laws to Be Relaxed." *The Argus,* p. 1.

Thornton, A. 1990. "The Courtship Process and Adolescent Sexuality." *Journal of Family Issues,* 11:239-73.

Underhill, G. 1995 (January 14). "All Quiet on the Water Front as Pros Lie Low." *Weekend Argus,* p. 7.

Van Rooyen, J. C. W. 1987. *Censorship in South Africa.* Cape Town: Juta.

PART 2: ANOTHER PERSPECTIVE

MERVYN BERNARD HURWITZ, M.D.

1. Basic Sexological Premises

A/B. Gender Roles and General Concepts of Sexuality and Love

The different ethnic groups have diverse concepts of gender role. In the black traditional community, the male plays a dominant role. He is allowed more than one wife. When his wife is no longer able to bear children, he is allowed to find a younger, fertile wife to bear more children. This lifestyle is more prevalent in the rural areas. In the urban areas, the blacks are more Westernized and polygamy is less prevalent, with the male having a monogamous relationship with only one wife (Burman and Preston-Whyte 1992).

Traditionally, the black woman does not demand sex from her partner, nor does she make advances towards him. There is little foreplay, and once the male has been satisfied, there is little afterplay. However, recently the urbanized black woman is becoming more demanding in her sexual relationship and the male is losing his secure dominant role. The women's liberation movement is gradually reaching the black urban woman. However, the man is still the traditional leader and plays a dominant role in decision making in the family, expecting his wife to be totally subservient (Monnig 1983).

Black males commonly become migrant laborers in the mines or in the city, leaving their wives in the rural areas to tend the farms and raise the children. The husband is usually the sole monetary supporter of the family.

He returns to his rural home if there is illness or bereavement in the family, usually visiting only once or twice a year. He seldom allows his wife or family to visit him in the city.

2. Religious and Ethnic Factors Affecting Sexuality

The South African community is made up of separate ethnic groups with different identities and affiliations and cannot be lumped together as one group. The white population is made up of two large groups, namely the Afrikaners (Boers) and the English-speaking people.

Afrikaners adhere to a strictly Calvinistic view. Sex is not taught at schools. Any discussion on sexuality is frowned upon and the topic is largely seen as taboo. In this male-dominated society, the woman has been assigned a secondary role. However, with the influence of the media and the gradual lifting of the censorship of sexually explicit information, the men are threatened by the changing role of women who are becoming more sexually assertive. In a 1987 survey comparing English-speaking and Afrikaans-speaking white South Africans, Louise Olivier found that 72.8 percent of Afrikaans-speaking women and 69.2 percent of English-speaking women could discuss sexual matters with their mothers. Only 4.4 percent of women could discuss sexual matters with their fathers.

In the black communities, 6 million out of nearly 18 million people are affiliated to the Church of Zion or other independent Protestant churches. Many blacks still subscribe to ancestor worship and tribal ritual, despite the strong influence of the missionaries who have tried to inculcate a Christian monotheism and ethic.

Moslem and Hindu influences are found among the Asian minorities.

3. Sexual Knowledge and Education

A. Government Policies and Programs

In the white population, sex education has been viewed as the parents' responsibility, with few health professionals becoming involved other than on a consultative basis.[1] Sometimes, sexual education is provided by the family doctor, who is approached when a young person becomes sexually active and wants counseling and instruction about the use of suitable contraception.

There is no formal sex education in either the white or black schools. Representation has been made to the Minister of Education in an effort to introduce sex education into the schools, but this has met with strong resistance. The Dutch Reformed Calvinistic approach indoctrinated by the church has been opposed to sex education in schools, and all discussion of sexuality is frowned upon. Private (nongovernment-controlled) schools do have sex-education classes. Lectures are given to pupils in the 11- to 17-year-old age group, usually by social workers and counselors at the Family Life Center, as well as by the author and other sex educators.

B. Informal Sources of Sexual Knowledge

In 1992, television programs on sexuality were initiated, directed primarily at the youth. Panel discussions sponsored by the media have been held to look at sex education and to expose various topics of sexual interest.

However, there is very strict censorship in South Africa, and many of the sex books that are freely available overseas are banned in South Africa. There is thus a very limited number of books on sex education or explicit books on sex. Talk shows are becoming frequent on television, and phone-in shows are available on radio. There is, however, a move afoot to ban all these sources of sexual information.

The ritual passage for black girls in the traditional tribal situation is very secretive. In the Pedi tribe, Monnig reports that these rituals are conducted by the girl's mother or grandmother. The girl is told about menstruation and informed that she must avoid sex during this time. She receives detailed instruction on the work and duties of a woman, particularly in her relationship with a man, and is instructed on sexual matters. The young Pedi girls assist one another in stretching their own labia minora, which is said to ensure greater sexual gratification for men.

4. Autoerotic Behaviors and Patterns

There is no literature or data pertaining to autoerotic behavior and patterns in South African children, adolescents, or adults. "Blue movies" and auto-erotic literature are banned. Pornographic programs and books are heavily censored. Studies of autoeroticism are discouraged by the church and schools. People returning from overseas with erotic literature have the publications confiscated at the airport and are liable to be punished.

In the English-speaking universities, some lectures and courses on sexuality have been introduced. Lectures in sexuality for medical students were introduced in the mid-1980s. Workshops on sexuality are given to doctors, nurses, social workers, and allied professionals to encourage them to feel more at ease with sexuality and to be able to discuss sexual problems with their patients.

5. Interpersonal Heterosexual Behaviors

A. Children

Forty percent of South Africa's population are under 15 years of age. Children of preprimary school age often attend nursery schools or crèches where the sexes are mixed. They share common toilet facilities, are taught

basic gender differences, and stereotypic gender-role models are reinforced. Both teachers and parents report that children play doctor-patient
games and tend to explore one another. This is often a source of great
anxiety to both parents and teachers.

In the black communities, there is overcrowding and a lack of privacy.
The children often have to sleep in the same room as their parents, and
many share a bed with parents or siblings. This early exposure to parental
sexual activity sometimes causes anxiety and confusion that can affect their
own sexual identity.

B. Adolescents

Puberty Rituals

Pubertal rituals are carried out in many black tribes. Male circumcision in
the black communities is common in both urban and rural areas and is
seen as a prerequisite for manhood. The age of circumcision varies in
different tribal groups from 9 to 22 years.[2] In the Xhosa tribe, for example,
males are circumcised between the age of 18 and 22 years, in a ritual
ceremony celebrated twice a year.[3] In most tribes, there is no anesthetic
given for pain; the boy is simply given only a piece of wood to bite on. The
youth is indoctrinated to believe that he has to endure pain to prove that
he is fit to be called a "man."

Due to poor techniques and inexperienced or poorly trained traditional
healers or "sangomas," the complications of circumcision are sometimes
serious, even functionally irreparable. Gangrene is not an infrequent complication following ritual circumcision.[4]

Courley and Kisner described forty-five cases of youths who required
hospitalization following ritual circumcision.[3] All forty-five cases were septic
on admission. In 5 percent of cases, the entire penis was necrotic; the
mortality rate was 9 percent. Septicemia and dehydration are frequent
causes of such mortality.

The chief cause of penile injury is a dressing that is too tight and applied
for too long. The hemorrhage is controlled by applying leaves around the
penile shaft and then binding the organ with a strip of sheepskin leather.
A concerned effort is being made to educate the traditional healers in the
use of commercial medicines and dressings rather than traditional leaves
and sheepskin.[3]

Female circumcision is not carried out in South Africa, although some
tribes, such as the Pedi, encourage the females at puberty to stretch the
labia minora.

Premarital Sexual Activities and Relationships

Focusing on adolescent black children and teenagers, Preston-Whyte and
Zondi found that both boys and girls admitted experiencing sex before
their 12th or 13th year.[5] Some had experienced penetration before they

reached physical maturity. By age 13, most had been sexually active, if not regularly, then at least on a number of occasions. Full penetration was the rule.

In a predominantly white South African survey, Olivier found that 30 percent of his respondents under age 17, twenty-four of eighty, were still virgins. In the colored community, Burman and Preston-Whyte (1992) found that 30.5 percent of all births occurred in teenagers, with 5 percent below the age of 16. Eighty-one percent of the teenage group had out-of-wedlock children.

There are no figures available on the number of teenagers who are involved in ongoing relationships while indulging in sexual activities. Peer pressure in the urban black community encourages sexual encounters that are often monitored by older teenagers.

The double standard is evident in the black communities. When a man's unmarried daughter becomes pregnant, he is enraged. Yet, when a son makes a girl pregnant, the father may be secretly and even overtly pleased. Among his peers, a boy who has many girlfriends, and who is known to have fathered a child or a number of children, is admired. His father often shares this attitude. The pressure is therefore towards, rather than away from, teenage sexual involvement. The relationship between a boy and girl who are "going together" is normally one that involves full intercourse (Burman and Preston-Whyte 1992).

C. Adults

Premarital Courtship, Dating, and Relationships

The formal ritual of dating and courtship familiar to Western civilization is more prevalent in the white South African community, which tends to be more affluent and able to afford movies, discos, and weekends away on vacation. There are several singles clubs, discos, and bars catering to adolescents and young adults looking for dates or a "one night stand." With the incidence of sexually transmitted diseases, the educated and affluent groups are more inclined to be selective and less promiscuous in their relationships than their less-educated brothers and sisters from a lower socioeconomic class.

Marriage and the Family

Monogamy is more commonly accepted amongst the white group than the black group. Traditional black men who have not accepted the doctrine of Christianity are allowed to have more than one wife. In the rural setting, a man's wealth is assessed by the number of children and cattle he owns, and thus he may take a second wife. Cohabitation is common in the white society in nonreligious couples, but is frowned on by the church, particularly the strong Calvinistic elements of the Dutch Reformed

Church. In the black traditional rural setting, marriage is not primarily concerned with legalizing sexual relations between two individuals, but rather with establishing paternity and giving the husband the right to sexual relations with his wife. In this value system, extramarital intercourse is possible and even socially accepted and provided for culturally (Monnig 1983).

Laws prohibiting interracial sex and marriage were repealed in 1985.

Incidence of Oral and Anal Sex

There are no figures available for the incidence of anal sex, fellatio, or cunnilingus. In my experience, anal intercourse is engaged in by a very small proportion of heterosexual couples. On the other hand, more than half the couples attending the Sexual Dysfunction Clinic at the Johannesburg Hospital reported engaging in cunnilingus and fellatio. Most men reported being happy to indulge in cunnilingus. Some women reported feeling uncomfortable with fellatio. In Olivier's 1987 survey, a surprising finding was that few women reported enjoying oral sex, only 9.2 percent in the 17- to 25-year age group and 5.9 percent in the over-age-25 cohort. From my personal experience in my private gynecological practice, I feel that these figures are low and that the overall figure is well over 30 percent.

6. Homoerotic, Homosexual, and Ambisexual Behaviors

In Olivier's survey of 2,842 women, 89.7 percent were heterosexual, 0.3 percent were lesbian, and 2.5 percent were bisexual. Most of the women in this survey, 2,711 of 2,842, were white females. There is no legal status for lesbian or homosexual couples in the South African society. In 1992, homosexuality was more acceptable and less frowned upon than previously. Gay advice bureaus are available, but there is no legislation to protect the rights of homosexuals.

The incidence of homosexuality in the black population is low. This is borne out by the low incidence of HIV-positive homosexual black males (0.6 percent), compared to 31 percent of homosexual or bisexual white males.[6,7]

7. Gender Conflicted Persons

Transvestites, transgenderists, and transsexuals have no legal standing. There are very few centers available in South Africa for the treatment of these patients, and surgical operations are very rarely performed. At least two years of psychiatric treatment and evaluation are needed before any operative procedure is considered.

8. Significant Unconventional Sexual Behaviors

A. Coercive Sex

Sexual Abuse

The Department of Health and Welfare keeps a social welfare register on all children who are abused. Legislation requires doctors, nurses, social workers, police officers, and members of the public to report cases of abuse. It would appear that sexual abuse is becoming more prevalent in all sectors of the community. This correlates with the escalating violence encountered throughout South Africa. Conviction for sexual abuse and rape carries a penalty of a lengthy prison sentence. In their study of teenage mothers, Burman and Preston-Whyte found that pregnancies occurred at a younger age among abused children than in the control group.

Incest

Incest is taboo in all groups in South Africa (Zulu report by Burman and Preston-Whyte; Pedi report by Monnig). If a pregnancy results from incest, a legal abortion may be performed.[8] There are no available statistics for the incidence of pedophilia, but it is a punishable offense.

Sexual Harassment

With the increase of feminism, more cases of sexual harassment are being reported in the workplace. South African men are known to be chauvinistic and to "put down" women both verbally and in terms of job opportunity. There is only recourse to the law in terms of discrimination and not in terms of harassment.

Rape

Rape cases are reported daily. However, in cases of family rape, they often are unreported. There is still a stigma attached to the rape victim and, despite attempts at educating the public, the rape victim is still often seen as inviting the sexual advances of the male. In black urban areas, two to three rapes are reported daily and many more are unreported. These rape cases are often committed by strangers or casual acquaintances.

B. Prostitution

Prostitution is rife, particularly in the larger cities. Escort agencies provide a front for prostitution, which is illegal in South Africa. No figures are available of the number of practicing prostitutes or their activities. With the present high rate of unemployment, estimated at over 25 percent in the black community, prostitution is on the increase. As prostitution is illegal, there are no facilities for regular medical examinations of prostitutes to control STDs or other infections.

C. Pornography and Erotica

As mentioned above in Sections 3B and 4, the Calvinist tradition has been very effective in maintaining severe restrictions on all pornographic and erotic material.

9. Contraception, Abortion, and Population Planning

A. Contraception and Teenage Unmarried Pregnancies

Family-planning clinics are available in many areas and provide a free service. There is a reluctance among the black males to allow their partners to use contraception. Among the more-educated population, there is an attempt to limit the size of the family and to use some form of contraception.

Adolescent pregnancies are common in the black communities. Contraception is seldom used. The reasons given for failure to use contraception include cost, not admitting sexual activity, unplanned coitus, a belief that they are too young to become pregnant, fear of the effect of contraceptive methods, and subconsciously wanting to become pregnant.

The earlier the age of menarche, the earlier the first coitus occurs.[8] Van Coeverden found that when the menarche occurred before the age of 12, 56 percent of teenagers attending a family-planning clinic experienced coitus by the age of 15.[9] If menarche occurred after the age of 13, then 42 percent were sexually active by the age of 17.

There are no statistics available as to whether the sexually active teenagers have multiple partners or are involved in steady exclusive relationships. Personal observation suggests that promiscuity is common. Peer pressure often forces teenagers to have sexual contact in order to avoid being ostracized by their peer group. Unstable home and socioeconomic factors, as well as poor school attendance, boredom, drugs, and alcohol abuse, are some factors related to the early onset of coitus.

Premarital sexual relations vary considerably between the various racial groups in South Africa. Children raised in crowded ghetto conditions often lack parental control and have fewer recreational facilities to occupy their spare time and energy. Above all, for many black girls, there is very little to look forward to except childbirth.[5]

B. Abortion

Although abortion was illegal in South Africa until late 1996, the Abortion and Sterilization Act of 1975 allowed for legal abortions under four well-defined circumstances:[8]

1. Where the continuation of a pregnancy poses a serious threat to the mother's physical and/or mental health;
2. Where a risk exists that the child will be seriously handicapped, physically or mentally;
3. In cases of rape or incest;
4. In cases of unlawful carnal intercourse with a woman who is permanently mentally handicapped.

A 1994 review covering a six-year period quotes the number of legal abortions in South Africa as being about 1,000 per annum and the registered number of instances where products of conception were found at surgery as being about 35,000 per annum.[10] The number of "back street abortions" performed annually is estimated at between 10,000 and 40,000. Many of the more-affluent patients travel overseas to countries where abortions are legal to have their pregnancies terminated. (See discussion of the new legislation adopted in November 1996, in Section 9C of Part 1.)

10. Sexually Transmitted Diseases

Sexually transmitted diseases constitute a major public health problem in South Africa. It has been estimated that over one million patients seek treatment for sexually transmitted diseases each year at community clinics, and that more are seen at hospital outpatient departments and primary health care clinics. STDs in South Africa conform largely to Third World patterns. Pelvic inflammatory disease, mainly due to STDs, is the commonest reason for acute emergency admission to the gynecological wards and is the most common disease syndrome seen in gynecological outpatient departments.[11]

A survey in Alexandra township, a poor urban black township in Johannesburg, estimates that 20 percent of the population over the age of 15 is treated at least once a year for an STD.[6] A second study of patients seen at a university clinic in Alexandra township revealed that 10 percent of all patients seen were referred with an STD, 53 percent being men and 47 percent women.[7] Fifty-four percent of the patients were between the ages of 20 and 29. Most men presented with urethritis or an ulcer, while the women presented with pelvic inflammatory disease or a discharge.

Gonorrhea remains the most common cause of acute urethritis. Twenty percent of all cases also harbor chlamydia trachomatis, the commonest cause of non-gonococcal urethritis (NGU).[11] The commonest organisms found in females with pelvic inflammatory disease are neisseria gonorrhoeae in 65 percent of cases, mycoplasma hominis in 53 percent of cases, and chlamydia trachomatis in 5 percent of cases.

Mixed infections are common and anaerobic superinfections occur in 82 percent of cases.[11] Men are more likely to be repeat attendants for STD, and are more likely to report multiple sex partners. Professor Ron Ballard states that there are upwards of three million new cases of STDs each year in our population of 26 million.[12]

There are poor resources available for the treatment of STDs. Attempts are being made for a wide-ranging communication campaign to attempt to educate the population to reduce the number of sexual partners.

A major factor affecting the availability of contraception, abortion, and the diagnosis and treatment of STDs and HIV/AIDS is the state of the country's national health care system. In the January 1995 annual health care and education report, the South African bishops conference warned that the country's national health care system is close to collapse. The system, the report stated, is in a chaotic state because of poor coordination of services, inadequate resources, and injustice. Only 19 percent of South Africa's 41 million people have medical coverage through private systems. Public hospitals that offer inexpensive care to uninsured patients are crowded and understaffed. Health Minister Nkosazana Zuma initiated a study of a national health insurance plan that would provide universal coverage. This study includes examination of successful models from Kenya and Namibia that stress preventing illness by teaching healthy living habits through community health organizations.

11. HIV/AIDS

In all of Africa, HIV infection is spread mainly through heterosexual intercourse.[13] Concomitant STDs, particularly genital ulcers, are implicated as cofactors in the transmission of the HIV virus.[14] The World Health Organization estimates that there are 5 million HIV-infected individuals in Africa. This epidemic has only recently reached South Africa, but there is every indication that the prevalence of HIV may reach alarming proportions in the future, and no field of medicine will remain unscathed.[15] It is estimated by the Department of National Health that there are currently 300,000 HIV-positive people in South Africa and 400 new cases per day.[16] The latest available statistics of AIDS in South Africa as of September 1992, total 27,389 confirmed cases.[17] However, AIDS is not a reportable disease in South Africa, and thus many cases are not recorded. (See Tables 22 and 23.)

A survey carried out at the Baragwanath Hospital, in Soweto, a black town adjoining Johannesburg, has revealed that between July 1988 and December 1990, 426 HIV-positive individuals were identified.[15] Eighty-five percent of these cases were traced to heterosexual transmission, 0.6 percent to homosexual contact, and 12.6 percent to perinatal maternal infection. In this study, a total of 111 HIV-positive women were diagnosed in the maternity units of Baragwanath Hospital, and 51 symptomatic children with perinatally acquired HIV infection were admitted to the pediatric wards.[18]

Table 22

AIDS Risk (as of September 1992)

AIDS Risk Category[16]	Percent of Total
Heterosexual	50
Homosexual/bisexual	31
Pediatric	15
Blood transfusion	1.9
Hemophiliacs	1.4
IV drug users	0.1

Table 23

Percent of AIDS Cases[14] (as of September 1992)

	Percentage of Cases by Race	Percentage of Nation's Population
Black	62.4	68.3
White	33.2	17.1
Colored (mixed race)	3.7	11.0
Asian	0.4	3.2

Late 1994 data from the Baragwanath Hospital showed that 8 percent of patients in the prenatal clinic were HIV-positive. At the Johannesburg Hospital, 10 percent of the prenatal clients were HIV-positive; a similar incidence was reported in late 1994 by the Johannesburg City Council for the inner-city population that was HIV-positive. In 1994, the number of HIV-positive South Africans doubled in 12 months.

According to McIntyre, the rate of HIV-positive pregnant women in 1992 was 4/100, with the rate doubling every nine to twelve months.[19] As a result of these alarming statistics, an HIV clinic has been started in the maternity unit of Baragwanath Hospital. The most-recent figures show that at least two HIV-positive women give birth daily at the hospital; 200 HIV-positive women were identified in the first eight months of 1992.

The major brunt of the HIV epidemic in South Africa is expected to be borne by black heterosexual adults and by infants.[20] A total of 181 HIV-positive black adults were admitted to the medical wards of Baragwanath Hospital between August 1987 and December 1990. Equal numbers of both sexes were seen, of which 34 percent have died.

There are no statistics of lesbian HIV-positive women in South Africa. All age groups in both sexes are at risk of acquiring HIV infections.[21] Tuberculosis is the commonest infectious complication of AIDS in South Africa.[22]

In South Africa, the HIV virus is most commonly transmitted by sexual intercourse. Transmission of the virus from mother to child is the second commonest mode of spread in all African countries, including South Africa.[23] Homosexuality is relatively uncommon among black South Africans, but is a common form of transmission of the HIV virus in the white population. Homosexuality, however, does not play a major role in the pandemic spread of the HIV virus in any African country.[24]

In the African context, black promiscuous men are very reluctant to use condoms and complain about the cost and inconvenience of the use of condoms. Since status is equated to fertility, the use of condoms and contraception is frowned upon. Condoms cannot be prescribed in the Health Service, but they can be obtained free of charge from Family Planning Clinics. Doubts have been expressed about the advisability of media advertisements on the use of condoms in South Africa, prompted by pervading Calvinistic reticence (Lachman 1990). AIDS education is available in many black schools but is not permitted in state-controlled schools for predominantly white pupils. In the conservative Calvinistic white community, AIDS is seen as a problem experienced only among homosexuals or the black community.

In a survey of 122 black mothers in the Durban area, it was found that these mothers were at a high risk of acquiring AIDS.[24] Urban black mothers seldom discuss the risk of unprotected sex with their daughters, despite their knowledge of transmission modes and of ways to prevent HIV infection. Fifty percent of these mothers had children by the same consort, whereas 44 percent had more than one partner. Ninety-two percent of these mothers stated that they would like their partners to use condoms, yet all the mothers said that they had not experienced intercourse where their partners had used condoms.

In 1989, the Johannesburg City Health embarked on an AIDS-awareness campaign using messages placed on the outside of thirty city buses.[25] The role of health education is to provide the entire community with a means to prevent HIV infection. A toll-free dial and listening service is available to anyone who has access to a telephone. Callers can choose to hear this information in any of the eight major languages in South Africa.

In recognition of the seriousness of the AIDS problem, the Department of National Health and Population Development recently established an AIDS unit. The unit consists of a multidisciplinary team. There are AIDS clinics in all the major cities of South Africa but these are already insufficient for the needs of the community. Counseling HIV-positive patients embodies the principles of counseling and care for all patients who have an incurable disease. It is different in that no other medical condition carries the stigma, moral censure, and societal consequences that accompany AIDS.[26]

An April 1995 Update: Early results of a Department of Health survey showed that two out of twenty-five South Africans are HIV-positive. In 1995, an estimated 850,000 to one million South Africans were infected, with over 700 new cases every day. The infection rate in Kwazulu Natal is almost three times that of the rest of the country; the number of AIDS cases for the first quarter of 1995 was double that for the same period in 1994. An estimated 15 percent to 19 percent of the people in Natal were infected in April 1995. The least-infected regions of the country were the North West and Northern Cape. The epidemiological director cautioned that the extent of underreporting was not known.

In a July 1996 report at the eleventh international conference on AIDS, South Africa had an estimated 1.8 million cases of HIV infection, second only to India's 3 million cases. In June 1996, Dr. Peter Piot, head of the United Nations Joint Program on HIV-AIDS, reported that 10 percent of the South African population is believed to be infected with HIV. In the province of Kwazulu Natal, the infection rate had reached 16 percent (Preston-Whyte 1995; Schoepf 1995). The rate was even higher in nearby Zambia and Zimbabwae, where 17 percent of the population live with the virus. In South Africa's northern neighbor, Botaswana, 18 percent of the people are infected. No one can explain this rapid rise in HIV infection in southern Africa, especially considering the fact that the infection reached South Africa later than it did other regions of Africa, and the efforts of the Mandela government in making AIDS prevention a national priority.

12. Sexual Dysfunctions, Counseling, and Therapies

A. Concepts of Sexual Dysfunction

Any problem related to sexuality that may negatively affect either the male or the female, both as individuals or in a relationship, is viewed as a sexual dysfunction. In the male, the most common reasons for referral to the Sexual Dysfunction Clinic or to a sex therapist are premature ejaculation and loss of libido. Orgasmic dysfunction in the female and loss of libido are the most common sexual dysfunctions seen at the Sexual Dysfunction Clinic. In the black population, most males are worried about their performance, their ability to sustain an erection for an often unrealistic length of time, or the inability to have intercourse up to four to five times a night.

B. Availability of Diagnosis and Treatment

The root of many of the problems is basic ignorance. Thus, patients are given information about basic sexual anatomy and physiology. At the Sexual Dysfunction Clinic in Johannesburg, patients are preferably seen as couples by the team consisting of a gynecologist, social worker, and nurse. All patients are examined physically, and the female patients are given a complete pelvic exam. The partners are encouraged to participate in these physical examinations.

All males attending the Sexual Dysfunction Clinic at the Johannesburg Hospital are checked by doppler flow for penile blood flow and penile blood pressure. Serum testosterone and prolactin levels are routinely carried out at the clinic on males with any form of sexual dysfunction. A consultant urologist is available for consultation. Some couples or individuals prefer to be counseled privately and are seen by a single therapist in private practice who may be a gynecologist, urologist, psychiatrist, psychologist, social worker, or general practitioner.

Sex therapists in South Africa have been trained locally and often internationally. They attend international workshops and congresses. Sex therapists in South Africa come from many disciplines, all of which have an interest in the field of sexology.

13. Sexual Research and Advanced Education

There is very little research in the field of sexology in South Africa. There are no facilities to carry out major research programs. However, some individuals conduct sporadic research into various aspects of sexual dysfunction.[27,28] There are no available institutes or programs for research.

Medical students at the various medical schools receive lectures on sexual dysfunction as part of their medical curriculum. Students at the University of the Witwatersrand are encouraged to attend the Sexual Dysfunction Clinic at the Johannesburg Hospital. There are sexual dysfunction clinics at the Johannesburg Hospital, Groote Schuur Hospital in Cape Town, and the H. F. Verwoerd Hospital in Pretoria. There are no postgraduate facilities available for the advanced study of human sexuality.

The Sex Society of South Africa is in the process of being formed at press time. *The Medical Sex Journal of South Africa* is published quarterly by the South African Academy of Family Practice and Primary Care. The address of the editorial offices is: P. O. Box 23195, Joubert Park, Johannesburg, South Africa.

The following organization is a source for additional information on sexuality: Planned Parenthood Association of South Africa, Third Floor, Marlborough House, 60 Eloff Street, Johannesburg 2001, South Africa. Phone: 27-11/331-2695.

Conclusion

In the early 1990s, South Africa is faced with a major upheaval, both politically, socially, and economically. The uncertain political, social, and economic future of South Africa, faced with the transition from a white-dominated government to a multiracial or black government, poses many

1132 · International Encyclopedia of Sexuality

challenges for the country. Violence has become a way of life. Sexual abuse is common, as is murder, rape, and anarchy. The future of the medical and paramedical services is in a state of flux. It is not likely that the situation of sexology will improve significantly in the near future, simply because most of the nation's resources and the people's energies will, of necessity, be devoted to more pressing and urgent challenges, including the need to provide primary health care, food, housing, and basic necessities to the underprivileged masses.

References and Suggested Readings

Burman, S., and E. Preston-Whyte, eds. 1992. *A Questionable Issue: Illegitimacy in South Africa.* Cape Town: Oxford University Press.
Lachman, S. J. 1990. *The Challenge of AIDS in the 1990's: South Africa.* Lennon Ltd. South Africa.
Monnig, H. V. 1983. *The Pedi.* Pretoria, South Africa: L. van Schaik.
Olivier, L. 1987. *Sex and the South Africa Woman.* Johannesburg: Lowry Publishers.
Preston-Whyte, E. M. 1995. "Half-Way There: Anthropology and Intervention-Oriented AIDS Research in KwaZulu/Natal, South Africa." In: Han ten Brummelhuis and Gilbert Herdt, ed. *Culture and Sexual Risk: Anthropological Perspectives on AIDS.* Amsterdam: Gordon and Breach Science Publishers.
Schoepf, Brooke Grundfest. 1995. "Culture, Sex Research and AIDS Prevention in Africa." In: Han ten Brummelhuis and Gilbert Herdt, ed. *Culture and Sexual Risk: Anthropological Perspectives on AIDS.* Amsterdam: Gordon and Breach Science Publishers.

Endnotes

1. Van Coeverden, H. A., S. de Groot, and E. E. Greathead. 1991. "Adolescent Sexuality and Contraception." *South Africa's Continuing Medical Education Monthly*, 9(11):1369-79.
2. Venter, A. J. 1974 (December 13). "Circumcision: The Silent Agony of Becoming a Man." *Personality Magazine.*
3. Cowley, I. P., and M. Kisner. 1970. "Ritual Circumcision (Umkhwethna) Amongst the Xhosa of Ciskei." *British Journal Urology*, 66:318-21
4. Du Toit, D. F., and W. J. Villet. 1979. "Gangrene of the Penis After Circumcision: Report of Three Cases." *South African Medical Journal*, 55(13):521-22.
5. Preston-Whyte, E., and M. Zondi. 1991. "Adolescent Sexuality and Its Implications for Teenage Pregnancy and AIDS." *South Africa's Continuing Medical Education Monthly*, 9(11):1389-94.
6. Frame, G., P. de L. G. M. Ferrinho, and I. D. Wilson. 1991. "The Care of Patients with STD's: Review of Previous Research and a Survey of General Practitioners." *South African Family Practice*, 12:887-92.
7. Frame, G., P. de L. G. M. Ferrinho, and G. Phakathi. 1991. "Patients with STD's at the Alexandra Health Centre and University Clinic." *South African Medical Journal*, 80(8):389-92.

8. Abortion and Sterilization Act No. 2, 1975. *Government Gazette.* No. 4608. March 12, 1975.

9. Van Coeverden, H. A., S. de Groot, and E. E. Greathead. 1987. "The Cape Teenage Clinic." *South African Medical Journal,* 71(6):434-36.

10. Nash, E. S., J. H. Brink, F. C. V. Potocnik, and B. L. Dirks. 1992. "South African Psychiatrists' Attitude to the Present Implementation of the Abortion and Sterilization Act of 1975." *South African Medical Journal,* 82(6):434-436.

11. Stevens J. 1990 (March). "South African Comment: Sexually Transmitted Disease." *Medicine International,* 72:5-7.

12. Ballard, R. (Professor, South Africa Institute for Medical Research). Personal communication.

13. Moodley, J., A. A. Hoosen, S. Naidoo, N. Nigil, and A. B. M. Klausman. 1992. "HIV Status and Sexually Transmitted Pathogens in Women Attending a Colposcopy Clinic." *Southern African Journal of Epidemiology and Infection,* 7(1):24-26

14. Piot, P., and M. Laga. 1989. "Genital Ulcers and Other Sexually Transmitted Diseases and the Sexual Transmission of HIV." *British Medical Journal,* 298:623-624.

15. Friedland, I. R., K. P. Klugman, A. S. Karstaedt, J. Patch, J. A. McIntyre, and C. A. Alwood. 1992. "AIDS—The Baragwanath Experience, Part 1. Epidemiology of HIV infection at Baragwanath Hospital 1988-1990." *South Africa Medical Journal,* 82(2):86-90.

16. Department of National Health and Population Development—AIDS Centre, SAIMR.

17. *Southern African Journal Epidemiology Infection.* 1992. 7(3):70.

18. Friedland, I. R., and J. A. McIntyre. 1992. "AIDS—The Baragwanath Experience, Part 2. HIV Infection in Pregnancy and Childhood." *South Africa Medical Journal,* 82(2):90-94.

19. McIntyre, J. A. (Consultant Obstetrician, Baragwanath Hospital). Personal communication.

20. Schoub, B. D. 1990. "The AIDS Epidemic in South Africa—Perceptions and Realities." *South Africa Medical Journal,* 77:607-9.

21. Karstaedt, A. S. 1992. "AIDS—The Baragwanath Experience, Part 3. HIV Infection at Baragwanath Hospital." *South Africa Medical Journal,* 82(2):95-97.

22. Fleming, A. F. 1990. "Opportunistic Infections in AIDS in Developed and Developing Countries." *Stevens Royal Society Tropical Medicine,* 84(1):1-6.

23. Schoub, B. D., et al. 1990. "Considerations on the Further Expansion of the AIDS Epidemic in South Africa." *South Africa Medical Journal,* 77:613-18.

24. Abdool Karim, Q., S. S. Abdool Karim, and J. Nkomokazi. 1991. "Sexual Behaviour and Knowledge of AIDS Among Urban Black Mothers." *South Africa Medical Journal,* 80(7):340-43.

25. Evian, C. R., M. de Beer, M. Crewe, G. N. Padayachee, and H. S. Hurwitz. 1991 "Evaluation of an AIDS Awareness Campaign Using City Buses in Johannesburg." *South Africa Medical Journal,.* 80(7):343-46.

26. Allwood, C. W., L. R. Friedland, A. S. Karstaedt, and J. A. McIntyre. 1992. "AIDS—The Baragwanath Experience, Part 4. Counseling and Ethical Issues." *South Africa Medical Journal,* 82(2):98-101.

27. Hurwitz, M. B. 1989. "Sexual Dysfunction with Infertility." *South Africa Medical Journal,* 76:58-62.

28. Hurwitz, M. B. 1992. "Breast Feeding and Sexuality." *Medical Sex Journal South Africa,* in press.